CALIFORNIA
VEHICLE
CODE

2014

ABRIDGED
CRIMINAL JUSTICE
EDITION

Also Includes:

Related Laws from the following California Codes:

Business & Professions • Fish & Game • Harbors & Navigation
Health & Safety • Public Resources • Public Utilities
and Streets & Highways

Contains New Legislation for 2014

LawTech Publishing
1060 Calle Cordillera, Ste. 105
San Clemente, CA 92673

1(800) 498-0911 | Fax: (949) 498-4858
E-mail: info@LawTechPublishing.com
www.LawTechPublishing.com

Comments and suggestions are welcome.

LEGAL ADVICE: The publisher is not engaged in the business of providing legal advice. For legal advice contact a licensed law practitioner.

ISBN: 978-1-56325-215-0

ABOUT THIS BOOK

This book consists primarily of the enforcement statutes from the Vehicle Code and an appendix of related penal provisions from other California Codes. It includes enactments through the end of the 2014 Regular Legislative Session.

General and permanent laws are enacted currently in California as additions to or amendments of the Codes. The code section numbers, as well as Title, Division, Part, Chapter, and Article headings, where appropriate, are included in the laws as enacted. However, section titles for LawTech's Codes are prepared by the LawTech editorial staff.

LEGEND

Section Numbers: Section numbers appear in **bold** type at the left margin on the line directly above the beginning of the text of each section. **Section Titles:** Section titles appear in **bold** type on the same line as Section Numbers. **Amended Sections:** Text added to sections by Legislation is underlined; text deleted from sections appears as three (3) asterisks ***. **Repealed or Renumbered Sections:** Sections repealed or renumbered by Legislation are represented by the section number, title and the word "Repealed"or "Renumbered" and the new section number. Repealed section numbers and titles will be retained in the book for two years. Sometimes the Legislature repeals a section and then adds it back in the same legislative session. The section they add back is typically the same subject matter, but with some changes. In these cases, the section has basically been amended. Therefore, we show the section with asterisks and underlining (as we do other amended sections) as a matter of convenience for the reader. If a section has been repealed and then added back as an entirely new subject , it will be shown as a newly added section, without underlining. **Legislative Histories**: Each section that has been affected by legislation is followed by the last year that it was affected, and the type of action that affected that section. For example: *(AM '12)*. **Table of Sections Affected** A table of sections affected by bills through the end of the regular session follows this page.

Emergency Legislation Notification: Emergency legislation is that which, due to the urgency thereof, becomes operative immediately instead of the following year. Check LawTech's web site frequently throughout the year for information concerning any emergency legislation that would impact this publication.

pg: 368

SECTIONS AFFECTED BY LEGISLATION IN 2013
VEHICLE CODE

165. . . . . AM	22508.5 . . . . AM/AD/RP
9400.1 . . . . AM	22651. . . . . AM
12505. . . . . AM	22651.05 . . . . AM
12804.11 . . . . AM	22658. . . . . AM
12804.9 . . . . AM	23112.5 . . . . AM
14606. . . . . AM	23124. . . . . AM
15250. . . . . AM	23612. . . . . AM
16028. . . . . AM	34501.12 . . . . AM/RP
21650. . . . . AM	34620. . . . . AM
21655.9 . . . . AM	34623 . . . . AM/RP
21750 . . . . AM/RP/AD	38603. . . . . AM
22352. . . . . AM	38604. . . . . AM

This page intentionally left blank.

TABLE OF CONTENTS

TABLE OF CONTENTS

SELECTED PENAL PROVISIONS FROM OTHER CALIFORNIA CODES

VEHICLE CODE
GENERAL PROVISIONS

20. False Statements

It is unlawful to use a false or fictitious name, or to knowingly make any false statement or knowingly conceal any material fact in any document filed with the department or the CHP.

27. Impersonation of CHP Member

Any person who without authority impersonates, or wears the badge of a member of the CHP with intention to deceive anyone is guilty of a misdemeanor.

28. Notification of Repossession

(a) Whenever possession is taken of any vehicle by or on behalf of any legal owner thereof under the terms of a security agreement or lease agreement, the person taking possession shall notify, within one hour after taking possession of the vehicle, and by the most expeditious means available, the city police department where the taking of possession occurred, if within an incorporated city, or the sheriff's department of the county where the taking of possession occurred, if outside an incorporated city, or the police department of a campus of the University of California or the California State University, if the taking of possession occurred on that campus, and shall within one business day forward a written notice to the city police or sheriff's department.

(b) If possession is taken of more than one vehicle, the possession of each vehicle shall be considered and reported as a separate event.

(c) Any person failing to notify the city police department, sheriff's department, or campus police department as required by this section is guilty of an infraction, and shall be fined a minimum of three hundred dollars ($300), and up to five hundred dollars ($500). The district attorney, city attorney, or city prosecutor shall promptly notify the Bureau of Security and Investigative Services of any conviction resulting from a violation of this section. *(AM '09)*

30. Legislative Policy: Red Lights and Sirens

It is declared as a matter of legislative policy that red lights and sirens on vehicles should be restricted to authorized emergency vehicles engaged in police, fire and lifesaving services; and that other types of vehicles which are engaged in activities which create special hazards upon the highways should be equipped with flashing amber warning lamps.

31. False Information to Peace Officer

No person shall give, either orally or in writing, information to a peace officer while in the performance of his duties under the provisions of this code when such person knows that the information is false.

DIVISION 1. WORDS AND PHRASES DEFINED

110. Alley

"Alley"is any highway having a roadway not exceeding 25 feet in width which is primarily used for access to the rear or side entrances of abutting property; provided, that the City and County of San Francisco may designate by ordinance or resolution as an "alley"any highway having a roadway not exceeding 25 feet in width.

165. Authorized Emergency Vehicle

An authorized emergency vehicle is:

(a) Any publicly owned and operated ambulance, lifeguard, or lifesaving equipment or any privately owned or operated ambulance licensed by the Commissioner of the California Highway Patrol to operate in response to emergency calls.

(b) Any publicly owned vehicle operated by the following persons, agencies, or organizations:

(1) Any federal, state, or local agency, department, or district employing peace officers as that term is defined in Chapter 4.5 (commencing with Section 830) of Part 2 of Title 3 of the Penal Code, for use by those officers in the performance of their duties.

(2) Any forestry or fire department of any public agency or fire department organized as provided in the Health and Safety Code.

(c) Any vehicle owned by the state, or any bridge and highway district, and equipped and used either for fighting fires, or towing or servicing other vehicles, caring for injured persons, or repairing damaged lighting or electrical equipment.

(d) Any state-owned vehicle used in responding to emergency fire, rescue, or communications calls and operated either by the ***Office of Emergency ***Services or by any public agency or industrial fire department to which the ***Office of Emergency ***Services has assigned the vehicle.

(e) Any vehicle owned or operated by any department or agency of the United States government when the vehicle is used in responding to emergency fire, ambulance, or lifesaving calls or is actively engaged in law enforcement work.

(f) Any vehicle for which an authorized emergency vehicle permit has been issued by the Commissioner of the California Highway Patrol. *(AM '13)*

175.   Autoette
An "autoette" is a motor vehicle, located on a natural island with an area in excess of 20,000 acres and that is within a county having a population in excess of 4,000,000, that meets all of the following requirements:

(a) Has three or more wheels in contact with the ground.

(b) Has an unladed weight of no greater than 1,800 pounds.

(c) Has an overall length of no more than 120 inches, including the front and rear bumpers.

(d) Has a width of no more than 55 inches, as measured from its widest part. *(AD '06)*

231.   Bicycle
A bicycle is a device upon which any person may ride, propelled exclusively by human power through a belt, chain, or gears, and having one or more wheels. Persons riding bicycles are subject to the provisions of this code specified in Sections 21200 and 21200.5.

233.   Bus
(a) Except as provided in subdivision (b), a "bus" is any vehicle, including a trailer bus, designed, used, or maintained for carrying more than 15 persons including the driver.

(b) A vehicle designed, used, or maintained for carrying more than 10 persons, including the driver, which is used to transport persons for compensation or profit, or is used by any nonprofit organization or group, is also a bus.

(c) This section does not alter the definition of a schoolbus, school pupil activity bus, general public paratransit vehicle, farm labor vehicle, or youth bus.

(d) A vanpool vehicle is not a bus.

231.5.   Bicycle Path
A "bicycle path" or "bike path" is a Class I bikeway, as defined in subdivision (a) of Section 890.4 of the Streets and Highways Code. *(AD '09)*

231.6.   Bicycle Path Crossing
(a) A "bicycle path crossing" is either of the following:

(1) That portion of a roadway included within the prolongation or connection of the boundary lines of a bike path at intersections where the intersecting roadways meet at approximately right angles.

(2) Any portion of a roadway distinctly indicated for bicycle crossing by lines or other markings on the surface.

(b) Notwithstanding subdivision (a), there shall not be a bicycle path crossing where local authorities have placed signs indicating no crossing. *(AD '09)*

235. Business District

A "business district"is that portion of a highway and the property contiguous thereto (a) upon one side of which highway, for a distance of 600 feet, 50 percent or more of the contiguous property fronting thereon is occupied by buildings in use for business, or (b) upon both sides of which highway, collectively, for a distance of 300 feet, 50 percent or more of the contiguous property fronting thereon is so occupied. A business district may be longer than the distances specified in this section if the above ratio of buildings in use for business to the length of the highway exists.

240. Business and Residence Districts: Determination

In determining whether a highway is within a business or residence district, the following limitations shall apply and shall qualify the definitions in Section 235 and 515:

(a) No building shall be regarded unless its entrance faces the highway and the front of the building is within 75 feet of the roadway.

(b) Where a highway is physically divided into two or more roadways only those buildings facing each roadway separately shall be regarded for the purpose of determining whether the roadway is within a district.

(c) All churches, apartments, hotels, multiple dwelling houses, clubs, and public buildings, other than schools, shall be deemed to be business structures.

(d) A highway or portion of a highway shall not be deemed to be within a district regardless of the number of buildings upon the contiguous property if there is no right of access to the highway by vehicles from the contiguous property.

260. Commercial Vehicle

(a) A "commercial vehicle"is a motor vehicle of a type required to be registered under this code used or maintained for the transportation of persons for hire, compensation, or profit or designed, used, or maintained primarily for the transportation of property.

(b) Passenger vehicles and house cars that are not used for the transportation of persons for hire, compensation, or profit are not commercial vehicles. This subdivision shall not apply to Chapter 4 (commencing with Section 6700) of Division 3.

(c) Any vanpool vehicle is not a commercial vehicle.

(d) The definition of a commercial vehicle in this section does not apply to Chapter 7 (commencing with Section 15200) of Division 6. *(AM '00, '03)*

275. Crosswalk

"Crosswalk"is either:

(a) That portion of a roadway included within the prolongation or connection of the boundary lines of sidewalks at intersection where the intersecting roadways meet at approximately right angles, except the prolongation of such lines from an alley across a street.

(b) Any portion of a roadway distinctly indicated for pedestrian crossing by lines or other markings on the surface.

Notwithstanding the foregoing provisions of this section, there shall not be a crosswalk where local authorities have placed signs indicating no crossing.

280. Darkness

"Darkness"is any time from one-half hour after sunset to one-half hour before sunrise and any other time when visibility is not sufficient to render clearly discernible any person or vehicle on the highway at a distance of 1000 feet.

305. Driver

A "driver"is a person who drives or is in actual physical control of a vehicle. The term "driver"does not include the tillerman or other person who, in an auxiliary capacity, assists the driver in the steering or operation of any articulated fire fighting apparatus.

313. Electric Personal Assistive Mobility Device

The term "electric personal assistive mobility device" or "EPAMD" means a self-balancing, nontandem two-wheeled device, that is not greater than 20 inches deep and 25 inches wide and can turn in place, designed to transport only one person, with an electric propulsion system averaging less than 750 watts (1 horsepower), the maximum speed of which, when powered solely by a propulsion system on a paved level surface, is no more than 12.5 miles per hour. *(AD '02; AM '07)*

332. Freeway

"Freeway" is a highway in respect to which the owners of abutting lands have no right or easement of access to or from their abutting lands or in respect to which such owners have only limited or restricted right or easement of access.

360. Highway

"Highway" is a way or place of whatever nature, publicly maintained and open to the use of the public for purposes of vehicular travel. Highway includes street.

365. Intersection

An "intersection" is the area embraced within the prolongation's of the lateral curb lines, or, if none, then the lateral boundary lines of the roadways, of two highways which join one another at approximately right angles or the area within which vehicles traveling upon different highways joining at any other angle may come in conflict.

377. Limit Line

A "limit line" is a solid white line not less than 12 nor more than 24 inches wide, extending across a roadway or any portion thereof to indicate the point at which traffic is required to stop in compliance with legal requirements.

385.2. Logging Dolly [Added Stats. 2013]

A "logging dolly" is a vehicle designed for carrying logs, having one or more axles that, if there are more than one, are not more than 54 inches apart, and used in connection with a motor truck solely for the purpose of transporting logs and securely connected with the towing vehicle both by a reach and by the load. *(AD '13)*

385.3. Logging Vehicle [Added Stats. 2013]

A "logging vehicle" is a vehicle used exclusively in the conduct of logging operations and not designed for the transportation of persons or property on a highway. *(AD '13)*

385.5. Low Speed Vehicle

(a) A "low-speed vehicle" is a motor vehicle that meets all of the following requirements:

(1) Has four wheels.

(2) Can attain a speed, in one mile, of more than 20 miles per hour and not more than 25 miles per hour, on a paved level surface.

(3) Has a gross vehicle weight rating of less than 3,000 pounds.

(b)(1) For the purposes of this section, a "low-speed vehicle" is not a golf cart, except when operated pursuant to Section 21115 or 21115.1.

(2) A "low-speed vehicle" is also known as a "neighborhood electric vehicle." *(AM '06)*

395.5. Mobile Billboard Advertising Display

A mobile billboard advertising display means an advertising display that is attached to a mobile, nonmotorized vehicle, device, or bicycle, that carries, pulls, or transports a sign or billboard, and is for the primary purpose of advertising. *(AM '11)*

400. Motorcycle

(a) A "motorcycle" is a motor vehicle having a seat or saddle for the use of the rider, designed to travel on not more than three wheels in contact with the ground.

(b) A motor vehicle that has four wheels in contact with the ground, two of which are a functional part of a sidecar, is a motorcycle if the vehicle otherwise comes within the definition of subdivision (a).

(c) A farm tractor is not a motorcycle.

(d) A three-wheeled motor vehicle that otherwise meets the requirements of subdivision (a), has a partially or completely enclosed seating area for the driver and passenger, is used by local public agencies for the enforcement of parking control provisions, and is operated at slow speeds on public streets, is not a motorcycle. However, a motor vehicle described in this subdivision shall comply with the applicable sections of this code imposing equipment installation requirements on motorcycles. *(AM '08)*

405. Motor-Driven Cycle

A "motor-driven cycle" is any motorcycle with a motor that displaces less than 150 cubic centimeters. A motor-driven cycle does not include a motorized bicycle, as defined in Section 406.

406. Motorized Bicycle

(a) A "motorized bicycle" or "moped" is any two-wheeled or three-wheeled device having fully operative pedals for propulsion by human power, or having no pedals if powered solely by electrical energy, and an automatic transmission and a motor which produces less than 2 gross brake horsepower and is capable of propelling the device at a maximum speed of not more than 30 miles per our on level ground.

(b) A "motorized bicycle" is also a device that has fully operative pedals for propulsion by human power and has an electric motor that meets all of the following requirements:

(1) Has a power output of not more than 1,000 watts.

(2) Is incapable of propelling the device at a speed of more than 20 miles per hour on ground level.

(3) Is incapable of further increasing the speed of the device when human power is used to propel the motorized bicycle faster than 20 miles per hour.

(4) Every manufacturer of motorized bicycles, as defined in this subdivision, shall provide a disclosure to buyers that advises buyers that their existing insurance policies may not provide coverage for these bicycles and that they should contact their insurance company or insurance agent to determine if coverage is provided.

(c) The disclosure required under paragraph (4) of subdivision (b) shall meet both of the following requirements:

(1) The disclosure shall be printed in not less than 14-point boldface type on a single sheet of paper that contains no information other than the disclosure.

(2) The disclosure shall include the following language in capital letters:

"YOUR INSURANCE POLICIES MAY NOT PROVIDE COVERAGE FOR ACCIDENTS INVOLVING THE USE OF THIS BICYCLE. TO DETERMINE IF COVERAGE IS PROVIDED YOU SHOULD CONTACT YOUR INSURANCE COMPANY OR AGENT."

407.5. Motorized Scooter

(a) A "motorized scooter" is any two-wheeled device that has handlebars, has a floorboard that is designed to be stood upon when riding, and is powered by an electric motor. This device may also have a driver seat that does not interfere with the ability of the rider to stand and ride and may also be designed to be powered by human propulsion. For purposes of this section, a motorcycle, as defined in Section 400, a motor-driven cycle, as defined in Section 405, or a motorized bicycle or moped, as defined in Section 406, is not a motorized scooter.

(b) A device meeting the definition in subdivision (a) that is powered by a source other than electrical power is also a motorized scooter.

(c)(1) A manufacturer of motorized scooters shall provide a disclosure to buyers that advises buyers that the buyers' existing insurance policies may not provide coverage for these scooters and that the buyers should contact their insurance company or insurance agent to determine if coverage is provided.

(2) The disclosure required under paragraph (1) shall meet both of the following requirements:

(A) The disclosure shall be printed in not less than 14-point boldface type on a single sheet of paper that contains no information other than the disclosure.

(B) The disclosure shall include the following language in capital letters: "YOUR INSURANCE POLICIES MAY NOT PROVIDE COVERAGE FOR ACCIDENTS INVOLVING THE USE OF THIS SCOOTER. TO DETERMINE IF COVERAGE IS PROVIDED, YOU SHOULD CONTACT YOUR INSURANCE COMPANY OR AGENT."

(d)(1) A manufacturer of motorized scooters shall provide a disclosure to a buyer that advises the buyer that the buyer may not modify or alter the exhaust system to cause that system to amplify or create an excessive noise, or to fail to meet applicable emission requirements.

(2) The disclosure required under paragraph (1) shall meet both of the following requirements:

(A) The disclosure shall be printed in not less than 14-point boldface type on a single sheet of paper that contains no information other than the disclosure.

(B) The disclosure shall include the following language in capital letters:

"YOU MAY NOT MODIFY OR ALTER THE EXHAUST SYSTEM OF THIS SCOOTER TO CAUSE IT TO AMPLIFY OR CREATE EXCESSIVE NOISE PER VEHICLE CODE SECTION 21226, OR TO FAIL TO MEET APPLICABLE EMISSION REQUIREMENTS PER VEHICLE CODE 27156."

(e) This section shall become operative on January 1, 2008. *(AD '02; AM '04)*

415. Motor Vehicle

(a) A "motor vehicle" is a vehicle that is self-propelled.

(b) "Motor vehicle" does not include a self-propelled wheelchair, motorized tricycle, or motorized quadricycle, if operated by a person who, by reason of physical disability, is otherwise unable to move about as a pedestrian.

(c) For purposes of Chapter 6 (commencing with Section 3000) of Division 2, "motor vehicle" includes a recreational vehicle as that term is defined in subdivision (a) of Section 18010 of the Health and Safety Code, but does not include a truck camper. *(AM '03, '04)*

463. Park or Parking

"Park or parking" shall mean the standing of a vehicle, whether occupied or not, otherwise than temporarily for the purpose of and while actually engaged in loading or unloading merchandise or passengers.

467. Pedestrian

(a) A "pedestrian" is a person who is afoot or who is using any of the following:

(1) A means of conveyance propelled by human power other than a bicycle.

(2) An electric personal assistive mobility device.

(b) "Pedestrian" includes a person who is operating a self-propelled wheelchair, motorized tricycle, or motorized quadricycle and, by reason of physical disability, is otherwise unable to move about as a pedestrian, as specified in subdivision (a). *(AD '02; AM '04, '07)*

467.5. Pedicab

"Pedicab" means either of the following:

(a) A bicycle that has three or more wheels, that transports, or is capable of transporting, passengers on seats attached to the bicycle, that is operated by a person, and that is being used for transporting passengers for hire.

(b) A bicycle that pulls a trailer, sidecar, or similar device, that transports, or is capable of transporting, passengers on seats attached to the trailer, sidecar, or similar device, that is operated by a person, and that is being used for transporting passengers for hire. *(AD '10)*

471 Pickup Truck

A "pickup truck" is a motor truck with a manufacturer's gross vehicle weight rating of less than 11,500 pounds, an unladen weight of less than 8,001 pounds, and which is equipped with an open box-type bed not exceeding 9 feet in length. "Pickup truck" does not include a motor vehicle otherwise meeting the above definition, that is equipped with a bed-mounted storage compartment unit commonly called a "utility body."

473. Pocket Bike

(a) A "pocket bike" is a two-wheeled motorized device that has a seat or saddle for the use of the rider, and that is not designed or manufactured for highway use. "Pocket bike" does not include an off-highway motorcycle, as defined in Section 436.

(b) For purposes of this section, a vehicle is designed for highway use if it meets the applicable Federal Motor Vehicle Safety Standards, as contained in Title 49 of the Code of Federal Regulations, and is equipped in accordance with the requirements of this code. *(AD '05)*

500. Recreational Off-Highway Vehicle

"Recreational off-highway vehicle" means a motor vehicle meeting all of the following criteria:

(a) Designed by the manufacturer for operation primarily off of the highway.

(b) Has a steering wheel for steering control.

(c) Has nonstraddle seating provided by the manufacturer for the operator and all passengers.

(d)(1) Has a maximum speed capability of greater than 30 miles per hour.

(2) A vehicle designed by the manufacturer with a maximum speed capability of 30 miles per hour or less but is modified so that it has a maximum speed capability of greater than 30 miles per hour satisfies the criteria set forth in this subdivision.

(e) Has an engine displacement equal to or less than 1,000cc (61 ci). *(AD '12)*

515. Residence District

A "residence district" is that portion of a highway and the property contiguous thereto, other than a business district, (a) upon one side of which highway, within a distance of a quarter of a mile, the contiguous property fronting thereon is occupied by 13 or more separate dwelling houses or business structures, or (b) upon both sides of which highway, collectively, within a distance of a quarter of a mile, the contiguous property fronting thereon is occupied by 16 or more separate dwelling houses or business structures. A residence district may be longer than one-quarter of a mile if the above ratio of separate dwelling houses or business structures to the length of the highway exists.

516. Resident

"Resident" means any person who manifests an intent to live or be located in this state on more than a temporary or transient basis. Presence in the state for six months or more in any twelve-month period gives rise to a rebuttable presumption of residency for the purposes of vehicle registration:

The following are evidence of residency:

(a) Address where registered to vote.

(b) Location of employment or place of business.

(c) Payment of resident tuition at a public institution of higher education.

(d) Attendance of dependents at a primary or secondary school.

(e) Filing a homeowner's property tax exemption.

(f) Renting or leasing a home for use as a residence.

(g) Declaration of residency to obtain a license or any other privilege or benefit not ordinarily extended to a nonresident.

(h) Possession of a Calif. driver's license.

(i) Other acts, occurrences, or events that indicate presence in the state is more than temporary or transient.

530. Roadway

A "roadway" is that portion of a highway improved, designed, or ordinarily used for vehicular travel.

531. Utility-Terrain Vehicle

"Utility-terrain vehicle" means a motor vehicle subject to subdivision (a) of Section 38010 that is all of the following:

(a) Designed for operation off of the highway.

(b) Suspended on four tires.

(c) Has a steering wheel for steering control.

(d) Has one seat to accommodate a driver and one passenger sitting side by side. *(AD '12)*

553. Shade Trailer
"Shade trailer"means a device designed and utilized to provide shade pursuant to Section 3395 of Title 8 of the California Code of Regulations.

555. Sidewalk
"Sidewalk"is that portion of a highway, other than the roadway, set apart by curbs, barriers, markings or other delineation for pedestrian travel.

590. Street
"Street"is a way or place of whatever nature, publicly maintained and open to the use of the public for purposes of vehicular travel. Street includes highway.

620. Traffic
The term "traffic"includes pedestrians, ridden animals, vehicles, street cars, and other conveyances, either singly or together, while using any highway for purposes of travel.

665.5. U-turn
A "U-turn"is the turning of a vehicle upon a highway so as to proceed in the opposite direction whether accomplished by one continuous movement or not.

667. Utility Trailer
(a) A "utility trailer"is a trailer or semitrailer used solely for the transportation of the user's personal property, not in commerce, which does not exceed a gross weight of 10,000 pounds or a manufacturer's gross vehicle weight rating of 10,000 pounds.

(b) Notwithstanding subdivision (a), a "utility trailer"includes a trailer or semitrailer designed and used for the transportation of livestock, not in commerce, which does not exceed a gross weight of 10,000 pounds or a manufacturer's gross vehicle weight rating of 10,000 pounds. *(AD '10)*

670. Vehicle
A "vehicle"is a device by which any person or property may be propelled, moved, or drawn upon a highway, excepting a device moved exclusively by human power or used exclusively upon stationary rails or tracks.

DIVISION 2. ADMINISTRATION

CHAPTER 1. DEPARTMENT OF MOTOR VEHICLES

1808.4. Confidential Department Records: Residence Address of Certain Public Officials
(a) For all of the following persons, his or her home address that appears in a record of the department is confidential if the person requests the confidentiality of that information:

(1) Attorney General.

(2) State Public Defender.

(3) A Member of the Legislature.

(4) A judge or court commissioner.

(5) A district attorney.

(6) A public defender.

(7) An attorney employed by the Department of Justice, the office of the State Public Defender, or a county office of the district attorney or public defender.

(8) A city attorney and an attorney who submits verification from his or her public employer that the attorney represents the city in matters that routinely place the attorney in personal contact with persons under investigation for, charged with, or convicted of, committing criminal acts, if that attorney is employed by a city attorney.

(9) A nonsworn police dispatcher.

(10) A child abuse investigator or social worker, working in child protective services within a social services department.

(11) An active or retired peace officer, as defined in Chapter 4.5 (commencing with Section 830) of Title 3 of Part 2 of the Penal Code.

(12) An employee of the Department of Corrections and Rehabilitation, Division of Juvenile Facilities, or the Prison Industry Authority specified in Sections 20403 and 20405 of the Government Code.

(13) A nonsworn employee of a city police department, a county sheriff's office, the Department of the California Highway Patrol, a federal, state, or local detention facility, or a local juvenile hall, camp, ranch, or home, who submits agency verification that, in the normal course of his or her employment, he or she controls or supervises inmates or is required to have a prisoner in his or her care or custody.

(14) A county counsel assigned to child abuse cases.

(15) An investigator employed by the Department of Justice, a county district attorney, or a county public defender.

(16) A member of a city council.

(17) A member of a board of supervisors.

(18) A federal prosecutor, criminal investigator, or National Park Service Ranger working in this state.

(19) An active or retired city enforcement officer engaged in the enforcement of the Vehicle Code or municipal parking ordinances.

(20) An employee of a trial court.

(21) A psychiatric social worker employed by a county.

(22) A police or sheriff department employee designated by the Chief of Police of the department or the sheriff of the county as being in a sensitive position. A designation pursuant to this paragraph shall, for purposes of this section, remain in effect for three years subject to additional designations that, for purposes of this section, shall remain in effect for additional three-year periods.

(23) A state employee in one of the following classifications:

(A) Licensing Registration Examiner, Department of Motor Vehicles.

(B) Motor Carrier Specialist I, Department of the California Highway Patrol.

(C) Museum Security Officer and Supervising Museum Security Officer.

(24)(A) The spouse or child of a person listed in paragraphs (1) to (23), inclusive, regardless of the spouse's or child's place of residence.

(B) The surviving spouse or child of a peace officer, as defined in Chapter 4.5 (commencing with Section 830) of Title 3 of Part 2 of the Penal Code, if the peace officer died in the line of duty.

(C)(i) Subparagraphs (A) and (B) shall not apply if the person listed in those subparagraphs was convicted of a crime and is on active parole or probation.

(ii) For requests made on or after January 1, 2011, the person requesting confidentiality for their spouse or child listed in subparagraph (A) or (B) shall declare, at the time of the request for confidentiality, whether the spouse or child has been convicted of a crime and is on active parole or probation.

(iii) Neither the listed person's employer nor the department shall be required to verify, or be responsible for verifying, that a person listed in subparagraph (A) or (B) was convicted of a crime and is on active parole or probation.

(b) The confidential home address of a person listed in subdivision (a) shall not be disclosed, except to any of the following:

(1) A court.

(2) A law enforcement agency.

(3) The State Board of Equalization.

(4) An attorney in a civil or criminal action that demonstrates to a court the need for the home address, if the disclosure is made pursuant to a subpoena.

(5) A governmental agency to which, under any provision of law, information is required to be furnished from records maintained by the department.

(c)(1) A record of the department containing a confidential home address shall be open to public inspection, as provided in Section 1808, if the address is completely obliterated or otherwise removed from the record.

(2) Following termination of office or employment, a confidential home address shall be withheld from public inspection for three years, unless the termination is the result of conviction of a criminal offense. If the termination or separation is the result of the filing of a criminal complaint, a confidential home address shall be withheld from public inspection during the time in which the terminated individual may file an appeal from termination, while an appeal from termination is ongoing, and until the appeal process is exhausted, after which confidentiality shall be at the discretion of the employing agency if the termination or separation is upheld. Upon reinstatement to an office or employment, the protections of this section are available.

(3) With respect to a retired peace officer, his or her home address shall be withheld from public inspection permanently upon request of confidentiality at the time the information would otherwise be opened. The home address of the surviving spouse or child listed in subparagraph (B) of paragraph (24) of subdivision (a) shall be withheld from public inspection for three years following the death of the peace officer.

(4) The department shall inform a person who requests a confidential home address what agency the individual whose address was requested is employed by or the court at which the judge or court commissioner presides.

(d) A violation of subdivision (a) by the disclosure of the confidential home address of a peace officer, as specified in paragraph (11) of subdivision (a), a nonsworn employee of the city police department or county sheriff's office, or the spouses or children of these persons, including, but not limited to, the surviving spouse or child listed in subparagraph (B) of paragraph (24) of subdivision (a), that results in bodily injury to the peace officer, employee of the city police department or county sheriff's office, or the spouses or children of these persons is a felony. *(AM '08-'10)*

1808.45. Unauthorized Disclosure: Misdemeanor

The willful, unauthorized disclosure of information from any department record to any person, or the use of any false representation to obtain information from a department record or any use of information obtained from any department record for a purpose other than the one stated in the request or the sale or other distribution of the information to a person or organization for purposes not disclosed in the request is a misdemeanor, punishable by a fine not exceeding five thousand dollars ($5,000) or by imprisonment in the county jail not exceeding one year, or both fine and imprisonment.

CHAPTER 2. CALIFORNIA HIGHWAY PATROL

2261. Wearing of Uniforms

A uniform substantially similar to the official uniform of members of the CHP shall not he worn by any other law enforcement officer or by any other person except duly appointed members of the CHP and persons authorized by the commissioner to wear such uniform in connection with a program of entertainment. A uniform shall be deemed substantially similar to the uniform of the CHP if it so resembles such official uniform as to cause an ordinary reasonable person to believe that the person wearing the uniform is a member of the CHP.

2402.6. Regulations and Standards: Compressed or Liquefied Gas and Liquefied Petroleum Gas

(a) The commissioner may adopt and enforce regulations and standards with respect to fuel containers and fuel systems on vehicles using compressed or liquefied natural gas and liquefied petroleum gas used in conjunction with a propulsion system certified by the State Air Resources Board as producing as few or fewer emissions as a State Air Resources Board approved system using compressed or liquefied natural gas or liquefied petroleum gas and with respect to the operation of vehicles using any of those fuels to ensure the safety of the equipment and vehicles and of persons and property using the highways.

(b) The commissioner may also adopt and enforce regulations and standards with respect to fuel containers and fuel systems on vehicles using compressed or liquefied hydrogen gas or liquid fuels that generate hydrogen gas.

(c) All motor vehicles with compressed natural gas fuel systems used for propulsion shall comply either with the regulations adopted pursuant to subdivision (a) or with National Fire Protection Administration Standard NFPA 52, "Compressed Natural Gas (CNG) Vehicular Fuel Systems" in effect at the time of manufacture, until standards for those fuel systems have been incorporated into the Federal Motor Vehicle Safety Standards by the United States Department of Transportation. Whenever those Federal Motor Vehicle Safety Standards include requirements for gaseous fuel systems, all motor vehicles with gaseous fuel systems which are manufactured after the effective date of those requirements shall comply with those requirements.

(d) It is an infraction for any person to operate any motor vehicle in violation of any provision of a regulation adopted pursuant to this section.

(e) The operator of every facility for filling portable liquefied natural gas or liquefied petroleum gas containers having a capacity of four pounds or more but not more than 200 pounds of gas shall post in a conspicuous place the regulations applicable to that filling procedure. *(AM '02)*

2436.3. Roadside Assistance Carrier Number

(a) On and after July 1, 1992, every employer shall obtain from the department a carrier identification number. Application for a carrier identification number shall be on forms furnished by the department. The number shall be displayed on both sides of each tow truck utilized in any freeway service patrol operation, in accordance with Section 27907.

(b) No employer shall operate a tow truck in any freeway service patrol operation if the carrier operation number issued pursuant to subdivision (a) has been suspended by the commissioner pursuant to Section 2432.1.

(c) The carrier identification number shall be removed before sale, transfer, or other disposal of the vehicle, or upon termination of an agreement or contract for freeway service patrol operations.

(d) A violation of this section is a misdemeanor.

2460. Definitions - Renderers and Transporters of Inedible Kitchen Grease

(a) The definitions set forth in Article 1 (commencing with Section 19200) of Chapter 5 of Part 3 of Division 9 of the Food and Agricultural Code apply for purposes of this article.

(b) A "licensed renderer" is a renderer licensed under Article 6 (commencing with Section 19300) of Chapter 5 of Part 3 of Division 9 of the Food and Agricultural Code.

(c) A "registered transporter" is a transporter of inedible kitchen grease registered under Article 6.5 (commencing with Section 19310) of Chapter 5 of Part 3 of Division 9 of the Food and Agricultural Code.

(d) A "peace officer" is any peace officer defined in Chapter 4.5 (commencing with Section 830) of Title 3 of Part 2 of the Penal Code. *(AD '98)*

2462. Records Required

(a) In addition to any other records required to be kept pursuant to Chapter 5 (commencing with Section 19200) of Part 3 of Division 9 of the Food and Agricultural Code, every licensed renderer shall record and keep for two years, in connection with the receipt of kitchen grease that is not intended for human food, all of the following information:

(1) The name, address, and registration number of every transporter of inedible kitchen grease who has delivered that material to the renderer.

(2) The total amount of inedible kitchen grease purchased in each transaction.

(3) The date of each transaction.

(b) Every registered transporter of inedible kitchen grease shall record and maintain for two years all of the following:

(1) The name and address of each location from which the transporter obtained the inedible kitchen grease.

(2) The quantity of material received from each location.

(3) The date on which the inedible kitchen grease was obtained from each location. *(AM '12)*

2464. Records to be Maintained at Regular Place of Business and Open to Inspection; Penalties

All records required to be retained pursuant to this article shall be maintained at the regular place of business of every licensed renderer and every registered transporter. Those records shall be exhibited on demand to any peace officer. *(AD '98)*

2466. Inspection of Premises by Peace Officer

Any peace officer may, during normal business hours, inspect any premises maintained by a licensed renderer or registered transporter, and any inedible kitchen grease located on the premises, for the purpose of determining whether that renderer or transporter is complying with the record maintenance requirements of this article. *(AD '98)*

2468. Failure to Keep or Exhibit Records; Penalties

(a) Any licensed renderer who fails in any respect to keep the written records required by this article, or to set out in that written record any matter required by this article to be set out in the record, is guilty of a misdemeanor.

(b) Every licensed renderer or registered transporter who refuses, upon demand of any peace officer, to exhibit any written record required by this article, or who destroys that record within two years after making the final entry of any information required by this article, is guilty of a misdemeanor.

(c) Any violation of subdivision (a) or (b) is punishable as follows:

(1) For a first offense, by a fine of not less than five hundred dollars ($500), or by imprisonment in the county jail for not more than 30 days, or by both that fine and imprisonment.

(2) For a second offense within a period of one year, by a fine of not less than one thousand dollars ($1,000), or by imprisonment in the county jail for not more than 30 days, or by both that fine and imprisonment. In addition to any other punishment imposed pursuant to this paragraph, the court may order the defendant to stop engaging in the business as a transporter or renderer for a period not to exceed 30 days.

(3) For a third or any subsequent offense within a period of two years, by a fine of not less than two thousand dollars ($2,000), or by imprisonment in the county jail for not more than six months, or by both that fine and imprisonment. In addition to any other sentence imposed pursuant to this paragraph, the court shall order the defendant to stop engaging in the business as a transporter or renderer for a period of 30 days. *(AM '12)*

2470. Unlawful to Transport Indelible Kitchen Grease Unless Registered

It is unlawful for any person to engage in the transportation of inedible kitchen grease without being registered with the Department of Food and Agriculture and without being in possession of a valid registration certificate issued by that department. *(AD '98)*

2472. Unlawful Transportation Out of California

It is unlawful for any person who is not a registered transporter or licensed renderer of inedible kitchen grease to transport that product from any place within this state to any place outside the borders of this state. *(AD '98)*

2474. Unlawful Theft, Contamination or Damage of Grease or Containers

It is unlawful for any person to steal, misappropriate, contaminate, or damage inedible kitchen grease, or containers thereof. *(AD '98)*

2476. Unlawful Possession from Unregistered Transporter

No licensed renderer, registered transporter, or any other person may take possession of inedible kitchen grease from an unregistered transporter or knowingly take possession of stolen inedible kitchen grease. *(AD '98)*

2504. Violation of Regulations

It is unlawful to violate any regulation adopted by the commissioner pursuant to this chapter.

CHAPTER 4. ADMINISTRATION & ENFORCEMENT

2800. Obedience to Traffic Officers

(a) It is unlawful to willfully fail or refuse to comply with a lawful order, signal, or direction of a peace officer, as defined in Chapter 4.5 (commencing with Section 830) of Title 3 of Part 2 of the Penal Code, when that peace officer is in uniform and is performing duties pursuant to any of the provisions of this code, or to refuse to submit to a lawful inspection pursuant to this code.

(b)(1) Except as authorized pursuant to Section 24004, it is unlawful to fail or refuse to comply with a lawful out-of-service order issued by an authorized employee of the Department of the California Highway Patrol or by an authorized enforcement officer as described in subdivision (d).

(2) It is unlawful for a driver transporting hazardous materials in a commercial motor vehicle that is required to display a placard pursuant to Section 27903 to violate paragraph (1).

(3) It is unlawful for a driver of a vehicle designed to transport 16 or more passengers, including the driver, to violate paragraph (1).

(c) It is unlawful to fail or refuse to comply with a lawful out-of-service order issued by the United States Secretary of the Department of Transportation.

(d) "Out-of-Service order"means a declaration by an authorized enforcement officer of a federal, state, Canadian, Mexican, or local jurisdiction that a driver, a commercial motor vehicle, or a motor carrier operation is out-of-service pursuant to Section 386.72, 392.5, 392.9a, 395.13, or 396.9 of Title 49 of the Code of Federal Regulations, state law, or the North American Standard Out-of-Service Criteria. *(AM '12)*

2800.1. Evading a Peace Officer

(a) Any person who, while operating a motor vehicle and with the intent to evade, willfully flees or otherwise attempts to elude a pursuing peace officer's motor vehicle, is guilty of a misdemeanor punishable by imprisonment in a county jail for not more than one year if all of the following conditions exist:

(1) The peace officer's motor vehicle is exhibiting at least one lighted red lamp visible from the front and the person either sees or reasonably should have seen the lamp.

(2) The peace officer's motor vehicle is sounding a siren as may be reasonably necessary.

(3) The peace officer's motor vehicle is distinctively marked.

(4) The peace officer's motor vehicle is operated by a peace officer, as defined in Chapter 4.5 (commencing with Section 830) of Title 3 of Part 2 of the Penal Code, and that peace officer is wearing a distinctive uniform.

(b) Any person who, while operating a motor vehicle and with the intent to evade, willfully flees or otherwise attempts to elude a pursuing peace officer's bicycle, is guilty of a misdemeanor punishable by imprisonment in a county jail for not more than one year if the following conditions exist:

(1) The peace officer's bicycle is distinctively marked.

(2) The peace officer's bicycle is operated by a peace officer, as defined in paragraph (4) of subdivision (a), and that peace officer is wearing a distinctive uniform.

(3) The peace officer gives a verbal command to stop.

(4) The peace officer sounds a horn that produces a sound of at least 115 decibels.

(5) The peace officer gives a hand signal commanding the person to stop.

(6) The person is aware or reasonably should have been aware of the verbal command, horn, and hand signal, but refuses to comply with the command to stop. *(AM '05)*

2800.2. Evading a Peace Officer: Reckless Driving

(a) If a person flees or attempts to elude a pursuing peace officer in violation of Section 2800.1 and the pursued vehicle is driven in a willful or wanton disregard for the safety of persons or property, the person driving the vehicle, upon conviction, shall be punished by imprisonment in the state prison, or by confinement in the county jail for not less than six months nor more than one year. The court may also impose a fine of not less than one thousand dollars ($1,000) nor more than ten thousand dollars ($10,000), or may impose both that imprisonment or confinement and fine.

(b) For purposes of this section, a willful or wanton disregard for the safety of persons or property includes, but is not limited to, driving while fleeing or attempting to elude a pursuing peace officer during which time either three or more violations that are assigned a traffic violation point count under Section 12810 occur, or damage to property occurs. *(AM '98)*

2800.3. Evading a Peace Officer Causing Injury or Death

(a) Whenever willful flight or attempt to elude a pursuing peace officer in violation of Section 2800.1 proximately causes serious bodily injury to any person, the person driving the pursued vehicle, upon conviction, shall be punished by imprisonment in the state prison for three, five, or seven years, by imprisonment in a county jail for not more than one year, or by a fine of not less than two thousand dollars ($2,000) nor more than ten thousand dollars ($10,000), or by both that fine and imprisonment.

(b) Whenever willful flight or attempt to elude a pursuing peace officer in violation of Section 2800.1 proximately causes death to a person, the person driving the pursued vehicle, upon conviction, shall be punished by imprisonment in the state prison for a term of 4, 6, or 10 years.

(c) Nothing in this section shall preclude the imposition of a greater sentence pursuant to Section 190 of the Penal Code or any other provisions of law applicable to punishment for an unlawful death.

(d) For the purposes of this section, "serious bodily injury" has the same meaning as defined in paragraph (4) of subdivision (f) of Section 243 of the Penal Code. *(AM '98, '05)*

2800.4. Flee or Attempt to Elude Pursuing Peace Officer; Driving Opposite Normal Traffic Flow

Whenever a person willfully flees or attempts to elude a pursuing peace officer in violation of Section 2800.1, and the person operating the pursued vehicle willfully drives that vehicle on a highway in a direction opposite to that in which the traffic lawfully moves upon that highway, the person upon conviction is punishable by imprisonment for not less than six months nor more than one year in a county jail or by imprisonment in the state prison, or by a fine of not less than one thousand dollars ($1,000) nor more than ten thousand dollars ($10,000), or by both that fine and imprisonment. *(AM '12)*

2801. Obedience to Firemen

It is unlawful to willfully fail or refuse to comply with any lawful order, signal, or direction of any member of any fire department, paid, volunteer, or company operated, when wearing the badge or insignia of a fireman and when in the course of his duties he is protecting the personnel and fire department equipment.

2803. Control of Illegal Size or Weight

(a) If the traffic officer determines that the vehicle is not safely loaded or that the height, width, length, or weight is unlawful, he may require the driver to stop in a suitable place and reload or remove such portion of the load as may be necessary to render the load safe or to reduce it to the limits permitted under this code. A suitable place is an area which allows the least obstruction to the highway and which requires the least travel on the highway by the vehicle. Determination of the suitability of an area shall be made by the traffic officer who requires the adjustment. All material so unloaded shall be cared for by the owner or operator of the vehicle at the risk of the owner or operator.

(b) If a certified weight certificate or bill of lading accompanies a vehicle which has been determined to be overweight due to the load on the vehicle, the driver shall submit the certified weight certificate or bill of lading, whichever is appropriate, to the traffic officer when the overweight load is removed in the presence of the officer. The officer may note on the certified weight certificate or bill of lading submitted by the driver the fact that a portion of the load has been removed to bring the vehicle and load within the allowable weight limit specified in this code, and the officer shall return the certificate or bill of lading to the driver.

(c) If the height, width or length of the vehicle is unlawful, irrespective of any load thereon, or if an unladen vehicle is overweight, the traffic officer may prohibit further movement of the vehicle until a permit is obtained as provided in Section 35780.

2805. Inspection of Vehicles

   (a) For the purpose of locating stolen vehicles, (1) any member of the California Highway Patrol, or (2) a member of a city police department, a member of a county sheriff's office, or a district attorney investigator, whose primary responsibility is to conduct vehicle theft investigations, may inspect any vehicle of a type required to be registered under this code, or any identifiable vehicle component thereof, on a highway or in any public garage, repair shop, terminal, parking lot, new or used car lot, automobile dismantler's lot, vehicle shredding facility, vehicle leasing or rental lot, vehicle equipment rental yard, vehicle salvage pool, or other similar establishment, or any agricultural or construction work location where work is being actively performed, and may inspect the title or registration of vehicles, in order to establish the rightful ownership or possession of the vehicle or identifiable vehicle component.

   As used in this subdivision, "identifiable vehicle component" means any component which can be distinguished from other similar components by a serial number or other unique distinguishing number, sign, or symbol.

   (b) A member of the California Highway Patrol, a member of a city police department or county sheriff's office, or a district attorney investigator whose primary responsibility is to conduct vehicle theft investigations, may also inspect, for the purposes specified in subdivision (a), implements of husbandry, special construction equipment, forklifts, and special mobile equipment in the places described in subdivision (a) or when that vehicle is incidentally operated or transported upon a highway.

   (c) Whenever possible, inspections conducted pursuant to subdivision (a) or (b) shall be conducted at a time and in a manner so as to minimize any interference with, or delay of, business operations. *(AM '00)*

2807. Schoolbus Inspection

   (a) The California Highway Patrol shall inspect every schoolbus at least once each school year to ascertain whether its construction, design, equipment, and color comply with all provisions of law.

   (b) No person shall drive any schoolbus unless there is displayed therein a certificate issued by the California Highway Patrol stating that on a certain date, which shall be within 13 months of the date of operation, an authorized employee of the California Highway Patrol inspected the bus and found that on the date of inspection the bus complied with the applicable provisions of state law relating to construction, design, equipment, and color. The Commissioner of the California Highway Patrol shall provide by rule or regulation for the issuance and display of distinctive inspection certificates.

2807.1. Inspection of School Pupil Activity Buses; Display of Inspection Certificates

   (a) The Department of the California Highway Patrol shall inspect and certify every school pupil activity bus specified in Section 546 at least once each year to ascertain whether its condition complies with all provisions of the law.

   (b) No person shall drive any motor vehicle specified in subdivision (a) unless there is displayed therein a certificate issued by the Department of the California Highway Patrol stating that on a certain date, which shall be within 13 months of the date of operation, an authorized employee of the Department of the California Highway Patrol inspected such motor vehicle and found that on the date of inspection such motor vehicle complied with the applicable provisions of the state law. The Commissioner of the California Highway Patrol shall provide by rule or regulation for the issuance and display of distinctive inspection certificates.

2810. Inspection to Prevent Theft

   (a) A member of the California Highway Patrol may stop any vehicle transporting any timber products, livestock, poultry, farm produce, crude oil, petroleum products, or inedible kitchen grease, and inspect the bills of lading, shipping or delivery papers, or other evidence to determine whether the driver is in legal possession of the load, and, upon reasonable belief that the driver of the vehicle is not in legal possession, shall take custody of the vehicle and load and turn them over to the custody of the sheriff of the county in which the timber products, livestock, poultry, farm produce, crude oil, petroleum products, or inedible kitchen grease, or any part thereof, is apprehended.

(b) The sheriff shall receive and provide for the care and safekeeping of the apprehended timber products, livestock, poultry, farm produce, crude oil, petroleum products, or inedible kitchen grease, or any part thereof, and immediately, in cooperation with the department, proceed with an investigation and its legal disposition.

(c) Any expense incurred by the sheriff in the performance of his or her duties under this section shall be a legal charge against the county. *(AM '99)*

2810.1. Inspection of Rental Commercial Vehicles; Compliance with Household Goods Carriers Act

(a) Any traffic officer may stop any commercial vehicle, as defined in Section 260, that is a rental vehicle and inspect the bills of lading, shipping, delivery papers, or other evidence to determine whether the driver is transporting household goods in violation of the Household Goods Carriers Act (Chapter 7 (commencing with Sec. 5101) of Division 2 of the Public Utilities Code). The officer may only stop and inspect where the officer has probable cause to believe that the vehicle is being operated in violation of that act.

(b) It is a public offense, for which an officer may issue a citation, for a driver to unlawfully transport household goods in violation of the Household Goods Carriers Act. That public offense is punishable as prescribed in Article 8 (commencing with Section 5311) of Chapter 7 of Division 2 of the Public Utilities Code. It is an infraction to refuse to submit to an inspection as authorized by subdivision (a).

(c) A copy of the citation for any offense described in subdivision (b) shall be sent by the department that employs the traffic officer to the Director of the Consumer Services Division of the California Public Utilities Commission. A copy of a citation shall be removed from any record of the commission upon a showing that the person was not convicted of the offense or that bail was not forfeited for that offense. A person for whom a copy of a citation has been sent to the commission and is on file with the commission may request the commission for an administrative hearing on that matter.

2813. Commercial Vehicle Inspection - Smoke Emissions

Every driver of a commercial vehicle shall stop and submit the vehicle to an inspection of the size, weight, equipment, and smoke emissions of the vehicle at any location where members of the CHP are conducting tests and inspections of commercial vehicles and when signs are displayed requiring the stop. Every driver who fails or refuses to stop and submit the vehicle to an inspection when signs are displayed requiring that stop is guilty of a misdemeanor.

2813.5. Commercial Vehicle: Inspection Stickers

(a) The commissioner shall have exclusive authority in the issuance of stickers as evidence that commercial vehicles have been inspected pursuant to Section 2813 and have been found to be in compliance with minimum safety standards established by the department. The commissioner may make and enforce regulations with respect to the issuance and display of the stickers upon commercial vehicles.

(b) It is unlawful for any unauthorized person, company, corporation, or public or private entity to possess, issue, or display upon a vehicle an unauthorized commercial vehicle safety inspection sticker or a sticker that is either a facsimile of, or is substantially similar to, that issued by the commissioner.

(c) Any violation of subdivision (b) is a misdemeanor. *(AM '04)*

2814.1. Combined Vehicle Inspection and Sobriety Checkpoints; Counties May Establish

(a) A board of supervisors of a county may, by ordinance, establish, on highways under its jurisdiction, a vehicle inspection checkpoint program to check for violations of Sections 27153 and 27153.5. The program shall be conducted by the local agency or department with the primary responsibility for traffic law enforcement.

(b) A driver of a motor vehicle shall stop and submit to an inspection conducted under subdivision (a) when signs and displays are posted requiring that stop.

(c) A county that elects to conduct the program described under subdivision (a) may fund that program through fine proceeds deposited with the county under Section 1463.15 of the Penal Code.

(d) State and local law enforcement agencies shall not conduct motorcycle only checkpoints. *(AM '12)*

2814.2. Sobriety Checkpoint Inspection – Stop Required; Removal of Vehicle

(a) A driver of a motor vehicle shall stop and submit to a sobriety checkpoint inspection conducted by a law enforcement agency when signs and displays are posted requiring that stop.

(b) Notwithstanding Section 14602.6 or 14607.6, a peace officer or any other authorized person shall not cause the impoundment of a vehicle at a sobriety checkpoint if the driver's only offense is a violation of Section 12500.

(c) During the conduct of a sobriety checkpoint, if the law enforcement officer encounters a driver who is in violation of Section 12500, the law enforcement officer shall make a reasonable attempt to identify the registered owner of the vehicle. If the registered owner is present, or the officer is able to identify the registered owner and obtain the registered owner's authorization to release the motor vehicle to a licensed driver by the end of the checkpoint, the vehicle shall be released to either the registered owner of the vehicle if he or she is a licensed driver or to the licensed driver authorized by the registered owner of the vehicle. If a notice to appear is issued, the name and driver's license number of the licensed driver to whom the vehicle was released pursuant to this subdivision shall be listed on the officer's copy of the notice to appear issued to the unlicensed driver. When a vehicle cannot be released, the vehicle shall be removed pursuant to subdivision (p) of Section 22651, whether a notice to appear has been issued or not. *(AD '11)*

2815. Disregard of Nonstudent Crossing Guard

Any person who shall disregard any traffic signal or direction given by a nonstudent school crossing guard, appointed pursuant to Section 21100, or authorized by any city police department, any board of supervisors of a county, or the CHP, when the guard is wearing the official insignia of such a school crossing guard, and when in the course of the guard's duties the guard is protecting any person in crossing a street or highway in the vicinity of a school or while returning thereafter to a place of safety, shall be guilty of an infraction and subject to the penalties provided in Section 42001.1.

2816. Discharge of Children from Youth Bus

It is unlawful to load or discharge children onto or from a youth bus upon a highway at any location where the children must cross the highway upon which the youth bus is stopped, unless traffic is controlled by a traffic officer or an official traffic control signal.

2817. Disregard of Peace Officer: Funeral Procession

Any person who disregards any traffic signal or direction given by a peace officer authorized pursuant to subdivision (d) of Section 70 of the Penal Code to escort funeral processions, if the peace officer is in a peace officer's uniform, and is in the process of escorting a funeral procession, shall be guilty of an infraction and subject to the penalties provided in subdivision (a) of Section 42001.

2818. Crossing Flare or Cone Patterns

It is unlawful to traverse an electronic beacon pattern, a flare pattern, cone pattern, or combination of electronic beacon, flare, or cone patterns, provided for the regulation of traffic, or provided in a situation where public safety personnel are engaged in traffic control or emergency scene management. *(AM '08)*

DIVISION 3. REGISTRATION OF VEHICLES AND CERTIFICATES OF TITLE

CHAPTER 1. ORIGINAL & RENEWAL REGISTRATION

4000. Registration Required

(a)(1) A person shall not drive, move, or leave standing upon a highway, or in an offstreet public parking facility, any motor vehicle, trailer, semitrailer, pole or pipe dolly, or logging dolly, unless it is registered and the appropriate fees have been paid under this code or registered under the permanent trailer identification program, except that an off-highway motor vehicle which displays an identification plate or device issued by the department pursuant to Section 38010 may be driven, moved, or left standing in an offstreet public parking facility without being registered or paying registration fees.

(2) For purposes of this subdivision, offstreet public parking facility means either of the following:

(A) Any publicly owned parking facility.

(B) Any privately owned parking facility for which no fee for the privilege to park is charged and which is held open for the common public use of retail customers.

(3) This subdivision does not apply to any motor vehicle stored in a privately owned offstreet parking facility by, or with the express permission of, the owner of the privately owned offstreet parking facility.

(4) Beginning July 1, 2011, the enforcement of paragraph (1) shall commence on the first day of the second month following the month of expiration of the vehicles registration. This paragraph shall become inoperative on January 1, 2012.

(b) No person shall drive, move, or leave standing upon a highway any motor vehicle, as defined in Chapter 2 (commencing with Section 39010) of Part 1 of Division 26 of the Health and Safety Code, which has been registered in violation of Part 5 (commencing with Section 43000) of that Division 26.

(c) Subdivisions (a) and (b) do not apply to off-highway motor vehicles operated pursuant to Sections 38025 and 38026.5.

(d) This section does not apply, following payment of fees due for registration, during the time that registration and transfer is being withheld by the department pending the investigation of any use tax due under the Revenue and Taxation Code.

(e) Subdivision (a) does not apply to a vehicle that is towed by a tow truck on the order of a sheriff, marshal, or other official acting pursuant to a court order or on the order of a peace officer acting pursuant to this code.

(f) Subdivision (a) applies to a vehicle that is towed from a highway or offstreet parking facility under the direction of a highway service organization when that organization is providing emergency roadside assistance to that vehicle. However, the operator of a tow truck providing that assistance to that vehicle is not responsible for the violation of subdivision (a) with respect to that vehicle. The owner of an unregistered vehicle that is disabled and located on private property, shall obtain a permit from the department pursuant to Section 4003 prior to having the vehicle towed on the highway.

(g) For purposes of this section, possession of a California drivers license by the registered owner of a vehicle shall give rise to a rebuttable presumption that the owner is a resident of California. *(AM '11)*

4000.38. Suspension, Revocation or Cancellation of Registration by DMV

(a) The department shall suspend, cancel, or revoke the registration of a vehicle when it determines that any of the following circumstances has occurred:

(1) The registration was obtained by providing false evidence of financial responsibility to the department.

(2) Upon notification by an insurance company that the required coverage has been canceled and a sufficient period of time has elapsed since the cancellation notification, as determined by the department, for replacement coverage to be processed and received by the department.

(3) Evidence of financial responsibility has not been submitted to the department within 30 days of the issuance of a registration certificate for the original registration or transfer of registration of a vehicle.

(b)(1) Prior to suspending, canceling, or revoking the registration of a vehicle, the department shall notify the vehicle owner of its intent to suspend, cancel, or revoke the registration, and shall provide the vehicle owner a reasonable time, not less than 45 days in cases under paragraph (2) of subdivision (a), to provide evidence of financial responsibility or to establish that the vehicle is not being operated.

(2) For the low-cost automobile insurance program established under Section 11629.7 of the Insurance Code, the department shall provide residents with information on the notification document, in plain, boldface type not less than 12 point in size, and in both English and Spanish, stating the following:

"California Low-Cost Auto Insurance: A program offering affordable automobile insurance is available. Visit (insert Internet Web site address provided by the Department of Insurance) or call toll free (insert toll-free telephone number for the California Automobile Assigned Risk Plan or its successor as provided by the Department of Insurance). Qualified applicants must be 19 years of age or older, have a driver's license for the past three years, and meet income eligibility requirements (insert income example provided by Department of Insurance)."

(c)(1) Notwithstanding any other provision of this code, before a registration is reinstated after suspension, cancellation, or revocation, there shall be paid to the department, in addition to any other fees required by this code, a fee sufficient to pay the cost of the reissuance as determined by the department.

(2) Commencing on January 1, 2011, the reissuance fee imposed by paragraph (1) shall not apply to a member of the California National Guard or the United States Armed Forces who was on active duty, serving outside of this state in a military conflict during a time of war, as defined in Section 18 of the Military and Veterans Code, at the time of the suspension, cancellation, or revocation of his or her vehicle registration. The person shall submit a copy of his or her official military orders upon requesting the registration reinstatement. *(AM '11)*

4000.4. Registration Required: Primary Use

(a) Except as provided in Sections 6700, 6702, and 6703, any vehicle which is registered to a nonresident owner, and which is based in Calif. or primarily used on Calif. highways, shall be registered in Calif.

(b) For purposes of this section, a vehicle is deemed to be primarily or regularly used on the highways of this state if the vehicle is located or operated in this state for a greater amount of time than it is located or operated in any other individual state during the registration period in question.

4000.6. Commercial Vehicles with Declared GVW Exceeding 10,000 Pounds

A commercial motor vehicle, singly or in combination, that operates with a declared gross or combined gross vehicle weight that exceeds 10,000 pounds shall be registered pursuant to Section 9400.1.

(a) A person submitting an application for registration of a commercial motor vehicle operated in combination with a semitrailer, trailer, or any combination thereof, shall include the declared combined gross weight of all units when applying for registration with the department, except as exempted under subdivision (a) of Section 9400.1.

(b) This section does not apply to pickups nor to any commercial motor vehicle or combination that does not exceed 10,000 pounds gross vehicle weight.

(c) A peace officer, as defined in Chapter 4.5 (commencing with Section 830) of Title 3 of Part 2 of the Penal Code, having reason to believe that a commercial motor vehicle is being operated, either singly or in combination, in excess of its registered declared gross or combined gross vehicle weight, may require the driver to stop and submit to an inspection or weighing of the vehicle or vehicles and an inspection of registration documents.

(d) A person shall not operate a commercial motor vehicle, either singly or in combination, in excess of its registered declared gross or combined gross vehicle weight.

(e) A violation of this section is an infraction punishable by a fine in an amount equal to the amount specified in Section 42030.1. *(AM '01, '04)*

4000.5. Autoette Registration; Removal from Island

(a) The department shall register an autoette, as defined in Section 175, as a motor vehicle.

(b) The owner of an autoette shall remove the license plates from the vehicle and return them to the department when the autoette is removed from a natural island, as described in Section 175. *(AD '06)*

4004. Foreign Commercial Vehicle - Temporary Operation

(a)(1) Commercial motor vehicles meeting the registration requirements of a foreign jurisdiction, and subject to registration but not entitled to exemption from registration or licensing under any of the provisions of this code or any agreements, arrangements, or declarations made under Article 3 (commencing with Section 8000) of Chapter 4, may, as an alternate to registration, secure a temporary registration to operate in this state for a period of not to exceed 90 days, or a trip permit to operate in this state for a period of four consecutive days.

(2) Each trip permit shall authorize the operation of a single commercial motor vehicle for a period of not more than four consecutive days, commencing with the day of first use and three consecutive days there-

after. Every permit shall identify, as the department may require, the commercial motor vehicle for which it is issued. Each trip permit shall be completed prior to operation of the commercial motor vehicle on any highway in this state and shall be carried in the commercial motor vehicle to which it applies and shall be readily available for inspection by a peace officer. Each permit shall be valid at the time of inspection by a peace officer only if it has been completed as required by the department and has been placed in the appropriate receptacle as required by this section. It is unlawful for any person to fail to comply with the provisions of this section.

(b) The privilege of securing and using a trip permit or a temporary registration not to exceed 90 days shall not extend to a vehicle that is based within this state and is operated by a person having an established place of business within this state. For purposes of this paragraph, a commercial motor vehicle shall be considered to be based in this state if it is primarily operated or dispatched from or principally garaged or serviced or maintained at a site with an address within this state.

(c) Any trailer or semitrailer identified in paragraph (1) of subdivision (a) of Section 5014.1 that enters the state without a currently valid license plate issued by California or another jurisdiction shall be immediately subject to full identification fees as specified in subdivision (e) of Section 5014.1. *(AM '11)*

4004.7. Permit for Unladen Operation of Expired or Terminated Apportioned Commercial Vehicle Registration

(a) If the apportioned registration issued under Article 4 (commencing with Section 8050) of Chapter 4 for a commercial vehicle or vehicle combination that was last registered by a California resident has expired or has been terminated, the department, upon receipt of a completed application, a fee of thirty dollars ($30), and proof of financial responsibility for the vehicle, may issue an unladen operation permit to authorize the unladen operation of that vehicle or vehicle combination for a period of not more than 15 continuous days.

(b) This section does not apply to any vehicle or vehicle combination for which any vehicle registration fees, other than those for the current year, vehicle license fees, or penalties, or any combination of those are due.

(c) Operation of a laden vehicle or vehicle combination under an unladen operation permit issued pursuant to this section is an infraction. *(AD '01)*

4014. Portable Dolly

Any portable or collapsible dolly carried in a tow truck or in a truck used by an automobile dismantler and used upon a highway exclusively for towing disabled vehicles is exempt from registration.

4020. Motorized Bicycles; Exempt From Registration

A motorized bicycle operated upon a highway is exempt from registration.

4022. Repossessed Vehicle

A vehicle repossessed pursuant to the terms of a security agreement is exempt from registration solely for the purpose of transporting the vehicle from the point of repossession to the storage facilities of the repossessor, and from the storage facilities to the legal owner or a licensed motor vehicle auction, provided that the repossessor transports with the vehicle the appropriate documents authorizing the repossession and makes them available to a law enforcement officer on request

4023. Low Speed Vehicle Exempt from Registration

A low-speed vehicle operated pursuant to Section 21115 or 21115.1 is exempt from registration. *(AD '99)*

4152.5. Foreign Vehicle Registration

Except as provided for in subdivision (c) of Section 9553, when California registration is required of a vehicle last registered in a foreign jurisdiction, an application for registration shall be made to the department within 20 days following the date registration became due. The application shall be deemed an original application. *(AM '00)*

4154. Farm Labor Vehicle Registration - Inspection Verification Required

The department may not issue or renew the registration of a farm labor vehicle unless the owner of the vehicle provides verification to the department that the inspection required by Section 31401 has been performed. For these purposes, the department shall determine what constitutes appropriate verification. *(AD '99)*

4159. Notice of Change of Address

Whenever any person after making application for the registration of a vehicle required to be registered under this code, or after obtaining registration either as owner or legal owner, moves or acquires a new address different from the address shown in the application or upon the certificate of ownership or registration card, such person shall, within 10 days thereafter, notify the department of his old and new address.

4160. Change of Address on Card

Any registered owner of a vehicle who moves or acquires a new address different from the address shown upon the registration card issued for the vehicle shall within 10 days mark out the former address shown on the face of the card and with pen and ink write or type the new address on the face of the card immediately below the former address with the initials of the registered owner.

4161. Engine or Motor Change: Distinguishing Vehicle Identification Number

(a) Whenever a motor vehicle engine or motor is installed, except temporarily, in a motor vehicle which is identified on the ownership and registration certificates by motor or engine number or by both the motor and frame numbers and subject to registration under this code, the owner of the motor vehicle shall, within 10 days thereafter, give notice to the department upon a form furnished by it containing a description of the motor vehicle engine or motor installed, including any identifying number thereon and the date of the installation. The owner of the motor vehicle shall also submit to the department with the notice the certificate of ownership and registration card covering the motor vehicle in which the motor vehicle engine or motor is installed and evidence of ownership covering the new or used motor vehicle engine or motor installed and such other documents as may be required by the department.

(b) Upon receipt of motor vehicle engine or motor change notification and other required documents, the department shall assign a distinguishing vehicle identification number to motor vehicles, other than motorcycles or motor-driven cycles registered under a motor number or motor and frame numbers. When the distinguishing vehicle identification number is placed on the vehicle as authorized, the vehicle shall thereafter be identified by the distinguishing identification number assigned.

(c) Notwithstanding any other provision of this section or any other provision of law, whenever an application is made to the department to register a replacement engine case for any motorcycle, the department shall request the Department of the California Highway Patrol to inspect the motorcycle to determine its proper identity. If the replacement engine case bears the same identifying numbers as the engine case being replaced, the original engine case shall be destroyed. A determination verifying proof of destruction shall be made by the Department of the California Highway Patrol. *(AM '01)*

4301. Surrender of Plates and Documents

The applicant shall surrender to the department all unexpired license plates, seals, certificates, or other evidence of foreign registration as may be in his possession or under his control. The department may require a certification from the jurisdiction of last registry when the applicant fails to surrender the last issued unexpired license plates.

4454. Registration Card Kept With Vehicle

(a) Every owner, upon receipt of a registration card, shall maintain the same or a facsimile copy thereof with the vehicle for which issued.

(b) This section does not apply when a registration card is necessarily removed from the vehicle for the purpose of application for renewal or transfer of registration, or when the vehicle is left unattended.

(c) Any violation of this section shall be cited in accordance with the provisions of Section 40610. *(AM '99)*

Asterisks (***) Denote Text Deleted By Legislation

4455. Display of Foreign Commercial Vehicle Permit
Any permit issued under Section 4004 shall be carried in the vehicle for which issued at all times while it is being operated in this State.

4456. Numbered Report-of-Sale Forms Required; Contents
(a) When selling a vehicle, dealers and lessor-retailers shall use numbered report-of-sale forms issued by the department. The forms shall be used in accordance with the following terms and conditions:

(1) The dealer or lessor-retailer shall attach for display a copy of the report of sale on the vehicle before the vehicle is delivered to the purchaser.

(2) The dealer or lessor-retailer shall submit to the department an application accompanied by all fees and penalties due for registration or transfer of registration of the vehicle within 30 days from the date of sale, as provided in subdivision (c) of Section 9553, if the vehicle is a used vehicle, and 20 days if the vehicle is a new vehicle. Penalties due for noncompliance with this paragraph shall be paid by the dealer or lessor-retailer. The dealer or lessor-retailer shall not charge the purchaser for the penalties.

(3) As part of an application to transfer registration of a used vehicle, the dealer or lessor-retailer shall include all of the following information on the certificate of title, application for a duplicate certificate of title, or form prescribed by the department:

(A) Date of sale and report of sale number.

(B) Purchaser's name and address.

(C) Dealer's name, address, number, and signature or signature of authorized agent.

(D) Salesperson number.

(4) If the department returns an application and the application was first received by the department within 30 days of the date of sale of the vehicle if the vehicle is a used vehicle, and 20 days if the vehicle is a new vehicle, the dealer or lessor-retailer shall submit a corrected application to the department within 50 days from the date of sale of the vehicle if the vehicle is a used vehicle, and 40 days if the vehicle is a new vehicle, or within 30 days from the date that the application is first returned by the department if the vehicle is a used vehicle, and 20 days if the vehicle is a new vehicle, whichever is later.

(5) If the department returns an application and the application was first received by the department more than 30 days from the date of sale of the vehicle if the vehicle is a used vehicle, and 20 days if the vehicle is a new vehicle, the dealer or lessor-retailer shall submit a corrected application to the department within 50 days from the date of sale of the vehicle if the vehicle is a used vehicle, and 40 days if the vehicle is a new vehicle.

(6) An application first received by the department more than 50 days from the date of sale of the vehicle if the vehicle is a used vehicle, and 40 days if the vehicle is a new vehicle, is subject to the penalties specified in subdivisions (a) and (b) of Section 4456.1.

(7) The dealer or lessor-retailer shall report the sale pursuant to Section 5901.

(b)(1) A transfer that takes place through a dealer conducting a wholesale vehicle auction shall be reported to the department by that dealer on a single form approved by the department. The completed form shall contain, at a minimum, all of the following information:

(A) The name and address of the seller.

(B) The seller's dealer number, if applicable.

(C) The date of delivery to the dealer conducting the auction.

(D) The actual mileage of the vehicle as indicated by the vehicle's odometer at the time of delivery to the dealer conducting the auction.

(E) The name, address, and occupational license number of the dealer conducting the auction.

(F) The name, address, and occupational license number of the buyer.

(G) The signature of the dealer conducting the auction.

(2) Submission of the completed form specified in paragraph (1) to the department shall fully satisfy the requirements of subdivision (a) and subdivision (a) of Section 5901 with respect to the dealer selling at auction and the dealer conducting the auction.

(3) The single form required by this subdivision does not relieve a dealer of any obligation or responsibility that is required by any other provision of law.

(c) A vehicle displaying a copy of the report of sale may be operated without license plates or registration card until either of the following, whichever occurs first:

(1) The license plates and registration card are received by the purchaser.

(2) A 90-day period, commencing with the date of sale of the vehicle, has expired.

(d) This section shall become operative on July 1, 2012. *(AD '11)*

4457. Stolen, Lost, or Damaged Cards and Plates

If any registration card or license plate is stolen, lost, mutilated, or illegible, the owner of the vehicle for which the same was issued, as shown by the records of the department, shall immediately make application for and may, upon the applicant furnishing information satisfactory to the department, obtain a duplicate or a substitute or a new registration under a new registration number, as determined to be most advisable by the department. An application for a duplicate registration card is not required in conjunction with any other application.

4458. Both Plates Lost or Stolen

If both license plates or a permanent trailer identification plate are lost or stolen, the registered owner shall immediately notify a law enforcement agency, and shall immediately apply to the department for new plates in lieu of the plates stolen or lost. The department shall in every proper case, except in the case of plates which are exempt from fees, cause to be issued applicable license plates of a different number and assign the registration number to the vehicle for which the plates are issued. *(AM '01)*

4459. Stolen, Lost, or Damaged Certificate

If any certificate of ownership is stolen, lost, mutilated or illegible, the legal owner or, if none, then the owner of the vehicle for which the same was issued as shown by the records of the department shall immediately make application for and may, upon the applicant furnishing information satisfactory to the department, obtain a duplicate.

4460. Seizure of Documents and Plates

(a) The Department of Motor Vehicles, the Traffic Adjudication Board, and the Department of the California Highway Patrol, any regularly employed and salaried police officer or deputy sheriff or any reserve police officer or reserve deputy sheriff listed in Section 830.6 of the Penal Code may take possession of any certificate, card, placard, permit, license, or license plate issued under this code, upon expiration, revocation, cancellation, or suspension thereof or which is fictitious or which has been unlawfully or erroneously issued. Any license plate which is not attached to the vehicle for which issued, when and in the manner required under this code, may be seized, and attachment to the proper vehicle may be made or required.

(b) Any document, placard, or license plate seized shall be delivered to the Department of Motor Vehicles. *(AM '03)*

4461. Unlawful Use of Evidences of Registration or Placards

(a) A person shall not lend a certificate of ownership, registration card, license plate, special plate, validation tab, or permit issued to him or her if the person desiring to borrow it would not be entitled to its use, and a person shall not knowingly permit its use by one not entitled to it.

(b) A person to whom a disabled person placard has been issued shall not lend the placard to another person, and a disabled person shall not knowingly permit the use for parking purposes of the placard or identification license plate issued pursuant to Section 5007 by one not entitled to it. A person to whom a disabled person placard has been issued may permit another person to use the placard only while in the presence or reasonable proximity of the disabled person for the purpose of transporting the disabled person. A violation of this subdivision is subject to the issuance of a notice of parking violation imposing a civil penalty of not less than two hundred fifty dollars ($250) and not more than one thousand dollars ($1,000), for which enforcement shall be governed by the procedures set forth in Article 3 (commencing with Section 40200) of Chapter 1 of Division 17 or is a misdemeanor punishable by a fine of not less than two hundred fifty dollars

($250) and not more than one thousand dollars ($1,000), imprisonment in the county jail for not more than six months, or both that fine and imprisonment.

(c) Except for the purpose of transporting a disabled person as specified in subdivision (b), a person shall not display a disabled person placard that was not issued to him or her or that has been canceled or revoked pursuant to Section 22511.6. A violation of this subdivision is subject to the issuance of a notice of parking violation imposing a civil penalty of not less than two hundred fifty dollars ($250) and not more than one thousand dollars ($1,000), for which enforcement shall be governed by the procedures set forth in Article 3 (commencing with Section 40200) of Chapter 1 of Division 17 or is a misdemeanor punishable by a fine of not less than two hundred fifty dollars ($250) and not more than one thousand dollars ($1,000), imprisonment in the county jail for not more than six months, or both that fine and imprisonment.

(d) Notwithstanding subdivisions (a), (b), and (c), a person using a vehicle displaying a special identification license plate issued to another pursuant to Section 5007 shall not park in those parking stalls or spaces designated for disabled persons pursuant to Section 22511.7 or 22511.8, unless transporting a disabled person. A violation of this subdivision is subject to the issuance of a notice of parking violation imposing a civil penalty of not less than two hundred fifty dollars ($250) and not more than one thousand dollars ($1,000), for which enforcement shall be governed by the procedures set forth in Article 3 (commencing with Section 40200) of Chapter 1 of Division 17 or is a misdemeanor punishable by a fine of not less than two hundred fifty dollars ($250) and not more than one thousand dollars ($1,000), imprisonment in the county jail for not more than six months, or both that fine and imprisonment.

(e) For the purposes of subdivisions (b) and (c), "disabled person placard" means a placard issued pursuant to Section 22511.55 or 22511.59. *(AM '00, '09)*

4462. Presentation of Evidence of Registration

(a) The driver of a motor vehicle shall present the registration or identification card or other evidence of registration of any or all vehicles under his or her immediate control for examination upon demand of any peace officer.

(b) No person shall display upon a vehicle, nor present to any peace officer, any registration card, identification card, temporary receipt, license plate, device issued pursuant to Section 4853, or permit not issued for that vehicle or not otherwise lawfully used thereon under this code. (c) This section shall become operative on January 1, 2001.

4462.5. Unlawful Display of Evidence of Registration

Every person who commits a violation of subdivision (b) of Section 4462, with intent to avoid compliance with vehicle registration requirements of Article 1 of Chapter 1 or Article 1 of Chapter 2, is guilty of a misdemeanor.

4463. False Evidences of Registration or Permits

(a) A person who, with intent to prejudice, damage, or defraud, commits any of the following acts is guilty of a felony and upon conviction thereof shall be punished by imprisonment pursuant to subdivision (h) of Section 1170 of the Penal Code for 16 months or two or three years, or by imprisonment in a county jail for not more than one year:

(1) Alters, forges, counterfeits, or falsifies a certificate of ownership, registration card, certificate, license, license plate, device issued pursuant to Section 4853, special plate, or permit provided for by this code or a comparable certificate of ownership, registration card, certificate, license, license plate, device comparable to that issued pursuant to Section 4853, special plate, or permit provided for by a foreign jurisdiction, or alters, forges, counterfeits, or falsifies the document, device, or plate with intent to represent it as issued by the department, or alters, forges, counterfeits, or falsifies with fraudulent intent an endorsement of transfer on a certificate of ownership or other document evidencing ownership, or with fraudulent intent displays or causes or permits to be displayed or have in his or her possession a blank, incomplete, canceled, suspended, revoked, altered, forged, counterfeit, or false certificate of ownership, registration card, certificate, license, license plate, device issued pursuant to Section 4853, special plate, or permit.

(2) Utters, publishes, passes, or attempts to pass, as true and genuine, a false, altered, forged, or counter-feited matter listed in paragraph (1) knowing it to be false, altered, forged, or counterfeited.

(b) A person who, with intent to prejudice, damage, or defraud, commits any of the following acts is guilty of a misdemeanor, and upon conviction thereof shall be punished by imprisonment in a county jail for six months, a fine of not less than five hundred dollars ($500) and not more than one thousand dollars ($1,000), or both that fine and imprisonment, which penalty shall not be suspended:

(1) Forges, counterfeits, or falsifies a disabled person placard or a comparable placard relating to park-ing privileges for disabled persons provided for by a foreign jurisdiction, or forges, counterfeits, or falsifies a disabled person placard with intent to represent it as issued by the department.

(2) Passes, or attempts to pass, as true and genuine, a false, forged, or counterfeit disabled person plac-ard knowing it to be false, forged, or counterfeited.

(3) Acquires, possesses, sells, or offers for sale a genuine or counterfeit disabled person placard.

(c) A person who, with fraudulent intent, displays or causes or permits to be displayed a forged, counter-feit, or false disabled person placard, is subject to the issuance of a notice of parking violation imposing a civil penalty of not less than two hundred fifty dollars ($250) and not more than one thousand dollars ($1,000), for which enforcement shall be governed by the procedures set forth in Article 3 (commencing with Section 40200) of Chapter 1 of Division 17 or is guilty of a misdemeanor punishable by imprison-ment in a county jail for six months, a fine of not less than two hundred fifty dollars ($250) and not more than one thousand dollars ($1,000), or both that fine and imprisonment, which penalty shall not be suspended.

(d) For purposes of subdivision (b) or (c), "disabled person placard"means a placard issued pursuant to Section 22511.55 or 22511.59.

(e) A person who, with intent to prejudice, damage, or defraud, commits any of the following acts is guilty of an infraction, and upon conviction thereof shall be punished by a fine of not less than one hun-dred dollars ($100) and not more than two hundred fifty dollars ($250) for a first offense, not less than two hundred fifty dollars ($250) and not more than five hundred dollars ($500) for a second offense, and not less than five hundred dollars ($500) and not more than one thousand dollars ($1,000) for a third or subsequent offense, which penalty shall not be suspended:

(1) Forges, counterfeits, or falsifies a Clean Air Sticker or a comparable clean air sticker relating to high occupancy vehicle lane privileges provided for by a foreign jurisdiction, or forges, counterfeits, or falsifies a Clean Air Sticker with intent to represent it as issued by the department.

(2) Passes, or attempts to pass, as true and genuine, a false, forged, or counterfeit Clean Air Sticker knowing it to be false, forged, or counterfeited.

(3) Acquires, possesses, sells, or offers for sale a counterfeit Clean Air Sticker.

(4) Acquires, possesses, sells, or offers for sale a genuine Clean Air Sticker separate from the vehicle for which the department issued that sticker.

(f) As used in this section, "Clean Air Sticker"means a label or decal issued pursuant to Sections 5205.5 and 21655.9. *(AM '11)*

4463.5. Facsimile License Plates

(a) No person shall manufacture or sell a decorative or facsimile license plate of a size substantially simi-lar to the license plate issued by the department.

(b) Notwithstanding subdivision (a), the director may authorize the manufacture and sale of decorative or facsimile license plates for special events or media productions.

(c) A violation of this section is a misdemeanor punishable by a fine of not less than five hundred dollars ($500).

4464. Altered license Plates

A person shall not display upon a vehicle a license plate that is altered from its original markings. *(AM '12)*

5004. Vehicles of Historic Value

(a) Notwithstanding any other provision of this code, any owner of a vehicle described in paragraph (1), (2), or (3) which is operated or moved over the highway primarily for the purpose of historical exhibition or other similar purpose shall, upon application in the manner and at the time prescribed by the department, be issued special identification plates for the vehicle:

(1) A motor vehicle with an engine of 16 or more cylinders manufactured prior to 1965.

(2) A motor vehicle manufactured in the year 1922 or prior thereto.

(3) A vehicle which was manufactured after 1922, is at least 25 years old, and is of historic interest.

(b) The special identification plates assigned to motor vehicles with an engine of 16 or more cylinders manufactured prior to 1965 and to any motor vehicle manufactured in the year 1922 and prior thereto shall run in a separate numerical series, commencing with "Horseless Carriage No. 1".

The special identification plates assigned to vehicles specified in paragraph (3) of subdivision (a) shall run in a separate numerical series, commencing with "Historical Vehicle No. 1".

Each series of plates shall have different and distinguishing colors.

(c) A fee of twenty-five dollars ($25) shall be charged for the initial issuance of the special identification plates. Such plates shall be permanent and shall not be required to be replaced. If such special identification plates become damaged or unserviceable in any manner, replacement for the plates may be obtained from the department upon proper application and upon payment of such fee as is provided for in Section 9265.

(d) All funds received by the department in payment for such identification plates or the replacement thereof shall be deposited in the California Environmental License Plate Fund.

(e) These vehicles shall not be exempt from the equipment provisions of Sections 26709, 27150, and 27600.

(f) As used in this section, a vehicle is of historic interest if it is collected, restored, maintained, and operated by a collector or hobbyist principally for purposes of exhibition and historic vehicle club activities.

5011. Identification Plate

Every piece of special construction equipment, special mobile equipment, cemetery equipment, trailer, semitrailer, and every logging vehicle shall display an identification plate issued pursuant to Section 5014 or 5014.1. *(AM '01)*

5011.5. Identification Plate: Charter Limousines

Every limousine operated by a charter-party carrier, as defined by Section 5371.4 of the Public Utilities Code, shall display a special identification license plate issued pursuant to Section 5385.6 of that code.

This section shall become operative on July 1, 1995. *(AM '04)*

5017. Display of Identification Plates; Carrying of Identification Card

(a) Each identification plate issued under Section 5016 shall bear a distinctive number to identify the equipment, logging vehicle, trailer, semitrailer, or implement of husbandry for which it is issued. The owner, upon being issued a plate, shall attach it to the equipment, logging vehicle, trailer, semitrailer, or implement of husbandry for which it is issued and shall carry the identification certificate issued by the department as provided by Section 4454. It shall be unlawful for any person to attach or use the plate upon any other equipment, logging vehicle, trailer, semitrailer, or implement of husbandry. If the equipment, logging vehicle, trailer, semitrailer, or implement of husbandry is destroyed or the ownership thereof transferred to another person, the person to whom the plate was issued shall, within 10 days, notify the department, on a form approved by the department, that the equipment, logging vehicle, trailer, semitrailer, or implement of husbandry has been destroyed or the ownership thereof transferred to another person.

(b) Upon the implementation of the permanent trailer identification plate program, all trailers except those exempted in paragraph (1) and (3) of subdivision (a) of Section 5014.1 may be assigned a single permanent plate for identification purposes. Upon issuance of the plate, it shall be attached to the vehicle pursuant to Sections 5200 and 5201.

(c) An identification certificate shall be issued for each trailer or semitrailer assigned an identification plate. The identification certificate shall contain upon its face, the date issued, the name and residence or business address of the registered owner or lessee and of the legal owner, if any, the vehicle identification number assigned to the trailer or semitrailer, and a description of the trailer or semitrailer as complete as that required in the application for registration of the trailer or semitrailer. For those trailers registered under Article 4 (commencing with Section 8050) of Chapter 4 on the effective date of the act adding this sentence that are being converted to the permanent trailer identification program, the identification card may contain only the name of the registrant, and the legal owner's name is not required to be shown. Upon transfer of those trailers, the identification card shall contain the name of the owner and legal owner, if any. When an identification certificate has been issued to a trailer or semitrailer, the owner or operator shall make that certificate available for inspection by a peace officer upon request.

(d) The application for transfer of ownership of a vehicle with a trailer plate or permanent trailer identification plate shall be made within 10 days of sale of the vehicle. The permanent trailer identification certificate is not a certificate of ownership as described in Section 38076. *(AM '02)*

5030. Special License Plate
A motorized bicycle, as defined in Section 406, is required to display a special license plate issued by the department.

5037. License Plate Required
(a) No motorized bicycle first sold on or after July 1, 1981, shall be moved or operated upon a highway unless the owner first makes application for a license plate and, when received, attaches it to the motorized bicycle as provided in this article.

(b) Motorized bicycles first sold prior to July 1, 1981, shall not be moved or operated upon a highway after January 1 1982, unless the owner makes application for a license plate and, when received, attaches it to the motorized bicycle as provided in this article.

(c) Any motorized bicycle currently licensed pursuant to Division 16.7 on July 1, 1981, may be operated upon a highway until July 1,1982.

5109. Transfer or Retention of Plates
When any person who has been issued environmental license plates sells, trades, or otherwise releases ownership of the vehicle upon which the personalized license plates have been displayed, such person shall immediately report the transfer of such plates to an acquired passenger vehicle, commercial vehicle, or trailer pursuant to Section 5108, unless such person determines to retain the plates pursuant to subdivision (c) of Section 5106.

5200. Display of License Plates
(a) When two license plates are issued by the department for use upon a vehicle, they shall be attached to the vehicle for which they were issued, one in the front and the other in the rear.

(b) When only one license plate is issued for use upon a vehicle, it shall be attached to the rear thereof, unless the license plate is issued for use upon a truck tractor, in which case the license plate shall be displayed in accordance with Section 4850.5. *(AM '03)*

5201. Positioning of Plates
(a) License plates shall at all times be securely fastened to the vehicle for which they are issued so as to prevent the plates from swinging, shall be mounted in a position so as to be clearly visible, and so that the characters are upright and display from left to right, and shall be maintained in a condition so as to be clearly legible. The rear license plate shall be mounted not less than 12 inches nor more than 60 inches from the ground, and the front license plate shall be mounted not more than 60 inches from the ground, except as follows:

(1) The rear license plate on a tow truck or repossessor's tow vehicle may be mounted on the left-hand side of the mast assembly at the rear of the cab of the vehicle, not less than 12 inches nor more than 90 inches from the ground.

(2) The rear license plate on a tank vehicle hauling hazardous waste, as defined in Section 25117 of the Health and Safety Code, or asphalt material may be mounted not less than 12 inches nor more than 90 inches from the ground.

(3) The rear license plate on a truck tractor may be mounted at the rear of the cab of the vehicle, but not less than 12 inches nor more than 90 inches from the ground.

(4) The rear license plate of a vehicle designed by the manufacturer for the collection and transportation of garbage, rubbish, or refuse that is used regularly for the collection and transportation of that material by a person or governmental entity employed to collect, transport, and dispose of garbage, rubbish, or refuse may be mounted not less than 12 inches nor more than 90 inches from the ground.

(5) The rear license plate on a two-axle livestock trailer may be mounted 12 inches or more, but not more than 90 inches, from the ground.

(6)(A) The rear license plate on a dump bed motortruck equipped with a trailing, load bearing swing axle shall be mounted more than 12 inches, but not more than 107 inches, from the ground.

(B) As used in this section, a trailing, load bearing swing axle is an axle which can be moved from a raised position to a position behind the vehicle that allows for the transfer of a portion of the weight of the vehicle and load to the trailing axle.

(b) A covering shall not be used on license plates except as follows:

(1) The installation of a cover over a lawfully parked vehicle to protect it from the weather and the elements does not constitute a violation of this subdivision. A peace officer or other regularly salaried employee of a public agency designated to enforce laws, including local ordinances, relating to the parking of vehicles may temporarily remove so much of the cover as is necessary to inspect any license plate, tab, or indicia of registration on a vehicle.

(2) The installation of a license plate security cover is not a violation of this subdivision if the device does not obstruct or impair the recognition of the license plate information, including, but not limited to, the issuing state, license plate number, and registration tabs, and the cover is limited to the area directly over the top of the registration tabs. No portion of a license plate security cover shall rest over the license plate number.

(c) A casing, shield, frame, border, product, or other device that obstructs or impairs the reading or recognition of a license plate by an electronic device operated by state or local law enforcement, an electronic device operated in connection with a toll road, high-occupancy toll lane, toll bridge, or other toll facility, or a remote emission sensing device, as specified in Sections 44081 and 44081.6 of the Health and Safety Code, shall not be installed on, or affixed to, a vehicle.

(d)(1) It is the intent of the Legislature that an accommodation be made to persons with disabilities and to those persons who regularly transport persons with disabilities, to allow the removal and relocation of wheelchair lifts and wheelchair carriers without the necessity of removing and reattaching the vehicle's rear license plate. Therefore, it is not a violation of this section if the reading or recognition of a rear license plate is obstructed or impaired by a wheelchair lift or wheelchair carrier and all of the following requirements are met:

(A) The owner of the vehicle has been issued a special identification license plate pursuant to Section 5007, or the person using the wheelchair that is carried on the vehicle has been issued a distinguishing placard under Section 22511.55.

(B)(i) The operator of the vehicle displays a decal, designed and issued by the department, that contains the license plate number assigned to the vehicle transporting the wheelchair.

(ii) The decal is displayed on the rear window of the vehicle, in a location determined by the department, in consultation with the Department of the California Highway Patrol, so as to be clearly visible to law enforcement.

(2) Notwithstanding any other law, if a decal is displayed pursuant to this subdivision, the requirements of this code that require the illumination of the license plate and the license plate number do not apply.

(3) The department shall adopt regulations governing the procedures for accepting and approving applications for decals, and issuing decals, authorized by this subdivision.

(4) This subdivision does not apply to a front license plate. *(AM '12)*

5202. Period of Display [Version Op 7-1-12]

(a) A license plate issued by this state or any other jurisdiction within or without the United States shall be attached upon receipt and remain attached during the period of its validity to the vehicle for which it is issued while being operated within this state or during the time the vehicle is being held for sale in this state, or until the time that a vehicle with special or identification plates is no longer entitled to those plates; and a person shall not operate, and an owner shall not knowingly permit to be operated, upon any highway, a vehicle unless the license plate is so attached. A special permit issued in lieu of plates shall be attached and displayed on the vehicle for which the permit was issued during the period of the permit's validity.

(b) This section shall become operative on July 1, 2012. *(AD '11)*

5204. Tabs

(a) Except as provided by subdivisions (b) and (c), a tab shall indicate the year of expiration and a tab shall indicate the month of expiration. Current month and year tabs shall be attached to the rear license plate assigned to the vehicle for the last preceding registration year in which license plates were issued, and, when so attached, the license plate with the tabs shall, for the purposes of this code, be deemed to be the license plate, except that truck tractors, and commercial motor vehicles having a declared gross vehicle weight of 10,001 pounds or more, shall display the current month and year tabs upon the front license plate assigned to the truck tractor or commercial motor vehicle. Vehicles that fail to display current month and year tabs or display expired tabs are in violation of this section.

(b) The requirement of subdivision (a) that the tabs indicate the year and the month of expiration does not apply to fleet vehicles subject to Article 9.5 (commencing with Section 5300) or vehicles defined in Section 468.

(c) Subdivision (a) does not apply when proper application for registration has been made pursuant to Section 4602 and the new indicia of current registration have not been received from the department.

(d) This section is enforceable against any motor vehicle that is driven, moved, or left standing upon a highway, or in an offstreet public parking facility, in the same manner as provided in subdivision (a) of Section 4000. *(AM '00)*

5206. Quarterly Certificates or Insignia

Vehicles for which weight fees are paid on a partial year basis shall display a certificate or insignia issued by the department, which shall state the end of the period for which the vehicle is licensed.

5302. Fleet Eligibility

(a) Motor vehicles registered in any state other than California shall not be permitted to participate in this program.

(b) Section 4604 does not apply to vehicles registered under this article.

(c) The department may conduct an audit of the records of each fleet owner or lessee of the vehicle fleets electing to participate in the program. The department shall be fully reimbursed by the fleet owner or lessee for the costs of conducting the audits.

(d) Vehicles registered under this article shall display in a conspicuous place on both the right and the left side of each motor vehicle the name, trademark, or logo of the company. The display of the name, trademark, or logo shall be in letters in sharp contrast to the background and shall be of a size, shape, and color that is readily legible during daylight hours from a distance of 50 feet.

(e) A motor vehicle under 6,000 pounds unladen weight that is owned or leased by a public utility may be registered under this article by displaying the permanent fleet registration number on both the right and left side or on the front and rear of the motor vehicle. The display shall be in sharp contrast to the background and shall be of a size, shape, and color that is readily legible during daylight hours from a distance of 50 feet. *(AM '00)*

5352. Registration
Subject to the exemptions stated in Section 5353, registration of any trailer coach in this state is required annually.

5500. Delivery of Evidence of Registration Before Disassembly: Penalties
(a) Any person, other than a licensed dismantler, desiring to disassemble a vehicle of a type required to be registered under this code, either partially or totally, with the intent to use as parts only, to reduce to scrap, or to construct another vehicle shall deliver to the department the certificate of ownership, the registration card, and the license plates last issued to the vehicle before dismantling may begin.

(b) Any person who is convicted of violating subdivision (a) shall be punished upon a first conviction by imprisonment in the county jail for not less than five days or more than six months, or by a fine of not less than fifty dollars ($50) or more than five hundred dollars ($500), or by both that fine and imprisonment; and, upon a second or any subsequent conviction, by imprisonment in the county jail for not less than 30 days or more than one year, or by a fine of not less than two hundred fifty Dollars ($250) or more than one thousand dollars ($1,000), or by both that fine and imprisonment.

5506. Sale by Rebuilder – Inspection and Certificate Required
No salvage vehicle rebuilder may resell or transfer ownership of any vehicle that is subject to inspection as provided in Section 5505, unless either a certificate of inspection issued by the Department of the California Highway Patrol, or vehicle verification form completed by an authorized employee of the Department of Motor Vehicles is provided to the buyer upon sale or transfer. Responsibility for compliance with this section shall rest with the salvage vehicle rebuilder selling or transferring the vehicle. This section shall not apply to a salvage vehicle rebuilder who has applied for and received a title in accordance with Section 5505. *(AD '02)*

CHAPTER 2. TRANSFERS OF TITLE OR INTEREST

5900. Notice of Sale or Transfer
(a) Whenever the owner of a vehicle registered under this code sells or transfers his or her title or interest in, and delivers the possession of, the vehicle to another, the owner shall, within five calendar days, notify the department of the sale or transfer giving the date thereof, the name and address of the owner and of the transferee, and the description of the vehicle that is required in the appropriate form provided for that purpose by the department.

(b) Except as otherwise provided in subdivision (c), pursuant to subsection (a) of Section 32705 of Title 49 of the United States Code, the owner shall also notify the department of the actual mileage of the vehicle as indicated by the vehicle's odometer at the time of sale or transfer. However, if the vehicle owner has knowledge that the mileage displayed on the odometer is incorrect, the owner shall indicate on the appropriate form the true mileage, if known, of the vehicle at the time of sale or transfer.

Providing false or inaccurate mileage is not a violation of this subdivision unless it is done with the intent to defraud.

(c) If the registered owner is not in possession of the vehicle that is sold or transferred, the person in physical possession of that vehicle shall give the notice required by subdivisions (a) and (b). If the registered owner sells or transfers the vehicle through a dealer conducting a wholesale motor vehicle auction, the owner shall furnish the information required by subdivisions (a) and (b) to that dealer. *(AM '00)*

5902. Application for Transfer
Whenever any person has received as transferee a properly endorsed certificate of ownership, that person shall, within 10 days thereafter, forward the certificate with the proper transfer fee to the department and thereby make application for a transfer of registration. The certificate of ownership shall contain a space for the applicant's driver's license or identification card number, and the applicant shall furnish that number, if any, in the space provided. *(AM '01)*

CHAPTER 4. PERMITS TO NONRESIDENT OWNERS

6700. Use of Foreign License Plates: Limitation

(a) Except as provided in Section 6700.2, the owner of any vehicle of a type otherwise subject to registration under this code, other than a commercial vehicle registered in a foreign jurisdiction, may operate the vehicle in this state until gainful employment is accepted in this state or until residency is established in this state, whichever occurs first, if the vehicle displays valid license plates and has a valid registration issued to the owner, and the owner was a resident of that state at the time of issuance. Application to register the vehicle shall be made within 20 days after gainful employment is accepted in this state or residency is established in this state.

(b) A nonresident owner of a vehicle, otherwise exempt from registration pursuant to this section or Section 6700.2, may operate or permit operation of the vehicle in this state without registering the vehicle in this state if the vehicle is registered in the place of residence of the owner and displays upon it valid license plates issued by that place. This exemption does not apply if the nonresident owner rents, leases, lends, or otherwise furnishes the vehicle to a California resident for regular use on the highways of this state, as defined in subdivision (b) of Section 4000.4.

(c) Any resident who operates upon a highway of this state a vehicle owned by a nonresident who furnished the vehicle to the resident operator for his or her regular use within this state, as defined in subdivision (b) of Section 4000.4, shall cause the vehicle to be registered in California within 20 days after its first operation within this state by the resident. *(AM '03)*

6700.2. Exemption for Nonresident Daily Commuters

(a) Notwithstanding Section 4000.4, subdivision (a) of Section 6700, or Section 6702, a nonresident daily commuter may operate a motor vehicle on the highways of this state only if all of the following conditions are met:

(1) The motor vehicle is a passenger vehicle or a commercial vehicle of less than 8,001 pounds unladen weight with not more than two axles of the type commonly referred to as a pickup truck.

(2) The motor vehicle is used regularly to transport passengers on the highways of this state principally between, and to and from, the place of residence in a contiguous state and the place of employment in this state by the owner of the motor vehicle and for no other business purpose.

(3) The motor vehicle is not used in the course of a business within this state, including the transportation of property other than incidental personal property between, and to or from, the place of residence in a contiguous state and the place of employment of the motor vehicle owner in this state.

(4) Nothing in paragraphs (2) and (3) prohibits a nonresident daily commuter operating a motor vehicle that displays currently valid external vehicle identification indicia and who possess a corresponding identification card issued pursuant to Section 6700.25 from using that vehicle for other lawful purposes.

(b) The exception to registration of a motor vehicle under the conditions specified in this section does not supersede any other exception to registration under other conditions provided by law.

(c) This section does not apply to a resident of a foreign country. *(AM '01)*

6700.4. Display of Indicia

A nonresident daily commuter indicia shall be displayed in a location on the vehicle which is clearly visible and adjacent to the rear license plate. The corresponding nonresident daily commuter identification card shall be carried at all times in the assigned vehicle and shall he presented to any Calif. peace officer upon demand.

6701. Exemption of Person in Military Service

(a) Any nonresident owner of a vehicle registered in a foreign state who is a member or spouse of a member of the armed forces of the United States on active duty within this state, and any resident owner of a vehicle registered in a foreign state who is a member or spouse of a member of the armed forces of the United States returning from active duty in a foreign state, may operate the vehicle in this state without securing California registration after satisfying all of the following requirements:

(1) The license plates displayed on the vehicle are valid plates issued by a foreign jurisdiction.

(2) The vehicle registration and license plates are issued to the military person or spouse of the military person.

(3) The vehicle registration and license plates were issued by the foreign jurisdiction where the military person was last regularly assigned and stationed for duty by military orders or a jurisdiction claimed by the nonresident military person as the permanent state of residence.

(4) If the vehicle is a motor vehicle, the owner or driver has in force one of the forms of financial responsibility specified in Section 16021.

(b) For purposes of paragraph (3) of subdivision (a), military orders do not include military orders for leave, for temporary duty, or for any other assignment of any nature requiring the military person's presence outside the foreign jurisdiction where the owner was regularly assigned and stationed for duty.

(c) This section applies to all vehicles owned by the military person or spouse except any commercial vehicle used in any business manner wherein the military person or spouse receives compensation.

CHAPTER 5.
REGISTRATION OFFENSES; SUSPENSION, REVOCATION, CANCELLATION

8802. Owner to Return Evidence of Registration
Whenever the department cancels, suspends, or revokes the registration of a vehicle or a certificate of ownership, registration card, or license plates, or any nonresident or other permit, the owner or person in possession shall immediately return the documents, plates, certificates, or other evidence of registration to the department.

8804. Resident Registering Vehicle in Foreign Jurisdiction: Misdemeanor
Every person who, while a resident, as defined in Section 516, of this state, with respect to any vehicle owned by him and operated in this state, registers or renews the registration for the vehicle in a foreign jurisdiction, without the payment of appropriate fees and taxes to this state, is guilty of a misdemeanor.

CHAPTER 6. REGISTRATION AND WEIGHT FEES

9102.5. Privately Owned Schoolbus: Exceptions
(a) In lieu of all other fees which are specified in this code, except fees for duplicate plates, certificates, or cards, a fee of fifteen dollars ($15) shall be paid for the registration and licensing of any privately owned schoolbus, as defined in Section 545, which is either of the following:

(1) Owned by a private nonprofit educational organization and operated in accordance with the rules and regulations of the Department of Education and the Department of the California Highway Patrol exclusively in transporting school pupils, or school pupils and employees, of the private nonprofit educational organization.

(2) Operated in accordance with the rules and regulations of the Department of Education and the Department of the California Highway Patrol exclusively in transporting school pupils, or school pupils and employees, of any public school or private nonprofit educational organization pursuant to a contract between a public school district or nonprofit educational organization and the owner or operator of the schoolbus.

This section does not apply to any schoolbus which is operated pursuant to any contract which requires the public school district or nonprofit educational organization to pay any amount representing the costs of registration and weight fees unless and until the contract is amended to require only the payment of an amount representing the fee required by this section.

(b) When a schoolbus under contract and registered pursuant to subdivision (a) is to be temporarily operated in such a manner that it becomes subject to full registration fees specified in this code, the owner may, prior to that operation, as an alternative to the full registration, secure a temporary permit to operate the vehicle in this state for any one or more calendar months. The permit shall be posted upon the windshield or other prominent place upon the vehicle, and shall identify the vehicle to which it is affixed. When so affixed, the permit shall serve as indicia of full registration for the period designated on the permit. Upon payment of the fees specified in Section 9266.5, the department may issue a temporary permit under this section.

(c) Notwithstanding any other provision, any schoolbus used exclusively to transport students at or below the 12th-grade level to or from any school, for an education-related purpose, or for an activity sponsored by a nonprofit organization shall be deemed to be a schoolbus for the purposes of this section and shall pay a fee of fifteen dollars ($15) in lieu of all other fees which are specified in this code, except fees for duplicate plates, certificates, or cards.

(d) This section does not apply to a schoolbus, operated to transport persons who are developmentally disabled, as defined by the Lanterman Developmental Disabilities Services Act (Division 4.5 (commencing with Section 4500) of the Welfare and Institutions Code), to or from vocational, prevocational, or work training centers sponsored by the State Department of Developmental Services. *(AM '03)*

9400. Weight Fees for Commercial Vehicles

Except as provided in Section 9400.1, and in addition to any other registration fee, there shall be paid the fees set forth in this section for the registration of any commercial motor vehicle that operates with unladen weight. Weight fees for pickup trucks are calculated under this section. Whenever a camper is temporarily attached to a motor vehicle designed to transport property, the motor vehicle shall be subject to the fees imposed by this section. The camper shall be deemed to be a load, and fees imposed by this section upon the motor vehicle shall be based upon the unladen weight of the motor vehicle, exclusive of the camper.

(a) For any electric vehicle designed, used, or maintained as described in this section, fees shall be paid according to the following schedule:

Unladen Weight	Fee
Less than 6,000 lbs.	$ 87
6,000 lbs. or more but less than 10,000 lbs.	266
10,000 lbs. or more	358

(b) For any motor vehicle having not more than two axles and designed, used, or maintained as described in this section, other than an electric vehicle, fees shall be paid according to the following schedule:

Unladen Weight	Fee
Less than 3,000 lbs.	$ 8
3,000 lbs. to and including 4,000 lbs.	24
4,001 lbs. to and including 5,000 lbs.	80
5,001 lbs. to and including 6,000 lbs.	154
6,001 lbs. to and including 7,000 lbs.	204
7,001 lbs. to and including 8,000 lbs.	257
8,001 lbs. to and including 9,000 lbs.	308
9,001 lbs. to and including 10,000 lbs.	360

(c) For any motor vehicle having three or more axles designed, used, or maintained as described in this section, other than an electric vehicle, fees shall be paid according to the following schedule:

Unladen Weight	Fee
2,000 lbs. to and including 3,000 lbs.	$ 43
3,001 lbs. to and including 4,000 lbs.	77
4,001 lbs. to and including 5,000 lbs.	154
5,001 lbs. to and including 6,000 lbs.	231
6,001 lbs. to and including 7,000 lbs.	308
7,001 lbs. to and including 8,000 lbs.	385
8,001 lbs. to and including 9,000 lbs.	462
9,001 lbs. to and including 10,000 lbs.	539

(d) This section is not applicable to any vehicle that is operated or moved over the highway exclusively for the purpose of historical exhibition or other similar noncommercial purpose.

(e) The fee changes effected by this section apply to (1) initial or original registration on or after January 1, 1995, and prior to December 31, 2001, of any commercial vehicle never before registered in this state and (2) to renewal of registration of any commercial vehicle whose registration expires on or after January 1, 1995, and prior to December 31, 2001.

(f) Commercial vehicles, other than those specified in Section 9400.1, with an initial registration or renewal of registration that is due on or after December 31, 2001, are subject to the payment of fees specified in this section. *(AM '01)*

9400.1. Fees; Commercial Motor Vehicles with GVW over 10,000 Pounds

(a)(1) In addition to any other required fee, there shall be paid the fees set forth in this section for the registration of commercial motor vehicles operated either singly or in combination with a declared gross vehicle weight of 10,001 pounds or more. Pickup truck and electric vehicle weight fees are not calculated under this section.

(2) The weight of a vehicle issued an identification plate pursuant to an application under Section 5014, and the weight of an implement of husbandry as defined in Section 36000, shall not be considered when calculating, pursuant to this section, the declared gross vehicle weight of a towing commercial motor vehicle that is owned and operated exclusively by a farmer or an employee of a farmer in the conduct of agricultural operations.

(3) Tow trucks that are utilized to render assistance to the motoring public or to tow or carry impounded vehicles shall pay fees in accordance with this section, except that the fee calculation shall be based only on the gross vehicle weight rating of the towing or carrying vehicle. Upon each initial or transfer application for registration of a tow truck described in this paragraph, the registered owner or lessee or that owner's or lessee's designee, shall certify to the department the gross vehicle weight rating of the tow truck:

Gross Vehicle Weight Range	Fee
10,001-15,000	$ 257
15,001-20,000	353
20,001-26,000	435
26,001-30,000	552
30,001-35,000	648
35,001-40,000	761
40,001-45,000	837
45,001-50,000	948
50,001-54,999	1,039
55,000-60,000	1,173
60,001-65,000	1,282
65,001-70,000	1,398
70,001-75,000	1,650
75,001-80,000	1,700

(b) The fees specified in subdivision (a) apply to both of the following:

(1) An initial or original registration occurring on or after December 31, 2001, to December 30, 2003, inclusive, of a commercial motor vehicle operated either singly or in combination with a declared gross vehicle weight of 10,001 pounds or more.

(2) The renewal of registration of a commercial motor vehicle operated either singly or in combination, with a declared gross vehicle weight of 10,001 pounds or more for which registration expires on or after December 31, 2001, to December 30, 2003, inclusive.

(c)(1) For both an initial or original registration occurring on or after December 31, 2003, of a commercial motor vehicle operated either singly or in combination with a declared gross vehicle weight of 10,001 pounds or more, and the renewal of registration of a commercial motor vehicle operated either singly or in combination, with a declared gross vehicle weight of 10,001 pounds or more for which registration expires on or after December 31, 2003, there shall be paid fees as follows:

Gross Vehicle Weight Range	Weight Code	Fee
10,001-15,000	A	$ 332
15,001-20,000	B	447
20,001-26,000	C	546
26,001-30,000	D	586
30,001-35,000	E	801
35,001-40,000	F	937
40,001-45,000	G	1,028
45,001-50,000	H	1,161
50,001-54,999	I	1,270
55,000-60,000	J	1,431
60,001-65,000	K	1,562
65,001-70,000	L	1,701
70,001-75,000	M	2,004
75,001-80,000	N	2,064

(2) For the purpose of obtaining "revenue neutrality"as described in Sections 1 and 59 of Senate Bill 2084 of the 1999-2000 Regular Session (Chapter 861 of the Statutes of 2000), the Director of Finance shall review the final 2003-04 Statement of Transactions of the State Highway Account. If that review indicates that the actual truck weight fee revenues deposited in the State Highway Account do not total at least seven hundred eighty-nine million dollars ($789,000,000), the Director of Finance shall instruct the department to adjust the schedule set forth in paragraph (1), but not to exceed the following fee amounts:

Gross Vehicle Weight Range	Weight Code	Fee
10,001-15,000	A	$ 354
15,001-20,000	B	482
20,001-26,000	C	591
26,001-30,000	D	746
30,001-35,000	E	874
35,001-40,000	F	1,024
40,001-45,000	G	1,125
45,001-50,000	H	1,272
50,001-54,999	I	1,393
55,000-60,000	J	1,571
60,001-65,000	K	1,716
65,001-70,000	L	1,870
70,001-75,000	M	2,204
75,001-80,000	N	2,271

(d)(1) In addition to the fees set forth in subdivision (a), a Cargo Theft Interdiction Program ***fee of three dollars ($3) shall be paid at the time of initial or original registration or renewal of registration of each motor vehicle subject to weight fees under this section.

(2) This subdivision does not apply to vehicles used or maintained for the transportation of persons for hire, compensation or profit, and tow trucks.

(3) For vehicles registered under Article 4 (commencing with Section 8050) of Chapter 4, the fee imposed under this subdivision shall be apportioned as required for registration fees under that article.

(4) Funds collected pursuant to the Cargo Theft Interdiction Program shall not be proportionately reduced for each month and shall be transferred to the Motor Carriers Safety Improvement Fund.

(e) Notwithstanding Section 42270 or any other provision of law, of the moneys collected by the department under this section, one hundred twenty- two dollars ($122) for each initial, original, and renewal registration shall be reported monthly to the Controller, and at the same time, deposited in the State Treasury to the credit of the Motor Vehicle Account in the State Transportation Fund. All other moneys collected by the department under this section shall be deposited to the credit of the State Highway Account in the State Transportation Fund, or directly to the credit of the Transportation Debt Service Fund as provided in paragraph (2) of subdivision (c) of Section 9400.4, as applicable. One hundred twenty-two dollars ($122) of the fee imposed under this section shall not be proportionately reduced for each month. For vehicles registered under Article 4 (commencing with Section 8050) of Chapter 4, the fee shall be apportioned as required for registration under that article.

(f)(1) The department, in consultation with the Department of the California Highway Patrol, shall design and make available a set of distinctive weight decals that reflect the declared gross combined weight or gross operating weight reported to the department at the time of initial registration, registration renewal, or when a weight change is reported to the department pursuant to Section 9406.1. A new decal shall be issued on each renewal or when the weight is changed pursuant to Section 9406.1. The decal for a tow truck that is subject to this section shall reflect the gross vehicle weight rating or weight code.

(2) The department may charge a fee, not to exceed ten dollars ($10), for the department***'s actual cost of producing and issuing each set of decals issued under paragraph (1).

(3) The weight decal shall be in sharp contrast to the background and shall be of a size, shape, and color that is readily legible during daylight hours from a distance of 50 feet.

(4) Each vehicle subject to this section shall display the weight decal on both the right and left sides of the vehicle.

(5) A person may not display upon a vehicle a decal issued pursuant to this subdivision that does not reflect the declared weight reported to the department.

(6) Notwithstanding subdivision (e) or any other provision of law, the moneys collected by the department under this subdivision shall be deposited in the State Treasury to the credit of the Motor Vehicle Account in the State Transportation Fund.

(7) This subdivision shall apply to vehicles subject to this section at the time of an initial registration, registration renewal, or reported weight change that occurs on or after July 1, 2004.

(8) The following shall apply to vehicles registered under the permanent fleet registration program pursuant to Article 9.5 (commencing with Section 5301) of Chapter 1:

(A) The department, in consultation with the Department of the California Highway Patrol, shall distinguish the weight decals issued to permanent fleet registration vehicles from those issued to other vehicles.

(B) The department shall issue the distinguishable weight decals only to the following:

(i) A permanent fleet registration vehicle that is registered with the department on January 1, 2005.

(ii) On and after January 1, 2005, a vehicle for which the department has an application for initial registration as a permanent fleet registration vehicle.

(iii) On and after January 1, 2005, a permanent fleet registration vehicle that has a weight change pursuant to Section 9406.1.

(C) The weight decal issued under this paragraph shall comply with the applicable provisions of paragraphs (1) to (6), inclusive. *(AM '13)*

9406. Alterations or Additions to Vehicles

Alterations or additions to registered vehicles for which fees have been paid under Section 9400 or 9400.1 placing the vehicles in weight fee classifications under Section 9400 or 9400.1 greater than the weight fees previously paid shall be reported to the department and at the same time the difference between the weight fee previously paid, reduced as provided in Section 9407, and the greater weight fee, reduced as provided in Section 9407, shall be paid to the department upon the operation of the vehicles in the greater weight fee classification under Section 9400 or 9400.1. *(AM '00)*

9406.1. Fees Due Prior to Operation of Vehicle

Prior to operation of a vehicle at a declared gross vehicle weight greater than reported to, and registered by, the department, the owner shall make application to the department and pay all appropriate fees. *(AD '00)*

9554.2. Operation of Vehicle at Greater GVW Than Reported; New Registration Application and Fees Due

Upon the operation of a commercial motor vehicle at a greater gross vehicle weight than had been reported to and registered by the department, a new registration application shall be made to the department. The greater declared gross vehicle weight fee as required in Section 9400.1 and any penalties defined in this code shall be paid to the department. *(AD '00)*

DIVISION 3.5. REGISTRATION AND TRANSFER OF VESSELS

9801. Seizure and Sale; Hearings

(a)(1) When the payment required for the registration or transfer of a vehicle is delinquent pursuant to subdivision (a) of Section 9800, the department may collect the amount of the lien on the vehicle plus costs, not to exceed two hundred fifty dollars ($250), by the filing of a certificate requesting judgment pursuant to Section 9805, or by appropriate civil action and by the seizure and sale of the vehicle or any other vehicle owned by the owner of the unregistered vehicle.

(2) In the case of a leased vehicle, the authority provided in paragraph (1) to seize and sell the vehicle or any other vehicle owned by the owner of that vehicle shall not apply to a lien for any delinquency for which only the lessee is liable pursuant to paragraph (1) of subdivision (a) of Section 10879 of the Revenue and Taxation Code.

(b) At least 10 days before the seizure, notice of the lien and of the intent to seize and sell the vehicle shall be given by the department to the registered and legal owners, and to any other person known to be claiming an interest in the vehicle, by registered mail addressed to those persons at the last known addresses appearing on the records of the department.

(c) Any person receiving the notice of the lien and the intent to seize and sell the vehicle may request a hearing to contest the existence or amount of the lien. If no hearing is requested, the vehicle shall be seized and sold.

(d) If a hearing is requested, 10 days' notice shall be given of the time and place of the hearing, which shall be held within the county of residence of the person requesting the hearing or of the registered owner. The hearing shall be conducted by a referee who shall submit findings and recommendations to the director or his or her authorized representative, who shall decide the matter. The decision shall be effective on notice thereof to the interested parties. However, the director or his or her authorized representative may rescind the decision and reconsider the matter for good cause shown at any time within three years after the date the disputed fee or tax first became due, or within one year from the hearing, whichever is later.

(e) At any time before seizure or sale, any registered owner, legal owner, or person claiming an interest in the vehicle may pay the department the amount of the lien, plus costs. In that event, the seizure or sale shall not be held and the vehicle, if seized, shall be returned by the department to the person entitled to its possession. This payment shall not constitute a waiver of the right to a hearing.

(f) When the department or an authorized agent has reasonable cause to believe that the lien may be jeopardized within the 10-day notice-of-intent period, the vehicle may be seized without prior notice to the registered or legal owner, upon obtaining authorization for the seizure from the Registrar of Vehicles or authorized representative. In all those cases, a notice of the lien and the intent to sell the vehicle shall be given by the department to the legal and registered owner, and to any other person known to be claiming an interest in the vehicle, within 48 hours after seizure excluding Saturdays, Sundays, and holidays specified in Section 6700 of the Government Code. Any hearing to contest the lien and the seizure shall be requested within 10 days following transmittal of that notice.

(g) When a lien exists against one or more vehicles owned by the same person or persons, the department may seize and sell a sufficient number of the vehicles to pay the lien, plus costs, on one or more of the vehicles in accordance with subdivision (a).

(h) The Department of the California Highway Patrol shall assist with the seizure and impounding of the vehicle. Any municipality or county law enforcement agency may assist with the seizure and impounding of the vehicle.

(i) Any property found by the department in any vehicle seized under the provisions of this article shall be handled by the department in the same manner as is provided in Sections 2414 and 2415. *(AD '82; AM '83, '89, '90, '92, '94)*

9853.2. Display of Number

The owner shall paint on or attach to each side of the forward half of the vessel the identification number in such manner as may be prescribed by rules and regulations of the department in order that it may be clearly visible. Any such rules and regulations shall be developed in cooperation with the Department of Boating and Waterways. The number shall be maintained in a legible condition. The certificate of number shall be pocket size and shall be available at all times for inspection on the vessel for which issued, whenever the vessel is in use, except as to those vessels subject to Section 9853.3.

9853.8. Operation of Certain Undocumented Vessels Requiring Numbering

(a) This section applies only to a sterndrive or inboard vessel that contains a spark-ignition marine engine below 373 kW (500 hp) rated power output that was manufactured on or after January 1, 2008, or contains a spark-ignition marine engine with any rated power output that was manufactured on or after January 1, 2009.

(b) It is an infraction, punishable by a fine of two hundred fifty dollars ($250), for a person to operate an undocumented vessel, requiring numbering by the state, that is not currently numbered by the state, and that does not comply with the emissions standards required by Section 2442 of Title 13 of the California Code of Regulations.

(c) As used in this section, "spark-ignition marine engine" has the same meaning as that term is defined in Section 9853.7. *(AD '07)*

9853.4. Stickers, Tabs or Other Devices

(a) The department may issue one or more stickers, tabs, or other suitable devices to identify vessels as being currently registered. The size, shape, and color of the sticker, tab, or other device and the positioning of the sticker, tab, or other device on the vessel shall be as determined by the department after consultation with the Department of Boating and Waterways, such consultation to consider the responsibilities and duties of the Department of Boating and Waterways as prescribed in the Harbors and Navigation Code.

(b) Whenever the department issues a sticker, tab, or other device pursuant to subdivision (a), the sticker, tab, or device shall only be displayed on the vessel for which it was issued.

9865. Change of Address

Any holder of a certificate of number shall notify the department within 15 days, if his address no longer conforms to the address appearing on the certificate and shall, as part of such notification, furnish the department with his new address. The department may provide for the surrender of the certificate bearing the former address and its replacement with a certificate bearing the new address or for the alteration of an outstanding certificate to show the new address of the holder.

9866. Display of Other Numbers on Bow

No number other than the number issued to an undocumented vessel or granted reciprocity pursuant to this chapter shall be painted, attached, or otherwise displayed on either side of the bow of such undocumented vessel.

9872. Defacing, Destroying or Altering Hull Identification Number

No person shall intentionally deface, destroy, or alter the hull identification number of a vessel required to be numbered under this chapter without written authorization from the department; nor shall any person place or stamp any serial or other number or mark upon an undocumented vessel which might interfere with identification of the hull identification number. This does not prohibit the restoration by an owner of an original number or mark when the restoration is authorized by the department, nor prevent any manufacturer from placing, in the ordinary course of business, numbers or marks upon new vessels or new parts thereof.

9872.1. Hull Identification Number: Violations

(a) No person shall knowingly buy, sell, offer for sale, receive, or have in his or her possession any vessel, or component part thereof, from which the hull identification number has been removed, defaced, altered, or destroyed, unless the vessel or component part has attached thereto a hull identification number assigned or approved by the department in lieu of the manufacturer's number.

(b) Whenever a vessel, or component part thereof, from which the hull identification number has been removed, defaced, altered, or destroyed, and which does not have attached thereto an assigned or approved number as described in subdivision (a), comes into the custody of a peace officer, the seized vessel or component part is subject, in accordance with the procedures specified in this section, to impoundment and to such disposition as may be provided by order of a court having jurisdiction. This subdivision does not apply with respect to a seized vessel or component part used as evidence in any criminal action or proceeding.

(c) Whenever a vessel or component part described in subdivision (a) comes into the custody of a peace officer, any person from whom the property was seized, and all claimants to the property whose interest or title is on registration records in the department, shall be notified within five days, excluding Saturdays, Sundays, and holidays, after the seizure, of the date, time, and place of the hearing required in subdivision (e). The notice shall contain the information specified in subdivision (d).

(d) Whenever a peace officer seizes a vessel or component part as provided in subdivision (b), any person from whom the property was seized shall be provided a notice of impoundment of the vessel or component part which shall serve as a receipt and contain the following information:

(1) Name and address of person from whom the property was seized.

(2) A statement that the vessel or component part seized has been impounded for investigation of a violation of this section and that the property will be released upon a determination that the hull identification number has not been removed, defaced, altered, or destroyed, or upon the presentation of satisfactory evidence of ownership of the vessel or component part, provided that no other person claims an interest in the property; otherwise, a hearing regarding the disposition of the vessel or component part shall take place in the proper court.

(3) A statement that any person from whom the property was seized, and all claimants to the property whose interest or title is on registration records in the department, will receive written notification of the date, time, and place of the hearing within five days, excluding Saturdays, Sundays, and holidays, after the seizure.

(4) Name and address of the law enforcement agency where evidence of ownership of the vessel or component part may be presented.

(5) A statement of the contents of this section.

(e) A hearing on the disposition of the property shall be held by the superior court within 60 days after the seizure. The hearing shall be before the court without a jury. A proceeding under this section is a limited civil case.

(1) If the evidence reveals either that the hull identification number has not been removed, altered, or destroyed or that the hull identification number has been removed, altered, or destroyed but satisfactory evidence of ownership has been presented to the seizing agency or court, the property shall be released to the person entitled thereto.

(2) If the evidence reveals that the hull identification number has been removed, altered, or destroyed, and satisfactory evidence of ownership has not been presented, the property shall be destroyed, sold, or otherwise disposed of as provided by court order.

(3) At the hearing, the seizing agency shall have the burden of establishing that the hull identification number has been removed, defaced, altered, or destroyed and that no satisfactory evidence of ownership has been presented.

(f) Nothing in this section precludes the return of a seized vessel or component part to the owner by the seizing agency following presentation of satisfactory evidence of ownership and, if determined necessary, upon the assignment of an identification number to the vessel or component part by the department. *(AM '98, '02)*

DIVISION 4. SPECIAL ANTI-THEFT LAWS

CHAPTER 1. REPORTS OF STOLEN VEHICLES

10501. False Report of Theft

(a) It is unlawful for any person to make or file a false or fraudulent report of theft of a vehicle required to be registered under this code with any law enforcement agency with intent to deceive.

(b) If a person has been previously convicted of a violation of subdivision (a), he or she is punishable by imprisonment pursuant to subdivision (h) of Section 1170 of the Penal Code for 16 months, or two or three years, or in a county jail for not to exceed one year. *(AM '11)*

CHAPTER 1.5. REPORTS OF STOLEN VESSELS

10552. False or Fraudulent Reports

It is unlawful for any person to make or file a false or fraudulent report of the theft of an undocumented vessel required to be numbered under this code with any law enforcement agents with intent to deceive.

CHAPTER 3. ALTERATION OR REMOVAL OF NUMBERS

10750. Altering or Changing Vehicle Numbers

(a) No person shall intentionally deface, destroy, or alter the motor number, other distinguishing number, or identification mark of a vehicle required for registration purposes without written authorization from the department, nor shall any person place or stamp any serial, motor, or other number or mark upon a vehicle, except one assigned thereto by the department.

(b) This section does not prohibit the restoration by an owner of the original vehicle identification number when the restoration is authorized by the department, nor prevent any manufacturer from placing in the ordinary course of business numbers or marks upon new motor vehicles or new parts thereof.

10751. Manufacturers' Serial or Identification Numbers

(a) No person shall knowingly buy, sell, offer for sale, receive, or have in his or her possession, any vehicle, or component part thereof, from which any serial or identification number, including, but not limited to, any number used for registration purposes, that is affixed by the manufacturer to the vehicle or component part, in whatever manner deemed proper by the manufacturer, has been removed, defaced, altered, or destroyed, unless the vehicle or component part has attached thereto an identification number assigned or approved by the department in lieu of the manufacturer's number.

(b) Whenever a vehicle described in subdivision (a), including a vehicle assembled with any component part which is in violation of subdivision (a), comes into the custody of a peace officer, it shall be destroyed, sold, or otherwise disposed of under the conditions as provided in an order by the court having jurisdiction. No court order providing for disposition shall be issued unless the person from whom the property was seized, and all claimants to the property whose interest or title is on registration records in the Department of Motor Vehicles, are provided a postseizure hearing by the court having jurisdiction within 90 days after the seizure. This subdivision shall not apply with respect to a seized vehicle or component part used as evidence in any criminal action or proceeding. Nothing in this section shall, however, preclude the return of a seized vehicle or a component part to the owner by the seizing agency following presentation of satisfactory evidence of ownership and, if determined necessary, upon the assignment of an identification number to the vehicle or component part by the department.

(c) Whenever a vehicle described in subdivision (a) comes into the custody of a peace officer, the person from whom the property was seized, and all claimants to the property whose interest or title is on registration records in the Department of Motor Vehicles, shall be notified within five days, excluding Saturdays, Sundays, and holidays, after the seizure, of the date, time, and place of the hearing required in subdivision (b). The notice shall contain the information specified in subdivision (d).

(d) Whenever a peace officer seizes a vehicle described in subdivision (a), the person from whom the property was seized shall be provided a notice of impoundment of the vehicle which shall serve as a receipt and contain the following information:

(1) Name and address of person from whom the property was seized.

(2) A statement that the vehicle seized has been impounded for investigation of a violation of Section 10751 of the California Vehicle Code and that the property will be released upon a determination that the serial or identification number has not been removed, defaced, altered, or destroyed, or upon the presentation of satisfactory evidence of ownership of the vehicle or a component part, if no other person claims an interest in the property; otherwise, a hearing regarding the disposition of the vehicle shall take place in the proper court.

(3) A statement that the person from whom the property was seized, and all claimants to the property whose interest or title is on registration records in the Department of Motor Vehicles, will receive written notification of the date, time, and place of the hearing within five days, excluding Saturdays, Sundays, and holidays, after the seizure.

(4) Name and address of the law enforcement agency where evidence of ownership of the vehicle or component part may be presented.

(5) A statement of the contents of Section 10751 of the Vehicle Code.

(e) A hearing on the disposition of the property shall be held by the superior court within 90 days after the seizure. The hearing shall be before the court without a jury. A proceeding under this section is a limited civil case.

(1) If the evidence reveals either that the serial or identification number has not been removed, defaced, altered, or destroyed or that the number has been removed, defaced, altered, or destroyed but satisfactory evidence of ownership has been presented to the seizing agency or court, the property shall be released to the person entitled thereto. Nothing in this section precludes the return of the vehicle or a component part to a good faith purchaser following presentation of satisfactory evidence of ownership thereof upon the assignment of an identification number to the vehicle or component part by the department.

(2) If the evidence reveals that the identification number has been removed, defaced, altered, or destroyed, and satisfactory evidence of ownership has not been presented, the vehicle shall be destroyed, sold, or otherwise disposed of as provided by court order.

(3) At the hearing, the seizing agency has the burden of establishing that the serial or identification number has been removed, defaced, altered, or destroyed and that no satisfactory evidence of ownership has been presented.

(f) This section does not apply to a scrap metal processor engaged primarily in the acquisition, processing, and shipment of ferrous and nonferrous scrap, and who receives dismantled vehicles from licensed dismantlers, licensed junk collectors, or licensed junk dealers as scrap metal for the purpose of recycling the dismantled vehicles for their metallic content, the end product of which is the production of material for recycling and remelting purposes for steel mills, foundries, smelters, and refiners. *(AM '98, '02)*

10752. Fraudulent Acquisition or Disposition of Vehicle Identification Number - Penalty

(a) No person shall, with intent to prejudice, damage, injure, or defraud, acquire, possess, sell, or offer for sale any genuine or counterfeit manufacturer's serial or identification number from or for, or purporting to be from or for, a vehicle or component part thereof.

(b) No person shall, with intent to prejudice, damage, injure, or defraud, acquire, possess, sell, or offer for sale any genuine or counterfeit serial or identification number issued by the department, the Department of the California Highway Patrol, or the vehicle registration and titling agency of any foreign jurisdiction which is from or for, or purports to be from or for, a vehicle or component part thereof.

(c) Every person convicted of a violation of subdivision (a) or (b) shall be punished by imprisonment pursuant to subdivision (h) of Section 1170 of the Penal Code, or in the county jail for not less than 90 days nor more than one year, and by a fine of not less than two hundred fifty dollars ($250) nor more than five thousand dollars ($5,000). *(AM '11)*

CHAPTER 4. THEFT AND INJURY OF VEHICLES

10801. Own or Operate a Chop Shop

Any person who knowingly and intentionally owns or operates a chop shop is guilty of a public offense and, upon conviction, shall be punished by imprisonment pursuant to subdivision (h) of Section 1170 of the Penal Code for two, three, or four years, or by a fine of not more than fifty thousand dollars ($50,000), or by both the fine and imprisonment, or by up to one year in the county jail, or by a fine of not more than one thousand dollars ($1,000), or by both the fine and imprisonment. *(AM '11)*

10802. Alter, Etc. Vehicle Identification Numbers

Any person who knowingly alters, counterfeits, defaces, destroys, disguises, falsifies, forges, obliterates, or removes vehicle identification numbers, with the intent to misrepresent the identity or prevent the identification of motor vehicles or motor vehicle parts, for the purpose of sale, transfer, import, or export, is guilty of a public offense and, upon conviction, shall be punished by imprisonment pursuant to subdivision (h) of Section 1170 of the Penal Code for 16 months, or two or three years, or by a fine of not more than twenty-five thousand dollars ($25,000), or by both the fine and imprisonment, or by up to one year in the county jail, or by a fine of not more than one thousand dollars ($1,000), or by both the fine and imprisonment. *(AM '11)*

10803. Chop Shop: Buyers and Sellers

(a) Any person who buys with the intent to resell, disposes of, sells, or transfers, more than one motor vehicle or parts from more than one motor vehicle, with the knowledge that the vehicle identification numbers of the motor vehicles or motor vehicle parts have been altered, counterfeited, defaced, destroyed, disguised, falsified, forged, obliterated, or removed for the purpose of misrepresenting the identity or preventing the identification of the motor vehicles or motor vehicle parts, is guilty of a public offense and, upon conviction, shall be punished by imprisonment pursuant to subdivision (h) of Section 1170 of the Penal Code for two, four, or six years, or by a fine of not more than sixty thousand dollars ($60,000), or by both the fine and imprisonment, or by up to one year in the county jail, or by a fine of not more than one thousand dollars ($1,000), or by both the fine and imprisonment.

(b) Any person who possesses, for the purpose of sale, transfer, import, or export, more than one motor vehicle or parts from more than one motor vehicle, with the knowledge that the vehicle identification numbers of the motor vehicles or motor vehicle parts have been altered, counterfeited, defaced, destroyed, disguised, falsified, forged, obliterated, or removed for the purpose of misrepresenting the identity or preventing the identification of the motor vehicles or motor vehicle parts, is guilty of a public offense and, upon conviction, shall be punished by imprisonment pursuant to subdivision (h) of Section 1170 of the Penal Code for 16 months, or two or three years, or by a fine of not more than thirty thousand dollars ($30,000), or by both the fine and imprisonment, or by imprisonment in the county jail not exceeding one year or by a fine of not more than one thousand dollars ($1,000) or by both the fine and imprisonment. *(AM '11)*

10851. Theft and Unlawful Driving or Taking of a Vehicle

(a) Any person who drives or takes a vehicle not his or her own, without the consent of the owner thereof, and with intent either to permanently or temporarily deprive the owner thereof of his or her title to or possession of the vehicle, whether with or without intent to steal the vehicle, or any person who is a party or an accessory to or an accomplice in the driving or unauthorized taking or stealing, is guilty of a public offense and, upon conviction thereof, shall be punished by imprisonment in a county jail for not more than one year or pursuant to subdivision (h) of Section 1170 of the Penal Code or by a fine of not more than five thousand dollars ($5,000), or by both the fine and imprisonment.

(b) If the vehicle is (1) an ambulance, as defined in subdivision (a) of Section 165, (2) a distinctively marked vehicle of a law enforcement agency or fire department, taken while the ambulance or vehicle is on an emergency call and this fact is known to the person driving or taking, or any person who is party or an accessory to or an accomplice in the driving or unauthorized taking or stealing, or (3) a vehicle which has been modified for the use of a disabled veteran or any other disabled person and which displays a distinguishing license plate or placard issued pursuant to Section 22511.5 or 22511.9 and this fact is known or should reasonably have been known to the person driving or taking, or any person who is party or an accessory in the driving or unauthorized taking or stealing, the offense is a felony punishable by imprisonment pursuant to subdivision (h) of Section 1170 of the Penal Code for two, three, or four years or by a fine of not more than ten thousand dollars ($10,000), or by both the fine and imprisonment.

(c) In any prosecution for a violation of subdivision (a) or (b), the consent of the owner of a vehicle to its taking or driving shall not in any case be presumed or implied because of the owner's consent on a previous occasion to the taking or driving of the vehicle by the same or a different person.

(d) The existence of any fact which makes subdivision (b) applicable shall be alleged in the accusatory pleading, and either admitted by the defendant in open court, or found to be true by the jury trying the issue of guilt or by the court where guilt is established by plea of guilty or nolo contendere or by trial by the court sitting without a jury.

(e) Any person who has been convicted of one or more previous felony violations of this section, or felony grand theft of a vehicle in violation of subdivision (d) of Section 487 of the Penal Code, former subdivision (3) of Section 487 of the Penal Code, as that section read prior to being amended by Section 4 of Chapter 1125 of the Statutes of 1993, or Section 487h of the Penal Code, is punishable as set forth in Section 666.5 of the Penal Code. The existence of any fact that would bring a person under Section 666.5 of the Penal Code shall be alleged in the information or indictment and either admitted by the defendant in open court, or found to be true by the jury trying the issue of guilt or by the court where guilt is established by plea of guilty or nolo contendere, or by trial by the court sitting without a jury.

(f) This section shall become operative on January 1, 1997. *(AM '11)*

10851.5. Theft of Binder Chains

Any person who takes binder chains, required under regulations adopted pursuant to Section 31510, having a value of nine hundred fifty dollars ($950) or less which chains are not his own, without the consent of the owner thereof, and with intent either permanently or temporarily to deprive the owner thereof of his title to or possession of the binder chains whether with or without intent to steal the same, or any person who is a party or accessory to or an accomplice in the unauthorized taking or stealing is guilty of a misdemeanor, and upon conviction thereof shall be punished by imprisonment in the county jail for not less than six months or by a fine of not less than one thousand dollars ($1,000) or by both such fine and imprisonment. The consent of the owner of the binder chain to its taking shall not in any case be presumed or implied because of such owner's consent on a previous occasion to the taking of the binder chain by the same or a different person. *(AM '09)*

10852. Breaking or Removing Vehicle Parts

No person shall either individually or in association with one or more other persons, willfully injure or tamper with any vehicle or the contents thereof or break or remove any part of a vehicle without the consent of the owner.

10853. Malicious Mischief to Vehicle

No person shall with intent to commit any malicious mischief, injury, or other crime, climb into or upon a vehicle whether it is in motion or at rest, nor shall any person attempt to manipulate any of the levers, starting mechanism, brakes, or other mechanism or device of a vehicle while the same is at rest and unattended, nor shall any person set in motion any vehicle while the same is at rest and unattended.

10854. Unlawful Use or Tampering by Bailee

Every person having the storage, care, safekeeping, custody, or possession of any vehicle of a type subject to registration under this code who, without the consent of the owner, takes, hires, runs, drives, or uses the vehicle or who takes or removes any part thereof is guilty of a misdemeanor and upon conviction shall be punished by a fine of not exceeding one thousand dollars ($1,000) or by imprisonment in the county jail for not exceeding one year or by both.

10855. Leased and Rented Vehicles
Whenever any person who has leased or rented a vehicle willfully and intentionally fails to return the vehicle to its owner within five days after the lease or rental agreement has expired, that person shall be presumed to have embezzled the vehicle.

DIVISION 5.
OCCUPATIONAL LICENSING AND BUSINESS REGULATIONS

CHAPTER 3.5. LESSOR-RETAILERS

11614. Violations by Licensed Lessor-Retailer
No lessor-retailer licensed under this chapter may do any of the following in connection with any activity for which this license is required:

(a) Make or disseminate, or cause to be made or disseminated, before the public in this state, in any newspaper or other publication, or any advertising device, or by oral representation, or in any other manner or means whatever, any statement that is untrue or misleading and that is known, or which by the exercise of reasonable care should be known, to be untrue or misleading; or make or disseminate, or cause to be made or disseminated, any statement as part of a plan or scheme with the intent not to sell any vehicle, or service so advertised, at the price stated therein, or as so advertised.

(b) Advertise, or offer for sale in any manner, any vehicle not actually for sale at the premises of the lessor-retailer or available within a reasonable time to the lessor-retailer at the time of the advertisement or offer.

(c) Fail within 48 hours to give, in writing, notification to withdraw any advertisement of a vehicle that has been sold or withdrawn from sale.

(d) Advertise any specific vehicle for sale without identifying the vehicle by its model, model year, and either its license number or that portion of the vehicle identification number that distinguishes the vehicle from all other vehicles of the same make, model, and model-year. Model-year is not required to be advertised for current model-year vehicles. Year models are no longer current when ensuing year models are available for purchase at retail in California.

(e) Advertise the total price of a vehicle without including all costs to the purchaser at the time of delivery at the lessor-retailer's premises, except sales tax, vehicle registration fees, finance charges, certificate of compliance or noncompliance fees not exceeding thirty-five dollars ($35) pursuant to any statute, and any dealer documentary preparation charge. The dealer documentary charge shall not exceed thirty-five dollars ($35).

(f)(1) Fail to disclose, in an advertisement of a vehicle for sale, that there will be added to the advertised total price, at the time of sale, charges for sales tax, vehicle registration fees, the fee charged by the state for the issuance of any certificate of compliance or noncompliance pursuant to any statute, finance charges, or any dealer documentary preparation charge.

(2) For purposes of paragraph (1), "advertisement" means any advertisement in a newspaper, magazine, direct mail publication, or handbill that is two or more columns in width or one column in width and more than seven inches in length, or on any Web page of a lessor-retailer's Web site that displays the price of a vehicle offered for sale on the Internet, as that term is defined in paragraph (6) of subdivision (e) of Section 17538 of the Business and Professions Code.

(g) Advertise or otherwise represent, or knowingly allow to be advertised or represented on the lessor-retailer's behalf or at the lessor-retailer's place of business, that no downpayment is required in connection with the sale of a vehicle when a downpayment is in fact required and the buyer is advised or induced to finance the downpayment by a loan in addition to any other loan financing the remainder of the purchase price of the vehicle. The terms "no downpayment," "zero down delivers," or similar terms shall not be advertised unless the vehicle will be sold to any qualified purchaser without a prior payment of any kind or trade-in.

(h) Refuse to sell a vehicle to any person at the advertised total price, exclusive of sales tax, vehicle registration fees, finance charges, certificate of compliance or noncompliance pursuant to any statute, and any dealer documentary preparation charge, which charges shall not exceed thirty-five dollars ($35) for the documentary preparation charge and thirty-five dollars ($35) for the certificate of compliance or noncompliance pursuant to any statute, while the vehicle remains unsold or unleased, unless the advertisement states the advertised total price is good only for a specified time and the time has elapsed.

(i) Engage in the business for which the licensee is licensed without having in force and effect a bond required by Section 11612.

(j) Engage in the business for which the lessor-retailer is licensed without at all times maintaining a principal place of business and any branch office location required by this chapter.

(k) Permit the use of the lessor-retailer license, supplies, or books by any other person for the purpose of permitting that person to engage in the sale of vehicles required to be registered under this code, or to permit the use of the lessor-retailer license, supplies, or books to operate a branch office location to be used by any other person, if, in either situation, the licensee has no financial or equitable interest or investment in the vehicles sold by, or the business of, or branch office location used by, the person, or has no interest or investment other than commissions, compensations, fees, or any other thing of value received for the use of the lessor-retailer license, supplies, or books to engage in the sale of vehicles.

(l) Violate any provision of Article 10 (commencing with Section 28050) of Chapter 5 of Division 12.

(m) Represent the dealer documentary preparation charge, or certificate of compliance or noncompliance fee, as a governmental fee.

(n) Advertise free merchandise, gifts, or services provided by a lessor-retailer contingent on the purchase of a vehicle. "Free"includes merchandise or services offered for sale at a price less than the lessor-retailer's cost of the merchandise or services.

(o) Advertise vehicles and related goods or services with the intent not to supply reasonably expectable demand, unless the advertisement discloses a limitation of quantity.

(p) Use the term "rebate"or similar words such as "cash back"in advertising the sale of a vehicle.

(q) Require a person to pay a higher price for a vehicle and related goods or services for receiving advertised credit terms than the cash price the same person would have to pay to purchase the same vehicle and related goods or services. For the purpose of this subdivision, "cash price"has the meaning as defined in subdivision (e) of Section 2981 of the Civil Code.

(r) Misrepresent the authority of a representative or agent to negotiate the final terms of a transaction.

(s) Violate any law prohibiting bait and switch advertising, including, but not limited to, the guides against bait advertising set forth in Part 238 of Title 16 of the Code of Federal Regulations, as those regulations read on January 1, 1988.

(t) Make any untrue or misleading statement indicating that a vehicle is equipped with all the factory installed optional equipment the manufacturer offers, including, but not limited to, a false statement that a vehicle is "fully factory equipped."

(u) Advertise any underselling claim, such as "we have the lowest prices"or "we will beat any dealer's price,"unless the lessor-retailer has conducted a recent survey showing that the lessor-retailer sells its vehicles at lower prices than any other licensee in its trade area and maintains records to adequately substantiate the claim. The substantiating records shall be made available to the department upon request.

(v) To display or offer for sale any used vehicle unless there is affixed to the vehicle the Federal Trade Commission's Buyer's Guide as required by Part 455 of Title 16 of the Code of Federal Regulations.

(w) This section shall become operative on July 1, 2001. *(AD '00; AM '02)*

11614.1. Prohibited Activity by Lessor-Retailer
No lessor-retailer licensed under this chapter may do any of the following in connection with any activity for which this license is required:

(a) Use a picture in connection with any advertisement of the price of a specific vehicle or class of vehicles, unless the picture is of the year, make, and model being offered for sale. The picture may not depict a vehicle with optional equipment or a design not actually offered at the advertised price.

(b) Advertise a vehicle for sale that was used by the selling lessor-retailer in its business as a demonstrator, executive vehicle, service vehicle, rental, loaner, or lease vehicle, unless the advertisement clearly and conspicuously discloses the previous use made by that licensee of the vehicle. An advertisement may not describe any of those vehicles as "new."

(c) Advertise any used vehicle of the current or prior model-year without expressly disclosing the vehicle as "used,""previously owned,"or a similar term that indicates that the vehicle is used, as defined in this code.

(d) Use the terms "on approved credit"or "on credit approval"in an advertisement for the sale of a vehicle unless those terms are clearly and conspicuously disclosed and unabbreviated.

(e) Advertise an amount described by terms such as "unpaid balance"or "balance can be financed"unless the total sale price is clearly and conspicuously disclosed and is in close proximity to the advertised balance.

(f) Advertise credit terms that fail to comply with the disclosure requirements of Section 226.24 of Title 12 of the Code of Federal Regulations. Advertisements of terms that include escalated payments, balloon payments, or deferred downpayments shall clearly and conspicuously identify those payments as to amounts and time due.

(g) Advertise claims such as "everyone financed,""no credit rejected,"or similar claims unless the dealer is willing to extend credit to any person under any and all circumstances.

(h) Advertise the amount of any downpayment unless it represents the total payment required of a purchaser prior to delivery of the vehicle, including any payment for sales tax or license. A statement such as "$_____ delivers,"is an example of an advertised downpayment.

(i) Fail to clearly and conspicuously disclose in an advertisement for the sale of a vehicle any disclosure required by this code or any qualifying term used in conjunction with advertised credit terms. Unless otherwise provided by statute, the specific size of disclosures or qualifying terms is not prescribed. *(AD '02; AM '03)*

CHAPTER 4. MANUFACTURERS, TRANSPORTERS, DEALERS & SALESMEN

11700.3. Aiding and Abetting Prohibited
No person may aid and abet a person in the performance of any act in violation of this chapter. *(AD '02)*

11713. Unlawful Acts by Licensee
No holder of any license issued under this article shall do any of the following:

(a) Make or disseminate, or cause to be made or disseminated, before the public in this state, in any newspaper or other publication, or any advertising device, or by public outcry or proclamation, or in any other manner or means whatever, any statement which is untrue or misleading and which is known, or which by the exercise of reasonable care should be known, to be untrue or misleading; or to so make or disseminate, or cause to be so disseminated, any statement as part of a plan or scheme with the intent not to sell any vehicle or service so advertised at the price stated therein, or as so advertised.

(b)(1)(A) Advertise or offer for sale or exchange in any manner, any vehicle not actually for sale at the premises of the dealer or available to the dealer directly from the manufacturer or distributor of the vehicle at the time of the advertisement or offer. However, a dealer who has been issued an autobroker's endorsement to his or her dealer's license may advertise his or her service of arranging or negotiating the purchase of a new motor vehicle from a franchised new motor vehicle dealer and may specify the line-makes and models of those new vehicles. Autobrokering service advertisements may not advertise the price or payment terms of any vehicle and shall disclose that the advertiser is an autobroker or auto buying service, and shall clearly and conspicuously state the following: "All new cars arranged for sale are subject to price and availability from the selling franchised new car dealer."

(B) As to printed advertisements, the disclosure statement required by subparagraph (A) shall be printed in not less than 10-point bold type size and shall be textually segregated from the other portions of the printed advertisement.

(2) Notwithstanding subparagraph (A), classified advertisements for autobrokering services that measure two column inches or less are exempt from the disclosure statement in subparagraph (A) pertaining to price and availability.

(3) Radio advertisements of a duration of less than 11 seconds that do not reference specific line-makes or models of motor vehicles are exempt from the disclosure statement required in subparagraph (A).

(c) Fail, within 48 hours, in writing to withdraw any advertisement of a vehicle that has been sold or withdrawn from sale.

(d) Advertise or represent a vehicle as a new vehicle if the vehicle is a used vehicle.

(e) Engage in the business for which the licensee is licensed without having in force and effect a bond as required by this article.

(f) Engage in the business for which the dealer is licensed without at all times maintaining an established place of business as required by this code.

(g) Include, as an added cost to the selling price of a vehicle, an amount for licensing or transfer of title of the vehicle, which is not due to the state unless, prior to the sale, that amount has been paid by a dealer to the state in order to avoid penalties that would have accrued because of late payment of the fees. However, a dealer may collect from the second purchaser of a vehicle a prorated fee based upon the number of months remaining in the registration year for that vehicle, if the vehicle had been previously sold by the dealer and the sale was subsequently rescinded and all the fees that were paid, as required by this code and Chapter 2 (commencing with Section 10751) of Division 2 of the Revenue and Taxation Code, were returned to the first purchaser of the vehicle.

(h) Employ any person as a salesperson who has not been licensed pursuant to Article 2 (commencing with Section 11800), and whose license is not displayed on the premises of the dealer as required by Section 11812, or willfully fail to notify the department by mail within 10 days of the employment or termination of employment of a salesperson.

(i) Deliver, following the sale, a vehicle for operation on California highways, if the vehicle does not meet all of the equipment requirements of Division 12 (commencing with Section 24000). This subdivision does not apply to the sale of a leased vehicle to the lessee if the lessee is in possession of the vehicle immediately prior to the time of the sale and the vehicle is registered in this state.

(j) Use, or permit the use of, the special plates assigned to him or her for any purpose other than as permitted by Section 11715.

(k) Advertise or otherwise represent, or knowingly allow to be advertised or represented on behalf of, or at the place of business of, the licenseholder that no downpayment is required in connection with the sale of a vehicle when a downpayment is in fact required and the buyer is advised or induced to finance the downpayment by a loan in addition to any other loan financing the remainder of the purchase price of the vehicle. The terms "no downpayment,""zero down delivers,"or similar terms shall not be advertised unless the vehicle will be sold to any qualified purchaser without a prior payment of any kind or trade-in.

(l) Participate in the sale of a vehicle required to be reported to the Department of Motor Vehicles under Section 5900 or 5901 without making the return and payment of the full sales tax due and required by Section 6451 of the Revenue and Taxation Code.

(m) Permit the use of the dealer's license, supplies, or books by any other person for the purpose of permitting that person to engage in the purchase or sale of vehicles required to be registered under this code, or permit the use of the dealer's license, supplies, or books to operate a branch location to be used by any other person, whether or not the licensee has any financial or equitable interest or investment in the vehicles purchased or sold by, or the business of, or branch location used by, the other person.

(n) Violate any provision of Article 10 (commencing with Section 28050) of Chapter 5 of Division 12.

(o) Sell a previously unregistered vehicle without disclosing in writing to the purchaser the date on which any manufacturer's or distributor's warranty commenced.

(p) Accept a purchase deposit relative to the sale of a vehicle, unless the vehicle is present at the premises of the dealer or available to the dealer directly from the manufacturer or distributor of the vehicle at the time the dealer accepts the deposit. Purchase deposits accepted by an autobroker when brokering a retail sale shall be governed by Sections 11736 and 11737.

(q) Consign for sale to another dealer a new vehicle.

(r) Display a vehicle for sale at a location other than an established place of business authorized by the department for that dealer or display a new motor vehicle at the business premises of another dealer registered as an autobroker. This subdivision does not apply to the display of a vehicle pursuant to subdivision (b) of Section 11709 or the demonstration of the qualities of a motor vehicle by way of a test drive.

(s) Use a picture in connection with any advertisement of the price of a specific vehicle or class of vehicles, unless the picture is of the year, make and model being offered for sale. The picture shall not depict a vehicle with optional equipment or a design not actually offered at the advertised price.

(t) Advertise a vehicle for sale that was used by the selling licensee in its business as a demonstrator, executive vehicle, service vehicle, rental, loaner, or lease vehicle, unless the advertisement clearly and conspicuously discloses the previous use made by that licensee of the vehicle. An advertisement shall not describe any of those vehicles as "new." *(AM '98, '02)*

11713.16. Prohibited Activities y Holder of Dealer's License

It is a violation of this code for the holder of any dealer's license issued under this article to do any of the following:

(a) Advertise any used vehicle of the current or prior model-year without expressly disclosing the vehicle as "used,""previously owned,"or a similar term that indicates that the vehicle is used, as defined in this code.

(b) Use the terms "on approved credit"or "on credit approval"in an advertisement for the sale of a vehicle unless those terms are clearly and conspicuously disclosed and unabbreviated.

(c) Advertise an amount described by terms such as "unpaid balance"or "balance can be financed"unless the total sale price is clearly and conspicuously disclosed and in close proximity to the advertised balance.

(d) Advertise credit terms that fail to comply with the disclosure requirements of Section 226.24 of Title 12 of the Code of Federal Regulations. Advertisements of terms that include escalated payments, balloon payments, or deferred downpayments shall clearly and conspicuously identify those payments as to amounts and time due.

(e) Advertise as the total sales price of a vehicle an amount that includes a deduction for a rebate. However, a dealer may advertise a separate amount that includes a deduction for a rebate provided that the advertisement clearly and conspicuously discloses, in close proximity to the amount advertised, the price of the vehicle before the rebate deduction and the amount of the rebate, each so identified.

(f) Advertise claims such as "everyone financed,""no credit rejected,"or similar claims unless the dealer is willing to extend credit to any person under any and all circumstances.

(g) Advertise the amount of any downpayment unless it represents the total payment required of a purchaser prior to delivery of the vehicle, including any payment for sales tax or license. Statements such as "$_____ delivers,""$_____ puts you in a new car"are examples of advertised downpayments.

(h) Advertise the price of a new vehicle or class of new vehicles unless the vehicle or vehicles have all of the equipment listed as standard by the manufacturer or distributor or the dealer has replaced the standard equipment with equipment of higher value.

(i) Fail to clearly and conspicuously disclose in an advertisement for the sale of a vehicle any disclosure required by this code or any qualifying term used in conjunction with advertised credit terms. Unless otherwise provided by statute, the specific size of disclosures or qualifying terms is not prescribed. *(AD '02)*

11715. Operation With Special Plates; Exceptions

(a) A manufacturer, remanufacturer, distributor, or dealer owning or lawfully possessing any vehicle of a type otherwise required to be registered under this code may operate or move the vehicle upon the highways without registering the vehicle upon condition that the vehicle displays special plates issued to the owner as provided in this chapter, in addition to other license plates or permits already assigned and attached to the vehicle in the manner prescribed in Sections 5200 to 5203, inclusive. A vehicle for sale or lease by a dealer may also be operated or moved upon the highways without registration for a period not to exceed seven days by a prospective buyer or lessee who is test-driving the vehicle for possible purchase or lease, if the vehicle is in compliance with this condition. The vehicle may also be moved or operated for the purpose of towing or transporting by any lawful method other vehicles.

(b) A transporter may operate or move any owned or lawfully possessed vehicle of like type by any lawful method upon the highways solely for the purpose of delivery, upon condition that there be displayed upon each vehicle in contact with the highway special license plates issued to the transporter as provided in this chapter, in addition to any license plates or permits already assigned and attached to the vehicle in the manner prescribed in Sections 5200 to 5203, inclusive. The vehicles may be used for the purpose of towing or transporting by any lawful method other vehicles when the towing or transporting vehicle is being delivered for sale or to the owner thereof.

(c) This section does not apply to any manufacturer, remanufacturer, transporter, distributor, or dealer operating or moving a vehicle as provided in Section 11716.

(d) This section does not apply to work or service vehicles owned by a manufacturer, remanufacturer, transporter, distributor, or dealer. This section does not apply to vehicles owned and leased by dealers, except those vehicles rented or leased to vehicle salespersons in the course of their employment for purposes of display or demonstration, nor to any unregistered vehicles used to transport more than one load of other vehicles for the purpose of sale.

(e) This section does not apply to vehicles currently registered in this state that are owned and operated by a licensed dealer when the notice of transfer has been forwarded to the department by the former owner of record pursuant to Section 5900 and when a copy of the notice is displayed as follows:

(1) For a motorcycle or motor-driven cycle, the notice is displayed in a conspicuous manner upon the vehicle.

(2) For a vehicle other than a motorcycle or motor-driven cycle, the notice is displayed in the lower right-hand corner of the windshield of the vehicle, as specified in paragraph (3) of subdivision (b) of Section 26708.

(f) Every owner, upon receipt of a registration card issued for special plates, shall maintain the same or a facsimile copy thereof with the vehicle bearing the special plates.

CHAPTER 9. TOWING

12110. Towing Service: Unlawful Acts

(a) Except as provided in subdivision (b), no towing service shall provide and no person or public entity shall accept any direct or indirect commission, gift, or any compensation whatever from a towing service in consideration of arranging or requesting the services of a tow truck. As used in this section, "arranging" does not include the activities of employees or principals of a provider of towing services in responding to a request for towing services.

(b) Subdivision (a) does not preclude a public entity otherwise authorized by law from requiring a fee in connection with the award of a franchise for towing vehicles on behalf of that public entity. However, the fee in those cases may not exceed the amount necessary to reimburse the public entity for its actual and reasonable costs incurred in connection with the towing program.

(c) Any towing service or any employee of a towing service that accepts or agrees to accept any money or anything of value from a repair shop and any repair shop or any employee of a repair shop that pays or agrees to pay any money or anything of value as a commission, referral fee, inducement, or in any manner a consideration, for the delivery or the arranging of a delivery of a vehicle, not owned by the repair shop or towing service, for the purpose of storage or repair, is guilty of a misdemeanor, punishable as set forth in subdivision (d). Nothing in this subdivision prevents a towing service from towing a vehicle to a repair shop owned by the same company that owns the towing service.

(d) Any person convicted of a violation of subdivision (a) or (c) shall be punished as follows:

(1) Upon first conviction, by a fine of not more than five thousand dollars ($5,000) or imprisonment in the county jail for not more than six months, or by both that fine and imprisonment. If the violation of subdivision (a) or (c) is committed by a tow truck driver, the person's privilege to operate a motor vehicle shall be suspended by the department under Section 13351.85. The clerk of the court shall send a certified abstract of the conviction to the department. If the violation of either subdivision (a) or (c) is committed by a tow truck driver, the court may order the impoundment of the tow truck involved for not more than 15 days.

(2) Upon a conviction of a violation of subdivision (a) or (c) that occurred within seven years of one or more separate convictions of violations of subdivision (a) or (c), by a fine of not more than ten thousand dollars ($10,000) or imprisonment in the county jail for not more than one year, or by both that fine and imprisonment. If the violation of subdivision (a) or (c) is committed by a tow truck driver, the person's privilege to operate a motor vehicle shall be suspended by the department under Section 13351.85. The clerk of the court shall send a certified abstract of the conviction to the department. If the violation of either subdivision (a) or (c) is committed by a tow truck owner, the court may order the impoundment of the tow truck involved for not less than 15 days but not more than 30 days. *(AM '00)*

CHAPTER 10. SALES OF VEHICLES BY PRIVATE PARTIES

12120. Sales of Vehicles
Only a dealer, a person described in Section 286, or the registered owner of record shall sell or offer for sale a vehicle of a type required to be registered pursuant to Division 3 or identified pursuant to Division 16.5, except as provided in Section 12121.

DIVISION 6. DRIVERS' LICENSES

CHAPTER 1. LICENSE ISSUANCE, EXPIRATION & RENEWAL

12500. Unlawful to Drive Unless Licensed
(a) A person may not drive a motor vehicle upon a highway, unless the person then holds a valid driver's license issued under this code, except those persons who are expressly exempted under this code.

(b) A person may not drive a motorcycle, motor-driven cycle, or motorized bicycle upon a highway, unless the person then holds a valid driver's license or endorsement issued under this code for that class, except those persons who are expressly exempted under this code, or those persons specifically authorized to operate motorized bicycles or motorized scooters with a valid driver's license of any class, as specified in subdivision (h) of Section 12804.9.

(c) A person may not drive a motor vehicle in or upon any offstreet parking facility, unless the person then holds a valid driver's license of the appropriate class or certification to operate the vehicle. As used in this subdivision, "offstreet parking facility"means any offstreet facility held open for use by the public for parking vehicles and includes any publicly owned facilities for offstreet parking, and privately owned facilities for offstreet parking where no fee is charged for the privilege to park and which are held open for the common public use of retail customers.

(d) A person may not drive a motor vehicle or combination of vehicles that is not of a type for which the person is licensed.

(e) A motorized scooter operated on public streets shall at all times be equipped with an engine that complies with the applicable State Air Resources Board emission requirements. *(AM '04, '07)*

12501. Persons Exempt
The following persons are not required to obtain a driver's license:

(a) An officer or employee of the United States, while operating a motor vehicle owned or controlled by the United States on the business of the United States, except when the motor vehicle being operated is a commercial motor vehicle, as defined in Section 15210.

(b) Any person while driving or operating implements of husbandry incidentally operated or moved over a highway, except as provided in Section 36300 or 36305.

(c) Any person driving or operating an off-highway motor vehicle subject to identification, as defined in Section 38012, while driving or operating such motor vehicle as provided in Section 38025. Nothing in this subdivision authorizes operation of a motor vehicle by a person without a valid driver's license upon any off-street parking facility, as defined in subdivision (d) of Section 12500.

12502. Nonresident Driver [Repeals 1-30-2014]

(a) The following persons may operate a motor vehicle in this state without obtaining a driver's license under this code:

(1) A nonresident over the age of 18 years having in his or her immediate possession a valid driver's license issued by a foreign jurisdiction of which he or she is a resident, except as provided in Section 12505.

(2) A nonresident, 21 years of age or older, if transporting hazardous material, as defined in Section 353, in a commercial vehicle, having in his or her immediate possession, a valid license with the appropriate endorsement issued by another state or other jurisdiction that is recognized by the department, or a Canadian driver's license and a copy of his or her current training certificate to transport hazardous material that complies with all federal laws and regulations with respect to hazardous materials, both of which shall be in his or her immediate possession.

(3) A nonresident having in his or her immediate possession a valid driver's license, issued by the Diplomatic Motor Vehicle Office of the Office of Foreign Missions of the United States Department of State, for the type of motor vehicle or combination of vehicles that the person is operating.

(b) Any person entitled to the exemption contained in subdivision (a), while operating, within this state, a commercial motor vehicle, as defined in subdivision (b) of Section 15210, shall have in his or her possession a current medical certificate of a type described in subdivision (c) of Section 12804.9, that has been issued within two years of the date of operation of the vehicle.

(c) A nonresident possessing a medical certificate in accordance with subdivision (b) shall comply with any restriction of the medical certificate issued to that nonresident.

(d) This section shall remain in effect only until January 30, 2014, and as of that date is repealed, unless a later enacted statute, that is enacted before January 30, 2014, deletes or extends that date. *(AM - RP - AD '12; A new version will be added 1-31-14)*

12502. Nonresident Driver [Op 1-31-2014]

(a) The following persons may operate a motor vehicle in this state without obtaining a driver's license under this code:

(1) A nonresident over the age of 18 years having in his or her immediate possession a valid driver's license issued by a foreign jurisdiction of which he or she is a resident, except as provided in Section 12505.

(2) A nonresident, 21 years of age or older, if transporting hazardous material, as defined in Section 353, in a commercial vehicle, having in his or her immediate possession, a valid license with the appropriate endorsement issued by another state or other jurisdiction that is recognized by the department, or a Canadian driver's license and a copy of his or her current training certificate to transport hazardous material that complies with all federal laws and regulations with respect to hazardous materials, both of which shall be in his or her immediate possession.

(3) A nonresident having in his or her immediate possession a valid driver's license, issued by the Diplomatic Motor Vehicle Office of the Office of Foreign Missions of the United States Department of State, for the type of motor vehicle or combination of vehicles that the person is operating.

(b)(1) A driver required to have a commercial driver's license under Part 383 of Title 49 of the Code of Federal Regulations who submits a current medical examiner's certificate to the licensing state in accordance with Section 383.71(h) of Subpart E of Part 383 of Title 49 of the Code of Federal Regulations, documenting that he or she meets the physical qualification requirements of Section 391.41 of Subpart E of Part 391 of Title 49 of the Code of Federal Regulations, is not required to carry on his or her person the medical examiner's certificate or a copy of that certificate.

(2) A driver may use the date-stamped receipt, given to the driver by the licensing state agency, for up to 15 days after the date stamped on the receipt, as proof of medical certification.

(c) A nonresident possessing a medical certificate in accordance with subdivision (b) shall comply with any restriction of the medical certificate issued to that nonresident.

(d) This section shall become operative on January 31, 2014. *(AD '12)*

12503. Unlicensed Nonresident

A nonresident over the age of 18 years whose home state or country does not require the licensing of drivers may operate a foreign vehicle owned by him for not to exceed 30 days without obtaining a license under this code.

12505. Residence or Employment

(a)(1) For purposes of this division only and notwithstanding Section 516, residency shall be determined as a person's state of domicile. "State of domicile" means the state where a person has his or her true, fixed, and permanent home and principal residence and to which he or she has manifested the intention of returning whenever he or she is absent.

Prima facie evidence of residency for driver's licensing purposes includes, but is not limited to, the following:

(A) Address where registered to vote.

(B) Payment of resident tuition at a public institution of higher education.

(C) Filing a homeowner's property tax exemption.

(D) Other acts, occurrences, or events that indicate presence in the state is more than temporary or transient.

(2) California residency is required of a person in order to be issued a commercial driver's license under this code.

(b) The presumption of residency in this state may be rebutted by satisfactory evidence that the licensee's primary residence is in another state.

(c) Any person entitled to an exemption under Section 12502, 12503, or 12504 may operate a motor vehicle in this state for not to exceed 10 days from the date he or she establishes residence in this state, except that ***a person shall not operate a motor vehicle for employment in this state after establishing residency without first obtaining a license from the department***.

(d) If the State of California is decertified by the federal government and prohibited from issuing an initial, renewal, or upgraded commercial driver's license pursuant to Section 384.405 of Title 49 of the Code of Federal Regulations, the following applies:

(1) An existing commercial driver's license issued pursuant to this code prior to the date that the state is notified of its decertification shall remain valid until its expiration date.

(2) A person who is a resident of this state may obtain a ***nondomiciled commercial learner's permit or commercial driver's license from any state that elects to issue a ***nondomiciled commercial learner's permit or commercial driver's license and that complies with the testing and licensing standards contained in subparts F, G, and H of Part 383 of Title 49 of the Code of Federal Regulations.

(3) For the purposes of this subdivision, a ***nondomiciled commercial learner's permit or commercial driver's license is a commercial learner's permit or commercial driver's license issued by a state to an individual domiciled in a foreign country or in another state.

(e) The department may issue a nondomiciled commercial learner's permit or nondomiciled commercial driver's license to a person who is domiciled in a state or jurisdiction that has been decertified by the federal government or not determined to be in compliance with the testing and licensing standards contained in subparts F, G, and H of Part 383 of Title 49 of the Code of Federal Regulations.

(f) Subject to Section 12504, a person over the age of 16 years who is a resident of a foreign jurisdiction other than a state, territory, or possession of the United States, the District of Columbia, the Commonwealth of Puerto Rico, or Canada, having a valid driver's license issued to him or her by any other foreign jurisdiction ***may operate a motor vehicle in this state without obtaining a license from the department,

***unless the department determines that the foreign jurisdiction does not meet the licensing standards imposed by this code.

(***g) ***A person who is 18 years of age or older and in possession of a valid commercial learner's permit or commercial driver's license issued by any state, territory, or possession of the United States, the District of Columbia, the Commonwealth of Puerto Rico, or ***a foreign jurisdiction that meets the licensing standards contained in subparts F, G, and H of Part 383 of Title 49 of the Code of Federal Regulations shall be granted reciprocity to operate vehicles of the appropriate class on the highways of this state.

(h) Any person from a foreign jurisdiction that does not meet the licensing standards contained in subparts F, G, and H of Part 383 of Title 49 of the Code of Federal Regulations shall obtain a commercial learner's permit or commercial driver's license from the department before operating on the highways a motor vehicle for which a ***commercial driver's license is required, as described in Section 12804.9. The medical examination form required for issuance of a ***commercial driver's license shall be completed by a health care professional, as defined in paragraph (2) of subdivision (a) of Section 12804.9, who is licensed, certified, or registered to perform physical examinations in the United States of America. This subdivision does not apply to (1) drivers of schoolbuses operated in California on a trip for educational purposes or (2) drivers of vehicles used to provide the services of a local public agency.

(***i) This section does not authorize the employment of a person in violation of Section 12515.
*** *(AM '13)*

12509. Instruction Permits

(a) Except as otherwise provided in subdivision (f) of Section 12514, the department, for good cause, may issue an instruction permit to a physically and mentally qualified person who meets one of the following requirements and who applies to the department for an instruction permit:

(1) Is 15 years and 6 months of age or older, and has successfully completed approved courses in automobile driver education and driver training as provided in paragraph (3) of subdivision (a) of Section 12814.6.

(2) Is 15 years and 6 months of age or older, and has successfully completed an approved course in automobile driver education and is taking driver training as provided in paragraph (3) of subdivision (a) of Section 12814.6.

(3) Is 15 years and 6 months of age and enrolled and participating in an integrated automobile driver education and training program as provided in subparagraph (B) of paragraph (3) of subdivision (a) of Section 12814.6.

(4) Is over 16 years of age and is applying for a restricted driver's license pursuant to Section 12814.7.

(5) Is over 17 years and 6 months of age.

(b) The applicant shall qualify for, and be issued, an instruction permit within 12 months from the date of the application.

(c) An instruction permit issued pursuant to subdivision (a) shall entitle the applicant to operate a vehicle, subject to the limitations imposed by this section and any other provisions of law, upon the highways for a period not exceeding 24 months from the date of the application.

(d) Except as provided in Section 12814.6, a person, while having in his or her immediate possession a valid permit issued pursuant to paragraphs (1) to (3), inclusive, of subdivision (a), may operate a motor vehicle, other than a motorcycle, motorized scooter, or a motorized bicycle, when accompanied by, and under the immediate supervision of, a California -licensed driver with a valid license of the appropriate class who is 18 years of age or over and whose driving privilege is not subject to probation. An accompanying licensed driver at all times shall occupy a position within the driver's compartment that would enable the accompanying licensed driver to assist the person in controlling the vehicle as may be necessary to avoid a collision and to provide immediate guidance in the safe operation of the vehicle.

(e) A person, while having in his or her immediate possession a valid permit issued pursuant to paragraph (4) of subdivision (a), may only operate a government -owned motor vehicle, other than a motorcycle, motorized scooter, or a motorized bicycle, when taking driver training instruction administered by the California National Guard.

(f) The department may also issue an instruction permit to a person who has been issued a valid driver's license to authorize the person to obtain driver training instruction and to practice that instruction in order to obtain another class of driver's license or an endorsement.

(g) The department may further restrict permits issued under subdivision (a) as it may determine to be appropriate to ensure the safe operation of a motor vehicle by the permittee. *(AM '11)*

12509.5. Instruction Permit Required to Operate 2-Wheel Vehicles; Requirements

(a) A person shall obtain an instruction permit issued pursuant to this section prior to operating, or being issued a class M1 or M2 driver's license to operate, a two-wheel motorcycle, motor-driven cycle, motorized scooter, motorized bicycle, moped, or bicycle with an attached motor. The person shall meet the following requirements to obtain an instruction permit for purposes of this section:

(1) If age 15 years and 6 months or older, but under the age of 18 years, the applicant shall meet all of the following requirements:

(A) Have a valid class C license or complete driver education and training pursuant to paragraph (3) of subdivision (a) of Section 12814.6.

(B) Successfully complete a motorcyclist safety program that is operated pursuant to Article 2 (commencing with Section 2930) of Chapter 5 of Division 2.

(C) Pass the motorcycle driver's written exam.

(2) If 18 years of age or older, but under 21 years of age, the applicant shall meet both of the following requirements:

(A) Successfully complete a motorcyclist safety program that is operated pursuant to Article 2 (commencing with Section 2930) of Chapter 5 of Division 2.

(B) Pass the motorcycle driver's written exam.

(3) If 21 years of age or older, pass the motorcycle driver's written exam.

(b) A person described in paragraph (1) or (2) of subdivision (a) shall hold an instruction permit issued pursuant to this section for a minimum of six months prior to being issued a class M1 or M2 license.

(c) A person issued an instruction permit pursuant to this section shall not operate a two-wheel motorcycle, motor-driven cycle, motorized scooter, motorized bicycle, moped, or bicycle with an attached motor during the hours of darkness, shall stay off any freeways that have full control of access and have no crossings at grade, and shall not carry any passenger except an instructor licensed under Chapter 1 (commencing with Section 11100) of Division 5 or a qualified instructor as defined in Section 41907 of the Education Code.

(d) An instruction permit issued pursuant to this section shall be valid for a period not exceeding 24 months from the date of application.

(e) The department may perform, during regularly scheduled computer system maintenance and upgrades, any necessary software updates related to the changes made by the addition, during the 2009-2010 Regular Session, of this section. *(AD '10)*

12511. Licensee Entitled to One license

No person shall have in his or her possession or otherwise under his or her control more than one driver's license.

12515. Driving for Hire or Truck Driving: Age Limit

(a) No person under the age of 18 years shall be employed for compensation by another for the purpose of driving a motor vehicle on the highways.

(b) No person under the age of 21 years shall be employed for compensation by another to drive, and no person under the age of 21 years may drive a motor vehicle, as defined in Section 34500 or subdivision (b) of Section 15210, that is engaged in interstate commerce, or any motor vehicle that is engaged in the interstate or intrastate transportation of hazardous material as defined in Section 353.

12516. Age for Driving Schoolbus

It is unlawful for an person under the age of 18 years to drive a school bus transporting pupils to or from school.

12517. Qualifications of Schoolbus or School Pupil Activity Bus Driver

(a)(1) A person may not operate a schoolbus while transporting pupils unless that person has in his or her immediate possession a valid driver's license for the appropriate class of vehicle to be driven endorsed for schoolbus and passenger transportation.

(2) When transporting one or more pupils at or below the 12th-grade level to or from a public or private school or to or from public or private school activities, the person described in paragraph (1) shall have in his or her immediate possession a certificate issued by the department to permit the operation of a schoolbus.

(b) A person may not operate a school pupil activity bus unless that person has in his or her immediate possession a valid driver's license for the appropriate class of vehicle to be driven endorsed for passenger transportation. When transporting one or more pupils at or below the 12th-grade level to or from public or private school activities, the person shall also have in his or her immediate possession a certificate issued by the department to permit the operation of school pupil activity buses.

(c) The applicant for a certificate to operate a schoolbus or school pupil activity bus shall meet the eligibility and training requirements specified for schoolbus and school pupil activity busdrivers in this code, the Education Code, and regulations adopted by the Department of the California Highway Patrol, and, in addition to the fee authorized in Section 2427, shall pay a fee of twenty-five dollars ($25) with the application for issuance of an original certificate, and a fee of twelve dollars ($12) for the renewal of that certificate. *(AM '06)*

12517.4. Restrictions

This section governs the issuance of a certificate to drive a schoolbus, school pupil activity bus, youth bus, general public paratransit vehicle, or farm labor vehicle.

(a) The driver certificate shall be issued only to applicants meeting all applicable provisions of this code and passing the examinations prescribed by the department and the Department of the California Highway Patrol. The examinations shall be conducted by the Department of the California Highway Patrol, pursuant to Sections 12517, 12519, 12522, 12523, and 12523.5.

(b) A temporary driver certificate shall be issued by the Department of the California Highway Patrol after an applicant has cleared a criminal history background check by the Department of Justice and, if applicable, the Federal Bureau of Investigation, and has passed the examinations and meets all other applicable provisions of this code.

(c) A permanent driver's certificate shall be issued by the department after an applicant has passed all tests and met all applicable provisions of this code. Certificates are valid for a maximum of five years and shall expire on the fifth birthday following the issuance of an original certificate or the expiration of the certificate renewed.

(d) A holder of a certificate may not violate any restriction placed on the certificate. Depending upon the type of vehicle used in the driving test and the abilities and physical condition of the applicant, the Department of the California Highway Patrol and the department may place restrictions on a certificate to assure the safe operation of a motor vehicle and safe transportation of passengers. These restrictions may include, but are not limited to, all of the following:

(1) Automatic transmission only.

(2) Hydraulic brakes only.

(3) Type 2 bus only.

(4) Conventional or type 2 bus only.

(5) Two-axle motor truck or passenger vehicle only.

(e) A holder of a certificate may not drive a motor vehicle equipped with a two-speed rear axle unless the certificate is endorsed: "May drive vehicle with two-speed rear axle."

(f) This section shall become operative on September 20, 2005. *(AM '04)*

12517.45. Requirements for Operating Certain Schoolbus Types while Transporting Pupils

(a) A person shall not operate a motor vehicle described in subdivision (k) of Section 545 while transporting school pupils at or below the 12th-grade level to or from a public or private school or to or from public or private school activities, unless all of the following requirements are met:

(1) The person has in his or her immediate possession all of the following:

(A) A valid driver's license of a class appropriate to the vehicle driven and that is endorsed for passenger transportation.

(B) Either a certificate to drive a schoolbus as described in Section 40082 of the Education Code, or a certificate to drive a school pupil activity bus as described in Section 40083 of the Education Code, issued by the department in accordance with eligibility and training requirements specified by the department, the State Department of Education, and the Department of the California Highway Patrol.

(C) A parental authorization form for each pupil signed by a parent or a legal guardian of the pupil that gives permission for that pupil to be transported to or from the school or school-related activity.

(2)(A) The motor vehicle has passed an annual inspection conducted by the Department of the California Highway Patrol and is in compliance with the charter-party carrier's responsibilities under Section 5374 of the Public Utilities Code.

(B) The Department of the California Highway Patrol may charge a charter-party carrier a reasonable fee sufficient to cover the costs incurred by the Department of the California Highway Patrol in conducting the annual inspection of a motor vehicle.

(b) A driver of a motor vehicle described in subdivision (k) of Section 545 shall comply with the duties specified in subdivision (a) of Section 5384.1 of the Public Utilities Code. *(AD '08)*

12517.5. Paratransit Vehicles; Driver Requirements

A person who is employed as a driver of a paratransit vehicle shall not operate that vehicle unless the person meets both of the following requirements:

(a) Has in his or her immediate possession a valid driver's license of a class appropriate to the vehicle driven.

(b) Successfully completes, during each calendar year, four hours of training administered by, or at the direction of, his or her employer or the employer's agent on the safe operation of paratransit vehicles and four hours of training on the special transportation needs of the persons he or she is employed to transport.

This subdivision may be satisfied if the driver receives transportation training or a certificate, or both, pursuant to Section 40082, 40083, 40085, 40085.5, or 40088 of the Education Code.

The employer shall maintain a record of the current training received by each driver in his or her employ and shall present that record on demand to any authorized representative of the Department of the California Highway Patrol. *(AM '99, '02)*

12519. Farm Labor Vehicle Driver's Certificate

(a) No person shall operate a farm labor vehicle unless the person has in his or her possession a driver's license for the appropriate class of vehicle to be driven, endorsed for passenger transportation, and, when transporting one or more farmworker passengers, a certificate issued by the department to permit the operation of farm labor vehicles.

(b) The applicants shall present evidence that they have successfully completed the driver training course developed by the Department of Education pursuant to Section 40081 of the Education Code, and approved by the department and the CHP before a permanent certificate will be issued.

(c) The certificate shall be issued only to applicants qualified by examinations prescribed by the department and the CHP. The examinations shall be conducted by the CHP.

(d) A person holding a valid certificate to permit the operation of a farm labor vehicle, issued prior to 1-1-91, shall not be required to reapply for a certificate to satisfy any additional requirements imposed by the act adding this subdivision until the certificate he or she holds expires or is canceled or revoked.

12520. Tow Truck Driver's Certificate

(a) No person employed as a tow truck driver, as defined in Section 2430.1, shall operate a tow truck unless that person has, in his or her immediate possession, a valid California driver's license of an appropriate class for the vehicle to be driven, and a tow truck driver certificate issued by the department or a temporary tow truck driver certificate issued by the Department of the California Highway Patrol, to permit the operation of the tow truck.

(b) When notified that the applicant has been cleared through the Department of Justice or the Federal Bureau of Investigation, or both, and if the applicant meets all other applicable provisions of this code, the department shall issue a permanent tow truck driver certificate. The permanent tow truck driver certificate shall be valid for a maximum of five years and shall expire on the same date as that of the applicant's driver's license.

12521. Tour Bus Operator - Requirements

An operator of a tour bus shall, at all times when operating the tour bus, do all of the following:

(a) Use a safety belt.

(b) Report any accidents involving the tour bus to the CHP.

12522. First Aid Exam for Schoolbus and Youth Bus Drivers

(a) Every person who operates a schoolbus or youth bus in the transportation of school pupils shall, in addition to any other requirement for a schoolbus or youth bus driver's certificate, qualify by an examination on first aid practices deemed necessary for schoolbus operator or youth bus operators. Standards for examination shall be determined by the Emergency Medical Services Authority after consultation with the State Department of Education, the department, and the CHP. The local school authority employing the applicant shall provide a course of instruction concerning necessary first aid practices.

(b) The CHP shall conduct the first aid examination as part of the examination of applicants for a schoolbus or youth bus driver's certificate and shall certify to the department that the applicant has satisfactorily demonstrated his or her qualifications in first aid practices, knowledge of schoolbus or youth bus laws and regulations, and ability to operate a schoolbus or youth bus. The first aid certifications shall be valid for the term of the schoolbus or youth bus driver's certificate.

(c) The first aid examination may be waived if the applicant possesses either of the following minimum qualifications:

(1) A current first aid certificate issued by the American Red Cross or by an organization whose first aid training program is at least equivalent to the American Red Cross first aid training program, as determined by the Emergency Medical Services Authority. The Emergency Medical Services Authority may charge a fee, sufficient to cover its administrative costs of approval, to an organization that applies to have its first aid training program approved for purposes of this paragraph.

(2) A current license as a physician and surgeon, osteopathic physician and surgeon, or registered nurse, or a current certificate as a physician's assistant or emergency medical technician. The first aid certificate or license shall be maintained throughout the term of the schoolbus or youth bus driver's certificate and shall be presented upon demand of any traffic officer. The schoolbus or youth bus driver's certificate shall not be valid during any time that the driver fails to maintain and possess that license or certificate after the first aid examination has been waived.

12523. Qualifications of Youth Bus Driver

(a) No person shall operate a youth bus without having in possession a valid driver's license of the appropriate class, endorsed for passenger transportation and a certificate issued by the department to permit the operation of a youth bus.

(d) An operator of a youth bus shall, at all times when operating a youth bus, do all of the following:

(1) Use seat belts.

(2) Refrain from smoking.

(3) Report any accidents reportable under Section 16000 to the CHP.

12523.5. General Public Paratransit Vehicle Certificate

(a) No person shall operate a general public paratransit vehicle unless he or she has in his or her possession a valid driver's license of the appropriate class endorsed for passenger transportation when operating a vehicle designed, used, or maintained for carrying more than 10 persons including the driver and either (1) a certificate issued by the department to permit the operation of a general public paratransit vehicle, or (2) a certificate issued by the department to drive a schoolbus or school pupil activity bus Pursuant to Section 12517.

(d) An operator of a general public paratransit vehicle shall do all of the following:

(1) Use seat belts.

(2) Refrain from smoking.

(3) Report any accident reportable under Section 16000 to the CHP.

12523.6. Driver of Vehicle for Hire Transporting Developmentally Disabled Persons; License Requirement

(a)(1) On and after March 1, 1998, no person who is employed primarily as a driver of a motor vehicle that is used for the transportation of persons with developmental disabilities, as defined in subdivision (a) of Section 4512 of the Welfare and Institutions Code, shall operate that motor vehicle unless that person has in his or her possession a valid driver's license of the appropriate class and a valid special driver certificate issued by the department.

(2) This subdivision only applies to a person who is employed by a business, a nonprofit organization, or a state or local public agency.

(b) The special driver certificate shall be issued only to an applicant who has cleared a criminal history background check by the Department of Justice and, if applicable, by the Federal Bureau of Investigation.

(1) In order to determine the applicant's suitability as the driver of a vehicle used for the transportation of persons with developmental disabilities, the Department of the California Highway Patrol shall require the applicant to furnish to that department, on a form provided or approved by that department for submission to the Department of Justice, a full set of fingerprints sufficient to enable a criminal background investigation.

(2) Except as provided in paragraph (3), an applicant shall furnish to the Department of the California Highway Patrol evidence of having resided in this state for seven consecutive years immediately prior to the date of application for the certificate.

(3) If an applicant is unable to furnish the evidence required under paragraph (2), the Department of the California Highway Patrol shall require the applicant to furnish an additional full set of fingerprints. That department shall submit those fingerprint cards to the Department of Justice. The Department of Justice shall, in turn, submit the additional full set of fingerprints required under this paragraph to the Federal Bureau of Investigation for a national criminal history record check.

(4) Applicant fingerprint forms shall be processed and returned to the area office of the Department of the California Highway Patrol from which they originated not later than 15 working days from the date on which the fingerprint forms were received by the Department of Justice, unless circumstances, other than the administrative duties of the Department of Justice, warrant further investigation. Upon implementation of an electronic fingerprinting system with terminals located statewide and managed by the Department of Justice, the Department of Justice shall ascertain the information required pursuant to this subdivision within three working days.

(5) The applicant shall pay, in addition to the fees authorized in Section 2427, a fee of twenty-five dollars ($25) for an original certificate and twelve dollars ($12) for the renewal of that certificate to the Department of the California Highway Patrol.

(c) A certificate issued under this section shall not be deemed a certification to operate a particular vehicle that otherwise requires a driver's license or endorsement for a particular class under this code.

(d) On or after March 1, 1998, no person who operates a business or a nonprofit organization or agency shall employ a person who is employed primarily as a driver of a motor vehicle for hire that is used for the transportation of persons with developmental disabilities unless the employed person operates the motor vehicle in compliance with subdivision (a).

(e) Nothing in this section precludes an employer of persons who are occasionally used as drivers of motor vehicles for the transportation of persons with developmental disabilities from requiring those persons, as a condition of employment, to obtain a special driver certificate pursuant to this section or precludes any volunteer driver from applying for a special driver certificate.

(f) As used in this section, a person is employed primarily as driver if that person performs at least 50 percent of his or her time worked including, but not limited to, time spent assisting persons onto and out of the vehicle, or at least 20 hours a week, whichever is less, as a compensated driver of a motor vehicle for hire for the transportation of persons with developmental disabilities.

(g) This section does not apply to any person who has successfully completed a background investigation prescribed by law, including, but not limited to, health care transport vehicle operators, or to the operator of a taxicab regulated pursuant to Section 21100. This section does not apply to a person who holds a valid certificate, other than a farm labor vehicle driver certificate, issued under Section 12517.4 or 12527. This section does not apply to a driver who provides transportation on a noncommercial basis to persons with developmental disabilities.

12524. Radioactive Materials Driver's Certificate

(a) No class A, class B, or class C driver's license holder shall operate a vehicle hauling fissile class III shipments or large quantity radioactive materials, as defined in Section 173.403 of Title 49 of the Code of Federal Regulations, unless the driver possesses a valid license of the appropriate class and a radioactive materials driver's certificate, issued by the department, which permits the driver to operate those vehicles.

(b) Applicants for the certificates shall present evidence to the department that they have successfully completed the radioactive materials hauler driving training course developed by the department and the CHP before a certificate may be issued. Either the employer of the driver or a driving school licensed pursuant to Chapter 1 (commencing with Section 11100) of Division 5 may administer the training course.

(c) The certificate shall be issued only to applicants qualified by examinations prescribed by the department and the CHP. These examinations shall be conducted by the department, and an examination fee if twelve dollars ($12) shall be paid by the applicant to the department.

(d) Any application for an original radioactive materials drivers certificate or renewal of the certificate and any radioactive materials drivers certificate issued pursuant to this section shall be subject to the provisions of Section 13369.

12804.6. Transit Bus Certificate

(a) A person shall not operate a transit bus transporting passengers unless that person has received from the department a certificate to operate a transit bus or is certified to drive a schoolbus or school pupil activity bus pursuant to Section 12517.

(b) All transit busdrivers shall comply with standards established in Section 40083 of the Education Code. The Department of Motor Vehicles shall establish an implementation program for transit busdrivers to meet these requirements. A transit busdriver who was employed as a busdriver on or before July 1, 1990, shall comply with Section 40085.5 of the Education Code instead of Section 40083 of that code in order to receive his or her original certificate.

(c) Implementation procedures for the issuance of transit busdrivers' certificates may be established by the Department of Motor Vehicles as necessary to implement an orderly transit busdriver training program.

(d) The department shall issue a transit busdriver certificate to a person who provides either of the following:

(1) Proof that he or she has complied with Section 40083 of the Education Code.

(2) Proof that he or she has complied with Section 40085.5 of the Education Code.

(e) The department may charge a fee of ten dollars ($10) to an applicant for an original or a duplicate or renewal certificate under this section.

(f) The department shall issue a certificate to the applicant. The status of the certificate shall also become part of the pull notice and periodic reports issued pursuant to Section 1808.1. The certificate or the pull notice or periodic reports shall become part of, the person's employee records for the purpose of inspection pursuant to Sections 1808.1 and 34501. It shall be unlawful for the employer to permit a person to drive a transit bus who does not have a valid certificate.

(g) The term of a certificate shall be a period not to exceed five years, and shall expire with the driver's license. *(AM '06)*

12804.9. Licenses: Test and Classifications

(a)(1) The examination shall include all of the following:

(A) A test of the applicant's knowledge and understanding of the provisions of this code governing the operation of vehicles upon the highways.

(B) A test of the applicant's ability to read and understand simple English used in highway traffic and directional signs.

(C) A test of the applicant's understanding of traffic signs and signals, including the bikeway signs, markers, and traffic control devices established by the Department of Transportation.

(D) An actual demonstration of the applicant's ability to exercise ordinary and reasonable control in operating a motor vehicle by driving it under the supervision of an examining officer. The applicant shall submit to an examination appropriate to the type of motor vehicle or combination of vehicles he or she desires a license to drive, except that the department may waive the driving test part of the examination for any applicant who submits a license issued by another state, territory, or possession of the United States, the District of Columbia, or the Commonwealth of Puerto Rico if the department verifies through any acknowledged national driver record data source that there are no stops, holds, or other impediments to its issuance. The examining officer may request to see evidence of financial responsibility for the vehicle prior to supervising the demonstration of the applicant's ability to operate the vehicle. The examining officer may refuse to examine an applicant who is unable to provide proof of financial responsibility for the vehicle, unless proof of financial responsibility is not required by this code.

(E) A test of the hearing and eyesight of the applicant, and of other matters that may be necessary to determine the applicant's mental and physical fitness to operate a motor vehicle upon the highways, and whether any grounds exist for refusal of a license under this code.

(2)(A) Before a class A or class B driver's license, or class C driver's license with a commercial endorsement, may be issued or renewed, the applicant shall have in his or her driver record a valid report of a medical examination of the applicant given not more than two years prior to the date of the application by a health care professional. As used in this paragraph, "health care professional" means a person who is licensed, certified, or registered in accordance with applicable state laws and regulations to practice medicine and perform physical examinations in the United States. Health care professionals are doctors of medicine, doctors of osteopathy, physician assistants, and registered advanced practice nurses, or doctors of chiropractic who are clinically competent to perform the medical examination presently required of motor carrier drivers by the United States Department of Transportation. The report shall be on a form approved by the department. In establishing the requirements, consideration may be given to the standards presently required of motor carrier drivers by the Federal Motor Carrier Safety Administration.

(B) The department may accept a federal waiver of one or more physical qualification standards if the waiver is accompanied by a report of a nonqualifying medical examination for a class A or class B driver's license, or class C driver's license with a commercial endorsement, pursuant to Section 391.41(a)(3)(ii) of Subpart E of Part 391 of Title 49 of the Code of Federal Regulations.

(3) A physical defect of the applicant that, in the opinion of the department, is compensated for to ensure safe driving ability, shall not prevent the issuance of a license to the applicant.

(b) In accordance with the following classifications, an applicant for a driver's license shall be required to submit to an examination appropriate to the type of motor vehicle or combination of vehicles the applicant desires a license to drive:

(1) Class A includes the following:

(A) Except as provided in subparagraph (H) of paragraph (3), a combination of vehicles, if a vehicle being towed has a gross vehicle weight rating or gross vehicle weight of more than 10,000 pounds.

(B) A vehicle towing more than one vehicle.

(C) A trailer bus.

(D) The operation of all vehicles under class B and class C.

(2) Class B includes the following:

(A) Except as provided in subparagraph (H) of paragraph (3), a single vehicle with a gross vehicle weight rating or gross vehicle weight of more than 26,000 pounds.

(B) A single vehicle with three or more axles, except any three-axle vehicle weighing less than 6,000 pounds.

(C) A bus with a gross vehicle weight rating or gross vehicle weight of more than 26,000 pounds, except a trailer bus.

(D) A farm labor vehicle.

(E) A single vehicle with three or more axles or a gross vehicle weight rating or gross vehicle weight of more than 26,000 pounds towing another vehicle with a gross vehicle weight rating or gross vehicle weight of 10,000 pounds or less.

(F) A house car over 40 feet in length, excluding safety devices and safety bumpers.

(G) The operation of all vehicles covered under class C.

(3) Class C includes the following:

(A) A two-axle vehicle with a gross vehicle weight rating or gross vehicle weight of 26,000 pounds or less, including when the vehicle is towing a trailer or semitrailer with a gross vehicle weight rating or gross vehicle weight of 10,000 pounds or less.

(B) Notwithstanding subparagraph (A), a two-axle vehicle weighing 4,000 pounds or more unladen when towing a trailer coach not exceeding 9,000 pounds gross.

(C) A house car of 40 feet in length or less.

(D) A three-axle vehicle weighing 6,000 pounds gross or less.

(E) A house car of 40 feet in length or less or a vehicle towing another vehicle with a gross vehicle weight rating of 10,000 pounds or less, including when a tow dolly is used. A person driving a vehicle may not tow another vehicle in violation of Section 21715.

(F)(i) A two-axle vehicle weighing 4,000 pounds or more unladen when towing either a trailer coach or a fifth-wheel travel trailer not exceeding 10,000 pounds gross vehicle weight rating, when the towing of the trailer is not for compensation.

(ii) A two-axle vehicle weighing 4,000 pounds or more unladen when towing a fifth-wheel travel trailer exceeding 10,000 pounds, but not exceeding 15,000 pounds, gross vehicle weight rating, when the towing of the trailer is not for compensation, and if the person has passed a specialized written examination provided by the department relating to the knowledge of this code and other safety aspects governing the towing of recreational vehicles upon the highway.

The authority to operate combinations of vehicles under this subparagraph may be granted by endorsement on a class C license upon completion of that written examination.

(G) A vehicle or combination of vehicles with a gross combination weight rating or a gross vehicle weight rating, as those terms are defined in subdivisions (j) and (k), respectively, of Section 15210, of 26,000 pounds or less, if all of the following conditions are met:

(i) Is operated by a farmer, an employee of a farmer, or an instructor credentialed in agriculture as part of an instructional program in agriculture at the high school, community college, or university level.

(ii) Is used exclusively in the conduct of agricultural operations.

(iii) Is not used in the capacity of a for-hire carrier or for compensation.

(H) Firefighting equipment, provided that the equipment is operated by a person who holds a firefighter endorsement pursuant to Section 12804.11.

(I) A motorized scooter.

(J) A bus with a gross vehicle weight rating or gross vehicle weight of 26,000 pounds or less, except a trailer bus.

(K) Class C does not include a two-wheel motorcycle or a two-wheel motor-driven cycle.

(4) Class M1. A two-wheel motorcycle or a motor-driven cycle. Authority to operate a vehicle included in a class M1 license may be granted by endorsement on a class A, B, or C license upon completion of an appropriate examination.

(5)(A) Class M2 includes the following:

(i) A motorized bicycle or moped, or a bicycle with an attached motor, except a motorized bicycle described in subdivision (b) of Section 406.

(ii) A motorized scooter.

(B) Authority to operate vehicles included in class M2 may be granted by endorsement on a class A, B, or C license upon completion of an appropriate examination, except that no endorsement is required for a motorized scooter. Persons holding a class M1 license or endorsement may operate vehicles included in class M2 without further examination.

(c) A driver's license or driver certificate is not valid for operating a commercial motor vehicle, as defined in subdivision (b) of Section 15210, any other motor vehicle defined in paragraph (1) or (2) of subdivision (b), or any other vehicle requiring a driver to hold any driver certificate or any driver's license endorsement under Section 15275, unless a medical certificate approved by the department that has been issued within two years of the date of the operation of that vehicle and a copy of the medical examination report from which the certificate was issued is on file with the department. Otherwise, the license is valid only for operating class C vehicles that are not commercial vehicles, as defined in subdivision (b) of Section 15210, and for operating class M1 or M2 vehicles, if so endorsed, that are not commercial vehicles, as defined in subdivision (b) of Section 15210.

(d) A license or driver certificate issued prior to the enactment of Chapter 7 (commencing with Section 15200) is valid to operate the class or type of vehicles specified under the law in existence prior to that enactment until the license or certificate expires or is otherwise suspended, revoked, or canceled. Upon application for renewal or replacement of a driver's license, endorsement, or certificate required to operate a commercial motor vehicle, a valid medical certificate on a form approved by the department shall be submitted to the department.

(e) The department may accept a certificate of driving skill that is issued by an employer, authorized by the department to issue a certificate under Section 15250, of the applicant, in lieu of a driving test, on class A or B applications, if the applicant has first qualified for a class C license and has met the other examination requirements for the license for which he or she is applying. The certificate may be submitted as evidence of the applicant's skill in the operation of the types of equipment covered by the license for which he or she is applying.

(f) The department may accept a certificate of competence in lieu of a driving test on class M1 or M2 applications, when the certificate is issued by a law enforcement agency for its officers who operate class M1 or M2 vehicles in their duties, if the applicant has met the other examination requirements for the license for which he or she is applying.

(g) The department may accept a certificate of satisfactory completion of a novice motorcyclist training program approved by the commissioner pursuant to Section 2932 in lieu of a driving test on class M1 or M2 applications, if the applicant has met the other examination requirements for the license for which he or she is applying. The department shall review and approve the written and driving test used by a program to determine whether the program may issue a certificate of completion.

(h) Notwithstanding subdivision (b), a person holding a valid California driver's license of any class may operate a short-term rental motorized bicycle without taking any special examination for the operation of a motorized bicycle, and without having a class M2 endorsement on that license. As used in this subdivision, "short-term" means 48 hours or less.

(i) A person under the age of 21 years shall not be issued a class M1 or M2 license or endorsement unless he or she provides evidence satisfactory to the department of completion of a motorcycle safety training program that is operated pursuant to Article 2 (commencing with Section 2930) of Chapter 5 of Division 2.

(j) A driver of a vanpool vehicle may operate with a class C license but shall possess evidence of a medical examination required for a class B license when operating vanpool vehicles. In order to be eligible to drive the vanpool vehicle, the driver shall keep in the vanpool vehicle a statement, signed under penalty of perjury, that he or she has not been convicted of reckless driving, drunk driving, or a hit-and-run offense in the last five years. *(AM '13)*

12804.10. Driving House Car Over 40 Feet Long; Class B License Required

(a) Notwithstanding any other provision of law, a person issued a class C license under paragraph (3) of subdivision (b) of Section 12804.9 may drive any house car of 40 feet in length or less without obtaining a noncommercial class B driver's license with house car endorsement as described in subdivision (b).

(b) Any person seeking to drive any house car over 40 feet in length, excluding safety devices and safety bumpers, shall obtain a noncommercial class B driver's license with house car endorsement as described in this subdivision. The applicant for that endorsement shall pass a specialized written examination and demonstrate the ability to exercise ordinary and reasonable control in operating that vehicle by driving it under the supervision of an examining officer. Upon satisfactory completion of the examination and demonstration, the applicant shall be issued a noncommercial class B driver's license with house car endorsement by the department. Upon application for an endorsement to operate this vehicle, and every two years thereafter, the applicant shall submit medical information on a form approved by the department.

12804.11. Operation of Firefighting Equipment

(a) To operate firefighting equipment, a driver, including a tiller operator, is required to do either of the following:

(1) Obtain and maintain a firefighter endorsement issued by the department and obtain and maintain a class C license as described in Section 12804.9, a restricted class A license as described in Section 12804.12, or a noncommercial class B license as described in Section 12804.10.

(2) Obtain and maintain a class A or B license as described in Section *** 12804.9 and, as appropriate, for the size and configuration of the firefighting equipment operated.

(b) To qualify for a firefighter endorsement the driver shall do all of the following:

(1)(A) Provide to the department proof of current employment as a firefighter or registration as a volunteer firefighter with a fire department and evidence of fire equipment operation training by providing a letter*** or other indication*** from the chief of the fire department*** or his or her designee.

(B) For purposes of this section, evidence of fire equipment operation training means the applicant has successfully completed Fire Apparatus Driver/Operator 1A taught by an instructor registered with the Office of the State Fire Marshal or fire department driver training that meets all of the following requirements:

(i) Meets or exceeds the standards outlined in NFPA 1002, Chapter 4 (2008 version) or the Fire Apparatus Driver/Operator 1A course adopted by the Office of the State Fire Marshal.

(ii) Prepares the applicant to safely operate the department's fire equipment that the applicant will be authorized to operate.

(iii) Includes a classroom (cognitive) portion of at least 16 hours.

(iv) Includes a manipulative portion of at least 14 hours, which includes directly supervised behind-the-wheel driver training.

(C) Driver training shall be conducted by a person who is registered with the Office of the State Fire Marshal to instruct a Fire Apparatus Driver/Operator 1A course or a person who meets all of the following criteria:

(i) Possesses a minimum of five years of fire service experience as an emergency vehicle operator, three of which must be at the rank of engineer or higher.

(ii) Possesses a valid California class A or B license or a class A or B license restricted to the operation of firefighting equipment.

(iii) Is certified as a qualified training instructor or training officer by the State of California, the federal government, or a county training officers'association.

(2) Pass the written firefighter examination developed by the department with the cooperation of the Office of the State Fire Marshal***.

(3) Upon application and every two years thereafter, submit medical information on a form approved by the department.

(c) There shall be no additional charge for adding a firefighter endorsement to an original license or when renewing a license. To add a firefighter endorsement to an existing license when not renewing the license, the applicant shall pay the fee for a duplicate license pursuant to Section 14901.

(d)(1) A driver of firefighting equipment is subject to the requirements of subdivision (a) if both of the following conditions exist:

(A) The equipment is operated by a person employed as a firefighter by a federal or state agency, by a regularly organized fire department of a city, county, city and county, or district, or by a tribal fire department or registered as a volunteer member of a regularly organized fire department having official recognition of the city, county, city and county, or district in which the department is located, or of a tribal fire department.

(B) The motor vehicle is used to travel to and from the scene of ***an emergency situation, or to transport equipment used in the control of ***an emergency situation, and which is owned, leased, or rented by, or under the exclusive control of, a federal or state agency, a regularly organized fire department of a city, county, city and county, or district, a volunteer fire department having official recognition of the city, county, city and county, or district in which the department is located, or a tribal fire department.

(2) A driver of firefighting equipment is not required to obtain and maintain a firefighter endorsement pursuant to paragraph (1) of subdivision (a) if the driver is operating the firefighting equipment for training purposes, during a nonemergency, while under the direct supervision of a fire department employee who is properly licensed to operate the equipment and is authorized by the fire department to provide training.

(e) For purposes of this section, a tiller operator is the driver of the rear free-axle portion of a ladder truck.

(f) For purposes of this section, "firefighting equipment"means a motor vehicle, that meets the definition of a class A or class B vehicle described in subdivision (b) of Section 12804.9, that is used to travel to and from the scene of an emergency situation, or to transport equipment used in the control of an emergency situation, and that is owned, leased, or rented by, or under the exclusive control of, a federal or state agency, a regularly organized fire department of a city, county, city and county, or district, or a volunteer fire department having official recognition of the city, county, city and county, or district in which the department is located.

(g) Notwithstanding paragraph (1) of subdivision (a), a regularly organized fire department, having official recognition of the city, county, city and county, or district in which the department is located, may require an employee or a volunteer of the fire department who is a driver or operator of firefighting equipment to hold a class A or B license.

(h) This section applies to a person hired by a fire department, or to a person renewing a driver's license, on or after January 1, 2011. *(AM '13)*

12804.15.   House Car: Defined; License Required

(a) Notwithstanding Section 362, for purposes of this section "house car"means a vehicle described in subdivision (b) of Section 12804.10.

(b)(1) Except as provided under paragraph (2), no person may operate a house car unless that person has in his or her possession a valid driver's license of the appropriate class and an endorsement thereto issued by the department to permit operation of the house car.

(2) A nonresident may not operate a house car in this state unless that person is in possession of an out-of-state driver's license authorizing the operation of that vehicle.

(c) An endorsement to drive a house car may be issued only if the applicant meets all of the following conditions:

(1) The applicant successfully completes an examination prescribed by the department to determine qualification for the endorsement.

(2) Upon initial application and every two years thereafter, the applicant submits medical information on a form approved by the department to verify that the person meets the minimum medical requirements established by the department for operation of a house car.

(3) Upon application for issuance of an original driver's license or renewal driver's license pursuant to subdivision (b) of Section 12804.10, there shall be paid to the department a fee of thirty-four dollars ($34) for a license that will expire on the applicant's fifth birthday following the date of the application.

(d) The department may deny, suspend, or revoke an endorsement to drive a house car when the applicant does not meet any requirement for the issuance or retention of the endorsement.

12814.6. Provisional Licenses for Minors; Distinctive Driver's License

(a) Except as provided in Section 12814.7, a driver's license issued to a person at least 16 years of age but under 18 years of age shall be issued pursuant to the provisional licensing program contained in this section. The program shall consist of all of the following components:

(1) Upon application for an original license, the applicant shall be issued an instruction permit pursuant to Section 12509. A person who has in his or her immediate possession a valid permit issued pursuant to Section 12509 may operate a motor vehicle, other than a motorcycle or motorized bicycle, only when the person is either taking the driver training instruction referred to in paragraph (3) or practicing that instruction, provided the person is accompanied by, and is under the immediate supervision of, a California licensed driver 25 years of age or older whose driving privilege is not on probation. The age requirement of this paragraph does not apply if the licensed driver is the parent, spouse, or guardian of the permitholder or is a licensed or certified driving instructor.

(2) The person shall hold an instruction permit for not less than six months prior to applying for a provisional driver's license.

(3) The person shall have complied with one of the following:

(A) Satisfactory completion of approved courses in automobile driver education and driver training maintained pursuant to provisions of the Education Code in any secondary school of California, or equivalent instruction in a secondary school of another state.

(B) Satisfactory completion of an integrated driver education and training program that is approved by the department and conducted by a driving instructor licensed under Chapter 1 (commencing with Section 11100) of Division 5. The program shall utilize segmented modules, whereby a portion of the educational instruction is provided by, and then reinforced through, specific behind-the-wheel training before moving to the next phase of driver education and training. The program shall contain a minimum of 30 hours of classroom instruction and six hours of behind-the-wheel training.

(C) Satisfactory completion of six hours or more of behind-the-wheel instruction by a driving school or an independent driving instructor licensed under Chapter 1 (commencing with Section 11100) of Division 5 and either an accredited course in automobile driver education in any secondary school of California pursuant to provisions of the Education Code or satisfactory completion of equivalent professional instruction acceptable to the department. To be acceptable to the department, the professional instruction shall meet minimum standards to be prescribed by the department, and the standards shall be at least equal to the requirements for driver education and driver training contained in the rules and regulations adopted by the State Board of Education pursuant to the Education Code. A person who has complied with this subdivision shall not be required by the governing board of a school district to comply with subparagraph (A) in order to graduate from high school.

(D) Except as provided under subparagraph (B), a student may not take driver training instruction, unless he or she has successfully completed driver education.

(4) The person shall complete 50 hours of supervised driving practice prior to the issuance of a provisional license, which is in addition to any other driver training instruction required by law. Not less than 10 of the required practice hours shall include driving during darkness, as defined in Section 280. Upon application for a provisional license, the person shall submit to the department the certification of a parent, spouse, guardian, or licensed or certified driving instructor that the applicant has completed the required amount of driving practice and is prepared to take the department's driving test. A person without a parent, spouse, guardian, or who is an emancipated minor, may have a licensed driver 25 years of age or older or a licensed or certified driving instructor complete the certification. This requirement does not apply to motorcycle practice.

(5) The person shall successfully complete an examination required by the department. Before retaking a test, the person shall wait for not less than one week after failure of the written test and for not less than two weeks after failure of the driving test.

(b) Except as provided in Section 12814.7, the provisional driver's license shall be subject to all of the following restrictions:

(1) Except as specified in paragraph (2), during the first 12 months after issuance of a provisional license the licensee may not do any of the following unless accompanied and supervised by a licensed driver who is the licensee's parent or guardian, a licensed driver who is 25 years of age or older, or a licensed or certified driving instructor:

(A) Drive between the hours of 11 p.m. and 5 a.m.

(B) Transport passengers who are under 20 years of age.

(2) A licensee may drive between the hours of 11 p.m. and 5 a.m. or transport an immediate family member without being accompanied and supervised by a licensed driver who is the licensee's parent or guardian, a licensed driver who is 25 years of age or older, or a licensed or certified driving instructor, in the following circumstances:

(A) Medical necessity of the licensee when reasonable transportation facilities are inadequate and operation of a vehicle by a minor is necessary. The licensee shall keep in his or her possession a signed statement from a physician familiar with the condition, containing a diagnosis and probable date when sufficient recovery will have been made to terminate the necessity.

(B) Schooling or school-authorized activities of the licensee when reasonable transportation facilities are inadequate and operation of a vehicle by a minor is necessary. The licensee shall keep in his or her possession a signed statement from the school principal, dean, or school staff member designated by the principal or dean, containing a probable date that the schooling or school-authorized activity will have been completed.

(C) Employment necessity of the licensee when reasonable transportation facilities are inadequate and operation of a vehicle by a minor is necessary. The licensee shall keep in his or her possession a signed statement from the employer, verifying employment and containing a probable date that the employment will have been completed.

(D) Necessity of the licensee or the licensee's immediate family member when reasonable transportation facilities are inadequate and operation of a vehicle by a minor is necessary to transport the licensee or the licensee's immediate family member. The licensee shall keep in his or her possession a signed statement from a parent or legal guardian verifying the reason and containing a probable date that the necessity will have ceased.

(E) The licensee is an emancipated minor.

(c) A law enforcement officer shall not stop a vehicle for the sole purpose of determining whether the driver is in violation of the restrictions imposed under subdivision (b).

(d) A law enforcement officer shall not stop a vehicle for the sole purpose of determining whether a driver who is subject to the license restrictions in subdivision (b) is in violation of Article 2.5 (commencing with Section 118947) of Chapter 4 of Part 15 of Division 104 of the Health and Safety Code.

(e)(1) Upon a finding that any licensee has violated paragraph (1) of subdivision (b), the court shall impose one of the following:

(A) Not less than eight hours nor more than 16 hours of community service for a first offense and not less than 16 hours nor more than 24 hours of community service for a second or subsequent offense.

(B) A fine of not more than thirty-five dollars ($35) for a first offense and a fine of not more than fifty dollars ($50) for a second or subsequent offense.

(2) If the court orders community service, the court shall retain jurisdiction until the hours of community service have been completed.

(3) If the hours of community service have not been completed within 90 days, the court shall impose a fine of not more than thirty-five dollars ($35) for a first offense and not more than fifty dollars ($50) for a second or subsequent offense.

(f) A conviction of paragraph (1) of subdivision (b), when reported to the department, may not be disclosed as otherwise specified in Section 1808 or constitute a violation point count value pursuant to Section 12810.

(g) Any term of restriction or suspension of the driving privilege imposed on a person pursuant to this subdivision shall remain in effect until the end of the term even though the person becomes 18 years of age before the term ends.

(1) The driving privilege shall be suspended when the record of the person shows one or more notifications issued pursuant to Section 40509 or 40509.5. The suspension shall continue until any notification issued pursuant to Section 40509 or 40509.5 has been cleared.

(2) A 30-day restriction shall be imposed when a driver's record shows a violation point count of two or more points in 12 months, as determined in accordance with Section 12810. The restriction shall require the licensee to be accompanied by a licensed parent, spouse, guardian, or other licensed driver 25 years of age or older, except when operating a class M vehicle, or so licensed, with no passengers aboard.

(3) A six-month suspension of the driving privilege and a one-year term of probation shall be imposed whenever a licensee's record shows a violation point count of three or more points in 12 months, as determined in accordance with Section 12810. The terms and conditions of probation shall include, but not be limited to, both of the following:

(A) The person shall violate no law which, if resulting in conviction, is reportable to the department under Section 1803.

(B) The person shall remain free from accident responsibility.

(h) Whenever action by the department under subdivision (g) arises as a result of a motor vehicle accident, the person may, in writing and within 10 days, demand a hearing to present evidence that he or she was not responsible for the accident upon which the action is based. Whenever action by the department is based upon a conviction reportable to the department under Section 1803, the person has no right to a hearing pursuant to Article 3 (commencing with Section 14100) of Chapter 3.

(i) The department shall require a person whose driving privilege is suspended or revoked pursuant to subdivision (g) to submit proof of financial responsibility as defined in Section 16430. The proof of financial responsibility shall be filed on or before the date of reinstatement following the suspension or revocation. The proof of financial responsibility shall be maintained with the department for three years following the date of reinstatement.

(j)(1) Notwithstanding any other provision of this code, the department may issue a distinctive driver's license, that displays a distinctive color or a distinctively colored stripe or other distinguishing characteristic, to persons at least 16 years of age and older but under 18 years of age, and to persons 18 years of age and older but under 21 years of age, so that the distinctive license feature is immediately recognizable. The features shall clearly differentiate between driver's licenses issued to persons at least 16 years of age or older but under 18 years of age and to persons 18 years of age or older but under 21 years of age.

(2) If changes in the format or appearance of driver's licenses are adopted pursuant to this subdivision, those changes may be implemented under any new contract for the production of driver's licenses entered into after the adoption of those changes.

(k) The department shall include, on the face of the provisional driver's license, the original issuance date of the provisional driver's license in addition to any other issuance date.

(l) This section shall be known and may be cited as the Brady-Jared Teen Driver Safety Act of 1997. *(AD '97, AM '00, '02, '03, '05, '07)*

12815. Licenses Lost, Destroyed, or Mutilated

(a) If a driver's license issued under this code is lost, destroyed or mutilated, or a new true, full name is acquired, the person to whom it was issued shall obtain a duplicate upon furnishing to the department (1) satisfactory proof of that loss, destruction, or mutilation and (2) if the licensee is a minor, evidence of permission to obtain a duplicate secured from the parents, guardian, or person having custody of the minor. Any person who loses a driver's license and who, after obtaining a duplicate, finds the original license shall immediately destroy the original license.

(b) A person in possession of a valid driver's license who has been informed either by the department or by a law enforcement agency that the document is mutilated shall surrender the license to the department not later than 10 days after that notification.

(c) For purposes of this section, a mutilated license is one that has been damaged sufficiently to render any or all of the elements of identity set forth in Sections 12800.5 and 12811 unreadable or unidentifiable through visual, mechanical, or electronic means. *(AM '99, '00)*

12951. Possession of License

(a) The licensee shall have the valid driver's license issued to him or her in his or her immediate possession at all times when driving a motor vehicle upon a highway.

Any charge under this subdivision shall be dismissed when the person charged produces in court a driver's license duly issued to that person and valid at the time of his or her arrest, except that upon a third or subsequent charge the court in its discretion may dismiss the charge. When a temporary, interim, or duplicate driver's license is produced in court, the charge shall not be dismissed unless the court has been furnished proof by the department that such temporary, interim, or duplicate license was issued prior to the arrest, that the driving privilege and license had not been suspended or revoked, and that the person was eligible for the temporary, interim, or duplicate license.

(b) The driver of a motor vehicle shall present his or her license for examination upon demand of a peace officer enforcing the provisions of this code.

13000.1. Issuance of Identification Card; Grounds for Refusal

(a) The department may refuse to issue or renew an identification card to any person for any of the following reasons:

(1) The department determines that the person has knowingly used a false or fictitious name in any application.

(2) The department determines that the person has impersonated another in making an application.

(3) The department determines that the person has knowingly made a false statement, knowingly concealed a material fact, or otherwise committed any fraud on any application.

(b) The department may declare an identification card invalid upon any of the grounds specified in subdivision (a) as reason to refuse to reissue or renew an identification card. The holder of an identification card that has been declared invalid shall surrender the identification card to the department. *(AD '00)*

13003. Duplicate Cards

(a) If an identification card issued under this code is lost, destroyed, mutilated, or a new true full name is acquired, the person to whom it was issued shall make application for an original identification card as specified in Section 13000. The fee provided in Section 14902 shall be paid to the department upon application for the card. Every identification card issued pursuant to this section shall expire as provided in Section 13002 and shall be deemed an original identification card for that purpose.(b) A person in possession of a valid identification card who has been informed either by the department or by a law enforcement agency that the document is mutilated shall surrender the identification card to the department not later than 10 days after that notification.

(c) For purposes of this section a mutilated identification card is one that has been damaged sufficiently to render any or all of the elements of identity set forth in Sections 13005 and 13005.5 unreadable or unidentifiable through visual, mechanical, or electronic means.

13004. Identification Cards; Unlawful Acts

It is unlawful for any person:

(a) To display or cause or permit to be displayed or have in his possession any canceled, fictitious, fraudulently altered, or fraudulently obtained identification card.

(b) To lend his identification card to any other person or knowingly permit the use thereof by another.

(c) To display or represent any identification card not issued to him as being his card.

(d) To permit any unlawful use of an identification card issued to him.

(e) To do any act forbidden or fail to perform any act required by this article.

(f) To photograph, photostat, duplicate, or in any way reproduce any identification card or facsimile thereof in such a manner that it could be mistaken for a valid identification card, or to display or have in his possession any such photograph, photostat, duplicate, reproduction, or facsimile unless authorized by the provisions of this code.

(g) To alter any identification card in any manner not authorized by this code.

13004.1. Identification Cards; Manufacture or Sell

(a) A person shall not manufacture or sell an identification document of a size and form substantially similar to, or that purports to confer the same privileges as, the identification cards issued by the department.

(b) A violation of this section is a misdemeanor punishable as follows:

(1) The court shall impose a fine of not less than two hundred fifty dollars ($250) and not more than one thousand dollars ($1,000), and 24 hours of community service, to be served when the person is not employed or is not attending school. No part of the fine or community service shall be suspended or waived.

(2) In lieu of the penalties imposed under paragraph (1), the court, in its discretion, may impose a jail term of up to one year and a fine of up to one thousand dollars ($1,000). In exercising its discretion the court shall consider the extent of the defendant's commercial motivation for the offense.

(c) Prosecution under this section shall not preclude prosecution under any other applicable provision of law. *(AM '07, '10)*

13007. Change of Address

Whenever any person after applying for or receiving an identification card acquires an address different from the address shown on the identification card issued to him, he shall within 10 days thereafter notify the department of his old and new address. The department may thereupon take such action as necessary to insure that the identification card reflects the proper address of the identification card holder.

CHAPTER 2. SUSPENSION OR REVOCATION OF LICENSES

13382. Notice of Order of Suspension; Service by Peace Officer

(a) If the chemical test results for a person who has been arrested for a violation of Section 23152 or 23153 show that the person has 0.08 percent or more, by weight, of alcohol in the person's blood, or if the chemical test results for a person who has been arrested for a violation of Section 23140 show that the person has 0.05 percent or more, by weight, of alcohol in the person's blood, the peace officer, acting on behalf of the department, shall serve a notice of order of suspension or revocation of the person's privilege to operate a motor vehicle personally on the arrested person.

(b) If the peace officer serves the notice of order of suspension or revocation, the peace officer shall take possession of any driver's license issued by this state which is held by the person. When the officer takes possession of a valid driver's license, the officer shall issue, on behalf of the department, a temporary driver's license. The temporary driver's license shall be an endorsement on the notice of the order of suspension or revocation and shall be valid for 30 days from the date of arrest.

(c) The peace officer shall immediately forward a copy of the completed notice of order of suspension form, and any driver's license taken into possession under subdivision (b), with the report required by Section 13380, to the department. For the purposes of this section, "immediately" means on or before the end of the fifth ordinary business day following the arrest. *(AD '98)*

13388. Preliminary Alcohol Screening Test; Driver Under 21 Years of Age

(a) If a peace officer lawfully detains a person under 21 years of age who is driving a motor vehicle, and the officer has reasonable cause to believe that the person is in violation of Section 23136, the officer shall request that the person take a preliminary alcohol screening test to determine the presence of alcohol in the person, if a preliminary alcohol screening test device is immediately available. If a preliminary alcohol screening test device is not immediately available, the officer may request the person to submit to chemical testing of his or her blood, breath, or urine, conducted pursuant to Section 23612.

(b) If the person refuses to take, or fails to complete, the preliminary alcohol screening test or refuses to take or fails to complete a chemical test if a preliminary alcohol device is not immediately available, or if the person takes the preliminary alcohol screening test and that test reveals a blood-alcohol concentration of 0.01 percent or greater, or if the results of a chemical test reveal a blood-alcohol concentration of 0.01 percent or greater, the officer shall proceed as follows:

(1) The officer, acting on behalf of the department, shall serve the person with a notice of an order of suspension of the person's driving privilege.

(2) The officer shall take possession of any driver's license issued by this state which is held by the person. When the officer takes possession of a valid driver's license, the officer shall issue, on behalf of the department, a temporary driver's license. The temporary driver's license shall be an endorsement on the notice of the order of suspension and shall be valid for 30 days from the date of issuance, or until receipt of the order of suspension from the department, whichever occurs first.

(3) The officer immediately shall forward a copy of the completed notice of order of suspension form, and any driver's license taken into possession under paragraph (2), with the report required by Section 13380, to the department. For the purposes of this paragraph, "immediately" means on or before the end of the fifth ordinary business day after the notice of order of suspension was served.

(c) For the purposes of this section, a preliminary alcohol screening test device is an instrument designed and used to measure the presence of alcohol in a person based on a breath sample. *(AD '98)*

13389. Preliminary Alcohol Screening; Person Previously Convicted of D.U.I.

(a) If a peace officer lawfully detains a person previously convicted of Section 23152 or 23153 who is driving a motor vehicle, while the person is on probation for a violation of Section 23152 or 23153, and the officer has reasonable cause to believe that the person is in violation of Section 23154, the officer shall request that the person take a preliminary alcohol screening test to determine the presence of alcohol in the person, if a preliminary alcohol screening test device is immediately available. If a preliminary alcohol screening test device is not immediately available, the officer may request the person to submit to chemical testing of his or her blood, breath, or urine, conducted pursuant to Section 23612.

(b) If the person refuses to take, or fails to complete, the preliminary alcohol screening test or refuses to take or fails to complete a chemical test if a preliminary alcohol device is not immediately available, or if the person takes the preliminary alcohol screening test and that test reveals a blood-alcohol concentration of 0.01 percent or greater, the officer shall proceed as follows:

(1) The officer, acting on behalf of the department, shall serve the person with a notice of an order of suspension of the person's driving privilege.

(2)(A) The officer shall take possession of any driver's license issued by this state that is held by the person. When the officer takes possession of a valid driver's license, the officer shall issue, on behalf of the department, a temporary driver's license.

(B) The temporary driver's license shall be an endorsement on the notice of the order of suspension and shall be valid for 30 days from the date of issuance, or until receipt of the order of suspension from the department, whichever occurs first.

(3)(A) The officer shall immediately forward a copy of the completed notice of order of suspension form, and any driver's license taken into possession under paragraph (2), with the report required by Section 13380, to the department.

(B) For the purposes of subparagraph (A), "immediately"means on or before the end of the fifth ordinary business day after the notice of order of suspension was served.

(c) For the purposes of this section, a preliminary alcohol screening test device is an instrument designed and used to measure the presence of alcohol in a person based on a breath sample. *(AD '07)*

CHAPTER 3. INVESTIGATION AND HEARING

Article 1. Investigation and Re-Examination

13803. Mandatory Re-Examination Upon Request of Family Member

(a) The department shall conduct a reexamination, including a demonstration of the person's ability to operate a motor vehicle as described in Section 12804.9, to determine whether the driving privilege of any person to operate a motor vehicle should be suspended or revoked, or whether terms or conditions of probation should be imposed upon receiving information from any member of the vehicle operator's family within 3 degrees of consanguinity, or the operator's spouse, who has reached 18 years of age, except that no person may report the same family member pursuant to this section more than one time during a 12-month period.

(b) The report described in subdivision (a) shall state that the person filing the report reasonably and in good faith believes that the operator cannot safely operate a motor vehicle. The report shall be based upon personal observation or physical evidence of a physical or medical condition that has the potential to impair the ability to drive safely, or upon personal knowledge of a driving record that, based on traffic citations or other evidence, indicates an unsafe driver. The observation or physical evidence, or the driving record, shall be described in the report, or the report shall be based upon an investigation by a law enforcement officer.

(c) No person who makes a report in good faith pursuant to this section shall be civilly or criminally liable for making that report.

(d) This section shall remain in effect only until January 1, 2011, and as of that date is repealed, unless a later enacted statute, that is enacted before January 1, 2011, deletes or extends that date. *(AD '00)*

CHAPTER 4. VIOLATION OF LICENSE PROVISIONS

14600. Change of Address

(a) Whenever any person after applying for or receiving a driver's license moves to a new residence, or acquires a new mailing address different from the address shown in the application or in the license as issued, he or she shall within 10 days thereafter notify the department of the old and new address. The department may issue a document to accompany the driver's license reflecting the new address of the holder of the license.

(b) When, pursuant to subdivision (b) of Section 12951, a driver presents his or her driver's license to a peace officer, he or she shall, if applicable, also present the document issued pursuant to subdivision (a) if the driver's license does not reflect the driver's current residence or mailing address.

14601. Driving When Privilege Suspended or Revoked

(a) No person shall drive a motor vehicle at any time when that person's driving privilege is suspended or revoked for reckless driving in violation of Section 23103, 23104, or 23105, any reason listed in subdivision (a) or (c) of Section 12806 authorizing the department to refuse to issue a license, negligent or incompetent operation of a motor vehicle as prescribed in subdivision (e) of Section 12809, or negligent operation as prescribed in Section 12810.5, if the person so driving has knowledge of the suspension or revocation. Knowledge shall be conclusively presumed if mailed notice has been given by the department to the person pursuant to Section 13106. The presumption established by this subdivision is a presumption affecting the burden of proof.

(b) A person convicted under this section shall be punished as follows:

(1) Upon a first conviction, by imprisonment in a county jail for not less than five days or more than six months and by a fine of not less than three hundred dollars ($300) or more than one thousand dollars ($1,000).

(2) If the offense occurred within five years of a prior offense that resulted in a conviction of a violation of this section or Section 14601.1, 14601.2, or 14601.5, by imprisonment in a county jail for not less than 10 days or more than one year and by a fine of not less than five hundred dollars ($500) or more than two thousand dollars ($2,000).

(c) If the offense occurred within five years of a prior offense that resulted in a conviction of a violation of this section or Section 14601.1, 14601.2, or 14601.5, and is granted probation, the court shall impose as a condition of probation that the person be confined in a county jail for at least 10 days.

(d) Nothing in this section prohibits a person from driving a motor vehicle, that is owned or utilized by the person's employer, during the course of employment on private property that is owned or utilized by the employer, except an offstreet parking facility as defined in subdivision (c) of Section 12500.

(e) When the prosecution agrees to a plea of guilty or nolo contendere to a charge of a violation of this section in satisfaction of, or as a substitute for, an original charge of a violation of Section 14601.2, and the court accepts that plea, except, in the interest of justice, when the court finds it would be inappropriate, the court shall, pursuant to Section 23575, require the person convicted, in addition to any other requirements, to install a certified ignition interlock device on any vehicle that the person owns or operates for a period not to exceed three years.

(f) This section also applies to the operation of an off-highway motor vehicle on those lands to which the Chappie-Z'berg Off-Highway Motor Vehicle Law of 1971 (Division 16.5 (commencing with Section 38000)) applies as to off-highway motor vehicles, as described in Section 38001. *(AM '00, '03, '04, '07)*

14601.1. Driving When Privilege Suspended or Revoked for Other Reasons

(a) No person shall drive a motor vehicle when his or her driving privilege is suspended or revoked for any reason other than those listed in Section 14601, 14601.2, or 14601.5, if the person so driving has knowledge of the suspension or revocation. Knowledge shall be conclusively presumed if mailed notice has been given by the department to the person pursuant to Section 13106. The presumption established by this subdivision is a presumption affecting the burden of proof.

(b) Any person convicted under this section shall be punished as follows:

(1) Upon a first conviction, by imprisonment in the county jail for not more than six months or by a fine of not less than three hundred dollars ($300) or more than one thousand dollars ($1,000), or by both that fine and imprisonment.

(2) If the offense occurred within five years of a prior offense which resulted in a conviction of a violation of this section or Section 14601, 14601.2, or 14601.5, by imprisonment in the county jail for not less than five days or more than one year and by a fine of not less than five hundred dollars ($500) or more than two thousand dollars ($2,000).

(c) Nothing in this section prohibits a person from driving a motor vehicle, which is owned or utilized by the person's employer, during the course of employment on private property which is owned or utilized by the employer, except an offstreet parking facility as defined in subdivision (d) of Section 12500.

(d) When the prosecution agrees to a plea of guilty or nolo contendere to a charge of a violation of this section in satisfaction of, or as a substitute for, an original charge of a violation of Section 14601.2, and the court accepts that plea, except, in the interest of justice, when the court finds it would be inappropriate, the court shall, pursuant to Section 23575, require the person convicted, in addition to any other requirements, to install a certified ignition interlock device on any vehicle that the person owns or operates for a period not to exceed three years.

(e) This section also applies to the operation of an off-highway motor vehicle on those lands to which the Chappie-Z'berg Off-Highway Motor Vehicle Law of 1971 (Division 16.5 (commencing with Section 38000)) applies as to off-highway motor vehicles, as described in Section 38001. *(AM '00, '04)*

14601.2. Driving When Privilege Suspended or Revoked for DUI, With Excessive Blood Alcohol, or When Addicted

(a) A person shall not drive a motor vehicle at any time when that person's driving privilege is suspended or revoked for a conviction of a violation of Section 23152 or 23153 if the person so driving has knowledge of the suspension or revocation.

(b) Except in full compliance with the restriction, a person shall not drive a motor vehicle at any time when that person's driving privilege is restricted if the person so driving has knowledge of the restriction.

(c) Knowledge of the suspension or revocation of the driving privilege shall be conclusively presumed if mailed notice has been given by the department to the person pursuant to Section 13106. Knowledge of the restriction of the driving privilege shall be presumed if notice has been given by the court to the person. The presumption established by this subdivision is a presumption affecting the burden of proof.

(d) A person convicted of a violation of this section shall be punished as follows:

(1) Upon a first conviction, by imprisonment in the county jail for not less than 10 days or more than six months and by a fine of not less than three hundred dollars ($300) or more than one thousand dollars ($1,000), unless the person has been designated a habitual traffic offender under subdivision (b) of Section 23546, subdivision (b) of Section 23550, or subdivision (d) of Section 23550.5, in which case the person, in addition, shall be sentenced as provided in paragraph (3) of subdivision (e) of Section 14601.3.

(2) If the offense occurred within five years of a prior offense that resulted in a conviction of a violation of this section or Section 14601, 14601.1, or 14601.5, by imprisonment in the county jail for not less than 30 days or more than one year and by a fine of not less than five hundred dollars ($500) or more than two thousand dollars ($2,000), unless the person has been designated a habitual traffic offender under subdivision (b) of Section 23546, subdivision (b) of Section 23550, or subdivision (d) of Section 23550.5, in which case the person, in addition, shall be sentenced as provided in paragraph (3) of subdivision (e) of Section 14601.3.

(e) If a person is convicted of a first offense under this section and is granted probation, the court shall impose as a condition of probation that the person be confined in the county jail for at least 10 days.

(f) If the offense occurred within five years of a prior offense that resulted in a conviction of a violation of this section or Section 14601, 14601.1, or 14601.5 and is granted probation, the court shall impose as a condition of probation that the person be confined in the county jail for at least 30 days.

(g) If a person is convicted of a second or subsequent offense that results in a conviction of this section within seven years, but over five years, of a prior offense that resulted in a conviction of a violation of this section or Section 14601, 14601.1, or 14601.5 and is granted probation, the court shall impose as a condition of probation that the person be confined in the county jail for at least 10 days.

(h) Pursuant to Section 23575, the court shall require a person convicted of a violation of this section to install a certified ignition interlock device on a vehicle the person owns or operates. Upon receipt of the abstract of a conviction under this section, the department shall not reinstate the privilege to operate a motor vehicle until the department receives proof of either the "Verification of Installation" form as described in paragraph (2) of subdivision (g) of Section 13386 or the Judicial Council Form I.D. 100.

(i) This section does not prohibit a person who is participating in, or has completed, an alcohol or drug rehabilitation program from driving a motor vehicle that is owned or utilized by the person's employer, during the course of employment on private property that is owned or utilized by the employer, except an offstreet parking facility as defined in subdivision (c) of Section 12500.

(j) This section also applies to the operation of an off-highway motor vehicle on those lands that the Chappie-Z'berg Off-Highway Motor Vehicle Law of 1971 (Division 16.5 (commencing with Section 38000)) applies as to off-highway motor vehicles, as described in Section 38001.

(k) If Section 23573 is applicable, then subdivision (h) is not applicable. *(AM '08)*

14601.3. Habitual Traffic Offender

(a) It is unlawful for a person whose driving privilege has been suspended or revoked to accumulate a driving record history which results from driving during the period of suspension or revocation. A person who violates this subdivision is designated an habitual traffic offender.

For purposes of this section, a driving record history means any of the following, if the driving occurred during any period of suspension or revocation:

(1) Two or more convictions within a 12-month period of an offense given a violation point count of two pursuant to Section 12810.

(2) Three or more convictions within a 12-month period of an offense given a violation point count of one pursuant to Section 12810.

(3) Three or more accidents within a 12-month period that are subject to the reporting requirements of Section 16000.

(4) Any combination of convictions or accidents, as specified in paragraphs (1) to (3), inclusive, which results during any 12-month period in a violation point count of three or more pursuant to Section 12810.

(b) Knowledge of suspension or revocation of the driving privilege shall be conclusively presumed if mailed notice has been given by the department to the person pursuant to Section 13106. The presumption established by this subdivision is a presumption affecting the burden of proof.

(c) The department, within 30 days of receipt of a duly certified abstract of the record of any court or accident report which results in a person being designated an habitual traffic offender, may execute and transmit by mail a notice of that designation to the office of the district attorney having jurisdiction over the location of the person's last known address as contained in the department's records.

(d)(1) The district attorney, within 30 days of receiving the notice required in subdivision (c), shall inform the department of whether or not the person will be prosecuted for being an habitual traffic offender.

(2) Notwithstanding any other provision of this section, any habitual traffic offender designated under subdivision (b) of Section 23546, subdivision (b) of Section 23550, or subdivision (b) of Section 23550.5, who is convicted of violating Section 14601.2 shall be sentenced as provided in paragraph (3) of subdivision (e).

(e) Any person convicted under this section of being an habitual traffic offender shall be punished as follows:

(1) Upon a first conviction, by imprisonment in the county jail for 30 days and by a fine of one thousand dollars ($1,000).

(2) Upon a second or any subsequent offense within seven years of a prior conviction under this section, by imprisonment in the county jail for 180 days and by a fine of two thousand dollars ($2,000).

(3) Any habitual traffic offender designated under Section 193.7 of the Penal Code or under subdivision (b) of Section 23546, subdivision (b) of Section 23550, subdivision (b) of Section 23550.5, or subdivision (d) of Section 23566 who is convicted of a violation of Section 14601.2 shall be punished by imprisonment in the county jail for 180 days and by a fine of two thousand dollars ($2,000). The penalty in this paragraph shall be consecutive to that imposed for the violation of any other law.

(f) This section also applies to the operation of an off-highway motor vehicle on those lands to which the Chappie-Z'berg Off-Highway Motor Vehicle Law of 1971 (Division 16.5 (commencing with Section 38000)) applies as to off-highway motor vehicles, as described in Section 38001. *(AM '99, '04)*

14601.4. Driving When Privilege Suspended or Revoked Causing Injury

(a) It is unlawful for a person, while driving a vehicle with a license suspended or revoked pursuant to Section 14601.2 to do an act forbidden by law or neglect a duty imposed by law in the driving of the vehicle, which act or neglect proximately causes bodily injury to a person other than the driver. In proving the person neglected a duty imposed by law in the driving of the vehicle, it is not necessary to prove that a specific section of this code was violated.

(b) A person convicted under this section shall be imprisoned in the county jail and shall not be released upon work release, community service, or other release program before the minimum period of imprisonment, prescribed in Section 14601.2, is served. If a person is convicted of that offense and is granted probation, the court shall require that the person convicted serve at least the minimum time of imprisonment, as specified in those sections, as a term or condition of probation.

(c) When the prosecution agrees to a plea of guilty or nolo contendere to a charge of a violation of this section in satisfaction of, or as a substitute for, an original charge of a violation of Section 14601.2, and the court accepts that plea, except, in the interest of justice, when the court finds it should be inappropriate, the court shall, pursuant to Section 23575, require the person convicted, in addition to other requirements, to install a certified ignition interlock device on a vehicle that the person owns or operates for a period not to exceed three years.

(d) This section also applies to the operation of an off-highway motor vehicle on those lands that the Chappie-Z'berg Off-Highway Motor Vehicle Law of 1971 (Division 16.5 (commencing with Section 38000)) applies as to off-highway motor vehicles, as described in Section 38001.

(e) Upon receipt of the abstract of a conviction under this section, the department shall not reinstate the privilege to operate a motor vehicle until the department receives proof of either the "Verification of Installation"form as described in paragraph (2) of subdivision (g) of Section 13386 or the Judicial Council Form I.D. 100.

(f) If Section 23573 is applicable, then subdivisions (c) and (e) are not applicable. *(AM '08)*

14601.5. Driving on Suspended or Revoked License: Penalties

(a) A person shall not drive a motor vehicle at any time when that person's driving privilege is suspended or revoked pursuant to Section 13353, 13353.1, or 13353.2 and that person has knowledge of the suspension or revocation.

(b) Except in full compliance with the restriction, a person shall not drive a motor vehicle at any time when that person's driving privilege is restricted pursuant to Section 13353.7 or 13353.8 and that person has knowledge of the restriction.

(c) Knowledge of suspension, revocation, or restriction of the driving privilege shall be conclusively presumed if notice has been given by the department to the person pursuant to Section 13106. The presumption established by this subdivision is a presumption affecting the burden of proof.

(d) A person convicted of a violation of this section is punishable, as follows:

(1) Upon a first conviction, by imprisonment in the county jail for not more than six months or by a fine of not less than three hundred dollars ($300) or more than one thousand dollars ($1,000), or by both that fine and imprisonment.

(2) If the offense occurred within five years of a prior offense that resulted in a conviction for a violation of this section or Section 14601, 14601.1, 14601.2, or 14601.3, by imprisonment in the county jail for not less than 10 days or more than one year, and by a fine of not less than five hundred dollars ($500) or more than two thousand dollars ($2,000).

(e) In imposing the minimum fine required by subdivision (d), the court shall take into consideration the defendant's ability to pay the fine and may, in the interest of justice, and for reasons stated in the record, reduce the amount of that minimum fine to less than the amount otherwise imposed.

(f) This section does not prohibit a person who is participating in, or has completed, an alcohol or drug rehabilitation program from driving a motor vehicle, that is owned or utilized by the person's employer, during the course of employment on private property that is owned or utilized by the employer, except an offstreet parking facility as defined in subdivision (c) of Section 12500.

(g) When the prosecution agrees to a plea of guilty or nolo contendere to a charge of a violation of this section in satisfaction of, or as a substitute for, an original charge of a violation of Section 14601.2, and the court accepts that plea, except, in the interest of justice, when the court finds it would be inappropriate, the court shall, pursuant to Section 23575, require the person convicted, in addition to other requirements, to install a certified ignition interlock device on a vehicle that the person owns or operates for a period not to exceed three years.

(h) This section also applies to the operation of an off-highway motor vehicle on those lands that the Chappie-Z'berg Off-Highway Motor Vehicle Law of 1971 (Division 16.5 (commencing with Section 38000)) applies as to off-highway motor vehicles, as described in Section 38001.

(i) Upon receipt of the abstract of a conviction under this section, the department shall not reinstate the privilege to operate a motor vehicle until the department receives proof of either the "Verification of Installation"form as described in paragraph (2) of subdivision (g) of Section 13386 or the Judicial Council Form I.D. 100.

(j) If Section 23573 is applicable, then subdivisions (g) and (i) are not applicable. *(AM '08)*

14602. Release of Vehicle Removed at Sobriety Checkpoint

In accordance with subdivision (p) of Section 22651, a vehicle removed pursuant to subdivision (c) of Section 2814.2 shall be released to the registered owner or his or her agent at any time the facility to which the vehicle has been removed is open upon presentation of the registered owner's or his or her agent's currently valid driver's license to operate the vehicle and proof of current vehicle registration. *(AD '11)*

14602.1. Vehicle Pursuit Data: Report

(a) Every state and local law enforcement agency, including, but not limited to, city police departments and county sheriffs'offices, shall report to the Department of the California Highway Patrol, on a paper or electronic form developed and approved by the Department of the California Highway Patrol, all motor vehicle pursuit data.

(b) Effective January 1, 2006, the form shall require the reporting of all motor vehicle pursuit data, which shall include, but not be limited to, all of the following:

(1) Whether any person involved in a pursuit or a subsequent arrest was injured, specifying the nature of that injury. For all purposes of this section, the form shall differentiate between the suspect driver, a suspect passenger, and the peace officers involved.

(2) The violations that caused the pursuit to be initiated.

(3) The identity of the peace officers involved in the pursuit.

(4) The means or methods used to stop the suspect being pursued.

(5) All charges filed with the court by the district attorney.

(6) The conditions of the pursuit, including, but not limited to, all of the following:

(A) Duration.

(B) Mileage.

(C) Number of peace officers involved.

(D) Maximum number of law enforcement vehicles involved.

(E) Time of day.

(F) Weather conditions.

(G) Maximum speeds.

(7) Whether a pursuit resulted in a collision, and a resulting injury or fatality to an uninvolved third party, and the corresponding number of persons involved.

(8) Whether the pursuit involved multiple law enforcement agencies.

(9) How the pursuit was terminated.

(c) In order to minimize costs, the department, upon updating the form, shall update the corresponding database to include all of the reporting requirements specified in subdivision (b).

(d) All motor vehicle pursuit data obtained pursuant to subdivision (b) shall be submitted to the Department of the California Highway Patrol no later than 30 days following a motor vehicle pursuit.

(e) The Department of the California Highway Patrol shall submit annually to the Legislature a report that includes, but is not limited to, the following information:

(1) The number of motor vehicle pursuits reported to the Department of the California Highway Patrol during that year.

(2) The number of those motor vehicle pursuits that reportedly resulted in a collision in which an injury or fatality to an uninvolved third party occurred.

(3) The total number of uninvolved third parties who were injured or killed as a result of those collisions during that year. *(AM '01, '05)*

14602.6. License Suspended, Revoked, or Never Issued: Arrest of Driver; Impounding Vehicle

(a)(1) Whenever a peace officer determines that a person was driving a vehicle while his or her driving privilege was suspended or revoked, driving a vehicle while his or her driving privilege is restricted pursuant to Section 13352 or 23575 and the vehicle is not equipped with a functioning, certified interlock device, or driving a vehicle without ever having been issued a driver's license, the peace officer may either immediately arrest that person and cause the removal and seizure of that vehicle or, if the vehicle is involved in a traffic collision, cause the removal and seizure of the vehicle without the necessity of arresting the person in accordance with Chapter 10 (commencing with Section 22650) of Division 11. A vehicle so impounded shall be impounded for 30 days.

(2) The impounding agency, within two working days of impoundment, shall send a notice by certified mail, return receipt requested, to the legal owner of the vehicle, at the address obtained from the department, informing the owner that the vehicle has been impounded. Failure to notify the legal owner within two working days shall prohibit the impounding agency from charging for more than 15 days' impoundment when the legal owner redeems the impounded vehicle. The impounding agency shall maintain a published telephone number that provides information 24 hours a day regarding the impoundment of vehicles and the rights of a registered owner to request a hearing. The law enforcement agency shall be open to issue a release to the registered owner or legal owner, or the agent of either, whenever the agency is open to serve the public for regular, nonemergency business.

(b) The registered and legal owner of a vehicle that is removed and seized under subdivision (a) or their agents shall be provided the opportunity for a storage hearing to determine the validity of, or consider any mitigating circumstances attendant to, the storage, in accordance with Section 22852.

(c) Any period in which a vehicle is subjected to storage under this section shall be included as part of the period of impoundment ordered by the court under subdivision (a) of Section 14602.5.

(d)(1) An impounding agency shall release a vehicle to the registered owner or his or her agent prior to the end of 30 days' impoundment under any of the following circumstances:

(A) When the vehicle is a stolen vehicle.

(B) When the vehicle is subject to bailment and is driven by an unlicensed employee of a business establishment, including a parking service or repair garage.

(C) When the license of the driver was suspended or revoked for an offense other than those included in Article 2 (commencing with Section 13200) of Chapter 2 of Division 6 or Article 3 (commencing with Section 13350) of Chapter 2 of Division 6.

(D) When the vehicle was seized under this section for an offense that does not authorize the seizure of the vehicle.

(E) When the driver reinstates his or her driver's license or acquires a driver's license and proper insurance.

(2) No vehicle shall be released pursuant to this subdivision without presentation of the registered owner's or agent's currently valid driver's license to operate the vehicle and proof of current vehicle registration, or upon order of a court.

(e) The registered owner or his or her agent is responsible for all towing and storage charges related to the impoundment, and any administrative charges authorized under Section 22850.5.

(f) A vehicle removed and seized under subdivision (a) shall be released to the legal owner of the vehicle or the legal owner's agent prior to the end of 30 days' impoundment if all of the following conditions are met:

(1) The legal owner is a motor vehicle dealer, bank, credit union, acceptance corporation, or other licensed financial institution legally operating in this state or is another person, not the registered owner, holding a security interest in the vehicle.

(2)(A)   The legal owner or the legal owner's agent pays all towing and storage fees related to the seizure of the vehicle. No lien sale processing fees shall be charged to the legal owner who redeems the vehicle prior to the 15th day of impoundment. Neither the impounding authority nor any person having possession of the vehicle shall collect from the legal owner of the type specified in paragraph (1), or the legal owner's agent any administrative charges imposed pursuant to Section 22850.5 unless the legal owner voluntarily requested a poststorage hearing.

(B)   A person operating or in charge of a storage facility where vehicles are stored pursuant to this section shall accept a valid bank credit card or cash for payment of towing, storage, and related fees by a legal or registered owner or the owner's agent claiming the vehicle. A credit card shall be in the name of the person presenting the card. "Credit card" means "credit card" as defined in subdivision (a) of Section 1747.02 of the Civil Code, except, for the purposes of this section, credit card does not include a credit card issued by a retail seller.

(C)   A person operating or in charge of a storage facility described in subparagraph (B) who violates subparagraph (B) shall be civilly liable to the owner of the vehicle or to the person who tendered the fees for four times the amount of the towing, storage, and related fees, but not to exceed five hundred dollars ($500).

(D)   A person operating or in charge of a storage facility described in subparagraph (B) shall have sufficient funds on the premises of the primary storage facility during normal business hours to accommodate, and make change in, a reasonable monetary transaction.

(E)   Credit charges for towing and storage services shall comply with Section 1748.1 of the Civil Code. Law enforcement agencies may include the costs of providing for payment by credit when making agreements with towing companies on rates.

(3)   The legal owner or the legal owner's agent presents a copy of the assignment, as defined in subdivision (b) of Section 7500.1 of the Business and Professions Code; a release from the one responsible governmental agency, only if required by the agency; a government-issued photographic identification card; and any one of the following, as determined by the legal owner or the legal owner's agent: a certificate of repossession for the vehicle, a security agreement for the vehicle, or title, whether paper or electronic, showing proof of legal ownership for the vehicle. Any documents presented may be originals, photocopies, or facsimile copies, or may be transmitted electronically. The law enforcement agency, impounding agency, or any other governmental agency, or any person acting on behalf of those agencies, shall not require any documents to be notarized. The law enforcement agency, impounding agency, or any person acting on behalf of those agencies may require the agent of the legal owner to produce a photocopy or facsimile copy of its repossession agency license or registration issued pursuant to Chapter 11 (commencing with Section 7500) of Division 3 of the Business and Professions Code, or to demonstrate, to the satisfaction of the law enforcement agency, impounding agency, or any person acting on behalf of those agencies, that the agent is exempt from licensure pursuant to Section 7500.2 or 7500.3 of the Business and Professions Code.

No administrative costs authorized under subdivision (a) of Section 22850.5 shall be charged to the legal owner of the type specified in paragraph (1), who redeems the vehicle unless the legal owner voluntarily requests a poststorage hearing. No city, county, city and county, or state agency shall require a legal owner or a legal owner's agent to request a poststorage hearing as a requirement for release of the vehicle to the legal owner or the legal owner's agent. The law enforcement agency, impounding agency, or other governmental agency, or any person acting on behalf of those agencies, shall not require any documents other than those specified in this paragraph. The law enforcement agency, impounding agency, or other governmental agency, or any person acting on behalf of those agencies, shall not require any documents to be notarized. The legal owner or the legal owner's agent shall be given a copy of any documents he or she is required to sign, except for a vehicle evidentiary hold logbook. The law enforcement agency, impounding agency, or any person acting on behalf of those agencies, or any person in possession of the vehicle, may photocopy and retain the copies of any documents presented by the legal owner or legal owner's agent.

(4) A failure by a storage facility to comply with any applicable conditions set forth in this subdivision shall not affect the right of the legal owner or the legal owner's agent to retrieve the vehicle, provided all conditions required of the legal owner or legal owner's agent under this subdivision are satisfied.

(g)(1) A legal owner or the legal owner's agent that obtains release of the vehicle pursuant to subdivision (f) shall not release the vehicle to the registered owner of the vehicle, or the person who was listed as the registered owner when the vehicle was impounded, or any agents of the registered owner, unless the registered owner is a rental car agency, until after the termination of the 30-day impoundment period.

(2) The legal owner or the legal owner's agent shall not relinquish the vehicle to the registered owner or the person who was listed as the registered owner when the vehicle was impounded until the registered owner or that owner's agent presents his or her valid driver's license or valid temporary driver's license to the legal owner or the legal owner's agent. The legal owner or the legal owner's agent or the person in possession of the vehicle shall make every reasonable effort to ensure that the license presented is valid and possession of the vehicle will not be given to the driver who was involved in the original impoundment proceeding until the expiration of the impoundment period.

(3) Prior to relinquishing the vehicle, the legal owner may require the registered owner to pay all towing and storage charges related to the impoundment and any administrative charges authorized under Section 22850.5 that were incurred by the legal owner in connection with obtaining custody of the vehicle.

(4) Any legal owner who knowingly releases or causes the release of a vehicle to a registered owner or the person in possession of the vehicle at the time of the impoundment or any agent of the registered owner in violation of this subdivision shall be guilty of a misdemeanor and subject to a fine in the amount of two thousand dollars ($2,000) in addition to any other penalties established by law.

(5) The legal owner, registered owner, or person in possession of the vehicle shall not change or attempt to change the name of the legal owner or the registered owner on the records of the department until the vehicle is released from the impoundment.

(h)(1) A vehicle removed and seized under subdivision (a) shall be released to a rental car agency prior to the end of 30 days'impoundment if the agency is either the legal owner or registered owner of the vehicle and the agency pays all towing and storage fees related to the seizure of the vehicle.

(2) The owner of a rental vehicle that was seized under this section may continue to rent the vehicle upon recovery of the vehicle. However, the rental car agency may not rent another vehicle to the driver of the vehicle that was seized until 30 days after the date that the vehicle was seized.

(3) The rental car agency may require the person to whom the vehicle was rented to pay all towing and storage charges related to the impoundment and any administrative charges authorized under Section 22850.5 that were incurred by the rental car agency in connection with obtaining custody of the vehicle.

(i) Notwithstanding any other provision of this section, the registered owner and not the legal owner shall remain responsible for any towing and storage charges related to the impoundment, any administrative charges authorized under Section 22850.5, and any parking fines, penalties, and administrative fees incurred by the registered owner.

(j) The law enforcement agency and the impounding agency, including any storage facility acting on behalf of the law enforcement agency or impounding agency, shall comply with this section and shall not be liable to the registered owner for the improper release of the vehicle to the legal owner or the legal owner's agent provided the release complies with the provisions of this section. The legal owner shall indemnify and hold harmless a storage facility from any claims arising out of the release of the vehicle to the legal owner or the legal owner's agent and from any damage to the vehicle after its release, including the reasonable costs associated with defending any such claims. A law enforcement agency shall not refuse to issue a release to a legal owner or the agent of a legal owner on the grounds that it previously issued a release. *(AM '06, '07, '09)*

14602.7.   Seizure of Vehicle Involved in Evading or Reckless Driving; Warrant Authorizing; Procedures

(a) A magistrate presented with the affidavit of a peace officer establishing reasonable cause to believe that a vehicle, described by vehicle type and license number, was an instrumentality used in the peace officer's presence in violation of Section 2800.1, 2800.2, 2800.3, or 23103, shall issue a warrant or order authorizing any peace officer to immediately seize and cause the removal of the vehicle. The warrant or court order may be entered into a computerized database. A vehicle so impounded may be impounded for a period not to exceed 30 days.

The impounding agency, within two working days of impoundment, shall send a notice by certified mail, return receipt requested, to the legal owner of the vehicle, at the address obtained from the department, informing the owner that the vehicle has been impounded and providing the owner with a copy of the warrant or court order. Failure to notify the legal owner within two working days shall prohibit the impounding agency from charging for more than 15 days impoundment when a legal owner redeems the impounded vehicle. The law enforcement agency shall be open to issue a release to the registered owner or legal owner, or the agent of either, whenever the agency is open to serve the public for regular, nonemergency business.

(b)(1) An impounding agency shall release a vehicle to the registered owner or his or her agent prior to the end of the impoundment period and without the permission of the magistrate authorizing the vehicle's seizure under any of the following circumstances:

(A) When the vehicle is a stolen vehicle.

(B) When the vehicle is subject to bailment and is driven by an unlicensed employee of the business establishment, including a parking service or repair garage.

(C) When the registered owner of the vehicle causes a peace officer to reasonably believe, based on the totality of the circumstances, that the registered owner was not the driver who violated Section 2800.1, 2800.2, or 2800.3, the agency shall immediately release the vehicle to the registered owner or his or her agent.

(2) No vehicle shall be released pursuant to this subdivision, except upon presentation of the registered owner's or agent's currently valid driver's license to operate the vehicle and proof of current vehicle registration, or upon order of the court.

(c)(1) Whenever a vehicle is impounded under this section, the magistrate ordering the storage shall provide the vehicle's registered and legal owners of record, or their agents, with the opportunity for a poststorage hearing to determine the validity of the storage.

(2) A notice of the storage shall be mailed or personally delivered to the registered and legal owners within 48 hours after issuance of the warrant or court order, excluding weekends and holidays, by the person or agency executing the warrant or court order, and shall include all of the following information:

(A) The name, address, and telephone number of the agency providing the notice.

(B) The location of the place of storage and a description of the vehicle, which shall include, if available, the name or make, the manufacturer, the license plate number, and the mileage of the vehicle.

(C) A copy of the warrant or court order and the peace officer's affidavit, as described in subdivision (a).

(D) A statement that, in order to receive their poststorage hearing, the owners, or their agents, are required to request the hearing from the magistrate issuing the warrant or court order in person, in writing, or by telephone, within 10 days of the date of the notice.

(3) The poststorage hearing shall be conducted within two court days after receipt of the request for the hearing.

(4) At the hearing, the magistrate may order the vehicle released if he or she finds any of the circumstances described in subdivision (b) or (e) that allow release of a vehicle by the impounding agency. The magistrate may also consider releasing the vehicle when the continued impoundment will cause undue hardship to persons dependent upon the vehicle for employment or to a person with a community property interest in the vehicle.

(5) Failure of either the registered or legal owner, or his or her agent, to request, or to attend, a scheduled hearing satisfies the poststorage hearing requirement.

(6) The agency employing the peace officer who caused the magistrate to issue the warrant or court order shall be responsible for the costs incurred for towing and storage if it is determined in the poststorage hearing that reasonable grounds for the storage are not established.

(d) The registered owner or his or her agent is responsible for all towing and storage charges related to the impoundment, and any administrative charges authorized under Section 22850.5.

(e) A vehicle removed and seized under subdivision (a) shall be released to the legal owner of the vehicle or the legal owner's agent prior to the end of the impoundment period and without the permission of the magistrate authorizing the seizure of the vehicle if all of the following conditions are met:

(1) The legal owner is a motor vehicle dealer, bank, credit union, acceptance corporation, or other licensed financial institution legally operating in this state or is another person, not the registered owner, holding a financial interest in the vehicle.

(2)(A) The legal owner or the legal owner's agent pays all towing and storage fees related to the seizure of the vehicle. No lien sale processing fees shall be charged to the legal owner who redeems the vehicle prior to the 15th day of impoundment. Neither the impounding authority nor any person having possession of the vehicle shall collect from the legal owner of the type specified in paragraph (1), or the legal owner's agent any administrative charges imposed pursuant to Section 22850.5 unless the legal owner voluntarily requested a poststorage hearing.

(B) A person operating or in charge of a storage facility where vehicles are stored pursuant to this section shall accept a valid bank credit card or cash for payment of towing, storage, and related fees by a legal or registered owner or the owner's agent claiming the vehicle. A credit card shall be in the name of the person presenting the card. "Credit card"means "credit card"as defined in subdivision (a) of Section 1747.02 of the Civil Code, except, for the purposes of this section, credit card does not include a credit card issued by a retail seller.

(C) A person operating or in charge of a storage facility described in subparagraph (B) who violates subparagraph (B) shall be civilly liable to the owner of the vehicle or to the person who tendered the fees for four times the amount of the towing, storage and related fees, but not to exceed five hundred dollars ($500).

(D) A person operating or in charge of a storage facility described in subparagraph (B) shall have sufficient funds on the premises of the primary storage facility during normal business hours to accommodate, and make change in, a reasonable monetary transaction.

(E) Credit charges for towing and storage services shall comply with Section 1748.1 of the Civil Code. Law enforcement agencies may include the costs of providing for payment by credit when making agreements with towing companies on rates.

(3) The legal owner or the legal owner's agent presents, to the law enforcement agency, impounding agency, person in possession of the vehicle, or any person acting on behalf of those agencies, a copy of the assignment, as defined in subdivision (b) of Section 7500.1 of the Business and Professions Code; a release from the one responsible governmental agency, only if required by the agency; a government-issued photographic identification card; and any one of the following, as determined by the legal owner or the legal owner's agent: a certificate of repossession for the vehicle, a security agreement for the vehicle, or title, whether paper or electronic, showing proof of legal ownership for the vehicle. Any documents presented may be originals, photocopies, or facsimile copies, or may be transmitted electronically. The law enforcement agency, impounding agency, or any other governmental agency, or any person acting on behalf of those agencies, shall not require any documents to be notarized. The law enforcement agency, impounding agency, or any person acting on behalf of those agencies, may require the agent of the legal owner to produce a photocopy or facsimile copy of its repossession agency license or registration issued pursuant to Chapter 11 (commencing with Section 7500) of Division 3 of the Business and Professions Code, or to demonstrate, to the satisfaction of the law enforcement agency, impounding agency, or any person acting on behalf of those agencies that the agent is exempt from licensure pursuant to Section 7500.2 or 7500.3 of the Business and Professions Code.

No administrative costs authorized under subdivision (a) of Section 22850.5 shall be charged to the legal owner of the type specified in paragraph (1), who redeems the vehicle unless the legal owner voluntarily requests a poststorage hearing. No city, county, city and county, or state agency shall require a legal owner or a legal owner's agent to request a poststorage hearing as a requirement for release of the vehicle to the legal owner or the legal owner's agent. The law enforcement agency, impounding agency, or other governmental agency, or any person acting on behalf of those agencies, shall not require any documents other than those specified in this paragraph. The law enforcement agency, impounding agency, or other governmental agency, or any person acting on behalf of those agencies, shall not require any documents to be notarized. The legal owner or the legal owner's agent shall be given a copy of any documents he or she is required to sign, except for a vehicle evidentiary hold logbook. The law enforcement agency, impounding agency, or any person acting on behalf of those agencies, or any person in possession of the vehicle, may photocopy and retain the copies of any documents presented by the legal owner or legal owner's agent.

(4) A failure by a storage facility to comply with any applicable conditions set forth in this subdivision shall not affect the right of the legal owner or the legal owner's agent to retrieve the vehicle, provided all conditions required of the legal owner or legal owner's agent under this subdivision are satisfied.

(f)(1) A legal owner or the legal owner's agent that obtains release of the vehicle pursuant to subdivision (e) shall not release the vehicle to the registered owner or the person who was listed as the registered owner when the vehicle was impounded of the vehicle or any agents of the registered owner, unless a registered owner is a rental car agency, until the termination of the impoundment period.

(2) The legal owner or the legal owner's agent shall not relinquish the vehicle to the registered owner or the person who was listed as the registered owner when the vehicle was impounded until the registered owner or that owner's agent presents his or her valid driver's license or valid temporary driver's license to the legal owner or the legal owner's agent. The legal owner or the legal owner's agent shall make every reasonable effort to ensure that the license presented is valid and possession of the vehicle will not be given to the driver who was involved in the original impoundment proceeding until the expiration of the impoundment period.

(3) Prior to relinquishing the vehicle, the legal owner may require the registered owner to pay all towing and storage charges related to the impoundment and the administrative charges authorized under Section 22850.5 that were incurred by the legal owner in connection with obtaining the custody of the vehicle.

(4) Any legal owner who knowingly releases or causes the release of a vehicle to a registered owner or the person in possession of the vehicle at the time of the impoundment or any agent of the registered owner in violation of this subdivision shall be guilty of a misdemeanor and subject to a fine in the amount of two thousand dollars ($2,000) in addition to any other penalties established by law.

(5) The legal owner, registered owner, or person in possession of the vehicle shall not change or attempt to change the name of the legal owner or the registered owner on the records of the department until the vehicle is released from the impoundment.

(g)(1) A vehicle impounded and seized under subdivision (a) shall be released to a rental car agency prior to the end of the impoundment period if the agency is either the legal owner or registered owner of the vehicle and the agency pays all towing and storage fees related to the seizure of the vehicle.

(2) The owner of a rental vehicle that was seized under this section may continue to rent the vehicle upon recovery of the vehicle. However, the rental car agency shall not rent another vehicle to the driver who used the vehicle that was seized to evade a police officer until 30 days after the date that the vehicle was seized.

(3) The rental car agency may require the person to whom the vehicle was rented and who evaded the peace officer to pay all towing and storage charges related to the impoundment and any administrative charges authorized under Section 22850.5 that were incurred by the rental car agency in connection with obtaining custody of the vehicle.

(h) Notwithstanding any other provision of this section, the registered owner and not the legal owner shall remain responsible for any towing and storage charges related to the impoundment and the administrative charges authorized under Section 22850.5 and any parking fines, penalties, and administrative fees incurred by the registered owner.

(i)(1) This section does not apply to vehicles abated under the Abandoned Vehicle Abatement Program pursuant to Sections 22660 to 22668, inclusive, and Section 22710, or to vehicles impounded for investigation pursuant to Section 22655, or to vehicles removed from private property pursuant to Section 22658.

(2) This section does not apply to abandoned vehicles removed pursuant to Section 22669 that are determined by the public agency to have an estimated value of three hundred dollars ($300) or less.

(j) The law enforcement agency and the impounding agency, including any storage facility acting on behalf of the law enforcement agency or impounding agency, shall comply with this section and shall not be liable to the registered owner for the improper release of the vehicle to the legal owner or the legal owner's agent provided the release complies with the provisions of this section. The legal owner shall indemnify and hold harmless a storage facility from any claims arising out of the release of the vehicle to the legal owner or the legal owner's agent and from any damage to the vehicle after its release, including the reasonable costs associated with defending any such claims. A law enforcement agency shall not refuse to issue a release to a legal owner or the agent of a legal owner on the grounds that it previously issued a release. *(AM '06, '07, '09)*

14602.8. Immediate Removal and Seizure of Vehicle; Requirements

(a)(1) If a peace officer determines that a person has been convicted of a violation of Section 23140, 23152, or 23153, that the violation occurred within the preceding 10 years, and that one or more of the following circumstances applies to that person, the officer may immediately cause the removal and seizure of the vehicle that the person was driving, under either of the following circumstances:

(A) The person was driving a vehicle when the person had 0.10 percent or more, by weight, of alcohol in his or her blood.

(B) The person driving the vehicle refused to submit to or complete a chemical test requested by the peace officer.

(2) A vehicle impounded pursuant to paragraph (1) shall be impounded for the following period of time:

(A) Five days, if the person has been convicted once of violating Section 23140, 23152, or 23153, and the violation occurred within the preceding 10 years.

(B) Fifteen days, if the person has been convicted two or more times of violating Section 23140, 23152, or 23153, or any combination thereof, and the violations occurred within the preceding 10 years.

(3) Within two working days after impoundment, the impounding agency shall send a notice by certified mail, return receipt requested, to the legal owner of the vehicle, at the address obtained from the department, informing the owner that the vehicle has been impounded. Failure to notify the legal owner within two working days shall prohibit the impounding agency from charging for more than five days' impoundment when the legal owner redeems the impounded vehicle. The impounding agency shall maintain a published telephone number that provides information 24 hours a day regarding the impoundment of vehicles and the rights of a registered owner to request a hearing. The law enforcement agency shall be open to issue a release to the registered owner or legal owner, or the agent of either, whenever the agency is open to serve the public for regular, nonemergency business.

(b) The registered and legal owner of a vehicle that is removed and seized under subdivision (a) or his or her agent shall be provided the opportunity for a storage hearing to determine the validity of, or consider any mitigating circumstances attendant to, the storage, in accordance with Section 22852.

(c) Any period during which a vehicle is subjected to storage under this section shall be included as part of the period of impoundment ordered by the court under Section 23594.

(d)(1) The impounding agency shall release the vehicle to the registered owner or his or her agent prior to the end of the impoundment period under any of the following circumstances:

(A) When the vehicle is a stolen vehicle.

(B) When the vehicle is subject to bailment and is driven by an unlicensed employee of a business establishment, including a parking service or repair garage.

(C) When the driver of the vehicle is not the sole registered owner of the vehicle and the vehicle is being released to another registered owner of the vehicle who agrees not to allow the driver to use the vehicle until after the end of the impoundment period.

(2) A vehicle shall not be released pursuant to this subdivision without presentation of the registered owner's or agent's currently valid driver's license to operate the vehicle and proof of current vehicle registration, or upon order of a court.

(e) The registered owner or his or her agent is responsible for all towing and storage charges related to the impoundment, and any administrative charges authorized under Section 22850.5.

(f) A vehicle removed and seized under subdivision (a) shall be released to the legal owner of the vehicle or the legal owner's agent prior to the end of the impoundment period if all of the following conditions are met:

(1) The legal owner is a motor vehicle dealer, bank, credit union, acceptance corporation, or other licensed financial institution legally operating in this state, or is another person who is not the registered owner and holds a security interest in the vehicle.

(2)(A) The legal owner or the legal owner's agent pays all towing and storage fees related to the seizure of the vehicle. A lien sale processing fee shall not be charged to the legal owner who redeems the vehicle prior to the 10th day of impoundment. The impounding authority or any person having possession of the vehicle shall not collect from the legal owner of the type specified in paragraph (1) or the legal owner's agent any administrative charges imposed pursuant to Section 22850.5 unless the legal owner voluntarily requested a poststorage hearing.

(B) A person operating or in charge of a storage facility where vehicles are stored pursuant to this section shall accept a valid bank credit card or cash for payment of towing, storage, and related fees by a legal or registered owner or the owner's agent claiming the vehicle. A credit card shall be in the name of the person presenting the card. "Credit card"means "credit card"as defined in subdivision (a) of Section 1747.02 of the Civil Code, except, for the purposes of this section, credit card does not include a credit card issued by a retail seller.

(C) A person operating or in charge of a storage facility described in subparagraph (B) who violates subparagraph (B) shall be civilly liable to the owner of the vehicle or to the person who tendered the fees for four times the amount of the towing, storage, and other related fees, but not to exceed five hundred dollars ($500).

(D) A person operating or in charge of a storage facility described in subparagraph (B) shall have sufficient funds on the premises of the primary storage facility during normal business hours to accommodate, and make change in, a reasonable monetary transaction.

(E) Credit charges for towing and storage services shall comply with Section 1748.1 of the Civil Code. Law enforcement agencies may include the costs of providing for payment by credit when making agreements with towing companies on rates.

(3)(A) The legal owner or the legal owner's agent presents to the law enforcement agency or impounding agency, or any person acting on behalf of those agencies, a copy of the assignment, as defined in subdivision (b) of Section 7500.1 of the Business and Professions Code; a release from the one responsible governmental agency, only if required by the agency; a government-issued photographic identification card; and any one of the following as determined by the legal owner or the legal owner's agent: a certificate of repossession for the vehicle, a security agreement for the vehicle, or title, whether paper or electronic, showing proof of legal ownership for the vehicle. The law enforcement agency, impounding agency, or any other governmental agency, or any person acting on behalf of those agencies, shall not require the presentation of any other documents.

(B) The legal owner or the legal owner's agent presents to the person in possession of the vehicle, or any person acting on behalf of the person in possession, a copy of the assignment, as defined in subdivision (b) of Section 7500.1 of the Business and Professions Code; a release from the one responsible governmental agency, only if required by the agency; a government-issued photographic identification card; and any one of the following as determined by the legal owner or the legal owner's agent: a certificate of repossession for the vehicle, a security agreement for the vehicle, or title, whether paper or electronic, showing proof of legal ownership for the vehicle. The person in possession of the vehicle, or any person acting on behalf of the person in possession, shall not require the presentation of any other documents.

(C) All presented documents may be originals, photocopies, or facsimile copies, or may be transmitted electronically. The law enforcement agency, impounding agency, or any person acting on behalf of them, shall not require a document to be notarized. The law enforcement agency, impounding agency, or any person in possession of the vehicle, or anyone acting on behalf of those agencies may require the agent of the legal owner to produce a photocopy or facsimile copy of its repossession agency license or registration issued pursuant to Chapter 11 (commencing with Section 7500) of Division 3 of the Business and Professions Code, or to demonstrate, to the satisfaction of the law enforcement agency, the impounding agency, any other governmental agency, or any person in possession of the vehicle, or anyone acting on behalf of them, that the agent is exempt from licensure pursuant to Section 7500.2 or 7500.3 of the Business and Professions Code.

(D) Administrative costs authorized under subdivision (a) of Section 22850.5 shall not be charged to the legal owner of the type specified in paragraph (1) who redeems the vehicle unless the legal owner voluntarily requests a poststorage hearing. A city, county, city and county, or state agency shall not require a legal owner or a legal owner's agent to request a poststorage hearing as a requirement for release of the vehicle to the legal owner or the legal owner's agent. The law enforcement agency, the impounding agency, any governmental agency, or any person acting on behalf of those agencies shall not require any documents other than those specified in this paragraph. The law enforcement agency, impounding agency, or other governmental agency, or any person acting on behalf of those agencies, shall not require any documents to be notarized. The legal owner or the legal owner's agent shall be given a copy of any documents he or she is required to sign, except for a vehicle evidentiary hold logbook. The law enforcement agency, impounding agency, or any person acting on behalf of those agencies, or any person in possession of the vehicle, may photocopy and retain the copies of any documents presented by the legal owner or legal owner's agent.

(4) A failure by a storage facility to comply with any applicable conditions set forth in this subdivision shall not affect the right of the legal owner or the legal owner's agent to retrieve the vehicle, provided all conditions required of the legal owner or legal owner's agent under this subdivision are satisfied.

(g)(1) A legal owner or the legal owner's agent who obtains release of the vehicle pursuant to subdivision (f) shall not release the vehicle to the registered owner of the vehicle or the person who was listed as the registered owner when the vehicle was impounded or any agents of the registered owner unless the registered owner is a rental car agency, until after the termination of the impoundment period.

(2) The legal owner or the legal owner's agent shall not relinquish the vehicle to the registered owner or the person who was listed as the registered owner when the vehicle was impounded until the registered owner or that owner's agent presents his or her valid driver's license or valid temporary driver's license to the legal owner or the legal owner's agent. The legal owner or the legal owner's agent or the person in possession of the vehicle shall make every reasonable effort to ensure that the license presented is valid and possession of the vehicle will not be given to the driver who was involved in the original impoundment proceeding until the expiration of the impoundment period.

(3) Prior to relinquishing the vehicle, the legal owner may require the registered owner to pay all towing and storage charges related to the impoundment and any administrative charges authorized under Section 22850.5 that were incurred by the legal owner in connection with obtaining custody of the vehicle.

(4) A legal owner who knowingly releases or causes the release of a vehicle to a registered owner or the person in possession of the vehicle at the time of the impoundment or an agent of the registered owner in violation of this subdivision is guilty of a misdemeanor and subject to a fine in the amount of two thousand dollars ($2,000) in addition to any other penalties established by law.

(5) The legal owner, registered owner, or person in possession of the vehicle shall not change or attempt to change the name of the legal owner or the registered owner on the records of the department until the vehicle is released from the impoundment.

(h)(1) A vehicle removed and seized under subdivision (a) shall be released to a rental car agency prior to the end of the impoundment period if the agency is either the legal owner or registered owner of the vehicle and the agency pays all towing and storage fees related to the seizure of the vehicle.

(2) The owner of a rental vehicle that was seized under this section may continue to rent the vehicle upon recovery of the vehicle. However, the rental car agency shall not rent another vehicle to the driver of the vehicle that was seized until the impoundment period has expired.

(3) The rental car agency may require the person to whom the vehicle was rented to pay all towing and storage charges related to the impoundment and any administrative charges authorized under Section 22850.5 that were incurred by the rental car agency in connection with obtaining custody of the vehicle.

(i) Notwithstanding any other provision of this section, the registered owner, and not the legal owner, shall remain responsible for any towing and storage charges related to the impoundment, any administrative charges authorized under Section 22850.5, and any parking fines, penalties, and administrative fees incurred by the registered owner.

(j) The law enforcement agency and the impounding agency, including any storage facility acting on behalf of the law enforcement agency or impounding agency, shall comply with this section and shall not be liable to the registered owner for the improper release of the vehicle to the legal owner or the legal owner's agent provided the release complies with the provisions of this section. The legal owner shall indemnify and hold harmless a storage facility from any claims arising out of the release of the vehicle to the legal owner or the legal owner's agent and from any damage to the vehicle after its release, including the reasonable costs associated with defending any such claims. A law enforcement agency shall not refuse to issue a release to a legal owner or the agent of a legal owner on the grounds that it previously issued a release. *(AM '11)*

14603. Violation of License Restrictions
No person shall operate a vehicle in violation of the provisions of a restricted license issued to him.

14604. Non-Owner Operation of Motor Vehicle: Owner Responsibility
(a) No owner of a motor vehicle may knowingly allow another person to drive the vehicle upon a highway unless the owner determines that the person possesses a valid driver's license that authorizes the person to operate the vehicle. For the purposes of this section, an owner is required only to make a reasonable effort or inquiry to determine whether the prospective driver possesses a valid driver's license before allowing him or her to operate the owner's vehicle. An owner is not required to inquire of the department whether the prospective driver possesses a valid driver's license.

(b) A rental company is deemed to be in compliance with subdivision (a) if the company rents the vehicle in accordance with Sections 14608 and 14609.

14605. Operation of Motor Vehicles in Parking Facility
(a) No person who owns or is in control of a motor vehicle shall cause or permit another person to operate the vehicle within or upon an off-street parking facility if the person has knowledge that the driver does not have a driver's license of the appropriate class or certification to operate the vehicle.

(b) No operator of an off-street parking facility shall hire or retain in his employment an attendant whose duties involve the operating of motor vehicles unless such attendant, at all times during such employment, is licensed as a driver under the provisions of this code.

(c) As used in this section, "off-street parking facility" means any off-street facility held open for use by the public for parking vehicles and includes all publicly owned facilities for off-street parking, and owned facilities for off-street parking where no fee is charged for the privilege to park and which are held open for the common public use of retail customers.

14606. Employment of Person to Drive Motor Vehicle; License and Medical Certificate [Repeals 1-30-2014]
(a) A person shall not employ or hire any person to drive a motor vehicle or knowingly permit or authorize the driving of a motor vehicle, owned by him or her or under his or her control, upon the highways by any person unless that person is licensed for the appropriate class of vehicle to be driven.

(b)(1) Whenever a person fails to qualify, on reexamination, to operate a commercial motor vehicle, an employer shall report that failure to the department within 10 days.

(2) Until January 30, 2014, if a driver has no medical certification status information in the Commercial Driver License Information System motor vehicle record obtained from the driver's state licensing agency, the employing motor carrier may accept as proof of medical certification a medical examiner's certificate issued to that driver prior to January 30, 2012, and shall retain a copy as part of a driver qualification file.

(c) This section shall remain in effect only until January 30, 2014, and as of that date is repealed, unless a later enacted statute, that is enacted before January 30, 2014, deletes or extends that date. *(AM - RP - AD '12; A new version will be operative 1-30-14)*

14606. Employment of Person to Drive Motor Vehicle; License and Medical Certificate [Op. 1-30-2014]

(a) A person shall not employ, hire, knowingly permit, or authorize any person to drive a motor vehicle owned by him or her or under his or her control upon the highways unless that person is licensed for the appropriate class of vehicle to be driven.

(b) Whenever a person fails to qualify, on reexamination, to operate a commercial motor vehicle, an employer shall report that failure to the department within 10 days.

(c) An employer shall obtain from a driver required to have a commercial driver's license or commercial endorsement a copy of the driver's medical certification before allowing the driver to operate a commercial motor vehicle. The employer shall retain the certification as part of a driver qualification file.

(d) This section shall become operative on January ***30, 2014. *(AM '13)*

14607. Permitting Unlicensed Minor to Drive

No person shall cause or knowingly permit his child, ward, or employee under the age of 18 years to drive a motor vehicle upon the highways unless such child, ward, or employee is then licensed under this code.

14607.6. Driving on License Suspended, Revoked, or Expired: Vehicle Forfeiture

(a) Notwithstanding any other provision of law, and except as provided in this section, a motor vehicle is subject to forfeiture as a nuisance if it is driven on a highway in this state by a driver with a suspended or revoked license, or by an unlicensed driver, who is a registered owner of the vehicle at the time of impoundment and has a previous misdemeanor conviction for a violation of subdivision (a) of Section 12500 or Section 14601, 14601.1, 14601.2, 14601.3, 14601.4, or 14601.5.

(b) A peace officer shall not stop a vehicle for the sole reason of determining whether the driver is properly licensed.

(c)(1) If a driver is unable to produce a valid driver's license on the demand of a peace officer enforcing the provisions of this code, as required by subdivision (b) of Section 12951, the vehicle shall be impounded regardless of ownership, unless the peace officer is reasonably able, by other means, to verify that the driver is properly licensed. Prior to impounding a vehicle, a peace officer shall attempt to verify the license status of a driver who claims to be properly licensed but is unable to produce the license on demand of the peace officer.

(2) A peace officer shall not impound a vehicle pursuant to this subdivision if the license of the driver expired within the preceding 30 days and the driver would otherwise have been properly licensed.

(3) A peace officer may exercise discretion in a situation where the driver without a valid license is an employee driving a vehicle registered to the employer in the course of employment. A peace officer may also exercise discretion in a situation where the driver without a valid license is the employee of a bona fide business establishment or is a person otherwise controlled by such an establishment and it reasonably appears that an owner of the vehicle, or an agent of the owner, relinquished possession of the vehicle to the business establishment solely for servicing or parking of the vehicle or other reasonably similar situations, and where the vehicle was not to be driven except as directly necessary to accomplish that business purpose. In this event, if the vehicle can be returned to or be retrieved by the business establishment or registered owner, the peace officer may release and not impound the vehicle.

(4) A registered or legal owner of record at the time of impoundment may request a hearing to determine the validity of the impoundment pursuant to subdivision (n).

(5) If the driver of a vehicle impounded pursuant to this subdivision was not a registered owner of the vehicle at the time of impoundment, or if the driver of the vehicle was a registered owner of the vehicle at the time of impoundment but the driver does not have a previous conviction for a violation of subdivision (a) of Section 12500 or Section 14601, 14601.1, 14601.2, 14601.3, 14601.4, or 14601.5, the vehicle shall be released pursuant to this code and is not subject to forfeiture.

(d)(1) This subdivision applies only if the driver of the vehicle is a registered owner of the vehicle at the time of impoundment. Except as provided in paragraph (5) of subdivision (c), if the driver of a vehicle impounded pursuant to subdivision (c) was a registered owner of the vehicle at the time of impoundment, the impounding agency shall authorize release of the vehicle if, within three days of impoundment, the driver of the vehicle at the time of impoundment presents his or her valid driver's license, including a valid temporary California driver's license or permit, to the impounding agency. The vehicle shall then be released to a registered owner of record at the time of impoundment, or an agent of that owner authorized in writing, upon payment of towing and storage charges related to the impoundment, and any administrative charges authorized by Section 22850.5, providing that the person claiming the vehicle is properly licensed and the vehicle is properly registered. A vehicle impounded pursuant to the circumstances described in paragraph (3) of subdivision (c) shall be released to a registered owner whether or not the driver of the vehicle at the time of impoundment presents a valid driver's license.

(2) If there is a community property interest in the vehicle impounded pursuant to subdivision (c), owned at the time of impoundment by a person other than the driver, and the vehicle is the only vehicle available to the driver's immediate family that may be operated with a class C driver's license, the vehicle shall be released to a registered owner or to the community property interest owner upon compliance with all of the following requirements:

(A) The registered owner or the community property interest owner requests release of the vehicle and the owner of the community property interest submits proof of that interest.

(B) The registered owner or the community property interest owner submits proof that he or she, or an authorized driver, is properly licensed and that the impounded vehicle is properly registered pursuant to this code.

(C) All towing and storage charges related to the impoundment and any administrative charges authorized pursuant to Section 22850.5 are paid.

(D) The registered owner or the community property interest owner signs a stipulated vehicle release agreement, as described in paragraph (3), in consideration for the nonforfeiture of the vehicle. This requirement applies only if the driver requests release of the vehicle.

(3) A stipulated vehicle release agreement shall provide for the consent of the signator to the automatic future forfeiture and transfer of title to the state of any vehicle registered to that person, if the vehicle is driven by a driver with a suspended or revoked license, or by an unlicensed driver. The agreement shall be in effect for only as long as it is noted on a driving record maintained by the department pursuant to Section 1806.1.

(4) The stipulated vehicle release agreement described in paragraph (3) shall be reported by the impounding agency to the department not later than 10 days after the day the agreement is signed.

(5) No vehicle shall be released pursuant to paragraph (2) if the driving record of a registered owner indicates that a prior stipulated vehicle release agreement was signed by that person.

(e)(1) The impounding agency, in the case of a vehicle that has not been redeemed pursuant to subdivision (d), or that has not been otherwise released, shall promptly ascertain from the department the names and addresses of all legal and registered owners of the vehicle.

(2) The impounding agency, within two days of impoundment, shall send a notice by certified mail, return receipt requested, to all legal and registered owners of the vehicle, at the addresses obtained from the department, informing them that the vehicle is subject to forfeiture and will be sold or otherwise disposed of pursuant to this section. The notice shall also include instructions for filing a claim with the district at-

torney, and the time limits for filing a claim. The notice shall also inform any legal owner of its right to conduct the sale pursuant to subdivision (g). If a registered owner was personally served at the time of impoundment with a notice containing all the information required to be provided by this paragraph, no further notice is required to be sent to a registered owner. However, a notice shall still be sent to the legal owners of the vehicle, if any. If notice was not sent to the legal owner within two working days, the impounding agency shall not charge the legal owner for more than 15-days'impoundment when the legal owner redeems the impounded vehicle.

(3) No processing charges shall be imposed on a legal owner who redeems an impounded vehicle within 15 days of the impoundment of that vehicle. If no claims are filed and served within 15 days after the mailing of the notice in paragraph (2), or if no claims are filed and served within five days of personal service of the notice specified in paragraph (2), when no other mailed notice is required pursuant to paragraph (2), the district attorney shall prepare a written declaration of forfeiture of the vehicle to the state. A written declaration of forfeiture signed by the district attorney under this subdivision shall be deemed to provide good and sufficient title to the forfeited vehicle. A copy of the declaration shall be provided on request to any person informed of the pending forfeiture pursuant to paragraph (2). A claim that is filed and is later withdrawn by the claimant shall be deemed not to have been filed.

(4) If a claim is timely filed and served, then the district attorney shall file a petition of forfeiture with the appropriate juvenile or superior court within 10 days of the receipt of the claim. The district attorney shall establish an expedited hearing date in accordance with instructions from the court, and the court shall hear the matter without delay. The court filing fee of one hundred dollars ($100) shall be paid by the claimant, but shall be reimbursed by the impounding agency if the claimant prevails. To the extent practicable, the civil and criminal cases shall be heard at the same time in an expedited, consolidated proceeding. A proceeding in the civil case is a limited civil case.

(5) The burden of proof in the civil case shall be on the prosecuting agency, by a preponderance of the evidence. All questions that may arise shall be decided and all other proceedings shall be conducted as in an ordinary civil action. A judgment of forfeiture does not require as a condition precedent the conviction of a defendant of an offense which made the vehicle subject to forfeiture. The filing of a claim within the time limits specified in paragraph (3) is considered a jurisdictional prerequisite for the availing of the action authorized by that paragraph.

(6) All right, title, and interest in the vehicle shall vest in the state upon commission of the act giving rise to the forfeiture.

(7) The filing fee in paragraph (4) shall be distributed as follows:

(A) To the county law library fund as provided in Section 6320 of the Business and Professions Code, the amount specified in Sections 6321 and 6322.1 of the Business and Professions Code.

(B) To the Trial Court Trust Fund, the remainder of the fee.

(f) Any vehicle impounded that is not redeemed pursuant to subdivision (d) and is subsequently forfeited pursuant to this section shall be sold once an order of forfeiture is issued by the district attorney of the county of the impounding agency or a court, as the case may be, pursuant to subdivision (e).

(g) Any legal owner who is a motor vehicle dealer, bank, credit union, acceptance corporation, or other licensed financial institution legally operating in this state, or the agent of that legal owner, may take possession and conduct the sale of the forfeited vehicle if the legal owner or agent notifies the agency impounding the vehicle of its intent to conduct the sale within 15 days of the mailing of the notice pursuant to subdivision (e). Sale of the vehicle after forfeiture pursuant to this subdivision may be conducted at the time, in the manner, and on the notice usually given for the sale of repossessed or surrendered vehicles. The proceeds of any sale conducted by or on behalf of the legal owner shall be disposed of as provided in subdivision (i). A notice pursuant to this subdivision may be presented in person, by certified mail, by facsimile transmission, or by electronic mail.

(h) If the legal owner or agent of the owner does not notify the agency impounding the vehicle of its intent to conduct the sale as provided in subdivision (g), the agency shall offer the forfeited vehicle for sale at public auction within 60 days of receiving title to the vehicle. Low value vehicles shall be disposed of pursuant to subdivision (k).

(i) The proceeds of a sale of a forfeited vehicle shall be disposed of in the following priority:

(1) To satisfy the towing and storage costs following impoundment, the costs of providing notice pursuant to subdivision (e), the costs of sale, and the unfunded costs of judicial proceedings, if any.

(2) To the legal owner in an amount to satisfy the indebtedness owed to the legal owner remaining as of the date of sale, including accrued interest or finance charges and delinquency charges, providing that the principal indebtedness was incurred prior to the date of impoundment.

(3) To the holder of any subordinate lien or encumbrance on the vehicle, other than a registered or legal owner, to satisfy any indebtedness so secured if written notification of demand is received before distribution of the proceeds is completed. The holder of a subordinate lien or encumbrance, if requested, shall furnish reasonable proof of its interest and, unless it does so upon request, is not entitled to distribution pursuant to this paragraph.

(4) To any other person, other than a registered or legal owner, who can reasonably establish an interest in the vehicle, including a community property interest, to the extent of his or her provable interest, if written notification is received before distribution of the proceeds is completed.

(5) Of the remaining proceeds, funds shall be made available to pay any local agency and court costs, that are reasonably related to the implementation of this section, that remain unsatisfied.

(6) Of the remaining proceeds, half shall be transferred to the Controller for deposit in the Vehicle Inspection and Repair Fund for the high-polluter repair assistance and removal program created by Article 9 (commencing with Section 44090) of Chapter 5 of Part 5 of Division 26 of the Health and Safety Code, and half shall be transferred to the general fund of the city or county of the impounding agency, or the city or county where the impoundment occurred. A portion of the local funds may be used to establish a reward fund for persons coming forward with information leading to the arrest and conviction of hit-and-run drivers and to publicize the availability of the reward fund.

(j) The person conducting the sale shall disburse the proceeds of the sale as provided in subdivision (i) and shall provide a written accounting regarding the disposition to the impounding agency and, on request, to any person entitled to or claiming a share of the proceeds, within 15 days after the sale is conducted.

(k) If the vehicle to be sold pursuant to this section is not of the type that can readily be sold to the public generally, the vehicle shall be conveyed to a licensed dismantler or donated to an eleemosynary institution. License plates shall be removed from any vehicle conveyed to a dismantler pursuant to this subdivision.

(l) No vehicle shall be sold pursuant to this section if the impounding agency determines the vehicle to have been stolen. In this event, the vehicle may be claimed by the registered owner at any time after impoundment, providing the vehicle registration is current and the registered owner has no outstanding traffic violations or parking penalties on his or her driving record or on the registration record of any vehicle registered to the person. If the identity of the legal and registered owners of the vehicle cannot be reasonably ascertained, the vehicle may be sold.

(m) Any owner of a vehicle who suffers any loss due to the impoundment or forfeiture of any vehicle pursuant to this section may recover the amount of the loss from the unlicensed, suspended, or revoked driver. If possession of a vehicle has been tendered to a business establishment in good faith, and an unlicensed driver employed or otherwise directed by the business establishment is the cause of the impoundment of the vehicle, a registered owner of the impounded vehicle may recover damages for the loss of use of the vehicle from the business establishment.

(n)(1) The impounding agency, if requested to do so not later than 10 days after the date the vehicle was impounded, shall provide the opportunity for a poststorage hearing to determine the validity of the storage to the persons who were the registered and legal owners of the vehicle at the time of impoundment, except that the hearing shall be requested within three days after the date the vehicle was impounded if personal service was provided to a registered owner pursuant to paragraph (2) of subdivision (e) and no mailed notice is required.

(2) The poststorage hearing shall be conducted not later than two days after the date it was requested. The impounding agency may authorize its own officer or employee to conduct the hearing if the hearing officer is not the same person who directed the storage of the vehicle. Failure of either the registered or legal owner to request a hearing as provided in paragraph (1) or to attend a scheduled hearing shall satisfy the poststorage hearing requirement.

(3) The agency employing the person who directed the storage is responsible for the costs incurred for towing and storage if it is determined that the driver at the time of impoundment had a valid driver's license.

(o) As used in this section, "days" means workdays not including weekends and holidays.

(p) Charges for towing and storage for any vehicle impounded pursuant to this section shall not exceed the normal towing and storage rates for other vehicle towing and storage conducted by the impounding agency in the normal course of business.

(q) The Judicial Council and the Department of Justice may prescribe standard forms and procedures for implementation of this section to be used by all jurisdictions throughout the state.

(r) The impounding agency may act as the agent of the state in carrying out this section.

(s) No vehicle shall be impounded pursuant to this section if the driver has a valid license but the license is for a class of vehicle other than the vehicle operated by the driver.

(t) This section does not apply to vehicles subject to Sections 14608 and 14609, if there has been compliance with the procedures in those sections.

(u) As used in this section, "district attorney" includes a city attorney charged with the duty of prosecuting misdemeanor offenses.

(v) The agent of a legal owner acting pursuant to subdivision (g) shall be licensed, or exempt from licensure, pursuant to Chapter 11 (commencing with Section 7500) of Division 3 of the Business and Professions Code. *(AM '98; '05)*

14608. Rental of Vehicles

(a) A person shall not rent a motor vehicle to another person unless both of the following requirements have been met:

(1) The person to whom the vehicle is rented is licensed under this code or is a nonresident who is licensed under the laws of the state or country of his or her residence.

(2) The person renting to another person has inspected the driver's license of the person to whom the vehicle is to be rented and compared either the signature thereon with that of the person to whom the vehicle is to be rented or the photograph thereon with the person to whom the vehicle is to be rented.

(b) This section does not prohibit a blind or disabled person who is a nondriver from renting a motor vehicle if both of the following conditions exist at the time of rental:

(1) The blind or disabled person either holds an identification card issued pursuant to this code or is not a resident of this state.

(2) The blind or disabled person has a driver present who is either licensed to drive a vehicle pursuant to this code or is a nonresident licensed to drive a vehicle pursuant to the laws of the state or country of the driver's residence. *(AM '12)*

14610. Unlawful Use of License

(a) It is unlawful for any person:

(1) To display or cause or permit to be displayed or have in his possession any canceled, revoked, suspended, fictitious, fraudulently altered, or fraudulently obtained driver's license.

(2) To lend his driver's license to any other person or knowingly permit the use thereof by another.

(3) To display or represent any driver's license not issued to him as being his license.

(4) To fail or refuse to surrender to the department upon its lawful demand any driver's license which has been suspended revoked or canceled.

(5) To permit any unlawful use of a driver's license issued to him.

(6) To do any act forbidden or fail to perform any act required by this division.

(7) To photograph, photostat, duplicate, or in any way reproduce any driver's license or facsimile thereof in such a manner that it could be mistaken for a valid license, or to display or have in his possession any such photograph, photostat, duplicate, reproduction, or facsimile unless authorized by the provisions of this code.

(8) To alter any driver's license in any manner not authorized by this code.

(b) For purposes of this section, "driver's license" includes a temporary permit to operate a motor vehicle.

14610.1. Identification Document - Manufacture or Sale

(a) A person shall not manufacture or sell an identification document of a size and form substantially similar to, or that purports to confer the same privileges as, the drivers'licenses issued by the department.

(b) A violation of this section is a misdemeanor punishable as follows:

(1) The court shall impose a fine of not less than two hundred fifty dollars ($250) and not more than one thousand dollars ($1,000), and 24 hours of community service, to be served when the person is not employed or is not attending school. No part of the fine or community service shall be suspended or waived.

(2) In lieu of the penalties imposed under paragraph (1), the court, in its discretion, may impose a jail term of up to one year and a fine of up to one thousand dollars ($1,000). In exercising its discretion the court shall consider the extent of the defendant's commercial motivation for the offense.

(c) Prosecution under this section shall not preclude prosecution under any other applicable provision of law. *(AM '07, '10)*

14611. Unlawful Direction of Vehicle With Radioactive Materials

(a) A person shall not knowingly direct the operation of a vehicle transporting a highway route controlled quantity of Class 7 radioactive materials, as defined in Section 173.403 of Title 49 of the Code of Federal Regulations, by a person who does not possess a training certificate pursuant to subdivision (b) of Section 12524 and a valid driver's license of the appropriate class.

(b) A person convicted under this section shall be punished by a fine of not less than five thousand dollars ($5,000) nor more than ten thousand dollars ($10,000). *(AM '10)*

15250. Commercial Driver's License Requirements

(a)(1) A person shall not operate a commercial motor vehicle unless that person has in his or her immediate possession a valid commercial driver's license of the appropriate class.

(2) A person shall not operate a commercial motor vehicle while transporting hazardous materials unless that person has in his or her possession a valid commercial driver's license with a hazardous materials endorsement. An instruction permit does not authorize the operation of a vehicle transporting hazardous materials.

(b)(1) Before an application for an original or renewal of a commercial driver's license with a hazardous materials endorsement is submitted to the United States Transportation Security Administration for the processing of a security threat assessment, as required under Part 1572 of Title 49 of the Code of Federal Regulations, the department shall complete a check of the applicant's driving record to ensure that the person is not subject to a disqualification under Part 383.51 of Title 49 of the Code of Federal Regulations.

(2)(A) A person shall not be issued a commercial driver's license until he or she has passed a written and driving test for the operation of a commercial motor vehicle that complies with the minimum federal standards established by the federal Commercial Motor Vehicle Safety Act of 1986 (Public Law 99-570) and Part 383 of Title 49 of the Code of Federal Regulations, and has satisfied all other requirements of that act as well as any other requirements imposed by this code.

(B) The driving skills test as specified in Section 383.113 of Title 49 of the Code of Federal Regulations may be waived for a commercial motor vehicle driver with military commercial motor vehicle experience who is currently licensed with the United States Armed Forces at the time of his or her application for a commercial driver's license, and whose driving record in combination with his or her driving experience meets, at a minimum, the conditions required by Section 383.77(a) and (b) of Title 49 of the Code of Federal Regulations.

(c) The tests shall be prescribed and conducted by ***or under the direction of the department. The department may allow a third-party tester to administer the driving test part of the examination required under this section and Section 15275 if all of the following conditions are met:

(1) The tests given by the third party are the same as those that would otherwise be given by the department.

(2) The third party has an agreement with the department that includes, but is not limited to, the following provisions:

(A) Authorization for the United States Secretary of Transportation, or his or her representative, and the department, or its representative, to conduct random examinations, inspections, and audits without prior notice.

(B) Permission for the department, or its representative, to conduct onsite inspections at least annually.

(C) A requirement that all third-party testers meet the same qualification and training standards as the department's examiners, to the extent necessary to conduct the driving skill tests in compliance with the requirements of Part 383 of Title 49 of the Code of Federal Regulations.

(D) The department may cancel, suspend, or revoke the agreement with a third-party tester if the third-party tester fails to comply with the standards for the commercial driver's license testing program, or with any other term of the third-party agreement, upon 15 days' prior written notice of the action to cancel, suspend, or revoke the agreement by the department to the third party. Any action to appeal or review any order of the department canceling, suspending, or revoking a third-party testing agreement shall be brought in a court of competent jurisdiction under Section 1085 of the Code of Civil Procedure, or as otherwise permitted by the laws of this state. The action shall be commenced within 90 days from the effective date of the order.

(E) Any third-party tester whose agreement has been canceled pursuant to subparagraph (D) may immediately apply for a third-party testing agreement.

(F) A suspension of a third-party testing agreement pursuant to subparagraph (D) shall be for a term of less than 12 months as determined by the department. After the period of suspension, the agreement shall be reinstated upon request of the third-party tester.

(G) A revocation of a third-party testing agreement pursuant to subparagraph (D) shall be for a term of not less than one year. A third-party tester may apply for a new third-party testing agreement after the period of revocation and upon submission of proof of correction of the circumstances causing the revocation.

(H) Authorization for the department to charge the third-party tester a fee, as determined by the department, that is sufficient to defray the actual costs incurred by the department for administering and evaluating the third-party testing program, and for carrying out any other activities deemed necessary by the department to ensure sufficient training for the drivers participating in the program.

(3) Except as provided in Section 15250.3, the tests given by the third party shall not be accepted in lieu of tests prescribed and conducted by the department for applicants for a passenger vehicle endorsement specified in paragraph (2) of subdivision (a) of Section 15278, if the applicant operates or will operate a tour bus.

(d) Commercial driver's license applicants who take and pass driving tests administered by a third party shall provide the department with certificates of driving skill satisfactory to the department that the applicant has successfully passed the driving tests administered by the third party.

(e) If a driving test is administered to a commercial driver's license applicant who is to be licensed in another state pursuant to Section 383.79 of Subpart E of Part 383 of Title 49 of the Code of Federal Regulations, the department may impose a fee on the applicant that does not exceed the reasonable cost of conducting the tests and reporting the results to the driver's state of record.

(f) Implementation dates for the issuance of a commercial driver's license pursuant to this chapter may be established by the department as it determines is necessary to accomplish an orderly commercial driver's license program.

(***g) Active duty members of the United States Armed Forces, members of the military reserves, members of the National Guard who are on active duty, including personnel on full-time National Guard duty, personnel on part-time National Guard training, and National Guard military technicians (civilians who are required to wear military uniforms), and active duty personnel of the United States Coast Guard are exempt from all commercial driver's license requirements and sanctions, as provided in Section 383.3(c) of Subpart A of Part 383 of Title 49 of the Code of Federal Regulations when operating motor vehicles for military purposes. This exception shall not apply to United States Armed Forces reserve technicians. *(AM '13)*

15275. Endorsements

(a) A person may not operate a commercial motor vehicle described in this chapter unless that person has in his or her possession a valid commercial driver's license for the appropriate class, and an endorsement issued by the department to permit the operation of the vehicle unless exempt from the requirement to obtain an endorsement pursuant to subdivision (b) of Section 15278.

(b)(1) An endorsement to drive vehicles specified in this article shall be issued only to applicants who are qualified by examinations prescribed by the department and who meet the minimum standards established in Part 383 of Title 49 of the Code of Federal Regulations.

(2) A hazardous materials endorsement shall be issued only to applicants who comply with paragraph (1) and the requirements set forth in Part 1572 of Title 49 of the Code of Federal Regulations.

(c) The department may deny, suspend, revoke, or cancel an endorsement to drive vehicles specified in this article when the applicant does not meet the qualifications for the issuance or retention of the endorsement.

(d) If the department denies, suspends, revokes, or cancels a hazardous materials endorsement because the department received notification that the applicant poses a security threat pursuant to Part 1572 of Title 49 of the Code of Federal Regulations, and, upon appeal by the United States Transportation Security Administration, that endorsement is ordered reinstated, the department shall issue or restore the hazardous materials endorsement to the applicant within the period specified under those federal regulations. *(AM '05)*

15311.1. Employer Knowingly Allow Employee to Drive in Violation of Out-of-Service Order

An employer that knowingly allows or requires an employee to operate a commercial motor vehicle in violation of an out-of-service order is, upon conviction, subject to a civil penalty of not less than two thousand seven hundred fifty dollars ($2,750) nor more than twenty-five thousand dollars ($25,000). *(AM '12)*

15312.1. Employer Knowingly Allow or Require Employee to Operate Commercial Vehicle in Violation Law or Regulation Pertaining to Railroad Crossings

(a) An employer that knowingly allows or requires an employee to operate a commercial motor vehicle in violation of a federal, state, or local law or regulation pertaining to railroad crossings is, upon conviction, subject to a civil penalty of not more than ten thousand dollars ($10,000).

(b) This section shall become operative on September 20, 2005. *(AD '04)*

15500. Acquisition of Vehicle by Minor: Driver's License Required

It is unlawful for any minor who does not possess a valid driver's license issued under this code to order, purchase or lease, attempt to purchase or lease, contract to purchase or lease, accept, or otherwise obtain, any vehicle of a type subject to registration.

15501. Unlawful for Minor to Present False Driver's License

It is unlawful for any minor to present or offer to any person offering for sale or lease or to give or otherwise furnish thereto any motor vehicle of a type subject to registration, a driver's license which is false, fraudulent, or not actually his own for the purpose of ordering, purchasing or leasing, attempting to purchase or lease, contracting to purchase or lease, accepting, or otherwise obtaining such a vehicle.

DIVISION 6.7.
UNATTENDED CHILD IN MOTOR VEHICLE SAFETY ACT

CHAPTER 1. GENERAL PROVISIONS

15602. Application of Division
This division applies to motor vehicles upon the highways and elsewhere throughout the state unless expressly provided otherwise. *(AD '01)*

CHAPTER 2. OFFENSES

15620. Leaving Child 6 Years of Age or Younger in Motor Vehicle; Circumstances
(a) A parent, legal guardian, or other person responsible for a child who is 6 years of age or younger may not leave that child inside a motor vehicle without being subject to the supervision of a person who is 12 years of age or older, under either of the following circumstances:

(1) Where there are conditions that present a significant risk to the child's health or safety.

(2) When the vehicle's engine is running or the vehicle's keys are in the ignition, or both.

(b) A violation of subdivision (a) is an infraction punishable by a fine of one hundred dollars ($100), except that the court may reduce or waive the fine if the defendant establishes to the satisfaction of the court that he or she is economically disadvantaged and the court, instead, refers the defendant to a community education program that includes education on the dangers of leaving young children unattended in motor vehicles, and provides certification of completion of that program. Upon completion of that program, the defendant shall provide that certification to the court. The court may, at its discretion, require any defendant described in this section to attend an education program on the dangers of leaving young children unattended in motor vehicles.

(c) Nothing in this section shall preclude prosecution under both this section and Section 192 of the Penal Code, or Section 273a of that code, or any other provision of law.

(d)(1) Subdivision (b) and Section 40000.1 do not apply if an unattended child is injured or medical services are rendered on that child because of a violation described in subdivision (a).

(2) Nothing in this subdivision precludes prosecution under any other provision of law. *(AM '02)*

DIVISION 7. FINANCIAL RESPONSIBILITY LAWS

CHAPTER 1. COMPULSORY FINANCIAL RESPONSIBILITY

16000. Accident Report
(a) The driver of a motor vehicle who is in any manner involved in an accident originating from the operation of the motor vehicle on a street or highway, or is involved in a reportable off-highway accident, as defined in Section 16000.1, that has resulted in damage to the property of any one person in excess of seven hundred fifty dollars ($750), or in bodily injury, or in the death of any person shall report the accident, within 10 days after the accident, either personally or through an insurance agent, broker, or legal representative, on a form approved by the department, to the office of the department at Sacramento, subject to this chapter. The driver shall identify on the form, by name and current residence address, if available, any person involved in the accident complaining of bodily injury.

(b) A report is not required under subdivision (a) if the motor vehicle involved in the accident was owned or leased by, or under the direction of, the United States, this state, another state, or a local agency.

(c) If none of the parties involved in an accident has reported the accident to the department under this section within one year following the date of the accident, the department is not required to file a report on the accident and the driver's license suspension requirements of Section 16004 or 16070 do not apply. *(AM '01-'03)*

16020. Financial Responsibility Evidence Required

(a) All drivers and all owners of a motor vehicle shall at all times be able to establish financial responsibility pursuant to Section 16021, and shall at all times carry in the vehicle evidence of the form of financial responsibility in effect for the vehicle.

(b) "Evidence of financial responsibility"means any of the following:

(1) A form issued by an insurance company or charitable risk pool, as specified by the department pursuant to Section 4000.37.

(2) If the owner is a self-insurer, as provided in Section 16052 or a depositor, as provided in Section 16054.2, the certificate of self-insurance or the assignment of deposit letter issued by the department.

(3) An insurance covering note or binder pursuant to Section 382 or 382.5 of the Insurance Code.

(4) A showing that the vehicle is owned or leased by, or under the direction of, the United States or a public entity, as defined in Section 811.2 of the Government Code.

(c) For purposes of this section, "evidence of financial responsibility"also may be obtained by a law enforcement officer and court personnel from an electronic reporting system when that system becomes available for use by law enforcement officers.

(d) For purposes of this section, "evidence of financial responsibility"also includes any of the following:

(1) The name of the insurance company and the number of an insurance policy or surety bond that was in effect at the time of the accident or at the time that evidence of financial responsibility is required to be provided pursuant to Section 16028, if that information is contained in the vehicle registration records of the department.

(2) The identifying motor carrier of property permit number issued by the Department of the California Highway Patrol to the motor carrier of property as defined in Section 34601, and displayed on the motor vehicle in the manner specified by the Department of the California Highway Patrol.

(3) The identifying number issued to the household goods carrier, passenger stage carrier, or transportation charter party carrier by the Public Utilities Commission and displayed on the motor vehicle in the manner specified by the commission.

(e) Evidence of financial responsibility does not include an identification number in paragraph (1), (2), or (3) of subdivision (d) if the carrier is currently suspended by the issuing agency for lack or lapse of insurance or other form of financial responsibility. *(AM '06)*

16020.3 Financial Responsibility Evidence Required for Vanpool

Notwithstanding any other provision of law, any employer that owns a vanpool vehicle, as described in paragraph (1) of subdivision (c) of Section 17149 of the Revenue and Taxation Code, shall maintain evidence of financial responsibility with respect to that vehicle in the same form and amount as described in Section 5391.2 of the Public Utilities Code.

16025. Exchange of Information by Parties to an Accident

(a) Every driver involved in the accident shall, unless rendered incapable, exchange with any other driver or property owner involved in the accident and present at the scene, all of the following information:

(1) Driver's name and current residence address, driver's license number, vehicle identification number, and current residence address of registered owner.

(2) Evidence of financial responsibility, as specified in Section 16020. If the financial responsibility of a person is a form of insurance, then that person shall supply the name and address of the insurance company and the number of the insurance policy.

(b) Any person failing to comply with all of the requirements of this section is guilty of an infraction punishable by a fine not to exceed two hundred fifty dollars ($250). *(AM '99)*

16028. Present Evidence of Financial Responsibility Upon Demand

(a) Upon the demand of a peace officer pursuant to subdivision (b) or upon the demand of a peace officer or traffic collision investigator pursuant to subdivision (c), every person who drives a motor vehicle upon a highway shall provide evidence of financial responsibility for the vehicle that is in effect at the time the demand is made. The evidence of financial responsibility may be provided using a mobile electronic device. However, a peace officer shall not stop a vehicle for the sole purpose of determining whether the vehicle is being driven in violation of this subdivision.

(b) If a notice to appear is issued for any alleged violation of this code, except a violation specified in Chapter 9 (commencing with Section 22500) of Division 11 or any local ordinance adopted pursuant to that chapter, the cited driver shall furnish written evidence of financial responsibility or may provide electronic verification of evidence of financial responsibility using a mobile electronic device upon request of the peace officer issuing the citation. The peace officer shall request and write the driver's evidence of financial responsibility on the notice to appear, except when the peace officer is unable to write the driver's evidence of financial responsibility on the notice to appear due to an emergency that requires his or her presence elsewhere. If the cited driver fails to provide evidence of financial responsibility at the time the notice to appear is issued, the peace officer may issue the driver a notice to appear for violation of subdivision (a). The notice to appear for violation of subdivision (a) shall be written on the same citation form as the original violation.

(c) If a peace officer, or a regularly employed and salaried employee of a city or county who has been trained as a traffic collision investigator, is summoned to the scene of an accident described in Section 16000, the driver of a motor vehicle that is in any manner involved in the accident shall furnish written evidence of financial responsibility or may provide electronic verification of evidence of financial responsibility using a mobile electronic device upon the request of the peace officer or traffic collision investigator. If the driver fails to provide evidence of financial responsibility when requested, the peace officer may issue the driver a notice to appear for violation of this subdivision. A traffic collision investigator may cause a notice to appear to be issued for a violation of this subdivision, upon review of that citation by a peace officer.

(d)(1) If, at the time a notice to appear for a violation of subdivision (a) is issued, the person is driving a motor vehicle owned or leased by the driver's employer, and the vehicle is being driven with the permission of the employer, this section shall apply to the employer rather than the driver. In that case, a notice to appear shall be issued to the employer rather than the driver, and the driver may sign the notice on behalf of the employer.

(2) The driver shall notify the employer of the receipt of the notice issued pursuant to paragraph (1) not later than five days after receipt.

(e) A person issued a notice to appear for a violation of subdivision (a) may personally appear before the clerk of the court, as designated in the notice to appear, and provide written evidence of financial responsibility in a form consistent with Section 16020, showing that the driver was in compliance with that section at the time the notice to appear for violating subdivision (a) was issued. In lieu of the personal appearance, the person may submit by mail to the court written evidence of having had financial responsibility at the time the notice to appear was issued. Upon receipt by the clerk of that written evidence of financial responsibility in a form consistent with Section 16020, further proceedings on the notice to appear for the violation of subdivision (a) shall be dismissed.

(f) For the purposes of this section, "mobile electronic device" means a portable computing and communication device that has a display screen with touch input or a miniature keyboard.

(g) For the purposes of this section, when a person provides evidence of financial responsibility using a mobile electronic device to a peace officer, the peace officer shall only view the evidence of financial responsibility and is prohibited from viewing any other content on the mobile electronic device.

(h) ***If a person presents a mobile electronic device pursuant to this section, that person assumes all liability for any damage to the mobile electronic device. *(AM '13)*

16030. Knowingly Providing False Evidence of Financial Responsibility: Punishment

(a) Except as provided in subdivision (c), any person who knowingly provides false evidence of financial responsibility (1) when requested by a peace officer pursuant to Section 16028 or (2) to the clerk of the court as permitted by subdivision (e) of Section 16028, including an expired or canceled insurance policy, bond, certificate of self-insurance, or assignment of deposit letter, is guilty of a misdemeanor punishable by a fine not exceeding seven hundred fifty dollars ($750) or imprisonment in the county jail not exceeding 30 days, or by both that fine and imprisonment. Upon receipt of the court's abstract of conviction, the department shall suspend the driving privilege, effective upon the date of conviction, for a period of one year. The court shall impose an interim suspension of the person's driving privileges pursuant to Section 13550, and shall notify the driver of the suspension pursuant to Section 13106, and all driver's licenses in the possession of the driver shall be surrendered to the court pursuant to Section 13550. Any driver's license surrendered to the court pursuant to this section shall be transmitted by the court, together with the required report of the conviction, to the department within 10 days of the conviction. The suspension may not be terminated until one year has elapsed from the date of the suspension and until the person files proof of financial responsibility, as provided in Chapter 3 (commencing with Section 16430) except that the suspension shall be reinstated if the person fails to maintain proof of financial responsibility for three years.

(b) However, in lieu of suspending a person's driving privileges pursuant to subdivision (a), the court shall restrict the person's driving privileges to driving that is required in the person's course of employment, if driving of a motor vehicle is necessary in order to perform the duties of the person's primary employment. The restriction shall remain in effect for the period of suspension otherwise required by subdivision (a). The court shall provide for endorsement of the restriction on the person's driver's license, and violation of the restriction constitutes a violation of Section 14603 and grounds for suspension or revocation of the license under Section 13360.

(c) This section does not apply to a driver who is driving a motor vehicle owned or leased by the employer of the driver and driven in the course of the driver's employment with the permission of the employer. *(AM '99)*

16050.5. Liability Insurance - Furnish Information
The owner of a vehicle, who has a liability insurance policy with respect to the vehicle, shall, upon request, furnish insurance information to a person who, while operating the vehicle with the owner's permission, is involved in a reportable accident with the insured vehicle, or to the department whenever the department is required to establish whether the permissive driver meets the financial responsibility requirements of Section 16020.

CHAPTER 3. PROOF OF ABILITY TO RESPOND IN DAMAGES

16430. Financial Responsibility: Proof Required
Proof of financial responsibility when required by this code means proof of financial responsibility resulting from the ownership or operation of a motor vehicle and arising by reason of personal injury to, or death of, any one person, of at least fifteen thousand dollars ($15,000), and, subject to the limit of fifteen thousand dollars ($15,000) for each person injured or killed, of at least thirty thousand dollars ($30,000) for the injury to, or the death of, two or more persons in any one accident, and for damages to property (in excess of seven hundred fifty dollars ($750)), of at least five thousand dollars ($5,000) resulting from any one accident. Proof of financial responsibility may be given in any manner authorized in this chapter. *(AM '02)*

CHAPTER 6. INTERSTATE HIGHWAY CARRIERS

16500. Proof Required: Commercial Passenger Vehicles
Every owner of a vehicle used in the transportation of passengers for hire, including taxicabs, when the operation of the vehicle is not subject to regulation by the Public Utilities Commission, shall maintain, whenever he or she may be engaged in conducting those operations, proof of financial responsibility resulting from the ownership or operation of the vehicle and arising by reason of personal injury to, or death of, any one person, of at least fifteen thousand dollars ($15,000), and, subject to the limit of fifteen thousand dollars ($15,000) for each person injured or killed, of at least thirty thousand dollars ($30,000) for such injury to, or the death of, two or more persons in any one accident, and for damages to property of at

least five thousand dollars ($5,000) resulting from any one accident. Proof of financial responsibility may be maintained by either:

(a) Being insured under a motor vehicle liability policy against that liability.

(b) Obtaining a bond of the same kind, and containing the same provisions, as those bonds specified in Section 16434.

(c) By depositing with the department thirty-five thousand dollars ($35,000), which amount shall be deposited in a special deposit account with the Controller for the purpose of this section.

(d) Qualifying as a self-insurer under Section 16053.

The department shall return the deposit to the person entitled thereto when he or she is no longer required to maintain proof of financial responsibility as required by this section or upon his or her death.

16500.5. Proof Required: Other Commercial Vehicles

(a) Except as specified in subdivision (b), the owner of the following commercial vehicles shall maintain proof of financial responsibility in the amount required by the director:

(1) A vehicle used to carry passengers for hire, except taxicabs as defined in subdivision (c) of Section 27908.

(2) A vehicle having an unladen weight of over 7,000 pounds which is used in the transportation of property in the conduct of a business.

(b) Subdivision (a) does not apply to the following vehicles:

(1) A schoolbus.

(2) A motor vehicle used by a farmer exclusively in the transportation of his or her livestock, implements of husbandry, and agricultural commodities or in the transportation of supplies to his or her farm.

(3) A motor vehicle used by a resident farmer of this state to occasionally transport from the place of production to a warehouse, regular market, place of storage, or place of shipment the farm products of neighboring farmers in exchange for like services, farm products, or other compensation.

(4) A vehicle used in for-hire transportation which is subject to regulation by the Public Utilities Commission.

(5) A rented vehicle used for noncommercial transportation of property.

(c) The director shall establish the amounts which are determined adequate to cover damages resulting from the ownership or operation of a commercial vehicle or vehicles subject to this section arising by reason of personal injury to, or death of, any person or damage to property, or both. The director shall establish the amounts at levels equal to those prescribed by the Public Utilities Commission for owners and operators of for-hire vehicles subject to its jurisdiction and control.

(d) Proof of financial responsibility may be maintained by any of the following:

(1) Being insured under one or more motor vehicle liability policies against that liability.

(2) Obtaining a bond of the same kind, and containing the same provisions, as those bonds specified in Section 16434.

(3) By depositing with the department five hundred thousand dollars ($500,000), which amount shall be deposited in a special deposit account with the Controller for the purpose of this section.

(4) Qualifying as a self-insurer under Section 16053.

(e) The department shall return the deposit made pursuant to paragraph (3) of subdivision (d) to the person entitled thereto when the owner is no longer required to maintain proof of financial responsibility as required by this section or upon the owner's death.

(f) An insurer, agent, or broker who has been incorrectly informed by an owner of a vehicle or his or her representative that the vehicle is 7,000 pounds or less unladen weight, or is incorrectly informed by the owner or his or her representative that the vehicle is exempt from the requirements of subdivisions (a) and (c) pursuant to the exemptions set forth in subdivision (b), may issue a policy of motor vehicle liability insurance in any amount less than that required by the director but not less than the amounts required under Section 16451. The policy of motor vehicle liability insurance when issued shall not be deemed to provide liability coverage amounts greater than that specifically set forth in the policy notwithstanding that the vehicle weighs in excess of 7,000 pounds unladen weight or is subsequently used in a manner which would have required the vehicle to be insured in the amounts established by the director pursuant to subdivision (c).

16502. Prohibited Use; Evidence of Financial Responsibility

(a) An owner shall not use, or with his or her consent permit the use of, a vehicle used in the transportation of persons or property in the conduct of a business, without maintaining proof of financial responsibility as required by this chapter.

(b) A motor vehicle from another country in which there is no evidence of financial responsibility required pursuant to this chapter or Part 387 (commencing with Section 387.1) of Title 49 of the Code of Federal Regulations shall be denied entry into the state. *(AM '06)*

16560. Interstate Highway Carriers

(a) Any person or corporation who operates or causes to be operated on the highways of this state any motor vehicle in the interstate or foreign transportation of property, other than household goods, for compensation without having first complied with the requirements of paragraph (1) of subdivision (g) of Section 7232 of the Revenue and Taxation Code is guilty of a misdemeanor, and is punishable by a fine of not more than one thousand dollars ($1,000), or by imprisonment in the county jail for not more than three months, or by both that fine and imprisonment.

(b) Any person or corporation who operates or causes to be operated on the highways of this state any motor vehicle in the interstate or foreign transportation of household goods or passengers for compensation without having first complied with the requirements of Chapter 1 (commencing with Section 3901) of Division 2 of the Public Utilities Code is guilty of a misdemeanor, and is punishable by a fine of not more than one thousand dollars ($1,000), or by imprisonment in the county jail for not more than three months, or both that fine and imprisonment. *(AM '99)*

DIVISION 10. ACCIDENTS AND ACCIDENT REPORTS

CHAPTER 1. ACCIDENTS & ACCIDENT REPORTS

20000. Application of Division

The provisions of this division apply upon highways and elsewhere throughout the State, unless expressly provided otherwise.

20001. Hit and Run: Injury or Fatal

(a) The driver of a vehicle involved in an accident resulting in injury to a person, other than himself or herself, or in the death of a person shall immediately stop the vehicle at the scene of the accident and shall fulfill the requirements of Sections 20003 and 20004.

(b)(1) Except as provided in paragraph (2), a person who violates subdivision (a) shall be punished by imprisonment in the state prison, or in a county jail for not more than one year, or by a fine of not less than one thousand dollars ($1,000) nor more than ten thousand dollars ($10,000), or by both that imprisonment and fine.

(2) If the accident described in subdivision (a) results in death or permanent, serious injury, a person who violates subdivision (a) shall be punished by imprisonment in the state prison for two, three, or four years, or in a county jail for not less than 90 days nor more than one year, or by a fine of not less than one thousand dollars ($1,000) nor more than ten thousand dollars ($10,000), or by both that imprisonment and fine. However, the court, in the interests of justice and for reasons stated in the record, may reduce or eliminate the minimum imprisonment required by this paragraph.

(3) In imposing the minimum fine required by this subdivision, the court shall take into consideration the defendant's ability to pay the fine and, in the interests of justice and for reasons stated in the record, may reduce the amount of that minimum fine to less than the amount otherwise required by this subdivision.

(c) A person who flees the scene of the crime after committing a violation of Section 191.5 of, or paragraph (1) of subdivision (c) of Section 192 of the Penal Code, upon conviction of any of those sections, in addition and consecutive to the punishment prescribed, shall be punished by an additional term of imprisonment of five years in the state prison. This additional term shall not be imposed unless the allegation is charged in the accusatory pleading and admitted by the defendant or found to be true by the trier of fact. The court shall not strike a finding that brings a person within the provisions of this subdivision or an allegation made pursuant to this subdivision.

(d) As used in this section, "permanent, serious injury" means the loss or permanent impairment of function of a bodily member or organ. *(AM '99, '07)*

20002. Hit and Run: Property Damaged

(a) The driver of any vehicle involved in an accident resulting only in damage to any property, including vehicles, shall immediately stop the vehicle at the nearest location that will not impede traffic or otherwise jeopardize the safety of other motorists. Moving the vehicle in accordance with this subdivision does not affect the question of fault. The driver shall also immediately do either of the following:

(1) Locate and notify the owner or person in charge of that property of the name and address of the driver and owner of the vehicle involved and, upon locating the driver of any other vehicle involved or the owner or person in charge of any damaged property, upon being requested, present his or her driver's license, and vehicle registration, to the other driver, property owner, or person in charge of that property. The information presented shall include the current residence address of the driver and of the registered owner. If the registered owner of an involved vehicle is present at the scene, he or she shall also, upon request, present his or her driver's license information, if available, or other valid identification to the other involved parties.

(2) Leave in a conspicuous place on the vehicle or other property damaged a written notice giving the name and address of the driver and of the owner of the vehicle involved and a statement of the circumstances thereof and shall without unnecessary delay notify the police department of the city wherein the collision occurred or, if the collision occurred in unincorporated territory, the local headquarters of the Department of the California Highway Patrol.

(b) Any person who parks a vehicle which, prior to the vehicle again being driven, becomes a runaway vehicle and is involved in an accident resulting in damage to any property, attended or unattended, shall comply with the requirements of this section relating to notification and reporting and shall, upon conviction thereof, be liable to the penalties of this section for failure to comply with the requirements.

(c) Any person failing to comply with all the requirements of this section is guilty of a misdemeanor and, upon conviction thereof, shall be punished by imprisonment in the county jail not exceeding six months, or by a fine not exceeding one thousand dollars ($1,000), or by both that imprisonment and fine. *(AM '01)*

20003. Present Information, Render Aid: Injury or Fatal

(a) The driver of any vehicle involved in an accident resulting in injury to or death of any person shall also give his or her name, current residence address, the names and current residence addresses of any occupant of the driver's vehicle injured in the accident, the registration number of the vehicle he or she is driving, and the name and current residence address of the owner to the person struck or the driver or occupants of any vehicle collided with, and shall give the information to any traffic or police officer at the scene of the accident. The driver also shall render to any person injured in the accident reasonable assistance, including transporting, or making arrangements for transporting, any injured person to a physician, surgeon, or hospital for medical or surgical treatment if it is apparent that treatment is necessary or if that transportation is requested by any injured person.

(b) Any driver or injured occupant of a driver's vehicle subject to the provisions of subdivision (a) shall also, upon being requested, exhibit his or her driver's license, if available, or, in the case of an injured occupant, any other available identification, to the person struck or to the driver or occupants of any vehicle collided with, and to any traffic or police officer at the scene of the accident.

20008. Duty to Report Accidents

(a) The driver of a vehicle, other than a common carrier vehicle, involved in any accident resulting in injuries to or death of any person shall within 24 hours after the accident make or cause to be made a written report of the accident to the CHP or, if the accident occurred within a city, to either the CHP or the police department of the city in which the accident occurred. If the agency which receives the report is not responsible for investigating the accident, it shall immediately forward the report to the law enforcement agency which is responsible for investigating the accident.

On or before the fifth day of each month, every police department which received a report during the previous calendar month of an accident which it is responsible for investigating shall forward the report or a copy thereof to the main office of the CHP at Sacramento.

(b) The owner or driver of a common carrier vehicle involved in any such accident shall make a like report to the CHP on or before the 10th day of the month following the accident.

DIVISION 11. RULES OF THE ROAD

CHAPTER 1. OBEDIENCE TO & EFFECT OF TRAFFIC LAWS

21050. Riding or Driving of Animal

Every person riding or driving an animal upon a highway has all of the rights and is subject to all of the duties applicable to the driver of a vehicle by this division and Division 10, except those provisions which by their very nature can have no application.

21055. Exemption of Authorized Emergency Vehicles

The driver of an authorized emergency vehicle is exempt from Chapter 2 (commencing with Section 21350), Chapter 3 (commencing with Section 21650), Chapter 4 (commencing with Section 21800), Chapter 5 (commencing with Section 21950), Chapter 6 (commencing with Section 22100), Chapter 7 (commencing with Section 22348), Chapter 8 (commencing with Section 22450), Chapter 9 (commencing with Section 22500), and Chapter 10 (commencing with Section 22650) of this division, and Article 3 (commencing with Section 38305) and Article 4 (commencing with Section 38312) of Chapter 5 of Division 16.5, under all of the following conditions:

(a) If the vehicle is being driven in response to an emergency call or while engaged in rescue operations or is being used in the immediate pursuit of an actual or suspected violator of the law or is responding to, but not returning from, a fire alarm, except that fire department vehicles are exempt whether directly responding to an emergency call or operated from one place to another as rendered desirable or necessary by reason of an emergency call and operated to the scene of the emergency or operated from one fire station to another or to some other location by reason of the emergency call.

(b) If the driver of the vehicle sounds a siren as may be reasonably necessary and the vehicle displays a lighted red lamp visible from the front as a warning to other drivers and pedestrians.

A siren shall not be sounded by an authorized emergency vehicle except when required under this section.

21056. Effect of Exemption

Section 21055 does not relieve the driver of a vehicle from the duty to drive with due regard for the safety of all persons using the highway, nor protect him from the consequences of an arbitrary exercise of the privileges granted in that section.

21057. Sirens and Illegal Speed of Escorts

Every police and traffic officer is hereby expressly prohibited from using a siren or driving at an illegal speed when serving as an escort of any vehicle, except when the escort or conveyance is furnished for the preservation of life or when expediting movements of supplies and personnel for any federal, state, or local governmental agency during a national emergency, or state of war emergency, or state of emergency, or local emergency as defined in Section 8558 of the Government Code.

21100.3. Local Regulation of Traffic

It is unlawful for any person to disobey the traffic directions of a person appointed or authorized by a local authority to regulate traffic pursuant to subdivision (e) of Section 21100 when such appointee is wearing an official insignia issued by the local authority and is acting in the course of his appointed duties.

21106. Establishment of Crosswalks

(a) Local authorities, by ordinance or resolution, may establish crosswalks between intersections.

(b) Local authorities may install signs at or adjacent to an intersection directing that pedestrians shall not cross in a crosswalk indicated at the intersection. It is unlawful for any pedestrian to cross at the crosswalk prohibited by a sign.

21107.9. Application of Code to Privately Owned and Maintained Roads Within a Mobilehome Park

(a) Any city or county, or city and county, may, by ordinance or resolution, find and declare that there are privately owned and maintained roads within a mobilehome park, as defined in Section 18214 of the Health and Safety Code, or within a manufactured housing community, as defined in Section 18801 of the Health and Safety Code, within the city or county, or city and county, that are generally not held open for use by the public for vehicular travel. Upon enactment of the ordinance or resolution, the provisions of this code shall apply to the privately owned and maintained roads within a mobilehome park or manufactured housing community if appropriate signs are erected at the entrance or entrances to the mobilehome park or manufactured housing community of the size, shape, and color as to be readily legible during daylight hours from a distance of 100 feet, to the effect that the roads within the park or community are subject to the provisions of this code. The city or county, or city and county, may impose reasonable conditions and may authorize the owners of the mobilehome park or manufactured housing community to erect traffic signs, markings, or devices which conform to the uniform standards and specifications adopted by the Department of Transportation.

(b) No ordinance or resolution shall be enacted unless there is first filed with the city or county a petition requested by the owner or owners of any privately owned and maintained roads within a mobilehome park or manufactured housing community, who are responsible for maintaining the roads.

(c) No ordinance or resolution shall be enacted without a public hearing thereon and 10 days'prior written notice to all owners of the roads within a mobilehome park or manufactured housing community proposed to be subject to the ordinance or resolution. At least seven days prior to the public hearing, the owner or manager of the mobilehome park or manufactured housing community shall post a written notice about the hearing in a conspicuous area in the park or community clubhouse, or if no clubhouse exists, in a conspicuous public place in the park or community.

(d) For purposes of this section, the prima facie speed limit on any road within a mobilehome park or manufactured housing community shall be 15 miles per hour. This section does not preclude a mobilehome park or manufactured housing community from requesting a higher or lower speed limit if an engineering and traffic survey has been conducted within the community supporting that request.

(e) The department is not required to provide patrol or enforce any provision of this code on any privately owned and maintained road within a mobilehome park or manufactured housing community, except those provisions applicable to private property other than by action under this section. *(AD '02)*

21113. Public Grounds

(a) A person shall not drive any vehicle or animal, or stop, park, or leave standing any vehicle or animal, whether attended or unattended, upon the driveways, paths, parking facilities, or the grounds of any public school, state university, state college, unit of the state park system, county park, municipal airport, rapid transit district, transit development board, transit district, joint powers agency operating or managing a commuter rail system, or any property under the direct control of the legislative body of a municipality, or any state, county, or hospital district institution or building, or any educational institution exempted, in whole or in part, from taxation, or any harbor improvement district or harbor district formed pursuant to Part 2 (commencing with Section 5800) or Part 3 (commencing with Section 6000) of Division 8 of the

Harbors and Navigation Code, a district organized pursuant to Part 3 (commencing with Section 27000) of Division 16 of the Streets and Highways Code, or state grounds served by the Department of the California Highway Patrol, or any property under the possession or control of a housing authority formed pursuant to Article 2 (commencing with Section 34240) of Part 2 of Division 24 of the Health and Safety Code, except with the permission of, and upon and subject to any condition or regulation that may be imposed by the legislative body of the municipality, or the governing board or officer of the public school, state university, state college, county park, municipal airport, rapid transit district, transit development board, transit district, joint powers agency operating or managing a commuter rail system, or state, county, or hospital district institution or building, or educational institution, or harbor district, or a district organized pursuant to Part 3 (commencing with Section 27000) of Division 16 of the Streets and Highways Code, or housing authority, or the Director of Parks and Recreation regarding units of the state park system or the state agency with jurisdiction over the grounds served by the Department of the California Highway Patrol.

(b) A governing board, legislative body, or officer shall erect or place appropriate signs giving notice of any special conditions or regulations that are imposed under this section and the governing board, legislative body, or officer shall also prepare and keep available at the principal administrative office of the governing board, legislative body, or officer, for examination by all interested persons, a written statement of all those special conditions and regulations adopted pursuant to this section.

(c) When a governing board, legislative body, or officer permits public traffic upon the driveways, paths, parking facilities, or grounds under their control then, except for those conditions imposed or regulations enacted by the governing board, legislative body, or officer applicable to the traffic, all the provisions of this code relating to traffic upon the highways shall be applicable to the traffic upon the driveways, paths, parking facilities, or grounds.

(d) A public transportation agency that imposes any condition or regulation upon a person who parks or leaves standing any vehicle, pursuant to subdivision (a), is authorized to do either of the following:

(1) Enforce that condition or regulation in the manner provided in Article 3 (commencing with Section 40200) of Chapter 1 of Division 17 of this code. The public transportation agency shall be considered the issuing agency for that purpose.

(2) Designate regularly employed and salaried employees, who are engaged in directing traffic or enforcing parking laws and regulations, for the purpose of removing any vehicle in the same manner as a city, county, or jurisdiction of a state agency pursuant to Chapter 10 (commencing with Section 22650) of Division 11 of this code.

(e) With respect to the permitted use of vehicles or animals on property under the direct control of the legislative body of a municipality, no change in the use of vehicles or animals on the property, that had been permitted on January 1, 1976, shall be effective unless and until the legislative body, at a meeting open to the general public, determines that the use of vehicles or animals on the property should be prohibited or regulated.

(f) A transit development board may adopt ordinances, rules, or regulations to restrict, or specify the conditions for, the use of bicycles, motorized bicycles, skateboards, and roller skates on property under the control of, or any portion of property used by, the board.

(g) A public agency, including, but not limited to, the Regents of the University of California and the Trustees of the California State University, may adopt rules or regulations to restrict, or specify the conditions for, the use of bicycles, motorized bicycles, skateboards, and roller skates on public property under the jurisdiction of that agency.

(h) "Housing authority," for the purposes of this section, means a housing authority located within a county with a population of over six million people, and any other housing authority that complies with the requirements of this section.

(i) "Public transportation agency," for purposes of this section, means a public agency that provides public transportation as defined in paragraph (1) of subdivision (f) of Section 1 of Article XIX A of the California Constitution. *(AM '12)*

21116. Levees, Banks of Waterways, and Pipeline Rights-of-Way

(a) No person shall drive any motor vehicle upon a roadway located on a levee, canal bank, natural watercourse bank, or pipeline right-of-way if the responsibility for maintenance of the levee, canal bank, natural watercourse bank, or pipeline right-of-way is vested in the state or in a reclamation, levee, drainage, water or irrigation district, or other local agency, unless such person has received permission to drive upon such roadway from the agency responsible for such maintenance, or unless such roadway has been dedicated as a public right-of-way.

(b) For this section to be applicable to a particular levee, canal bank, natural watercourse bank, or pipeline right-of-way, the state or other agency having responsibility for maintenance of the levee, canal bank, natural watercourse bank, or pipeline right-of-way, shall erect or place appropriate signs giving notice that permission is required to be obtained to drive a motor vehicle thereon and giving notice of any special conditions or regulations that are imposed pursuant to this section and shall prepare and keep available at the principal office of the state agency or other agency affected or of the board of such agency, for examination by all interested persons, a written statement, in conformity with the existing rights of such agency to control access to the roadway, describing the nature of the vehicles, if any, to which such permission might be granted and the conditions, regulations, and procedure for the acquisition of such permission adopted pursuant to this section.

(c) Nothing in this section prohibits the establishment of bicycle paths or routes (as prescribed by Article 6.5 of Chapter 1 of Division 5 of the Public Resources Code) on levees, canal banks, natural watercourse banks, or pipeline rights-of-way.

21200. Laws Applicable to Bicycle Use

(a) A person riding a bicycle or operating a pedicab upon a highway has all the rights and is subject to all the provisions applicable to the driver of a vehicle by this division, including, but not limited to, provisions concerning driving under the influence of alcoholic beverages or drugs, and by Division 10 (commencing with Section 20000), Section 27400, Division 16.7 (commencing with Section 39000), Division 17 (commencing with Section 40000.1), and Division 18 (commencing with Section 42000), except those provisions which by their very nature can have no application.

(b)(1) A peace officer, as defined in Chapter 4.5 (commencing with Section 830) of Title 3 of Part 2 of the Penal Code, operating a bicycle during the course of his or her duties is exempt from the requirements of subdivision (a), except as those requirements relate to driving under the influence of alcoholic beverages or drugs, if the bicycle is being operated under any of the following circumstances:

(A) In response to an emergency call.

(B) While engaged in rescue operations.

(C) In the immediate pursuit of an actual or suspected violator of the law.

(2) This subdivision does not relieve a peace officer from the duty to operate a bicycle with due regard for the safety of all persons using the highway. *(AM '10)*

21200.5. Riding Bicycle Under Influence of Alcohol or Drugs

Notwithstanding Section 21200, it is unlawful for any person to ride a bicycle upon a highway while under the influence of an alcoholic beverage or any drug, or under the combined influence of an alcoholic beverage and any drug. Any person arrested for a violation of this section may request to have a chemical test made of the person's blood, breath, or urine for the purpose of determining the alcoholic or drug content of that person's blood pursuant to Section 23612, and, if so requested, the arresting officer shall have the test performed. A conviction of a violation of this section shall be punished by a fine of not more than two hundred fifty dollars ($250). Violations of this section are subject to Section 13202.5. *(AM '99)*

21201. Equipment Requirements

(a) No person shall operate a bicycle on a roadway unless it is equipped with a brake which will enable the operator to make one braked wheel skid on dry, level, clean pavement.

(b) No person shall operate on the highway a bicycle equipped with handlebars so raised that the operator must elevate his hands above the level of his shoulders in order to grasp the normal steering grip area.

(c) No person shall operate upon a highway a bicycle that is of a size that prevents the operator from safely stopping the bicycle, supporting it in an upright position with at least one foot on the ground, and restarting it in a safe manner.

(d) A bicycle operated during darkness upon a highway, a sidewalk where bicycle operation is not prohibited by the local jurisdiction, or a bikeway, as defined in Section 890.4 of the Streets and Highways Code, shall be equipped with all of the following:

(1) A lamp emitting a white light that, while the bicycle is in motion, illuminates the highway, sidewalk, or bikeway in front of the bicyclist and is visible from a distance of 300 feet in front and from the sides of the bicycle.

(2) A red reflector on the rear that shall be visible from a distance of 500 feet to the rear when directly in front of lawful upper beams of headlamps on a motor vehicle.

(3) A white or yellow reflector on each pedal, shoe, or ankle visible from the front and rear of the bicycle from a distance of 200 feet.

(4) A white or yellow reflector on each side forward of the center of the bicycle, and a white or red reflector on each side to the rear of the center of the bicycle, except that bicycles that are equipped with reflectorized tires on the front and the rear need not be equipped with these side reflectors.

The reflectors and reflectorized tires shall be of a type meeting requirements established by the department.

(e) A lamp or lamp combination, emitting a white light, attached to the operator and visible from a distance of 300 feet in front and from the sides of the bicycle, may be used in lieu of the lamp required by paragraph (1) of subdivision (d). *(AM '07)*

21201.3. Blue Lights on Bicycle or Motorized Bicycle Prohibited; Peace Officer Exception

(a) A bicycle or motorized bicycle used by a peace officer, as defined in Section 830.1 of, subdivision (a), (b), (c), (d), (e), (f), (g), or (i) of Section 830.2 of, subdivision (b) or (d) of Section 830.31 of, subdivision (a) or (b) of Section 830.32 of, Section 830.33 of, subdivision (a) of Section 830.36 of, subdivision (a) of Section 830.4 of, or Section 830.6 of, the Penal Code, in the performance of the peace officer's duties, may display a steady or flashing blue warning light that is visible from the front, sides, or rear of the bicycle or motorized bicycle.

(b) No person shall display a steady or flashing blue warning light on a bicycle or motorized bicycle except as authorized under subdivision (a).

(e) A lamp or lamp combination, emitting a white light, attached to the operator and visible from a distance of 300 feet in front and from the sides of the bicycle, may he used in lieu of the lamp required by clause (1) of subdivision (d). *(AD '98)*

21202. Operation on Roadway

(a) Any person operating a bicycle upon a roadway at a speed less than the normal speed of traffic moving in the same direction at that time shall ride as close as practicable to the right-hand curb or edge of the roadway except under any of the following situations:

(1) When overtaking and passing another bicycle or vehicle proceeding in the same direction.

(2) When preparing for a left turn at an intersection or into a private road or driveway.

(3) When reasonably necessary to avoid conditions (including, but not limited to, fixed or moving objects, vehicles, bicycles, pedestrians, animals, surface hazards, or substandard width lanes) that make it unsafe to continue along the right-hand curb or edge, subject to the provisions of Section 21656. For purposes of this section, a "substandard width lane" is a lane that is too narrow for a bicycle and a vehicle to travel safely side by side within the lane.

(4) When approaching a place where a right turn is authorized.

(b) Any person operating a bicycle upon a roadway of a highway, which highway carries traffic in one direction only and has two or more marked traffic lanes, may ride as near the left-hand curb or edge of that roadway as practicable.

21203. Hitching Rides

No person riding upon any motorcycle, motorized bicycle, bicycle, coaster, roller skates, sled, or toy vehicle shall attach the same or himself to any streetcar or vehicle on the roadway.

21204. Riding on Bicycle

(a) A person operating a bicycle upon a highway shall not ride other than upon or astride a permanent and regular seat attached thereto, unless the bicycle was designed by the manufacturer to be ridden without a seat.

(b) An operator shall not allow a person riding as a passenger, and a person shall not ride as a passenger, on a bicycle upon a highway other than upon or astride a separate seat attached thereto. If the passenger is four years of age or younger, or weighs 40 pounds or less, the seat shall have adequate provision for retaining the passenger in place and for protecting the passenger from the moving parts of the bicycle. *(AM '09)*

21205. Carrying Articles

No person operating a bicycle shall carry any package, bundle or article which prevents the operator from keeping at least one hand upon the handlebars.

21207.5. Motorized Bicycles: Prohibited Operation

Notwithstanding Sections 21207 and 23127 of this code, or any other provision of law, no motorized bicycle may be operated on a bicycle path or trail, bikeway, bicycle lane established pursuant to Section 21207, equestrian trail, or hiking or recreational trail, unless it is within or adjacent to a roadway or unless the local authority or the governing body of a public agency having jurisdiction over such path or trail permits, by ordinance, such operation.

21208. Permitted Movements from Bicycle Lanes

(a) Whenever a bicycle lane has been established on a roadway pursuant to Section 21207, any person operating a bicycle upon the roadway at a speed less than the normal speed of traffic moving in the same direction at that time shall ride within the bicycle lane, except that the person may move out of the lane under any of the following situations:

(1) When overtaking and passing another bicycle, vehicle, or pedestrian within the lane or about to enter the lane if the overtaking and passing cannot be done safely within the lane.

(2) When preparing for a left turn at an intersection or into a private road or driveway.

(3) When reasonably necessary to leave the bicycle lane to avoid debris or other hazardous conditions.

(4) When approaching a place where a right turn is authorized.

(b) No person operating a bicycle shall leave a bicycle lane until the movement can be made with reasonable safety and then only after giving an appropriate signal in the manner provided in Chapter 6 (commencing with Section 22100) in the event that any vehicle may be affected by the movement.

21209. Motor Vehicles and Motorized Bicycles in Bicycle Lanes

(a) No person shall drive a motor vehicle in a bicycle lane established on a roadway pursuant to Section 21207 except as follows:

(1) To park where parking is permitted.

(2) To enter or leave the roadway.

(3) To prepare for a turn within a distance of 200 feet from the intersection.

(b) This section does not prohibit the use of a motorized bicycle in a bicycle lane, pursuant to Section 21207.5, at a speed no greater than is reasonable or prudent, having due regard for visibility, traffic conditions, and the condition of the roadway surface of the bicycle lane, and in a manner which does not endanger the safety of bicyclists.

21210. Bicycle Parking

No person shall leave a bicycle lying on its side on any sidewalk, or shall park a bicycle on a sidewalk in any other position, so that there is not an adequate path for pedestrian traffic. Local authorities may, by ordinance or resolution, prohibit bicycle parking in designated areas of the public highway, provided that appropriate signs are erected.

21211. Obstruction of Bikeways or Bicycle Paths or Trails

(a) No person may stop, stand, sit, or loiter upon any class I bikeway, as defined in subdivision (a) of Section 890.4 of the Streets and Highways Code, or any other public or private bicycle path or trail, if the stopping, standing, sitting, or loitering impedes or blocks the normal and reasonable movement of any bicyclist.

(b) No person may place or park any bicycle, vehicle, or any other object upon any bikeway or bicycle path or trail, as specified in subdivision (a), which impedes or blocks the normal and reasonable movement of any bicyclist unless the placement or parking is necessary for safe operation or is otherwise in compliance with the law.

(c) This section does not apply to drivers or owners of utility or public utility vehicles, as provided in Section 22512.

(d) This section does not apply to owners or drivers of vehicles who make brief stops while engaged in the delivery of newspapers to customers along the person's route.

(e) This section does not apply to the driver or owner of a rubbish or garbage truck while actually engaged in the collection of rubbish or garbage within a business or residence district if the front turn signal lamps at each side of the vehicle are being flashed simultaneously and the rear turn signal lamps at each side of the vehicle are being flashed simultaneously.

(f) This section does not apply to the driver or owner of a tow vehicle while actually engaged in the towing of a vehicle if the front turn signal lamps at each side of the vehicle are being flashed simultaneously and the rear turn signal lamps at each side of the vehicle are being flashed simultaneously. *(AM '01)*

21212. Bicycle Helmet Requirements

(a) A person under 18 years of age shall not operate a bicycle, a nonmotorized scooter, or a skateboard, nor shall they wear in-line or roller skates, nor ride upon a bicycle, a nonmotorized scooter, or a skateboard as a passenger, upon a street, bikeway, as defined in Section 890.4 of the Streets and Highways Code, or any other public bicycle path or trail unless that person is wearing a properly fitted and fastened bicycle helmet that meets the standards of either the American Society for Testing and Materials (ASTM) or the United States Consumer Product Safety Commission (CPSC), or standards subsequently established by those entities. This requirement also applies to a person who rides upon a bicycle while in a restraining seat that is attached to the bicycle or in a trailer towed by the bicycle.

(b) Any helmet sold or offered for sale for use by operators and passengers of bicycles, nonmotorized scooters, skateboards, or in-line or roller skates shall be conspicuously labeled in accordance with the standard described in subdivision (a) which shall constitute the manufacturer's certification that the helmet conforms to the applicable safety standards.

(c) No person shall sell, or offer for sale, for use by an operator or passenger of a bicycle, nonmotorized scooter, skateboard, or in-line or roller skates any safety helmet which is not of a type meeting requirements established by this section.

(d) Any charge under this subdivision shall be dismissed when the person charged alleges in court, under oath, that the charge against the person is the first charge against that person under this subdivision, unless it is otherwise established in court that the charge is not the first charge against the person.

(e) Except as provided in subdivision (d), a violation of this section is an infraction punishable by a fine of not more than twenty-five dollars ($25).

The parent or legal guardian having control or custody of an unemancipated minor whose conduct violates this section shall be jointly and severally liable with the minor for the amount of the fine imposed pursuant to this subdivision.

(f) Notwithstanding Section 1463 of the Penal Code or any other provision of law, the fines collected for a violation of this section shall be allocated as follows:

(1) Seventy-two and one-half percent of the amount collected shall be deposited in a special account of the county health department, to be used for bicycle, nonmotorized scooter, skateboard, and in-line and roller skate safety education and for assisting low-income families in obtaining approved bicycle helmets for

children under the age of 18 years, either on a loan or purchase basis. The county may contract for the implementation of this program, which, to the extent practicable, shall be operated in conjunction with the child passenger restraint program pursuant to Section 27360.

(2) Two and one-half percent of the amount collected shall be deposited in the county treasury to be used by the county to administer the program described in paragraph (1).

(3) If the violation occurred within a city, 25 percent of the amount collected shall be transferred to and deposited in the treasury of that city. If the violation occurred in an unincorporated area, this 25 percent shall be deposited and used pursuant to paragraph (1). *(AM '02)*

21220.5. Motor Scooter Defined
For the purposes of this article, a motorized scooter is defined in Section 407.5. *(AD '99)*

21221. Operator of Motorized Scooter - Rights and Responsibilities
Every person operating a motorized scooter upon a highway has all the rights and is subject to all the provisions applicable to the driver of a vehicle by this division, including, but not limited to, provisions concerning driving under the influence of alcoholic beverages or drugs, and by Division 10 (commencing with Section 20000), Division 17 (commencing with Section 40000.1), and Division 18 (commencing with Section 42000), except those provisions which, by their very nature, can have no application. *(AD '99)*

21221.5. Operation of Motorized Scooter While Under the Influence of Alcoholic Beverage or Drug
Notwithstanding Section 21221, it is unlawful for any person to operate a motorized scooter upon a highway while under the influence of an alcoholic beverage or any drug, or under the combined influence of an alcoholic beverage and any drug. Any person arrested for a violation of this section may request to have a chemical test made of the person's blood or breath for the purpose of determining the alcoholic or drug content of that person's blood pursuant to subdivision (d) of Section 23612, and, if so requested, the arresting officer shall have the test performed. A conviction of a violation of this section shall be punished by a fine of not more than two hundred fifty dollars ($250). *(AD '99; AM '00)*

21223. Motorized Scooter; Equipment Requirements
(a) Every motorized scooter operated upon any highway during darkness shall be equipped with the following:

(1) Except as provided in subdivision (b), a lamp emitting a white light which, while the motorized scooter is in motion, illuminates the highway in front of the operator and is visible from a distance of 300 feet in front and from the sides of the motorized scooter.

(2) Except as provided in subdivision (c), a red reflector on the rear that is visible from a distance of 500 feet to the rear when directly in front of lawful upper beams of headlamps on a motor vehicle.

(3) A white or yellow reflector on each side visible from the front and rear of the motorized scooter from a distance of 200 feet.

(b) A lamp or lamp combination, emitting a white light, attached to the operator and visible from a distance of 300 feet in front and from the sides of the motorized scooter, may be used in lieu of the lamp required by paragraph (1) of subdivision (a).

(c) A red reflector, or reflectorized material meeting the requirements of Section 25500, attached to the operator and visible from a distance of 500 feet to the rear when directly in front of lawful upper beams of headlamps on a motor vehicle, may be used in lieu of the reflector required by paragraph (2) of subdivision (a). *(AD '99)*

21224. Exemption from Financial Responsibility; Registration and License Plate Requirements
(a) A person operating a motorized scooter is not subject to the provisions of this code relating to financial responsibility, registration, and license plate requirements, and, for those purposes, a motorized scooter is not a motor vehicle.

(b) A motorized scooter is exempt from the equipment requirements in Division 12 (commencing with Section 24000), except for Sections 24003 and 27400, Article 4 (commencing with Section 27450) of Chapter 5 of Division 12, and Section 27602.

(c) Notwithstanding subdivision (b), any motorized scooter may be equipped with equipment authorized by Division 12 (commencing with Section 24000).

(d) Any motorized scooter equipped with lighting equipment that is authorized by Division 12 (commencing with Section 24000) shall meet the lighting requirements in Article 1 (commencing with Section 24250) of Chapter 2 of Division 12 for that equipment. *(AD '99)*

21225. Local Authorities May Enact Ordinances
This article does not prevent a local authority, by ordinance, from regulating the registration of motorized scooters and the parking and operation of motorized scooters on pedestrian or bicycle facilities and local streets and highways, if that regulation is not in conflict with this code. *(AD '99; AM '04)*

21226. Motorized Scooters; Noise, Muffler and Exhaust System Requirements; Sale When Noise Limits Exceeded is Prohibited
(a) A person shall not sell or offer for sale a motorized scooter that produces a maximum noise level exceeding 80 dbA at a distance of 50 feet from the centerline of travel when tested in accordance with Society of Automotive Engineers (SAE) Recommended Practice J331 JAN00.

(b) A motorized scooter, as defined in subdivision (b) of Section 407.5, shall at all times be equipped with a muffler meeting the requirements of this section, in constant operation and properly maintained to prevent any excessive or unusual noise, and a muffler or exhaust system shall not be equipped with a cutout, bypass, or similar device.

(c) A motorized scooter, as defined in subdivision (b) of Section 407.5, operated off the highways shall at all times be equipped with a muffler meeting the requirements of this section, in constant operation and properly maintained to prevent any excessive or unusual noise, and a muffler or exhaust system shall not be equipped with a cutout, bypass, or similar device.

(d) A person shall not modify the exhaust system of a motorized scooter in a manner that will amplify or increase the noise level emitted by the motor of the scooter so that it is not in compliance with this section or exceeds the noise level limit established by subdivision (a). A person shall not operate a motorized scooter with an exhaust system so modified. *(AD '04)*

21227. Motorized Scooter - Operation Requirements
(a) A motorized scooter shall comply with one of the following:

(1) Operate in a manner so that the electric motor is disengaged or ceases to function when the brakes are applied.

(2) Operate in a manner so that the motor is engaged through a switch or mechanism that, when released, will cause the electric motor to disengage or cease to function.

(b) It is unlawful for a person to operate a motorized scooter that does not meet one of the requirements of subdivision (a). *(AD '99)*

21228. Motorized Scooter - Operate at Right Hand Curb or Roadway Edge; Exceptions
Any person operating a motorized scooter upon a highway at a speed less than the normal speed of traffic moving in the same direction at that time shall ride as close as practicable to the right-hand curb or right edge of the roadway, except under the following situations:

(a) When overtaking and passing another vehicle proceeding in the same direction.

(b) When preparing for a left turn, the operator shall stop and dismount as close as practicable to the right-hand curb or right edge of the roadway and complete the turn by crossing the roadway on foot, subject to the restrictions placed on pedestrians in Chapter 5 (commencing with Section 21950).

(c)(1) When reasonably necessary to avoid conditions, including, but not limited to, fixed or moving objects, vehicles, bicycles, pedestrians, animals, surface hazards, or substandard width lanes, which make it unsafe to continue along the right-hand curb or right edge of the roadway, subject to Section 21656.

(2) For the purposes of paragraph (1), a "substandard width lane" is a lane that is too narrow for a motorized scooter and another vehicle to travel safely side by side within the lane.

(d) Any person operating a motorized scooter upon a highway that carries traffic in one direction only and has two or more marked traffic lanes may operate the motorized scooter as near the left-hand curb or left edge of that roadway as practicable.

However, when preparing for a right turn, the operator shall stop and dismount as close as practicable to the left-hand curb or left edge of the highway and complete the turn by crossing the roadway on foot, subject to the restrictions placed on pedestrians in Chapter 5 (commencing with Section 21950). *(AD '99; AM '03)*

21229. Motorized Scooter - Operation in Bicycle Lane; Exceptions
(a) Whenever a class II bicycle lane has been established on a roadway, any person operating a motorized scooter upon the roadway shall ride within the bicycle lane, except that the person may move out of the lane under any of the following situations:

(1) When overtaking and passing another vehicle or pedestrian within the lane or when about to enter the lane if the overtaking and passing cannot be done safely within the lane.

(2) When preparing for a left turn, the operator shall stop and dismount as close as practicable to the right-hand curb or right edge of the roadway and complete the turn by crossing the roadway on foot, subject to the restrictions placed on pedestrians in Chapter 5 (commencing with Section 21950).

(3) When reasonably necessary to leave the bicycle lane to avoid debris or other hazardous conditions.

(4) When approaching a place where a right turn is authorized.

(b) No person operating a motorized scooter shall leave a bicycle lane until the movement can be made with reasonable safety and then only after giving an appropriate signal in the manner provided in Chapter 6 (commencing with Section 22100) in the event that any vehicle may be affected by the movement. *(AD '99)*

21230. Motorized Scooter - Operation on Bicycle Path or Trail Permitted; Exception
Notwithstanding any other provision of law, a motorized scooter may be operated on a bicycle path or trail or bikeway, unless the local authority or the governing body of a local agency having jurisdiction over that path, trail, or bikeway prohibits that operation by ordinance. *(AD '99)*

21235. Motorized Scooter - Prohibited Operation
The operator of a motorized scooter shall not do any of the following:

(a) Operate a motorized scooter unless it is equipped with a brake that will enable the operator to make a braked wheel skid on dry, level, clean pavement.

(b) Operate a motorized scooter on a highway with a speed limit in excess of 25 miles per hour unless the motorized scooter is operated within a class II bicycle lane.

(c) Operate a motorized scooter without wearing a properly fitted and fastened bicycle helmet that meets the standards described in Section 21212.

(d) Operate a motorized scooter without a valid driver's license or instruction permit.

(e) Operate a motorized scooter with any passengers in addition to the operator.

(f) Operate a motorized scooter carrying any package, bundle, or article that prevents the operator from keeping at least one hand upon the handlebars.

(g) Operate a motorized scooter upon a sidewalk, except as may be necessary to enter or leave adjacent property.

(h) Operate a motorized scooter on the highway with the handlebars raised so that the operator must elevate his or her hands above the level of his or her shoulders in order to grasp the normal steering grip area.

(i) Leave a motorized scooter lying on its side on any sidewalk, or park a motorized scooter on a sidewalk in any other position, so that there is not an adequate path for pedestrian traffic.

(j) Attach the motorized scooter or himself or herself while on the roadway, by any means, to any other vehicle on the roadway. *(AD '99; AM '04)*

21250. Low Speed Vehicle Defined
For the purposes of this article, a low-speed vehicle means a vehicle as defined in Section 385.5. A "low-speed vehicle"is also known as a "neighborhood electric vehicle." *(AD '99; AM '04)*

21251. Low Speed Vehicle Subject to All Provisions
Except as provided in Chapter 6.2 (commencing with Section 1962), Chapter 7 (commencing with Section 1963), Chapter 7.1 (commencing with Section 1964), Chapter 8 (commencing with Section 1965), and Chapter 8.1 (commencing with Section 1966) of Division 2.5 of the Streets and Highways Code, and Sections 4023, 21115, and 21115.1, a low-speed vehicle is subject to all the provisions applicable to a motor vehicle, and the driver of a low-speed vehicle is subject to all the provisions applicable to the driver of a motor vehicle or other vehicle, when applicable, by this code or another code, with the exception of those provisions that, by their very nature, can have no application. *(AM '11)*

21252. Disclosure Statement Required
A vehicle dealer, selling a low-speed vehicle, shall provide to the buyer a disclosure statement regarding the operation of the vehicle that is in compliance with existing provisions of the California Code of Regulations. *(AD '99)*

21253. Low Speed Vehicle Must Meet Federal Standards
A low-speed vehicle operated or parked on the roadway shall at all times meet federal Motor Vehicle Safety Standards established for low-speed vehicles in Section 571.500 of Title 49 of the Code of Federal Regulations. *(AD '99)*

21254. Modification to Increase Vehicle Speed; Applicability of Federal Standards
A motor vehicle that was originally designated as a low-speed vehicle and that has been modified or altered to exceed 25 miles per hour shall not qualify for the relaxed federal Motor Vehicle Safety Standards established for low-speed vehicles and instead shall meet all federal Motor Vehicle Safety Standards for a passenger vehicle. *(AD '99)*

21260. Low Speed Vehicle - Maximum Speed; Crossing at Intersections
(a) Except as provided in paragraph (1) of subdivision (b), or in an area where a neighborhood electric vehicle transportation plan has been adopted pursuant to Chapter 6.2 (commencing with Section 1962), Chapter 7 (commencing with Section 1963), Chapter 7.1 (commencing with Section 1964), Chapter 8 (commencing with Section 1965), or Chapter 8.1 (commencing with Section 1966) of Division 2.5 of the Streets and Highways Code, the operator of a low-speed vehicle shall not operate the vehicle on any roadway with a speed limit in excess of 35 miles per hour.

(b)(1) The operator of a low-speed vehicle may cross a roadway with a speed limit in excess of 35 miles per hour if the crossing begins and ends on a roadway with a speed limit of 35 miles per hour or less and occurs at an intersection of approximately 90 degrees.

(2) Notwithstanding paragraph (1), the operator of a low-speed vehicle shall not traverse an uncontrolled intersection with any state highway unless that intersection has been approved and authorized by the agency having primary traffic enforcement responsibilities for that crossing by a low-speed vehicle. *(AM '11)*

21266. Low Speed Vehicles - Local Authorities May Prohibit or Restrict Use
(a) Notwithstanding Section 21260, local authorities, by ordinance or resolution, may restrict or prohibit the use of low-speed vehicles.

(b) Notwithstanding Section 21260, a local law enforcement agency with primary traffic enforcement responsibilities or the Department of the California Highway Patrol may prohibit the operation of a low-speed vehicle on any roadway under that agency's or department's jurisdiction when the agency or the department deems the prohibition to be in the best interest of public safety. Any such prohibition shall become effective when appropriate signs giving notice thereof are erected upon the roadway. *(AD '99)*

Article 6. Electric Personal Assistive Mobility Devices

21281. Required Safety Equipment

Every electric personal assistive mobility device, or EPAMD, shall be equipped with the following safety mechanisms:

(a) Front, rear, and side reflectors.

(b) A system that enables the operator to bring the device to a controlled stop.

(c) If the EPAMD is operated between one-half hour after sunset and one-half hour before sunrise, a lamp emitting a white light that, while the EPAMD is in motion, illuminates the area in front of the operator and is visible from a distance of 300 feet in front of the EPAMD.

(d) A sound emitting device that can be activated from time to time by the operator, as appropriate, to alert nearby persons. *(AD '02)*

21281.5. Operate EPAMD; Unsafe Speed, Endanger Person or Property; Disregard for Safety of Persons or Property, Yield Right-of-Way

(a) A person shall not operate an EPAMD on a sidewalk, bike path, pathway, trail, bike lane, street, road, or highway at a speed greater than is reasonable and prudent having due regard for weather, visibility, pedestrians, and other conveyance traffic on, and the surface, width, and condition of, the sidewalk, bike path, pathway, trail, bike lane, street, road, or highway.

(b) A person shall not operate an EPAMD at a speed that endangers the safety of persons or property.

(c) A person shall not operate an EPAMD on a sidewalk, bike path, pathway, trail, bike lane, street, road, or highway with willful or wanton disregard for the safety of persons or property.

(d) A person operating an EPAMD on a sidewalk, bike path, pathway, trail, bike lane, street, road, or highway shall yield the right-of-way to all pedestrians on foot, including persons with disabilities using assistive devices and service animals that are close enough to constitute a hazard. *(AD '07)*

21282. Local Jurisdictions May Regulate Use

Notwithstanding Section 21966, for the purpose of assuring the safety of pedestrians, including seniors, persons with disabilities, and others using sidewalks, bike paths, pathways, trails, bike lanes, streets, roads, and highways, a city, county, or city and county may, by ordinance, regulate the time, place, and manner of the operation of electric personal assistive mobility devices as defined in Section 313, and their use as a pedestrian pursuant to paragraph (2) of subdivision (a) of Section 467, including limiting, prohibiting entirely in the local jurisdiction, or prohibiting use in specified areas as determined to be appropriate by local entities. State agencies may limit or prohibit the time, place, and manner of use on state property. *(AD '02)*

CHAPTER 2. TRAFFIC SIGNS, SIGNALS, AND MARKINGS

21367. Traffic Control: Highway Construction

(a) As provided in Section 125 of the Streets and Highways Code and in Section 21100 of this code, respectively, the duly authorized representative of CalTrans or local authorities, with respect to highways under their respective jurisdictions, including, but not limited to, persons contracting to perform construction, maintenance, or repair of a highway, may, with the approval of the department or local authority, as the case may be, and when engaged in the performance of that work, restrict the use of, and regulate the movement of traffic through or around, the affected area whenever the traffic would endanger the safety of workers or the work would interfere with or endanger the movement of traffic through the area. Traffic may be regulated by warning signs, lights, appropriate control devices, or by a person or persons controlling and directing the flow of traffic.

(b) It is unlawful to disobey the instructions of a person controlling and directing traffic pursuant to subdivision (a).

(c) It is unlawful to fail to comply with the directions of warning signs, lights, or other control devices provided for the regulation of traffic pursuant to subdivision (a).

21451. Circular Green or Green Arrow

(a) A driver facing a circular green signal shall proceed straight through or turn right or left or make a U-turn unless a sign prohibits a U-turn. Any driver, including one turning, shall yield the right-of-way to other traffic and to pedestrians lawfully within the intersection or an adjacent crosswalk.

(b) A driver facing a green arrow signal, shown alone or in combination with another indication, shall enter the intersection only to make the movement indicated by that green arrow or any other movement that is permitted by other indications shown at the same time. A driver facing a left green arrow may also make a U-turn unless prohibited by a sign. A driver shall yield the right-of-way to other traffic and to pedestrians lawfully within the intersection or an adjacent crosswalk.

(c) A pedestrian facing a circular green signal, unless prohibited by sign or otherwise directed by a pedestrian control signal as provided in Section 21456, may proceed across the roadway within any marked or unmarked crosswalk, but shall yield the right-of-way to vehicles lawfully within the intersection at the time that signal is first shown.

(d) A pedestrian facing a green arrow turn signal, unless otherwise directed by a pedestrian control signal as provided in Section 21456, shall not enter the roadway.

21452. Circular Yellow or Yellow Arrow

(a) A driver facing a steady circular yellow or yellow arrow signal is, by that signal, warned that the related green movement is ending or that a red indication will be shown immediately thereafter.

(b) A pedestrian facing a steady circular yellow or a yellow arrow signal, unless otherwise directed by a pedestrian control signal as provided in Section 21456, is, by that signal, warned that there is insufficient time to cross the roadway and shall not enter the roadway.

21453. Circular Red or Red Arrow

(a) A driver facing a steady circular red signal alone shall stop at a marked limit line, but if none, before entering the crosswalk on the near side of the intersection or, if none, then before entering the intersection, and shall remain stopped until an indication to proceed is shown, except as provided in subdivision (b).

(b) Except when a sign is in place prohibiting a turn, a driver, after stopping as required by subdivision (a), facing a steady circular red signal, may turn right, or turn left from a one-way street onto a one-way street. A driver making that turn shall yield the right-of-way to pedestrians lawfully within an adjacent crosswalk and to any vehicle that has approached or is approaching so closely as to constitute an immediate hazard to the driver, and shall continue to yield the right-of-way to that vehicle until the driver can proceed with reasonable safety.

(c) A driver facing a steady red arrow signal shall not enter the intersection to make the movement indicated by the arrow and, unless entering the intersection to make a movement permitted by another signal, shall stop at a clearly marked limit line, but if none, before entering the crosswalk on the near side of the intersection, or if none, then before entering the intersection, and shall remain stopped until an indication permitting movement is shown.

(d) Unless otherwise directed by a pedestrian control signal as provided in Section 21456, a pedestrian facing a steady circular red or red arrow signal shall not enter the roadway. *(AM '01)*

21454. Lane Use Control Signals

When lane use control signals are placed over individual lanes, those signals shall indicate and apply to drivers of vehicles as follows:

(a) Green indication: A driver may travel in any lane over which a green signal is shown.

(b) Steady yellow indication: A driver is thereby warned that a lane control change is being made.

(c) Steady red indication: A driver shall not enter or travel in any lane over which a red signal is shown.

(d) Flashing yellow indication: A driver may use the lane only for the purpose of making a left turn to or from the highway.

21455. Signal at Other Places

When an official traffic control signal is erected and maintained at a place other than an intersection, the provisions of this article shall be applicable except those provisions which by their nature can have no application. Any stop required shall be made at a sign or crosswalk or limit line indicating where the stop shall be made, but in the absence of any such sign or marking the stop shall be made at the signal.

21456. Walk, Wait, or Don't Walk

Whenever a pedestrian control signal showing the words "WALK" or "WAIT" or "DON'T WALK" or other approved symbol is in place, the signal shall indicate as follows:

(a) "WALK" or approved "Walking Person" symbol. A pedestrian facing the signal may proceed across the roadway in the direction of the signal, but shall yield right-of-way to vehicles lawfully within the intersection at the time that signal is first shown.

(b) Flashing or steady "DON'T WALK" or "WAIT" or approved "Upraised Hand" symbol. No pedestrian shall start to cross the roadway in the direction of the signal, but any pedestrian who has partially completed crossing shall proceed to a sidewalk or safety zone or otherwise leave the roadway while the "WAIT" or "DON'T WALK" or approved "Upraised Hand" symbol is showing.

21456.2. Official Traffic Control Signal - Bicycle Operator to Obey

(a) Unless otherwise directed by a bicycle signal as provided in Section 21456.3, an operator of a bicycle shall obey the provisions of this article applicable to the driver of a vehicle.

(b) Whenever an official traffic control signal exhibiting different colored bicycle symbols is shown concurrently with official traffic control signals exhibiting different colored lights or arrows, an operator of a bicycle facing those traffic control signals shall obey the bicycle signals as provided in Section 21456.3. *(AD '99; AM '05)*

21456.3. Bicycle Signals

(a) An operator of a bicycle facing a green bicycle signal shall proceed straight through or turn right or left or make a U-turn unless a sign prohibits a U-turn. An operator of a bicycle, including one turning, shall yield the right-of-way to other traffic and to pedestrians lawfully within the intersection or an adjacent crosswalk.

(b) An operator of a bicycle facing a steady yellow bicycle signal is, by that signal, warned that the related green movement is ending or that a red indication will be shown immediately thereafter.

(c) Except as provided in subdivision (d), an operator of a bicycle facing a steady red bicycle signal shall stop at a marked limit line, but if none, before entering the crosswalk on the near side of the intersection, or, if none, then before entering the intersection, and shall remain stopped until an indication to proceed is shown.

(d) Except when a sign is in place prohibiting a turn, an operator of a bicycle, after stopping as required by subdivision (c), facing a steady red bicycle signal, may turn right, or turn left from a one-way street onto a one-way street. An operator of a bicycle making a turn shall yield the right-of-way to pedestrians lawfully within an adjacent crosswalk and to traffic lawfully using the intersection.

(e) A bicycle signal may be used only at those locations that meet geometric standards or traffic volume standards, or both, as adopted by the Department of Transportation. *(AD '99; AM '05)*

21457. Flashing Signals

Whenever an illuminated flashing red or yellow light is used in a traffic signal or with a traffic sign, it shall require obedience by drivers as follows:

(a) Flashing red (stop signal): When a red lens is illuminated with rapid intermittent flashes, a driver shall stop at a clearly marked limit line, but if none, before entering the crosswalk on the near side of the intersection, or if none, then at the point nearest the intersecting roadway where the driver has a view of approaching traffic on the intersecting roadway before entering it, and the driver may proceed subject to the rules applicable after making a stop at a stop sign.

(b) Flashing yellow (caution signal): When a yellow lens is illuminated with rapid intermittent flashes, a driver may proceed through the intersection or past the signal only with caution.

21458. Curb Markings

(a) Whenever local authorities enact local parking regulations and indicate them by the use of paint upon curbs, the following colors only shall be used, and the colors indicate as follows:

(1) Red indicates no stopping, standing, or parking, whether the vehicle is attended or unattended, except that a bus may stop in a red zone marked or signposted as a bus loading zone.

(2) Yellow indicates stopping only for the purpose of loading or unloading passengers or freight for the time as may be specified by local ordinance.

(3) White indicates stopping for either of the following purposes:

(A) Loading or unloading of passengers for the time as may be specified by local ordinance.

(B) Depositing mail in an adjacent mailbox.

(4) Green indicates time limit parking specified by local ordinance.

(5) Blue indicates parking limited exclusively to the vehicles of disabled persons and disabled veterans.

(b) Regulations adopted pursuant to subdivision (a) shall be effective on days and during hours or times as prescribed local ordinances.

21460. Double Lines

(a) If double parallel solid yellow lines are in place, a person driving a vehicle shall not drive to the left of the lines, except as permitted in this section.

(b) If double parallel solid white lines are in place, a person driving a vehicle shall not cross any part of those double solid white lines, except as permitted in this section or Section 21655.8.

(c) If the double parallel lines, one of which is broken, are in place, a person driving a vehicle shall not drive to the left of the lines, except as follows:

(1) If the driver is on the side of the roadway in which the broken line is in place, the driver may cross over the double lines or drive to the left of the double lines when overtaking or passing other vehicles.

(2) As provided in Section 21460.5.

(d) The markings as specified in subdivision (a), (b), or (c) do not prohibit a driver from crossing the marking if (1) turning to the left at an intersection or into or out of a driveway or private road, or (2) making a U-turn under the rules governing that turn, and the markings shall be disregarded when authorized signs have been erected designating offcenter traffic lanes as permitted pursuant to Section 21657.

(e) Raised pavement markers may be used to simulate painted lines described in this section if the markers are placed in accordance with standards established by the Department of Transportation. *(AM'11)*

21460.5. Two-Way Left-Turn Lanes

(a) CalTrans and local authorities in their respective jurisdictions may designate a two-way left-turn lane on a highway. A two-way left-turn lane is a lane near the center of the highway set aside for use by vehicles making left turns in both directions from or into the highway.

(b) Two-way left-turn lanes shall be designated by distinctive roadway markings consisting of parallel double yellow lines, interior line dashed and exterior line solid, on each side of the lane. CalTrans may determine and prescribe standards and specifications governing length, width, and positioning of the distinctive pavement markings. All pavement markings designating a two-way left-turn lane shall conform to such standards and specifications.

(c) A vehicle shall not be driven in a designated two-way left-turn lane except when preparing for or making a left turn from or into a highway or when preparing for or making a U-turn when otherwise permitted by law, and shall not be driven in that lane for more than 200 feet while preparing for and making the turn or while preparing to merge into the adjacent lanes of travel. A left turn or U-turn shall not be made from any other lane where a two-way left-turn lane has been designated.

(d) This section shall not prohibit driving across a two-way left-turn lane.

(e) Raised pavement markers may be used to simulate painted lines described in this section when such markers are placed in accordance with standards established by CalTrans.

21461. Obedience by Driver to Official Traffic Control Devices

(a) It is unlawful for a driver of a vehicle to fail to obey a sign or signal defined as regulatory in the federal Manual on Uniform Traffic Control Devices, or a Department of Transportation approved supplement to that manual of a regulatory nature erected or maintained to enhance traffic safety and operations or to indicate and carry out the provisions of this code or a local traffic ordinance or resolution adopted pursuant to a local traffic ordinance, or to fail to obey a device erected or maintained by lawful authority of a public body or official.

(b) Subdivision (a) does not apply to acts constituting violations under Chapter 9 (commencing with Section 22500) of this division or to acts constituting violations of a local traffic ordinance adopted pursuant to Chapter 9 (commencing with Section 22500). *(AM '04)*

21461.5. Obedience by Pedestrian to Official Traffic Control Devices

It shall be unlawful for any pedestrian to fail to obey any sign or signal erected or maintained to carry out the provisions of this code or any local traffic ordinance or resolution adopted pursuant to a local traffic ordinance, or to fail to obey any device erected or maintained pursuant to Section 21352.

21462. Obedience to Traffic Control Signals

The driver of any vehicle, the person in charge of any animal, any pedestrian, and the motorman of any streetcar shall obey the instructions of any official traffic signal applicable to him and placed as provided by law, unless otherwise directed by a police or traffic officer or when it is necessary for the purpose of avoiding a collision or in case of other emergency, subject to the exemptions granted by Section 21055.

21463. Illegal Operation of Signals

No person shall operate a manually or traffic actuated signal other than for the purpose of permitting a pedestrian or vehicle to cross a roadway.

21464. Interference With Traffic Devices

(a) A person, without lawful authority, may not deface, injure, attach any material or substance to, knock down, or remove, nor may a person shoot at, any official traffic control device, traffic guidepost, traffic signpost, motorist callbox, or historical marker placed or erected as authorized or required by law, nor may a person without lawful authority deface, injure, attach any material or substance to, or remove, nor may a person shoot at, any inscription, shield, or insignia on any device, guide, or marker.

(b) A person may not use, and a vehicle, other than an authorized emergency vehicle or a public transit passenger vehicle, may not be equipped with, any device, including, but not limited to, a mobile infrared transmitter, that is capable of sending a signal that interrupts or changes the sequence patterns of an official traffic control signal unless that device or use is authorized by the Department of Transportation pursuant to Section 21350 or by local authorities pursuant to Section 21351.

(c) A person may not buy, possess, manufacture, install, sell, offer for sale, or otherwise distribute a device described in subdivision (b), including, but not limited to, a mobile infrared transmitter (MIRT), unless the purchase, possession, manufacture, installation, sale, offer for sale, or distribution is for the use of the device by a peace officer or other person authorized to operate an authorized emergency vehicle or a public transit passenger vehicle, in the scope of his or her duties.

(d) Any willful violation of subdivision (a), (b), or (c) that results in injury to, or the death of, a person is punishable by imprisonment pursuant to subdivision (h) of Section 1170 of the Penal Code, or by imprisonment in a county jail for a period of not more than six months, and by a fine of not less than five thousand dollars ($5,000) nor more than ten thousand dollars ($10,000).

(e) Any willful violation of subdivision (a), (b), or (c) that does not result in injury to, or the death of, a person is punishable by a fine of not more than five thousand dollars ($5,000).

(f) The court shall allow the offender to perform community service designated by the court in lieu of all or part of any fine imposed under this section. *(AM '11)*

21465. Unauthorized Traffic Devices

No person shall place, maintain, or display upon, or in view of, any highway any unofficial sign, signal, device, or marking, or any sign, signal, device, or marking which purports to be or is an imitation of, or resembles, an official traffic control device or which attempts to direct the movement of traffic or which hides from view any official traffic control device.

21466. Light Preventing Recognition of Official Traffic Control Device

No person shall place or maintain or display upon or in view of any highway any light in such position as to prevent the driver of a vehicle from readily recognizing any official traffic control device.

21466.5. Light Impairing Drivers Vision

No person shall place or maintain or display, upon or in view of any highway, any light of any color of such brilliance as to impair the vision of drivers upon the highway. A light source shall be considered vision impairing when its brilliance exceeds the values listed below.

The brightness reading of an objectionable light source shall be measured with a 1½-degree photoelectric brightness meter placed at the driver's point of view. The maximum measured brightness of the light source within 10 degrees from the driver's normal line of sight shall not be more than 1,000 times the minimum measured brightness in the driver's field of view, except that when the minimum measured brightness in the field of view is 10 foot-lamberts or less, the measured brightness of the light source in foot-lambert shall not exceed 500 plus 100 times the angle, in degrees, between the driver's line of sight and the light source.

The provisions of this section shall not apply to railroads as defined in Section 229 of the Public Utilities Code.

CHAPTER 3. DRIVING, OVERTAKING, & PASSING

21650. Right Side of Roadway

Upon all highways, a vehicle shall be driven upon the right half of the roadway, except as follows:

(a) When overtaking and passing another vehicle proceeding in the same direction under the rules governing that movement.

(b) When placing a vehicle in a lawful position for, and when the vehicle is lawfully making, a left turn.

(c) When the right half of a roadway is closed to traffic under construction or repair.

(d) Upon a roadway restricted to one-way traffic.

(e) When the roadway is not of sufficient width.

(f) When the vehicle is necessarily traveling so slowly as to impede the normal movement of traffic, that portion of the highway adjacent to the right edge of the roadway may be utilized temporarily when in a condition permitting safe operation.

(g) This section does not prohibit the operation of bicycles on any shoulder of a highway, on any sidewalk, on any bicycle path within a highway, or along any crosswalk or bicycle path crossing, where the operation is not otherwise prohibited by this code or local ordinance.

(h) This section does not prohibit the operation of a transit bus on the shoulder of a state highway in conjunction with the implementation of a program authorized pursuant to Section 148.1 of the Streets and Highways Code on state highways within the areas served by the transit services of the Monterey-Salinas Transit District or the Santa Cruz Metropolitan Transit District. *(AM '13)*

21650.1. Bicycle Operated on Roadway or Highway Shoulder

A bicycle operated on a roadway, or the shoulder of a highway, shall be operated in the same direction as vehicles are required to be driven upon the roadway.

21651. Divided Highways

(a) Whenever a highway has been divided into two or more roadways by means of intermittent barriers or by means of a dividing section of not less than two feet in width, either unpaved or delineated by curbs, double-parallel lines, or other markings on the roadway, it is unlawful to do either of the following:

(1) To drive any vehicle over, upon, or across the dividing section.

(2) To make any left, semicircular, or U-turn with the vehicle on the divided highway, except through an opening in the barrier designated and intended by public authorities for the use of vehicles or through a plainly marked opening in the dividing section.

(b) It is unlawful to drive any vehicle upon a highway, except to the right of an intermittent barrier or a dividing section which separates two or more opposing lanes of traffic. Except as otherwise provided in subdivision (c), a violation of this subdivision is a misdemeanor.

(c) Any willful violation of subdivision (b) which results in injury to, or death of, a person shall be punished by imprisonment pursuant to subdivision (h) of Section 1170 of the Penal Code, or imprisonment in a county jail for a period of not more than six months. *(AM '11)*

21652. Entrance to Public Highway from Service Road
When any service road has been constructed on or along any public highway and the main thoroughfare of the highway has been separated from the service road, it is unlawful for any person to drive any vehicle into the main thoroughfare from the service road or from the main thoroughfare into the service road except through an opening in the dividing curb, section, separation, or line.

21654. Slow-Moving Vehicles
(a) Notwithstanding the prima facie speed limits, any vehicle proceeding upon a highway at a speed less than the normal speed of traffic moving in the same direction at such time shall be driven in the right-hand lane for traffic or as close as practicable to the right-hand edge or curb, except when overtaking and passing another vehicle proceeding in the same direction or when preparing for a left turn at an intersection or into a private road or driveway.

(b) If a vehicle is being driven at a speed less than the normal speed of traffic moving in the same direction at such time, and is not being driven in the right-hand lane for traffic or as close as practicable to the right-hand edge or curb, it shall constitute prima facie evidence that the driver is operating the vehicle in violation of subdivision (a) of this section.

(c) CalTrans, with respect to state highways, and local authorities, with respect to highways under their jurisdiction, may place and maintain upon highways official signs directing slow-moving traffic to use the right-hand traffic lane except when overtaking and passing another vehicle or preparing for a left turn.

21655. Designated Lanes for Certain Vehicles
(a) Whenever CalTrans or local authorities with respect to highways under their respective jurisdictions determines upon the basis of an engineering and traffic investigation that the designation of a specific lane or lanes for the travel of vehicles required to travel at reduced speeds would facilitate the safe and orderly movement of traffic, the department or local authority may designate a specific lane or lanes for the travel of vehicles which are subject to the provisions of Section 22406 and shall erect signs at reasonable intervals giving notice thereof.

(b) Any trailer bus, except as provided in Section 21655.5, and any vehicle subject to the provisions of Section 22406 shall be driven in the lane or lanes designated pursuant to subdivision (a) whenever signs have been erected of that designation. Except as otherwise provided in this subdivision, when a specific lane or lanes have not been so designated, any of those vehicles shall be driven in the right-hand lane for traffic or as close as practicable to the right edge or curb. If however, a specific lane or lanes have not been designated on a divided highway having four or more clearly marked lanes for traffic in one direction, any of those vehicles may also be driven in the lane to the immediate left of that right-hand lane, unless otherwise prohibited under this code. When overtaking and passing another When overtaking and passing another vehicle proceeding in the same direction, the driver shall use either the designated lane, the lane to the immediate left of the right-hand lane, or the right-hand lane for traffic as permitted under this code.

This subdivision does not apply to a driver who is preparing for a left-or right-hand turn or who is entering into or exiting from a highway or to a driver who must necessarily drive in a lane other than the right-hand lane to continue on his or her intended route.

21655.5.   Exclusive or Preferential Use Lanes for High Occupancy Vehicles

(a)   The Department of Transportation and local authorities, with respect to highways under their respective jurisdictions, may authorize or permit exclusive or preferential use of highway lanes for high-occupancy vehicles. Prior to establishing the lanes, competent engineering estimates shall be made of the effect of the lanes on safety, congestion, and highway capacity.

(b)   The Department of Transportation and local authorities, with respect to highways under their respective jurisdictions, shall place and maintain, or cause to be placed and maintained, signs and other official traffic control devices to designate the exclusive or preferential lanes, to advise motorists of the applicable vehicle occupancy levels, and, except where ramp metering and bypass lanes are regulated with the activation of traffic signals, to advise motorists of the hours of high-occupancy vehicle usage. No person shall drive a vehicle upon those lanes except in conformity with the instructions imparted by the official traffic control devices. A motorcycle, a mass transit vehicle, or a paratransit vehicle that is clearly and identifiably marked on all sides of the vehicle with the name of the paratransit provider may be operated upon those exclusive or preferential use lanes unless specifically prohibited by a traffic control device.

(c)   When responding to an existing emergency or breakdown in which a mass transit vehicle is blocking an exclusive or preferential use lane, a clearly marked mass transit vehicle, mass transit supervisor's vehicle, or mass transit maintenance vehicle that is responding to the emergency or breakdown may be operated in the segment of the exclusive or preferential use lane being blocked by the mass transit vehicle, regardless of the number of persons in the vehicle responding to the emergency or breakdown, if both vehicles are owned or operated by the same agency, and that agency provides public mass transit services.

(d)   For purposes of this section, a "paratransit vehicle" is defined in Section 462.

(e)   For purposes of this section, a "mass transit vehicle" means a transit bus regularly used to transport paying passengers in mass transit service.

(f)   It is the intent of the Legislature, in amending this section, to stimulate and encourage the development of ways and means of relieving traffic congestion on California highways and, at the same time, to encourage individual citizens to pool their vehicular resources and thereby conserve fuel and lessen emission of air pollutants.

(g)   The provisions of this section regarding mass transit vehicles and paratransit vehicles shall only apply if the Director of Transportation determines that the application will not subject the state to a reduction in the amount of federal aid for highways. *(AM '02)*

21655.8.   Entering or Exiting Exclusive or Preferential Use Lanes

(a)   Except as required under subdivision (b), when exclusive or preferential use lanes for high-occupancy vehicles are established pursuant to Section 21655.5 and double parallel solid lines are in place to the right thereof, no person driving a vehicle may cross over these double lines to enter into or exit from the exclusive or preferential use lanes, and entrance or exit may be made only in areas designated for these purposes or where a single broken line is in place to the right of the exclusive or preferential use lanes.

(b)   Upon the approach of an authorized emergency vehicle displaying a red light or siren, as specified in Section 21806, a person driving a vehicle in an exclusive or preferential use lane shall exit that lane immediately upon determining that the exit can be accomplished with reasonable safety.

(c)   Raised pavement markers may be used to simulate painted lines described in this section.

21655.9.   Preferential Highway Lanes; Special Identifier Required; Misuse of Identifier [Repeals 1-1-2019]

(a)(1)   Whenever the Department of Transportation or a local authority authorizes or permits exclusive or preferential use of highway lanes or highway access ramps for high-occupancy vehicles pursuant to Section 21655.5, the use of those lanes or ramps shall also be extended to vehicles that are issued distinctive decals, labels, or other identifiers pursuant to Section 5205.5 regardless of vehicle occupancy or ownership.

(2)   A local authority during periods of peak congestion shall suspend for a lane the access privileges extended pursuant to paragraph (1) for those vehicles issued distinctive decals, labels, or other identifiers pur-

suant to Section 5205.5, if a periodic review of lane performance by that local authority discloses both of the following factors regarding the lane:

(A) The lane, or a portion ***of the lane, exceeds a level of service C, as described in subdivision (b) of Section 65089 of the Government Code.

(B) The operation or projected operation of vehicles in the lane, or a portion ***of the lane, will significantly increase congestion.

(b) A person shall not drive a vehicle described in subdivision (a) of Section 5205.5 with a single occupant upon a high-occupancy vehicle lane pursuant to this section unless the decal, label, or other identifier issued pursuant to Section 5205.5 is properly displayed on the vehicle, and the vehicle registration described in Section 5205.5 is with the vehicle.

(c) A person shall not operate or own a vehicle displaying a decal, label, or other identifier, as described in Section 5205.5, if that decal, label, or identifier was not issued for that vehicle pursuant to Section 5205.5. A violation of this subdivision is a misdemeanor.

(d) If the provisions in Section 5205.5 authorizing the department to issue decals, labels, or other identifiers to hybrid and alternative fuel vehicles are repealed, vehicles displaying those decals, labels, or other identifiers shall not access high-occupancy vehicle lanes without meeting the occupancy requirements otherwise applicable to those lanes.

(e) This section shall ***become inoperative on January 1, ***2019, or ***the date the federal authorization pursuant to Section 166 of Title 23 of the United States Code expires, or the date the Secretary of State receives the notice described in subdivision (i) of Section 5205.5, whichever occurs first, and***, as of January 1, 2019, is repealed, unless a later enacted statute, that becomes operative on or before January 1, 2019, deletes or extends the dates on which it becomes inoperative and is repealed. *(AM '13)*

21656. Turning Out of Slow-Moving Vehicles

On a two-lane highway where passing is unsafe because of traffic in the opposite direction or other conditions, a slow-moving vehicle, including a passenger vehicle, behind which five or more vehicles are formed in line, shall turn off the roadway at the nearest place designated as a turnout by signs erected by the authority having jurisdiction over the highway, or wherever sufficient area for a safe turnout exists, in order to permit the vehicles following it to proceed. As used in this section a slow-moving vehicle is one which is proceeding at a rate of speed less than the normal flow of traffic at the particular time and place.

21657. Designated Traffic Direction

The authorities in charge of any highway may designate any highway, roadway, part of a roadway, or specific lanes upon which vehicular traffic shall proceed in one direction at all or such times as shall be indicated by official traffic control devices. When a roadway has been so designated, a vehicle shall be driven only in the direction designated at all or such times as shall be indicated by traffic control devices.

21658. Laned Roadways

Whenever any roadway has been divided into two or more clearly marked lanes for traffic in one direction, the following rules apply:

(a) A vehicle shall be driven as nearly as practical entirely within a single lane and shall not be moved from the lane until such movement can be made with reasonable safety.

(b) Official signs may be erected directing slow-moving traffic to use a designated lane or allocating specified lanes to traffic moving in the same direction, and drivers of vehicles shall obey the directions of the traffic device.

21659. Three-Lane Highways

Upon a roadway which is divided into three lanes a vehicle shall not be driven in the extreme left lane at any time, nor in the center lane except when overtaking and passing another vehicle where the roadway ahead is clearly visible and the center lane is clear of traffic within a safe distance, or in preparation for a left turn, or where the center lane is at the time allocated exclusively to traffic moving in the direction the vehicle is proceeding and is signposted to give notice of such allocation. This section does not apply upon a one-way roadway.

21660. Approaching Vehicles

Drivers of vehicles proceeding in opposite directions shall pass each other to the right, and, except when a roadway has been divided into traffic lanes, each driver shall give to the other at least one-half of the main traveled portion of the roadway whenever possible.

21661. Narrow Roadways

Whenever upon any grade the width of the roadway is insufficient to permit the passing of vehicles approaching from opposite directions at the point of meeting, the driver of the vehicle descending the grade shall yield the right-of-way to the vehicle ascending the grade and shall, if necessary, back his vehicle to a place in the highway where it is possible for the vehicles to pass.

21662. Mountain Driving

The driver of a motor vehicle traveling through defiles or canyons or upon mountain highways shall hold the motor vehicle under control at all times and shall do the following when applicable:

(a) If the roadway has no marked centerline, the driver shall drive as near the right-hand edge of the roadway as is reasonably possible.

(b) If the roadway has insufficient width to permit a motor vehicle to be driven entirely to the right of the center of the roadway, the driver shall give audible warning with the horn of the motor vehicle upon approaching a curve where the view is obstructed within a distance of 200 feet along the highway.

21663. Driving on Sidewalk

Except as expressly permitted pursuant to this code, including Sections 21100.4, and 21114.5, no person shall operate or move a motor vehicle upon a sidewalk except as may be necessary to enter or leave adjacent property.

21664. Freeway Entry or Exit

It is unlawful for the driver of any vehicle to enter or exit any freeway which has full control of access and no crossing at grade, except upon a designated on-ramp with respect to entering the freeway or a designated off-ramp with respect to exiting the freeway.

21700. Obstruction to Driving

No person shall drive a vehicle when it is so loaded, or when there are in the front seat such number of persons as to obstruct the view of the driver to the front or sides of the vehicle or as to interfere with the driver's control over the driving mechanism of the vehicle.

21700.5. Buses Transporting School Pupils in City of San Diego

No person shall knowingly drive a bus within the City of San Diego which is transporting any private school pupil who is enrolled in kindergarten or any of grades 1 to 12, inclusive, to or from a public or private school, unless every such pupil is seated in a seat.

21701. Interference With Driver or Mechanism

No person shall willfully interfere with the driver of a vehicle or with the mechanism thereof in such manner as to affect the driver's control of the vehicle. The provisions of this section shall not apply to a drivers' license examiner or other employee of the department when conducting the road driving test of an applicant for a driver's license nor to a person giving instruction as a part of a course in driver training conducted by a public school, educational institution or a driver training school licensed by the department.

21702. Limitation on Driving Hours

(a) No person shall drive upon any highway any vehicle designed or used for transporting persons for compensation for more than 10 consecutive hours nor for more than 10 hours spread over a total of 15 consecutive hours. Thereafter, such person shall not drive any such vehicle until eight consecutive hours have elapsed. Regardless of aggregate driving time, no driver shall drive for more than 10 hours in any 24-hour period unless eight consecutive hours off duty have elapsed.

(b) No person shall drive upon any highway any vehicle designed or used for transporting merchandise, freight, materials or other property for more than 12 consecutive hours nor for more than 12 hours spread over a total of 15 consecutive hours. Thereafter, such person shad not drive any such vehicle until eight consecutive hours have elapsed. Regardless of aggregate driving time, no driver shall drive for more than 12 hours in any 24-hour period unless eight consecutive hours off duty have elapsed.

(c) This section does not apply in any case of casualty or unavoidable accident or an act of God.

(d) In computing the number of hours under this section, any time spent by a person in driving such a vehicle outside this state shall, upon the vehicle entering this state, be included.

(e) Any person who violates any provision of this section is guilty of a misdemeanor and is punishable by a fine of not less than one hundred dollars ($100) nor more than one thousand dollars ($1,000) for each offense.

(f) This section shall not apply to the driver of a vehicle which is subject to the provisions of Section 34500.

21703. Following Too Closely

The driver of a motor vehicle shall not follow another vehicle more closely than is reasonable and prudent, having due regard for the speed of such vehicle and the traffic upon, and the condition of, the roadway.

21704. Distance Between Vehicles

(a) The driver of any motor vehicle subject to the speed restriction of Section 22406 that is operated outside of a business or residence district, shall keep the vehicle he is driving at a distance of not less than 300 feet to the rear of any other motor vehicle subject to such speed restriction which is preceding it.

(b) The provisions of this section shall not prevent overtaking and passing nor shall they apply upon a highway with two or more lanes for traffic in the direction of travel.

21705. Caravans

Motor vehicles being driven outside of a business or residence district in a caravan or motorcade, whether or not towing other vehicles, shall be so operated as to allow sufficient space and in no event less than 100 feet between each vehicle or combination of vehicles so as to enable any other vehicle to overtake or pass.

21706. Following Emergency Vehicles

No motor vehicle, except an authorized emergency vehicle, shall follow within 300 feet of any authorized emergency vehicle being operated under the provisions of Section 21055.

This section shall not apply to a police or traffic officer when serving as an escort within the purview of Section 21057.

21706.5. Emergency Incident Zone; Unsafe Operation

(a) For purposes of this section, the following terms have the following meanings:

(1) "Emergency incident zone"means an area on a freeway that is within 500 feet of, and in the direction of travel of, a stationary authorized emergency vehicle that has its emergency lights activated. Traffic in the opposite lanes of the freeway is not in an "emergency incident zone."

(2) "Operate a vehicle in an unsafe manner"means operating a motor vehicle in violation of an act made unlawful under this division, except a violation of Section 21809.

(b) A person shall not operate a vehicle in an unsafe manner within an emergency incident zone. *(AD '06)*

21707. Fire Areas

No motor vehicle, except an authorized emergency vehicle or a vehicle of a duly authorized member of a fire or police department, shall be operated within the block wherein an emergency situation responded to by any fire department vehicle exists, except that in the event the nearest intersection to the emergency is more than 300 feet therefrom, this section shall prohibit operation of vehicles only within 300 feet of the emergency, unless directed to do so by a member of the fire department or police department, sheriff, deputy sheriff, or member of the CHP.The emergency shall be deemed to have ceased to exist when the official of the fire department in charge at the scene of the emergency shall so indicate. Officials of the fire department or police department or the CHP who are present shall make every effort to prevent the closing off entirely of congested highway traffic passing the scene of any such emergency.

21708. Fire Hoses

No person shall drive or propel any vehicle or conveyance upon, over, or across, or in any manner damage any fire hose or chemical hose used by or under the supervision and control of any organized fire department. However, any vehicle may cross a hose provided suitable jumpers or other appliances are installed to protect the hose.

21709. Safety Zones

No vehicle shall at any time be driven through or within a safety zone.

21710. Coasting Prohibited

The driver of a motor vehicle when traveling on down grade upon any highway shall not coast with the gears of such vehicle in neutral.

21711. Towed Vehicles Swerving

No person shall operate a train of vehicles when any vehicle being towed whips or swerves from side to side or fails to follow substantially in the path of the towing vehicle.

21712. Unlawful Riding and Towing

(a) A person driving a motor vehicle shall not knowingly permit a person to ride on a vehicle or upon a portion of a vehicle that is not designed or intended for the use of passengers.

(b) A person shall not ride on a vehicle or upon a portion of a vehicle that is not designed or intended for the use of passengers.

(c) A person driving a motor vehicle shall not knowingly permit a person to ride in the trunk of that motor vehicle.

(d) A person shall not ride in the trunk of a motor vehicle.

(e) A person violating subdivision (c) or (d) shall be punished as follows:

(1) By a fine of one hundred dollars ($100).

(2) For a second violation occurring within one year of a prior violation that resulted in a conviction, a fine of two hundred dollars ($200).

(3) For a third or a subsequent violation occurring within one year of two or more prior violations that resulted in convictions, a fine of two hundred fifty dollars ($250).

(f) Subdivisions (a) and (b) do not apply to an employee engaged in the necessary discharge of his or her duty or in the case of persons riding completely within or upon vehicle bodies in the space intended for a load on the vehicle.

(g) A person shall not drive a motor vehicle that is towing a trailer coach, camp trailer, or trailer carrying a vessel, containing a passenger, except when a trailer carrying or designed to carry a vessel is engaged in the launching or recovery of the vessel.

(h) A person shall not knowingly drive a motor vehicle that is towing a person riding upon a motorcycle, motorized bicycle, bicycle, coaster, roller skates, sled, skis, or toy vehicle.

(i) Subdivision (g) does not apply to a trailer coach that is towed with a fifth-wheel device if the trailer coach is equipped with safety glazing materials wherever glazing materials are used in windows or doors, with an audible or visual signaling device that a passenger inside the trailer coach can use to gain the attention of the motor vehicle driver, and with at least one unobstructed exit capable of being opened from both the interior and exterior of the trailer coach. *(AM '06)*

21713. Armored Car

No person shall operate on any highway any privately owned armored car unless a license to operate such car has first been obtained from the commissioner in accordance with Chapter 2.5 of Division 2.

Violation of this section is a misdemeanor and upon conviction is punishable by a fine not exceeding one thousand dollars ($1,000) or by imprisonment in the county jail for not to exceed six months or by both such fine and imprisonment.

21714. Use of HOV Lanes or Lane Splitting by Fully Enclosed 3-Wheel Motor Vehicle
The driver of a vehicle described in subdivision (f) of Section 27803 shall not operate the vehicle in either of the following areas:

(a) On, or immediately adjacent to, the striping or other markers designating adjacent traffic lanes.

(b) Between two or more vehicles that are traveling in adjacent traffic lanes. *(AM '08)*

21715. Passenger Vehicle Combinations: Number and Weight Limits
(a) No passenger vehicle regardless of weight, or any other motor vehicle under 4,000 pounds unladen, shall draw or tow more than one vehicle in combination, except that an auxiliary dolly or tow dolly may be used with the towed vehicle.

(b) No motor vehicle under 4,000 pounds unladen shall tow any vehicle weighing 6,000 pounds or more gross.

21716. Golf Cart Operation
Except as provided in Section 21115.1 and Chapter 6 (commencing with Section 1950) of Division 2.5 of the Streets and Highways Code, no person shall operate a golf cart on any highway except in a speed zone of 25 miles per hour or less. *(AM '00)*

21717. Turning Across Bicycle Lane
Whenever it is necessary for the driver of a motor vehicle to cross a bicycle lane that is adjacent to his lane of travel to make a turn, the driver shall drive the motor vehicle into the bicycle lane prior to making the turn and shall make the turn pursuant to Section 22100.

21718. Stopping, Parking on Freeway Prohibited; Exceptions
(a) No person shall stop, park, or leave standing any vehicle upon a freeway which has full control of access and no crossings at grade except:

(1) When necessary to avoid injury or damage to persons or property.

(2) When required by law or in obedience to a peace officer or official traffic control device.

(3) When any person is actually engaged in maintenance or construction on freeway property or any employee of a public agency is actually engaged in the performance of official duties.

(4) When any vehicle is so disabled that it is impossible to avoid temporarily stopping and another vehicle has been summoned to render assistance to the disabled vehicle or driver of the disabled vehicle. This paragraph applies when the vehicle summoned to render assistance is a vehicle owned by the donor of free emergency assistance that has been summoned by display upon or within a disabled vehicle of a placard or sign given to the driver of the disabled vehicle by the donor for the specific purpose of summoning assistance, other than towing service, from the donor.

(5) Where stopping, standing, or parking is specifically permitted. However, buses may not stop on freeways unless sidewalks are provided with shoulders of sufficient width to permit stopping without interfering with the normal movement of traffic and without the possibility of crossing over fast lanes to reach the bus stop.

(6) Where necessary for any person to report a traffic accident or other situation or incident to a peace officer or any person specified in paragraph (3), either directly or by means of an emergency telephone or similar device.

(7) When necessary for the purpose of rapid removal of impediments to traffic by the owner or operator of a tow truck operating under an agreement with the Department of the California Highway Patrol.

(b) A conviction of a violation of this section is a conviction involving the safe operation of a motor vehicle upon the highway if a notice to appear for the violation was issued by a peace officer described in Section 830.1 or 830.2 of the Penal Code.

21720. Pocket Bike Operation Prohibited
A pocket bike shall not be operated on a sidewalk, roadway, or any other part of a highway, or on a bikeway, bicycle path or trail, equestrian trail, hiking or recreational trail, or on public lands open to off-highway motor vehicle use. *(AD '05)*

21721. Removal and Seizure of Pocket Bike; Conditions for Release

(a) A peace officer, as defined in Chapter 4.5 (commencing with Section 830) of Title 3 of Part 2 of the Penal Code, may cause the removal and seizure of a pocket bike, upon the notice to appear for a violation of Section 21720. A pocket bike so seized shall be held for a minimum of 48 hours.

(b) A violator of this section shall be responsible for all costs associated with the removal, seizure, and storage of the pocket bike.

(c) A city, county, or city and county may adopt a regulation, ordinance, or resolution imposing charges equal to its administrative costs relating to the removal, seizure, and storage costs of a pocket bike. The charges shall not exceed the actual costs incurred for the expenses directly related to removing, seizing, and storing a pocket bike.

(d) An agency shall release a seized pocket bike to the owner, violator, or the violator's agent after 48 hours, if all of the following conditions are met:

(1) The violator or authorized agent's request is made during normal business hours.

(2) The applicable removal, seizure, and storage costs have been paid by the owner, or any other responsible party. *(AD '05)*

21750. Overtake and Pass to Left [Inop. 9-16-14]

(a) The driver of a vehicle overtaking another vehicle or a bicycle proceeding in the same direction shall pass to the left at a safe distance without interfering with the safe operation of the overtaken vehicle or bicycle, subject to the limitations and exceptions ***set forth in this article.

(b) This section shall become inoperative on September 16, 2014, and, as of January 1, 2015, is repealed, unless a later enacted statute, that becomes operative on or before January 1, 2015, deletes or extends the dates on which it becomes inoperative and is repealed. *(AM-RP-AD '13)*

21750. Overtake and Pass to Left [Added Stats. 2013]

(a) The driver of a vehicle overtaking another vehicle proceeding in the same direction shall pass to the left at a safe distance without interfering with the safe operation of the overtaken vehicle, subject to the limitations and exceptions set forth in this article.

(b) This section shall become operative on September 16, 2014. *(AD '13, Op 9-16-14)*

21751. Passing Without Sufficient Clearance

On a two-lane highway, no vehicle shall be driven to the left side of the center of the roadway in overtaking and passing another vehicle proceeding in the same direction unless the left side is clearly visible and free of oncoming traffic for a sufficient distance ahead to permit such overtaking and passing to be completely made without interfering with the safe operation of any vehicle approaching from the opposite direction.

21752. When Driving on Left Prohibited

No vehicle shall be driven to the left side of the roadway under the following conditions:

(a) When approaching or upon the crest of a grade or a curve in the highway where the driver's view is obstructed within such distance as to create a hazard in the event another vehicle might approach from the opposite direction.

(b) When the view is obstructed upon approaching within 100 feet of any bridge, viaduct, or tunnel.

(c) When approaching within 100 feet of or when traversing any railroad grade crossing.

(d) When approaching within 100 feet of or when traversing any intersection.

This section shall not apply upon a one-way roadway. *(AM '00)*

21753. Yielding for Passing

Except when passing on the right is permitted, the driver of an overtaken vehicle shall safely move to the right-hand side of the highway in favor of the overtaking vehicle after an audible signal or a momentary flash of headlights by the overtaking vehicle, and shall not increase the speed of his or her vehicle until completely passed by the overtaking vehicle. This section does not require the driver of an overtaken vehicle to drive on the shoulder of the highway in order to allow the overtaking vehicle to pass. *(AM '99)*

21754. Passing on the Right
The driver of a vehicle may overtake and pass to the right of another vehicle only under the following conditions:

(a) When the vehicle overtaken is making or about to make a left turn.

(b) Upon a highway within a business or residence district with unobstructed pavement of sufficient width for two or more lines of moving vehicles in the direction of travel.

(c) Upon any highway outside of a business or residence district with unobstructed pavement of sufficient width and clearly marked for two or more lines of moving traffic in the direction of travel.

(d) Upon a one-way street.

(e) Upon a highway divided into two roadways where traffic is restricted to one direction upon each of such roadways.

The provisions of this section shall not relieve the driver of a slow moving vehicle from the duty to drive as closely as practicable to the right hand edge of the roadway. *(AM '10)*

21755. Pass on Right Safely
(a) The driver of a vehicle may overtake and pass another vehicle upon the right only under conditions permitting that movement in safety. In no event shall that movement be made by driving off the paved or main-traveled portion of the roadway.

(b) This section does not prohibit the use of a bicycle in a bicycle lane or on a shoulder. *(AM '10)*

21756. Passing Standing Streetcar, Trolley Coach, or Bus
(a) The driver of a vehicle overtaking any interurban electric or streetcar stopped or about to stop for the purpose of receiving or discharging any passenger shall stop the vehicle to the rear of the nearest running board or door of such car and thereupon remain standing until all passengers have boarded the car or upon alighting have reached a place of safety, except as provided in subdivision (b) hereof.

(b) Where a safety zone has been established or at an intersection where traffic is controlled by an officer or a traffic control signal device, a vehicle need not be brought to a stop before passing any interurban electric or streetcar but may proceed past such car at a speed not greater than 10 miles per hour and with due caution for the safety of pedestrians.

(c) Whenever any trolley coach or bus has stopped at a safety zone to receive or discharge passengers, a vehicle may proceed past such trolley coach or bus at a speed not greater than 10 miles per hour.

21757. Passing Streetcar on Left
The driver of a vehicle shall not overtake and pass upon the left, nor shall any driver of a vehicle drive upon the left side of any interurban electric or streetcar proceeding in the same direction whether the street car is actually in motion or temporarily at rest, except:

(a) When so directed by a police or traffic officer.

(b) When upon a one-way street.

(c) When upon a street where the tracks are so located as to prevent compliance with this section.

21758. Passing on Grades
In the event any vehicle is being operated on any grade outside of a business or residence district at a speed of less than 20 miles per hour, no person operating any other motor vehicle shall attempt to overtake and pass such slow moving vehicle unless the overtaking vehicle is operated at a speed of at least 10 miles per hour in excess of the speed of the overtaken vehicle, nor unless the passing movement is completed within a total distance not greater than one-quarter of a mile.

21759. Caution in Passing Animals
The driver of any vehicle approaching any horse drawn vehicle, any ridden animal, or any livestock shall exercise proper control of his vehicle and shall reduce speed or stop as may appear necessary or as may be signaled or otherwise requested by any person driving, riding or in charge of the animal or livestock to safeguard the animal or livestock and to insure the safety of any person driving or riding the animal or in charge of the livestock.

21760.   Three Feet for Safety Act [Operative 9-16-2014] [Added Stats. 2013]

(a) This section shall be known and may be cited as the Three Feet for Safety Act.

(b) The driver of a motor vehicle overtaking and passing a bicycle that is proceeding in the same direction on a highway shall pass in compliance with the requirements of this article applicable to overtaking and passing a vehicle, and shall do so at a safe distance that does not interfere with the safe operation of the overtaken bicycle, having due regard for the size and speed of the motor vehicle and the bicycle, traffic conditions, weather, visibility, and the surface and width of the highway.

(c) A driver of a motor vehicle shall not overtake or pass a bicycle proceeding in the same direction on a highway at a distance of less than three feet between any part of the motor vehicle and any part of the bicycle or its operator.

(d) If the driver of a motor vehicle is unable to comply with subdivision (c), due to traffic or roadway conditions, the driver shall slow to a speed that is reasonable and prudent, and may pass only when doing so would not endanger the safety of the operator of the bicycle, taking into account the size and speed of the motor vehicle and bicycle, traffic conditions, weather, visibility, and surface and width of the highway.

(e)(1) A violation of subdivision (b), (c), or (d) is an infraction punishable by a fine of thirty-five dollars ($35).

(2) If a collision occurs between a motor vehicle and a bicycle causing bodily injury to the operator of the bicycle, and the driver of the motor vehicle is found to be in violation of subdivision (b), (c), or (d), a two-hundred-twenty-dollar ($220) fine shall be imposed on that driver.

(f) This section shall become operative on September 16, 2014. *(AD '13, Op 9-16-14)*

CHAPTER 4. RIGHT-OF-WAY

21800.   Intersections

(a) The driver of a vehicle approaching an intersection shall yield the right-of-way to any vehicle which has entered the intersection from a different highway.

(b)(1) When two vehicles enter an intersection from different highways at the same time, the driver of the vehicle on the left shall yield the right-of-way to the vehicle on his or her immediate right, except that the driver of any vehicle on a terminating highway shall yield the right-of-way to any vehicle on the intersecting continuing highway.

(2) For the purposes of this section, "terminating highway" means a highway which intersects, but does not continue beyond the intersection, with another highway which does continue beyond the intersection.

(c) When two vehicles enter an intersection from different highways at the same time and the intersection is controlled from all directions by stop signs, the driver of the vehicle on the left shall yield the right-of-way to the vehicle on his or her immediate right.

(d)(1) The driver of any vehicle approaching an intersection which has official traffic control signals that are inoperative shall stop at the intersection, and may proceed with caution when it is safe to do so.

(2) When two vehicles enter an intersection from different highways at the same time, and the official traffic control signals for the intersection are inoperative, the driver of the vehicle on the left shall yield the right-of-way to the vehicle on his or her immediate right, except that the driver of any vehicle on a terminating highway shall yield the right-of-way to any vehicle on the intersecting continuing highway.

(e) This section does not apply to any of the following:

(1) Any intersection controlled by an official traffic control signal or yield right-of-way sign.

(2) Any intersection controlled by stop signs from less than all directions.

(3) When vehicles are approaching each other from opposite directions and the driver of one of the vehicles intends to make, or is making, a left turn. *(AM'01, '09)*

21801.   Left-Turn or U-Turn

(a) The driver of a vehicle intending to turn to the left or to complete a U-turn upon a highway, or to turn left into public or private property, or an alley, shall yield the right-of-way to all vehicles approaching from the opposite direction which are close enough to constitute a hazard at any time during the turning movement, and shall continue to yield the right-of-way to the approaching vehicles until the left turn or U-turn can be made with reasonable safety.

(b) A driver having yielded as prescribed in subdivision (a), and having given a signal when and as required by this code, may turn left or complete a U-turn, and the drivers of vehicles approaching the intersection or the entrance to the property or alley from the opposite direction shall yield the right-of-way to the turning vehicle.

21802. Stop Signs: Intersections

(a) The driver of any vehicle approaching a stop sign at the entrance to, or within, an intersection shall stop as required by Section 22450. The driver shall then yield the right-of-way to any vehicles which have approached from another highway, or which are approaching so closely as to constitute an immediate hazard, and shall continue to yield the right-of-way to those vehicles until he or she can proceed with reasonable safety.

(b) A driver having yielded as prescribed in subdivision (a) may proceed to enter the intersection, and the drivers of all other approaching vehicles shall yield the right-of-way to the vehicle entering or crossing the intersection.

(c) This section does not apply where stop signs are erected upon all approaches to an intersection.

21803. Yield Signs: Intersections

(a) The driver of any vehicle approaching any intersection which is controlled by a yield right-of-way sign shall, upon arriving at the sign, yield the right-of-way to any vehicles which have entered the intersection, or which are approaching on the intersecting highway close enough to constitute an immediate hazard, and shall continue to yield the right-of-way to those vehicles until he or she can proceed with reasonable safety.

(b) A driver having yielded as prescribed in subdivision (a) may proceed to enter the intersection, and the drivers of all other approaching vehicles shall yield the right-of-way to the vehicle entering or crossing the intersection.

21804. Entry Onto Highway

(a) The driver of any vehicle about to enter or cross a highway from any public or private property, or from an alley, shall yield the right-of-way to all traffic, as defined in Section 620, approaching on the highway close enough to constitute an immediate hazard, and shall continue to yield the right-of-way to that traffic until he or she can proceed with reasonable safety.

(b) A driver having yielded as prescribed in subdivision (a) may proceed to enter or cross the highway, and the drivers of all other vehicles approaching on the highway shall yield the right-of-way to the vehicle entering or crossing the intersection.

21805. Equestrian Crossings

(a) CalTrans, and local authorities with respect to highways under their jurisdiction, may designate any intersection of a highway as a bridle path or equestrian crossing by erecting appropriate signs. The signs shall be erected on the highway at or near the approach to the intersection, and shall be of a type approved by CalTrans. The signs shall indicate the crossing and any crosswalks, safety devices, or signals the authorities deem necessary to safeguard vehicular and equestrian traffic at the intersection.

(b) The driver of any vehicle shall yield the right-of-way to any horseback rider who is crossing the highway at any designated equestrian crossing which is marked by signs as prescribed in subdivision (a).

(c) Subdivision (b) does not relieve any horseback rider from the duty of using due care for his or her own safety. No horseback rider shall leave a curb or other place of safety and proceed suddenly into the path of a vehicle which is close enough to constitute an immediate hazard.

21806. Authorized Emergency Vehicles

Upon the immediate approach of an authorized emergency vehicle which is sounding a siren and which has at least one lighted lamp exhibiting red light that is visible, under normal atmospheric conditions, from a distance of 1,000 feet to the front of the vehicle, the surrounding traffic shall, except as otherwise directed by a traffic officer, do the following:

(a)(1) Except as required under paragraph (2), the driver of every other vehicle shall yield the right-of-way and shall immediately drive to the right-hand edge or curb of the highway, clear of any intersection, and thereupon shall stop and remain stopped until the authorized emergency vehicle has passed.

(2) A person driving a vehicle in an exclusive or preferential use lane shall exit that lane immediately upon determining that the exit can be accomplished with reasonable safety.

(b) The operator of every street car shall immediately stop the street car, clear of any intersection, and remain stopped until the authorized emergency vehicle has passed.

(c) All pedestrians upon the highway shall proceed to the nearest curb or place of safety and remain there until the authorized emergency vehicle has passed.

21809. Passing Stationary Emergency Vehicle or Tow Truck

(a) A person driving a vehicle on a freeway approaching a stationary authorized emergency vehicle that is displaying emergency lights, a stationary tow truck that is displaying flashing amber warning lights, or a stationary marked Department of Transportation vehicle that is displaying flashing amber warning lights, shall approach with due caution and, before passing in a lane immediately adjacent to the authorized emergency vehicle, tow truck, or Department of Transportation vehicle, absent other direction by a peace officer, proceed to do one of the following:

(1) Make a lane change into an available lane not immediately adjacent to the authorized emergency vehicle, tow truck, or Department of Transportation vehicle, with due regard for safety and traffic conditions, if practicable and not prohibited by law.

(2) If the maneuver described in paragraph (1) would be unsafe or impracticable, slow to a reasonable and prudent speed that is safe for existing weather, road, and vehicular or pedestrian traffic conditions.

(b) A violation of subdivision (a) is an infraction, punishable by a fine of not more than fifty dollars ($50).

(c) The requirements of subdivision (a) do not apply if the stationary authorized emergency vehicle that is displaying emergency lights, the stationary tow truck that is displaying flashing amber warning lights, or the stationary marked Department of Transportation vehicle that is displaying flashing amber warning lights is not adjacent to the freeway or is separated from the freeway by a protective physical barrier. *(AD '06; AM '09)*

CHAPTER 5. PEDESTRIANS' RIGHTS AND DUTIES

21950. Right-of-Way at Crosswalks

(a) The driver of a vehicle shall yield the right-of-way to a pedestrian crossing the roadway within any marked crosswalk or within any unmarked crosswalk at an intersection, except as otherwise provided in this chapter.

(b) This section does not relieve a pedestrian from the duty of using due care for his or her safety. No pedestrian may suddenly leave a curb or other place of safety and walk or run into the path of a vehicle that is so close as to constitute an immediate hazard. No pedestrian may unnecessarily stop or delay traffic while in a marked or unmarked crosswalk.

(c) The driver of a vehicle approaching a pedestrian within any marked or unmarked crosswalk shall exercise all due care and shall reduce the speed of the vehicle or take any other action relating to the operation of the vehicle as necessary to safeguard the safety of the pedestrian.

(d) Subdivision (b) does not relieve a driver of a vehicle from the duty of exercising due care for the safety of any pedestrian within any marked crosswalk or within any unmarked crosswalk at an intersection. *(AM '00)*

21951. Vehicles Stopped for Pedestrians

Whenever any vehicle has stopped at a marked crosswalk or at any unmarked crosswalk at an intersection to permit a pedestrian to cross the roadway the driver of any other vehicle approaching from the rear shall not overtake and pass the stopped vehicle.

21952. Right-of-Way on Sidewalk

The driver of any motor vehicle, prior to driving over or upon any sidewalk, shall yield the right-of-way to any pedestrian approaching thereon.

21953. Tunnel or Overhead Crossing

Whenever any pedestrian crosses a roadway other than by means of a pedestrian tunnel or overhead pedestrian crossing, if a pedestrian tunnel or overhead crossing serves the place where the pedestrian is crossing the roadway, such pedestrian shall yield the right-of-way to all vehicles on the highway so near as to constitute an immediate hazard.

This section shall not be construed to mean that a marked crosswalk, with or without a signal device, cannot be installed where a pedestrian tunnel or overhead crossing exists.

21954. Pedestrian Outside Crosswalks

(a) Every pedestrian upon a roadway at any point other than within a marked crosswalk or within an unmarked crosswalk at an intersection shall yield the right-of-way to all vehicles upon the roadway so near as to constitute an immediate hazard.

(b) The provisions of this section shall not relieve the driver of a vehicle from the duty to exercise due care for the safety of any pedestrian upon a roadway.

21955. Crossing Between Controlled Intersections

Between adjacent intersections controlled by traffic control signal devices or by police officers, pedestrians shall not cross the roadway at any place except in a crosswalk.

21956. Pedestrian on Roadway

(a) No pedestrian may walk upon any roadway outside of a business or residence district otherwise than close to his or her left-hand edge of the roadway.

(b) A pedestrian may walk close to his or her right-hand edge of the roadway if a crosswalk or other means of safely crossing the roadway is not available or if existing traffic or other conditions would compromise the safety of a pedestrian attempting to cross the road. *(AM '00)*

21957. Hitchhiking

No person shall stand in a roadway for the purpose of soliciting a ride from the driver of any vehicle.

21959. Skiing or Tobogganing

It is unlawful for any person to ski or toboggan on or across any roadway in such manner as to interfere with the movement of vehicles thereon.

A person on skis proceeding on or across a highway at a pace no greater than a walk is not within the prohibition of this section and shall be considered to be a pedestrian with all the rights and duties thereof as prescribed in this code.

21962. Pedestrian on Bridge

Any peace officer having reasonable cause to believe that any pedestrian is stopped or standing on any bridge or overpass for the purpose of violating Section 23110, may lawfully order such person from the bridge or overpass.

21963. Visually Handicapped Pedestrian

A totally or partially blind pedestrian who is carrying a predominantly white cane (with or without a red tip), or using a guide dog, shall have the right-of-way, and the driver of any vehicle approaching such pedestrian, who fails to yield the right-of-way, or to take all reasonably necessary precautions to avoid injury to this blind pedestrian, is guilty of a misdemeanor, punishable by imprisonment in the county jail not exceeding six months, or by a fine of not less than five hundred dollars ($500) no more than one thousand dollars ($1,000), or both. This section shall not preclude prosecution under any other applicable provision of law.

21964. White Canes

No person, other than those totally or partially blind, shall carry or use on any highway or in any public building, public facility, or other public place, a predominantly white cane (with or without a red tip).

21966. Pedestrian in Bicycle Lane

No pedestrian shall proceed along a bicycle path or lane where there is an adjacent adequate pedestrian facility.

21968. Motorized Skateboard Prohibited

No motorized skateboard may be propelled on any sidewalk, roadway, or any other part of a highway or on any bikeway, bicycle path or trail, equestrian trail, or hiking or recreational trail.

21970. Vehicle Blocking Crosswalk

(a) No person may stop a vehicle unnecessarily in a manner that causes the vehicle to block a marked or unmarked crosswalk or sidewalk.

(b) Subdivision (a) does not preclude the driver of a vehicle facing a steady circular red light from turning right or turning left from a one-way street onto a one-way street pursuant to subdivision (b) of Section 21453. *(AD '00)*

21971. Violations Causing Bodily Injury Punishable Under Section 42001.18

Notwithstanding any other provision of law, any person who violates subdivision (a) or (b) of Section 21451, subdivision (b) of Section 21453, subdivision (a) of Section 21950, or Section 21952, and causes the bodily injury of anyone other than the driver is guilty of an infraction punishable under Section 42001.18.

CHAPTER 6. TURNING, STOPPING & TURNING SIGNALS

22100. Turning Upon a Highway

Except as provided in Section 22100.5 or 22101, the driver of any vehicle intending to turn upon a highway shall do so as follows:

(a) Right Turns. Both the approach for a right-hand turn and a right-hand turn shall be made as close as practicable to the right-hand curb or edge of the roadway except:

(1) Upon a highway having three marked lanes for traffic moving in one direction that terminates at an intersecting highway accommodating traffic in both directions, the driver of a vehicle in the middle lane may turn right into any lane lawfully available to traffic moving in that direction upon the roadway being entered.

(2) If a right-hand turn is made from a one-way highway at an intersection, a driver shall approach the turn as provided in this subdivision and shall complete the turn in any lane lawfully available to traffic moving in that direction upon the roadway being entered.

(3) Upon a highway having an additional lane or lanes marked for a right turn by appropriate signs or markings, the driver of a vehicle may turn right from any lane designated and marked for that turning movement.

(b) Left Turns. The approach for a left turn shall be made as close as practicable to the left-hand edge of the extreme left-hand lane or portion of the roadway lawfully available to traffic moving in the direction of travel of the vehicle and, when turning at an intersection, the left turn shall not be made before entering the intersection. After entering the intersection, the left turn shall be made so as to leave the intersection in a lane lawfully available to traffic moving in that direction upon the roadway being entered, except that upon a highway having three marked lanes for traffic moving in one direction that terminates at an intersecting highway accommodating traffic in both directions, the driver of a vehicle in the middle lane may turn left into any lane lawfully available to traffic moving in that direction upon the roadway being entered. *(AM '04)*

22100.5. U-Turn at Controlled Intersection
No driver shall make a U-turn at an intersection controlled by official traffic signals except as provided in Section 21451, and then only from the far left-hand lane that is lawfully available to traffic moving in the direction of travel from which the turn is commenced. No driver shall make a U-turn at an intersection controlled by official traffic control devices except from the far left-hand lane that is lawfully available to traffic moving in the direction of travel from which the turn is commenced.

22101. Regulation of Turns at Intersection
(a) CalTrans or local authorities in respect to highways under their respective jurisdictions, may cause official traffic control devices to be placed or erected within or adjacent to intersections to regulate or prohibit turning movements at such intersections.

(b) When turning movements are required at an intersection notice of shall be given by erection of a sign, unless an additional clearly marked traffic lane is provided for the approach to the turning movement, in which event notice as applicable to such additional traffic lane shall be given by any official traffic control device.

(c) When right- or left-hand turns are prohibited at an intersection notice of such prohibition shall be given by erection of a sign.

(d) When official traffic control devices are placed as required in subdivisions (b) or (c), it shall be unlawful for any driver of a vehicle to disobey the directions of such official traffic control devices.

22102. U-Turn in Business District
No person in a business district shall make a U-turn, except at an intersection, or on a divided highway where an opening has been provided in accordance with Section 21651. This turning movement shall be made as close as practicable to the extreme left-hand edge of the lanes moving in the driver's direction of travel immediately prior to the initiation of the turning movement, when more than one lane in the direction of travel is present.

22103. U-Turn in Residence District
No person in a residence district shall make a U-turn when any other vehicle is approaching from either direction within 200 feet, except at an intersection when the approaching vehicle is controlled by an official traffic control device.

22104. Turning Near Fire Stations
No person shall make a U-turn in front of the driveway entrance or approaches to a fire station. No person shall use the driveway entrance or approaches to a fire station for the purpose of turning a vehicle so as to proceed in the opposite direction.

22105. Unobstructed View Necessary for U-Turn
No person shall make a U-turn upon any highway where the driver of such vehicle does not have an unobstructed view for 200 feet in both directions along the highway and of any traffic thereon.

22106. Starting Parked Vehicles or Backing
No person shall start a vehicle stopped, standing, or parked on a highway, nor shall any person back a vehicle on a highway until such movement can be made with reasonable safety.

22107. Turning Movements and Required Signals
No person shall turn a vehicle from a direct course or move right or left upon a roadway until such movement can be made with reasonable safety and then only after the giving of an appropriate signal in the manner provided in this chapter in the event any other vehicle may be affected by the movement.

22108. Duration of Signal
Any signal of intention to turn right or left shall be given continuously during the last 100 feet traveled by the vehicle before turning.

22109.   Signal When Stopping

No person shall stop or suddenly decrease the speed of a vehicle on a highway without first giving an appropriate signal in the manner provided in this chapter to the driver of any vehicle immediately to the rear when there is opportunity to give the signal.

22110.   Method of Signaling

(a) The signals required by this chapter shall be given by signal lamp, unless a vehicle is not required to be and is not equipped with turn signals. Drivers of vehicles not required to be and not equipped with turn signals shall give a hand and arm signal when required by this chapter.

(b) In the event the signal lamps become inoperable while driving, hand and arm signals shall be used in the manner required in this chapter. *(AM '99)*

22111.   Hand Signals

All required signals given by hand and arm shall be given from the left side of a vehicle in the following manner:

(a) Left turn - hand and arm extended horizontally beyond the side of the vehicle.

(b) Right turn - hand and arm extended upward beyond the side of the vehicle, except that a bicyclist may extend the right hand and arm horizontally to the right side of the bicycle.

(c) Stop or sudden decrease of speed signal - hand and arm extended downward beyond the side of the vehicle.

22112.   Schoolbus Signal

(a) On approach to a schoolbus stop where pupils are loading or unloading from a schoolbus, the schoolbus driver shall activate an approved amber warning light system, if the schoolbus is so equipped, beginning 200 feet before the schoolbus stop. The schoolbus driver shall deactivate the amber warning light system after reaching the schoolbus stop. The schoolbus driver shall operate the flashing red light signal system and stop signal arm, as required on the schoolbus, at all times when the schoolbus is stopped for the purpose of loading or unloading pupils. The flashing red light signal system, amber warning lights system, and stop signal arm shall not be operated at any place where traffic is controlled by a traffic officer or at any location identified in subdivision (e) of this section. The schoolbus flashing red light signal system, amber warning lights system, and stop signal arm shall not be operated at any other time.

(b) The schoolbus driver shall stop to load or unload pupils only at a schoolbus stop designated for pupils by the school district superintendent or the head or principal of a private school, or authorized by any of those individuals for school activity trips.

(c) When a schoolbus is stopped on a highway or private road for the purpose of loading or unloading pupils, at a location where traffic is not controlled by a traffic officer, the driver shall, before opening the door, ensure that the flashing red light signal system and stop signal arm are activated, and that it is safe to enter or exit the schoolbus.

(d) When a schoolbus is stopped on a highway or private road for the purpose of loading or unloading pupils, at a location where traffic is not controlled by a traffic officer or official traffic control signal, the schoolbus driver shall do all of the following:

(1) Escort all pupils in pre-kindergarten, kindergarten, or any of grades 1 to 8, inclusive, who need to cross the highway or private road upon which the schoolbus is stopped. The driver shall use an approved hand-held "STOP"sign while escorting all pupils.

(2) Require all pupils who need to cross the highway or private road upon which the schoolbus is stopped to walk in front of the bus as they cross.

(3) Ensure that all pupils who need to cross the highway or private road upon which the schoolbus is stopped have crossed safely, and that all other pupils and pedestrians are a safe distance from the schoolbus before setting the schoolbus in motion.

(e) Except at a location where pupils are loading or unloading from a schoolbus and must cross a highway or private road upon which the schoolbus is stopped, the schoolbus driver may not activate the amber warning light system, the flashing red light signal system and stop signal arm at any of the following locations:

(1) Schoolbus loading zones on or adjacent to school grounds or during an activity trip, if the schoolbus is lawfully stopped or parked.

(2) Where the schoolbus is disabled due to mechanical breakdown. The driver of a relief bus that arrives at the scene to transport pupils from the disabled schoolbus shall not activate the amber warning light system, the flashing red light system, and stop signal arm.

(3) Where a pupil requires physical assistance from the driver or authorized attendant to board or leave the schoolbus and providing the assistance extends the length of time the schoolbus is stopped beyond the time required to load or unload a pupil that does not require physical assistance.

(4) Where the roadway surface on which the bus is stopped is partially or completely covered by snow or ice and requiring traffic to stop would pose a safety hazard as determined by the schoolbus motor carrier.

(5) On a state highway with a posted speed limit of 55 miles per hour or higher where the schoolbus is completely off the main traveled portion of the highway.

(6) Any location determined by a school district or a private school, with the approval of the Department of the California Highway Patrol, to present a traffic or safety hazard.

(f) Notwithstanding subdivisions (a) to (d), inclusive, the Department of the California Highway Patrol may require the activation of an approved flashing amber warning light system, if the schoolbus is so equipped, or the flashing red light signal system and stop signal arm, as required on the schoolbus, at any location where the department determines that the activation is necessary for the safety of school pupils loading or unloading from a schoolbus. *(AM '12)*

CHAPTER 7. SPEED LAWS

22348. Excessive Speed and Designated Lane Use

(a) Notwithstanding subdivision (b) of Section 22351, a person shall not drive a vehicle upon a highway with a speed limit established pursuant to Section 22349 or 22356 at a speed greater than that speed limit.

(b) A person who drives a vehicle upon a highway at a speed greater than 100 miles per hour is guilty of an infraction punishable, as follows:

(1) Upon a first conviction of a violation of this subdivision, by a fine of not to exceed five hundred dollars ($500). The court may also suspend the privilege of the person to operate a motor vehicle for a period not to exceed 30 days pursuant to Section 13200.5.

(2) Upon a conviction under this subdivision of an offense that occurred within three years of a prior offense resulting in a conviction of an offense under this subdivision, by a fine of not to exceed seven hundred fifty dollars ($750). The person's privilege to operate a motor vehicle shall be suspended by the Department of Motor Vehicles pursuant to subdivision (a) of Section 13355.

(3) Upon a conviction under this subdivision of an offense that occurred within five years of two or more prior offenses resulting in convictions of offenses under this subdivision, by a fine of not to exceed one thousand dollars ($1,000). The person's privilege to operate a motor vehicle shall be suspended by the Department of Motor Vehicles pursuant to subdivision (b) of Section 13355.

(c) A vehicle subject to Section 22406 shall be driven in a lane designated pursuant to Section 21655, or if a lane has not been so designated, in the right-hand lane for traffic or as close as practicable to the right-hand edge or curb. When overtaking and passing another vehicle proceeding in the same direction, the driver shall use either the designated lane, the lane to the immediate left of the right-hand lane, or the right-hand lane for traffic as permitted under this code. If, however, specific lane or lanes have not been designated on a divided highway having four or more clearly marked lanes for traffic in one direction, a vehicle may also be driven in the lane to the immediate left of the right-hand lane, unless otherwise prohibited under this code. This subdivision does not apply to a driver who is preparing for a left- or right-hand turn or who is in the process of entering into or exiting from a highway or to a driver who is required necessarily to drive in a lane other than the right-hand lane to continue on his or her intended route. *(AM '04)*

22349. Maximum Speed Limit

(a) Except as provided in Section 22356, no person may drive a vehicle upon a highway at a speed greater than 65 miles per hour.

(b) Notwithstanding any other provision of law, no person may drive a vehicle upon a two-lane, undivided highway at a speed greater than 55 miles per hour unless that highway, or portion thereof, has been posted for a higher speed by the Department of Transportation or appropriate local agency upon the basis of an engineering and traffic survey. For purposes of this subdivision, the following apply:

(1) A two-lane, undivided highway is a highway with not more than one through lane of travel in each direction.

(2) Passing lanes may not be considered when determining the number of through lanes.

(c) It is the intent of the Legislature that there be reasonable signing on affected two-lane, undivided highways described in subdivision (b) in continuing the 55 miles-per-hour speed limit, including placing signs at county boundaries to the extent possible, and at other appropriate locations. *(AM '99)*

22350. Basic Speed Law

No person shall drive a vehicle upon a highway at a speed greater than is reasonable or prudent having due regard for weather, visibility, the traffic on, and the surface and width of, the highway, and in no event at a speed which endangers the safety of persons or property.

22352. Prima Facie Speed Limits

***The prima facie limits are as follows and shall be applicable unless changed as authorized in this code and, if so changed, only when signs have been erected giving notice thereof:

(***a) Fifteen miles per hour:

(***1) When traversing a railway grade crossing, if during the last 100 feet of the approach to the crossing the driver does not have a clear and unobstructed view of the crossing and of any traffic on the railway for a distance of 400 feet in both directions along the railway. This subdivision does not apply in the case of any railway grade crossing where a human flagman is on duty or a clearly visible electrical or mechanical railway crossing signal device is installed but does not then indicate the immediate approach of a railway train or car.

(***2) When traversing any intersection of highways if during the last 100 feet of the driver's approach to the intersection the driver does not have a clear and unobstructed view of the intersection and of any traffic upon all of the highways entering the intersection for a distance of 100 feet along all those highways, except at an intersection protected by stop signs or yield right-of-way signs or controlled by official traffic control signals.

(***3) On any alley.

(***b) Twenty-five miles per hour:

(***1) On any highway other than a state highway, in any business or residence district unless a different speed is determined by local authority under procedures set forth in this code.

(***2) When approaching or passing a school building or the grounds thereof, contiguous to a highway and posted with a standard "SCHOOL" warning sign, while children are going to or leaving the school either during school hours or during the noon recess period. The prima facie limit shall also apply when approaching or passing any school grounds which are not separated from the highway by a fence, gate, or other physical barrier while the grounds are in use by children and the highway is posted with a standard "SCHOOL" warning sign. For purposes of this subparagraph, standard "SCHOOL" warning signs may be placed at any distance up to 500 feet away from school grounds.

(***3) When passing a senior center or other facility primarily used by senior citizens, contiguous to a street other than a state highway and posted with a standard "SENIOR" warning sign. A local authority ***may erect ***a sign pursuant to this paragraph ***when the local agency makes a determination that the proposed signing should be implemented. A local authority may*** request grant funding from the Pedestrian Safety Account pursuant to Section 894.7 of the Streets and Highways Code, or any other grant funding available to it, and use that grant funding to pay for the erection of those signs, or may utilize any other

funds available to it to pay for the erection of those signs, including, but not limited to, donations from private sources.
*** *(AM '13)*

22356. Increase of Freeway Speed Limit

Whenever CalTrans, after consultation with the CHP, determines upon the basis of an engineering and traffic survey on existing freeway segments, or upon the basis of appropriate design standards and projected traffic volumes in the case of newly constructed freeway segments, that a speed greater than 55 miles per hour would facilitate the orderly movement of vehicular traffic and would be reasonable and safe upon any state highway, or portion thereof, which is a freeway with full control of access and without crossings at grade otherwise subject to a maximum speed limit of 55 miles per hour, CalTrans, with the approval of the CHP, may declare a higher maximum speed of 60 or 65 miles per hour, and shall cause appropriate signs to be erected giving notice thereof. CalTrans shall only make a determination under this section that is fully consistent with, and in full compliance with, federal law.

(a) No person shall drive a vehicle upon that highway at a speed greater than 60 or 65 miles per hour, as posted.

(c) This section shall remain in effect only until the date specified in subdivision (c) of Section 22366, and as of that date is repealed.

22362. Speed Limit Where Persons at Work

It is prima facie a violation of the basic speed law for any person to operate a vehicle in excess of the posted speed limit upon any portion of a highway where officers or employees of the agency having jurisdiction of the same, or any contractor of the agency or his employees, are at work on the roadway or within the right-of-way so close thereto as to be endangered by passing traffic. This section applies only when appropriate signs, indicating the limits of the restricted zone, and the speed limit applicable therein, are placed by such agency within 400 feet of each end of such zone. The signs shall display the figures indicating the applicable limit, which shall not be less than 25 miles per hour, and shall indicate the purpose of the speed restriction. Nothing in this section shall be deemed to relieve any operator of a vehicle from complying with the basic speed law.

22400. Minimum Speed Law

(a) No person shall drive upon a highway at such a slow speed as to impede or block the normal and reasonable movement of traffic, unless the reduced speed is necessary for safe operation, because of a grade, or in compliance with law.

No person shall bring a vehicle to a complete stop upon a highway so as to impede or block the normal and reasonable movement of traffic unless the stop is necessary for safe operation or in compliance with law.

(b) Whenever CalTrans determines on the basis of an engineering and traffic survey that slow speeds on any part of a state highway consistently impede the normal and reasonable movement of traffic, the department may determine and declare a minimum speed limit below which no person shall drive a vehicle, except when necessary for safe operation or in compliance with law, when appropriate signs giving notice thereof are erected along the part of the highway for which a minimum speed limit is established.

Subdivision (b) of this section shall apply only to vehicles subject to registration.

22405. Violations on Bridges and Structures

(a) No person shall drive a vehicle on any bridge, elevated structure, tube, or tunnel constituting a part of a highway, at a speed which is greater than the maximum speed which can be maintained with safety to such structure.

(b) Upon the trial of any person charged with a violation of this section with respect to a sign erected under Section 22404, proof of the determination of the maximum speed by CalTrans or local authority and the erection and maintenance of the speed signs shall constitute prima facie evidence of the maximum speed which can be maintained with safety to the bridge, elevated structure, tube, or tunnel.

22406. Maximum Speed for Designated Vehicles

No person may drive any of the following vehicles on a highway at a speed in excess of 55 miles per hour:

(a) A motortruck or truck tractor having three or more axles or any motortruck or truck tractor drawing any other vehicle.

(b) A passenger vehicle or bus drawing any other vehicle.

(c) A schoolbus transporting any school pupil.

(d) A farm labor vehicle when transporting passengers.

(e) A vehicle transporting explosives.

(f) A trailer bus, as defined in Section 636. *(AM '99, '00)*

22406.1. Operation of Commercial Vehicle at Speed Exceeding Maximum Speed by 15 MPH or More

(a) A person who operates a commercial motor vehicle, as defined in subdivision (b) of Section 15210, upon a highway at a speed exceeding a posted speed limit established under this code by 15 miles per hour or more, is guilty of a misdemeanor.

(b) A person who holds a commercial driver's license, as defined in subdivision (a) of Section 15210, and operates a noncommerical motor vehicle upon a highway at a speed exceeding a posted speed limit established under this code by 15 miles per hour or more, is guilty of an infraction.

(c) A violation of either subdivision (a) or (b) is a "serious traffic violation," as defined in subdivision (p) of Section 15210, and is subject to the sanctions provided under Section 15306 or 15308, in addition to any other penalty provided by law.

(d) This section shall become operative on September 20, 2005. *(AD '00; AM '04)*

22406.5. Tank Vehicle Driver Penalties

Any person who drives a tank vehicle subject to Div. 14.7 (commencing with Section 34000) while transporting more than 500 gallons of flammable liquid at a speed greater than the applicable speed limit or in willful or wanton disregard for the safety of persons or property is, in addition to any other applicable penalty, subject to a fine of not less than five hundred dollars ($500) for a first offense and, for a second or subsequent offense within two years of a prior offense, to a fine of not less than two thousand dollars ($2,000) and a suspension of up to six months of a hazardous materials or cargo tank endorsement, or both.

22407. Decreasing Truck Speed Limit

Whenever the Department of Transportation or local authority determines upon the basis of engineering studies and a traffic survey that the speed of 55 miles per hour is more than is reasonable or safe for vehicles mentioned in subdivision (a) of Section 22406 which have a manufacturer's gross vehicle weight rating of 10,000 pounds or more, in descending a grade upon any portion of a highway, the department or local authority, with respect to highways under their respective jurisdiction, may determine and declare a speed limit of 50, 45, 40, 35, 30, 25 or 20 miles per hour, whichever is found most appropriate to facilitate the orderly movement of traffic and is reasonable and safe, which declared speed limit shall be effective for such vehicles when appropriate signs giving notice thereof are erected upon the highway.

22409. Solid Tire

No person shall operate any vehicle equipped with any solid tire when such vehicle has a gross weight as set forth in the following table at any speed in excess of the speed set forth opposite such gross weight:

10,000 lbs. or more but less than 16,000 lbs	25 mph
16,000 lbs. or more but less than 22,000 lbs	15 mph
22,000 lbs. or more	12 mph

22410. Metal Tires

No person shall operate any vehicle equipped with any metal tire in contact with the surface of the highway at a speed in excess of six miles per hour.

22411. Maximum Speed Limit - Motorized Scooter

No person shall operate a motorized scooter at a speed in excess of 15 miles per hour. *(AD '99)*

CHAPTER 8. SPECIAL STOPS REQUIRED

22450. Stop Requirements

(a) The driver of any vehicle approaching a stop sign at the entrance to, or within, an intersection shall stop at a limit line, if marked, otherwise before entering the crosswalk on the near side of the intersection.

If there is no limit line or crosswalk, the driver shall stop at the entrance to the intersecting roadway.

(b) The driver of a vehicle approaching a stop sign at a railroad grade crossing shall stop at a limit line, if marked, otherwise before crossing the first track or entrance to the railroad grade crossing.

(c) Notwithstanding any other provision of law, a local authority may adopt rules and regulations by ordinance or resolution providing for the placement of a stop sign at any location on a highway under its jurisdiction where the stop sign would enhance traffic safety. *(AM '07)*

22451. Stops for Train Signals

(a) The driver of any vehicle or pedestrian approaching a railroad or rail transit grade crossing shall stop not less than 15 feet from the nearest rail and shall not proceed until he or she can do so safely, whenever the following conditions exist:

(1) A clearly visible electric or mechanical signal device or a flagman gives warning of the approach or passage of a train or car.

(2) An approaching train or car is plainly visible or is emitting an audible signal and, by reason of its speed or nearness, is an immediate hazard.

(b) No driver or pedestrian shall proceed through, around, or under any railroad or rail transit crossing gate while the gate is closed.

(c) Whenever a railroad or rail transit crossing is equipped with an automated enforcement system, a notice of a violation of this section is subject to the procedures provided in Section 40518. *(AM '98, '00)*

22452. Railroad Crossings

(a) Subdivisions (b) and (d) apply to the operation of the following vehicles:

(1) A bus or farm labor vehicle carrying passengers.

(2) A motortruck transporting employees in addition to those riding in the cab.

(3) A schoolbus and a school pupil activity bus transporting school pupils, except as otherwise provided in paragraph (4) of subdivision (d).

(4) A commercial motor vehicle transporting any quantity of a Division 2.3 chlorine, as classified by Title 49 of the Code of Federal Regulations.

(5) A commercial motor vehicle that is required to be marked or placarded in accordance with the regulations of Title 49 of the Code of Federal Regulations with one of the following federal classifications:

(A) Division 1.1.

(B) Division 1.2, or Division 1.3.

(C) Division 2.3 Poison gas.

(D) Division 4.3.

(E) Class 7.

(F) Class 3 Flammable.

(G) Division 5.1.

(H) Division 2.2.

(I) Division 2.3 Chlorine.

(J) Division 6.1 Poison.

(K) Division 2.2 Oxygen.

(L) Division 2.1.

(M) Class 3 Combustible liquid.

(N) Division 4.1.

(O) Division 5.1.

(P) Division 5.2.

(Q) Class 8.

(R) Class Division 1.4.

(S) A cargo tank motor vehicle, whether loaded or empty, used for the transportation of a hazardous material, as defined in Parts 107 to 180, inclusive, of Title 49 of the Code of Federal Regulations.

(6) A cargo tank motor vehicle transporting a commodity that at the time of loading has a temperature above its flashpoint, as determined under Section 173.120 of Title 49 of the Code of Federal Regulations.

(7) A cargo tank motor vehicle, whether loaded or empty, transporting a commodity under exemption in accordance with Subpart B of Part 107 of Title 49 of the Code of Federal Regulations.

(b) Before traversing a railroad grade crossing, the driver of a vehicle described in subdivision (a) shall stop that vehicle not less than 15 nor more than 50 feet from the nearest rail of the track and while so stopped shall listen, and look in both directions along the track, for an approaching train and for signals indicating the approach of a train, and shall not proceed until he or she can do so safely. Upon proceeding, the gears shall not be shifted manually while crossing the tracks.

(c) The driver of a commercial motor vehicle, other than those listed in subdivision (a), upon approaching a railroad grade crossing, shall be driven at a rate of speed that allows the commercial vehicle to stop before reaching the nearest rail of that crossing, and shall not be driven upon, or over, the crossing until due caution is taken to ascertain that the course is clear.

(d) A stop need not be made at a crossing in the following circumstances:

(1) Of railroad tracks running along and upon the roadway within a business or residence district.

(2) Where a traffic officer or an official traffic control signal directs traffic to proceed.

(3) Where an exempt sign was authorized by the Public Utilities Commission prior to January 1, 1978.

(4) Where an official railroad crossing stop exempt sign in compliance with Section 21400 has been placed by the Department of Transportation or a local authority pursuant to Section 22452.5. This paragraph does not apply with respect to a schoolbus or to a school pupil activity bus transporting school pupils. *(AM '10)*

22454. Schoolbus

(a) The driver of any vehicle, upon meeting or overtaking, from either direction, any schoolbus equipped with signs as required in this code, that is stopped for the purpose of loading or unloading any schoolchildren and displays a flashing red light signal and stop signal arm, as defined in paragraph (4) of subdivision (b) of Section 25257, if equipped with a stop signal arm, visible from front or rear, shall bring the vehicle to a stop immediately before passing the schoolbus and shall not proceed past the schoolbus until the flashing red light signal and stop signal arm, if equipped with a stop signal arm, cease operation.

(b)(1) The driver of a vehicle upon a divided highway or multiple-lane highway need not stop upon meeting or passing a schoolbus that is upon the other roadway.

(2) For the purposes of this subdivision, a multiple-lane highway is any highway that has two or more lanes of travel in each direction.

(c)(1) If a vehicle was observed overtaking a schoolbus in violation of subdivision (a), and the driver of the schoolbus witnessed the violation, the driver may, within 24 hours, report the violation and furnish the vehicle license plate number and description and the time and place of the violation to the local law enforcement agency having jurisdiction of the offense. That law enforcement agency shall issue a letter of warning prepared in accordance with paragraph (2) with respect to the alleged violation to the registered owner of the vehicle. The issuance of a warning letter under this paragraph shall not be entered on the driving record of the person to whom it is issued, but does not preclude the imposition of any other applicable penalty.

(2) The Attorney General shall prepare and furnish to every law enforcement agency in the state a form letter for purposes of paragraph (1), and the law enforcement agency may issue those letters in the exact form prepared by the Attorney General. The Attorney General may charge a fee to any law enforcement agency that requests a copy of the form letter to recover the costs of preparing and providing that copy.

(d) This section also applies to a roadway upon private property. *(AM '99)*

22455. Vending from Vehicles

(a) The driver of any commercial vehicle engaged in vending upon a street may vend products on a street in a residence district only after bringing the vehicle to a complete stop and lawfully parking adjacent to the curb, consistent with the requirements of Chapter 9 (commencing with Section 22500) and local ordinances adopted pursuant thereto.

(b) Notwithstanding subdivision (a) of Section 114315 of the Health and Safety Code or any other provision of law, a local authority may, by ordinance or resolution, adopt additional requirements for the public safety regulating the type of vending and the time, place, and manner of vending from vehicles upon any street. *(AM '08)*

22456. Destiny Nicole Stout Memorial Act; Signs Required on Ice Cream Truck Vending in Residential Area

(a) This section shall be known and may be cited as the Destiny Nicole Stout Memorial Act.

(b) The Legislature finds and declares that motor vehicles engaged in vending ice cream and similar food items in residential neighborhoods can increase the danger to children, and it is necessary that these vehicles are clearly seen and noticed by motorists and pedestrians to protect public safety.

(c) As used in this section, the term "ice cream truck" means a motor vehicle engaged in the curbside vending or sale of frozen or refrigerated desserts, confections, or novelties commonly known as ice cream, or prepackaged candies, prepackaged snack foods, or soft drinks, primarily intended for the sale to children under 12 years of age.

(d) Any ice cream truck shall be equipped at all times, while engaged in vending in a residential area, with signs mounted on both the front and the rear and clearly legible from a distance of 100 feet under daylight conditions, incorporating the words "WARNING" and "CHILDREN CROSSING." Each sign shall be at least 12 inches high by 48 inches wide, with letters of a dark color and at least four inches in height, a one-inch wide solid border, and a sharply contrasting background.

(e) A person may not vend from an ice cream truck that is stopped, parked, or standing on any public street, alley, or highway under any of the following conditions:

(1) On a street, alley, or highway with a posted speed limit greater than 25 miles per hour.

(2) If the street, alley, or highway is within 100 feet of an intersection with an opposing highway that has a posted speed limit greater than 25 miles per hour.

(3) If the vendor does not have an unobstructed view for 200 feet in both directions along the highway and of any traffic on the highway. *(AD '00)*

CHAPTER 9. STOPPING, STANDING, & PARKING

22500. Prohibited Stopping, Standing, or Parking

No person shall stop, park, or leave standing any vehicle whether attended or unattended, except when necessary to avoid conflict with other traffic or in compliance with the directions of a peace officer or official traffic control device, in any of the following places:

(a) Within an intersection, except adjacent to curbs as may be permitted by local ordinance.

(b) On a crosswalk, except that a bus engaged as a common carrier or a taxicab may stop in an unmarked crosswalk to load or unload passengers when authorized by the legislative body of any city pursuant to an ordinance.

(c) Between a safety zone and the adjacent right-hand curb or within the area between the zone and the curb as may be indicated by a sign or red paint on the curb, which sign or paint was erected or placed by local authorities pursuant to an ordinance.

(d) Within 15 feet of the driveway entrance to any fire station. This subdivision does not apply to any vehicle owned or operated by a fire department and clearly marked as a fire department vehicle.

(e) In front of a public or private driveway, except that a bus engaged as a common carrier, schoolbus, or a taxicab may stop to load or unload passengers when authorized by local authorities pursuant to an ordinance.

In unincorporated territory, where the entrance of a private road or driveway is not delineated by an opening in a curb or by other curb construction, so much of the surface of the ground as is paved, surfaced, or otherwise plainly marked by vehicle use as a private road or driveway entrance, shall constitute a driveway.

(f) On any portion of a sidewalk, or with the body of the vehicle extending over any portion of a sidewalk, except electric carts when authorized by local ordinance, as specified in Section 21114.5. Lights, mirrors, or devices that are required to be mounted upon a vehicle under this code may extend from the body of the vehicle over the sidewalk to a distance of not more than 10 inches.

(g) Alongside or opposite any street or highway excavation or obstruction when stopping, standing, or parking would obstruct traffic.

(h) On the roadway side of any vehicle stopped, parked, or standing at the curb or edge of a highway, except for a schoolbus when stopped to load or unload pupils in a business or residence district where the speed limit is 25 miles per hour or less.

(i) Except as provided under Section 22500.5, alongside curb space authorized for the loading and unloading of passengers of a bus engaged as a common carrier in local transportation when indicated by a sign or red paint on the curb erected or painted by local authorities pursuant to an ordinance.

(j) In a tube or tunnel, except vehicles of the authorities in charge, being used in the repair, maintenance, or inspection of the facility.

(k) Upon a bridge, except vehicles of the authorities in charge, being used in the repair, maintenance, or inspection of the facility, and except that buses engaged as a common carrier in local transportation may stop to load or unload passengers upon a bridge where sidewalks are provided, when authorized by local authorities pursuant to an ordinance, and except that local authorities pursuant to an ordinance or the Department of Transportation pursuant to an order, within their respective jurisdictions, may permit parking on bridges having sidewalks and shoulders of sufficient width to permit parking without interfering with the normal movement of traffic on the roadway. Local authorities, by ordinance or resolution, may permit parking on these bridges on state highways in their respective jurisdictions if the ordinance or resolution is first approved in writing by the Department of Transportation. Parking shall not be permitted unless there are signs in place, as may be necessary, to indicate the provisions of local ordinances or the order of the Department of Transportation.

(l) In front of or upon that portion of a curb that has been cut down, lowered, or constructed to provide wheelchair accessibility to the sidewalk. *(AM '98, '02)*

22500.1. Additional Prohibited Stopping, Standing, or Parking: Fire Lane

In addition to Section 22500, no person shall stop, park, or leave standing any vehicle, whether attended or unattended, except when necessary to avoid conflict with other traffic or in compliance with the directions of a peace officer or official traffic control device along the edge of any highway, at any curb, or in any location in a publicly or privately owned or operated off-street parking facility, designated as a fire lane by the fire department or fire district with jurisdiction over the area in which the place is located.

The designation shall be indicated (1) by a sign posted immediately adjacent to, and visible from, the designated space clearly stating in letters not less than one inch in height the place is a fire lane, (2) by outlining or painting the place in red and, in contrasting color, marking the place with the words "FIRE LANE", which are clearly visible from a vehicle, or (3) by a red curb or red paint on the edge of the roadway upon which is clearly marked the words "FIRE LANE".

22502. Curb Parking

(a) Except as otherwise provided in this chapter, a vehicle stopped or parked upon a roadway where there are adjacent curbs shall be stopped or parked with the right-hand wheels of the vehicle parallel with and within 18 inches of the right-hand curb, except that a motorcycle shall be parked with at least one wheel or fender touching the right-hand curb. Where no curbs or barriers bound a two-way roadway, right-hand parallel parking is required unless otherwise indicated.

(b)(1) The provisions of subdivision (a) or (e) do not apply to a commercial vehicle if a variation from the requirements of subdivision (a) or (e) is reasonably necessary to accomplish the loading or unloading of merchandise or passengers on, or from, a vehicle and while anything connected with the loading, or unloading, is being executed.

(2) This subdivision does not permit a vehicle to stop or park upon a roadway in a direction opposite to that in which traffic normally moves upon that half of the roadway on which the vehicle is stopped or parked.

(c) Notwithstanding subdivision (b), a local authority may, by ordinance, prohibit a commercial vehicle from stopping, parking, or standing on one side of a roadway in a business district with the wheels of the vehicle more than 18 inches from the curb. The ordinance shall be effective only if signs are placed in the areas to which it is applicable clearly indicating the prohibition.

(d) This section does not apply to vehicles of a public utility when the vehicles are being used in connection with the operation, maintenance, or repair of facilities of the public utility or are being used in connection with providing public utility service.

(e)(1) Upon a one-way roadway, a vehicle may be stopped or parked as provided in subdivision (a) or with the left-hand wheels parallel to and within 18 inches of the left-hand curb, except that a motorcycle, if parked on the left-hand side, shall have either one wheel or one fender touching the curb. Where no curb or barriers bound a one-way roadway, parallel parking on either side is required unless otherwise indicated.

(2) This subdivision does not apply upon a roadway of a divided highway.

(f)(1) The City of Long Beach may, by ordinance or resolution, implement a pilot program to authorize vehicles to park on the left-hand side of the roadway parallel to and within 18 inches of the left-hand curb on two-way local residential streets that dead-end with no cul-de-sac or other designated area in which to turn around, if the City of Long Beach has first made a finding, supported by a professional engineering study, that the ordinance or resolution is justified by the need to facilitate the safe and orderly movement of vehicles on the roadways affected by the resolution or ordinance. The area covered by the ordinance or resolution shall be limited to the streets perpendicular to Ocean Boulevard beginning at Balboa Place and ending at 72nd Place, but shall not cover 62nd Place. The ordinance or resolution permitting that parking shall not apply until signs or markings giving adequate notice have been placed near the designated roadways. The city shall submit to the Legislature, two years from the date of the enactment of the ordinance or resolution that establishes the pilot program, a report that outlines the advantages and disadvantages of the pilot program. The report submitted pursuant to this subdivision shall be submitted in compliance with Section 9795 of the Government Code.

(2) The pilot program authorized under this subdivision shall terminate, and this subdivision shall become inoperative, three years from the date of enactment of the ordinance or resolution that establishes the pilot program. *(AM '10)*

22504. Unincorporated Area Parking; School Bus Stops

(a) Upon any highway in unincorporated areas, a person shall not stop, park, or leave standing any vehicle, whether attended or unattended, upon the roadway when it is practicable to stop, park, or leave the vehicle off such portion of the highway, but in every event an unobstructed width of the highway opposite a standing vehicle shall be left for the free passage of other vehicles and a clear view of the stopped vehicle shall be available from a distance of 200 feet in each direction upon the highway. This section shall not apply upon a highway where the roadway is bounded by adjacent curbs.

(b) This section does not apply to the driver of any vehicle which is disabled in such a manner and to such extent that it is impossible to avoid stopping and temporarily leaving the disabled vehicle on the roadway.

(c)(1) A schoolbus stop shall not be designated where there is not a clear view of a proposed or existing schoolbus stop from a distance of 200 feet in each direction along a highway, or upon the main traveled portion of a highway where there is not a clear view of the stop from 500 feet in each direction along the highway and the speed limit is more than 25 miles per hour, unless approved by the Department of the California Highway Patrol upon the request of the school district superintendent or the head or principal of a private school. If the schoolbus stop is approved by the Department of the California Highway Patrol, the Department of Transportation, in respect to state highways, and local authorities, in respect to highways under their jurisdiction, shall place sufficient signs along the highway to give adequate notice to motorists that they are approaching such bus stops.

(2) A school bus stop shall not be designated on any divided or multiple-lane highway where pupils must cross the highway to board or after exiting the bus, unless traffic is controlled by a traffic officer or official traffic control signal. For purposes of this section, a multiple-lane highway is defined as any highway having two or more lanes of travel in each direction. *(AM '12)*

22505. Stopping, Standing, or Parking on State Highway Segments

(a) CalTrans with respect to highways under its jurisdiction may place markings prohibiting or restricting the stopping, standing, or parking of vehicles, including, but not limited to, vehicles which are six feet or more in height (including any load thereon), in any of the following areas and under the following conditions:

(1) In areas where, in its opinion, stopping, standing, or parking is dangerous to those using the highway or where the stopping, standing, or parking of vehicles would unduly interfere with the free movement of traffic thereon.

(2) In areas within one-half mile of the boundary of any unit of the state park system which the Director of Conservation has determined are unusually high fire hazard areas, upon notification of CalTrans of such determination by the Director of Conservation.

(3) In areas within one-half mile of the boundary of any unit of the state park system which the county health officer has determined are areas where a substantial public health hazard would result if camping were allowed, upon notification of CalTrans of such determination by the county health officer.

(b) No person shall stop, park, or leave standing any vehicle in violation of the restrictions stated on the signs or markings.

(c) This section does not apply to any of the following;

(1) Public utility vehicles while performing a work operation.

(2) The driver of any vehicle which is disabled in such a manner and to such an extent that it is impossible to avoid stopping, parking, or leaving the disabled vehicle standing on the roadway.

22507.8. Parking in Spaces for the Disabled

(a) It is unlawful for any person to park or leave standing any vehicle in a stall or space designated for disabled persons and disabled veterans pursuant to Section 22511.7 or 22511.8 of this code or Section 14679 of the Government Code, unless the vehicle displays either a special identification license plate issued pursuant to Section 5007 or a distinguishing placard issued pursuant to Section 22511.55 or 22511.59.

(b) It is unlawful for any person to obstruct, block, or otherwise bar access to those parking stalls or spaces except as provided in subdivision (a).

(c) It is unlawful for any person to park or leave standing any vehicle, including a vehicle displaying a special identification license plate issued pursuant to Section 5007 or a distinguishing placard issued pursuant to Section 22511.55 or 22511.59, in either of the following places:

(1) On the lines marking the boundaries of a parking stall or space designated for disabled persons or disabled veterans.

(2) In any area of the pavement adjacent to a parking stall or space designated for disabled persons or disabled veterans that is marked by crosshatched lines and is thereby designated, pursuant to any local ordinance, for the loading and unloading of vehicles parked in the stall or space.

(d) Subdivisions (a), (b), and (c) apply to all offstreet parking facilities owned or operated by the state, and to all offstreet parking facilities owned or operated by a local authority. Subdivisions (a), (b), and (c) also apply to any privately owned and maintained offstreet parking facility. *(AM '09)*

22508.5.   Inoperable Parking Meters; Local Authorities May Prohibit Parking [Inop. 1-1-14 through 12-31-16]

(a)   Except as provided in subdivision (b), a vehicle may park, for up to the posted time limit, in any parking space that is ***regulated by an inoperable parking meter or an inoperable parking payment center.

(b)   ***A local authority may, by ordinance or resolution, prohibit or restrict the parking of vehicles ***in a parking space regulated by an inoperable parking ***meter or inoperable parking payment ***center. ***An ordinance or resolution adopted by a local authority pursuant to this section shall not become effective until signs or markings giving adequate notice of the restriction or prohibition on parking have been placed at parking locations, parking meters, or parking payment centers.

(c)   For purposes of this section:

(1)   "Inoperable parking meter"means a meter located next to and designated for an individual parking space, which has become inoperable and cannot accept payment in any form or cannot register that a payment in any form has been made.

(2)   "Inoperable parking payment center"means an electronic parking meter or pay station serving one or more parking spaces that is closest to the space where a person has parked and that cannot accept payment in any form, cannot register that a payment in any form has been made, or cannot issue a receipt that is required to be displayed in a conspicuous location on or in the vehicle.

(d)   This section shall become inoperative on January 1, 2014, and shall remain inoperative until January 1, 2017. *(AM-AD-RP '13*

22508.5.   Inoperable Parking Meters; Local Authorities May Not Prohibit Parking   [Added Stats. 2013]

(a)   A vehicle may park, for up to the posted time limit, in any parking space that is regulated by an inoperable parking meter or an inoperable parking payment center.

(b)   A local authority shall not, by ordinance or resolution, prohibit or restrict the parking of vehicles in a space that is regulated by an inoperable parking meter or inoperable parking payment center.

(c)   For purposes of this section:

(1)   "Inoperable parking meter"means a meter located next to and designated for an individual parking space, which has become inoperable and cannot accept payment in any form or cannot register that a payment in any form has been made.

(2)   "Inoperable parking payment center"means an electronic parking meter or pay station serving one or more parking spaces that is closest to the space where a person has parked and that cannot accept payment in any form, cannot register that a payment in any form has been made, or cannot issue a receipt that is required to be displayed in a conspicuous location on or in the vehicle.

(d)   This section shall remain in effect only until January 1, 2017, and as of that date is repealed, unless a later enacted statute, that is enacted before January 1, 2017, deletes or extends that date. *(AM-AD-RP '13)*

22510.   Parking in Snow Areas

(a)   Local authorities may, by ordinance or resolution, prohibit or restrict the parking or standing of vehicles on designated streets or highways within their jurisdiction, or portions thereof, for the purpose of snow removal. The ordinance or resolution shall not be effective until the street or highway, or portion thereof, has been sign-posted in accordance with the uniform standards and specifications of the CalTrans, or until the local authorities have caused to be posted in a conspicuous place at each entrance to the street or highway, a notice not less than 17 inches by 22 inches in size, with lettering not less than one inch in height, setting forth the days parking is prohibited. The signs shall, at a minimum, be placed on each affected street or highway, at the boundary of the local authority, and at the beginning and end of each highway or highway segment included in that area. No person shall stop, park, or leave standing any vehicle, whether attended or unattended, within the area marked by signs, except when necessary to avoid conflict with other traffic or in compliance with the directions of a traffic or peace officer.

(b) No ordinance or resolution authorized by subdivision (a) which affects a state highway shall be effective until it is submitted to, and approved by, the CalTrans.

(c) The CalTrans, with respect to state highways, may restrict the parking or standing of vehicles for purposes of snow removal. The restrictions shall not be effective until the highway, or portion thereof, has been posted with signs in accordance with the uniform standards and specifications of the department. No person shall stop, park, or leave standing any vehicle, whether attended or unattended, within the area marked by parking restriction signs, except when necessary to avoid conflict with other traffic or in compliance with the directions of a traffic or peace officer.

22511.　Zero-Emission Vehicles – Designated Parking

(a) A local authority, by ordinance or resolution, and a person in lawful possession of an offstreet parking facility may designate stalls or spaces in an offstreet parking facility owned or operated by that local authority or person for the exclusive purpose of charging and parking a vehicle that is connected for electric charging purposes.

(b) If posted in accordance with subdivision (d) or (e), the owner or person in lawful possession of a privately owned or operated offstreet parking facility, after notifying the police or sheriff's department, may cause the removal of a vehicle from a stall or space designated pursuant to subdivision (a) in the facility to the nearest public garage if the vehicle is not connected for electric charging purposes.

(c) If posted in accordance with subdivision (d), the local authority owning or operating an offstreet parking facility, after notifying the police or sheriff's department, may cause the removal of a vehicle from a stall or space designated pursuant to subdivision (a) in the facility to the nearest garage, as defined in Section 340, that is owned, leased, or approved for use by a public agency if the vehicle is not connected for electric charging purposes.

(d) The posting required for an offstreet parking facility owned or operated either privately or by a local authority shall consist of a sign not less than 17 by 22 inches in size with lettering not less than one inch in height that clearly and conspicuously states the following: "Unauthorized vehicles not connected for electric charging purposes will be towed away at owner's expense. Towed vehicles may be reclaimed at

_____
(Address)
　or by telephoning

_____."
(Telephone number of local law enforcement agency)

The sign shall be posted in either of the following locations:

(1) Immediately adjacent to, and visible from, the stall or space.

(2) In a conspicuous place at each entrance to the offstreet parking facility.

(e) If the parking facility is privately owned and public parking is prohibited by the posting of a sign meeting the requirements of paragraph (1) of subdivision (a) of Section 22658, the requirements of subdivision (b) may be met by the posting of a sign immediately adjacent to, and visible from, each stall or space indicating that a vehicle not meeting the requirements of subdivision (a) will be removed at the owner's expense and containing the telephone number of the local traffic law enforcement agency.

(f) This section does not interfere with existing law governing the ability of local authorities to adopt ordinances related to parking programs within their jurisdiction, such as programs that provide free parking in metered areas or municipal garages for electric vehicles. *(AM '11)*

22511.1.　Designated Zero-Emission Vehicle Parking; Violations

(a) A person shall not park or leave standing a vehicle in a stall or space designated pursuant to Section 22511 unless the vehicle is connected for electric charging purposes.

(b) A person shall not obstruct, block, or otherwise bar access to parking stalls or spaces described in subdivision (a) except as provided in subdivision (a).

(AM '11)

22511.3. Veteran with Special Plates may Park in Metered Parking Space Without Charge; Local Authority's Option

(a) A veteran displaying special license plates issued under Section 5101.3, 5101.4, 5101.5, 5101.6, or 5101.8 may park his or her motor vehicle, weighing not more than 6,000 pounds gross weight, without charge, in a metered parking space.

(b) Nothing in this section restricts the rights of a person displaying either a special identification license plate issued pursuant to Section 5007 or a distinguishing placard issued pursuant to Section 22511.55 or 22511.59.

(c)(1) This section does not exempt a vehicle displaying special license plates issued under Section 5101.3, 5101.4, 5101.5, 5101.6, or 5101.8 from compliance with any other state law or ordinance, including, but not limited to, vehicle height restrictions, zones that prohibit stopping, parking, or standing of all vehicles, parking time limitations, street sweeping, restrictions of the parking space to a particular type of vehicle, or the parking of a vehicle that is involved in the operation of a street vending business.

(2) This section does not authorize a vehicle displaying special license plates issued under Section 5101.3, 5101.4, 5101.5, 5101.6, or 5101.8 to park in a state parking facility that is designated only for state employees.

(3) This section does not authorize a vehicle displaying special license plates issued under Section 5101.3, 5101.4, 5101.5, 5101.6, or 5101.8 to park during time periods other than the normal business hours of, or the maximum time allotted by, a state or local authority parking facility.

(4) This section does not require the state or a local authority to designate specific parking spaces for vehicles displaying special license plates issued under Section 5101.3, 5101.4, 5101.5, 5101.6, or 5101.8.

(d) A local authority's compliance with subdivision (a) is solely contingent upon the approval of its governing body. *(AD '08)*

22511.5. Parking Exemption for Disabled Persons

(a)(1) A disabled person or disabled veteran displaying special license plates issued under Section 5007 or a distinguishing placard issued under Section 22511.55 or 22511.59 is allowed to park for unlimited periods in any of the following zones:

(A) In any restricted zone described in paragraph (5) of subdivision (a) of Section 21458 or on streets upon which preferential parking privileges and height limits have been given pursuant to Section 22507.

(B) In any parking zone that is restricted as to the length of time parking is permitted as indicated by a sign erected pursuant to a local ordinance.

(2) A disabled person or disabled veteran is allowed to park in any metered parking space without being required to pay parking meter fees.

(3) This subdivision does not apply to a zone for which state law or ordinance absolutely prohibits stopping, parking, or standing of all vehicles, or which the law or ordinance reserves for special types of vehicles, or to the parking of a vehicle that is involved in the operation of a street vending business.

(b) A disabled person or disabled veteran is allowed to park a motor vehicle displaying a special disabled person license plate or placard issued by a foreign jurisdiction with the same parking privileges authorized in this code for any motor vehicle displaying a special license plate or a distinguishing placard issued by the Department of Motor Vehicles. *(AM '04, '10)*

22511.55. Placards; Issuance; Substitute

(a)(1) A disabled person or disabled veteran may apply to the department for the issuance of a distinguishing placard. The placard may be used in lieu of the special license plate or plates issued under Section 5007 for parking purposes described in Section 22511.5 when (A) suspended from the rearview mirror, (B) if there is no rearview mirror, when displayed on the dashboard of a vehicle, or (C) inserted in a clip designated for a distinguishing placard and installed by the manufacturer on the driver's side of the front window. It is the intent of the Legislature to encourage the use of distinguishing placards because they provide law enforcement officers with a more readily recognizable symbol for distinguishing vehicles qualified for the parking privilege. The placard shall be the size, shape, and color determined by the department and shall bear the International Symbol of Access adopted pursuant to Section 3 of Public Law 100-641, commonly known as the "wheelchair symbol." The department shall incorporate instructions for the lawful use of a placard, and a summary of the penalties for the unlawful use of a placard, into the identification card issued to the placard owner.

(2)(A) The department may establish procedures for the issuance and renewal of the placards. The procedures shall include, but are not limited to, advising an applicant in writing on the application for a placard of the procedure to apply for a special license plate or plates, as described in Section 5007, and the fee exemptions established pursuant to Section 9105 and in subdivision (a) of Section 10783 of the Revenue and Taxation Code. The placards shall have a fixed expiration date of June 30 every two years. A portion of the placard shall be printed in a contrasting color that shall be changed every two years. The size and color of this contrasting portion of the placard shall be large and distinctive enough to be readily identifiable by a law enforcement officer in a passing vehicle.

(B) As used in this section, "year" means the period between the inclusive dates of July 1 through June 30.

(C) Prior to the end of each year, the department shall, for the most current three years available, compare its record of disability placards issued against the records of the Office of Vital Records of the State Department of Public Health, or its successor, and withhold any renewal notices that otherwise would have been sent for a placardholder identified as deceased.

(3) Except as provided in paragraph (4), a person shall not be eligible for more than one placard at a time.

(4) Organizations and agencies involved in the transportation of disabled persons or disabled veterans may apply for a placard for each vehicle used for the purpose of transporting disabled persons or disabled veterans.

(b)(1) Except as provided in paragraph (4), prior to issuing an original distinguishing placard to a disabled person or disabled veteran , the department shall require the submission of a certificate, in accordance with paragraph (2), signed by the physician and surgeon, or to the extent that it does not cause a reduction in the receipt of federal aid highway funds, by a nurse practitioner, certified nurse midwife, or physician assistant, substantiating the disability, unless the applicant's disability is readily observable and uncontested. The disability of a person who has lost, or has lost use of, one or more lower extremities or one hand, for a disabled veteran, or both hands, for a disabled person, or who has significant limitation in the use of lower extremities, may also be certified by a licensed chiropractor. The blindness of an applicant shall be certified by a licensed physician and surgeon who specializes in diseases of the eye or a licensed optometrist. The physician and surgeon, nurse practitioner, certified nurse midwife, physician assistant, chiropractor, or optometrist certifying the qualifying disability shall provide a full description of the illness or disability on the form submitted to the department.

(2) The physician and surgeon, nurse practitioner, certified nurse midwife, physician assistant, chiropractor, or optometrist who signs a certificate submitted under this subdivision shall retain information sufficient to substantiate that certificate and, upon request of the department, shall make that information available for inspection by the Medical Board of California or the appropriate regulatory board.

(3) The department shall maintain in its records all information on an applicant's certification of permanent disability and shall make that information available to eligible law enforcement or parking control agencies upon a request pursuant to Section 22511.58.

(4) For a disabled veteran, the department shall accept, in lieu of the certificate described in paragraph (1), a certificate from the United States Department of Veterans Affairs that certifies that the applicant is a disabled veteran as described in Section 295.7.

(c) A person who is issued a distinguishing placard pursuant to subdivision (a) may apply to the department for a substitute placard without recertification of eligibility, if that placard is lost or stolen.

(d) The distinguishing placard shall be returned to the department not later than 60 days after the death of the disabled person or disabled veteran to whom the placard was issued.

(e) The department shall print on any distinguishing placard issued on or after January 1, 2005, the maximum penalty that may be imposed for a violation of Section 4461. For purposes of this subdivision, the "maximum penalty"is the amount derived from adding all of the following:

(1) The maximum fine that may be imposed under Section 4461.

(2) The penalty required to be imposed under Section 70372 of the Government Code.

(3) The penalty required to be levied under Section 76000 of the Government Code.

(4) The penalty required to be levied under Section 1464 of the Penal Code.

(5) The surcharge required to be levied under Section 1465.7 of the Penal Code.

(6) The penalty authorized to be imposed under Section 4461.3. *(AM '06, '10)*

22511.56. Placard: Show ID and Evidence of Authenticity

(a) A person using a distinguishing placard issued under Section 22511.55 or 22511.59, or a special license plate issued under Section 5007, for parking as permitted by Section 22511.5 shall, upon request of a peace officer or person authorized to enforce parking laws, ordinances, or regulations, present identification and evidence of the issuance of that placard or plate to that person, or that vehicle if the plate was issued pursuant to paragraph (3) of subdivision (a) of Section 5007.

(b) Failure to present the requested identification and evidence of the issuance of that placard or plate shall be a rebuttable presumption that the placard or plate is being misused and that the associated vehicle has been parked in violation of Section 22507.8, or has exercised a disabled person's parking privilege pursuant to Section 22511.5.

(c) In addition to any other applicable penalty for the misuse of a placard, the officer or parking enforcement person may confiscate a placard being used for parking purposes that benefit a person other than the person to whom the placard was issued by the Department of Motor Vehicles. A placard lawfully used by a person transporting a disabled person pursuant to subdivision (b) of Section 4461 may not be confiscated.

(d) In addition to any other applicable penalty for the misuse of a special license plate issued under Section 5007, a peace officer may confiscate the plate being used for parking purposes that benefit a person other than the person to whom the plate was issued by the Department of Motor Vehicles.

(e) After verification with the Department of Motor Vehicles that the user of the placard or plate is not the registered owner of the placard or plate, the appropriate agency that confiscated the placard or plate shall notify the department of the placard or plate number and the department shall cancel the placard or plate. A placard or plate canceled by the department pursuant to this subdivision may be destroyed by the agency that confiscated the placard or plate. *(AM '06)*

22511.7. Parking for the Disabled - Marking Spaces

(a) In addition to Section 22511.8 for offstreet parking, a local authority may, by ordinance or resolution, designate onstreet parking spaces for the exclusive use of a vehicle that displays either a special identification license plate issued pursuant to Section 5007 or a distinguishing placard issued pursuant to Section 22511.55 or 22511.59.

(b)(1) Whenever a local authority so designates a parking space, it shall be indicated by blue paint on the curb or edge of the paved portion of the street adjacent to the space. In addition, the local authority shall post immediately adjacent to and visible from the space a sign consisting of a profile view of a wheelchair with occupant in white on a blue background.

(2) The sign required pursuant to paragraph (1) shall clearly and conspicuously state the following: "Minimum Fine $250."This paragraph applies only to signs for parking spaces constructed on or after July 1, 2008, and signs that are replaced on or after July 1, 2008.

(3) If the loading and unloading area of the pavement adjacent to a parking stall or space designated for disabled persons or disabled veterans is to be marked by a border and hatched lines, the border shall be painted blue and the hatched lines shall be painted a suitable contrasting color to the parking space. Blue or white paint is preferred. In addition, within the border the words "No Parking"shall be painted in white letters no less than 12 inches high. This paragraph applies only to parking spaces constructed on or after July 1, 2008, and painting that is done on or after July 1, 2008.

(c) This section does not restrict the privilege granted to disabled persons and disabled veterans by Section 22511.5. *(AM '07, '09)*

22511.8. Offstreet Parking for the Disabled: Removal of Vehicles

(a) A local authority, by ordinance or resolution, and a person in lawful possession of an offstreet parking facility may designate stalls or spaces in an offstreet parking facility owned or operated by the local authority or person for the exclusive use of a vehicle that displays either a special license plate issued pursuant to Section 5007 or a distinguishing placard issued pursuant to Section 22511.55 or 22511.59. The designation shall be made by posting a sign as described in paragraph (1), and by either of the markings described in paragraph (2) or (3):

(1)(A) By posting immediately adjacent to, and visible from, each stall or space, a sign consisting of a profile view of a wheelchair with occupant in white on a blue background.

(B) The sign shall also clearly and conspicuously state the following: "Minimum Fine $250."This subparagraph applies only to signs for parking spaces constructed on or after July 1, 2008, and signs that are replaced on or after July 1, 2008, or as the State Architect deems necessary when renovations, structural repair, alterations, and additions occur to existing buildings and facilities on or after July 1, 2008.

(2)(A) By outlining or painting the stall or space in blue and outlining on the ground in the stall or space in white or suitable contrasting color a profile view depicting a wheelchair with occupant.

(B) The loading and unloading area of the pavement adjacent to a parking stall or space designated for disabled persons or disabled veterans shall be marked by a border and hatched lines. The border shall be painted blue and the hatched lines shall be painted a suitable contrasting color to the parking space. Blue or white paint is preferred. In addition, within the border the words "No Parking"shall be painted in white letters no less than 12 inches high. This subparagraph applies only to parking spaces constructed on or after July 1, 2008, and painting that is done on or after July 1, 2008, or as the State Architect deems necessary when renovations, structural repair, alterations, and additions occur to existing buildings and facilities on or after July 1, 2008.

(3) By outlining a profile view of a wheelchair with occupant in white on a blue background, of the same dimensions as in paragraph (2). The profile view shall be located so that it is visible to a traffic enforcement officer when a vehicle is properly parked in the space.

(b) The Department of General Services under the Division of the State Architect shall develop pursuant to Section 4450 of the Government Code, as appropriate, conforming regulations to ensure compliance with subparagraph (B) of paragraph (1) of subdivision (a) and subparagraph (B) of paragraph (2) of subdivision (a). Initial regulations to implement these provisions shall be adopted as emergency regulations. The adoption of these regulations shall be considered by the Department of General Services to be an emergency necessary for the immediate preservation of the public peace, health and safety, or general welfare.

(c) If posted in accordance with subdivision (e) or (f), the owner or person in lawful possession of a privately owned or operated offstreet parking facility, after notifying the police or sheriff's department, may cause the removal of a vehicle from a stall or space designated pursuant to subdivision (a) in the facility to the nearest public garage unless a special license plate issued pursuant to Section 5007 or distinguishing placard issued pursuant to Section 22511.55 or 22511.59 is displayed on the vehicle.

(d) If posted in accordance with subdivision (e), the local authority owning or operating an offstreet parking facility, after notifying the police or sheriff's department, may cause the removal of a vehicle from a stall or space designated pursuant to subdivision (a) in the facility to the nearest public garage unless a special license plate issued pursuant to Section 5007 or a distinguishing placard issued pursuant to Section 22511.55 or 22511.59 is displayed on the vehicle.

(e) Except as provided in Section 22511.9, the posting required for an offstreet parking facility owned or operated either privately or by a local authority shall consist of a sign not less than 17 by 22 inches in size with lettering not less than one inch in height which clearly and conspicuously states the following: "Unauthorized vehicles parked in designated accessible spaces not displaying distinguishing placards or special license plates issued for persons with disabilities will be towed away at the owner's expense. Towed vehicles may be reclaimed at:

(Address)_____ or by telephoning

_____ "

(Telephone number of local law enforcement agency)
The sign shall be posted in either of the following locations:
(1) Immediately adjacent to, and visible from, the stall or space.
(2) In a conspicuous place at each entrance to the offstreet parking facility.

(f) If the parking facility is privately owned and public parking is prohibited by the posting of a sign meeting the requirements of paragraph (1) of subdivision (a) of Section 22658, the requirements of subdivision (c) may be met by the posting of a sign immediately adjacent to, and visible from, each stall or space indicating that a vehicle not meeting the requirements of subdivision (a) will be removed at the owner's expense and containing the telephone number of the local traffic law enforcement agency.

(g) This section does not restrict the privilege granted to disabled persons and disabled veterans by Section 22511.5. *(AM '04, '07, '09)*

22511.85. Parking in Two Adjacent Stalls – When Permitted

A vehicle, identified with a special license plate issued pursuant to Section 5007 or a distinguishing placard issued pursuant to Section 22511.55 or 22511.59, which is equipped with a lift, ramp, or assistive equipment that is used for the loading and unloading of a person with a disability may park in not more than two adjacent stalls or spaces on a street or highway or in a public or private off-street parking facility if the equipment has been or will be used for loading or unloading a person with a disability, and if there is no single parking space immediately available on the street or highway or within the facility that is suitable for that purpose, including, but not limited to, when there is not sufficient space to operate a vehicle lift, ramp, or assistive equipment, or there is not sufficient room for a person with a disability to exit the vehicle or maneuver once outside the vehicle. *(AD '00; AM '08)*

22513. Tow Trucks

(a) Except as provided in subdivision (b) or (c), the owner or operator of a tow truck who complies with the requirements of this code relating to tow trucks may stop or park the tow truck upon a highway for the purpose of rendering assistance to a disabled vehicle.

(b) It is a misdemeanor for the owner or operator of a tow truck to stop at the scene of an accident or near a disabled vehicle for the purpose of soliciting an engagement for towing services, either directly or indirectly, or to furnish any towing service, unless summoned to the scene, requested to stop, or flagged down by the owner or operator of a disabled vehicle or requested to perform the service by a law enforcement officer or public agency pursuant to that agency's procedures.

(c) It is a misdemeanor for the owner or operator of a tow truck to move any vehicle from a highway, street, or public property without the express authorization of the owner or operator of the vehicle or a law enforcement officer or public agency pursuant to that agency's procedures, when the vehicle has been left unattended or when there is an injury as the result of an accident.

(d) This section does not apply to any of the following:

(1) A vehicle owned or operated by, or under contract to, a motor club, as defined by Section 12142 of the Insurance Code, which stops to provide services for which compensation is neither requested nor received, provided that those services may not include towing other than that which may be necessary to remove the vehicle to the nearest safe shoulder. The owner or operator of such a vehicle may contact a law enforcement agency or other public agency on behalf of a motorist, but may not refer a motorist to a tow truck owner or operator, unless the motorist is a member of the motor club, the motorist is referred to a tow truck owner or operator under contract to the motor club, and, if there is a dispatch facility which services the area and is owned or operated by the motor club, the referral is made through that dispatch facility.

(2) A tow truck operator employed by a law enforcement agency or other public agency.

(3) A tow truck owner or operator acting under contract with a law enforcement or other public agency to abate abandoned vehicles, or to provide towing service or emergency road service to motorists while involved in freeway service patrol operations, to the extent authorized by law.

22514. Fire Hydrants

No person shall stop, park, or leave standing any vehicle within 15 feet of a fire hydrant except as follows:

(a) If the vehicle is attended by a licensed driver who is seated in the front seat and who can immediately move such vehicle in case of necessity.

(b) If the local authority adopts an ordinance or resolution reducing that distance. If the distance is less than 10 feet total length when measured along the curb or edge of the street, the distance shall be indicated by signs or markings.

(c) If the vehicle is owned or operated by a fire department and is clearly marked as a fire department vehicle.

22515. Unattended Vehicles

(a) No person driving, or in control of, or in charge of, a motor vehicle shall permit it to stand on any highway unattended without first effectively setting the brakes thereon and stopping the motor thereof.

(b) No person in control of, or in charge of, any vehicle, other than a motor vehicle, shall permit it to stand on any highway without first effectively setting the brakes thereon, or blocking the wheels thereof, to effectively prevent the movement of the vehicle.

22516. Locked Vehicle

No person shall leave standing a locked vehicle in which there is any person who cannot readily escape therefrom.

22517. Opening and Closing Doors

No person shall open the door of a vehicle on the side available to moving traffic unless it is reasonably safe to do so and can be done without interfering with the movement of such traffic, nor shall any person leave a door open upon the side of a vehicle available to moving traffic for a period of time longer than necessary to load or unload passengers.

22520.5. Vending On or Near Freeways

(a) No person shall solicit, display, sell, offer for sale, or otherwise vend or attempt to vend any merchandise or service while being wholly or partly within any of the following:

(1) The right-of-way of any freeway, including any on ramp, off ramp, or roadway shoulder which lies within the right-of-way of the freeway.

(2) Any roadway or adjacent shoulder within 500 feet of a freeway off ramp or on ramp.

(3) Any sidewalk within 500 feet of a freeway off ramp or on ramp, when vending or attempting to vend to vehicular traffic.

(b) Subdivision (a) does not apply to a roadside rest area or vista point located within a freeway right-of-way which is subject to Section 22520.6, to a tow truck or service vehicle rendering assistance to a disabled vehicle, or to a person issued a permit to vend upon the freeway pursuant to Section 670 of the Streets and Highways Code.

(c) A violation of this section is an infraction. A second or subsequent conviction of a violation of this section is a misdemeanor.

22520.6. Prohibited Activity: Roadside Rest or Vista Point

(a) No person shall engage in any activity within a highway roadside rest area or vista point prohibited by rules and regulations adopted pursuant to Section 225 of the Streets and Highways Code.

(b) A violation of this section is an infraction. A second or subsequent conviction of a violation of this section is a misdemeanor.

22521. Parking Upon or Near Railroad Track

No person shall park a vehicle upon any railroad track or within 7½ feet of the nearest rail.

22522. Parking Near Sidewalk Access Ramps

No person shall park a vehicle within three feet of any sidewalk access ramp constructed at, or adjacent to, a crosswalk or at any other location on a sidewalk so as to be accessible to and usable by the physically disabled, if the area adjoining the ramp is designated by either a sign or red paint. *(AM '99)*

22523. Abandonment Prohibited

(a) No person shall abandon a vehicle upon any highway.

(b) No person shall abandon a vehicle upon public or private property without the express or implied consent of the owner or person in lawful possession or control of the property.

(c) Any person convicted of a violation of this section shall be punished by a fine of not less than one hundred dollars ($100) and shall provide proof that the costs of removal and disposition of the vehicle have been paid. No part of any fine imposed shall be suspended. The fine may be paid in installments if the court determines that the defendant is unable to pay the entire amount in one payment.

(d) Proof that the costs of removal and disposition of the vehicle have been paid shall not be required if proof is provided to the court that the vehicle was stolen prior to abandonment. That proof may consist of a police report or other evidence acceptable to the court.

(e) The costs required to be paid for the removal and disposition of any vehicle determined to be abandoned pursuant to Section 22669 shall not exceed those for towing and seven days of storage. This subdivision does not apply if the registered owner or legal owner has completed and returned to the lienholder a "Declaration of Opposition"form within the time specified in Section 22851.8.

(f)(1) If a vehicle is abandoned in violation of subdivision (b) and is not redeemed after impound, the last registered owner is guilty of an infraction. In addition to any other penalty, the registered owner shall be liable for any deficiency remaining after disposal of the vehicle under Section 3071 or 3072 of the Civil Code or Section 22851.10 of this code.

(2) The filing of a report of sale or transfer of the vehicle pursuant to Section 5602, the filing of a vehicle theft report with a law enforcement agency, or the filing of a form or notice with the department pursuant to subdivision (b) of Section 4456 or Section 5900 or 5901 relieves the registered owner of liability under this subdivision.

22526. Entering Occupied Intersection or Marked Crosswalk

(a) Notwithstanding any official traffic control signal indication to proceed, a driver of a vehicle shall not enter an intersection or marked crosswalk unless there is sufficient space on the other side of the intersection or marked crosswalk to accommodate the vehicle driven without obstructing the through passage of vehicles from either side.

(b) A driver of a vehicle which is making a turn at an intersection who is facing a steady circular yellow or yellow arrow signal shall not enter the intersection or marked crosswalk unless there is sufficient space on the other side of the intersection or marked crosswalk to accommodate the vehicle driven without obstructing the through passage of vehicles from either side.

(c) A driver of a vehicle shall not enter a railroad or rail transit crossing, notwithstanding any official traffic control device or signal indication to proceed, unless there is sufficient undercarriage clearance to cross the intersection without obstructing the through passage of a railway vehicle, including, but not limited to, a train, trolley, or city transit vehicle.

(d) A driver of a vehicle shall not enter a railroad or rail transit crossing, notwithstanding any official traffic control device or signal indication to proceed, unless there is sufficient space on the other side of the railroad or rail transit crossing to accommodate the vehicle driven and any railway vehicle, including, but not limited to, a train, trolley, or city transit vehicle.

(e) A local authority may post appropriate signs at the entrance to intersections indicating the prohibition in subdivisions (a), (b), and (c).

(f) A violation of this section is not a violation of a law relating to the safe operation of vehicles and is the following:

(1) A stopping violation when a notice to appear has been issued by a peace officer described in Section 830.1, 830.2, or 830.33 of the Penal Code.

(2) A parking violation when a notice of parking violation is issued by a person, other than a peace officer described in paragraph (1), who is authorized to enforce parking statutes and regulations.

(g) This section shall be known and may be cited as the Anti-Gridlock Act of 1987. *(AM '01, '05, '10)*

CHAPTER 10. REMOVAL OF PARKED & ABANDONED VEHICLES

22650. Prohibition of Removal

It is unlawful for any peace officer or any unauthorized person to remove any unattended vehicle from a highway to a garage or to any other place, except as provided in this code.

(a) Those law enforcement and other agencies identified in this chapter as having the authority to remove vehicles shall also have the authority to provide hearings in compliance with the provisions of Section 22852. During these hearings the storing agency shall have the burden of establishing the authority and the validity of, the removal.

(b) Nothing in this section shall be deemed to prevent a review or other action as may be permitted by the laws of this state by a court of competent jurisdiction.

22651. Circumstances Permitting Removal

A peace officer, as defined in Chapter 4.5 (commencing with Section 830) of Title 3 of Part 2 of the Penal Code, or a regularly employed and salaried employee, who is engaged in directing traffic or enforcing parking laws and regulations, of a city, county, or jurisdiction of a state agency in which a vehicle is located, may remove a vehicle located within the territorial limits in which the officer or employee may act, under the following circumstances:

(a) When a vehicle is left unattended upon a bridge, viaduct, or causeway or in a tube or tunnel where the vehicle constitutes an obstruction to traffic.

(b) When a vehicle is parked or left standing upon a highway in a position so as to obstruct the normal movement of traffic or in a condition so as to create a hazard to other traffic upon the highway.

(c) When a vehicle is found upon a highway or public land and a report has previously been made that the vehicle is stolen or a complaint has been filed and a warrant thereon is issued charging that the vehicle was embezzled.

(d) When a vehicle is illegally parked so as to block the entrance to a private driveway and it is impractical to move the vehicle from in front of the driveway to another point on the highway.

(e) When a vehicle is illegally parked so as to prevent access by firefighting equipment to a fire hydrant and it is impracticable to move the vehicle from in front of the fire hydrant to another point on the highway.

(f) When a vehicle, except highway maintenance or construction equipment, is stopped, parked, or left standing for more than four hours upon the right-of-way of a freeway that has full control of access and no crossings at grade and the driver, if present, cannot move the vehicle under its own power.

(g) When the person in charge of a vehicle upon a highway or public land is, by reason of physical injuries or illness, incapacitated to an extent so as to be unable to provide for its custody or removal.

(h)(1) When an officer arrests a person driving or in control of a vehicle for an alleged offense and the officer is, by this code or other law, required or permitted to take, and does take, the person into custody.

(2) When an officer serves a notice of an order of suspension or revocation pursuant to Section 13388 or 13389.

(i)(1) When a vehicle, other than a rented vehicle, is found upon a highway or public land, or is removed pursuant to this code, and it is known that the vehicle has been issued five or more notices of parking violations to which the owner or person in control of the vehicle has not responded within 21 calendar days of notice of citation issuance or citation issuance or 14 calendar days of the mailing of a notice of delinquent parking violation to the agency responsible for processing notices of parking violations, or the registered owner of the vehicle is known to have been issued five or more notices for failure to pay or failure to appear in court for traffic violations for which a certificate has not been issued by the magistrate or clerk of the court hearing the case showing that the case has been adjudicated or concerning which the registered owner's record has not been cleared pursuant to Chapter 6 (commencing with Section 41500) of Division 17, the vehicle may be impounded until that person furnishes to the impounding law enforcement agency all of the following:

(A) Evidence of his or her identity.

(B) An address within this state at which he or she can be located.

(C) Satisfactory evidence that all parking penalties due for the vehicle and all other vehicles registered to the registered owner of the impounded vehicle, and all traffic violations of the registered owner, have been cleared.

(2) The requirements in subparagraph (C) of paragraph (1) shall be fully enforced by the impounding law enforcement agency on and after the time that the Department of Motor Vehicles is able to provide access to the necessary records.

(3) A notice of parking violation issued for an unlawfully parked vehicle shall be accompanied by a warning that repeated violations may result in the impounding of the vehicle. In lieu of furnishing satisfactory evidence that the full amount of parking penalties or bail has been deposited, that person may demand to be taken without unnecessary delay before a magistrate, for traffic offenses, or a hearing examiner, for parking offenses, within the county in which the offenses charged are alleged to have been committed and who has jurisdiction of the offenses and is nearest or most accessible with reference to the place where the vehicle is impounded. Evidence of current registration shall be produced after a vehicle has been impounded, or, at the discretion of the impounding law enforcement agency, a notice to appear for violation of subdivision (a) of Section 4000 shall be issued to that person.

(4) A vehicle shall be released to the legal owner, as defined in Section 370, if the legal owner does all of the following:

(A) Pays the cost of towing and storing the vehicle.

(B) Submits evidence of payment of fees as provided in Section 9561.

(C) Completes an affidavit in a form acceptable to the impounding law enforcement agency stating that the vehicle was not in possession of the legal owner at the time of occurrence of the offenses relating to standing or parking. A vehicle released to a legal owner under this subdivision is a repossessed vehicle for purposes of disposition or sale. The impounding agency shall have a lien on any surplus that remains upon sale of the vehicle to which the registered owner is or may be entitled, as security for the full amount of the parking penalties for all notices of parking violations issued for the vehicle and for all local administrative charges imposed pursuant to Section 22850.5. The legal owner shall promptly remit to, and deposit with, the agency responsible for processing notices of parking violations from that surplus, on receipt of that surplus, the full amount of the parking penalties for all notices of parking violations issued for the vehicle and for all local administrative charges imposed pursuant to Section 22850.5.

(5) The impounding agency that has a lien on the surplus that remains upon the sale of a vehicle to which a registered owner is entitled pursuant to paragraph (4) has a deficiency claim against the registered owner for the full amount of the parking penalties for all notices of parking violations issued for the vehicle and for all local administrative charges imposed pursuant to Section 22850.5, less the amount received from the sale of the vehicle.

(j) When a vehicle is found illegally parked and there are no license plates or other evidence of registration displayed, the vehicle may be impounded until the owner or person in control of the vehicle furnishes the impounding law enforcement agency evidence of his or her identity and an address within this state at which he or she can be located.

(k) When a vehicle is parked or left standing upon a highway for 72 or more consecutive hours in violation of a local ordinance authorizing removal.

(l) When a vehicle is illegally parked on a highway in violation of a local ordinance forbidding standing or parking and the use of a highway, or a portion thereof, is necessary for the cleaning, repair, or construction of the highway, or for the installation of underground utilities, and signs giving notice that the vehicle may be removed are erected or placed at least 24 hours prior to the removal by a local authority pursuant to the ordinance.

(m) When the use of the highway, or a portion of the highway, is authorized by a local authority for a purpose other than the normal flow of traffic or for the movement of equipment, articles, or structures of unusual size, and the parking of a vehicle would prohibit or interfere with that use or movement, and signs giving notice that the vehicle may be removed are erected or placed at least 24 hours prior to the removal by a local authority pursuant to the ordinance.

(n) Whenever a vehicle is parked or left standing where local authorities, by resolution or ordinance, have prohibited parking and have authorized the removal of vehicles. Except as provided in subdivisions (v) and (w), a vehicle shall not be removed unless signs are posted giving notice of the removal.

(o)(1) When a vehicle is found or operated upon a highway, public land, or an offstreet parking facility under the following circumstances:

(A) With a registration expiration date in excess of six months before the date it is found or operated on the highway, public lands, or the offstreet parking facility.

(B) Displaying in, or upon, the vehicle, a registration card, identification card, temporary receipt, license plate, special plate, registration sticker, device issued pursuant to Section 4853, or permit that was not issued for that vehicle, or is not otherwise lawfully used on that vehicle under this code.

(C) Displaying in, or upon, the vehicle, an altered, forged, counterfeit, or falsified registration card, identification card, temporary receipt, license plate, special plate, registration sticker, device issued pursuant to Section 4853, or permit.

(2) When a vehicle described in paragraph (1) is occupied, only a peace officer, as defined in Chapter 4.5 (commencing with Section 830) of Title 3 of Part 2 of the Penal Code, may remove the vehicle.

(3) For the purposes of this subdivision, the vehicle shall be released under either of the following circumstances:

(A) To the registered owner or person in control of the vehicle only after the owner or person furnishes the storing law enforcement agency with proof of current registration and a currently valid driver's license to operate the vehicle.

(B) To the legal owner or the legal owner's agency, without payment of any fees, fines, or penalties for parking tickets or registration and without proof of current registration, if the vehicle will only be transported pursuant to the exemption specified in Section 4022 and if the legal owner does all of the following:

(i) Pays the cost of towing and storing the vehicle.

(ii) Completes an affidavit in a form acceptable to the impounding law enforcement agency stating that the vehicle was not in possession of the legal owner at the time of occurrence of an offense relating to standing or parking. A vehicle released to a legal owner under this subdivision is a repossessed vehicle for purposes of disposition or sale. The impounding agency has a lien on any surplus that remains upon sale of the vehicle to which the registered owner is or may be entitled, as security for the full amount of parking penalties for any notices of parking violations issued for the vehicle and for all local administrative charges imposed pursuant to Section 22850.5. Upon receipt of any surplus, the legal owner shall promptly remit to, and deposit with, the agency responsible for processing notices of parking violations from that surplus, the full amount of the parking penalties for all notices of parking violations issued for the vehicle and for all local administrative charges imposed pursuant to Section 22850.5.

(4) The impounding agency that has a lien on the surplus that remains upon the sale of a vehicle to which a registered owner is entitled has a deficiency claim against the registered owner for the full amount of parking penalties for any notices of parking violations issued for the vehicle and for all local administrative charges imposed pursuant to Section 22850.5, less the amount received from the sale of the vehicle.

(5) As used in this subdivision, "offstreet parking facility" means an offstreet facility held open for use by the public for parking vehicles and includes a publicly owned facility for offstreet parking, and a privately owned facility for offstreet parking if a fee is not charged for the privilege to park and it is held open for the common public use of retail customers.

(p) When the peace officer issues the driver of a vehicle a notice to appear for a violation of Section 12500, 14601, 14601.1, 14601.2, 14601.3, 14601.4, 14601.5, or 14604 and the vehicle is not impounded pursuant to Section 22655.5. A vehicle so removed from the highway or public land, or from private property after having been on a highway or public land, shall not be released to the registered owner or his or her agent, except upon presentation of the registered owner's or his or her agent's currently valid driver's license to operate the vehicle and proof of current vehicle registration, to the impounding law enforcement agency, or upon order of a court.

(q) When a vehicle is parked for more than 24 hours on a portion of highway that is located within the boundaries of a common interest development, as defined in Section 4100 or 6534 of the Civil Code, and signs, as required by paragraph (1) of subdivision (a) of Section 22658 of this code, have been posted on that portion of highway providing notice to drivers that vehicles parked thereon for more than 24 hours will be removed at the owner's expense, pursuant to a resolution or ordinance adopted by the local authority.

(r) When a vehicle is illegally parked and blocks the movement of a legally parked vehicle.

(s)(1) When a vehicle, except highway maintenance or construction equipment, an authorized emergency vehicle, or a vehicle that is properly permitted or otherwise authorized by the Department of Transportation, is stopped, parked, or left standing for more than eight hours within a roadside rest area or viewpoint.

(2) Notwithstanding paragraph (1), when a commercial motor vehicle, as defined in paragraph (1) of subdivision (b) of Section 15210, is stopped, parked, or left standing for more than 10 hours within a roadside rest area or viewpoint.

(3) For purposes of this subdivision, a roadside rest area or viewpoint is a publicly maintained vehicle parking area, adjacent to a highway, utilized for the convenient, safe stopping of a vehicle to enable motorists to rest or to view the scenery. If two or more roadside rest areas are located on opposite sides of the highway, or upon the center divider, within seven miles of each other, then that combination of rest areas is considered to be the same rest area.

(t) When a peace officer issues a notice to appear for a violation of Section 25279.

(u) When a peace officer issues a citation for a violation of Section 11700 and the vehicle is being offered for sale.

(v)(1) When a vehicle is a mobile billboard advertising display, as defined in Section 395.5, and is parked or left standing in violation of a local resolution or ordinance adopted pursuant to subdivision (m) of Section 21100, if the registered owner of the vehicle was previously issued a warning citation for the same offense, pursuant to paragraph (2).

(2) Notwithstanding subdivision (a) of Section 22507, a city or county, in lieu of posting signs noticing a local ordinance prohibiting mobile billboard advertising displays adopted pursuant to subdivision (m) of Section 21100, may provide notice by issuing a warning citation advising the registered owner of the vehicle that he or she may be subject to penalties upon a subsequent violation of the ordinance, that may include the removal of the vehicle as provided in paragraph (1). A city or county is not required to provide further notice for a subsequent violation prior to the enforcement of penalties for a violation of the ordinance.

(w)(1) When a vehicle is parked or left standing in violation of a local ordinance or resolution adopted pursuant to subdivision (p) of Section 21100, if the registered owner of the vehicle was previously issued a warning citation for the same offense, pursuant to paragraph (2).

(2) Notwithstanding subdivision (a) of Section 22507, a city or county, in lieu of posting signs noticing a local ordinance regulating advertising signs adopted pursuant to subdivision (p) of Section 21100, may provide notice by issuing a warning citation advising the registered owner of the vehicle that he or she may be subject to penalties upon a subsequent violation of the ordinance that may include the removal of the vehicle as provided in paragraph (1). A city or county is not required to provide further notice for a subsequent violation prior to the enforcement of penalties for a violation of the ordinance. *(AM '13)*

22651.05. Removal of Vehicles by Trained Volunteers; Requirements

(a) A trained volunteer of a state or local law enforcement agency, who is engaged in directing traffic or enforcing parking laws and regulations, of a city, county, or jurisdiction of a state agency in which a vehicle is located, may remove or authorize the removal of a vehicle located within the territorial limits in which an officer or employee of that agency may act, under any of the following circumstances:

(1) When a vehicle is parked or left standing upon a highway for 72 or more consecutive hours in violation of a local ordinance authorizing the removal.

(2) When a vehicle is illegally parked or left standing on a highway in violation of a local ordinance forbidding standing or parking and the use of a highway, or a portion thereof, is necessary for the cleaning, repair, or construction of the highway, or for the installation of underground utilities, and signs giving notice that the vehicle may be removed are erected or placed at least 24 hours prior to the removal by local authorities pursuant to the ordinance.

(3) Wherever the use of the highway, or a portion thereof, is authorized by local authorities for a purpose other than the normal flow of traffic or for the movement of equipment, articles, or structures of unusual size, and the parking of a vehicle would prohibit or interfere with that use or movement, and signs giving notice that the vehicle may be removed are erected or placed at least 24 hours prior to the removal by local authorities pursuant to the ordinance.

(4) Whenever a vehicle is parked or left standing where local authorities, by resolution or ordinance, have prohibited parking and have authorized the removal of vehicles. A vehicle may not be removed unless signs are posted giving notice of the removal.

(5) Whenever a vehicle is parked for more than 24 hours on a portion of highway that is located within the boundaries of a common interest development, as defined in ***Section ***4100 or 6534 of the Civil Code, and signs, as required by Section 22658.2, have been posted on that portion of highway providing notice to drivers that vehicles parked thereon for more than 24 hours will be removed at the owner***'s expense, pursuant to a resolution or ordinance adopted by the local authority.

(b) The provisions of this chapter that apply to a vehicle removed pursuant to Section 22651 apply to a vehicle removed pursuant to subdivision (a).

(c) For purposes of subdivision (a), a "trained volunteer" is a person who, of his or her own free will, provides services, without any financial gain, to a local or state law enforcement agency, and who is duly trained and certified to remove a vehicle by a local or state law enforcement agency. *(AM '13; Op 1-1-2014)*

22651.1. Towing or Storage Charges

Persons operating or in charge of any storage facility where vehicles are stored pursuant to Section 22651 shall accept a valid bank credit card or cash for payment of towing and storage by the registered owner, legal owner, or the owner's agent claiming the vehicle. A credit card shall be in the name of the person presenting the card. "Credit card" means "credit card" as defined in subdivision (a) of Section 1747.02 of the Civil Code, except, for the purposes of this section, credit card does not include a credit card issued by a retail seller. A person operating or in charge of any storage facility who refuses to accept a valid bank credit card shall be liable to the owner of the vehicle or to the person who tendered the fees for four times the amount of the towing and storage charges, but not to exceed five hundred dollars ($500). In addition, persons operating or in charge of the storage facility shall have sufficient funds on the premises to accommodate and make change in a reasonable monetary transaction.

Credit charges for towing and storage services shall comply with Section 1748.1 of the Civil Code. Law enforcement agencies may include the costs of providing for payment by credit when agreeing with a towing or storage provider on rates. *(AM '09)*

22651.2. Removal of Vehicle

(a) Any peace officer, as defined in Chapter 4.5 (commencing with Section 830) of Title 3 of Part 2 of the Penal Code, or any regularly employed and salaried employee, who is engaged in directing traffic or enforcing parking laws and regulations of a city, county, or jurisdiction of a state agency in which a vehicle is located, may remove a vehicle located within the territorial limits in which the officer or employee may act when the vehicle is found upon a highway or any public lands, and if all of the following requirements are satisfied:

(1) Because of the size and placement of signs or placards on the vehicle, it appears that the primary purpose of parking the vehicle at that location is to advertise to the public an event or function on private property or on public property hired for a private event or function to which the public is invited.

(2) The vehicle is known to have been previously issued a notice of parking violation that was accompanied by a notice warning that an additional parking violation may result in the impoundment of the vehicle.

(3) The registered owner of the vehicle has been mailed a notice advising of the existence of the parking violation and that an additional violation may result in the impoundment of the vehicle.

(b) Subdivision (a) does not apply to a vehicle bearing any sign or placard advertising any business or enterprise carried on by or through the use of that vehicle.

(c) Section 22852 applies to the removal of any vehicle pursuant to this section.

22651.3. Offstreet Parking Facility: Removal and Impoundment

(a) Any peace officer, as that term is defined in Chapter 4.5 (commencing with Section 830) of Title 3 of Part 2 of the Penal Code, or any regularly employed and salaried employee, who is engaged in directing traffic or enforcing parking laws and regulations, of a city, county, or jurisdiction of a state agency in which any vehicle, other than a rented vehicle, is located may remove the vehicle from an offstreet public parking facility located within the territorial limits in which the officer or employee may act when the vehicle is known to have been issued five or more notices of parking violation over a period of five or more days, to which the owner or person in control of the vehicle has not responded or when any vehicle is illegally parked so as to prevent the movement of a legally parked vehicle.

A notice of parking violation issued to a vehicle which is registered in a foreign jurisdiction or is without current California registration and is known to have been issued five or more notices of parking violation over a period of five or more days shall be accompanied by a warning that repeated violations may result in the impounding of the vehicle.

(b) The vehicle may be impounded until the owner or person in control of the vehicle furnishes to the impounding law enforcement agency evidence of his or her identity and an address within this state at which he or she can be located and furnishes satisfactory evidence that bail has been deposited for all notices of parking violation issued for the vehicle. In lieu of requiring satisfactory evidence that the bail has been deposited, the impounding law enforcement agency may, in its discretion, issue a notice to appear for the offenses charged, as provided in Article 2 (commencing with Section 40500) of Chapter 2 of Division 17. In lieu of either furnishing satisfactory evidence that the bail has been deposited or accepting the notice to appear, the owner or person in control of the vehicle may demand to be taken without unnecessary delay before a magistrate within the county in which the offenses charged are alleged to have been committed and who has jurisdiction of the offenses and is nearest or most accessible with reference to the place where the vehicle is impounded.

(c) Evidence of current registration shall be produced after a vehicle has been impounded. At the discretion of the impounding law enforcement agency, a notice to appear for violation of subdivision (a) of Section 4000 may be issued to the owner or person in control of the vehicle, if the two days immediately following the day of impoundment are weekend days or holidays.

22651.4. Foreign Commercial Vehicle Impound

(a) A peace officer, as defined in Chapter 4.5 (commencing with Section 830) of Title 3 of Part 2 of the Penal Code, may impound a vehicle and its cargo pursuant to Section 34517.

(b) A member of the department may impound a vehicle and its cargo pursuant to Section 34518.

(c) A member of the department may store or impound a vehicle upon determination that the registrant of the vehicle or the driver of the vehicle has failed to pay registration, regulatory, fuel permit, or other fees, or has an outstanding warrant in a county in the state. The impoundment charges are the responsibility of the owner of the vehicle. The stored or impounded vehicle shall be released upon payment of those fees or fines or the posting of bail. The driver or owner of the vehicle may request a hearing to determine the validity of the seizure. *(AM '06)*

22651.5. Additional Circumstances Permitting Removal

(a) Any peace officer, as defined in Chapter 4.5 (commencing with Section 830) of Title 3 of Part 2 of the Penal Code, or any regularly employed and salaried employee who is engaged in directing traffic or enforcing parking laws or regulations, may, upon the complaint of any person, remove a vehicle parked within 500 feet of any occupied building of a school, community college, or university during normal hours of operation, or a vehicle parked within a residence or business district, from a highway or from public or private property, if an alarm device or horn has been activated within the vehicle, whether continuously activated or intermittently and repeatedly activated, the peace officer or designated employee is unable to locate the owner of the vehicle within 20 minutes from the time of arrival at the vehicle's location, and the alarm device or horn has not been completely silenced prior to removal.

(b) Upon removal of a vehicle from a highway or from public or private property pursuant to this section, the peace officer or designated employee ordering the removal shall immediately report the removal and the location to which the vehicle is removed to the Stolen Vehicle System of the Department of Justice.

22651.6. Removal of Vehicle Used in Speed Contest

A peace officer or employee specified in Section 22651 may remove a vehicle located within the territorial limits in which the officer or employee may act when the vehicle was used by a person who was engaged in a motor vehicle speed contest, as described in subdivision (a) of Section 23109, and the person was arrested and taken into custody for that offense by a peace officer.

22651.7. Immobilization

(a) In addition to, or as an alternative to, removal, a peace officer, as defined in Chapter 4.5 (commencing with Section 830) of Title 3 of Part 2 of the Penal Code, or a regularly employed and salaried employee who is engaged in directing traffic or enforcing parking laws and regulations, of a jurisdiction in which a vehicle is located may immobilize the vehicle with a device designed and manufactured for the immobilization of vehicles, on a highway or any public lands located within the territorial limits in which the officer or employee may act if the vehicle is found upon a highway or public lands and it is known to have been issued five or more notices of parking violations that are delinquent because the owner or person in control of the vehicle has not responded to the agency responsible for processing notices of parking violation within 21 calendar days of notice of citation issuance or citation issuance or 14 calendar days of the mailing of a notice of delinquent parking violation, or the registered owner of the vehicle is known to have been issued five or more notices for failure to pay or failure to appear in court for traffic violations for which no certificate has been issued by the magistrate or clerk of the court hearing the case showing that the case has been adjudicated or concerning which the registered owner's record has not been cleared pursuant to Chapter 6 (commencing with Section 41500) of Division 17. The vehicle may be immobilized until that person furnishes to the immobilizing law enforcement agency all of the following:

(1) Evidence of his or her identity.

(2) An address within this state at which he or she can be located.

(3) Satisfactory evidence that the full amount of parking penalties has been deposited for all notices of parking violation issued for the vehicle and any other vehicle registered to the registered owner of the immobilized vehicle and that bail has been deposited for all traffic violations of the registered owner that have not been cleared. The requirements in this paragraph shall be fully enforced by the immobilizing law enforcement agency on and after the time that the Department of Motor Vehicles is able to provide access to the necessary records. A notice of parking violation issued to the vehicle shall be accompanied by a warning that repeated violations may result in the impounding or immobilization of the vehicle. In lieu of furnishing satisfactory evidence that the full amount of parking penalties or bail, or both, have been deposited that person may demand to be taken without unnecessary delay before a magistrate, for traffic offenses, or a hearing examiner, for parking offenses, within the county in which the offenses charged are alleged to have been committed and who has jurisdiction of the offenses and is nearest or most accessible with reference to

the place where the vehicle is immobilized. Evidence of current registration shall be produced after a vehicle has been immobilized or, at the discretion of the immobilizing law enforcement agency, a notice to appear for violation of subdivision (a) of Section 4000 shall be issued to that person.

(b) A person, other than a person authorized under subdivision (a), shall not immobilize a vehicle. *(AM '06)*

22651.8. "Satisfactory Evidence" of Parking Violation Bail

For purposes of paragraph (1) of subdivision (i) of Section 22651 and Section 22651.7, "satisfactory evidence" includes, but is not limited to, a copy of a receipt issued by the department pursuant to subdivision (a) of Section 4760 for payment of notices of parking violations appearing on the department's records at the time of payment. The processing agency shall, within 72 hours of receiving that satisfactory evidence, update its records to reflect the payments made to the department. If the processing agency does not receive the amount of the parking penalties and administrative fees from the department within four months of the date of issuance of that satisfactory evidence, the processing agency may revise its records to reflect that no payments were received for the notices of parking violation.

22651.9 Removal of Advertised "For Sale" Parked Vehicle

(a) Any peace officer, as defined in Chapter 4.5 (commencing with Section 830) of Title 3 of Part 2 of the Penal Code, or any regularly employed and salaried employee, who is engaged in directing traffic or enforcing parking laws and regulations, of a city, county, or city and county in which a vehicle is located, may remove a vehicle located within the territorial limits in which the officer or employee may act when the vehicle is found upon a street or any public lands, if all of the following requirements are satisfied:

(1) Because of a sign or placard on the vehicle, it appears that the primary purpose of parking the vehicle at that location is to advertise to the public the private sale of that vehicle.

(2) Within the past 30 days, the vehicle is known to have been previously issued a notice of parking violation, under local ordinance, which was accompanied by a notice containing all of the following:

(A) A warning that an additional parking violation may result in the impounding of the vehicle.

(B) A warning that the vehicle may be impounded pursuant to this section, even if moved to another street, so long as the signs or placards offering the vehicle for sale remain on the vehicle.

(C) A listing of the streets or public lands subject to the resolution or ordinance adopted pursuant to paragraph (4), or if all streets covered, a statement to that effect.

(3) The notice of parking violation was issued at least 24 hours prior to the removal of the vehicle.

(4) The local authority of the city, county, or city and county has, by resolution or ordinance, authorized the removal of vehicles pursuant to this section from the street or public lands on which the vehicle is located.

22652. Removal from Handicapped Persons' Parking Spaces

(a) A peace officer, as defined in Chapter 4.5 (commencing with Section 830) of Title 3 of Part 2 of the Penal Code, or any regularly employed and salaried employee engaged in directing traffic or enforcing parking laws and regulations of a city, county, or jurisdiction of a state agency may remove any vehicle from a stall or space designated for physically disabled persons pursuant to Section 22511.7 or 22511.8, located within the jurisdictional limits in which the officer or employee is authorized to act, if the vehicle is parked in violation of Section 22507.8 and if the police or sheriff's department or the Department of the California Highway Patrol is notified.

(b) In a privately or publicly owned or operated offstreet parking facility, this section applies only to those stalls and spaces if the posting requirements under subdivisions (a) and (d) of Section 22511.8 have been complied with and if the stalls or spaces are clearly signed or marked. *(AM '04)*

22652.6. Vehicle Removal; Violation of Local Ordinance or Resolution

Any peace officer, as defined in Chapter 4.5 (commencing with Section 830) of Title 3 of Part 2 of the Penal Code, or any regularly employed and salaried employee engaged in directing traffic or enforcing parking laws and regulations of a city or county, may remove any vehicle parked or standing on the streets or highways or from a stall or space of a privately or publicly owned or operated offstreet parking facility within the jurisdiction of the city or county when the vehicle is in violation of a local ordinance or resolution adopted pursuant to Section 22511.57. *(AD '94)*

22653. Removal From Private Property: Stolen Vehicle

(a) Any peace officer, other than an employee directing traffic or enforcing parking laws and regulations, may remove a vehicle from private property located within the territorial limits in which the officer is empowered to act, when a report has previously been made that the vehicle has been stolen or a complaint has been filed and a warrant thereon issued charging that the vehicle has been embezzled.

(b) Any peace officer may, after a reasonable period of time, remove a vehicle from private property located within the territorial limits in which the officer is empowered to act, if the vehicle has been involved in, and left at the scene of, a traffic accident and no owner is available to grant permission to remove the vehicle. This subdivision does not authorize the removal of a vehicle where the owner has been contacted and has refused to grant permission to remove the vehicle.

(c) Any peace officer may, at the request of the property owner or person in lawful possession of any private property, remove a vehicle from private property located within the territorial limits in which the officer is empowered to act when an officer arrests any person driving or in control of a vehicle for an alleged offense and the officer is, by this code or other law, required or authorized to take, and does take the person arrested before a magistrate without unnecessary delay.

22654. Authorization for Moving a Vehicle

(a) Whenever any peace officer, or other employee directing traffic or enforcing parking laws and regulations, finds a vehicle standing upon a highway, located within the territorial limits in which the officer or employee is empowered to act, in violation of Sections 22500 and 22504, the officer or employee may move the vehicle or require the driver or other person in charge of the vehicle to move it to the nearest available position off the roadway or to the nearest parking location, or may remove and store the vehicle if moving it off the roadway to a parking location is impracticable.

(b) Whenever the officer or employee finds a vehicle standing upon a street, located within the territorial limits in which the officer or employee is empowered to act, in violation of a traffic ordinance enacted by local authorities to prevent flooding of adjacent property, he or she may move the vehicle or require the driver or person in charge of the vehicle to move it to the nearest available location in the vicinity where parking is permitted.

(c) Any state, county, or city authority charged with the maintenance of any highway may move any vehicle which is disabled or abandoned or which constitutes an obstruction to traffic from the place where it is located on a highway to the nearest available position on the same highway as may be necessary to keep the highway open or safe for public travel. In addition, employees of CalTrans may remove any disabled vehicle which constitutes an obstruction to traffic on a freeway from the place where it is located to the nearest available location where parking is permitted; and, if the vehicle is unoccupied, the department shall comply with the notice requirements of subdivision (d).

(d) Any state, county, or city authority charged with the maintenance or operation of any highway, highway facility, or public works facility, in cases necessitating the prompt performance of any work on or service to the highway, highway facility, or public works facility, may move to the nearest available location where parking is permitted, any unattended vehicle which obstructs or interferes with the performance of the work or service or may remove and store the vehicle if moving it off the roadway to a location where parking is permitted would be impracticable. If the vehicle is moved to another location where it is not readily visible from its former parked location or it is stored, the person causing the movement or storage of the vehicle shall immediately, by the most expeditious means, notify the owner of the vehicle of its location. If for any reason the vehicle owner cannot be so notified, the person causing the vehicle to be moved or stored shall immediately, by the most expeditious means, notify the police department of the city in which the vehicle was parked, or, if the vehicle had been parked in an unincorporated area of a county, notify the sheriffs department and nearest office of the CHP in that county. No vehicle may be removed and stored pursuant to this subdivision unless signs indicating that no person shall stop, park, or leave standing any vehicle within the areas marked by the signs because the work or service would be done, were placed at least 24 hours prior to the movement or removal and storage.

(e) Whenever any peace officer finds a vehicle parked or standing upon a highway in a manner so as to obstruct necessary emergency services, or the routing of traffic at the scene of a disaster, the officer may move the vehicle or require the driver or other person in charge of the vehicle to move it to the nearest available parking location. If the vehicle is unoccupied, and moving the vehicle to a parking location is impractical, the officer may store the vehicle pursuant to Sections 22850 and 22852 and subdivision (a) or (b) of Section 22853. If the vehicle so moved or stored was otherwise lawfully parked, no moving or storage charges shall be assessed against or collected from the driver or owner.

22655. Impounding Vehicle for Investigation

(a) When any peace officer, as that term is defined in Chapter 4.5 (commencing with Section 830) of Title 3 of Part 2 of the Penal Code or any regularly employed and salaried employee who is engaged in directing traffic or enforcing parking statutes and regulations, has reasonable cause to believe that a motor vehicle on a highway or on private property open to the general public onto which the public is explicitly or implicitly invited, located within the territorial limits in which the officer is empowered to act, has been involved in a hit-and-run accident, and the operator of the vehicle has failed to stop and comply with Sections 20002 to 20006, inclusive, the officer may remove the vehicle from the highway or from public or private property for the purpose of inspection.

(b) Unless sooner released, the vehicle shall be released upon the expiration of 48 hours after the removal from the highway or private property upon demand of the owner. When determining the 48-hour period, weekends, and holidays shall not be included.

(c) Notwithstanding subdivision (b), when a motor vehicle to be inspected pursuant to subdivision (a) is a commercial vehicle, any cargo within the vehicle may be removed or transferred to another vehicle.

This section shall not be construed to authorize the removal of any vehicle from an enclosed structure on private property that is not open to the general public.

22655.3. Removal for Investigation

Any peace officer pursuing a fleeing or evading person in a motor vehicle may remove and store, or cause to be removed and stored, any vehicle used in violation of Section 2800.1 or 2800.2 from property other than that of the registered owner of the vehicle for the purposes of investigation, identification, or apprehension of the driver if the driver of the vehicle abandons the vehicle and leaves it unattended. All towing and storage fees for a vehicle removed under this section shall be paid by the owner, unless the vehicle was stolen or taken without permission.

No vehicle shall be impounded under this section if the driver is arrested before arrival of the towing equipment or if the registered owner is in the vehicle.

As used in this section, "remove and store a vehicle" means that the peace officer may cause the removal of a vehicle to, and storage of a vehicle in, a private lot where the vehicle may be secured by the owner of the facility or by the owner's representative.

This section is not intended to change current statute and case law governing searches and seizures.

22655.5. Impounding for Evidence

A peace officer, as defined in Chapter 4.5 (commencing with Section 830) of Title 3 of Part 2 of the Penal Code, may remove a motor vehicle from the highway or from public or private property within the territorial limits in which the officer may act under the following circumstances:

(a) When any vehicle is found upon a highway or public or private property and a peace officer has probable cause to believe that the vehicle was used as the means of committing a public offense.

(b) When any vehicle is found upon a highway or public or private property and a peace officer has probable cause to believe that the vehicle is itself evidence which tends to show that a crime has been committed or that the vehicle contains evidence, which cannot readily be removed, which tends to show that a crime has been committed.

(c) Notwithstanding Section 3068 of the Civil Code or Section 22851 of this code, no lien shall attach to a vehicle removed under this section unless the vehicle was used by the alleged perpetrator of the crime with the express or implied permission of the owner of the vehicle.

(d) In any prosecution of the crime for which a vehicle was impounded pursuant to this section, the prosecutor may request, and the court may order, the perpetrator of the crime, if convicted, to pay the costs of towing and storage of the vehicle, and any administrative charges imposed pursuant to Section 22850.5.

(e) This section shall become operative on January 1, 1993.

22656. Removal from Railroad Right-of-Way

Any peace officer, as that term is defined in Chapter 4.5 (commencing with Section 830) of Title 3 of Part 2 of the Penal Code, may remove a vehicle from the right-of-way of a railroad, street railway, or light rail line located within the territorial limits in which the officer is empowered to act if the vehicle is parked or abandoned upon any track or within 7½ feet of the nearest rail. The officer may also remove a vehicle that is parked beyond 7½ feet of the nearest rail but within the right-of-way of a railroad, street railway, or light rail if signs are posted giving notice that vehicles may be removed. *(AM '02)*

22658. Removal From Private Property: When Sign Posted

(a) The owner or person in lawful possession of private property, including an association of a common interest development as defined in Sections 4080 and 4100 or Sections 6528 and 6534 of the Civil Code, may cause the removal of a vehicle parked on the property to a storage facility that meets the requirements of subdivision (n) under any of the following circumstances:

(1) There is displayed, in plain view at all entrances to the property, a sign not less than 17 inches by 22 inches in size, with lettering not less than one inch in height, prohibiting public parking and indicating that vehicles will be removed at the owner's expense, and containing the telephone number of the local traffic law enforcement agency and the name and telephone number of each towing company that is a party to a written general towing authorization agreement with the owner or person in lawful possession of the property. The sign may also indicate that a citation may also be issued for the violation.

(2) The vehicle has been issued a notice of parking violation, and 96 hours have elapsed since the issuance of that notice.

(3) The vehicle is on private property and lacks an engine, transmission, wheels, tires,

doors, windshield, or any other major part or equipment necessary to operate safely on the highways, the owner or person in lawful possession of the private property has notified the local traffic law enforcement agency, and 24 hours have elapsed since that notification.

(4) The lot or parcel upon which the vehicle is parked is improved with a single-family dwelling.

(b) The tow truck operator removing the vehicle, if the operator knows or is able to ascertain from the property owner, person in lawful possession of the property, or the registration records of the Department of Motor Vehicles the name and address of the registered and legal owner of the vehicle, shall immediately give, or cause to be given, notice in writing to the registered and legal owner of the fact of the removal, the grounds for the removal, and indicate the place to which the vehicle has been removed. If the vehicle is stored in a storage facility, a copy of the notice shall be given to the proprietor of the storage facility. The notice provided for in this section shall include the amount of mileage on the vehicle at the time of removal and the time of the removal from the property. If the tow truck operator does not know and is not able to ascertain the name of the owner or for any other reason is unable to give the notice to the owner as provided in this section, the tow truck operator shall comply with the requirements of subdivision (c) of Section 22853 relating to notice in the same manner as applicable to an officer removing a vehicle from private property.

(c) This section does not limit or affect any right or remedy that the owner or person in lawful possession of private property may have by virtue of other provisions of law authorizing the removal of a vehicle parked upon private property.

(d) The owner of a vehicle removed from private property pursuant to subdivision (a) may recover for any damage to the vehicle resulting from any intentional or negligent act of a person causing the removal of, or removing, the vehicle.

(e)(1) An owner or person in lawful possession of private property, or an association of a common interest development, causing the removal of a vehicle parked on that property is liable for double the storage or towing charges whenever there has been a failure to comply with paragraph (1), (2), or (3) of subdivision (a) or to state the grounds for the removal of the vehicle if requested by the legal or registered owner of the vehicle as required by subdivision (f).

(2) A property owner or owner's agent or lessee who causes the removal of a vehicle parked on that property pursuant to the exemption set forth in subparagraph (A) of paragraph (1) of subdivision (l) and fails to comply with that subdivision is guilty of an infraction, punishable by a fine of one thousand dollars ($1,000).

(f) An owner or person in lawful possession of private property, or an association of a common interest development, causing the removal of a vehicle parked on that property shall notify by telephone or, if impractical, by the most expeditious means available, the local traffic law enforcement agency within one hour after authorizing the tow. An owner or person in lawful possession of private property, an association of a common interest development, causing the removal of a vehicle parked on that property, or the tow truck operator who removes the vehicle, shall state the grounds for the removal of the vehicle if requested by the legal or registered owner of that vehicle. A towing company that removes a vehicle from private property in compliance with subdivision (l) is not responsible in a situation relating to the validity of the removal. A towing company that removes the vehicle under this section shall be responsible for the following:

(1) Damage to the vehicle in the transit and subsequent storage of the vehicle.

(2) The removal of a vehicle other than the vehicle specified by the owner or other person in lawful possession of the private property.

(g)(1)(A) Possession of a vehicle under this section shall be deemed to arise when a vehicle is removed from private property and is in transit.

(B) Upon the request of the owner of the vehicle or that owner's agent, the towing company or its driver shall immediately and unconditionally release a vehicle that is not yet removed from the private property and in transit.

(C) A person failing to comply with subparagraph (B) is guilty of a misdemeanor.

(2) If a vehicle is released to a person in compliance with subparagraph (B) of paragraph (1), the vehicle owner or authorized agent shall immediately move that vehicle to a lawful location.

(h) A towing company may impose a charge of not more than one-half of the regular towing charge for the towing of a vehicle at the request of the owner, the owner's agent, or the person in lawful possession of the private property pursuant to this section if the owner of the vehicle or the vehicle owner's agent returns to the vehicle after the vehicle is coupled to the tow truck by means of a regular hitch, coupling device, drawbar, portable dolly, or is lifted off the ground by means of a conventional trailer, and before it is removed from the private property. The regular towing charge may only be imposed after the vehicle has been removed from the property and is in transit.

(i)(1)(A) A charge for towing or storage, or both, of a vehicle under this section is excessive if the charge exceeds the greater of the following:

(i) That which would have been charged for that towing or storage, or both, made at the request of a law enforcement agency under an agreement between a towing company and the law enforcement agency that exercises primary jurisdiction in the city in which is located the private property from which the vehicle was, or was attempted to be, removed, or if the private property is not located within a city, then the law enforcement agency that exercises primary jurisdiction in the county in which the private property is located.

(ii) That which would have been charged for that towing or storage, or both, under the rate approved for that towing operator by the Department of the California Highway Patrol for the jurisdiction in which the private property is located and from which the vehicle was, or was attempted to be, removed.

(B) A towing operator shall make available for inspection and copying his or her rate approved by the Department of the California Highway Patrol, if any, within 24 hours of a request without a warrant to law enforcement, the Attorney General, district attorney, or city attorney.

(2) If a vehicle is released within 24 hours from the time the vehicle is brought into the storage facility, regardless of the calendar date, the storage charge shall be for only one day. Not more than one day's storage charge may be required for a vehicle released the same day that it is stored.

(3) If a request to release a vehicle is made and the appropriate fees are tendered and documentation establishing that the person requesting release is entitled to possession of the vehicle, or is the owner's insurance representative, is presented within the initial 24 hours of storage, and the storage facility fails to comply with the request to release the vehicle or is not open for business during normal business hours, then only one day's storage charge may be required to be paid until after the first business day. A business day is any day in which the lienholder is open for business to the public for at least eight hours. If a request is made more than 24 hours after the vehicle is placed in storage, charges may be imposed on a full calendar day basis for each day, or part thereof, that the vehicle is in storage.

(j)(1) A person who charges a vehicle owner a towing, service, or storage charge at an excessive rate, as described in subdivision (h) or (i), is civilly liable to the vehicle owner for four times the amount charged.

(2) A person who knowingly charges a vehicle owner a towing, service, or storage charge at an excessive rate, as described in subdivision (h) or (i), or who fails to make available his or her rate as required in subparagraph (B) of paragraph (1) of subdivision (i), is guilty of a misdemeanor, punishable by a fine of not more than two thousand five hundred dollars ($2,500), or by imprisonment in ***a county jail for not more than three months, or by both that fine and imprisonment.

(k)(1) A person operating or in charge of a storage facility where vehicles are stored pursuant to this section shall accept a valid bank credit card or cash for payment of towing and storage by a registered owner, the legal owner, or the owner's agent claiming the vehicle. A credit card shall be in the name of the person presenting the card. "Credit card"means "credit card"as defined in subdivision (a) of Section 1747.02 of the Civil Code, except, for the purposes of this section, credit card does not include a credit card issued by a retail seller.

(2) A person described in paragraph (1) shall conspicuously display, in that portion of the storage facility office where business is conducted with the public, a notice advising that all valid credit cards and cash are acceptable means of payment.

(3) A person operating or in charge of a storage facility who refuses to accept a valid credit card or who fails to post the required notice under paragraph (2) is guilty of a misdemeanor, punishable by a fine of not more than two thousand five hundred dollars ($2,500), or by imprisonment in ***a county jail for not more than three months, or by both that fine and imprisonment.

(4) A person described in paragraph (1) who violates paragraph (1) or (2) is civilly liable to the registered owner of the vehicle or the person who tendered the fees for four times the amount of the towing and storage charges.

(5) A person operating or in charge of the storage facility shall have sufficient moneys on the premises of the primary storage facility during normal business hours to accommodate, and make change in, a reasonable monetary transaction.

(6) Credit charges for towing and storage services shall comply with Section 1748.1 of the Civil Code. Law enforcement agencies may include the costs of providing for payment by credit when making agreements with towing companies as described in subdivision (i).

(l)(1)(A) A towing company shall not remove or commence the removal of a vehicle from private property without first obtaining the written authorization from the property owner or lessee, including an association of a common interest development, or an employee or agent thereof, who shall be present at the time of removal and verify the alleged violation, except that presence and verification is not required if the person authorizing the tow is the property owner, or the owner's agent who is not a tow operator, of a residential rental property of 15 or fewer units that does not have an onsite owner, owner's agent or employee, and the tenant has verified the violation, requested the tow from that tenant's assigned parking space, and provided a signed request or electronic mail, or has called and provides a signed request or electronic mail within 24 hours, to the property owner or owner's agent, which the owner or agent shall provide to the towing company within 48 hours of authorizing the tow. The signed request or electronic mail shall contain the name and address of the tenant, and the date and time the tenant requested the tow. A towing company shall obtain, within 48 hours of receiving the written authorization to tow, a copy of a tenant request required pursuant to this subparagraph. For the purpose of this subparagraph, a person providing the written authorization who is required to be present on the private property at the time of the tow does not have to be physically present at the specified location of where the vehicle to be removed is located on the private property.

(B) The written authorization under subparagraph (A) shall include all of the following:

(i) The make, model, vehicle identification number, and license plate number of the removed vehicle.

(ii) The name, signature, job title, residential or business address, and working telephone number of the person, described in subparagraph (A), authorizing the removal of the vehicle.

(iii) The grounds for the removal of the vehicle.

(iv) The time when the vehicle was first observed parked at the private property.

(v) The time that authorization to tow the vehicle was given.

(C)(i) When the vehicle owner or his or her agent claims the vehicle, the towing company prior to payment of a towing or storage charge shall provide a photocopy of the written authorization to the vehicle owner or the agent.

(ii) If the vehicle was towed from a residential property, the towing company shall redact the information specified in clause (ii) of subparagraph (B) in the photocopy of the written authorization provided to the vehicle owner or the agent pursuant to clause (i).

(iii) The towing company shall also provide to the vehicle owner or the agent a separate notice that provides the telephone number of the appropriate local law enforcement or prosecuting agency by stating "If you believe that you have been wrongfully towed, please contact the local law enforcement or prosecuting agency at _insert appropriate telephone number]."The notice shall be in English and in the most populous language, other than English, that is spoken in the jurisdiction.

(D) A towing company shall not remove or commence the removal of a vehicle from private property described in subdivision (a) of Section 22953 unless the towing company has made a good faith inquiry to determine that the owner or the property owner's agent complied with Section 22953.

(E)(i) General authorization to remove or commence removal of a vehicle at the towing company's discretion shall not be delegated to a towing company or its affiliates except in the case of a vehicle unlawfully parked within 15 feet of a fire hydrant or in a fire lane, or in a manner which interferes with an entrance to, or exit from, the private property.

(ii) In those cases in which general authorization is granted to a towing company or its affiliate to undertake the removal or commence the removal of a vehicle that is unlawfully parked within 15 feet of a fire hydrant or in a fire lane, or that interferes with an entrance to, or exit from, private property, the towing company and the property owner, or owner's agent, or person in lawful possession of the private property shall have a written agreement granting that general authorization.

(2) If a towing company removes a vehicle under a general authorization described in subparagraph (E) of paragraph (1) and that vehicle is unlawfully parked within 15 feet of a fire hydrant or in a fire lane, or in a manner that interferes with an entrance to, or exit from, the private property, the towing company shall take, prior to the removal of that vehicle, a photograph of the vehicle that clearly indicates that parking violation. Prior to accepting payment, the towing company shall keep one copy of the photograph taken pursuant to this paragraph, and shall present that photograph and provide, without charge, a photocopy to the owner or an agent of the owner, when that person claims the vehicle.

(3) A towing company shall maintain the original written authorization, or the general authorization described in subparagraph (E) of paragraph (1) and the photograph of the violation, required pursuant to this section, and any written requests from a tenant to the property owner or owner's agent required by subparagraph (A) of paragraph (1), for a period of three years and shall make them available for inspection and copying within 24 hours of a request without a warrant to law enforcement, the Attorney General, district attorney, or city attorney.

(4) A person who violates this subdivision is guilty of a misdemeanor, punishable by a fine of not more than two thousand five hundred dollars ($2,500), or by imprisonment in ***a county jail for not more than three months, or by both that fine and imprisonment.

(5) A person who violates this subdivision is civilly liable to the owner of the vehicle or his or her agent for four times the amount of the towing and storage charges.

(m)(1) A towing company that removes a vehicle from private property under this section shall notify the local law enforcement agency of that tow after the vehicle is removed from the private property and is in transit.

(2) A towing company is guilty of a misdemeanor if the towing company fails to provide the notification required under paragraph (1) within 60 minutes after the vehicle is removed from the private property and is in transit or 15 minutes after arriving at the storage facility, whichever time is less.

(3) A towing company that does not provide the notification under paragraph (1) within 30 minutes after the vehicle is removed from the private property and is in transit is civilly liable to the registered owner of the vehicle, or the person who tenders the fees, for three times the amount of the towing and storage charges.

(4) If notification is impracticable, the times for notification, as required pursuant to paragraphs (2) and (3), shall be tolled for the time period that notification is impracticable. This paragraph is an affirmative defense.

(n) A vehicle removed from private property pursuant to this section shall be stored in a facility that meets all of the following requirements:

(1)(A) Is located within a 10-mile radius of the property from where the vehicle was removed.

(B) The 10-mile radius requirement of subparagraph (A) does not apply if a towing company has prior general written approval from the law enforcement agency that exercises primary jurisdiction in the city in which is located the private property from which the vehicle was removed, or if the private property is not located within a city, then the law enforcement agency that exercises primary jurisdiction in the county in which is located the private property.

(2)(A) Remains open during normal business hours and releases vehicles after normal business hours.

(B) A gate fee may be charged for releasing a vehicle after normal business hours, weekends, and state holidays. However, the maximum hourly charge for releasing a vehicle after normal business hours shall be one-half of the hourly tow rate charged for initially towing the vehicle, or less.

(C) Notwithstanding any other provision of law and for purposes of this paragraph, "normal business hours" are Monday to Friday, inclusive, from 8 a.m. to 5 p.m., inclusive, except state holidays.

(3) Has a public pay telephone in the office area that is open and accessible to the public.

(o)(1) It is the intent of the Legislature in the adoption of subdivision (k) to assist vehicle owners or their agents by, among other things, allowing payment by credit cards for towing and storage services, thereby expediting the recovery of towed vehicles and concurrently promoting the safety and welfare of the public.

(2) It is the intent of the Legislature in the adoption of subdivision (l) to further the safety of the general public by ensuring that a private property owner or lessee has provided his or her authorization for the removal of a vehicle from his or her property, thereby promoting the safety of those persons involved in ordering the removal of the vehicle as well as those persons removing, towing, and storing the vehicle.

(3) It is the intent of the Legislature in the adoption of subdivision (g) to promote the safety of the general public by requiring towing companies to unconditionally release a vehicle that is not lawfully in their possession, thereby avoiding the likelihood of dangerous and violent confrontation and physical injury to vehicle owners and towing operators, the stranding of vehicle owners and their passengers at a dangerous time and location, and impeding expedited vehicle recovery, without wasting law enforcement's limited resources.

(p) The remedies, sanctions, restrictions, and procedures provided in this section are not exclusive and are in addition to other remedies, sanctions, restrictions, or procedures that may be provided in other provisions of law, including, but not limited to, those that are provided in Sections 12110 and 34660.

(q) A vehicle removed and stored pursuant to this section shall be released by the law enforcement agency, impounding agency, or person in possession of the vehicle, or any person acting on behalf of them, to the legal owner or the legal owner's agent upon presentation of the assignment, as defined in subdivision (b) of Section 7500.1 of the Business and Professions Code; a release from the one responsible governmental agency, only if required by the agency; a government-issued photographic identification card; and any one of the following as determined by the legal owner or the legal owner's agent: a certificate of repossession for the vehicle, a security agreement for the vehicle, or title, whether paper or electronic, showing proof of legal ownership for the vehicle. Any documents presented may be originals, photocopies, or facsimile copies, or may be transmitted electronically. The storage facility shall not require any documents to be notarized. The storage facility may require the agent of the legal owner to produce a photocopy or facsimile copy of its repossession agency license or registration issued pursuant to Chapter 11 (commencing with Section 7500) of Division 3 of the Business and Professions Code, or to demonstrate, to the satisfaction of the storage facility, that the agent is exempt from licensure pursuant to Section 7500.2 or 7500.3 of the Business and Professions Code. *(AM '13; Op. 1-1-2014)*

22658.1. Notification: Damage to Fences

(a) Any towing company that, in removing a vehicle, cuts, removes, otherwise damages, or leaves open a fence without the prior approval of the property owner or the person in charge of the property shall then and there do either of the following:

(1) Locate and notify the owner or person in charge of the property of the damage or open condition of the fence, the name and address of the towing company, and the license, registration, or identification number of the vehicle being removed.

(2) Leave in a conspicuous place on the property the name and address of the towing company, and the license, registration, or identification number of the vehicle being removed, and shall without unnecessary delay, notify the police department of the city in which the property is located, or if the property is located in unincorporated territory, either the sheriff or the local headquarters of the CHP, of that information and the location of the damaged or opened fence.

(b) Any person failing to comply with all the requirements of this section is guilty of an infraction.

22659. Removal From State Property

Any peace officer of the Department of the California Highway Patrol or any person duly authorized by the state agency in possession of property owned by the state, or rented or leased from others by the state and any peace officer of the Department of the California Highway Patrol providing policing services to property of a district agricultural association may, subsequent to giving notice to the city police or county sheriff, whichever is appropriate, cause the removal of a vehicle from the property to the nearest public garage, under any of the following circumstances:

(a) When the vehicle is illegally parked in locations where signs are posted giving notice of violation and removal.

(b) When an officer arrests any person driving or in control of a vehicle for an alleged offense and the officer is by this code or other law required to take the person arrested before a magistrate without unnecessary delay.

(c) When any vehicle is found upon the property and report has previously been made that the vehicle has been stolen or complaint has been filed and a warrant thereon issued charging that the vehicle has been embezzled.

(d) When the person or persons in charge of a vehicle upon the property are by reason of physical injuries or illness incapacitated to that extent as to be unable to provide for its custody or removal.

The person causing removal of the vehicle shall comply with the requirements of Sections 22852 and 22853 relating to notice.

22669. Removal of Abandoned Vehicles

(a) Any peace officer or any other employee of the state, county, or city designated by an agency or department of the state or the board of supervisors or city council to perform this function, in the territorial limits in which the officer or employee is authorized to act, who has reasonable grounds to believe that the vehicle has been abandoned, as determined pursuant to Section 22523, may remove the vehicle from a highway or from public or private property.

(b) Any person performing a franchise or contract awarded pursuant to subdivision (a) of Section 22710, may remove a vehicle from a highway or place to which it has been removed pursuant to subdivision (c) of Section 22654 or from public or private property, after a determination by a peace officer or other designated employee of the state, county, or city in which the vehicle is located that the vehicle is abandoned, as determined pursuant to Section 22523.

(c) A state, county, or city employee, other than a peace officer or employee of a sheriff's department or a city police department, designated to remove vehicles pursuant to this section may do so only after he or she has mailed or personally delivered a written report identifying the vehicle and its location to the office of the CHP located nearest to the vehicle.

(d) Motor vehicles which are parked, resting, or otherwise immobilized on any highway or public right-of-way and which lack an engine, transmission, wheels, tires, doors, windshield, or any other part or equipment necessary to operate safely on the highways of his state, are hereby declared a hazard to public health, safety, and welfare and may be removed immediately upon discovery by a peace officer or other designated employee of the state, county, or city.

CHAPTER 12. PUBLIC OFFENSES

23103. Reckless Driving

(a) A person who drives a vehicle upon a highway in willful or wanton disregard for the safety of persons or property is guilty of reckless driving.

(b) A person who drives a vehicle in an offstreet parking facility, as defined in subdivision (c) of Section 12500, in willful or wanton disregard for the safety of persons or property is guilty of reckless driving.

(c) Except as otherwise provided in Section 40008, persons convicted of the offense of reckless driving shall be punished by imprisonment in a county jail for not less than five days nor more than 90 days or by a fine of not less than one hundred forty-five dollars ($145) nor more than one thousand dollars ($1,000), or by both that fine and imprisonment, except as provided in Section 23104 or 23105. *(AM '01, '07, '10)*

23104. Reckless Driving: Bodily Injury

(a) Except as provided in subdivision (b), whenever reckless driving of a vehicle proximately causes bodily injury to a person other than the driver, the person driving the vehicle shall, upon conviction thereof, be punished by imprisonment in the county jail for not less than 30 days nor more than six months or by a fine of not less than two hundred twenty dollars ($220) nor more than one thousand dollars ($1,000), or by both the fine and imprisonment.

(b) A person convicted of reckless driving that proximately causes great bodily injury, as defined in Section 12022.7 of the Penal Code, to a person other than the driver, who previously has been convicted of a violation of Section 23103, 23104, 23105, 23109, 23109.1, 23152, or 23153, shall be punished by imprisonment pursuant to subdivision (h) of Section 1170 of the Penal Code, by imprisonment in the county jail for not less than 30 days nor more than six months or by a fine of not less than two hundred twenty dollars ($220) nor more than one thousand dollars ($1,000) or by both the fine and imprisonment. *(AM '11)*

23109. Speed Contests

(a) A person shall not engage in a motor vehicle speed contest on a highway. As used in this section, a motor vehicle speed contest includes a motor vehicle race against another vehicle, a clock, or other timing device. For purposes of this section, an event in which the time to cover a prescribed route of more than 20 miles is measured, but where the vehicle does not exceed the speed limits, is not a speed contest.

(b) A person shall not aid or abet in any motor vehicle speed contest on any highway.

(c) A person shall not engage in a motor vehicle exhibition of speed on a highway, and a person shall not aid or abet in a motor vehicle exhibition of speed on any highway.

(d) A person shall not, for the purpose of facilitating or aiding or as an incident to any motor vehicle speed contest or exhibition upon a highway, in any manner obstruct or place a barricade or obstruction or assist or participate in placing a barricade or obstruction upon any highway.

(e)(1) A person convicted of a violation of subdivision (a) shall be punished by imprisonment in a county jail for not less than 24 hours nor more than 90 days or by a fine of not less than three hundred fifty-five dollars ($355) nor more than one thousand dollars ($1,000), or by both that fine and imprisonment. That person shall also be required to perform 40 hours of community service. The court may order the privilege to operate a motor vehicle suspended for 90 days to six months, as provided in paragraph (8) of subdivision (a) of Section 13352. The person's privilege to operate a motor vehicle may be restricted for 90 days to six months to necessary travel to and from that person's place of employment and, if driving a motor vehicle is necessary to perform the duties of the person's employment, restricted to driving in that person's scope of employment. This subdivision does not interfere with the court's power to grant probation in a suitable case.

(2) If a person is convicted of a violation of subdivision (a) and that violation proximately causes bodily injury to a person other than the driver, the person convicted shall be punished by imprisonment in a county jail for not less than 30 days nor more than six months or by a fine of not less than five hundred dollars ($500) nor more than one thousand dollars ($1,000), or by both that fine and imprisonment.

(f)(1) If a person is convicted of a violation of subdivision (a) for an offense that occurred within five years of the date of a prior offense that resulted in a conviction of a violation of subdivision (a), that person shall be punished by imprisonment in a county jail for not less than four days nor more than six months, and by a fine of not less than five hundred dollars ($500) nor more than one thousand dollars ($1,000).

(2) If the perpetration of the most recent offense within the five-year period described in paragraph (1) proximately causes bodily injury to a person other than the driver, a person convicted of that second violation shall be imprisoned in a county jail for not less than 30 days nor more than six months and by a fine of not less than five hundred dollars ($500) nor more than one thousand dollars ($1,000).

(3) If the perpetration of the most recent offense within the five-year period described in paragraph (1) proximately causes serious bodily injury, as defined in paragraph (4) of subdivision (f) of Section 243 of the Penal Code, to a person other than the driver, a person convicted of that second violation shall be imprisoned in the state prison, or in a county jail for not less than 30 days nor more than one year, and by a fine of not less than five hundred dollars ($500) nor more than one thousand dollars ($1,000).

(4) The court shall order the privilege to operate a motor vehicle of a person convicted under paragraph (1), (2), or (3) suspended for a period of six months, as provided in paragraph (9) of subdivision (a) of Section 13352. In lieu of the suspension, the person's privilege to operate a motor vehicle may be restricted for six months to necessary travel to and from that person's place of employment and, if driving a motor vehicle is necessary to perform the duties of the person's employment, restricted to driving in that person's scope of employment.

(5) This subdivision does not interfere with the court's power to grant probation in a suitable case.

(g) If the court grants probation to a person subject to punishment under subdivision (f), in addition to subdivision (f) and any other terms and conditions imposed by the court, which may include a fine, the court shall impose as a condition of probation that the person be confined in a county jail for not less than 48 hours nor more than six months. The court shall order the person's privilege to operate a motor vehicle to be suspended for a period of six months, as provided in paragraph (9) of subdivision (a) of Section 13352 or restricted pursuant to subdivision (f).

(h) If a person is convicted of a violation of subdivision (a) and the vehicle used in the violation is registered to that person, the vehicle may be impounded at the registered owner's expense for not less than one day nor more than 30 days.

(i) A person who violates subdivision (b), (c), or (d) shall upon conviction of that violation be punished by imprisonment in a county jail for not more than 90 days, by a fine of not more than five hundred dollars ($500), or by both that fine and imprisonment.

(j) If a person's privilege to operate a motor vehicle is restricted by a court pursuant to this section, the court shall clearly mark the restriction and the dates of the restriction on that person's driver's license and promptly notify the Department of Motor Vehicles of the terms of the restriction in a manner prescribed by the department. The Department of Motor Vehicles shall place that restriction in the person's records in the Department of Motor Vehicles and enter the restriction on a license subsequently issued by the Department of Motor Vehicles to that person during the period of the restriction.

(k) The court may order that a person convicted under this section, who is to be punished by imprisonment in a county jail, be imprisoned on days other than days of regular employment of the person, as determined by the court.

(l) This section shall be known and may be cited as the Louis Friend Memorial Act. *(AM '06, '09-'10)*

23109.2. Motor Vehicle Speed Contest; Arrest of Driver and Removal of Vehicle

(a)(1) Whenever a peace officer determines that a person was engaged in any of the activities set forth in paragraph (2), the peace officer may immediately arrest and take into custody that person and may cause the removal and seizure of the motor vehicle used in that offense in accordance with Chapter 10 (commencing with Section 22650). A motor vehicle so seized may be impounded for not more than 30 days.

(2)(A) A motor vehicle speed contest, as described in subdivision (a) of Section 23109.

(B) Reckless driving on a highway, as described in subdivision (a) of Section 23103.

(C) Reckless driving in an offstreet parking facility, as described in subdivision (b) of Section 23103.

(D) Exhibition of speed on a highway, as described in subdivision (c) of Section 23109.

(b) The registered and legal owner of a vehicle removed and seized under subdivision (a) or their agents shall be provided the opportunity for a storage hearing to determine the validity of the storage in accordance with Section 22852.

(c)(1) Notwithstanding Chapter 10 (commencing with Section 22650) or any other provision of law, an impounding agency shall release a motor vehicle to the registered owner or his or her agent prior to the conclusion of the impoundment period described in subdivision (a) under any of the following circumstances:

(A) If the vehicle is a stolen vehicle.

(B) If the person alleged to have been engaged in the motor vehicle speed contest, as described in subdivision (a), was not authorized by the registered owner of the motor vehicle to operate the motor vehicle at the time of the commission of the offense.

(C) If the registered owner of the vehicle was neither the driver nor a passenger of the vehicle at the time of the alleged violation pursuant to subdivision (a), or was unaware that the driver was using the vehicle to engage in any of the activities described in subdivision (a).

(D) If the legal owner or registered owner of the vehicle is a rental car agency.

(E) If, prior to the conclusion of the impoundment period, a citation or notice is dismissed under Section 40500, criminal charges are not filed by the district attorney because of a lack of evidence, or the charges are otherwise dismissed by the court.

(2) A vehicle shall be released pursuant to this subdivision only if the registered owner or his or her agent presents a currently valid driver's license to operate the vehicle and proof of current vehicle registration, or if ordered by a court.

(3) If, pursuant to subparagraph (E) of paragraph (1) a motor vehicle is released prior to the conclusion of the impoundment period, neither the person charged with a violation of subdivision (a) of Section 23109 nor the registered owner of the motor vehicle is responsible for towing and storage charges nor shall the motor vehicle be sold to satisfy those charges.

(d) A vehicle seized and removed under subdivision (a) shall be released to the legal owner of the vehicle, or the legal owner's agent, on or before the 30th day of impoundment if all of the following conditions are met:

(1) The legal owner is a motor vehicle dealer, bank, credit union, acceptance corporation, or other licensed financial institution legally operating in this state, or is another person, not the registered owner, holding a security interest in the vehicle.

(2) The legal owner or the legal owner's agent pays all towing and storage fees related to the impoundment of the vehicle. No lien sale processing fees shall be charged to a legal owner who redeems the vehicle on or before the 15th day of impoundment.

(3) The legal owner or the legal owner's agent presents foreclosure documents or an affidavit of repossession for the vehicle.

(e)(1) The registered owner or his or her agent is responsible for all towing and storage charges related to the impoundment, and any administrative charges authorized under Section 22850.5.

(2) Notwithstanding paragraph (1), if the person convicted of engaging in the activities set forth in paragraph (2) of subdivision (a) was not authorized by the registered owner of the motor vehicle to operate the motor vehicle at the time of the commission of the offense, the court shall order the convicted person to reimburse the registered owner for any towing and storage charges related to the impoundment, and any administrative charges authorized under Section 22850.5 incurred by the registered owner to obtain possession of the vehicle, unless the court finds that the person convicted does not have the ability to pay all or part of those charges.

(3) If the vehicle is a rental vehicle, the rental car agency may require the person to whom the vehicle was rented to pay all towing and storage charges related to the impoundment and any administrative charges authorized under Section 22850.5 incurred by the rental car agency in connection with obtaining possession of the vehicle.

(4) The owner is not liable for any towing and storage charges related to the impoundment if acquittal or dismissal occurs.

(5) The vehicle may not be sold prior to the defendant's conviction.

(6) The impounding agency is responsible for the actual costs incurred by the towing agency as a result of the impoundment should the registered owner be absolved of liability for those charges pursuant to paragraph (3) of subdivision (c). Notwithstanding this provision, nothing shall prohibit impounding agencies from making prior payment arrangements to satisfy this requirement.

(f) Any period when a vehicle is subjected to storage under this section shall be included as part of the period of impoundment ordered by the court under subdivision (h) of Section 23109. *(AD '02; RP/AD '07)*

23110. Throwing Substances at Vehicles

(a) Any person who throws any substance at a vehicle or any occupant thereof on a highway is guilty of a misdemeanor.

(b) Any person who with intent to do great bodily injury maliciously and willfully throws or projects any rock, brick, bottle, metal or other missile, or projects any other substance capable of doing serious bodily harm at such vehicle or occupant thereof is guilty of a felony and upon conviction shall be punished by imprisonment in the state prison.

23111. Throwing Substances on Highways or Adjoining Areas

No person in any vehicle and no pedestrian shall throw or discharge from or upon any road or highway or adjoining area, public or private, any lighted or nonlighted cigarette, cigar, match, or any flaming or glowing substance. This section shall be known as the Paul Buzzo Act.

23112. Throwing, Depositing, or Dumping Matter on Highway

(a) No person shall throw or deposit, nor shall the registered owner or the driver, if such owner is not then present in the vehicle, aid or abet in the throwing or depositing upon any highway any bottle, can, garbage, glass, nail, offal, paper, wire, any substance likely to injure or damage traffic using the highway, or any noisome, nauseous, or offensive matter of any kind.

(b) No person shall place, deposit or dump, or cause to be placed, deposited or dumped, any rocks, refuse, garbage, or dirt in or upon any highway, including any portion of the right-of-way thereof without the consent of the state or local agency having jurisdiction over the highway.

23112.5. Notification of Hazardous Spill

(a) Any person who dumps, spills, or causes the release of hazardous material, as defined by Section 353, or hazardous waste, as defined by Section 25117 of the Health and Safety Code, upon any highway shall notify the Department of the California Highway Patrol or the agency having traffic jurisdiction for that highway of the dump, spill, or release, as soon as the person has knowledge of the dump, spill, or release and notification is possible. Upon receiving notification pursuant to this section, the Department of the California Highway Patrol shall, as soon as possible, notify the ***Office of Emergency ***Services of the dump, spill, or release, except for petroleum spills of less than 42 gallons from vehicular fuel tanks.

(b) Any person who is convicted of a violation of this section shall be punished by a mandatory fine of not less than two thousand dollars ($2,000). *(AM '13)*

23112.7. Motor Vehicle Used for Illegal Dumping of Waste; Impoundment and Civil Forfeiture

(a)(1) A motor vehicle used for illegal dumping of waste matter on public or private property is subject to impoundment pursuant to subdivision (c).

(2) A motor vehicle used for illegal dumping of harmful waste matter on public or private property is subject to impoundment and civil forfeiture pursuant to subdivision (d).

(b) For the purposes of this section, the following terms have the following meanings:

(1) "Illegal dumping" means the willful or intentional depositing, dropping, dumping, placing, or throwing of any waste matter onto public or private property that is not expressly designated for the purpose of disposal of waste matter. "Illegal dumping" does not include the discarding of small quantities of waste matter related to consumer goods and that are reasonably understood to be ordinarily carried on or about the body of a living person, including, but not limited to, beverage containers and closures, packaging, wrappers, wastepaper, newspaper, magazines, or other similar waste matter that escapes or is allowed to escape from a container, receptacle, or package.

(2) "Waste matter" means any form of tangible matter described by any of the following:

(A) All forms of garbage, refuse, rubbish, recyclable materials, and solid waste.

(B) Dirt, soil, rock, decomposed rock, gravel, sand, or other aggregate material dumped or deposited as refuse.

(C) Abandoned or discarded furniture; or commercial, industrial, or agricultural machinery, apparatus, structure, or other container; or a piece, portion, or part of these items.

(D) All forms of liquid waste not otherwise defined in or deemed to fall within the purview of Section 25117 of the Health and Safety Code, including, but not limited to, water-based or oil-based paints, chemical solutions, water contaminated with any substance rendering it unusable for irrigation or construction, oils, fuels, and other petroleum distillates or byproducts.

(E) Any form of biological waste not otherwise designated by law as hazardous waste, including, but not limited to, body parts, carcasses, and any associated container, enclosure, or wrapping material used to dispose these matters.

(F) A physical substance used as an ingredient in any process, now known or hereafter developed or devised, to manufacture a controlled substance specified in Section 11054, 11055, 11056, 11057, or 11058 of the Health and Safety Code, or that is a byproduct or result of the manufacturing process of the controlled substance.

(3) "Harmful waste matter" is a hazardous substance as defined in Section 374.8 of the Penal Code; a hazardous waste as defined in Section 25117 of the Health and Safety Code; waste that, pursuant to Division 30 (commencing with Section 40000) of the Public Resources Code, cannot be disposed in a municipal solid waste landfill without special handling, processing, or treatment; or waste matter in excess of one cubic yard.

(c)(1) Whenever a person, who has one or more prior convictions of Section 374.3 or 374.8 of the Penal Code that are not infractions, is convicted of a misdemeanor violation of Section 374.3 of the Penal Code, or of a violation of Section 374.8 of the Penal Code, for illegally dumping waste matter or harmful waste matter that is committed while driving a motor vehicle of which he or she is the registered owner of the vehicle, or is the registered owner's agent or employee, the court at the time of sentencing may order the motor vehicle impounded for a period of not more than six months.

(2) In determining the impoundment period imposed pursuant to paragraph (1), the court shall consider both of the following factors:

(A) The size and nature of the waste matter dumped.

(B) Whether the dumping occurred for a business purpose.

(3) The cost of keeping the vehicle is a lien on the vehicle pursuant to Chapter 6.5 (commencing with Section 3067) of Title 14 of Part 4 of Division 3 of the Civil Code.

(4) Notwithstanding paragraph (1), a vehicle impounded pursuant to this subdivision shall be released to the legal owner or his or her agent pursuant to subdivision (b) of Section 23592.

(5) The impounding agency shall not be liable to the registered owner for the release of the vehicle to the legal owner or his or her agent when made in compliance with paragraph (4).

(6) This subdivision does not apply if there is a community property interest in the vehicle that is owned by a person other than the defendant and the vehicle is the only vehicle available to the defendant's immediate family that may be operated on the highway with a class A, class B, or class C driver's license.

(d)(1) Notwithstanding Section 86 of the Code of Civil Procedure and any other provision of law otherwise prescribing the jurisdiction of the court based upon the value of the property involved, whenever a person, who has two or more prior convictions of Section 374.3 or 374.8 of the Penal Code that are not infractions, is charged with a misdemeanor violation of Section 374.3 of the Penal Code, or of a violation of Section 374.8 of the Penal Code, for illegally dumping harmful waste matter, the court with jurisdiction over the offense may, upon a motion of the prosecutor or the county counsel in a criminal action, declare a motor vehicle if used by the defendant in the commission of the violation, to be a nuisance, and upon conviction order the vehicle sold pursuant to Section 23596, if the person is the registered owner of the vehicle or the registered owner's employee or agent.

(2) The proceeds of the sale of the vehicle pursuant to this subdivision shall be distributed and used in decreasing order of priority, as follows:

(A) To satisfy all costs of the sale, including costs incurred with respect to the taking and keeping of the vehicle pending sale.

(B) To the legal owner in an amount to satisfy the indebtedness owed to the legal owner remaining as of the date of the sale, including accrued interest or finance charges and delinquency charges.

(C) To recover the costs made, incurred, or associated with the enforcement of this section, the abatement of waste matter, and the deterrence of illegal dumping.

(3) A vehicle shall not be sold pursuant to this subdivision in either of the following circumstances:

(A) The vehicle is owned by the employer or principal of the defendant and the use of the vehicle was made without the employer's or principal's knowledge and consent, and did not provide a direct benefit to the employer's or principal's business.

(B) There is a community property interest in the vehicle that is owned by a person other than the defendant and the vehicle is the only vehicle available to the defendant's immediate family that may be operated on the highway with a class A, class B, or class C driver's license. *(AD '06)*

23113. Removal of Material From Highway

(a) Any person who drops, dumps, deposits, places, or throws, or causes or permits to be dropped, dumped, deposited, placed, or thrown, upon any highway or street any material described in Section 23112 or in subdivision (d) of Section 23114 shall immediately remove the material or cause the material to be removed.

(b) If the person fails to comply with subdivision (a), the governmental agency responsible for the maintenance of the street or highway on which the material has been deposited may remove the material and collect, by civil action, if necessary, the actual cost of the removal operation in addition to any other damages authorized by law from the person made responsible under subdivision (a).

(c) A member of the Department of the California Highway Patrol may direct a responsible party to remove the aggregate material described in subdivision (d) of Section 23114 from a highway when that material has escaped or been released from a vehicle.

(d) Notwithstanding any other provision of law, a government agency described in subdivision (b), the Department of the California Highway Patrol, or the employees or officers of those agencies, may not be held liable for any damage to material, to cargo, or to personal property caused by a negligent act or omission of the employee or officer when the employee or officer is acting within the scope and purpose of subdivision (b) or (c). Nothing in this subdivision affects liability for purposes of establishing gross negligence or willful misconduct. This subdivision applies to the negligent performance of a ministerial act, and does not affect liability under any provision of law, including liability, if any, derived from the failure to preserve evidence in a civil or criminal action. *(AM '99)*

23114. Spilling Loads on Highways

(a) Except as provided in Subpart I (commencing with Section 393.100) of Title 49 of the Code of Federal Regulations related to hay and straw, a vehicle shall not be driven or moved on any highway unless the vehicle is so constructed, covered, or loaded as to prevent any of its contents or load other than clear water or feathers from live birds from dropping, sifting, leaking, blowing, spilling, or otherwise escaping from the vehicle.

(b)(1) Aggregate material shall only be carried in the cargo area of a vehicle. The cargo area shall not contain any holes, cracks, or openings through which that material may escape, regardless of the degree to which the vehicle is loaded, except as provided in paragraph (2).

(2) Every vehicle used to transport aggregate materials, regardless of the degree to which the vehicle is loaded, shall be equipped with all of the following:

(A) Properly functioning seals on any openings used to empty the load, including, but not limited to, bottom dump release gates and tailgates.

(B) Splash flaps behind every tire, or set of tires, regardless of the position on the truck, truck tractor, or trailer.

(C) Center flaps at a location to the rear of each bottom dump release gate as to trucks or trailers equipped with bottom dump release gates. The center flap may be positioned directly behind the bottom dump release gate and in front of the rear axle of the vehicle, or it may be positioned to the rear of the rear axle in line with the splash flaps required behind the tires. The width of the center flap may extend not more than one inch from one sidewall to the opposite sidewall of the inside tires and shall extend to within five inches of the pavement surface, and may be not less than 24 inches from the bottom edge to the top edge of that center flap.

(D) Fenders starting at the splash flap with the leading edge of the fenders extending forward at least six inches beyond the center of the axle that cover the tops of tires not already covered by the truck, truck tractor, or trailer body.

(E) Complete enclosures on all vertical sides of the cargo area, including, but not limited to, tailgates.

(F) Shed boards designed to prevent aggregate materials from being deposited on the vehicle body during top loading.

(c) Vehicles comprised of full rigid enclosures are exempt only from subparagraphs (C) and (F) of paragraph (2) of subdivision (b).

(d) For purposes of this section, "aggregate material" means rock fragments, pebbles, sand, dirt, gravel, cobbles, crushed base, asphalt, and other similar materials.

(e)(1) In addition to subdivisions (a) and (b), a vehicle may not transport any aggregate material upon a highway unless the material is covered.

(2) Vehicles transporting loads composed entirely of asphalt material are exempt only from the provisions of this section requiring that loads be covered.

(3) Vehicles transporting loads composed entirely of petroleum coke material are not required to cover their loads if they are loaded using safety procedures, specialized equipment, and a chemical surfactant designed to prevent materials from blowing, spilling, or otherwise escaping from the vehicle.

(4) Vehicles transporting loads of aggregate materials are not required to cover their loads if the load, where it contacts the sides, front, and back of the cargo container area, remains six inches from the upper edge of the container area, and if the load does not extend, at its peak, above any part of the upper edge of the cargo container area.

(f) A person who provides a location for vehicles to be loaded with an aggregate material or other material shall provide a location for vehicle operators to comply with this section before entering a highway.

(1) A person is exempt from the requirements of this subdivision if the location that he or she provides for vehicles to be loaded with the materials described in this subdivision has 100 yards or less between the scale houses where the trucks carrying aggregate material are weighed and the point of egress to a public road.

(2) A driver of a vehicle loaded with aggregate material leaving locations exempted from the requirements of this subdivision is authorized to operate on public roads only until that driver is able to safely cover the load at a site near the location's point of egress to the public road. Except as provided under paragraph (4) of subdivision (e), an uncovered vehicle described in this paragraph may not operate more than 200 yards from the point of egress to the public road. *(AM '08)*

23115. Rubbish Vehicles

(a) No vehicle transporting garbage, swill, used cans or bottles, wastepapers, waste cardboard, ashes, refuse, trash, or rubbish, or any noisome, nauseous, or offensive matter, or anything being transported for disposal or recycling shall be driven or moved upon any highway unless the load is totally covered in a manner that will prevent the load or any part of the load from spilling or falling from the vehicle.

(b) Subdivision (a) does not prohibit a rubbish vehicle from being without cover while in the process of acquiring its load if no law, administrative regulation, or local ordinance requires that it be covered in those circumstances.

(c) Vehicles transporting wastepaper, waste cardboard, or used cans or bottles, are in compliance with subdivision (a) if appropriate binders including, but not limited to, bands, wires, straps, or netting are used to prevent the load, or any part of the load, from spilling or falling from the vehicle.

(d) This section does not apply to any vehicle engaged in transporting wet waste fruit or vegetable matter, or waste products to or from a food processing establishment. *(AM '01)*

23116. Carry Passenger in Back of Truck

(a) No person driving a pickup truck or a flatbed motortruck on a highway shall transport any person in or on the back of the truck.

(b) No person shall ride in or on the back of a truck or flatbed motortruck being driven on a highway.

(c) Subdivisions (a) and (b) do not apply if the person in the back of the truck is secured with a restraint system. The restraint system shall meet or exceed the federal motor vehicle safety standards published in Sections 571.207, 571.209, and 571.210 of Title 49 of the Code of Federal Regulations.

(d) Subdivisions (a), (b), and (c) do not apply to any person transporting one or more persons in the back of a truck or flatbed motortruck owned by a farmer or rancher, if that vehicle is used exclusively within the boundaries of lands owned or managed by that farmer or rancher, including the incidental use of that vehicle on not more than one mile of highway between one part of the farm or ranch to another part of that farm or ranch.

(e) Subdivisions (a), (b), and (c) do not apply if the person in the back of the truck or the flatbed is being transported in an emergency response situation by a public agency or pursuant to the direction or authority of a public agency.

As used in this subdivision, "emergency response situation" means instances in which necessary measures are needed in order to prevent injury or death to persons or to prevent, confine, or mitigate damage or destruction to property.

(f) Subdivisions (a) and (b) do not apply if the person in the back of the truck or flatbed motortruck is being transported in a parade that is supervised by a law enforcement agency and the speed of the truck while in the parade does not exceed eight miles per hour. *(AM '00)*

23117. Carrying Animal in Truck Bed

(a) No person driving a motor vehicle shall transport any animal in the back of the vehicle in a space intended for any load on the vehicle on a highway unless the space is enclosed or has side and tail racks to a height of at least 46 inches extending vertically from the floor, the vehicle has installed means of preventing the animal from being discharged, or the animal is cross tethered to the vehicle, or is protected by a secured container or cage, in a manner which will prevent the animal from being thrown, falling, or jumping from the vehicle.

(b) This section does not apply to any of the following:

(1) The transportation of livestock.

(2) The transportation of a dog whose owner either owns or is employed by a ranching or farming operation who is traveling on a road in a rural area or who is traveling to and from a livestock auction.

(3) The transportation of a dog for purposes associated with ranching or farming.

23118. Unlicensed Repossession Vehicle; Court Order and Impound

(a)(1) A magistrate presented with the affidavit of a peace officer establishing reasonable cause to believe that a vehicle, described by vehicle type and license number, is being used or operated in violation of Section 7502.1 of the Business and Professions Code shall issue a warrant or order authorizing any peace officer to immediately seize and cause the removal of the vehicle.

(2) The warrant or court order may be entered into a computerized database.

(3) Any vehicle so impounded may be impounded until such time as the owner of the property, or the person in possession of the property at the time of the impoundment, produces proof of licensure pursuant to Chapter 11 (commencing with Section 7500) of Division 3 of the Business and Professions Code, or proof of an exemption from licensure pursuant to Section 7500.2 or 7500.3 of the Business and Professions Code.

(4) The impounding agency, within two working days of impoundment, shall send a notice by certified mail, return receipt requested, to the legal owner of the vehicle, at an address obtained from the department, informing the owner that the vehicle has been impounded and providing the owner with a copy of the warrant or court order. Failure to notify the legal owner within two working days shall prohibit the impounding agency from charging for more than 15 days impoundment when a legal owner redeems the impounded vehicle. The law enforcement agency shall be open to issue a release to the registered owner or legal owner, or the agent of either, whenever the agency is open to serve the public for regular, nonemergency business.

(b)(1) An impounding agency shall release a vehicle to the registered owner or his or her agent prior to the end of the impoundment period and without the permission of the magistrate authorizing the vehicle's seizure under any of the following circumstances:

(A) When the vehicle is a stolen vehicle.

(B) When the vehicle was seized under this section for an offense that does not authorize the seizure of the vehicle.

(2) No vehicle may be released under this subdivision, except upon presentation of the registered owner's or agent's currently valid license to operate the vehicle, and proof of current vehicle registration, or upon order of the court.

(c)(1) Whenever a vehicle is impounded under this section, the magistrate ordering the storage shall provide the vehicle's registered and legal owners of record, or their agents, with the opportunity for a poststorage hearing to determine the validity of the storage.

(2) A notice of the storage shall be mailed or personally delivered to the registered and legal owners within 48 hours after issuance of the warrant or court order, excluding weekends and holidays, by the person or agency executing the warrant or court order, and shall include all of the following information:

(A) The name, address, and telephone number of the agency providing the notice.

(B) The location of the place of storage and a description of the vehicle, which shall include, if available, the name or make, the manufacturer, the license plate number, and the mileage of the vehicle.

(C) A copy of the warrant or court order and the peace officer's affidavit, as described in subdivision (a).

(D) A statement that, in order to receive their poststorage hearing, the owners, or their agents, are required to request the hearing from the magistrate issuing the warrant or court order in person, in writing, or by telephone, within 10 days of the date of the notice.

(3) The poststorage hearing shall be conducted within two court days after receipt of the request for the hearing.

(4) At the hearing, the magistrate may order the vehicle released if he or she finds any of the circumstances described in subdivision (b) or (e) that allow release of a vehicle by the impounding agency.

(5) Failure of either the registered or legal owner, or his or her agent, to request, or to attend, a scheduled hearing satisfies the poststorage hearing requirement.

(6) The agency employing the peace officer who caused the magistrate to issue the warrant or court order shall be responsible for the costs incurred for towing and storage if it is determined in the poststorage hearing that reasonable grounds for the storage are not established.

(d) The registered owner or his or her agent is responsible for all towing and storage charges related to the impoundment, and any administrative charges authorized under Section 22850.5.

(e) A vehicle removed and seized under subdivision (a) shall be released to the legal owner of the vehicle or the legal owner's agent prior to the end of the impoundment period and without the permission of the magistrate authorizing the seizure of the vehicle if all of the following conditions are met:

(1) The legal owner is a motor vehicle dealer, bank, credit union, acceptance corporation, or other licensed financial institution legally operating in this state or is another person, not the registered owner, holding a security interest in the vehicle.

(2)(A) The legal owner or the legal owner's agent pays all towing and storage fees related to the seizure of the vehicle. Except as specifically authorized by this subdivision, no other fees shall be charged to the legal owner or the agent of the legal owner. No lien sale processing fees shall be charged to the legal owner who redeems the vehicle prior to the 15th day of impoundment. Neither the impounding authority nor any person having possession of the vehicle shall collect from the legal owner of the type specified in paragraph (1), or the legal owner's agent any administrative charges imposed pursuant to Section 22850.5 unless the legal owner voluntarily requested a poststorage hearing.

(B) A person operating or in charge of a storage facility where vehicles are stored pursuant to this section shall accept a valid bank credit card or cash for payment of towing, storage, and related fees by a legal or registered owner or the owner's agent claiming the vehicle. A credit card shall be in the name of the person presenting the card. "Credit card" means "credit card" as defined in subdivision (a) of Section 1747.02 of the Civil Code, except, for the purposes of this section, credit card does not include a credit card issued by a retail seller.

(C) A person operating or in charge of a storage facility described in subparagraph (B) who violates subparagraph (B) shall be civilly liable to the owner of the vehicle or to the person who tendered the fees for four times the amount of the towing, storage, and related fees, but not to exceed five hundred dollars ($500).

(D) A person operating or in charge of the storage facility shall have sufficient funds on the premises of the primary storage facility during normal business hours to accommodate, and make change in, a reasonable monetary transaction.

(E) Credit charges for towing and storage services shall comply with Section 1748.1 of the Civil Code. Law enforcement agencies may include the costs of providing for payment by credit when making agreements with towing companies on rates.

(3)(A) The legal owner or the legal owner's agent presents to the law enforcement agency or impounding agency, or any person acting on behalf of those agencies, a copy of the assignment, as defined in subdivision (b) of Section 7500.1 of the Business and Professions Code; a release from the one responsible governmental agency, only if required by the agency; a government-issued photographic identification card; and any one of the following as determined by the legal owner or the legal owner's agent: a certificate of repossession for the vehicle, a security agreement for the vehicle, or title, whether paper or electronic, showing proof of legal ownership for the vehicle. The law enforcement agency, impounding agency, or any other governmental agency, or any person acting on behalf of those agencies, shall not require the presentation of any other documents.

(B) The legal owner or the legal owner's agent presents to the person in possession of the vehicle, or any person acting on behalf of the person in possession, a copy of the assignment, as defined in subdivision (b) of Section 7500.1 of the Business and Professions Code; a release from the one responsible governmental agency, only if required by the agency; a government-issued photographic identification card; and any one of the following as determined by the legal owner or the legal owner's agent: a certificate of repossession for the vehicle, a security agreement for the vehicle, or title, whether paper or electronic, showing proof of legal ownership for the vehicle. The person in possession of the vehicle, or any person acting on behalf of the person in possession, shall not require the presentation of any other documents.

(C) All presented documents may be originals, photocopies, or facsimile copies, or may be transmitted electronically. The law enforcement agency, impounding agency, or any person in possession of the vehicle, or anyone acting on behalf of them, shall not require a document to be notarized. The law enforcement agency, impounding agency, or any person acting on behalf of those agencies, may require the agent of the legal owner to produce a photocopy or facsimile copy of its repossession agency license or registration issued pursuant to Chapter 11 (commencing with Section 7500) of Division 3 of the Business and Professions Code, or to demonstrate, to the satisfaction of the law enforcement agency, impounding agency, or any person in possession of the vehicle, or anyone acting on behalf of them, that the agent is exempt from licensure pursuant to Section 7500.2 or 7500.3 of the Business and Professions Code.

(D) No administrative costs authorized under subdivision (a) of Section 22850.5 shall be charged to the legal owner of the type specified in paragraph (1), who redeems the vehicle unless the legal owner voluntarily requests a poststorage hearing. No city, county, city and county, or state agency shall require a legal owner or a legal owner's agent to request a poststorage hearing as a requirement for release of the vehicle to the legal owner or the legal owner's agent. The law enforcement agency, impounding agency, or any other governmental agency, or any person acting on behalf of those agencies, shall not require any documents other than those specified in this paragraph. The law enforcement agency, impounding agency, or other governmental agency, or any person acting on behalf of those agencies, may not require any documents to be notarized. The legal owner or the legal owner's agent shall be given a copy of any documents he or she is required to sign, except for a vehicle evidentiary hold logbook. The law enforcement agency, impounding agency, or any person acting on behalf of those agencies, or any person in possession of the vehicle, may photocopy and retain the copies of any documents presented by the legal owner or legal owner's agent.

(4) A failure by a storage facility to comply with any applicable conditions set forth in this subdivision shall not affect the right of the legal owner or the legal owner's agent to retrieve the vehicle, provided all conditions required of the legal owner or legal owner's agent under this subdivision are satisfied.

(f)(1) A legal owner or the legal owner's agent that obtains release of the vehicle pursuant to subdivision (e) shall not release the vehicle to the registered owner of the vehicle or the person who was listed as the registered owner when the vehicle was impounded or the person in possession of the vehicle at the time of the impound or any agents of the registered owner until the termination of the impoundment period.

(2) The legal owner or the legal owner's agent shall not relinquish the vehicle to the registered owner or the person who was listed as the registered owner when the vehicle was impounded until the registered owner or that owner's agent presents his or her valid driver's license or valid temporary driver's license to the legal owner or the legal owner's agent. The legal owner or the legal owner's agent or the person in possession of the vehicle shall make every reasonable effort to ensure that the licenses presented are valid and possession of the vehicle will not be given to the driver who was involved in the original impound proceeding until the expiration of the impoundment period.

(3) Prior to relinquishing the vehicle, the legal owner may require the registered owner to pay all towing and storage charges related to the impoundment and the administrative charges authorized under Section 22850.5 that were incurred by the legal owner in connection with obtaining the custody of the vehicle.

(4) Any legal owner who knowingly releases or causes the release of a vehicle to a registered owner or the person in possession of the vehicle at the time of the impound or any agent of the registered owner in violation of this subdivision shall be guilty of a misdemeanor and subject to a fine in the amount of two thousand dollars ($2,000) in addition to any other penalties established by law.

(5) The legal owner, registered owner, or person in possession of the vehicle shall not change or attempt to change the name of the legal owner or the registered owner on the records of the department until the vehicle is released from the impound.

(g) Notwithstanding any other provision of this section, the registered owner and not the legal owner shall remain responsible for any towing and storage charges related to the impoundment and the administrative charges authorized under Section 22850.5 and any parking fines, penalties, and administrative fees incurred by the registered owner.

(h) The law enforcement agency and the impounding agency, including any storage facility acting on behalf of the law enforcement agency or impounding agency, shall comply with this section and shall not be liable to the registered owner for the improper release of the vehicle to the legal owner or the legal owner's agent provided the release complies with the provisions of this section. The legal owner shall indemnify and hold harmless a storage facility from any claims arising out of the release of the vehicle to the legal owner or the legal owner's agent and from any damage to the vehicle after its release, including the reasonable costs associated with defending any such claims. A law enforcement agency shall not refuse to issue a release to a legal owner or the agent of a legal owner on the grounds that it previously issued a release. *(AD '09)*

23120. Temple Width of Glasses
No person shall operate a motor vehicle while wearing glasses having a temple width of one-half inch or more if any part of such temple extends below the horizontal center of the lens so as to interfere with lateral vision.

23123. Use of Wireless Telephone While Driving; Hands-Free Operation Required; Exceptions
(a) A person shall not drive a motor vehicle while using a wireless telephone unless that telephone is specifically designed and configured to allow hands-free listening and talking, and is used in that manner while driving.

(b) A violation of this section is an infraction punishable by a base fine of twenty dollars ($20) for a first offense and fifty dollars ($50) for each subsequent offense.

(c) This section does not apply to a person using a wireless telephone for emergency purposes, including, but not limited to, an emergency call to a law enforcement agency, health care provider, fire department, or other emergency services agency or entity.

(d) This section does not apply to an emergency services professional using a wireless telephone while operating an authorized emergency vehicle, as defined in Section 165, in the course and scope of his or her duties.

(e) This section does not apply to a person driving a schoolbus or transit vehicle that is subject to Section 23125.

(f) This section does not apply to a person while driving a motor vehicle on private property.

(g) This section shall become operative on July 1, 2011. *(AD '06; AM '07)*

23123.5. Text-Based Communication While Driving Prohibited; Exceptions
(a) A person shall not drive a motor vehicle while using an electronic wireless communications device to write, send, or read a text-based communication, unless the electronic wireless communications device is specifically designed and configured to allow voice-operated and hands-free operation to dictate, send, or listen to a text-based communication, and it is used in that manner while driving.

(b) As used in this section "write, send, or read a text-based communication" means using an electronic wireless communications device to manually communicate with any person using a text-based communication, including, but not limited to, communications referred to as a text message, instant message, or electronic mail.

(c) For purposes of this section, a person shall not be deemed to be writing, reading, or sending a text-based communication if the person reads, selects, or enters a telephone number or name in an electronic wireless communications device for the purpose of making or receiving a telephone call or if a person otherwise activates or deactivates a feature or function on an electronic wireless communications device.

(d) A violation of this section is an infraction punishable by a base fine of twenty dollars ($20) for a first offense and fifty dollars ($50) for each subsequent offense.

(e) This section does not apply to an emergency services professional using an electronic wireless communications device while operating an authorized emergency vehicle, as defined in Section 165, in the course and scope of his or her duties. *(AM '12)*

23124. Use of Wireless Telephone or Mobile Service Device by Driver Under 18 Prohibited

(a) This section applies to a person under the age of 18 years.

(b) Notwithstanding ***Sections 23123 and 23123.5, a person described in subdivision (a) shall not drive a motor vehicle while using a wireless telephone or an electronic wireless communications device, even if equipped with a hands-free*** device.

(c) A violation of this section is an infraction punishable by a base fine of twenty dollars ($20) for a first offense and fifty dollars ($50) for each subsequent offense.

(d) A law enforcement officer shall not stop a vehicle for the sole purpose of determining whether the driver is violating subdivision (b).

(e) Subdivision (d) does not prohibit a law enforcement officer from stopping a vehicle for a violation of Section ***23123 or 23123.5.

(f) This section does not apply to a person using a wireless telephone or a mobile service device for emergency purposes, including, but not limited to, an emergency call to a law enforcement agency, health care provider, fire department, or other emergency services agency or entity.

(g) For the purposes of this section, "***electronic wireless communications device"includes, but is not limited to, a broadband personal communication device, specialized mobile radio device, handheld device or laptop computer with mobile data access, pager, and two-way messaging device.
*** *(AM '13)*

23125. Use of Wireless Telephone Prohibited While Driving Schoolbus or Transit Vehicle Prohibited; Exceptions

(a) A person may not drive a schoolbus or transit vehicle, as defined in subdivision (g) of Section 99247 of the Public Utilities Code, while using a wireless telephone.

(b) This section does not apply to a driver using a wireless telephone for work-related purposes, or for emergency purposes, including, but not limited to, an emergency call to a law enforcement agency, health care provider, fire department, or other emergency service agency or entity.

(c) Notwithstanding any other provision of law, a violation of subdivision (a) does not constitute a serious traffic violation within the meaning of subdivision (i) of Section 15210. *(AD '04)*

23127. Trails and Paths

No person shall operate an unauthorized motor vehicle on any state, county, city, private, or district hiking or horseback riding trail or bicycle path that is clearly marked by an authorized agent or owner with signs at all entrances and exits and at intervals of not more than one mile indicating no unauthorized motor vehicles are permitted on the hiking or horseback riding trail, or bicycle path, except bicycle paths which are contiguous or adjacent to a roadway dedicated solely to motor vehicle use.

For the purpose of this section "unauthorized motor vehicle"means any motor vehicle that is driven upon a hiking or horseback riding trail without the written permission of an agent or the owner of the trail or path.

This section does not apply to the operation of an authorized emergency or maintenance vehicle on a hiking or horseback riding trail or bicycle path whenever necessary in furtherance of the purpose for which the vehicle has been classed as an authorized emergency vehicle. Any person who violates this section is guilty of a misdemeanor.

23128. Snowmobiles

It is unlawful for any person to operate a snowmobile in the following manner:

(a) On a highway except as provided in Section 38025.

(b) In a careless or negligent manner so as to endanger a person or property.

(c) For the purpose of pursuing deer or other game mammal with intent to harass such animals.

(d) For the propose of violating Section 602 of the Penal Code.

23129. Camper Exits

No person shall drive a motor vehicle upon which is mounted a camper containing any passengers unless there is at least one unobstructed exit capable of being opened from both the interior and exterior of such camper.

23135. Operation of Modified Motorized Bicycle

It is unlawful for any person to operate upon a highway any vehicle which was originally manufactured as a motorized bicycle, as defined in Section 406, and which has been modified in such a manner that it no longer conforms to the definition of a motorized bicycle.

23136. Person Under 21 With Blood-Alcohol of 0.01 Percent or Greater

(a) Notwithstanding Sections 23152 and 23153, it is unlawful for a person under the age of 21 years who has a blood-alcohol concentration of 0.01 percent or greater, as measured by a preliminary alcohol screening test or other chemical test, to drive a vehicle. However, this section shall not be a bar to prosecution under Section 23152 or 23153 or any other provision of law.

(b) A person shall be found to be in violation of subdivision (a) if the person was, at the time of driving, under the age of 21 years, and the trier of fact finds that the person had consumed an alcoholic beverage and was driving a vehicle with a blood-alcohol concentration of 0.01 percent or greater, as measured by a preliminary alcohol screening test or other chemical test.

(c)(1) Any person under the age of 21 years who drives a motor vehicle is deemed to have given his or her consent to a preliminary alcohol screening test or other chemical test for the purpose of determining the presence of alcohol in the person, if lawfully detained for an alleged violation of subdivision (a).

(2) The testing shall be incidental to a lawful detention and administered at the direction of a peace officer having reasonable cause to believe the person was driving a motor vehicle in violation of subdivision (a).

(3) The person shall be told that his or her failure to submit to, or the failure to complete, a preliminary alcohol screening test or other chemical test as requested will result in the suspension or revocation of the person's privilege to operate a motor vehicle for a period of one year to three years, as provided in Section 13353.1.

23140. Alcohol: Minor Driver

(a) It is unlawful for a person under the age of 21 years who has 0.05 percent or more, by weight, of alcohol in his or her blood to drive a vehicle.

(b) A person may be found to be in violation of subdivision (a) if the person was, at the time of driving, under the age of 21 years and under the influence of, or affected by, an alcoholic beverage regardless of whether a chemical test was made to determine that person's blood-alcohol concentration and if the trier of fact finds that the person had consumed an alcoholic beverage and was driving a vehicle while having a concentration of 0.05 percent or more, by weight, of alcohol in his or her blood.

(c) Notwithstanding any provision of law to the contrary, upon a finding that a person has violated this section, the clerk of the court shall prepare within 10 days after the finding and immediately forward to the department an abstract of the record of the court in which the finding is made. That abstract shall be a public record and available for public inspection in the same manner as other records reported under Section 1803. *(AM '07)*

ALCOHOL & DRUG OFFENSES

23152.   DUI: Drive Vehicle While Under Influence of Alcohol and/or Drugs [Op 1-1-2014]

(a) It is unlawful for a person who is under the influence of any alcoholic beverage to drive a vehicle.

(b) It is unlawful for a person who has 0.08 percent or more, by weight, of alcohol in his or her blood to drive a vehicle.

For purposes of this article and Section 34501.16, percent, by weight, of alcohol in a person's blood is based upon grams of alcohol per 100 milliliters of blood or grams of alcohol per 210 liters of breath.

In any prosecution under this subdivision, it is a rebuttable presumption that the person had 0.08 percent or more, by weight, of alcohol in his or her blood at the time of driving the vehicle if the person had 0.08 percent or more, by weight, of alcohol in his or her blood at the time of the performance of a chemical test within three hours after the driving.

(c) It is unlawful for a person who is addicted to the use of any drug to drive a vehicle. This subdivision shall not apply to a person who is participating in a narcotic treatment program approved pursuant to Article 3 (commencing with Section 11875) of Chapter 1 of Part 3 of Division 10.5 of the Health and Safety Code.

(d) It is unlawful for a person who has 0.04 percent or more, by weight, of alcohol in his or her blood to drive a commercial motor vehicle, as defined in Section 15210.

In any prosecution under this subdivision, it is a rebuttable presumption that the person had 0.04 percent or more, by weight, of alcohol in his or her blood at the time of driving the vehicle if the person had 0.04 percent or more, by weight, of alcohol in his or her blood at the time of the performance of a chemical test within three hours after the driving.

(e) It is unlawful for a person who is under the influence of any drug to drive a vehicle.

(f) It is unlawful for a person who is under the combined influence of any alcoholic beverage and drug to drive a vehicle.

(g) This section shall become operative on January 1, 2014. *(AM '12)*

23153.   DUI Causing Injury [Op 1-1-2014]

(a) It is unlawful for a person, while under the influence of any alcoholic beverage to drive a vehicle and concurrently do any act forbidden by law, or neglect any duty imposed by law in driving the vehicle, which act or neglect proximately causes bodily injury to any person other than the driver.

(b) It is unlawful for a person, while having 0.08 percent or more, by weight, of alcohol in his or her blood to drive a vehicle and concurrently do any act forbidden by law, or neglect any duty imposed by law in driving the vehicle, which act or neglect proximately causes bodily injury to any person other than the driver.

In any prosecution under this subdivision, it is a rebuttable presumption that the person had 0.08 percent or more, by weight, of alcohol in his or her blood at the time of driving the vehicle if the person had 0.08 percent or more, by weight, of alcohol in his or her blood at the time of the performance of a chemical test within three hours after driving.

(c) In proving the person neglected any duty imposed by law in driving the vehicle, it is not necessary to prove that any specific section of this code was violated.

(d) It is unlawful for a person, while having 0.04 percent or more, by weight, of alcohol in his or her blood to drive a commercial motor vehicle, as defined in Section 15210, and concurrently to do any act forbidden by law or neglect any duty imposed by law in driving the vehicle, which act or neglect proximately causes bodily injury to any person other than the driver.

In any prosecution under this subdivision, it is a rebuttable presumption that the person had 0.04 percent or more, by weight, of alcohol in his or her blood at the time of driving the vehicle if the person had 0.04 percent or more, by weight, of alcohol in his or her blood at the time of performance of a chemical test within three hours after driving.

(e) It is unlawful for a person, while under the influence of any drug, to drive a vehicle and concurrently do any act forbidden by law, or neglect any duty imposed by law in driving the vehicle, which act or neglect proximately causes bodily injury to any person other than the driver.

(f) It is unlawful for a person, while under the combined influence of any alcoholic beverage and drug, to drive a vehicle and concurrently do any act forbidden by law, or neglect any duty imposed by law in driving the vehicle, which act or neglect proximately causes bodily injury to any person other than the driver.

(g) This section shall become operative on January 1, 2014. *(AM '12)*

23154. Person on Probation for D.U.I. - Operate Motor Vehicle with Blood Alcohol Concentration of 0.01 or Greater

(a) It is unlawful for a person who is on probation for a violation of Section 23152 or 23153 to operate a motor vehicle at any time with a blood-alcohol concentration of 0.01 percent or greater, as measured by a preliminary alcohol screening test or other chemical test.

(b) A person may be found to be in violation of subdivision (a) if the person was, at the time of driving, on probation for a violation of Section 23152 or 23153, and the trier of fact finds that the person had consumed an alcoholic beverage and was driving a vehicle with a blood-alcohol concentration of 0.01 percent or greater, as measured by a preliminary alcohol screening test or other chemical test.

(c)(1) A person who is on probation for a violation of Section 23152 or 23153 who drives a motor vehicle is deemed to have given his or her consent to a preliminary alcohol screening test or other chemical test for the purpose of determining the presence of alcohol in the person, if lawfully detained for an alleged violation of subdivision (a).

(2) The testing shall be incidental to a lawful detention and administered at the direction of a peace officer having reasonable cause to believe the person is driving a motor vehicle in violation of subdivision (a).

(3) The person shall be told that his or her failure to submit to, or the failure to complete, a preliminary alcohol screening test or other chemical test as requested will result in the suspension or revocation of the person's privilege to operate a motor vehicle for a period of one year to three years, as provided in Section 13353.1. *(AD '07)*

23157. Implied Consent For Chemical Testing [Renumbered to 23162]

23162. Implied Consent For Chemical Testing

(a)(1)(A) Any person who drives a motor vehicle is deemed to have given his or her consent to chemical testing of his or her blood or breath for the purpose of determining the alcoholic content of his or her blood, if lawfully arrested for any offense allegedly committed in violation of Section 23140, 23152, or 23153. If a blood or breath test, or both, are unavailable, then paragraph (2) of subdivision (d) applies.

(B) Any person who drives a motor vehicle is deemed to have given his or her consent to chemical testing of his or her blood or urine for the purpose of determining the drug content of his or her blood, if lawfully arrested for any offense allegedly committed in violation of Section 23140, 23152, or 23153.

(C) The testing shall be incidental to a lawful arrest and administered at the direction of a peace officer having reasonable cause to believe the person was driving a motor vehicle in violation of Section 23140, 23152, or 23153.

(D) The person shall be told that his or her failure to submit to, or the failure to complete, the required chemical testing will result in a fine, mandatory imprisonment if the person is convicted of a violation of Section 23152 or 23153, and (i) the suspension of the person's privilege to operate a motor vehicle for a period of one year, (ii) the revocation of the person's privilege to operate a motor vehicle for a period of two years if the refusal occurs within seven years of a separate violation of Section 23103 as specified in Section 23103.5, or of Section 23140, 23152, or 23153, or of Section 191.5 or paragraph (3) of subdivision (c) of Section 192 of the Penal Code which resulted in a conviction, or if the person's privilege to operate a motor vehicle has been suspended or revoked pursuant to Section 13353, 13353.1, or 13353.2 for an offense which occurred on a separate occasion, or (iii) the revocation of the person's privilege to operate a motor vehicle for a period of three years if the refusal occurs within seven years of two or more separate violations of Section 23103 as specified in Section 23103.5, or of Section 23140, 23152, or 23153, or of

Section 191.5 or paragraph (3) of subdivision (c) of Section 192 of the Penal Code, or any combination thereof, which resulted in convictions, or if the person's privilege to operate a motor vehicle has been suspended or revoked two or more times pursuant to Section 13353, 13353.1, or 13353.2 for offenses which occurred on separate occasions, or if there is any combination of those convictions or administrative suspensions or revocations.

(2)(A) If the person is lawfully arrested for driving under the influence of an alcoholic beverage, the person has the choice of whether the test shall be of his or her blood or breath and the officer shall advise the person that he or she has that choice. If the person arrested either is incapable, or states that he or she is incapable, of completing the chosen test, the person shall submit to the remaining test. If a blood or breath test, or both, are unavailable, then paragraph (2) of subdivision (d) applies.

(B) If the person is lawfully arrested for driving under the influence of any drug or the combined influence of an alcoholic beverage and any drug, the person has the choice of whether the test shall be of his or her blood, breath, or urine, and the officer shall advise the person that he or she has that choice.

(C) A person who chooses to submit to a breath test may also be requested to submit to a blood or urine test if the officer has reasonable cause to believe that the person was driving under the influence of any drug or the combined influence of an alcoholic beverage and any drug and if the officer has a clear indication that a blood or urine test will reveal evidence of the person being under the influence. The officer shall state in his or her report the facts upon which that belief and that clear indication are based. The person has the choice of submitting to and completing a blood or urine test, and the officer shall advise the person that he or she is required to submit to an additional test and that he or she may choose a test of either blood or urine. If the person arrested either is incapable, or states that he or she is incapable, of completing either chosen test, the person shall submit to and complete the other remaining test.

(3) If the person is lawfully arrested for an offense allegedly committed in violation of Section 23140, 23152, or 23153, and, because of the need for medical treatment, the person is first transported to a medical facility where it is not feasible to administer a particular test of, or to obtain a particular sample of, the person's blood, breath, or urine, the person has the choice of those tests which are available at the facility to which that person has been transported. In that case, the officer shall advise the person of those tests which are available at the medical facility and that the person's choice is limited to those tests which are available.

(4) The officer shall also advise the person that he or she does not have the right to have an attorney present before stating whether he or she will submit to a test or tests, before deciding which test or tests to take, or during administration of the test or tests chosen, and that, in the event of refusal to submit to a test or tests, the refusal may be used against him or her in a court of law.

(5) Any person who is unconscious or otherwise in a condition rendering him or her incapable of refusal is deemed not to have withdrawn his or her consent and a test or tests may be administered whether or not the person is told that his or her failure to submit to, or the noncompletion of, the test or tests will result in the suspension or revocation of his or her privilege to operate a motor vehicle. Any person who is dead is deemed not to have withdrawn his or her consent and a test or tests may be administered at the direction of a peace officer.

(b) Any person who is afflicted with hemophilia is exempt from the blood test required by this section.

(c) Any person who is afflicted with a heart condition and is using an anticoagulant under the direction of a licensed physician and surgeon is exempt from the blood test required by this section.

(d)(1) A person lawfully arrested for any offense allegedly committed while the person was driving a motor vehicle in violation of Section 23140, 23152, or 23153 may request the arresting officer to have a chemical test made of the arrested person's blood or breath for the purpose of determining the alcoholic content of that person's blood, and, if so requested, the arresting officer shall have the test performed.

(2) If a blood or breath test is not available under subparagraph (A) of paragraph (1) of subdivision (a), or under subparagraph (A) of paragraph (2) of subdivision (a), or under paragraph (1) of this subdivision, the person shall submit to the remaining test in order to determine the percent, by weight, of alcohol in the person's blood. If both the blood and breath tests are unavailable, the person shall be deemed to have given his or her consent to chemical testing of his or her urine and shall submit to a urine test.

(e) If the person, who has been arrested for a violation of Section 23140, 23152, or 23153, refuses or fails to complete a chemical test or tests, or requests that a blood or urine test be taken, the peace officer, acting on behalf of the department, shall serve the notice of the order of suspension or revocation of the person's privilege to operate a motor vehicle personally on the arrested person. The notice shall be on a form provided by the department.

(f) If the peace officer serves the notice of the order of suspension or revocation of the person's privilege to operate a motor vehicle, the peace officer shall take possession of any driver's license issued by this state which is held by the person. The temporary driver's license shall be an endorsement on the notice of the order of suspension and shall be valid for 30 days from the date of arrest.

(g) The peace officer shall immediately forward a copy of the completed notice of suspension or revocation form and any driver's license taken into possession under subdivision (f), with the report required by Section 23158.2, to the department. If the person submitted to a blood or urine test, the peace officer shall forward the results immediately to the appropriate forensic laboratory. The forensic laboratory shall forward the results of the chemical tests to the department within 15 calendar days of the date of the arrest.

(h) A preliminary alcohol screening test that indicates the presence or concentration of alcohol based on a breath sample in order to establish reasonable cause to believe the person was driving a vehicle in violation of Section 23140, 23152, or 23153 is a field sobriety test and may be used by an officer as a further investigative tool.

(i) If the officer decides to use a preliminary alcohol screening test, the officer shall advise the person that he or she is requesting that person to take a preliminary alcohol screening test to assist the officer in determining if that person is under the influence of alcohol or drugs, or a combination of alcohol and drugs. The person's obligation to submit to a blood, breath, or urine test, as required by this section, for the purpose of determining the alcohol or drug content of that person's blood, is not satisfied by the person submitting to a preliminary alcohol screening test. The officer shall advise the person of that fact and of the person's right to refuse to take the preliminary alcohol screening test. *(AM '99)*

23220. Drinking While Driving

(a) No person shall drink any alcoholic beverage while driving a motor vehicle upon any highway or on any lands described in subdivision (b).

(b) As used in subdivision (a), "lands" means those lands to which the Chappie-Z'berg Off-Highway Motor Vehicle Law of 1971 (Division 16.5 (commencing with Section 38000)) applies as to off-highway motor vehicles, as described in Section 38001. *(AM '98)*

23221. Drinking in Motor Vehicle

(a) No driver shall drink any alcoholic beverage while in a motor vehicle upon a highway.

(b) No passenger shall drink any alcoholic beverage while in a motor vehicle upon a highway. *(AM '99)*

23222. Possession of Marijuana or Open Container While Driving

(a) No person shall have in his or her possession on his or her person, while driving a motor vehicle upon a highway or on lands, as described in subdivision (b) of Section 23220, any bottle, can, or other receptacle, containing any alcoholic beverage which has been opened, or a seal broken, or the contents of which have been partially removed.

(b) Except as authorized by law, every person who possesses, while driving a motor vehicle upon a highway or on lands, as described in subdivision (b) of Section 23220, not more than one avoirdupois ounce of marijuana, other than concentrated cannabis as defined by Section 11006.5 of the Health and Safety Code, is guilty of an infraction punishable by a fine of not more than one hundred dollars ($100). *(AM '98, '10)*

23223. Possession of Open Container in Motor Vehicle

(a) No driver shall have in his or her possession, while in a motor vehicle upon a highway or on lands, as described in subdivision (b) of Section 23220, any bottle, can, or other receptacle, containing any alcoholic beverage that has been opened, or a seal broken, or the contents of which have been partially removed.

(b) No passenger shall have in his or her possession, while in a motor vehicle upon a highway or on lands, as described in subdivision (b) of Section 23220, any bottle, can, or other receptacle containing any alcoholic beverage that has been opened or a seal broken, or the contents of which have been partially removed. *(AM '99)*

23224. Possession of Alcohol in Vehicle: Person Under 21

(a) No person under the age of 21 years shall knowingly drive any motor vehicle carrying any alcoholic beverage, unless the person is accompanied by a parent, responsible adult relative, any other adult designated by the parent, or legal guardian for the purpose of transportation of an alcoholic beverage, or is employed by a licensee under the Alcoholic Beverage Control Act (Division 9 of the Business and Professions Code), and is driving the motor vehicle during regular hours and in the course of the person's employment. If the driver was unaccompanied, he or she shall have a complete defense if he or she was following, in a timely manner, the reasonable instructions of his or her parent, legal guardian, responsible adult relative, or adult designee relating to disposition of the alcoholic beverage.

(b) No passenger in any motor vehicle who is under the age of 21 years shall knowingly possess or have under that person's control any alcoholic beverage, unless the passenger is accompanied by a parent, legal guardian, responsible adult relative, any other adult designated by the parent, or legal guardian for the purpose of transportation of an alcoholic beverage, or is employed by a licensee under the Alcoholic Beverage Control Act (Division 9 of the Business and Professions Code), and the possession or control is during regular hours and in the course of the passenger's employment. If the passenger was unaccompanied, he or she shall have a complete defense if he or she was following, in a timely manner, the reasonable instructions of his or her parent, legal guardian, responsible adult relative or adult designee relating to disposition of the alcoholic beverage.

(c) If the vehicle used in any violation of subdivision (a) or (b) is registered to an offender who is under the age of 21 years, the vehicle may be impounded at the owner's expense for not less than one day nor more than 30 days for each violation.

(d) Any person under 21 years of age convicted of a violation of this section is subject to Section 13202.5.

(e) Any person convicted for a violation of subdivision (a) or (b) is guilty of a misdemeanor and shall be punished upon conviction by a fine of not more than one thousand dollars ($1,000) or by imprisonment in the county jail for not more than six months, or by both that fine and imprisonment.

23225. Storage of Opened Container

(a)(1) It is unlawful for the registered owner of any motor vehicle to keep in a motor vehicle, when the vehicle is upon any highway or on lands, as described in subdivision (b) of Section 23220, any bottle, can, or other receptacle containing any alcoholic beverage that has been opened, or a seal broken, or the contents of which have been partially removed, unless the container is kept in the trunk of the vehicle.

(2) If the vehicle is not equipped with a trunk and is not an off-highway motor vehicle subject to identification, as defined in Section 38012, the bottle, can, or other receptacle described in paragraph (1) shall be kept in some other area of the vehicle that is not normally occupied by the driver or passengers. For the purposes of this paragraph, a utility compartment or glove compartment shall be deemed to be within the area occupied by the driver and passengers.

(3) If the vehicle is not equipped with a trunk and is an off-highway motor vehicle subject to identification, as defined in subdivision (a) of Section 38012, the bottle, can, or other receptacle described in paragraph (1) shall be kept in a locked container. As used in this paragraph, "locked container" means a secure container that is fully enclosed and locked by a padlock, key lock, combination lock, or similar locking device.

(b) Subdivision (a) is also applicable to a driver of a motor vehicle if the registered owner is not present in the vehicle.

(c) This section shall not apply to the living quarters of a housecar or camper. *(AM '99)*

23226. Storage of Opened Container in Passenger Compartment

(a) It is unlawful for any driver to keep in the passenger compartment of a motor vehicle, when the vehicle is upon any highway or on lands, as described in subdivision (b) of Section 23220, any bottle, can, or other receptacle containing any alcoholic beverage that has been opened, or a seal broken, or the contents of which have been partially removed.

(b) It is unlawful for any passenger to keep in the passenger compartment of a motor vehicle, when the vehicle is upon any highway or on lands, as described in subdivision (b) of Section 23220, any bottle, can, or other receptacle containing any alcoholic beverage that has been opened or a seal broken, or the contents of which have been partially removed.

(c) This section shall not apply to the living quarters of a housecar or camper. *(AM '99)*

23229. Possession of Alcoholic Beverages: Exceptions

(a) Except as provided in Section 23229.1, Sections 23221 and 23223 do not apply to passengers in any bus, taxicab, or limousine for hire licensed to transport passengers pursuant to the Public Utilities Code or proper local authority, or the living quarters of a housecar or camper.

(b) Except as provided in Section 23229.1, Section 23225 does not apply to the driver or owner of a bus, taxicab, or limousine for hire licensed to transport passengers pursuant to the Public Utilities Code or proper local authority.

23229.1. Possession of Alcohol in Limousine: Passengers Under Age 21

(a) Subject to subdivision (b), Sections 23223 and 23225 apply to any driver providing transportation services on a prearranged basis as a charter-party carrier of passengers, as defined in Section 5360 of the Public Utilities Code, when the driver of the vehicle transports any passenger under 21 years of age and fails to comply with the requirements of Section 5384.1 of the Public Utilities Code.

(b) For purposes of subdivision (a), it is not a violation of Section 23225 for any driver providing transportation services on a prearranged basis as a charter-party carrier of passengers that is licensed pursuant to the Public Utilities Code to keep any bottle, can, or other receptacle containing any alcoholic beverage in a locked utility compartment within the area occupied by the driver and passengers.

(c) In addition to the requirements of Section 1803, every clerk of a court in which any driver in subdivision (a) was convicted of a violation of Section 23225 shall prepare within 10 days after conviction, and immediately forward to the Public Utilities Commission at its office in San Francisco, an abstract of the record of the court covering the case in which the person was convicted. If sentencing is not pronounced in conjunction with the conviction, the abstract shall be forwarded to the commission within 10 days after sentencing, and the abstract shall be certified, by the person required to prepare it, to be true and correct. For the purposes of this subdivision, a forfeiture of bail is equivalent to a conviction. *(AM '12)*

IGNITION INTERLOCK DEVICE

23247. Ignition Interlock Device: Punishment/Defense for Violation of Section 23246

(a) It is unlawful for a person to knowingly rent, lease, or lend a motor vehicle to another person known to have had his or her driving privilege restricted as provided in Section 13352 or 13352, 23575, or 23700, unless the vehicle is equipped with a functioning, certified ignition interlock device. AnyA person, whose driving privilege is restricted pursuant to Section 13352 or 2357513352, 23575, or 23700 shall notify any other person who rents, leases, or loans a motor vehicle to him or her of the driving restriction imposed under that section.

(b) It is unlawful for any person whose driving privilege is restricted pursuant to Section 1335213352, 23575, or 23575 23700 to request or solicit any other person to blow into an ignition interlock device or to start a motor vehicle equipped with the device for the purpose of providing the person so restricted with an operable motor vehicle.

(c) It is unlawful to blow into an ignition interlock device or to start a motor vehicle equipped with the device for the purpose of providing an operable motor vehicle to a person whose driving privilege is restricted pursuant to Section 1335213352, 23575, or 23575. 23700.

(d) It is unlawful to remove, bypass, or tamper with, an ignition interlock device.

(e) It is unlawful for any person whose driving privilege is restricted pursuant to Section 1335213352, 23575, or 23575 23700 to operate any vehicle not equipped with a functioning ignition interlock device.

(f) Any person convicted of a violation of this section shall be punished by imprisonment in the county jail for not more than six months or by a fine of not more than five thousand dollars ($5,000), or by both that fine and imprisonment.

(g)(1) If any person whose driving privilege is restricted pursuant to Section 13352 is convicted of a violation of subdivision (e), the court shall notify the Department of Motor Vehicles, which shall immediately terminate the restriction and shall suspend or revoke the person's driving privilege for the remaining period of the originating suspension or revocation and until all reinstatement requirements in Section 13352 are met.

(2) If any person who is restricted pursuant to subdivision (a) or (l) of Section 23575 or Section 23700 is convicted of a violation of subdivision (e), the department shall suspend the person's drivingsdriving privilege for one year from the date of the conviction.

(h) Notwithstanding any other provision of law, if a vehicle in which an ignition interlock device has been installed is impounded, the manufacturer or installer of the device shall have the right to remove the device from the vehicle during normal business hours. No charge shall be imposed for the removal of the device nor shall the manufacturer or installer be liable for any removal, towing, impoundment, storage, release, or administrative costs or penalties associated with the impoundment. Upon request, the person seeking to remove the device shall present documentation to justify removal of the device from the vehicle. Any damage to the vehicle resulting from the removal of the device is the responsibility of the person removing it. *(AM '99, '10)*

CHAPTER 13. VEHICULAR CROSSINGS & TOLL HIGHWAYS

23251. Authority of the Calif. Highway Patrol
(a) The CHP shall provide for proper and adequate policing of all toll highways and all vehicular crossings to insure the enforcement thereon of this code and of any other law relating to the use and operation of vehicles upon toll highways, highways or vehicular crossings, and of the rules and regulations of the California Department of Transportation in respect thereto, and to cooperate with the California Department of Transportation to the end that vehicular crossings be operated at all times in a manner as to carry traffic efficiently. The authority of the CHP is exclusive except as to the authority conferred by law upon the California Department of Transportation in respect to vehicular crossings.

(b) Notwithstanding subdivision (a), a private operator of all toll highway may make temporary arrangements, not to exceed 30 days, for traffic enforcement services with an agency that employees peace officers as described in Section 830.1 of the Penal Code, if the CHP cannot fulfill its responsibilities as described in this section, as determined by the Secretary of the Business, Transportation and Housing Agency.

(c) The services provided by the CHP for all toll highways that are operated by a private entity shall be reimbursed pursuant to Section 30809.1 of the Streets and Highways Code. If the private operator of a toll highway and the CHP reach an impasse in negotiating an agreement for reimbursement, the Secretary of the Business, Transportation and Housing Agency shall assist in resolving the impasse.

23253. Obedience to Officers
All persons in, or upon, any toll highway or vehicular crossing shall at all times comply with any lawful order, signal, or direction by voice or hand of any member of the CHP or an employee of the California Department of Transportation who is a peace officer.

23254. Vehicular Crossing
A "vehicular crossing" is any toll bridge or toll highway crossing and the approaches thereto, constructed or acquired by the Department of Transportation under the provisions of the California Toll Bridge Authority Act.

23270. Unauthorized Towing; Maximum Towing Fee; Permits

(a) No person shall commence to tow any vehicle or other object on any vehicular crossing unless authorized to do so by the California Department of Transportation and unless such towing is done by means of a tow car as defined in Section 615. No person, other than a member of the CHP or an employee of the California Department of Transportation, shall, by means of pushing with another vehicle, propel any vehicle or object on a vehicular crossing. No person, other than an employee of the California Department of Transportation, shall, on any vehicular crossing, tow any vehicle or other object except a vehicle or object constructed and designed to be towed by a vehicle of a type similar to that being used for such purpose.

(b) The Calif. Transportation Commission shall, by regulation, establish the maximum towing fee which may be charged by any person authorized to tow a vehicle pursuant to subdivision (a). No such authorized person shall charge a fee for towing a vehicle which is in excess of such maximum fee established by the Calif. Transportation Commission.

(c) The Director of Transportation may grant a special permit to any person to tow any vehicle or object over and completely across any vehicular crossing when in his judgment the towing vehicle is so constructed and equipped that the vehicle or object can be towed across the vehicular crossing without endangering persons or property and without interrupting the orderly traffic across the vehicular crossing.

(d) The prohibitions of this section shall apply only on those vehicular crossings upon which a towing service is maintained by the California Department of Transportation.

23302. Evasion of Toll

(a)(1) It is unlawful for a driver to fail to pay tolls or other charges on any vehicular crossing or toll highway. Except as otherwise provided in subdivision (b), (c), or (d), it is prima facie evidence of a violation of this section for a person to drive a vehicle onto any vehicular crossing or toll highway without either lawful money of the United States in the driver's immediate possession in an amount sufficient to pay the prescribed tolls or other charges due from that driver or a transponder or other electronic toll payment device associated with a valid Automatic Vehicle Identification account with a balance sufficient to pay those tolls.

(2) Except as specified in paragraph (3), if a transponder or other electronic toll payment device is used to pay tolls or other charges due, the device shall be located in or on the vehicle in a location so as to be visible for the purpose of enforcement at all times when the vehicle is located on the vehicular crossing or toll highway. Where required by the operator of a vehicular crossing or toll highway, this requirement applies even if the operator offers free travel or nontoll accounts to certain classes of users.

(3) If a motorcyclist uses a transponder or other electronic toll payment device to lawfully enter a vehicle crossing or toll highway, the motorcyclist shall use any one of the following methods as long as the transponder or device is able to be read by the toll operator's detection equipment:

(A) Place the transponder or other electronic toll payment device in the motorcyclist's pocket.

(B) Place the transponder or other electronic toll payment device inside a cycle net that drapes over the gas tank of the motorcycle.

(C) Mount the transponder or other electronic toll payment device on license plate devices provided by the toll operator, if the toll operator provides those devices.

(D) Keep the transponder or other electronic toll payment device in the glove or storage compartment of the motorcycle.

(E) Mount the transponder or other electronic toll payment device on the windshield of the motorcycle.

(b) For vehicular crossings and toll highways that use electronic toll collection as the only method of paying tolls or other charges, it is prima facie evidence of a violation of this section for a driver to drive a vehicle onto the vehicular crossing or toll highway without a transponder or other electronic toll payment device associated with a valid Automatic Vehicle Identification account with a balance sufficient to pay those tolls.

(c) For vehicular crossings and toll highways where the issuing agency, as defined in Section 40250, permits pay-by-plate payment of tolls and other charges, in accordance with policies adopted by the issuing agency, it is prima facie evidence of a violation of this section for a driver to drive a vehicle onto the vehicular crossing or toll highway without at least one of the following:

(1) Lawful money of the United States in the driver's immediate possession in an amount sufficient to pay the prescribed tolls or other charges due from that person.

(2) A transponder or other electronic toll payment device associated with a valid Automatic Vehicle Identification account with a balance sufficient to pay those tolls.

(3) Valid vehicle license plates properly attached pursuant to Section 4850.5 or 5200 to the vehicle in which that driver enters onto the vehicular crossing or toll highway.

(d) For vehicular crossings and toll highways where the issuing agency, as defined in Section 40250, permits pay-by-plate payment of tolls and other charges in accordance with policies adopted by the issuing agency, and where electronic toll collection is the only other method of paying tolls or other charges, it is prima facie evidence of a violation of this section for a driver to drive a vehicle onto the vehicular crossing or toll highway without either a transponder or other electronic toll payment device associated with a valid Automatic Vehicle Identification account with a balance sufficient to pay those tolls or valid vehicle license plates properly attached to the vehicle pursuant to Section 4850.5 or 5200 in which that driver enters onto the vehicular crossing or toll highway.

(e) As used in this article, "pay-by-plate toll payment"means an issuing agency's use of on-road vehicle license plate identification recognition technology to accept payment of tolls in accordance with policies adopted by the issuing agency.

(f) This section does not require an issuing agency to offer pay-by-plate toll processing as a method for paying tolls. *(AM '12)*

23302.5. Evade Payment of Tolls

(a) No person shall evade or attempt to evade the payment of tolls or other charges on any vehicular crossing or toll highway.

(b) A violation of subdivision (a) is subject to civil penalties and is neither an infraction nor a public offense, as defined in Section 15 of the Penal Code. The enforcement of those civil penalties shall be governed by the civil administrative procedures set forth in Article 4 (commencing with Section 40250) of Chapter 1 of Division 17.

23330. Animals, Vehicles, Bicycles, and Motorized Bicycles

Except where a special permit has been obtained from the Department of Transportation under the provisions of Article 6 (commencing with Section 35780) of Chapter 5 of Division 15, none of the following shall be permitted on any vehicular crossing:

(a) Animals while being led or driven, even though tethered or harnessed.

(b) Bicycles, motorized bicycles, or motorized scooters, unless the department by signs indicates that bicycles, motorized bicycles, or motorized scooters, or any combination thereof, are permitted upon all or any portion of the vehicular crossing.

(c) Vehicles having a total width of vehicle or load exceeding 102 inches.

(d) Vehicles carrying items prohibited by regulations promulgated by the Department of Transportation. *(AM '99)*

23331. Pedestrians

Pedestrians shall not be permitted upon any vehicular crossing, unless unobstructed sidewalks of more than three feet in width are constructed and maintained and signs indicating that pedestrians are permitted are in place.

23332. Trespass Prohibited

It is unlawful for any person to be upon any portion of a vehicular crossing which is not intended for public use without the permission of the California Department of Transportation. This section does not apply to a person engaged in the operation, maintenance, or repair of a vehicular crossing or any facility thereon nor to any person attempting to effect a rescue.

23333. Stopping and Parking

No vehicle shall stop, stand, or be parked in or upon any vehicular crossing except:

(a) When necessary to avoid injury or damage to persons or property.

(b) When necessary for the repair, maintenance or operation of a publicly owned toll bridge.

(c) In compliance with the direction of a member of the CHP or an employee of the California Department of Transportation who is a peace officer or with the direction of a sign or signal.

(d) In such places as may be designated by the Director of Transportation.

23336. Violation of Rules and Regulations

It is unlawful to violate any rules or regulations adopted under Section 23334, notice of which has been given either by a sign on a vehicular crossing or by publication as provided in Section 23335.

DIVISION 11.5.
SENTENCING FOR DRIVING WHILE UNDER THE INFLUENCE

23550. Fourth Offense Within Seven Years; Penalty

(a) If a person is convicted of a violation of Section 23152 and the offense occurred within 10 years of three or more separate violations of Section 23103, as specified in Section 23103.5, or Section 23152 or 23153, or any combination thereof, that resulted in convictions, that person shall be punished by imprisonment pursuant to subdivision (h) of Section 1170 of the Penal Code, or in a county jail for not less than 180 days nor more than one year, and by a fine of not less than three hundred ninety dollars ($390) nor more than one thousand dollars ($1,000). The person's privilege to operate a motor vehicle shall be revoked by the Department of Motor Vehicles pursuant to paragraph (7) of subdivision (a) of Section 13352. The court shall require the person to surrender the driver's license to the court in accordance with Section 13550.

(b) A person convicted of a violation of Section 23152 punishable under this section shall be designated as a habitual traffic offender for a period of three years, subsequent to the conviction. The person shall be advised of this designation pursuant to subdivision (b) of Section 13350. *(AM '11)*

23550.5. Felony Provisions

(a) A person is guilty of a public offense, punishable by imprisonment in the state prison or confinement in a county jail for not more than one year and by a fine of not less than three hundred ninety dollars ($390) nor more than one thousand dollars ($1,000) if that person is convicted of a violation of Section 23152 or 23153, and the offense occurred within 10 years of any of the following:

(1) A prior violation of Section 23152 that was punished as a felony under Section 23550 or this section, or both, or under former Section 23175 or former Section 23175.5, or both.

(2) A prior violation of Section 23153 that was punished as a felony.

(3) A prior violation of paragraph (1) of subdivision (c) of Section 192 of the Penal Code that was punished as a felony.

(b) Each person who, having previously been convicted of a violation of subdivision (a) of Section 191.5 of the Penal Code, a felony violation of subdivision (b) of Section 191.5, or a violation of subdivision (a) of Section 192.5 of the Penal Code, is subsequently convicted of a violation of Section 23152 or 23153 is guilty of a public offense punishable by imprisonment in the state prison or confinement in a county jail for not more than one year and by a fine of not less than three hundred ninety dollars ($390) nor more than one thousand dollars ($1,000).

(c) The privilege to operate a motor vehicle of a person convicted of a violation that is punishable under subdivision (a) or (b) shall be revoked by the department under paragraph (7) of subdivision (a) of Section 13352, unless paragraph (6) of subdivision (a) of Section 13352 is also applicable, in which case the privilege shall be revoked under that provision. The court shall require the person to surrender the driver's license to the court in accordance with Section 13550.

(d) A person convicted of a violation of Section 23152 or 23153 that is punishable under this section shall be designated as a habitual traffic offender for a period of three years, subsequent to the conviction.

The person shall be advised of this designation under subdivision (b) of Section 13350. *(AM '01, '02, '07, '09-'10)*

23560.   Second Conviction within Seven Years; Penalty

If a person is convicted of a violation of Section 23153 and the offense occurred within 10 years of a separate violation of Section 23103, as specified in Section 23103.5, 23152, or 23153 that resulted in a conviction, that person shall be punished by imprisonment in the state prison, or in a county jail for not less than 120 days nor more than one year, and by a fine of not less than three hundred ninety dollars ($390) nor more than five thousand dollars ($5,000). The person's privilege to operate a motor vehicle shall be revoked by the Department of Motor Vehicles pursuant to paragraph (4) of subdivision (a) of Section 13352. The court shall require the person to surrender the driver's license to the court in accordance with Section 13550. *(AD '98; AM '02, '04)*

23566.   Third Conviction within Seven Years; Penalty

(a) If a person is convicted of a violation of Section 23153 and the offense occurred within 10 years of two or more separate violations of Section 23103, as specified in Section 23103.5, or Section 23152 or 23153, or any combination of these violations, that resulted in convictions, that person shall be punished by imprisonment in the state prison for a term of two, three, or four years and by a fine of not less than one thousand fifteen dollars ($1,015) nor more than five thousand dollars ($5,000). The person's privilege to operate a motor vehicle shall be revoked by the Department of Motor Vehicles pursuant to paragraph (6) of subdivision (a) of Section 13352. The court shall require the person to surrender the driver's license to the court in accordance with Section 13550.

(b) If a person is convicted of a violation of Section 23153, and the act or neglect proximately causes great bodily injury, as defined in Section 12022.7 of the Penal Code, to any person other than the driver, and the offense occurred within 10 years of two or more separate violations of Section 23103, as specified in Section 23103.5, or Section 23152 or 23153, or any combination of these violations, that resulted in convictions, that person shall be punished by imprisonment in the state prison for a term of two, three, or four years and by a fine of not less than one thousand fifteen dollars ($1,015) nor more than five thousand dollars ($5,000). The person's privilege to operate a motor vehicle shall be revoked by the Department of Motor Vehicles pursuant to paragraph (6) of subdivision (a) of Section 13352. The court shall require the person to surrender the driver's license to the court in accordance with Section 13550.

(c) If a person is convicted under subdivision (b), and the offense for which the person is convicted occurred within 10 years of four or more separate violations of Section 23103, as specified in Section 23103.5, or Section 23152 or 23153, or any combination of these violations, that resulted in convictions, that person shall, in addition and consecutive to the sentences imposed under subdivision (b), be punished by an additional term of imprisonment in the state prison for three years.

The enhancement allegation provided in this subdivision shall be pleaded and proved as provided by law.

(d) A person convicted of Section 23153 punishable under this section shall be designated as a habitual traffic offender for a period of three years, subsequent to the conviction. The person shall be advised of this designation pursuant to subdivision (b) of Section 13350.

(e) A person confined in state prison under this section shall be ordered by the court to participate in an alcohol or drug program, or both, that is available at the prison during the person's confinement. Completion of an alcohol or drug program under this section does not meet the program completion requirement of paragraph (6) of subdivision (a) of Section 13352, unless the drug or alcohol program is licensed under Section 11836 of the Health and Safety Code, or is a program specified in Section 8001 of the Penal Code. *(AM '99, '02, '04, '10)*

23573.   Interlock Requirements and Terms of Requirement; DMV to Inform Persons Convicted

(a) The Department of Motor Vehicles, upon receipt of the court's abstract of conviction for a violation listed in subdivision (j), shall inform the convicted person of the requirements of this section and the term for which the person is required to have a certified ignition interlock device installed. The records of the department shall reflect the mandatory use of the device for the term required and the time when the device is required to be installed pursuant to this code.

(b) The department shall advise the person that installation of an ignition interlock device on a vehicle does not allow the person to drive without a valid driver's license.

(c) A person who is notified by the department pursuant to subdivision (a) shall, within 30 days of notification, complete all of the following:

(1) Arrange for each vehicle owned or operated by the person to be fitted with an ignition interlock device by a certified ignition interlock device provider under Section 13386.

(2) Notify the department and provide to the department proof of installation by submitting the "Verification of Installation"form described in paragraph (2) of subdivision (g) of Section 13386.

(3) Pay to the department a fee sufficient to cover the costs of administration of this section, including startup costs, as determined by the department.

(d) The department shall place a restriction on the driver's license record of the convicted person that states the driver is restricted to driving only vehicles equipped with a certified ignition interlock device.

(e)(1) A person who is notified by the department pursuant to subdivision (a) shall arrange for each vehicle with an ignition interlock device to be serviced by the installer at least once every 60 days in order for the installer to recalibrate and monitor the operation of the device.

(2) The installer shall notify the department if the device is removed or indicates that the person has attempted to remove, bypass, or tamper with the device, or if the person fails three or more times to comply with any requirement for the maintenance or calibration of the ignition interlock device.

(f) The department shall monitor the installation and maintenance of the ignition interlock device installed pursuant to subdivision (a).

(g)(1) A person who is notified by the department, pursuant to subdivision (a), is exempt from the requirements of subdivision (c) if all of the following circumstances occur:

(A) Within 30 days of the notification, the person certifies to the department all of the following:

(i) The person does not own a vehicle.

(ii) The person does not have access to a vehicle at his or her residence.

(iii) The person no longer has access to the vehicle being driven by the person when he or she was arrested for a violation that subsequently resulted in a conviction for a violation listed in subdivision (j).

(iv) The person acknowledges that he or she is only allowed to drive a vehicle that is fitted with an operating ignition interlock device and that he or she is required to have a valid driver's license before he or she can drive.

(v) The person is subject to the requirements of this section when he or she purchases or has access to a vehicle.

(B) The person's driver's license record has been restricted pursuant to subdivision (d).

(C) The person complies with this section immediately upon commencing ownership or operation of a vehicle subject to the required installation of an ignition interlock device.

(2) A person who has been granted an exemption pursuant to this subdivision and who subsequently drives a vehicle in violation of the exemption is subject to the penalties of subdivision (i) in addition to any other applicable penalties in law.

(h) This section does not permit a person to drive without a valid driver's license.

(i) A person who is required under subdivision (c) to install an ignition interlock device who willfully fails to install the ignition interlock device within the time period required under subdivision (c) is guilty of a misdemeanor and shall be punished by imprisonment in the county jail for not more than six months or by a fine of not more than five thousand dollars ($5,000), or by both that fine and imprisonment.

(j) In addition to all other requirements of this code, a person convicted of any of the following violations shall be punished as follows:

(1) Upon a conviction of a violation of Section 14601.2, 14601.4, or 14601.5 subsequent to one prior conviction of a violation of Section 23103.5, 23152, or 23153, within a 10-year period, the person shall

immediately install a certified ignition interlock device, pursuant to this section, in all vehicles owned or operated by that person for a term of one year.

(2) Upon a conviction of a violation of Section 14601.2, 14601.4, or 14601.5 subsequent to two prior convictions of a violation of Section 23103.5, 23152, or 23153, within a 10-year period, or one prior conviction of Section 14601.2, 14601.4, or 14601.5, within a 10-year period, the person shall immediately install a certified ignition interlock device, pursuant to this section, in all vehicles owned or operated by that person for a term of two years.

(3) Upon a conviction of a violation of Section 14601.2, 14601.4, or 14601.5 subsequent to three or more prior convictions of a violation of Section 23103.5, 23152, or 23153, within a 10-year period, or two or more prior convictions of Section 14601.2, 14601.4, or 14601.5, within a 10-year period, the person shall immediately install a certified ignition interlock device, pursuant to this section, in all vehicles owned or operated by that person for a term of three years.

(k) The department shall notify the court if a person subject to this section has failed to show proof of installation within 30 days of the department informing the person he or she is required to install a certified ignition interlock device.

(l) Subdivisions (j), (k), (m), (n), and (o) of Section 23575 apply to this section.

(m) The requirements of this section are in addition to any other requirements of law.

(n) This section shall become operative on July 1, 2009. *(AD '08)*

23610. Presumptions

(a) Upon the trial of any criminal action, or preliminary proceeding in a criminal action, arising out of acts alleged to have been committed by any person while driving a vehicle while under the influence of an alcoholic beverage in violation of subdivision (a) of Section 23152 or subdivision (a) of Section 23153, the amount of alcohol in the person's blood at the time of the test as shown by chemical analysis of that person's blood, breath, or urine shall give rise to the following presumptions affecting the burden of proof:

(1) If there was at that time less than 0.05 percent, by weight, of alcohol in the person's blood, it shall be presumed that the person was not under the influence of an alcoholic beverage at the time of the alleged offense.

(2) If there was at that time 0.05 percent or more but less than 0.08 percent, by weight, of alcohol in the person's blood, that fact shall not give rise to any presumption that the person was or was not under the influence of an alcoholic beverage, but the fact may be considered with other competent evidence in determining whether the person was under the influence of an alcoholic beverage at the time of the alleged offense.

(3) If there was at that time 0.08 percent or more, by weight, of alcohol in the person's blood, it shall be presumed that the person was under the influence of an alcoholic beverage at the time of the alleged offense.

(b) Percent, by weight, of alcohol in the person's blood shall be based upon grams of alcohol per 100 milliliters of blood or grams of alcohol per 210 liters of breath.

(c) This section shall not be construed as limiting the introduction of any other competent evidence bearing upon the question of whether the person ingested any alcoholic beverage or was under the influence of an alcoholic beverage at the time of the alleged offense.

23612. Implied Consent

(a)(1)(A) A person who drives a motor vehicle is deemed to have given his or her consent to chemical testing of his or her blood or breath for the purpose of determining the alcoholic content of his or her blood, if lawfully arrested for an offense allegedly committed in violation of Section 23140, 23152, or 23153. If a blood or breath test, or both, are unavailable, then paragraph (2) of subdivision (d) applies.

(B) A person who drives a motor vehicle is deemed to have given his or her consent to chemical testing of his or her blood for the purpose of determining the drug content of his or her blood, if lawfully arrested for an offense allegedly committed in violation of Section 23140, 23152, or 23153. If a blood test is unavailable, the person shall be deemed to have given his or her consent to chemical testing of his or her urine and shall submit to a urine test.

(C) The testing shall be incidental to a lawful arrest and administered at the direction of a peace officer having reasonable cause to believe the person was driving a motor vehicle in violation of Section 23140, 23152, or 23153.

(D) The person shall be told that his or her failure to submit to, or the failure to complete, the required chemical testing will result in a fine, mandatory imprisonment if the person is convicted of a violation of Section 23152 or 23153, and (i) the suspension of the person's privilege to operate a motor vehicle for a period of one year, (ii) the revocation of the person's privilege to operate a motor vehicle for a period of two years if the refusal occurs within 10 years of a separate violation of Section 23103 as specified in Section 23103.5, or of Section 23140, 23152, or 23153 of this code, or of Section 191.5 or subdivision (a) of Section 192.5 of the Penal Code that resulted in a conviction, or if the person's privilege to operate a motor vehicle has been suspended or revoked pursuant to Section 13353, 13353.1, or 13353.2 for an offense that occurred on a separate occasion, or (iii) the revocation of the person's privilege to operate a motor vehicle for a period of three years if the refusal occurs within 10 years of two or more separate violations of Section 23103 as specified in Section 23103.5, or of Section 23140, 23152, or 23153 of this code, or of Section 191.5 or subdivision (a) of Section 192.5 of the Penal Code, or any combination thereof, that resulted in convictions, or if the person's privilege to operate a motor vehicle has been suspended or revoked two or more times pursuant to Section 13353, 13353.1, or 13353.2 for offenses that occurred on separate occasions, or if there is any combination of those convictions***, administrative suspensions, or revocations.

(2)(A) If the person is lawfully arrested for driving under the influence of an alcoholic beverage, the person has the choice of whether the test shall be of his or her blood or breath and the officer shall advise the person that he or she has that choice. If the person arrested either is incapable, or states that he or she is incapable, of completing the chosen test, the person shall submit to the remaining test. If a blood or breath test, or both, are unavailable, then paragraph (2) of subdivision (d) applies.

(B) If the person is lawfully arrested for driving under the influence of any drug or the combined influence of an alcoholic beverage and any drug, the person has the choice of whether the test shall be of his or her blood or breath, and the officer shall advise the person that he or she has that choice.

(C) A person who chooses to submit to a breath test may also be requested to submit to a blood test if the officer has reasonable cause to believe that the person was driving under the influence of a drug or the combined influence of an alcoholic beverage and a drug and if the officer has a clear indication that a blood test will reveal evidence of the person being under the influence. The officer shall state in his or her report the facts upon which that belief and that clear indication are based. The officer shall advise the person that he or she is required to submit to an additional test. The person shall submit to and complete a blood test. If the person arrested is incapable of completing the blood test, the person shall submit to and complete a urine test.

(3) If the person is lawfully arrested for an offense allegedly committed in violation of Section 23140, 23152, or 23153, and, because of the need for medical treatment, the person is first transported to a medical facility where it is not feasible to administer a particular test of, or to obtain a particular sample of, the person's blood or breath, the person has the choice of those tests, including a urine test, that are available at the facility to which that person has been transported. In that case, the officer shall advise the person of those tests that are available at the medical facility and that the person's choice is limited to those tests that are available.

(4) The officer shall also advise the person that he or she does not have the right to have an attorney present before stating whether he or she will submit to a test or tests, before deciding which test or tests to take, or during administration of the test or tests chosen, and that, in the event of refusal to submit to a test or tests, the refusal may be used against him or her in a court of law.

(5) A person who is unconscious or otherwise in a condition rendering him or her incapable of refusal is deemed not to have withdrawn his or her consent and a test or tests may be administered whether or not the person is told that his or her failure to submit to, or the noncompletion of, the test or tests will result in the suspension or revocation of his or her privilege to operate a motor vehicle. A person who is dead is deemed

not to have withdrawn his or her consent and a test or tests may be administered at the direction of a peace officer.

(b) A person who is afflicted with hemophilia is exempt from the blood test required by this section, but shall submit to, and complete, a urine test.

(c) A person who is afflicted with a heart condition and is using an anticoagulant under the direction of a licensed physician and surgeon is exempt from the blood test required by this section, but shall submit to, and complete, a urine test.

(d)(1) A person lawfully arrested for an offense allegedly committed while the person was driving a motor vehicle in violation of Section 23140, 23152, or 23153 may request the arresting officer to have a chemical test made of the arrested person's blood or breath for the purpose of determining the alcoholic content of that person's blood, and, if so requested, the arresting officer shall have the test performed.

(2) If a blood or breath test is not available under subparagraph (A) of paragraph (1) of subdivision (a), or under subparagraph (A) of paragraph (2) of subdivision (a), or under paragraph (1) of this subdivision, the person shall submit to the remaining test in order to determine the percent, by weight, of alcohol in the person's blood. If both the blood and breath tests are unavailable, the person shall be deemed to have given his or her consent to chemical testing of his or her urine and shall submit to a urine test.

(e) If the person, who has been arrested for a violation of Section 23140, 23152, or 23153, refuses or fails to complete a chemical test or tests, or requests that a blood or urine test be taken, the peace officer, acting on behalf of the department, shall serve the notice of the order of suspension or revocation of the person's privilege to operate a motor vehicle personally on the arrested person. The notice shall be on a form provided by the department.

(f) If the peace officer serves the notice of the order of suspension or revocation of the person's privilege to operate a motor vehicle, the peace officer shall take possession of all driver's licenses issued by this state that are held by the person. The temporary driver's license shall be an endorsement on the notice of the order of suspension and shall be valid for 30 days from the date of arrest.

(g)(1) The peace officer shall immediately forward a copy of the completed notice of suspension or revocation form and any driver's license taken into possession under subdivision (f), with the report required by Section 13380, to the department. If the person submitted to a blood or urine test, the peace officer shall forward the results immediately to the appropriate forensic laboratory. The forensic laboratory shall forward the results of the chemical tests to the department within 15 calendar days of the date of the arrest.

(2)(A) Notwithstanding any other law, a document containing data prepared and maintained in the governmental forensic laboratory computerized database system that is electronically transmitted or retrieved through public or private computer networks to or by the department is the best available evidence of the chemical test results in all administrative proceedings conducted by the department. In addition, any other official record that is maintained in the governmental forensic laboratory, relates to a chemical test analysis prepared and maintained in the governmental forensic laboratory computerized database system, and is electronically transmitted and retrieved through a public or private computer network to or by the department is admissible as evidence in the department's administrative proceedings. In order to be admissible as evidence in administrative proceedings, a document described in this subparagraph shall bear a certification by the employee of the department who retrieved the document certifying that the information was received or retrieved directly from the computerized database system of a governmental forensic laboratory and that the document accurately reflects the data received or retrieved.

(B) Notwithstanding any other law, the failure of an employee of the department to certify under subparagraph (A) is not a public offense.

(h) A preliminary alcohol screening test that indicates the presence or concentration of alcohol based on a breath sample in order to establish reasonable cause to believe the person was driving a vehicle in violation of Section 23140, 23152, or 23153 is a field sobriety test and may be used by an officer as a further investigative tool.

(i) If the officer decides to use a preliminary alcohol screening test, the officer shall advise the person that he or she is requesting that person to take a preliminary alcohol screening test to assist the officer in determining if that person is under the influence of alcohol or drugs, or a combination of alcohol and drugs. The person's obligation to submit to a blood, breath, or urine test, as required by this section, for the purpose of determining the alcohol or drug content of that person's blood, is not satisfied by the person submitting to a preliminary alcohol screening test. The officer shall advise the person of that fact and of the person's right to refuse to take the preliminary alcohol screening test. *(AM '13)*

23614. Breath Tests; Admonishment that Sample not Retained
   (a) In addition to the requirements of Section 23612, a person who chooses to submit to a breath test shall be advised before or after the test that the breath-testing equipment does not retain any sample of the breath and that no breath sample will be available after the test which could be analyzed later by that person or any other person.

   (b) The person shall also be advised that, because no breath sample is retained, the person will be given an opportunity to provide a blood or urine sample that will be retained at no cost to the person so that there will be something retained that may be subsequently analyzed for the alcoholic content of the person's blood. If the person completes a breath test and wishes to provide a blood or urine sample to be retained, the sample shall be collected and retained in the same manner as if the person had chosen a blood or urine test initially.

   (c) The person shall also be advised that the blood or urine sample may be tested by either party in any criminal prosecution. The failure of either party to perform this test shall place neither a duty upon the opposing party to perform the test nor affect the admissibility of any other evidence of the alcoholic content of the blood of the person arrested.

   (d) No failure or omission to advise pursuant to this section shall affect the admissibility of any evidence of the alcoholic content of the blood of the person arrested.

DIVISION 12. EQUIPMENT OF VEHICLES

CHAPTER 1. GENERAL PROVISIONS

24002. Vehicle Not Equipped or Unsafe
   (a) It is unlawful to operate any vehicle or combination of vehicles which is in an unsafe condition, or which is not safely loaded, and which presents an immediate safety hazard.

   (b) It is unlawful to operate any vehicle or combinations of vehicles which is not equipped as provided in this code.

24002.5. Operation of Farm Labor Vehicle that is Safety Hazard
   (a) No person may operate a farm labor vehicle that is in a condition that presents an immediate safety hazard or in violation of Section 24004 or 31402.

   (b) A violation of this section is a misdemeanor punishable by a fine of not less than one thousand dollars ($1,000) and not more than five thousand dollars ($5,000), or both that fine and a sentence of confinement for not more than six months in the county jail. No part of any fine imposed under this section may be suspended.

   (c) As used in this section, an "immediate safety hazard" is any equipment violation described in subdivision (a) of Section 31401 or Section 31405, including any violation of a regulation adopted pursuant to those provisions.

   (d) Any member of the Department of the California Highway Patrol may impound a farm labor vehicle operated in violation of this section pursuant to Section 34506.4. *(AD '00)*

24003. Vehicle With Unlawful Lamps
   No vehicle shall be equipped with any lamp or illuminating device not required or permitted in this code, nor shall any lamp or illuminating device be mounted inside a vehicle unless specifically permitted this code. This section does not apply to:

(a) Interior lamps such as door, brake and instrument lamps, and map, dash, and dome lamps designed and used for the purpose of illuminating the interior of the vehicle.

(b) Lamps needed in the operation or utilization of those vehicles mentioned in Section 25501, or vehicles used by public utilities in the repair or maintenance of their service, or used only for the illumination of cargo space of a vehicle while loading or unloading.

(c) Warning lamps mounted inside an authorized emergency vehicle and meeting requirements established by the department.

24004. Unlawful Operation After Notice by Officer

No person shall operate any vehicle or combination of vehicles after notice by a peace officer that the vehicle is in an unsafe condition or is not equipped as required by this code, except as may be necessary to return the vehicle or combination of vehicles to the residence or place of business of the owner or driver or to a garage, until the vehicle and its equipment have been made to conform with the requirements of this code.

The provisions of this section shall not apply to an employee who does not know that such notice has been issued, and in such event the provisions of Section 40001 shall be applicable.

24005. Sale, Transfer or Installation of Unlawful Equipment

It is unlawful for any person to sell, offer for sale, lease, install, or replace, either for himself or as the agent or employee of another, or through such agent or employee, any glass, lighting equipment, signal devices, brakes, vacuum or pressure hose, muffler, exhaust, or any kind of equipment whatsoever for use, or with knowledge that any such equipment is intended for eventual use, in any vehicle, that is not in conformity with this code or regulations made thereunder.

24008. Modification of Vehicles - Road Clearance

It is unlawful to operate any passenger vehicle, or commercial vehicle under 6,000 pounds, which has been modified from the original design so that any portion of the vehicle, other than the wheels, has less clearance from the surface of a level roadway than the clearance between the roadway and the lowermost portion of any rim of any wheel in contact with the roadway.

24008.5. Frame and Floor Height

(a) No person shall operate any motor vehicle with a frame height or body floor height greater than specified in subdivisions (b) and (c).

(b) The maximum frame height is as follows:

(1) Passenger vehicles, except housecars:23 inches

(2) All other motor vehicles, including housecars, as follows:

Up to 4,500 pounds GVWR . . . . .27 inches
4,501 to 7,500 pounds GVWR. . . . . .30 inches
7,501 to 10,000 pounds GVWR. . . . . .31 inches

(c) The lowest portion of the body floor shall not be more than five inches above the top of the frame.

(d) The following definitions govern the construction of this section:

(1) "Frame"means the main longitudinal structural members of the chassis of the vehicle or, for vehicles with unitized body construction, the lowest main longitudinal structural members of the vehicle.

(2) "Frame height"means the vertical distance between the ground and the lowest point on the frame, measured when the vehicle is unladen on a level surface at the lowest point on the frame midway between the front axle and the second axle on the vehicle.

(3) "GVWR"means the manufacturer's gross vehicle weight rating, as defined in Section 390, whether or not the vehicle is modified by use of parts not originally installed by the manufacturer.

24009. Manufacturer's Name and GVW Rating

No person shall sell or offer for sale a new motor truck, truck tractor, or bus that is not equipped with an identification plate or marking bearing the manufacturer's name and the manufacturer's gross vehicle weight rating of such vehicle.

24010. Vehicle Rental Responsibility

(a) No person engaged in the rental of any vehicle, for periods of 30 days or less, shall rent, lease or otherwise allow the operation of such vehicle unless all of the following requirements are met:

(1) All necessary equipment required by this code and regulations adopted pursuant to this code for the operation of the vehicle upon a highway has been provided or offered to the lessee for his or her use.

(2) The vehicle conforms to all applicable federal motor vehicle safety standards established under the National Traffic and Motor Vehicle Safety Act of 1966 and the regulations adopted under that act.

(3) The vehicle is mechanically sound and safe to operate within the meaning of Section 24002.

(b) In order to ensure compliance with this section, the department may conduct periodic inspections, without prior notice, of the business premises of persons engaged in the rental of vehicles for periods of 30 days or less and of the vehicles themselves, for the purpose of ascertaining that the vehicles are in compliance with this section. Any vehicle which is found not in compliance shall not be rented or leased until proof of full compliance with this section is made to the satisfaction of the department.

(c) The contract or rental agreement shall include the name of the person from whom the vehicle is rented, leased or obtained, the address of that person's place of business in this state where the vehicle is rented, leased, or delivered, and a statement of any required equipment refused by the person to whom the vehicle is rented, leased, or delivered.

24012. Compliance With Lighting Equipment Mounting Regulations

All lighting equipment or devices subject to requirements established by the department shall comply with the engineering requirements and specifications, including mounting and aiming instructions, determined and publicized by the department.

24015. Motorized Bicycle: Safety and Equipment Requirements

(a) Motorized bicycles shall comply with those federal motor vehicle safety standards established under the National Traffic and Motor Vehicle Safety Act of 1965 (15 U.S.C., Section 1381, et seq.) which are applicable to a motor-driven cycle, as that term is defined in such federal standards. Such standards include, but are not limited to, provisions requiring a headlamp, taillamp, stoplamp, side and rear reflex reflectors, and adequate brakes.

(b) In addition to equipment required in subdivision (a), all motorized bicycles operated upon a highway shall be equipped with a mirror as required in subdivision (a) of Section 26709, a horn as required in Section 27000, and an adequate muffler as required in subdivision (a) of Section 27150.

(c) Except as provided in subdivisions (a) and (b), none of the provisions of this chapter relating to motorcycles and motor-driven cycles, as defined in this code, shall apply to a motorized bicycle.

24016. Motorized Bicycle - Requirements

(a) A motorized bicycle described in subdivision (b) of Section 406 shall meet the following criteria:

(1) Comply with the equipment and manufacturing requirements for bicycles adopted by the Consumer Product Safety Commission (16 C.F.R. 1512.1, et seq.) or the requirements adopted by the National Highway Traffic Safety Administration (49 C.F.R. 571.1, et seq.) in accordance with the National Traffic and Motor Vehicle Safety Act of 1966 (15 U.S.C. Sec. 1381, et seq.) for motor driven cycles.

(2) Operate in a manner so that the electric motor is disengaged or ceases to function when the brakes are applied, or operate in a manner such that the motor is engaged through a switch or mechanism that, when released, will cause the electric motor to disengage or cease to function.

(b) All of the following apply to a motorized bicycle described in subdivision (b) of Section 406:

(1) No person shall operate a motorized bicycle unless the person is wearing a properly fitted and fastened bicycle helmet that meets the standards described in Section 21212.

(2) A person operating a motorized bicycle is subject to Sections 21200 and 21200.5.

(3) A person operating a motorized bicycle is not subject to the provisions of this code relating to financial responsibility, driver's licenses, registration, and license plate requirements, and a motorized bicycle is not a motor vehicle.

(4) A motorized bicycle shall only be operated by a person 16 years of age or older.

(5) Every manufacturer of a motorized bicycle shall certify that it complies with the equipment and manufacturing requirements for bicycles adopted by the Consumer Product Safety Commission (16 C.F.R. 1512.1, et seq.).

(c) No person shall tamper with or modify a motorized bicycle described in subdivision (b) of Section 406 so as to increase the speed capability of the bicycle.

24017. Transit Bus – Speedometer Required

A transit bus operated by a motor carrier, whether the motor carrier is a private company or a public agency, that provides public transportation services shall be equipped with a speedometer that shall be maintained in good working order. *(AD '11)*

24018. Two-Way Communication Device Required on All Transit Busses

(a) Every transit bus operated by a motor carrier, whether that motor carrier is a private company or a public agency, that provides public transportation services shall be equipped with a two-way communication device that enables the driver to contact the motor carrier in the event of an emergency. The two-way communication devices shall be maintained in good working order.

(b) For the purposes of this section, "two-way communication device" is a radio, cellular telephone, or other similar device permitting communication between the transit bus driver and personnel responsible for the safety of operations of the motor carrier, including, but not limited to, the motor carrier's dispatcher.

(c) This section does not apply to buses operated by a school district or on behalf of a school district.

(d) The commissioner shall upon request grant a nonrenewable one year extension to any motor carrier to comply with the requirements of this section.

(e) Nothing in this section shall require a motor carrier to replace an existing two-way communication device that currently meets the requirements of this section. *(AD '02)*

CHAPTER 2. LIGHTING EQUIPMENT

24250. Lighting During Darkness

During darkness, a vehicle shall be equipped with lighted lighting equipment as required for the vehicle by this chapter.

24252. Lighting Equipment Requirements

(a) All lighting equipment of a required type installed on a vehicle shall at all times be maintained in good working order. Lamps shall be equipped with bulbs of the correct voltage rating corresponding to the nominal voltage at the lamp socket.

(b) The voltage at any tail, side marker or clearance lamp socket on a vehicle shall not be less than 85 percent of the design voltage of the bulb. Voltage tests shall be conducted with the engine operating.

(c) Two or more lamp or reflector functions may be combined, provided each function subject to requirements established by the department meets such requirements.

(1) No turn signal lamp may be combined optically with a stoplamp unless the stoplamp is extinguished when the turn signal is flashing.

(2) No clearance lamp may be combined optically with any taillamp or identification lamp.

24253. Taillamps Which Remain Lighted

(a) All motor vehicles manufactured and first registered after January 1, 1970, shall be equipped so all taillamps are capable of remaining lighted for a period of at least one-quarter hour with the engine inoperative. This requirement shall be complied with by an energy storing system which is recharged by energy produced by the vehicle.

(b) All motorcycles manufactured and first registered after January 1, 1971, shall be equipped so all taillamps, when turned on, will remain lighted automatically for a period of at least one-quarter hour if the engine stops.

24255. Supplemental Infrared Vision System; Requirements

(a) A vehicle may be equipped with a system to supplement the driver's visibility of the roadway to the front or rear of the vehicle during darkness. This system may incorporate an illuminating device that emits radiation predominantly in the infrared region of the electromagnetic spectrum and a display monitor to provide an image visible to the driver of the vehicle. The system, or any portion of it, shall not obstruct the vision of the driver, and shall not emit any glaring light visible in any direction or to any person. The illuminating device may be mounted inside the vehicle, if it is constructed and mounted so as to prevent any direct or reflected light, other than a monitorial indicator emitted from the device, from being visible to the driver.

(b) The system shall be operated only with the headlamps lighted. An illuminating device for the system shall be interlocked with the headlamp switch so that it is operable only when the headlamps are lighted.

(c)(1) No part of the illuminating device may be physically or optically combined with any other required or permitted lighting device.

(2) The illuminating device may be installed within a housing containing other required or permitted lighting devices, if the function of the other devices is not impaired thereby. *(AD '04)*

24400. Headlamps on Motor Vehicles

(a) A motor vehicle, other than a motorcycle, shall be equipped with at least two headlamps, with at least one on each side of the front of the vehicle, and, except as to vehicles registered prior to January 1, 1930, they shall be located directly above or in advance of the front axle of the vehicle. The headlamps and every light source in any headlamp unit shall be located at a height of not more than 54 inches nor less than 22 inches.

(b) A motor vehicle, other than a motorcycle, shall be operated during darkness, or inclement weather, or both, with at least two lighted headlamps that comply with subdivision (a).

(c) As used in subdivision (b), "inclement weather" is a weather condition that is either of the following:

(1) A condition that prevents a driver of a motor vehicle from clearly discerning a person or another motor vehicle on the highway from a distance of 1,000 feet.

(2) A condition requiring the windshield wipers to be in continuous use due to rain, mist, snow, fog, or other precipitation or atmospheric moisture. *(AM '06, '10)*

24401. Dimmed Lights on Parked Vehicles

Whenever any motor vehicle is parked or standing upon a highway any headlamp that is lighted shall dimmed or on the lower beam.

24402. Auxiliary Driving and Passing Lamps

(a) Any motor vehicle may be equipped with not to exceed two auxiliary driving lamps mounted on the front at a height of not less than 16 inches nor more than 42 inches. Driving lamps are lamps designed for supplementing the upper beam from headlamps and may not be lighted with the lower beam.

(b) Any motor vehicle may be equipped with not to exceed two auxiliary passing lamps mounted on the front at a height of not less than 24 inches nor more than 42 inches. Passing lamps are lamps designed for supplementing the lower beam from headlamps and may also be lighted with the upper beam.

24403. Foglamps

(a) A motor vehicle may be equipped with not more than two foglamps that may be used with, but may not be used in substitution of, headlamps.

(b) On a motor vehicle other than a motorcycle, the foglamps authorized under this section shall be mounted on the front at a height of not less than 12 inches nor more than 30 inches and aimed so that when the vehicle is not loaded none of the high-intensity portion of the light to the left of the center of the vehicle projects higher than a level of four inches below the level of the center of the lamp from which it comes, for a distance of 25 feet in front of the vehicle.

(c) On a motorcycle, the foglamps authorized under this section shall be mounted on the front at a height of not less than 12 inches nor more than 40 inches and aimed so that when the vehicle is not loaded none of the high-intensity portion of the light to the left of the center of the vehicle projects higher than a level of four inches below the level of the center of the lamp from which it comes, for a distance of 25 feet in front of the vehicle. *(AM '03)*

24404. Spotlamps

(a) A motor vehicle may be equipped with not to exceed two white spotlamps, which shall not be used in substitution of headlamps.

(b) No spotlamp shall be equipped with any lamp source exceeding 32 standard candlepower or 30 watts nor project any glaring light into the eyes of an approaching driver.

(c) Every spotlamp shall be so directed when in use:

That no portion of the main substantially parallel beam of light will strike the roadway to the left of the prolongation of the left side line of the vehicle.

That the top of the beam will not strike the roadway at a distance in excess of 300 feet from the vehicle.

(d) This section does not apply to spotlamps on authorized emergency vehicles.

(e) No spotlamp when in use shall be directed so as to illuminate any other moving vehicle.

24405. Maximum Number of Lamps

(a) Not more than four lamps of the following types showing to the front of a vehicle may be lighted at any one time:

(1) Headlamps.

(2) Auxiliary driving or passing lamps.

(3) Fog lamps.

(4) Warning lamps.

(5) Spot lamps.

(6) Gaseous discharge lamps specified in Section 25258.

(b) For the purpose of this section each pair of a dual headlamp system shall be considered as one lamp.

(c) Subdivision (a) does not apply to any authorized emergency vehicle.

24406. Multiple Beams

Except as otherwise provided, the headlamps, or other auxiliary driving lamps, or a combination thereof, on a motor vehicle during darkness shall be so arranged that the driver may select at will between distributions of light projected to different elevations, and the lamps may, in addition, be so arranged that the selection can be made automatically.

24407. Upper and Lower Beam

Multiple-beam road lighting equipment shall be designed and aimed as follows:

(a) There shall be an uppermost distribution of light, or composite beam, so aimed and of such intensity as to reveal persons and vehicles at a distance of at least 350 feet ahead for all conditions of loading.

(b) There shall be a lowermost distribution of light, or composite beam so aimed and of sufficient intensity to reveal a person or vehicle at a distance of at least 100 feet ahead. On a straight level road under any condition of loading none of the high intensity portion of the beam shall be directed to strike the eyes of an approaching driver.

24408. Beam Indicator

(a) Every new motor vehicle registered in this state after January 1, 1940, which has multiple-beam road lighting equipment shall be equipped with a beam indicator, which shall be lighted whenever the uppermost distribution of light from the headlamps is in use, and shall not otherwise be lighted.

(b) The indicator shall be so designed and located that when lighted it will be readily visible without glare to the driver of the vehicle so equipped. Any such lamp on the exterior of the vehicle shall have a light source not exceeding two candlepower, and the light shall not show to the front or sides of the vehicle.

24409. Use of Multiple Beams

Whenever a motor vehicle is being operated during darkness, the driver shall use a distribution of light, or composite beam, directed high enough and of sufficient intensity to persons and vehicles at a safe distance in advance of the vehicle, subject to the following requirements and limitations:

(a) Whenever the driver of a vehicle approaches an oncoming vehicle within 500 feet, he shall use a distribution of light or composite beam so aimed that the glaring rays are not projected into the eyes of the oncoming driver. The lowermost distribution of light specified in this article shall be deemed to avoid glare at all times regardless of road contour.

(b) Whenever the driver of a vehicle follows another vehicle within 300 feet to the rear, he shall use the lowermost distribution of light specified in this article.

24410. Single Beams

Headlamps arranged to provide a single distribution of light not supplemented by auxiliary driving lamps are permitted on motor vehicles manufactured and sold prior to September 19, 1940, in lieu of multiple-beam road lighting equipment if the single distribution of light complies with the following requirements and limitations:

(a) The headlamps shall be so aimed that when the vehicle is not loaded none of the high intensity portion of the light shall at a distance of 25 feet ahead project higher than a level of five inches below the level of the center of the lamp from which it comes, and in no case higher than 42 inches above the level on which the vehicle stands at a distance of 75 feet ahead.

(b) The intensity shall be sufficient to reveal persons and vehicles at a distance of at least 200 feet.

24411. Auxiliary Lamps: Off-Highway Use

Notwithstanding any other provision of law, a vehicle may be equipped with not more than eight lamps for use as headlamps while the vehicle is operated or driven off the highway. The lamps shall be mounted at a height of not less than 16 inches from the ground, or more than 12 inches above the top of the passenger compartment, at any place between the front of the vehicle an a line lying on a point 40 inches to the rear of the seat occupied by the driver, shall be wired independently of all other lighting circuits, and, whenever the vehicle is operated or driven upon a highway, shall be covered or hooded with an opaque hood or cover, and turned off.

24600. Taillamps

During darkness every motor vehicle which is not in combination with any other vehicle and every vehicle at the end of a combination of vehicles shall be equipped with lighted taillamps mounted on the rear as follows:

(a) Every vehicle shall be equipped with one or more taillamps.

(b) Every vehicle, other than a motorcycle, manufactured and first registered on or after January 1, 1958, shall be equipped with not less than two taillamps, except that trailers and semitrailers manufactured after July 23, 1973, which are less than 30 inches wide, may be equipped with one taillamp which shall be mounted at or near the vertical centerline of the vehicles. If a vehicle is equipped with two taillamps, they shall be mounted as specified in subdivision (d).

(c) Every vehicle or vehicle at the end of a combination of vehicles, subject to subdivision (a) of Section 22406 shall be equipped with not less than two taillamps.

(d) When two taillamps are required, at least one shall be mounted at the left and one at the right side respectively at the same level.

(e) Taillamps shall be red in color and shall be plainly visible from all distances within 500 feet to the rear except that taillamps on vehicles manufactured after January 1, 1969, shall be plainly visible from all distances within 1,000 feet to the rear.

(f) Taillamps on vehicles manufactured on or after January 1, 1969, mounted not lower than 15 inches nor higher than 72 inches, except that a tow truck, in addition to being equipped with the required taillamps, may also be equipped with two taillamps which may be mounted not lower than 15 inches nor higher than the maximum allowable vehicle height and as far forward as the rearmost portion of the driver's seat in the rearmost position. The additional taillamps on a tow truck shall be lighted whenever the headlamps are lighted.

24601. License Plate Lamp

Either the taillamp or a separate lamp shall be so constructed and placed as to illuminate with a white light the rear license plate during darkness and render it clearly legible from a distance of 50 feet to the rear. When the rear license plate is illuminated by a lamp other than a required taillamp, the two lamps shall be turned on or off only by the same control switch at all times.

24602. Fog Taillamps

(a) A vehicle may be equipped with not more than two red fog taillamps mounted on the rear which may be lighted, in addition to the required taillamps, only when atmospheric conditions, such as fog, rain, snow, smoke, or dust, reduce the daytime or nighttime visibility of other vehicles to less than 500 feet.

(b) The lamps authorized under subdivision (a) shall be installed as follows:

(1) When two lamps are installed, one shall be mounted at the left side and one at the right side at the same level and as close as practical to the sides. When one lamp is installed, it shall be mounted as close as practical to the left side or on the center of the vehicle.

(2) The lamps shall be mounted not lower than 12 inches nor higher than 60 inches.

(3) The edge of the lens of the lamp shall be no closer than four inches from the edge of the lens of any stoplamp.

(4) The lamps shall be wired so they can be turned on only when the headlamps are on and shall have a switch that allows them to be turned off when the headlamps are on.

(5) A nonflashing amber pilot light that is lighted when the lamps are turned on shall be mounted in a location readily visible to the driver. *(AM '04, '05)*

24603. Stoplamps

Every motor vehicle that is not in combination with any other vehicle and every vehicle at the end of a combination of vehicles shall at all times be equipped with stoplamps mounted on the rear as follows:

(a) Every such vehicle shall be equipped with one or more stoplamps.

(b) Every such vehicle, other than a motorcycle, manufactured and first registered on or after January 1, 1958, shall be equipped with two stoplamps, except that trailers and semitrailers manufactured after July 23, 1973, which are less than 30 inches wide, may be equipped with one stoplamp which shall be mounted at or near the vertical centerline of the trailer. If such vehicle is equipped with two stoplamps, they shall be mounted as specified in subdivision (d).

(c) Except as provided in subdivision (h), stoplamps on vehicles manufactured on or after January 1, 1969, shall be mounted not lower than 15 inches nor higher than 72 inches, except that a tow truck or a repossessor's tow vehicle, in addition to being equipped with the required stoplamps, may also be equipped with two stoplamps which may be mounted not lower than 15 inches nor higher than the maximum allowable vehicle height and as far forward as the rearmost portion of the driver's seat in the rearmost position.

(d) Where two stoplamps are required, at least one shall be mounted at the left and one at the right side, respectively, at the same level.

(e) Stoplamps on vehicles manufactured on or after January 1, 1979, shall emit a red light. Stoplamps on vehicles manufactured before January 1, 1979, shall emit a red or yellow light. All stoplamps shall be plainly visible and understandable from a distance of 300 feet to the rear both during normal sunlight and at nighttime, except that stoplamps on a vehicle of a size required to be equipped with clearance lamps shall be visible from a distance of 500 feet during those times.

(f) Stoplamps shall be activated upon application of the service (foot) brake and the hand control head for air, vacuum, or electric brakes. In addition, all stoplamps may be activated by a mechanical device designed to function only upon sudden release of the accelerator while the vehicle is in motion. Stoplamps on vehicles equipped with a manual transmission may be manually activated by a mechanical device when the vehicle is downshifted if the device is automatically rendered inoperative while the vehicle is accelerating.

(g) Any vehicle may be equipped with supplemental stoplamps mounted to the rear of the rearmost portion of the driver's seat in its rearmost position in addition to the lamps required to be mounted on the rear of the vehicle. Supplemental stoplamps installed after January 1, 1979, shall be red in color and mounted not lower than 15 inches above the roadway. The supplemental stoplamp on that side of a vehicle toward which a turn will be made may flash as part of the supplemental turn signal lamp.

A supplemental stoplamp may be mounted inside the rear window of a vehicle, if it is mounted at the centerline of the vehicle and is constructed and mounted so as to prevent any light, other than a monitorial indicator emitted from the device, either direct or reflected, from being visible to the driver.

(h) Any supplemental stoplamp installed after January 1, 1987, shall comply with Federal Motor Vehicle Safety Standard No. 108 (49 C.F.R. 571.108). Any vehicle equipped with a stoplamp that complies with the federal motor vehicle safety standards applicable to that make and model vehicle shall conform to that applicable safety standard unless modified to comply with the federal motor vehicle safety standard designated in this subdivision. *(AM '09)*

24604. Lamp or Flag on Projections
Whenever the load upon any vehicle extends, or whenever any integral part of any vehicle projects, to the rear four feet or more beyond the rear of the vehicle, as measured from the taillamps, there shall be displayed at the extreme end of the load or projecting part of the vehicle during darkness, in addition to the required taillamp, two red lights with a bulb rated not in excess of six candlepower plainly visible from a distance of at least 500 feet to the sides and rear. At any other time there shall be displayed at the extreme end of the load or projecting part of the vehicle a solid red or fluorescent orange flag or cloth not less than 12 inches square. *(AM '98, '00)*

24605. Tow Trucks and Towed Vehicles
(a) A tow truck or an automobile dismantler's tow vehicle used to tow a vehicle shall be equipped with and carry a taillamp, a stoplamp, and turn signal lamps for use on the rear of a towed vehicle.

(b) Whenever a tow truck or an automobile dismantler's tow vehicle is towing a vehicle and a stoplamp and turn signal lamps cannot be lighted and displayed on the rear of the towed vehicle, the operator of the tow truck or the automobile dismantler's tow vehicle shall display to the rear a stoplamp and turn signal lamps mounted on the towed vehicle, except as provided in subdivision (c). During darkness, if a taillamp on the towed vehicle cannot be lighted, the operator of the tow truck or the automobile dismantler's tow vehicle shall display to the rear a taillamp mounted on the towed vehicle. No other lighting equipment need be displayed on the towed vehicle.

(c) Whenever any motor vehicle is towing another motor vehicle, stoplamps and turn signal lamps are not required on the towed motor vehicle, but only if a stoplamp and a turn signal lamp on each side of the rear of the towing vehicle is plainly visible to the rear of the towed vehicle. This subdivision does not apply to driveaway-towaway operations. *(AM '09)*

24606. Backup Lamps
(a) Every motor vehicle, other than a motorcycle, of a type subject to registration and manufactured on and after January 1, 1969, shall be equipped with one or more backup lamps either separately or in combination with another lamp. Any vehicle may be equipped with backup lamps.

(b) Backup lamps shall be so directed as to project a white light illuminating the highway to the rear of the vehicle for a distance not to exceed 75 feet. A backup lamp may project incidental red, amber, or white light through reflectors or lenses that are adjacent or close to, or a part of, the lamp assembly.

(c) Backup lamps shall not be lighted except when the vehicle is about to be or is backing or except in conjunction with a lighting system which activates the lights for a temporary period after the ignition system is turned off.

(d) Any motor vehicle may be equipped with a lamp emitting white light on each side near or on the rear of the vehicle which is designed to provide supplemental illumination in an area to the side and rear not lighted by the backup lamps. These lamps shall be lighted only with the backup lamps.

24607. Reflectors on Rear
Every vehicle subject to registration under this code shall at all times be equipped with red reflectors mounted on the rear as follows:

(a) Every vehicle shall be equipped with at least one reflector so maintained as to be plainly visible at night from all distances within 350 to 100 feet from the vehicle when directly in front of the lawful upper headlamp beams.

(b) Every vehicle, other than a motorcycle or a low-speed vehicle, manufactured and first registered on or after January 1, 1965, shall be equipped with at least two reflectors meeting the visibility requirements of subdivision (a), except that trailers and semitrailers manufactured after July 23, 1973, that are less than 30 inches wide, may be equipped with one reflector which shall be mounted at or near the vertical centerline of the trailer. If the vehicle is equipped with two reflectors, they shall be mounted as specified in subdivision (d).

(c) Every motortruck having an unladen weight of more than 5,000 pounds, every trailer coach, every camp trailer, every vehicle, or vehicle at the end of a combination of vehicles, subject to subdivision (a) of Section 22406, and every vehicle 80 or more inches in width manufactured on or after January 1, 1969, shall be equipped with at least two reflectors maintained so as to be plainly visible at night from all distances within 600 feet to 100 feet from the vehicle when directly in front of lawful upper headlamp beams.

(d) When more than one reflector is required, at least one shall be mounted at the left side and one at the right side, respectively, at the same level. Required reflectors shall be mounted not lower than 15 inches nor higher than 60 inches, except that a tow truck, in addition to being equipped with the required reflectors, may also be equipped with two reflectors which may be mounted not lower than 15 inches nor higher than the maximum allowable vehicle height and as far forward as the rearmost portion of the driver's seat in the rearmost position. Additional reflectors of a type meeting requirements established by the department may be mounted at any height.

(e) Reflectors on truck tractors may be mounted on the rear of the cab. Any reflector installed on a vehicle as part of its original equipment prior to January 1, 1941, need not meet the requirements of the department provided it meets the visibility requirements of subdivision (a).

(f) Area reflectorizing material may be used in lieu of the reflectors required or permitted in subdivisions (a), (b), (c), (d), and (e), provided each installation is of sufficient size to meet the photometric requirement for those reflectors. *(AM '99)*

24608. Reflectors on Front and Sides

(a) Motortrucks, trailers, semitrailers, and buses 80 or more inches in width manufactured on or after January 1, 1958, shall be equipped with an amber reflector on each side at the front and a red reflector on each side at the rear. Any vehicle may be so equipped.

(b) Motortrucks, trailers, semitrailers, housecars, and buses 80 or more inches in width and 30 or more feet in length manufactured on or after January 1, 1958, shall be equipped with an amber reflector mounted on each side at the approximate midpoint of the vehicle. Any such vehicle manufactured prior to January 1, 1958, may be so equipped.

(c) Required reflectors on the sides of vehicles shall be mounted not lower than 15 inches nor higher than 60 inches. Additional reflectors of a type meeting requirements established by the department may be mounted at any height.

(d) Reflectors required or permitted in subdivisions (a) and (b) shall be so maintained as to be plainly visible at night from all distances within 600 feet to 100 feet from the vehicle when directly in front of lawful upper headlamp beams.

(e) Area reflectorizing material may be used in lieu of the reflectors required or permitted in subdivisions (a) and (b), provided each installation is of sufficient size to meet the photometric requirement for such reflectors.

24609. Vehicle Reflectors

(a) A vehicle may be equipped with white or amber reflectors that are mounted on the front of the vehicle at a height of 15 inches or more, but not more than 60 inches from the ground.

(b) A schoolbus may be equipped with a set of two devices, with each device in the set consisting of an amber reflector integrated into the lens of an amber light that is otherwise permitted under this code, if the set is mounted with one device on the left side and one on the right side of the vehicle, and with each device at the same level. *(AM '03)*

24611. Reflectors Not Required

Trailers that are equipped with red and white reflective sheeting or reflectors on both the sides and rear and displayed in accordance with federal Motor Vehicle Safety Standard regulations (49 C.F.R. 571.108) for trailers with a width of 80 inches or more and having a gross vehicle weight rating of over 10,000 pounds need not be equipped with the reflectors required by Section 24607 or 24608.

24612. Conspicuity System Required; Trailers and Semi-Trailers

(a) All trailers and semitrailers having an overall width of 80 inches or more and a gross vehicle weight rating of more than 10,000 pounds, and manufactured on or after December 1, 1993, except those designed exclusively for living or office use, and all truck tractors manufactured on or after July 1, 1997, shall be equipped with the conspicuity system specified in federal Motor Vehicle Safety Standard No. 108 (49 C.F.R. 571.108). The conspicuity system shall consist of either retroreflective sheeting or reflex reflectors, or a combination of retroreflective sheeting and reflex reflectors, as specified in the federal standard applicable on the date of manufacture of the vehicle.

(b) Any trailer, semitrailer, or motor truck having an overall width of 80 inches or more and manufactured prior to December 1, 1993, and any truck tractor manufactured prior to July 1, 1997, may be equipped with the conspicuity system described in subdivision (a).

24615. Slow-Moving Vehicle Emblem

It is unlawful to operate upon a public highway any vehicle or combination of vehicles, which is designed to be and is operated at a speed of 25 miles per hour or less, unless the rearmost vehicle displays a "slow-moving vehicle emblem," except upon vehicles used by a utility, whether publicly or for the construction, maintenance, or repair of its own facilities or upon vehicles used by highway authorities or bridge or highway districts in highway maintenance, inspection, survey, or construction work, while such vehicle is engaged in work at the job site upon a highway. Any other vehicle or combination of vehicles, when operated at a speed of 25 miles per hour or less, may display such emblem. The emblem shall be mounted on the rear of the vehicle, base down, and at a height of not less than three nor more than five feet from ground to base. Such emblem shall consist of a truncated equilateral triangle having a minimum height of 14 inches with a red reflective border not less than 1¾ inches in width and a fluorescent orange center. This emblem shall not be displayed except as permitted or required by this section.

24616. Rear Facing Auxiliary Lamps

(a) A motor vehicle may be equipped with one or two rear-facing auxiliary lamps. For the purposes of this section, a rear-facing auxiliary lamp is a lamp that is mounted on the vehicle facing rearward. That lamp shall meet the photometric and performance requirements of the Society of Automotive Engineers Standard J1424 for cargo lamps.

(b) A rear-facing auxiliary lamp may project only a white light, with the main cone of light projecting both rearward and downward. The main cone of light shall illuminate the road surface or ground immediately rearward of a line parallel to the rear of the vehicle for a distance not greater than 50 feet. The main cone of light may not project to the front or sides of the vehicle.

(c) A rear-facing auxiliary lamp may be activated only when the vehicle is stopped. A vehicle equipped with a rear-facing auxiliary lamp shall also be equipped with a system that allows activation of the lamp only when the vehicle is in the "park" setting, if the vehicle is equipped with an automatic transmission, or in the "neutral" setting with the parking brake engaged, if the vehicle is equipped with a manual transmission.

(d) A vehicle equipped with a rear-facing auxiliary lamp may have an activation switch accessible to the operator from the rear of the vehicle.

24800. Lighted Parking Lamps
No vehicle shall be driven at any time with the parking lamps lighted except when the lamps are being used as turn signal lamps or when the headlamps are also lighted.

24950. Turn Signal System Required
Whenever any motor vehicle is towing a trailer coach or a camp trailer the combination of vehicles shall be equipped with a lamp-type turn signal system.

24951. Turn Signal System
(a) Any vehicle may be equipped with a lamp-type turn signal system capable of clearly indicating any intention to turn either to the right or to the left.

(b) The following vehicles shall be equipped with a lamp-type turn signal system meeting the requirements of this chapter.

(1) Motor trucks, truck tractors, buses and passenger vehicles, other than motorcycles, manufactured and first registered on or after January 1, 1958.

(2) Trailers and semitrailers manufactured and first registered between December 31, 1957, and January 1, 1969, having a gross weight of 6,000 pounds or more.

(3) Trailers and semitrailers 80 or more inches in width manufactured on or after January 1,1969.

(4) Motorcycles manufactured and first registered on or after January 1, 1973, except motor-driven cycles whose speed attainable in one mile is 30 miles per hour or less.

The requirements of this subdivision shall not apply to special mobile equipment, or auxiliary dollies.

(c) Turn signal lamps on vehicles manufactured on or after January 1, 1969, shall be mounted not lower than 15 inches.

24952. Visibility Requirements of Signals
A lamp-type turn signal shall be plainly visible and understandable in normal sunlight and at nighttime from a distance of at least 300 feet to the front and rear of the vehicle, except that turn signal lamps on vehicles of a size required to be equipped with clearance lamps shall be visible from a distance of 500 feet during such times.

24953. Turn Signal Lamps
(a) Any turn signal system used to give a signal of intention to turn right or left shall project a flashing white or amber light visible to the front and a flashing red or amber light visible to the rear.

(b) Side-mounted turn signal lamps projecting a flashing amber light to either side may be used to supplement the front and rear turn signals. Side-mounted turn signal lamps mounted to the rear of the center of the vehicle may project a flashing red light no part of which shall be visible from the front.

(c) In addition to any required turn signal lamps, any vehicle may be equipped with supplemental rear turn signal lamps mounted to the rear of the rearmost portion of the driver's seat in its rearmost position.

(d) In addition to any required or authorized turn signal lamps, any vehicle may be equipped with supplemental rear turn signal lamps that are mounted on, or are an integral portion of, the outside rearview mirrors, so long as the lamps flash simultaneously with the rear turn signal lamps, the light emitted from the lamps is projected only to the rear of the vehicle and is not visible to the driver under normal operating conditions, except for a visual indicator designed to allow monitoring of lamp operation, and the lamps do not project a glaring light.

25100. Clearance and Side-Marker Lamps
(a) Except as provided in subdivisions (b) and (d), every vehicle 50 inches or more in overall width shall be equipped during darkness as follows:

(1) At least one amber clearance lamp on each side mounted on a forward-facing portion of the vehicle and visible from the front and at least one red clearance lamp at each side mounted on a rearward facing portion of the vehicle and visible from the rear.

(2) At least one amber side-marker lamp on each side near the front and at least one red side-marker lamp on each side near the rear.

(3) At least one amber side-marker lamp on each side at or near the center on trailers and semitrailers 30 feet or more in length and which are manufactured and first registered after January 1, 1962. Any such vehicle manufactured and first registered prior to January 1, 1962, may be so equipped.

(4) At east one amber side-marker lamp mounted at approximate midpoint of housecars, motortrucks, and buses 30 or more feet in length and manufactured on or after January 1, 1969. Any such vehicle manufactured prior to January 1,1969, may be so equipped.

(5) Combination clearance and sidemarker lamps mounted as sidemarker lamps and meeting the visibility requirements for both types of lamps may be used in lieu of required individual clearance or side-marker lamps.

(b) The following vehicles when 80 inches or more in overall width and not equipped as provided in subdivision (a) shall be equipped during darkness as follows:

(1) Truck tractors shall be equipped with at least one amber clearance lamp on each side on the front of the cab or sleeper and may be equipped with amber side-marker lamps on each side.

(2) Truck tractors manufactured on or after January 1, 1969, shall be equipped with one amber side-marker lamp on each side near the front.

(3) Pole or pipe dollies, or logging dollies, shall be equipped with at least one combination clearance and side-marker lamp on each side showing red to the front, side, and rear.

(4) Vehicles, except truck tractors, which are 80 inches or more in width over a distance not exceeding three feet from front to rear shall be equipped with at least one amber combination clearance lamp and side-marker lamp on each side visible from the front, side, and rear if the projection is near the front of the vehicle and at least one red lamp if the projection is near the rear of the vehicle.

(5) Towing motor vehicles engaged in driveaway-towaway operations shall be equipped with at least one amber clearance lamp at each side on the front and at least one amber side-marker lamp on each side near the front.

(6) Towed motor vehicles engaged in driveaway-towaway operations shall be equipped with at least one amber side-marker lamp on each side of intermediate vehicles, and the rearmost vehicle shall be equipped with at least one red side-marker lamp on each side and at least one red clearance lamp on each side on the rear.

(7) Trailers and semitrailers designed for transporting single boats in a cradle-type mounting and for launching the boat from the rear of the trailer need not be equipped with font and rear clearance lamps provided amber clearance lamps showing to the front and red clearance lamps showing to the rear are located on each side at or near the midpoint between the front and rear of the trailer to indicate the extreme width of the trailer.

(c) Loads extending beyond the side of a vehicle where the overall width of the vehicle and load is 80 inches or more shall be equipped with an amber combination clearance and side-marker lamp on the side at the front and a red combination clearance and side-marker lamp on the side at the rear. In lieu of the foregoing requirement, projecting loads not exceeding three feet from front to rear at the extreme width shall be equipped with at least one amber combination clearance and side-marker lamp on the side visible from the front, side, and rear if the projection is near the front of the vehicle and at least one red lamp if projection is near the rear of the vehicle.

(d) Clearance and side-marker lamps are not required on auxiliary dollies or on passenger vehicles other than a housecar.

(e) Clearance lamps shall be visible from all distances between 500 feet and 50 feet to the front or rear of the vehicle, and side-marker lamps shall be visible from all distances between 500 feet and 50 feet to the side of the vehicle.

(f) Clearance lamps shall, so far as is practicable, be mounted to the extreme width of the vehicle. Side-marker lamps shall be mounted not lower than 15 inches on vehicles manufactured on and after January 1, 1968. Combination clearance and side-marker lamps required on loads shall be mounted so the lenses project to the outer extremity of the vehicle or load.

25102. Lamps on Sides of Vehicles

In addition to the lamps otherwise permitted by this chapter, any motor vehicle may be equipped with lamps on the sides thereof visible from the side of the vehicle but not from the front or rear thereof, which lamps, together with mountings or receptacles, shall be set into depressions or recesses in the body of the vehicle and shall not protrude beyond or outside the body of the vehicle. The light source in each of the lamps shall not exceed two candlepower and shall emit diffused light of any color, except that the color red is permitted only on authorized emergency vehicles.

25102.5. Lamps on Sides of School Buses

(a) A school bus may be equipped with lamps mounted so as to be visible from the sides of the bus which may be lighted, in addition to other required lights, when, and only when, atmospheric conditions such as fog, rain, snow, smoke, or dust, reduce the visibility of other vehicles to less than 500 feet.

(b) The type and mounting requirements of such lamps shall be established by regulations adopted by the department. The regulations shall be adopted by January 1, 1980.

25103. Lamp on Projecting Load

Whenever the load upon any vehicle extends from the left side of the vehicle one foot or more, there shall be displayed at the extreme left side of the load during darkness:

(a) An amber lamp plainly visible for 300 feet to the front and rear of the vehicle.

(b) An amber lamp at the front visible for 300 feet to the front and a red lamp at the rear plainly visible for 300 feet to the rear of the vehicle if the projecting load exceeds 120 inches in length.

The lamp shall not contain a bulb rated in excess of six candlepower.

25104. Red Flag on Wide Vehicles

Any vehicle or equipment that requires a permit issued pursuant to Article 6 (commencing with Section 35780) of Chapter 5 of Division 15 because it is wider than permitted under Chapter 2 (commencing with Section 35100) of Division 15 shall display a solid red or fluorescent orange flag or cloth not less than 12 inches square at the extreme left front and left rear of the vehicle or equipment, if the vehicle or equipment is being operated other than during darkness. *(AM '98)*

25105. Courtesy Lamps

(a) Any motor vehicle may be equipped with running board or door-mounted courtesy lamps. The bulbs in the lamps shall not exceed six standard candlepower and shall emit either a green or white light without glare. The beams of the lamps shall not be visible to the front or rear of the vehicle.

(b) Any motor vehicle may be equipped with inside door-mounted red lamps or red reflectorizing devices or material visible to the rear of the vehicle when the doors are open. The bulbs in the lamps shall not exceed six standard candlepower.

(c) Any motor vehicle may be equipped with exterior lamps for the purpose of lighting the entrances and exits of the vehicles, which lamps may be lighted only when the vehicles are not in motion. The lamp source of the exterior lamps shall not exceed 32 standard candlepower, or 30 watts, nor project any glaring light into the eyes of an approaching driver.

25106. Side, Cowl, or Fender Lamps

(a) Any motor vehicle may be equipped with lighted white or amber cowl or fender lamps on the front. Any vehicle may be equipped with not more than one amber side lamp on each side near the front, nor more than one red side lamp on each side near the rear. The light source of each such lamp shall not exceed four standard candlepower.

(b) Lamps meeting requirements established by the department for side-marker or combination clearance and side-marker lamps may be installed on the sides of vehicles at any location, but any lamp installed within 24 inches of the rear of the vehicle shall be red and any lamp installed at any other location shall be amber.

25107. Cornering Lamps on Fenders
Any motor vehicle may be equipped with not more than two cornering lamps designed and of sufficient intensity for the purpose of revealing objects on in the direction of turn while the vehicle is turning or while the turn signal lamps are operating to signal an intention to turn. The lamps shall be designed so that no glaring light is projected into the eyes of an approaching driver.

25108. Pilot Indicator
(a) Any motor vehicle may be equipped with not more than two amber turn-signal pilot indicators mounted on the exterior. The light output from any indicator shall not exceed five candlepower unless a provision is made for operating the indicator at reduced intensity during darkness in which event the light output shall not exceed five candlepower during darkness or 15 candlepower at any other time. The center of the beam shall be projected toward the driver.

(b) Any vehicle may be equipped with pilot indicators visible from the front to monitor the functioning or condition of parts essential to the operation of the vehicle or of equipment attached to the vehicle that is necessary for protection of the cargo or load. The pilot indicators shall be steady-burning, having a projected lighted lens area of not more than three-quarters of a square inch and have a light output of not more than five candlepower. The pilot indicator may be of any color except red.

(c) Other exterior pilot indicators of any color may be used for monitoring exterior lighting devices, provided that the area of each indicator is less than 0.20 square inches, the intensity of each indicator does not exceed 0.10 candlepower, and the color red is not visible to the front.

(d) Any towed vehicle may be equipped with an exterior-mounted indicator lamp used only to indicate the functional status of an antilock braking system providing that either of the following conditions are met:

(1) The indicator lamp complies with the applicable requirements of the federal motor vehicle safety standards.

(2) The indicator lamp is designed and located so that it will be readily visible, with the assistance of a rearview mirror if necessary, to the driver of the towing motor vehicle and the indicator lamp has a light source not exceeding five candlepower. The light shall not show to the sides or rear of the vehicle and the indicator lamp may emit any color except red.

(e)(1) Notwithstanding any other provision of law, any motor vehicle may be equipped with not more than two exterior-lighted data monitors that transmit information to the driver of the vehicle regarding the efficient or safe operation, or both the efficient and safe operation, of the vehicle.

(2) Data monitors shall comply with all of the following conditions:

(A) Be mounted to the vehicle in a manner so that they are readily visible to the driver of the vehicle when the driver is seated in the normal driving position. Data monitors shall not be designed to convey information to any person other than the driver of the vehicle.

(B) Be limited in size to not more than two square inches of lighted area each.

(C) Not emit a light brighter than reasonably necessary to convey the intended information.

(D) Not project a glaring light to the driver or, to other motorists, or to any other person.

(3) Data monitors may incorporate flashing or changing elements only as necessary to convey the intended information. Data monitors shall not resemble any official traffic-control device or required lighting device or be combined with any required lighting device.

(4) Data monitors may display any color, except that the color red shall not be visible to the front of the vehicle. *(AM '01)*

25109. Running Lamps
Any motor vehicle may be equipped with two white or amber running lamps mounted on the front, one at each side, which shall not be lighted during darkness except while the motor vehicle is parked.

25110. Utility Flood and Loading Lamps

(a) The following vehicles may be equipped with utility flood or loading lamps mounted on the rear, and sides, that project a white light illuminating an area to the side or rear of the vehicle for a distance not to exceed 75 feet at the level of the roadway:

(1) Tow trucks that are used to tow disabled vehicles may display utility floodlights, but only during the period of preparation for towing at the location from which a disabled vehicle is to be towed.

(2) Ambulances used to respond to emergency calls may display utility flood and loading lights, but only at the scene of an emergency or while loading or unloading patients.

(3) Firefighting equipment designed and operated exclusively as such may display utility floodlamps only at the scene of an emergency.

(4) Vehicles used by law enforcement agencies or organizations engaged in the detoxification of alcoholics may display utility flood or loading lights when loading or unloading persons under the influence of intoxicants for transportation to detoxification centers or places of incarceration.

(5) Vehicles used by law enforcement agencies for mobile blood alcohol testing, drug evaluation, or field sobriety testing.

(6) Vehicles used by publicly or privately owned public utilities may display utility flood or loading lights when engaged in emergency roadside repair of electric, gas, telephone, telegraph, water, or sewer facilities.

(b) Lamps permitted under subdivision (a) shall not be lighted during darkness, except while the vehicle is parked, nor project any glaring light into the eyes of an approaching driver.

25250. Flashing Lights

Flashing lights are prohibited on vehicles except as otherwise permitted.

25251. Permitted Flashing Lights

(a) Flashing lights are permitted on vehicles as follows:

(1) To indicate an intention to turn or move to the right or left upon a roadway, turn signal lamps and turn signal exterior pilot indicator lamps and side lamps permitted under Section 25106 may be flashed on the side of a vehicle toward which the turn or movement is to be made.

(2) When disabled or parked off the roadway but within 10 feet of the roadway, or when approaching, stopped at, or departing from, a railroad grade crossing, turn signal lamps may be flashed as warning lights if the front turn signal lamps at each side are being flashed simultaneously and the rear turn signal lamps at each side are being flashed simultaneously.

(3) To warn other motorists of accidents or hazards on a roadway, turn signal lamps may be flashed as warning lights while the vehicle is approaching, overtaking, or passing the accident or hazard on the roadway if the front turn signal lamps at each side are being flashed simultaneously and the rear turn signal lamps at each side are being flashed simultaneously.

(4) For use on authorized emergency vehicles.

(5) To warn other motorists of a funeral procession, turn signal lamps may be flashed as warning lights on all vehicles actually engaged in a funeral procession, if the front turn signal lamps at each side are being flashed simultaneously and the rear turn signal lamps at each side are being flashed simultaneously.

(b) Turn signal lamps shall be flashed as warning lights whenever a vehicle is disabled upon the roadway and the vehicle is equipped with a device to automatically activate the front turn signal lamps at each side to flash simultaneously and the rear turn signal lamps at each side to flash simultaneously, if the device and the turn signal lamps were not rendered inoperative by the event which caused the vehicle to be disabled.

(c) Side lamps permitted under Section 25106 and used in conjunction with turn signal lamps may be flashed with the turn signal lamps as part of the warning light system, as provided in paragraphs (2) and (3) of subdivision (a).

(d) Required or permitted lamps on a trailer or semitrailer may flash when the trailer or semitrailer has broken away from the towing vehicle and the connection between the vehicles is broken.

(e) Hazard warning lights, as permitted by paragraphs (2) and (3) of subdivision (a) may be flashed in a repeating series of short and long flashes when the driver is in need of help.

25251.2. Motorcycles: Headlamp Flasher

Any motorcycle may be equipped with a means of modulating the upper beam of the headlamp between a high and a lower brightness at a rate of 200 to 280 flashes per minute. Such headlamps shall not be so modulated during darkness.

25251.5. Deceleration Warning Lights

(a) Any motor vehicle may also be equipped with a system in which an amber light is center mounted on the rear of a vehicle to communicate a component of deceleration of the vehicle, and which light pulses in a controlled fashion at a rate which varies exponentially with a component of deceleration.

(b) Any motor vehicle may be equipped with two amber lamps on the rear of the vehicle which operate simultaneously with not more than four flashes within four seconds after the accelerator pedal is in the deceleration position and which are not lighted at any other time. The lamps shall be mounted at the same height, with one lamp located on each side of the vertical centerline of the vehicle, not higher than the bottom of the rear window, or if the vehicle has no rear window, not higher than 60 inches. The light output from each of the lamps shall not exceed 200 candlepower at any angle horizontal or above. The amber lamps may be used either separately or in combination with another lamp.

(c) Any stoplamp or supplemental stoplamp required or permitted by Section 24603 may be equipped so as to flash not more than four times within the first four seconds after actuation by application of the brakes.

25252. Warning Lamps on Authorized Emergency Vehicles

Every authorized emergency vehicle shall be equipped with at least one steady burning red warning lamp visible from at least 1000 feet to the front of the vehicle to be used as provided in this code.

In addition, authorized emergency vehicles may display revolving, flashing, or steady red warning lights to the front, sides or rear of the vehicles.

25253. Warning Lamps on Tow Trucks

(a) Tow trucks used to tow disabled vehicles shall be equipped with flashing amber warning lamps. This subdivision does not apply to a tractor-trailer combination.

(b) Tow trucks may display flashing amber warning lamps while providing service to a disabled vehicle. A flashing amber warning lamp upon a tow truck may be displayed to the rear when the tow truck is towing a vehicle and moving at a speed slower than the normal flow of traffic.

(c) This section shall become operative on January 1, 2010. *(AD '06)*

25257. Schoolbus Warning Signal System

(a) Every school bus when operated for the transportation of schoolchildren, shall be equipped with a flashing red light signal system.

(b)(1) Every schoolbus manufactured on or after September 1, 1992, shall also be equipped with a stop signal arm. Any schoolbus manufactured before September 1, 1992, may be equipped with a stop signal arm.

(2) Any schoolbus manufactured on or after July 1, 1993, shall also be equipped with an amber warning light system, in addition to the flashing red light signal system. Any schoolbus manufactured before July 1, 1993, may be equipped with an amber warning light system.

(3) On or before September 1, 1992, the department shall adopt regulations governing the specifications, installation, and use of stop signal arms, to comply with federal standards.

(4) A "stop signal arm" is a device that can be extended outward from the side of a schoolbus to provide a signal to other motorists not to pass the bus because it has stopped to load or unload passengers, that is manufactured pursuant to the specifications of Federal Motor Vehicle Safety Standard No. 131, issued on April 25, 1991.

25257.2. Transportation of Disabled Persons on Schoolbus

If a schoolbus is used for the transportation of persons of any age who are developmentally disabled, as defined by the Lanterman Developmental Disabilities Services Act Division 4.5 (commencing with Section

4500) of the Welfare and Institutions Code), the amber light signal system, flashing red light signal system, and stop signal arm shall not be used other than as required by Sections 22112 and 22454.

25258. Authorized Emergency Vehicles; Additional Lights

(a) An authorized emergency vehicle operating under the conditions specified in Section 21055 may display a flashing white light from a gaseous discharge lamp designed and used for the purpose of controlling official traffic control signals.

(b) An authorized emergency vehicle used by a peace officer, as defined in Section 830.1 of, subdivision (a), (b), (c), (d), (e), (f), (g), or (i) of Section 830.2 of, subdivision (n) of Section 830.3 of, subdivision (b) of Section 830.31 of, subdivision (a) or (b) of Section 830.32 of, Section 830.33 of, subdivision (a) of Section 830.36 of, subdivision (a) of Section 830.4 of, or Section 830.6 of, the Penal Code, in the performance of the peace officer's duties, may, in addition, display a steady or flashing blue warning light visible from the front, sides, or rear of the vehicle.

(c) Except as provided in subdivision (a), a vehicle shall not be equipped with a device that emits any illumination or radiation that is designed or used for the purpose of controlling official traffic control signals. *(AM '98, '04, '10)*

25259. Additional Warning Lights on Authorized Emergency Vehicles

(a) Any authorized emergency vehicle may display flashing amber warning lights to the front, sides, or rear.

(b) A vehicle operated by a police or traffic officer while in the actual performance of his or her duties may display steady burning or flashing white lights to either side mounted above the roofline of the vehicle.

(c) Any authorized emergency vehicle may display not more than two flashing white warning lights to the front mounted above the roofline of the vehicle and not more than two flashing white warning lights to the front mounted below the roofline of the vehicle. These lamps may be in addition to the flashing headlamps permitted under Section 25252.5.

25259.1. Display of Flashing Lights - Vehicle Operated by Disaster Service Worker; Requirements

(a) Any vehicle operated by a disaster service worker who has received training in accordance with subdivision (b) and used by that worker in the performance of emergency or disaster services ordered by lawful authority during a state of war emergency, a state of emergency, or a local emergency, as those terms are defined in Section 8558 of the Government Code, may display flashing amber warning lights to the front, sides, or rear while at the scene of the emergency or disaster.

(b) Any disaster service worker operating a vehicle that displays flashing amber warning lights shall receive a training course from the public agency, disaster council, or emergency organization described in Section 3101 of the Government Code concerning the safe operation of the use of flashing amber warning lights prior to operating a vehicle that displays flashing amber warning lights.

(c) A person operating a vehicle that is authorized to display flashing amber warning lights under this section shall either completely cover or remove those lights when the lights are not in use.

25259.5. Warning Lights or Red Cross Vehicles

An emergency response or disaster service vehicle owned or leased and operated by the American National Red Cross, or any chapter or branch thereof, and equipped and clearly marked as a Red Cross emergency service or disaster service vehicle, may display flashing amber warning lights to the front, sides, or rear of the vehicle while at the scene of an emergency or disaster operation. Vehicles not used on emergency response shall not be included.

25260.4. Warning Lamps: Hazardous Substance Spill Response Vehicle

Any hazardous substance spill response vehicle, under contract to the Department of Transportation for the cleanup of hazardous substance spills, may display flashing amber warning lights to the front, sides, or rear of the vehicle while it is engaged in the actual cleanup of the spill. The warning lights shall be removed or covered with opaque material whenever the vehicle is not actually engaged in the cleanup of a hazardous substance at the scene of the spill.

25262. Armored Cars
An armored car may be equipped with red lights which may be used while resisting armed robbery. At all other times the red lights shall not be lighted. The authority to use red lights granted by this section does not constitute an armored car an authorized emergency vehicle, and all other provisions of this code applicable to drivers of vehicles apply to drivers of armored cars.

25265. Warning Lights on Sanitation District Repair Vehicles
Repair vehicles of sanitary districts or county sanitation districts necessarily parked other than adjacent to the curb in a highway for purposes of repairing district facilities, may display flashing amber warning lights to the front, sides or rear, but these lights shall not be lighted when the vehicle is in motion.

25268. Use of Flashing Amber Warning Light
No person shall display a flashing amber warning light on a vehicle as permitted by this code except when an unusual traffic hazard exists.

25269. Use of Red Warning Light
No person shall display a flashing or steady burning red warning light on a vehicle except as permitted by Section 21055 or when an extreme hazard exists.

25270. Warning Lights on Pilot Cars
Any pilot car required by the permit referred to in Section 35780 or 35790, or any vehicle or combination of vehicles subject to the permit if specified in the permit, shall be equipped with flashing amber warning lights to the front, sides or rear. The pilot car and any vehicles required by the permit to have flashing amber warning lights, shall display the flashing amber warning lights while actually engaged in the movement described in the permit. The warning lamps shall be removed or covered with opaque material whenever the pilot car is not escorting the movement described in the permit.

25275. Warning Lamps on Trucks With Long Loads
Any truck or truck tractor which is primarily used in the transportation of loads specified in subdivision (a) of Section 35414, may be equipped with a flashing amber warning lamp. Such lamp may be displayed to the front, sides, or rear of the combination only when its length exceeds 75 feet and when an unusual traffic hazard exists.

25275.5. Buses: Crime Alarm Lights
Any bus operated either by a public agency or under the authority of a certificate of public convenience and necessity issued by the PUC may be equipped with a system of crime alarm lights. The system of crime alarm lights shall consist of the installation of additional lamp sources, not exceeding 32 standard candlepower or 30 watts, in the front and rear clearance lamps required or permitted by Section 25100. Such lamps shall be operated by a flasher unit or units that are not audible inside the bus. When actuated, both rear crime alarm lights shall flash simultaneously and both front crime alarm lights shall flash simultaneously. Crime alarm lights shall be actuated only when a crime is in progress on board the bus or has recently been committed on board the bus.

25279. Warning Lights on Private Security Agency Vehicles
(a) Vehicles owned and operated by private security agencies and utilized exclusively on privately owned and maintained roads to which this code is made applicable by local ordinance or resolution, may display flashing amber warning lights to the front, sides, or rear, while being operated in response to emergency calls for the immediate preservation of life or property.

(b)(1) Vehicles owned by a private security agency and operated by personnel who are registered with the Department of Consumer Affairs under Article 3 (commencing with Section 7582) of Chapter 11.5 of Div. 3 of the Business and Professions Code may be equipped with a flashing amber warning light system while the vehicle is operated on a highway, if the vehicle is in compliance with Section 27605 and is distinctively marked with the words "PRIVATE SECURITY" or "SECURITY PATROL" on the rear and both sides of the vehicle in a size that is legible from a distance of not less than 50 feet.

(2) The flashing amber warning light system authorized under paragraph (1) shall not be activated while the vehicle is on the highway, unless otherwise directed by a peace officer, as defined in Chapter 4.5 (commencing with Section 830) of Title 3 of Part 2 of the Penal Code.

(c) A peace officer may order that the flashing amber warning light system of a vehicle that is found to be in violation of this section be immediately removed at the place of business of the vehicle's owner or a garage.

(d) A flashing amber warning light system shall not be installed on a vehicle that has been found to be in violation of this section, unless written authorization is obtained from the Commissioner of the California Highway Patrol. *(AM '96)*

25300. Warning Devices on Disabled or Parked Vehicles

(a) Every vehicle which, if operated during darkness, would be subject to the provisions of Section 25100, and every truck tractor, irrespective of width, shall at all times be equipped with at least three red emergency reflectors. The reflectors need be carried by only one vehicle in a combination. All reflectors shall be maintained in good working condition.

(b) When any such vehicle is disabled on the roadway during darkness, reflectors of the type specified in subdivision (a) shall be immediately placed as follows:

(1) One at the traffic side of the disabled vehicle, not more than 10 feet to the front or rear thereof;

(2) One at distance of approximately 100 feet to the rear of the disabled vehicle in the center of the traffic lane occupied by such vehicle; and

(3) One at a distance of approximately 100 feet to the front of the disabled vehicle in the center of the traffic lane occupied by such vehicle.

(4) If disablement of any such vehicle occurs within 500 feet of a curve, crest of a hill, or other obstruction to view, the driver shall so place the reflectors in that direction as to afford ample warning to other users of the highway, but in no case less than 100 nor more than 500 feet from the disabled vehicle.

(5) If disablement of the vehicle occurs upon any roadway of a divided or one-way highway, the driver shall place one reflector at a distance of a proximately 200 feet and one such reflector at a distance of approximately 100 feet to the rear of the vehicle in the center of the lane occupied by the stopped vehicle, and one such reflector at the traffic side of the vehicle not more than 10 feet to the rear of the vehicle.

(c) When any such vehicle is disabled or parked off the roadway but within 10 feet thereof during darkness, warning reflectors of the type specified in subdivision (a) shall be immediately placed by the driver as follows: one at a distance of approximately 200 feet and one at a distance of approximately 100 feet to the rear of the vehicle, and one at the traffic side of the vehicle not more than 10 feet to the rear of the vehicle. The reflectors shall, if possible, be placed between the edge of the roadway and the vehicle, but in no event less than two feet to the left of the widest portion of the vehicle or load thereon.

(d) Until the reflectors required by this section can be placed properly, the requirements of this section may be complied with temporarily by either placing lighted red fusees in the required locations or by use of turn signal lamps but only if front turn signal lamps at each side are being flashed simultaneously and rear turn signal lamps at each side are being flashed simultaneously.

(e) The reflectors shall be displayed continuously during darkness while the vehicle remains disabled upon the roadway or parked or disabled within 10 feet thereof.

(f) Subdivisions (b), (c), (d), and (e) do not apply to a vehicle under either of the following circumstances:

(1) Parked in a legal position within the corporate limits of any city.

(2) Parked in a legal position within upon a roadway bounded by adjacent curbs.

(g) In addition to the reflectors specified in subdivision (a), an emergency warning sign or banner may be attached to a vehicle which is disabled upon the roadway or which is parked or disabled within 10 feet of a roadway.

25301. Utility and Public Utility Vehicles

When utility or public utility vehicles are parked, stopped or standing at the site of work as described in Section 22512, warning devices shall be displayed as follows:

(a) During daylight warning devices shall consist of either:

A warning flag or barricade striping on the front and rear of the vehicle.

A warning flag, sign, or barrier on the highway not more than 50 feet in advance of the vehicle and not more than 50 feet to the rear thereof, except that in zones where the speed limit is in excess of 25 miles per hour the 50-foot distance may be increased up to 500 feet from the vehicle as circumstances may warrant.

(b) During darkness the warning devices shall consist of either:

One or more flashing amber warning lights on the vehicle giving warning to approaching traffic from each direction.

A warning light, flare, fusee, or reflector on the highway not more than 50 feet in advance of the vehicle and not more than 50 feet to the rear thereof, except that in zones where the speed limit is in excess of 25 miles per hour the 50-foot distance may be increased up to 500 feet from the vehicle where circumstances may warrant.

(c) The provisions of subdivisions (a) or (b) do not prevent the display of both types of the warning devices during daylight or darkness.

(d) During either daylight or darkness, no warning device is necessary if the vehicle is equipped with the flashing warning lights visible to approaching traffic from each direction as provided in subdivision (b).

25305. Use of Fusees

(a) No person shall place, deposit, or display upon or adjacent to any highway any lighted fusee, except as a warning to approaching vehicular traffic or railroad trains, or both, of an existing hazard upon or adjacent to the highway or highway-railroad crossing.

(b) It is unlawful to use any fusee which produces other than a red light. The provisions of this subdivision shall not apply to any railroad, as defined in Section 229 of the Public Utilities Code.

25350. Identification of Lamps and Signs

Any passenger common carrier motor vehicle manufactured prior to January 1, 1968, may be equipped with green identification lamps. Any bus may be equipped with an illuminated termini sign, an illuminated identification sign, or any combination thereof, which shall not project any glaring light. Internally illuminated termini signs, identification signs, or any combination thereof, meeting the requirements of Section 25400 may be mounted inside a bus. Any commercial vehicle, other than a passenger common carrier motor vehicle, may be equipped with an illuminated identification sign upon the front thereof which shall not exceed 24 inches in length or 8 inches in width and which emits diffused white light without glare.

25351. Identification Lamps

(a) A commercial vehicle and, except as provided in subdivision (d), any other vehicle 80 or more inches in width may be equipped with identification lamps mounted on the front or rear. No part of any such lamps or their mountings on the front of a motor vehicle shall extend below the top of the windshield.

(b) Identification lamps on such vehicles manufactured prior to January 1, 1968, may exhibit either amber, green, or white light to the front and red light to the rear.

(c) Identification lamps on such vehicles manufactured on or after January 1, 1968, may exhibit only amber light to the front and red light to the rear.

(d) Identification lamps are not permitted on passenger vehicles, except housecars and ambulances, regardless of width.

25353. Illuminated Signs on Public Transit System Busses; Requirements

(a) Notwithstanding Sections 25400 and 25950, a bus operated by a publicly owned transit system on regularly scheduled service may be equipped with illuminated signs that include destination signs, route-number signs, run-number signs, public service announcement signs, or a combination thereof, visible from any direction of the vehicle, that emit any light color, other than the color red emitted from forward-facing signs, pursuant to the following conditions:

(1) Each illuminated sign shall emit diffused nonglaring light.

(2) Each illuminated sign shall be limited in size to a display area of not greater than 720 square inches.

(3) Each illuminated sign shall not resemble nor be installed in a position that interferes with the visibility or effectiveness of a required lamp, reflector, or other device upon the vehicle.

(4) Each illuminated sign shall display information directly related to public transit service, including, but not limited to, route number, destination description, run number, and public service announcements.

(5) The mixing of individually colored light emitting diode elements, including red, is allowed as long as the emitted color formed by the combination of light emitting diode elements is not red.

(b)(1) An illuminated sign may be operated as a dynamic message sign in a paging or streaming mode.

(2) The following definitions shall govern the construction of paragraph (1):

(A) "Paging," meaning character elements or other information presented for a period of time and then disappearing all at once before the same or new elements are presented, is permitted if the display time of each message is between 2.7 and 10 seconds. Blanking times between each message shall be between 0.5 and 25 seconds.

(B) "Streaming," meaning character elements or other information moving smoothly and continuously across the display, is permitted if the character movement time, from one end of the display to the other, is at least 2.7 seconds, and the movement time of the entire message does not exceed 10 seconds.

(c) A regulation adopted pursuant to this section shall comply with applicable federal law, including, but not limited to, the federal Americans with Disabilities Act of 1990 (42 U.S.C. Sec. 12101 et seq.). *(AD '06)*

25400. Lighting Requirements

(a) Any vehicle may be equipped with a lamp or device on the exterior of the vehicle that emits a diffused nonglaring light of not more than 0.05 candela per square inch of area.

(b) Any diffused nonglaring light shall not display red to the front, but may display other colors. A diffused nonglaring light shall not resemble nor be installed within 12 inches or in such position as to interfere with the visibility or effectiveness of any required lamp, reflector, or other device upon the vehicle.

(c) A diffused nonglaring lamp or device, other than a display sign authorized by subdivision (d), shall be limited in size to an area of 720 square inches and where any lease, rental, or donation is involved the installation of the lamp or device shall be limited to those vehicles operated either primarily within business or residential districts or municipalities, or between business districts, residential districts, and municipalities in close proximity.

(d) An internally illuminated sign emitting not more than 0.25 candela per square inch and possessing copy which does not contain a white background may be displayed on each side, but not on the front or rear, of a trolley coach or of a bus being operated in urban or suburban service as described in Section 35107 of this code.

25401. Diffused Lights Resembling Signs

No diffused nonglaring light on a vehicle shall resemble any official traffic control device.

25500. Use of Reflectorizing Material

(a) Area reflectorizing material may be displayed on any vehicle, provided: the color red is not displayed on the front; designs do not tend to distort the length or width of the vehicle; and designs do not resemble official traffic control devices, except that alternate striping resembling a barricade pattern may be used.

No vehicle shall be equipped with area reflectorizing material contrary to these provisions.

(b) The provisions of this section shall not apply to license plate stickers or tabs affixed to license plates as authorized by the department.

25650. Headlamps on Motorcycles

Every motorcycle during darkness shall be equipped with at least one and not more than two lighted headlamps which shall conform to the requirements and limitations of this division.

25650.5. Headlamps on Motorcycles Manufactured After 1978

Every motorcycle manufactured and first registered on and after January 1, 1978, shall be equipped with at least one and not more than two headlamps which automatically turn on when the engine of the motorcycle is started and which remain lighted as long as the engine is running. This section does not preclude equipping motorcycles used as authorized emergency vehicles with a switch to be used to turn off the headlamp during emergency situations or when the light would interfere with law enforcement, if the switch is removed prior to resale of the motorcycle.

25651. Headlamps on Motor-driven Cycles

The headlamp upon a motor-driven cycle may be of the single-beam or multiple-beam type, but in either event, when the vehicle is operated during darkness, the headlamp shall comply with the requirements and limitations as follows:

(a) The headlamp shall be of sufficient intensity to reveal a person or a vehicle at a distance of not less than 100 feet when the motor-driven cycle is operated at any speed less than 25 miles per hour and at a distance of not less than 200 feet when operated at a speed of 25 to not exceeding 35 miles per hour, and at a distance of 300 feet when operated at a speed greater than 35 miles per hour.

(b) In the event the motor-driven cycle is equipped with a multiple-beam headlamp, the upper beam shall meet the minimum requirements set forth above and the lowermost beam shall meet the requirements applicable to a lowermost distribution of light as set forth in subdivision (b) of Section 24407.

(c) In the event the motor-driven cycle is equipped with a single-beam lamp, it shall be so aimed that when the vehicle is loaded none of the high intensity portion of light, at a distance of 25 feet ahead, shall project higher than the level of the center of the lamp from which it comes.

25803. Lamps on Other Vehicles

(a) All vehicles not otherwise required to be equipped with headlamps, rear lights, or reflectors by this chapter shall, if operated on a highway during darkness, be equipped with a lamp exhibiting a red light visible from a distance of 500 feet to the rear of the vehicle. In addition, all of these vehicles operated alone or as the first vehicle in a combination of vehicles, shall be equipped with at least one lighted lamp exhibiting a white light visible from a distance of 500 feet to the front of the vehicle.

(b) A vehicle shall also be equipped with an amber reflector on the front near the left side and a red reflector on the rear near the left side. The reflectors shall be mounted on the vehicle not lower than 16 inches nor higher than 60 inches above the ground and so designed and maintained as to be visible during darkness from all distances within 500 feet from the vehicle when directly in front of a motor vehicle displaying lawful lighted headlamps undimmed.

(c) In addition, if a vehicle described in subdivision (a) or the load thereon has a total outside width in excess of 100 inches there shall be displayed during darkness at the left outer extremity at least one amber light visible under normal atmospheric conditions from a distance of 500 feet to the front, sides, and rear. At all other times there shall be displayed at the left outer extremity a solid red or fluorescent orange flag or cloth not less than 12 inches square. *(AM '98, '04)*

25805. Lamps on Forklift Trucks

Notwithstanding any other provision of this article, a forklift truck which is towed upon the highway at the end of a combination of vehicles shall at all times be equipped with at least one stop lamp mounted upon the rear of the vehicle and shall be equipped with lamp-type turn signals. Such vehicle shall, during the hours of darkness, be equipped with at least one taillamp and one red reflector mounted upon the rear of the vehicle and shall be equipped with clearance lamps if the vehicle is 50 or more inches in width.

25950. Color of Lamps and Reflectors

This section applies to the color of lamps and to any reflector exhibiting or reflecting perceptible light of 0.05 candela or more per foot-candle of incident illumination. Unless provided otherwise, the color of lamps and reflectors upon a vehicle shall be as follows:

(a) The emitted light from all lamps and the reflected light from all reflectors, visible from in front of a vehicle, shall be white or yellow, except as follows:

(1) Rear side marker lamps required by Section 25100 may show red to the front.

(2) The color of foglamps described in Section 24403 may be in the color spectrum from white to yellow.

(3) An illuminating device, as permitted under Section 24255, shall emit radiation predominantly in the infrared region of the electromagnetic spectrum. Any incidental visible light projecting to the front of the vehicle shall be predominantly yellow to white. Any incidental visible light projecting to the rear of the vehicle shall be predominantly red. Any incidental visible light from an illuminating device, as permitted under Section 24255, shall not resemble any other required or permitted lighting device or official traffic control device.

(b) The emitted light from all lamps and the reflected light from all reflectors, visible from the rear of a vehicle, shall be red except as follows:

(1) Stoplamps on vehicles manufactured before January 1, 1979, may show yellow to the rear.

(2) Turn signal lamps may show yellow to the rear.

(3) Front side marker lamps required by Section 25100 may show yellow to the rear.

(4) Backup lamps shall show white to the rear.

(5) The rearward facing portion of a front-mounted double-faced turn signal lamp may show amber to the rear while the headlamps or parking lamps are lighted, if the intensity of the light emitted is not greater than the parking lamps and the turn signal function is not impaired.

(6) A reflector meeting the requirements of, and installed in accordance with, Section 24611 shall be red or white, or both.

(c) All lamps and reflectors visible from the front, sides, or rear of a vehicle, except headlamps, may have any unlighted color, provided the emitted light from all lamps or reflected light from all reflectors complies with the required color. Except for backup lamps, the entire effective projected luminous area of lamps visible from the rear or mounted on the sides near the rear of a vehicle shall be covered by an inner lens of the required color when the unlighted color differs from the required emitted light color. Taillamps, stoplamps, and turn signal lamps that are visible to the rear may be white when unlighted on vehicles manufactured before January 1, 1974. *(AM '04)*

25951. Direction of Beam
Any lighted lamp or device upon a motor vehicle other than headlamps, spot lamps, signal lamps, or auxiliary driving lamps, warning lamps which projects a beam of light of an intensity greater than 300 candlepower shall be so directed that no part of the beam will strike the level of the roadway at a distance of more than 75 feet from the vehicle.

25952. Lamps and Reflectors on Loads
(a) Lamps, reflectors, and area reflectorizing material of a type required or permitted on a vehicle may be mounted on a load carried by the vehicle in lieu of or in addition to, such equipment on the vehicle.

Such equipment shall be mounted on the load in a manner that would comply with the requirements of this code and regulations adopted pursuant to this code if the load were an integral part of the vehicle.

(b) Lamps on vehicles carried as a load shall not be lighted unless such lamps are mounted in accordance with subdivision (a).

26100. Vehicle Equipment
(a) A person shall not sell or offer for sale for use upon or as part of the equipment of a vehicle any lighting equipment, safety glazing material, or other device that does not meet the provisions of Section 26104.

(b) A person shall not use upon a vehicle, and a person shall not drive a vehicle upon a highway that is equipped with, any lighting equipment, safety glazing material, or other device that is not in compliance with Section 26104.

(c) This section does not apply to a taillamp or stop lamp in use on or prior to December 1, 1935. *(AM '10)*

26101. Modification of Vehicle Equipment

(a) A person shall not sell or offer for sale for use upon or as part of the equipment of a vehicle any device that is intended to modify the original design or performance of any lighting equipment, safety glazing material, or other device, unless the modifying device meets the provisions of Section 26104.

(b) A person shall not use upon a vehicle, and a person shall not drive a vehicle upon a highway that has installed a device that is intended to modify the original design or performance of a lighting, safety glazing material, or other device, unless the modifying device complies with Section 26104.

(c) This section does not apply to a taillamp or stop lamp in use on or prior to December 1, 1935, or to lamps installed on authorized emergency vehicles. *(AM '10)*

CHAPTER 3. BRAKES

26301. Motor Vehicles Over Seven Tons

Any motor vehicle first registered in this state after January 1, 1940, shall be equipped with power brakes if its gross weight exceeds 14,000 pounds, except that any such vehicle having a gross weight of less than 18,000 pounds may, in lieu of power brakes, be equipped with two-stage hydraulic actuators of a type designed to increase braking effect of its brakes.

26301.5. Emergency Brake System

Every passenger vehicle manufactured and first registered after January 1, 1973, except motorcycles, shall be equipped with an emergency brake system so constructed that rupture or leakage-type failure of any single component of the service brake system, except structural failures of the brake master cylinder body or effectiveness indicator body, shall not result in complete loss of function of the vehicle's brakes when force on the brake pedal is continued.

26302. Trailers

(a) Every trailer or semitrailer, manufactured and first registered after January 1, 1940, and having a gross weight of 6,000 pounds or more and which is operated at a speed of 20 miles per hour or over shall be equipped with brakes.

(b) Every trailer or semitrailer manufactured and first registered after January 1, 1966, and having a gross weight of 3,000 pounds or more shall be equipped with brakes on at least two wheels.

(c) Every trailer or semitrailer manufactured after January 1, 1982, and equipped with air brakes shall be equipped with brakes on all wheels.

(d) Brakes required on trailers or semitrailers shall be adequate, supplemental to the brakes on the towing vehicle, to enable the combination of vehicles to comply with the stopping distance requirements of Section 26454.

(e) The provisions of this section shall not apply to any vehicle being used to support the boom or mast attached to a mobile crane or shovel.

26303. Trailer Coaches and Camp Trailers

Every trailer coach and every camp trailer having a gross weight of 1,500 pounds or more, but exclusive of passengers, shall be equipped with brakes on at least two wheels which are adequate, supplemental to the brakes on the towing vehicle, to enable the combination of vehicles to comply with the stopping distance requirements of Section 26454.

26304. Breakaway Brakes

(a) Power brakes on any trailer or semitrailer manufactured after December 31, 1955, operated over public highways and required to be equipped with brakes shall be designed to be automatically applied upon breakaway from the towing vehicle and shall be capable of stopping and holding such vehicle stationary for not less than 15 minutes.

(b) Every new truck or truck tractor manufactured after December 31, 1955, operated over public highways and used in towing a vehicle shall be equipped with service brakes capable of stopping the truck or truck tractor in the event of breakaway of the towed vehicle.

26307. Forklift Truck Brakes

No forklift truck manufactured after January 1, 1970, shall be towed behind another vehicle unless it is equipped with brakes on the wheels of the rearmost axle when the forklift truck is in the towing position, which brakes shall be adequate, supplemental to the brakes on the towing vehicle, to enable the combination of vehicles to comply with the stopping distance requirements of Section 26454.

26311. Service Brakes on All Wheels

(a) Every motor vehicle shall be equipped with service brakes on all wheels, except as follows:

(1) Trucks and truck tractors manufactured before January 1, 1982, having three or more axles need not have brakes on the front wheels, except when such vehicles are equipped with at least two steerable axles, the wheels of one such axle need not be equipped with brakes.

(2) Any vehicle being towed in a driveaway-towaway operation.

(3) Any vehicle manufactured prior to 1930.

(4) Any two-axle truck tractor manufactured prior to 1964.

(5) Any sidecar attached to a motorcycle.

(6) Any motorcycle manufactured prior to 1966. Such motorcycle shall be equipped with brakes on at least one wheel.

(b) Any bus, truck, or truck tractor may be equipped with a manual or automatic means for reducing the braking effort on the front wheels. The manual means shall be used only when operating under adverse road conditions, such as wet, snowy, or icy roads,

(c) Vehicles and combinations of vehicles exempted in subdivisions (a) and (b) from the requirements of brakes on all wheels shall comply with the stopping distance requirements of Section 26454.

26450. Required Brake Systems

Every motor vehicle shall be equipped with a service brake system and every motor vehicle, other than a motorcycle, shall be equipped with a parking brake system. Both the service brake and parking brake shall be separately applied.

If the two systems are connected in any way, they shall be so constructed that failure of any one part, except failure in the drums, brakeshoes, or other mechanical parts of the wheel brake assemblies, shall not leave the motor vehicle without operative brakes.

26451. Parking Brake System

The parking brake system of every motor vehicle shall comply with the following requirements:

(a) The parking brake shall be adequate to hold the vehicle or combination of vehicles stationary on any grade on which it is operated under all conditions of loading on a surface free from snow, ice or loose material. In any event the parking brake shall be capable of locking the braked wheels to the limit of traction.

(b) The parking brake shall be applied either by the driver's muscular efforts, by spring action, or by other energy which is isolated and used exclusively for the operation of the parking brake or the combination parking brake and emergency stopping system.

(c) The parking brake shall be held in the applied position solely by mechanical means.

26452. Brakes After Engine Failure

All motor vehicles shall be so equipped as to permit application of the brakes at least once for the purpose of bringing the vehicle to a stop within the legal stopping distance after the engine has become inoperative.

26453. Condition of Brakes

All brakes and component parts thereof shall be maintained in good condition and in good working order. The brakes shall be so adjusted as to operate as equally as practicable with respect to the wheels on opposite sides of the vehicle.

26454. Control and Stopping Requirements

(a) The service brakes of every motor vehicle or combination of vehicles shall be adequate to control the movement of and to stop and hold such vehicle or combination of vehicles under all conditions of loading on any grade on which it is operated.

(b) Every motor vehicle or combination of vehicles, at any time and under all conditions of loading, shall, upon application of the service brake, be capable of stopping from an initial speed of 20 miles per hour according to the following requirements:

(1) Any passenger vehicle: 25 feet.

(2) Any single motor vehicle with a manufacturer's gross vehicle weight rating of less than 10,000 lbs: 30 feet.

(3) Any combination of vehicles consisting of a passenger vehicle or any motor vehicle with a manufacturer's gross vehicle weight rating of less than 10,000 lbs. in combination with any trailer, semitrailer or trailer coach: 40 feet.

(4) Any single motor vehicle with a manufacturer's gross vehicle weight rating of 10,000 lbs. or more or any bus: 40 feet.

(5) All other combinations of vehicles: 50 feet.

26457. Exemptions

Special mobile equipment, logging vehicles, equipment operated under special permit, and any chassis without body or load are not subject to stopping distance requirements, but if any such vehicle or equipment cannot be stopped within 32 feet from an initial speed of 15 miles per hour, it shall not be operated at a speed in excess of that permitting a stop in 32 feet.

26458. Power Brake: Single Control

(a) The braking system on every motor vehicle used to tow another vehicle shall be so arranged that one control on the towing vehicle shall, when applied, operate all the service brakes on the power unit and combination of vehicles when either or both of the following conditions exist:

(1) The towing vehicle is required to be equipped with power brakes.

(2) The towed vehicle is required to be equipped with brakes and is equipped with power brakes.

(b) Subdivision (a) shall not be construed to prohibit motor vehicles from being equipped with an additional control to be used to operate the brakes on the trailer or trailers.

(c) Subdivision (a) does not apply to any of the following combinations of vehicles, if the combination of vehicles meets the stopping distance requirements of Section 26454:

(1) Vehicle engaged in driveaway-towaway operations.

(2) Disabled vehicles, while being towed.

(3) Towed motor vehicles.

(4) Trailers equipped with inertially controlled brakes which are designed to be applied automatically upon breakaway from the towing vehicle and which are capable of stopping and holding the trailer stationary for not less than 15 minutes.

26458.5. Operation of Trailer Brakes

Pursuant to Section 26458, whenever a motor vehicle is equipped with an additional control to operate the brakes on a trailer, that control shall not be used in lieu of the service brake control except in the case of failure of the service rake system.

26502. Adjustment and Use of Special Devices

(a) Airbrakes of every motor vehicle and combination of vehicles shall be so adjusted and maintained as to be capable of providing full service brake application at all times except as provided in subdivision (b) of Section 26311. A full service brake shall deliver to all brake chambers not less than 90 percent of reservoir pressure remaining with the brakes applied.

(b) The department may by regulation authorize the use of special devices or systems to automatically reduce the maximum air pressure delivered to the brake chambers in order to compensate for load variation and to obtain balanced braking. Permitted systems shall be of the fail safe type and shall not increase the vehicle stopping distance.

26503. Safety Valve

Every motor vehicle equipped with airbrakes or equipped to operate airbrakes on towed vehicles shall be equipped with a standard type safety valve which shall be installed so as to have an uninterrupted connection with the air reservoir or tank. It shall be adjusted and maintained so that it will open and discharge the air system under any condition at a pressure of not to exceed 150 pounds per square inch and close and re-seat itself at a point above the maximum air governor setting. The department may by regulation prescribe a higher maximum opening pressure for air pressure systems designed for, and capable of safely operating with, pressure safety valves with a higher opening pressure.

26504. Air Governor

The air governor cut-in and cut-out pressures of every motor vehicle equipped with airbrakes or equipped to operate airbrakes on towed vehicles shall be adjusted so that the maximum pressure in the air system and the minimum cut-in pressure shall be within limits prescribed by the department. In adopting regulations specifying such pressures the department shall consider the safe operating capacities of the various air brake systems which are now or may be used on motor vehicles and shall be guided by the designed capabilities of those systems.

26505. Pressure Gauge

A motor vehicle equipped with airbrakes or equipped to operate airbrakes on towed vehicles shall be equipped with a pressure gauge of reliable and satisfactory construction and maintained in an efficient working condition, accurate within 10 percent of the actual air reservoir pressure, and visible and legible to a person when seated in the driving position. *(AM '10)*

26506. Warning Device

(a) Every motor vehicle airbrake system used to operate the brakes on the motor vehicle or on a towed vehicle shall be equipped with a low air pressure warning device that complies with either the requirements set forth in the Federal Motor Vehicle Safety Standards in effect at the time of manufacture or the requirements of subdivision (b).

(b) The device shall be readily visible or audible to the driver and shall give a satisfactory continuous warning when the air supply pressure drops below a fixed pressure, which shall be not more than 75 pounds per square inch nor less than 55 pounds per square inch with the engine running. A gauge indicating pressure shall not satisfy this requirement.

26507. Check Valve

A check valve shall be installed and properly maintained in the air supply piping of every motor vehicle equipped with airbrakes, either between the air compressor and the first reservoir or tank immediately adjacent to the air intake of said reservoir, or between No. 1 reservoir (wet tank) and No. 2 reservoir (dry tank) immediately adjacent to the air intake of the No. 2 reservoir; provided, that the air supply for the brakes is not drawn from the No. 1 reservoir and that the No. 1 and No. 2 reservoirs are connected by only one pipeline.

26508. Emergency Stopping System

Every vehicle or combination of vehicles using compressed air at the wheels for applying the service brakes shall be equipped with an emergency stopping system meeting the requirements of this section and capable of stopping the vehicle or combination of vehicles in the event of failure in the service brake air system as follows:

(a) Every motor vehicle operated either singly or in a combination of vehicles and every towed vehicle shall be equipped with an emergency stopping system.

(b) Motor vehicles used to tow vehicles which use compressed air at the wheels for applying the service brakes shall be equipped with a device or devices with both a manual and automatic means of actuating the emergency stopping system on the towed vehicle as follows:

(1) The automatic device shall operate automatically in the event of reduction of the service brake air supply of the towing vehicle to a fixed pressure which shall be not lower than 20 pounds per square inch nor higher than 45 pounds per square inch.

(2) The manual device shall be readily operable by a person seated in the driver's seat, with its emergency position or method of operation clearly indicated. In no instance may the manual means be so arranged as to permit its use to prevent operation of the automatic means.

(c) Motor vehicles manufactured prior to 1964 shall be deemed to be in compliance with subdivisions (e) and (f) when equipped with axle-by-axle protected airbrakes using a separate air tank system for each of at least two axles, provided that each system independently meets all other requirements of this section. Each system shall be capable of being manually applied, released, and reapplied from the driver's seat but shall not be capable of being released from the driver's seat after any reapplication unless there is available a means which can be applied from the driver's seat to stop and hold the vehicle or combination of vehicles.

(d) Towed vehicles shall be deemed to be in compliance with this section when:

(1) The towed vehicle is equipped with a no-bleed-back relay-emergency valve or equivalent device, so designed that the supply reservoir used to provide air for the brakes is safeguarded against backflow of air from the reservoir through the supply line.

(2) The brakes are applied automatically and promptly upon breakaway from the towing vehicle and maintain application for at least 15 minutes, and

(3) The combination of vehicles is capable of stopping within the distance and under the conditions specified in subdivisions (k) and (l).

(e) If the service brake system and the emergency stopping system are connected in any way, they shall be so constructed that a failure or malfunction in any one part of either system, including brake chamber diaphragm failure but not including failure in the drums, brakeshoes, or other mechanical parts of the wheel brakes, shall not leave the vehicle without one operative stopping system capable of complying with the performance requirements in subdivision (k).

(f) Every emergency stopping system shall be designed so that it is capable of being manually applied, released, and reapplied by a person seated in the driver's seat. The system shall be designed so that it cannot be released from the driver's seat after any reapplication unless immediate further application can be made from the driver's seat to stop and hold the vehicle or combination of vehicles. The emergency stopping system may also be applied automatically.

(g) No vehicle or combination of vehicles upon failure of the service brake air system shall be driven on a highway under its own power except to the extent necessary to move the vehicles off the roadway to the nearest place of safety.

(h) No vehicle or combination of vehicles shall be equipped with an emergency stopping system that creates a hazard on the highway, or increases the service brake stopping distance of a vehicle or combination of vehicles, or interferes in any way with the application of the service brakes on any vehicle or combination of vehicles.

(i) Any energy-storing device which is a part of the emergency stopping system shall be designed so that it is recharged or reset from the source of compressed air or other energy produced by the vehicle, except that energy to release the emergency stopping system may be produced by the driver's muscular effort from the driver's seat. No device shall be used which can be set to prevent automatic delivery of air to protected air supply reservoirs of motor vehicle emergency stopping systems when air is available in the service brake air supply system.

(j) Any vehicle manufactured on or after January 1, 1964, which uses axle-by-axle protected airbrakes as the emergency stopping system shall use a separate air tank system for each axle, except that motor vehicles equipped with a dual or tandem treadle valve system need have no more than two protected air tanks in such system, one for each valve.

(k) Every motor vehicle or combination of vehicles, at all times and under all conditions of loading, upon application of the emergency stopping system, shall be capable of:

(1) Developing stopping force that is not less than the percentage of its gross weight tabulated herein for its classification.

(2) Decelerating in a stop from 20 miles per hour at not less than the feet per second per second tabulated herein for its classification, and

(3) Stopping from a speed of 20 miles per hour in not more than the distance tabulated herein for its classification, such distance to be measured from the point at which movement of the emergency stopping system control begins. (See Code for table of stopping distances.)

(l) Tests for deceleration and stopping distance shall be made on a substantially level, dry, smooth, hard surface that is free from loose material and where the grade does not exceed plus or minus 1 percent. No test of emergency stopping system performance shall be made upon a highway at a speed in excess of 25 miles per hour.

(m) The provisions of this section shall not apply to:

(1) Auxiliary dollies, special mobile equipment, or special construction equipment.

(2) Motor vehicles which are operated in a driveaway-towaway operation and not registered in this State.

(3) Disabled vehicles when being towed.

(4) Vehicles which are operated under a one-trip permit as provided in Section 4003.

(5) Vehicles which because of unladen width, length, height or weight may not be moved upon the highway without the permit specified in Section 35780.

(n) The emergency stopping system requirements specified in subdivision (k) shall not apply to a vehicle or combination of vehicles being operated under a special weight permit nor to any overweight authorized emergency vehicle operated under the provisions of Section 35002.

(o) Every owner or lessee shall instruct and require that the driver be thoroughly familiar with the requirements of this section. The driver of a vehicle or combination of vehicles required to comply with the requirements of this section shall be able to demonstrate the application and release of the emergency system on the vehicle and each vehicle in the combination.

26520. Vacuum Gauge

Motor vehicles required to be equipped with power brakes and which are equipped with vacuum or vacuum-assisted brakes shall be equipped with a properly maintained vacuum gauge of reliable and satisfactory construction, accurate within 10 percent of the actual vacuum in the supply reservoir, and visible and legible to the driver at all times.

This section shall not apply to a two-axle motor truck operated singly.

26521. Warning Device

Motor vehicles required to be equipped with power brakes and equipped with vacuum or vacuum-assisted brakes and motor vehicles used to tow vehicles equipped with vacuum brakes or vacuum-assisted brakes shall be equipped with either an audible or visible warning signal to indicate readily to the driver when the vacuum drops to eight inches of mercury and less. A vacuum gauge shall not be deemed to meet this requirement. This section shall not apply to a two-axle motor truck operated singly nor to any motor vehicle manufactured prior to 1964.

26522. Check Valve

Vehicles required to be equipped with power brakes and equipped with vacuum or vacuum-assisted brakes shall have a check valve installed and properly maintained in the vacuum system between the source of vacuum and the vacuum reserve.

CHAPTER 4. WINDSHIELDS & MIRRORS

26700. Windshields: Exception

(a) Except as provided in subdivision (b), a passenger vehicle, other than a motorcycle, and every bus, motortruck or truck tractor, and every firetruck, fire engine or other fire apparatus, whether publicly or privately owned, shall be equipped with an adequate windshield.

(b) Subdivision (a) does not apply to any vehicle issued identification plates pursuant to Section 5004 which was not required to be equipped with a windshield at the time it was first sold or registered under the laws of this state, another state, or foreign jurisdiction.

26701. Safety Glazing Material

(a) No person shall sell, offer for sale, or operate any motor vehicle, except a motorcycle, manufactured after January 1, 1936, unless it is equipped with safety glazing material wherever glazing materials are used in partitions, doors, windows, windshields, auxiliary wind deflectors, or openings in the roof.

(b) No person shall sell or offer for sale any camper manufactured after January 1, 1968, nor shall any person operate a motor vehicle registered in this state which is equipped with such a camper, unless the camper is equipped with safety glazing materials wherever glazing materials are used in outside windows and doors, interior partitions, and openings in the roof.

(c) No person shall operate a motorcycle manufactured after January 1, 1969, equipped with a windshield containing glazing material unless it is safety glazing material.

(d) No person shall sell, offer for sale, or operate any motor vehicle equipped with red, blue or amber translucent aftermarket material in any partitions, windows, windshields, or wind deflectors.

(e) No person shall sell, offer for sale, or operate any trailer coach manufactured after January 1, 1977, that is capable of being towed with a fifth-wheel device unless the trailer coach is equipped with safety glazing materials wherever glazing materials are used in windows or doors, interior partitions, and openings in the roof.

26703. Replacement of Glazing Material

(a) No person shall replace any glazing materials used in interior partitions, doors, windows, or openings in the roof in any motor vehicle, in the outside windows, doors, interior partitions, or openings in the roof of any camper, or in windows, doors, interior partitions, or openings in the roof of a trailer coach capable of being towed with a fifth-wheel device, with any glazing material other than safety glazing material.

(b) No person shall replace any glazing material used in the windshield, rear window, auxiliary wind deflectors, or windows to the left and right of the driver with any material other than safety glazing material.

26705. Motorcycle Windshields

On or after January 1, 1969, no person shall sell or offer for sale on or as part of the equipment of a motorcycle any motorcycle windshield unless the glazing material used therein is safety glazing material.

26706. Windshield Wipers

(a) Every motor vehicle, except motorcycles, equipped with a windshield shall also be equipped with a self-operating windshield wiper.

(b) Every new motor vehicle first registered after December 31, 1949, except motorcycles, shall be equipped with two such windshield wipers, one mounted on the right half and one on the left half of the windshield, except that any motor vehicle may be equipped with a single wiper so long as it meets the wiped area requirements in Federal Motor Vehicle Safety Standards Governing Windshield Wiping and Washing Systems.

(c) This section does not apply to snow removal equipment equipped with adequate manually operated windshield wipers.

26707. Condition and Use of Windshield Wipers

Windshield wipers required by this code shall be maintained in good operating condition and shall provide clear vision through the windshield for the driver. Wipers shall be operated under conditions of fog, snow, or rain and shall be capable of effectively clearing the windshield under all ordinary storm or load conditions while the vehicle is in operation.

26708.   Material Obstructing or Reducing Drivers View

(a)(1)   A person shall not drive any motor vehicle with any object or material placed, displayed, installed, affixed, or applied upon the windshield or side or rear windows.

(2)   A person shall not drive any motor vehicle with any object or material placed, displayed, installed, affixed, or applied in or upon the vehicle that obstructs or reduces the driver's clear view through the windshield or side windows.

(3)   This subdivision applies to a person driving a motor vehicle with the driver's clear vision through the windshield, or side or rear windows, obstructed by snow or ice.

(b)   This section does not apply to any of the following:

(1)   Rearview mirrors.

(2)   Adjustable nontransparent sunvisors that are mounted forward of the side windows and are not attached to the glass.

(3)   Signs, stickers, or other materials that are displayed in a seven-inch square in the lower corner of the windshield farthest removed from the driver, signs, stickers, or other materials that are displayed in a seven-inch square in the lower corner of the rear window farthest removed from the driver, or signs, stickers, or other materials that are displayed in a five-inch square in the lower corner of the windshield nearest the driver.

(4)   Side windows that are to the rear of the driver.

(5)   Direction, destination, or terminus signs upon a passenger common carrier motor vehicle or a schoolbus, if those signs do not interfere with the driver's clear view of approaching traffic.

(6)   Rear window wiper motor.

(7)   Rear trunk lid handle or hinges.

(8)   The rear window or windows, if the motor vehicle is equipped with outside mirrors on both the left- and right-hand sides of the vehicle that are so located as to reflect to the driver a view of the highway through each mirror for a distance of at least 200 feet to the rear of the vehicle.

(9)   A clear, transparent lens affixed to the side window opposite the driver on a vehicle greater than 80 inches in width and that occupies an area not exceeding 50 square inches of the lowest corner toward the rear of that window and that provides the driver with a wide-angle view through the lens.

(10)   Sun screening devices meeting the requirements of Section 26708.2 installed on the side windows on either side of the vehicle's front seat, if the driver or a passenger in the front seat has in his or her possession a letter or other document signed by a licensed physician and surgeon certifying that the person must be shaded from the sun due to a medical condition, or has in his or her possession a letter or other document signed by a licensed optometrist certifying that the person must be shaded from the sun due to a visual condition. The devices authorized by this paragraph shall not be used during darkness.

(11)   An electronic communication device affixed to the center uppermost portion of the interior of a windshield within an area that is not greater than five inches square, if the device provides either of the following:

(A)   The capability for enforcement facilities of the Department of the California Highway Patrol to communicate with a vehicle equipped with the device.

(B)   The capability for electronic toll and traffic management on public or private roads or facilities.

(12)   A portable Global Positioning System (GPS), which may be mounted in a seven-inch square in the lower corner of the windshield farthest removed from the driver or in a five-inch square in the lower corner of the windshield nearest to the driver and outside of an airbag deployment zone, if the system is used only for door-to-door navigation while the motor vehicle is being operated.

(13)(A)   A video event recorder with the capability of monitoring driver performance to improve driver safety, which may be mounted in a seven-inch square in the lower corner of the windshield farthest removed from the driver, in a five-inch square in the lower corner of the windshield nearest to the driver and outside of an airbag deployment zone, or in a five-inch square mounted to the center uppermost portion of the interior of the windshield. As used in this section, "video event recorder" means a video recorder that continuously records in a digital loop, recording audio, video, and G-force levels, but saves video only when triggered by an unusual motion or crash or when operated by the driver to monitor driver performance.

(B) A vehicle equipped with a video event recorder shall have a notice posted in a visible location which states that a passenger's conversation may be recorded.

(C) Video event recorders shall store no more than 30 seconds before and after a triggering event.

(D) The registered owner or lessee of the vehicle may disable the device.

(E) The data recorded to the device is the property of the registered owner or lessee of the vehicle.

(F) When a person is driving for hire as an employee in a vehicle with a video event recorder, the person's employer shall provide unedited copies of the recordings upon the request of the employee or the employee's representative. These copies shall be provided free of charge to the employee and within five days of the request.

(14)(A) A video event recorder in a commercial motor vehicle with the capability of monitoring driver performance to improve driver safety, which may be mounted no more than two inches below the upper edge of the area swept by the windshield wipers, and outside the driver's sight lines to the road and highway signs and signals. Subparagraphs (B) to (F), inclusive, of paragraph (13) apply to the exemption provided by this paragraph.

(B) Except as provided in subparagraph (C), subparagraph (A) shall become inoperative on the following dates, whichever date is later:

(i) The date that the Department of the California Highway Patrol determines is the expiration date of the exemption from the requirements of paragraph (1) of subdivision (e) of Section 393.60 of Title 49 of the Code of Federal Regulations, as renewed in the notice of the Federal Motor Carrier Safety Administration on pages 21791 and 21792 of Volume 76 of the Federal Register (April 18, 2011).

(ii) The date that the Department of the California Highway Patrol determines is the expiration date for a subsequent renewal of an exemption specified in clause (i).

(C) Notwithstanding subparagraph (B), subparagraph (A) shall become operative on the date that the Department of the California Highway Patrol determines is the effective date of regulations revising paragraph (1) of subdivision (e) of Section 393.60 of Title 49 of the Code of Federal Regulations to allow the placement of a video event recorder at the top of the windshield on a commercial motor vehicle.

(c) Notwithstanding subdivision (a), transparent material may be installed, affixed, or applied to the topmost portion of the windshield if the following conditions apply:

(1) The bottom edge of the material is at least 29 inches above the undepressed driver's seat when measured from a point five inches in front of the bottom of the backrest with the driver's seat in its rearmost and lowermost position with the vehicle on a level surface.

(2) The material is not red or amber in color.

(3) There is no opaque lettering on the material and any other lettering does not affect primary colors or distort vision through the windshield.

(4) The material does not reflect sunlight or headlight glare into the eyes of occupants of oncoming or following vehicles to any greater extent than the windshield without the material.

(d) Notwithstanding subdivision (a), clear, colorless, and transparent material may be installed, affixed, or applied to the front side windows, located to the immediate left and right of the front seat if the following conditions are met:

(1) The material has a minimum visible light transmittance of 88 percent.

(2) The window glazing with the material applied meets all requirements of Federal Motor Vehicle Safety Standard No. 205 (49 C.F.R. 571.205), including the specified minimum light transmittance of 70 percent and the abrasion resistance of AS-14 glazing, as specified in that federal standard.

(3) The material is designed and manufactured to enhance the ability of the existing window glass to block the sun's harmful ultraviolet A rays.

(4) The driver has in his or her possession, or within the vehicle, a certificate signed by the installing company certifying that the windows with the material installed meet the requirements of this subdivision and the certificate identifies the installing company and the material's manufacturer by full name and street address, or, if the material was installed by the vehicle owner, a certificate signed by the material's manufacturer certifying that the windows with the material installed according to manufacturer's instructions meet the requirements of this subdivision and the certificate identifies the material's manufacturer by full name and street address.

(5) If the material described in this subdivision tears or bubbles, or is otherwise worn to prohibit clear vision, it shall be removed or replaced. *(AM '12)*

26708.2. Sun Screening Devices

Sun screening devices permitted by paragraph (10) of subdivision (b) of Section 26708 shall meet the following requirements:

(a) The devices shall be held in place by means allowing ready removal from the window area, such as a frame, a rigid material with temporary fasteners, or a flexible roller shade.

(b) Devices utilizing transparent material shall be green, gray, or a neutral smoke in color and shall have a luminous transmittance of not less than 35 percent.

(c) Devices utilizing nontransparent louvers or other alternating patterns of opaque and open sections shall have an essentially uniform pattern over the entire surface, except for framing and supports. At least 35 percent of the device area shall be open and no individual louver or opaque section shall have a projected vertical dimension exceeding 1/16 inch.

(d) The devices shall not have a reflective quality exceeding 35 percent on either the inner or outer surface. *(AD '84)*

26708.5. Transparent Materials

(a) No person shall place, install, affix, or apply any transparent material upon the windshield, or side or rear windows, of any motor vehicle if the material alters the color or reduces the light transmittance of the windshield or side or rear windows, except as provided in subdivision (b), (c), or (d) of Section 26708.

(b) Tinted safety glass may be installed in a vehicle if (1) the glass complies with motor vehicle safety standards of the United States Department of Transportation for safety glazing materials, and (2) the glass is installed in a location permitted by those standards for the particular type of glass used. *(AM '98)*

26708.7. Federal, State or Local Law Enforcement Vehicles Exempt

Notwithstanding any other law, a vehicle operated and owned or leased by a federal, state, or local agency, department, or district, that employs peace officers, as defined by Chapter 4.5 (commencing with Section 830) of Title 3 of Part 2 of the Penal Code, for use by those peace officers in the performance of their duties, is exempt from California law, and regulations adopted pursuant thereto, prohibiting or limiting material that may be placed, displayed, installed, affixed, or applied to the side or rear windows, commonly referred to as window tinting or glazing. *(AD '12)*

26709. Mirrors

(a) Every motor vehicle registered in a foreign jurisdiction and every motorcycle subject to registration in this state shall be equipped with a mirror so located as to reflect to the driver a view of the highway for a distance of at least 200 feet to the rear of such vehicle.

Every motor vehicle subject to registration in this state, except a motorcycle, shall be equipped with not less than two such mirrors, including one affixed to the left-hand side.

(b) The following described types of motor vehicles, of a type subject to registration, shall be equipped with mirrors on both the left- and right-hand sides of the vehicle so located as to reflect to the driver a view of the highway through each mirror for a distance of at least 200 feet to the rear of such vehicle:

(1) A motor vehicle so constructed or loaded as to obstruct the driver's view to the rear.

(2) A motor vehicle towing a vehicle and the towed vehicle or load thereon obstructs the driver's view to the rear.

(3) A bus or trolley coach.

(c) The provisions of subdivision (b) shall not apply to a passenger vehicle when the load obstructing the driver's view consists of passengers.

26710. Defective Windshields and Rear Windows

It is unlawful to operate any motor vehicle upon a highway when the windshield or rear window is in such a defective condition as to impair the driver's vision either to the front or rear. In the event any windshield or rear window fails to comply with this code the officer making the inspection shall direct the driver to make the windshield and rear window conform to the requirements of this code within 48 hours. The officer may also arrest the driver and give him notice to appear and further require the driver or the owner of the vehicle to produce in court satisfactory evidence that the windshield or rear window has been made to conform to the requirements of this code.

26711. Eyeshades on Bus or Trolley Coach

Every bus or trolley coach, except those first registered prior to January 1, 1960, and engaged in urban and suburban service as defined in Section 35107, shall be equipped with movable eyeshades of sufficient size to shade the eyes of the operator of a bus or trolley coach while it is being driven facing the sun.

26712. Defroster Required

Every passenger vehicle used or maintained for the transportation of persons for hire, compensation, or profit shall be equipped with a defrosting device which is adequate to remove snow, ice, frost, fog, or internal moisture from the windshield.

CHAPTER 5. OTHER EQUIPMENT

27000. Horns or Warning Devices

(a) A motor vehicle, when operated upon a highway, shall be equipped with a horn in good working order and capable of emitting sound audible under normal conditions from a distance of not less than 200 feet, but no horn shall emit an unreasonably loud or harsh sound. An authorized emergency vehicle may be equipped with, and use in conjunction with the siren on that vehicle, an air horn that emits sounds that do not comply with the requirements of this section.

(b) A refuse or garbage truck shall be equipped with an automatic backup audible alarm that sounds on backing and is capable of emitting sound audible under normal conditions from a distance of not less than 100 feet or shall be equipped with an automatic backup device that is in good working order, located at the rear of the vehicle and that immediately applies the service brake of the vehicle on contact by the vehicle with any obstruction to the rear. The backup device or alarm shall also be capable of operating automatically when the vehicle is in neutral or a forward gear but rolls backward.

(c) A refuse or garbage truck, except a vehicle, known as a rolloff vehicle, that is used for the express purpose of transporting waste containers such as open boxes or compactors, purchased after January 1, 2010, shall also be equipped with a functioning camera providing a video display for the driver that enhances or supplements the driver's view behind the truck for the purpose of safely maneuvering the truck.

(d)(1) A construction vehicle with a gross vehicle weight rating (GVWR) in excess of 14,000 pounds that operates at, or transports construction or industrial materials to and from, a mine or construction site, or both, shall be equipped with an automatic backup audible alarm that sounds on backing and is capable of emitting sound audible under normal conditions from a distance of not less than 200 feet.

(2) As used in this subdivision, "construction vehicle" includes, but is not limited to, all of the following:

(A) A vehicle designed to transport concrete, cement, clay, limestone, aggregate material as defined in subdivision (d) of Section 23114, or other similar construction or industrial material, including a transfer truck or a tractor trailer combination used exclusively to pull bottom dump, end dump, or side dump trailers.

(B) A vehicle that is a concrete mixer truck, a truck with a concrete placing boom, a water tank truck, a single engine crane with a load rating of 35 tons or more, or a tractor that exclusively pulls a low-boy trailer. *(AM '11)*

27001. Use of Horns

(a) The driver of a motor vehicle when reasonably necessary to insure safe operation shall give audible warning with his horn.

(b) The horn shall not otherwise be used, except as a theft alarm system which operates as specified in Article 13 of this chapter.

27002. Sirens

No vehicle, except an authorized emergency vehicle, shall be equipped with, nor shall any person use upon a vehicle any siren except that an authorized emergency vehicle shall be equipped with a siren meeting requirements established by the department.

27003. Sirens on Armored Cars

An armored car may be equipped with a siren which may be used while resisting armed robbery. At all other times, the siren shall not be sounded. The authority to use a siren granted by this section does not constitute an armored car an authorized emergency vehicle, and all other provisions of this code applicable to drivers of vehicles apply to drivers of armored cars.

27007. Sound Amplification Devices

No driver of a vehicle shall operate, or permit the operation of, any sound amplification system which can be heard outside the vehicle from 50 or more feet when the vehicle is being operated upon a highway, unless that system is being operated to request assistance or warn of a hazardous situation. This section shall not apply to authorized emergency vehicles or vehicles operated by gas, electric, communications, or water utilities. This section does not apply to the sound systems of vehicles used for advertising, or in parades, political or other special events, except that use of sound systems on those vehicles may be prohibited by a local authority by ordinance or resolution.

27150. Adequate Muffler Required

(a) Every motor vehicle subject to registration shall at all times be equipped with an adequate muffler in constant operation and properly maintained to prevent any excessive or unusual noise, and no muffler or exhaust system shall be equipped with a cutout, bypass, or similar device.

(b) Except as provided in Division 16.5 with respect to off-highway motor vehicles subject to identification, every passenger vehicle operated off the highways shall at all times be equipped with an adequate muffler in constant operation and properly maintained so as to meet the requirements of Article 2.5, and no muffler or exhaust system shall be equipped with a cutout, bypass, or similar device.

(c) The provisions of subdivision (b) shall not be applicable to passenger vehicles being operated off the highways in an organized racing or competitive event conducted under the auspices of a recognized sanctioning body or by permit issued by the local governmental authority having jurisdiction.

27150.1. Sale of Exhaust Systems

No person engaged in a business that involves the selling of motor vehicle exhaust systems, or parts thereof, including, but not limited to, mufflers, shall offer for sale, sell, or install, a motor vehicle exhaust system, or part thereof, including, but not limited to, a muffler, unless it meets the regulations and standards applicable pursuant to this article. Motor vehicle exhaust systems or parts thereof include, but are not limited to, nonoriginal exhaust equipment.

A violation of this section is a misdemeanor. *(AM '01, '02)*

27150.3. Whistle-Tip Prohibited

(a) A person may not modify the exhaust system of a motor vehicle with a whistle-tip.

(b) A person may not operate a motor vehicle if that vehicle's exhaust system is modified in violation of subdivision (a).

(c) A person may not engage in the business of installing a whistle-tip onto a motor vehicle's exhaust system.

(d) For purposes of subdivisions (a) and (c), a "whistle-tip" is a device that is applied to, or is a modification of, a motor vehicle's exhaust pipe for the sole purpose of creating a high-pitched or shrieking noise when the motor vehicle is operated. *(AD '03)*

27151. Modification of Exhaust Systems

(a) No person shall modify the exhaust system of a motor vehicle in a manner which will amplify or increase the noise emitted by the motor of the vehicle so that the vehicle is not in compliance with the provisions of Section 27150 or exceeds the noise limits established for the type of vehicle in Article 2.5 (commencing with Section 27200). No person shall operate a motor vehicle with an exhaust system so modified.

(b) For the purposes of exhaust systems installed on motor vehicles with a manufacturer's gross vehicle weight rating of less than 6,000 pounds, other than motorcycles, a sound level of 95 dbA or less, when tested in accordance with Society of Automotive Engineers Standard J1169 May 1998, complies with this section. Motor vehicle exhaust systems or parts thereof include, but are not limited to, nonoriginal exhaust equipment. *(AM '01)*

27152. Exhaust Pipes

The exhaust gases from a motor vehicle shall not be directed to the side of the vehicle between 2 feet and 11 feet above the ground.

27153. Exhaust Products

No motor vehicle shall be operated in a manner resulting in the escape of excessive smoke, flame, gas, oil, or fuel residue The provisions of this section apply to motor vehicles of the United States or its agencies, to the extent authorized by federal law.

27153.5. Motor Vehicle Exhaust Standards

(a) No motor vehicle first sold or registered as a new motor vehicle on or after January 1, 1971, shall discharge into the atmosphere at elevation of less than 4,000 feet any air contaminant for a period of more than 10 seconds which is:

(1) As dark or darker in shade as that designated as No. 1 on the Ringelmann Chart, as published by the United States Bureau of Mines, or

(2) Of such opacity as to obscure an observer's view to a degree equal to or greater than does smoke described in paragraph (1) of this subdivision.

(b) No motor vehicle first sold or registered prior to January 1, 1971, shall discharge into the atmosphere at elevation of less than 4,000 feet any air contaminant for a period of more than 10 seconds which is:

(1) As dark or darker in shade than that designated as No. 2 on the Ringelmann Chart, as published by the United States Bureau of Mines, or

(2) Of such opacity as to obscure an observer's view to a degree equal to or greater than does smoke described in paragraph (1) of this subdivision.

(c) The provisions of this section apply to motor vehicles of the United States or its agencies, to the extent authorized by federal law.

27154. Gases and Fumes

The cab of any motor vehicle shall be reasonably tight against the penetration of gases and fumes from the engine or exhaust system. The exhaust system, including the manifold, muffler, and exhaust pipes shall be so constructed as to be capable of being maintained and shall be maintained in a reasonably gastight condition.

27155. Fuel Tank Caps

No motor vehicle shall be operated or parked on any highway unless the filling spout for the fuel tank is closed by a cap or cover of noncombustible material.

27156. Air Pollution Control Device

(a) No person shall operate or leave standing upon a highway a motor vehicle that is a gross polluter, as defined in Section 39032.5 of the Health and Safety Code.

(b) No person shall operate or leave standing upon a highway a motor vehicle that is required to be equipped with a motor vehicle pollution control device under Part 5 (commencing with Section 43000) of Division 26 of the Health and Safety Code or any other certified motor vehicle pollution control device required by any other state law or any rule or regulation adopted pursuant to that law, or required to be equipped with a motor vehicle pollution control device pursuant to the National Emission Standards Act (42 U.S.C. Secs. 7521 to 7550, inclusive) and the standards and regulations adopted pursuant to that federal act, unless the motor vehicle is equipped with the required motor vehicle pollution control device that is correctly installed and in operating condition. No person shall disconnect, modify, or alter any such required device.

(c) No person shall install, sell, offer for sale, or advertise any device, apparatus, or mechanism intended for use with, or as a part of, a required motor vehicle pollution control device or system that alters or modifies the original design or performance of the motor vehicle pollution control device or system.

(d) If the court finds that a person has willfully violated this section, the court shall impose the maximum fine that may be imposed in the case, and no part of the fine may be suspended.

(e) "Willfully," as used in this section, has the same meaning as the meaning of that word prescribed in Section 7 of the Penal Code.

(f) No person shall operate a vehicle after notice by a traffic officer that the vehicle is not equipped with the required certified motor vehicle pollution control device correctly installed in operating condition, except as may be necessary to return the vehicle to the residence or place of business of the owner or driver or to a garage, until the vehicle has been properly equipped with such a device.

(g) The notice to appear issued or complaint filed for a violation of this section shall require that the person to whom the notice to appear is issued, or against whom the complaint is filed, produce proof of correction pursuant to Section 40150 or proof of exemption pursuant to Section 4000.1 or 4000.2.

(h) This section shall not apply to an alteration, modification, or modifying device, apparatus, or mechanism found by resolution of the State Air Resources Board to do either of the following:

(1) Not to reduce the effectiveness of a required motor vehicle pollution control device.

(2) To result in emissions from the modified or altered vehicle that are at levels that comply with existing state or federal standards for that model -year of the vehicle being modified or converted.

(i) Aftermarket and performance parts with valid State Air Resources Board Executive Orders may be sold and installed concurrent with a motorcycle's transfer to an ultimate purchaser.

(j) This section applies to motor vehicles of the United States or its agencies, to the extent authorized by federal law. *(AM '07)*

27158. Certificates of Compliance; Vehicle Inspection

After notice by a traffic officer that a vehicle does not comply with any regulation adopted pursuant to Section 27157, no person shall operate, and no owner shall permit the operation of, such vehicle for more than 30 days thereafter unless a certificate of compliance has been issued for such vehicle in accordance with the provisions of Section 9889.18 of the Business and Professions Code or unless the department has checked the vehicle and determined that the vehicle has been made to comply with such regulation adopted pursuant to Section 27157. A certificate of compliance issued for such vehicle shall, for a period of one year from date of issue, constitute proof of compliance with any regulations adopted pursuant to Section 27157 provided that no required pollution control device has been disconnected, or altered or as been adjusted by other than a licensed installer in a licensed motor vehicle pollution control device installation and inspection station subsequent to the issuance of the certificate of compliance. The provisions of this section shall apply to the United States an its agencies to the extent authorized by federal law.

27158.5. Certificates of Compliance or Inspection: 1955 Through 1965 Model Year Motor Vehicles
After notice by a traffic officer that a motor vehicle does not comply with any standard adopted pursuant to Section 27157.5, no person shall operate, and no owner shall permit the operation of, such motor vehicle for more than 30 days thereafter unless a certificate of compliance has been issued for such vehicle in accordance with the provisions of Section 9889.18 of the Business and Professions Code or unless the department has checked the vehicle and determined that the vehicle has been made to comply with such standard adopted pursuant to Section 27157.5. A certificate of compliance issued for such vehicle shall, for a period of one year from date of issue, constitute proof of compliance with the standards determined pursuant to Section 27157.5.

27159. Diesel Vehicles; Excessive Pollution; Removal from Service
Any uniformed member of the California Highway Patrol may order a vehicle stored when it is located within the territorial limits in which the member may act if requested by a representative of the State Air Resources Board to remove the vehicle from service pursuant to subdivision (f) of Section 44011.6 of the Health and Safety Code. All towing and storage fees for a vehicle removed under this section shall be paid by the owner.

27202.1. Motorcycle Exhaust EPA Certification Label Required
(a) Notwithstanding any other law, a person shall not park, use, or operate a motorcycle, registered in the State of California, that does not bear the required applicable federal Environmental Protection Agency exhaust system label pursuant to Subparts D (commencing with Section 205.150) and E (commencing with Section 205.164) of Part 205 of Title 40 of the Code of Federal Regulations. A violation of this section shall be considered a mechanical violation and a peace officer shall not stop a motorcycle solely on a suspicion of a violation of this section. A peace officer shall cite a violation of this section as a secondary infraction.

(b) A violation of this section is punishable as follows:

(1) For a first conviction, by a fine of not less than fifty dollars ($50), nor more than one hundred dollars ($100).

(2) For a second or subsequent conviction, by a fine of not less than one hundred dollars ($100), nor more than two hundred fifty dollars ($250).

(c)(1) The notice to appear issued or complaint filed for a violation of this section shall require that the person to whom the notice to appear is issued, or against whom the complaint is filed, produce proof of correction pursuant to Section 40150.

(2) Upon producing proof of correction to the satisfaction of the court, the court may dismiss the penalty imposed pursuant to subdivision (b) for a first violation of this section.

(d)(1) This section is applicable to a person operating a motorcycle that is manufactured on or after January 1, 2013, or a motorcycle with aftermarket exhaust system equipment that is manufactured on or after January 1, 2013.

(2) Penalties imposed pursuant to this section are in addition to penalties imposed pursuant to any other applicable laws or regulations.

(3) This section does not supersede, negate, or otherwise alter any other applicable laws or regulations. *(AD '10)*

27305. Fire Fighting Vehicles
All publicly owned firefighting vehicles designed for and used in responding to emergency fire calls and in combating fires shall be equipped with seatbelts for each seat utilized by personnel when such vehicles are being operated. Such seatbelts shall comply with requirements established by the department.

27314.5. Notice: Safety Belts
(a)(1) Subject to paragraph (3), no dealer shall sell or offer for sale any used passenger vehicle of a model year of 1972 to 1990, inclusive, unless there is affixed to the window of the left front door or, if there is no

window, to another suitable location so that it may be seen and read by a person standing outside the vehicle at that location, a notice, printed in 14-point type, which reads as follows:

"WARNING: While use of all seat belts reduces the chance of ejection, failure to install and use shoulder harnesses with lap belts can result in serious or fatal injuries in some crashes. Lap-only belts increase the chance of head and neck injury by allowing the upper torso to move unrestrained in a crash and increase the chance of spinal column and abdominal injuries by concentrating excessive force on the lower torso. Because children carry a disproportionate amount of body weight above the waist, they are more likely to sustain those injuries. Shoulder harnesses may be available that can be retrofitted in this vehicle. For more information call the Auto Safety Hotline at 1-800-424-9393."

(2) The notice shall remain affixed to the vehicle pursuant to paragraph (1) at all times that the vehicle is for sale.

(3) The notice is not required to be affixed to any vehicle equipped with both a lap belt and a shoulder harness for the driver and one passenger in the front seat of the vehicle and for at least two passengers in the rear seat of the vehicle.

(b)(1) In addition to the requirements of subdivision (a), and subject to paragraph (3) and subdivision (c), the dealer shall affix, to one rear seat lap belt buckle of every used passenger vehicle of a model year of 1972 to 1990, inclusive, that has a rear seat, a notice, printed in 10-point type, that reads as follows:

"WARNING: While use of all seat belts reduces the chance of ejection, failure to install and use shoulder harnesses with lap belts can result in serious or fatal injuries in some crashes. Shoulder harnesses may be available that can be retrofitted in this vehicle. For more information, call the Auto Safety Hotline at 1-800-424-9393."

(2) The notice shall remain affixed to the vehicle pursuant to paragraph (1) at all times that the vehicle is for sale.

(3) The message is not required to be affixed to any vehicle either equipped with both a lap belt and a shoulder harness for at least two passengers in the rear seat or having no rear seat lap belts.

(c) A dealer is not in violation of subdivision (b) unless a private nonprofit entity has furnished a supply of the appropriate notices suitable for affixing as required free of charge or, having requested a resupply of notices, has not received the resupply.

(d) The department shall furnish, to a nonprofit private entity for purposes of this section, for a fee not to exceed its costs in so furnishing, at least once every six months, a list of all licensed dealers who sell used passenger vehicles.

27315. Safety Belts

(a) The Legislature finds that a mandatory seatbelt law will contribute to reducing highway deaths and injuries by encouraging greater usage of existing manual seatbelts, that automatic crash protection systems that require no action by vehicle occupants offer the best hope of reducing deaths and injuries, and that encouraging the use of manual safety belts is only a partial remedy for addressing this major cause of death and injury. The Legislature declares that the enactment of this section is intended to be compatible with support for federal motor vehicle safety standards requiring automatic crash protection systems and should not be used in any manner to rescind federal requirements for installation of automatic restraints in new cars.

(b) This section shall be known and may be cited as the Motor Vehicle Safety Act.

(c)(1) As used in this section, motor vehicle means a passenger vehicle, a motortruck, or a truck tractor, but does not include a motorcycle.

(2) For purposes of this section, a motor vehicle also means a farm labor vehicle, regardless of the date of certification under Section 31401.

(d)(1) A person shall not operate a motor vehicle on a highway unless that person and all passengers 16 years of age or over are properly restrained by a safety belt. This paragraph does not apply to the operator of a taxicab, as defined in Section 27908, when the taxicab is driven on a city street and is engaged in the transportation of a fare-paying passenger. The safety belt requirement established by this paragraph is the minimum safety standard applicable to employees being transported in a motor vehicle. This paragraph does not preempt more stringent or restrictive standards imposed by the Labor Code or another state or federal regulation regarding the transportation of employees in a motor vehicle.

(2) For purposes of this section the phrase, properly restrained by a safety belt means that the lower (lap) portion of the belt crosses the hips or upper thighs of the occupant and the upper (shoulder) portion of the belt, if present, crosses the chest in front of the occupant.

(3) The operator of a limousine for hire or the operator of an authorized emergency vehicle, as defined in subdivision (a) of Section 165, shall not operate the limousine for hire or authorized emergency vehicle unless the operator and any passengers eight years of age or over in the front seat, are properly restrained by a safety belt.

(4) The operator of a taxicab shall not operate the taxicab unless any passengers eight years of age or over in the front seat, are properly restrained by a safety belt.

(e) A person 16 years of age or over shall not be a passenger in a motor vehicle on a highway unless that person is properly restrained by a safety belt. This subdivision does not apply to a passenger in a sleeper berth, as defined in subdivision (x) of Section 1201 of Title 13 of the California Code of Regulations.

(f) An owner of a motor vehicle, including an owner or operator of a taxicab, as defined in Section 27908, or a limousine for hire, operated on a highway shall maintain safety belts in good working order for the use of the occupants of the vehicle. The safety belts shall conform to motor vehicle safety standards established by the United States Department of Transportation. This subdivision, however, does not require installation or maintenance of safety belts if it is not required by the laws of the United States applicable to the vehicle at the time of its initial sale.

(g) This section does not apply to a passenger or operator with a physically disabling condition or medical condition that would prevent appropriate restraint in a safety belt, if the condition is duly certified by a licensed physician and surgeon or by a licensed chiropractor who shall state the nature of the condition, as well as the reason the restraint is inappropriate. This section also does not apply to a public employee, if the public employee is in an authorized emergency vehicle as defined in paragraph (1) of subdivision (b) of Section 165, or to a passenger in a seat behind the front seat of an authorized emergency vehicle as defined in paragraph (1) of subdivision (b) of Section 165 operated by the public employee, unless required by the agency employing the public employee.

(h) Notwithstanding subdivision (a) of Section 42001, a violation of subdivision (d), (e), or (f) is an infraction punishable by a fine of not more than twenty dollars ($20) for a first offense, and a fine of not more than fifty dollars ($50) for each subsequent offense. In lieu of the fine and any penalty assessment or court costs, the court, pursuant to Section 42005, may order that a person convicted of a first offense attend a school for traffic violators or another court-approved program in which the proper use of safety belts is demonstrated.

(i) In a civil action, a violation of subdivision (d), (e), or (f), or information of a violation of subdivision (h), does not establish negligence as a matter of law or negligence per se for comparative fault purposes, but negligence may be proven as a fact without regard to the violation.

(j) If the United States Secretary of Transportation fails to adopt safety standards for manual safety belt systems by September 1, 1989, a motor vehicle manufactured after that date for sale or sold in this state shall not be registered unless it contains a manual safety belt system that meets the performance standards applicable to automatic crash protection devices adopted by the United States Secretary of Transportation pursuant to Federal Motor Vehicle Safety Standard No. 208 (49 C.F.R. 571.208) as in effect on January 1, 1985.

(k) A motor vehicle offered for original sale in this state that has been manufactured on or after September 1, 1989, shall comply with the automatic restraint requirements of Section S4.1.2.1 of Federal Motor Vehicle Safety Standard No. 208 (49 C.F.R. 571.208), as published in Volume 49 of the Federal Register, No. 138, page 29009. An automobile manufacturer that sells or delivers a motor vehicle subject to this subdivision, and fails to comply with this subdivision, shall be punished by a fine of not more than five hundred dollars ($500) for each sale or delivery of a noncomplying motor vehicle.

(l) Compliance with subdivision (j) or (k) by a manufacturer shall be made by self-certification in the same manner as self-certification is accomplished under federal law.

(m) This section does not apply to a person actually engaged in delivery of newspapers to customers along the person's route if the person is properly restrained by a safety belt prior to commencing and subsequent to completing delivery on the route.

(n) This section does not apply to a person actually engaged in collection and delivery activities as a rural delivery carrier for the United States Postal Service if the person is properly restrained by a safety belt prior to stopping at the first box and subsequent to stopping at the last box on the route.

(o) This section does not apply to a driver actually engaged in the collection of solid waste or recyclable materials along that driver's collection route if the driver is properly restrained by a safety belt prior to commencing and subsequent to completing the collection route.

(p) Subdivisions (d), (e), (f), (g), and (h) shall become inoperative immediately upon the date that the United States Secretary of Transportation, or his or her delegate, determines to rescind the portion of the Federal Motor Vehicle Safety Standard No. 208 (49 C.F.R. 571.208) that requires the installation of automatic restraints in new motor vehicles, except that those subdivisions shall not become inoperative if the secretary's decision to rescind that Standard No. 208 is not based, in any respect, on the enactment or continued operation of those subdivisions. *(AM '11)*

27315.1. Applicability of Section 27315 - Fully Enclosed 3-Wheel Motor Vehicle

Section 27315 applies to any person in a fully enclosed three-wheeled motor vehicle that is not less than seven feet in length and not less than four feet in width, and has an unladen weight of 900 pounds or more.

27315.3. Safety Belts for Police Patrol Vehicles Mandated

(a) As used in this section, "passenger motor vehicle"means a passenger vehicle as defined in Section 465 and a motortruck as defined in Section 410 of less than 6,001 pounds unladen weight, but does not include a motorcycle as defined in Section 400.

(b) Every sheriff's department and city police department and the Department of the California Highway Patrol shall maintain safety belts in good working order for the use of occupants of a vehicle that it operates on a highway for the purpose of patrol. The safety belts shall conform to motor vehicle safety standards established by the United States Department of Transportation. This subdivision does not, however, require installation or maintenance of safety belts where not required by the laws of the United States applicable to the vehicle at the time of its initial sale.

(c) Notwithstanding subdivision (a) of Section 42001, a violation of subdivision (b) is an infraction punishable by a fine, including all penalty assessments and court costs imposed on the convicted department, of not more than twenty dollars ($20) for a first offense, and a fine, including all penalty assessments and court costs imposed on the convicted department, of not more than fifty dollars ($50) for each subsequent offense.

(d)(1) For a violation of subdivision (b), in addition to the fines provided for pursuant to subdivision (c) and the penalty assessments provided for pursuant to Section 1464 of the Penal Code, an additional penalty assessment of two dollars ($2) shall be levied for a first offense, and an additional penalty assessment of five dollars ($5) shall be levied for any subsequent offense.

(2) All money collected pursuant to this subdivision shall be utilized in accordance with Section 1464 of the Penal Code.

(e) In a civil action, a violation of subdivision (b) or information of a violation of subdivision (c) shall not establish negligence as a matter of law or negligence per se for comparative fault purposes, but negligence may be proven as a fact without regard to the violation.

(f) Subdivisions (b) and (c) shall become inoperative immediately upon the date that the Secretary of the United States Department of Transportation, or his or her delegate, determines to rescind the portion of the Federal Motor Vehicle Safety Standard No. 208 (49 C.F.R. 571.208) that requires the installation of automatic restraints in new passenger motor vehicles, except that those subdivisions shall not become inoperative if the secretary's decision to rescind Standard No. 208 is not based, in any respect, on the enactment or continued operation of those subdivisions or subdivisions (d) to (h), inclusive, of Section 27315. *(AM '11)*

27316. Safety Belts; Schoolbuses; Study

(a) Unless specifically prohibited by the National Highway Transportation Safety Administration, all schoolbuses purchased or leased for use in California shall be equipped at all designated seating positions with a combination pelvic and upper torso passenger restraint system, if the schoolbus is either of the following:

(1) Type 1, as defined in paragraph (1) of subdivision (b) of Section 1201 of Title 13 of the California Code of Regulations, and is manufactured on or after July 1, 2005.

(2) Type 2, as defined in paragraph (2) of subdivision (b) of Section 1201 of Title 13 of the California Code of Regulations, and is manufactured on or after July 1, 2004.

(b) For purposes of this section, a "passenger restraint system" means any of the following:

(1) A restraint system that is in compliance with Federal Motor Vehicle Safety Standard 209, for a type 2 seatbelt assembly, and with Federal Motor Vehicle Safety Standard 210, as those standards were in effect on the date the schoolbus was manufactured.

(2) A restraint system certified by the schoolbus manufacturer that is in compliance with Federal Motor Vehicle Safety Standard 222 and incorporates a type 2 lap/shoulder restraint system.

(c) No person, school district, or organization, with respect to a schoolbus equipped with passenger restraint systems pursuant to this section, may be charged for a violation of this code or any regulation adopted thereunder requiring a passenger to use a passenger restraint system, if a passenger on the schoolbus fails to use or improperly uses the passenger restraint system.

(d) It is the intent of the Legislature, in implementing this section, that school pupil transportation providers work to prioritize the allocation of schoolbuses purchased, leased, or contracted for on or after July 1, 2004, for type 2 schoolbuses, or on or after July 1, 2005, for type 1 schoolbuses, to ensure that elementary -level schoolbus passengers receive first priority for new schoolbuses whenever feasible. *(RP & AD '99; AM '01)*

27316.5. Type 2 Pupil Activity Buses; Passenger Restraint System Required

(a) Unless specifically prohibited by the National Highway Transportation Safety Administration, all type 2 school pupil activity buses, manufactured on or after July 1, 2004, purchased or leased for use in California shall be equipped at all designated seating positions with a combination pelvic and upper torso passenger restraint system.

(b) For purposes of this section, a "passenger restraint system" is either of the following:

(1) A restraint system that is in compliance with Federal Motor Vehicle Safety Standard 209, for a type 2 seatbelt assembly, and with Federal Motor Vehicle Safety Standard 210, as those standards were in effect on the date that the school pupil activity bus was manufactured.

(2) A restraint system certified by the school pupil activity bus manufacturer that is in compliance with Federal Motor Vehicle Safety Standard 222 and incorporates a type 2 lap-shoulder restraint system.

(c) No person, school district, or organization, with respect to a type 2 school pupil activity bus equipped with passenger restraint systems pursuant to this section, may be charged for a violation of this code or any regulation adopted thereunder requiring a passenger to use a passenger restraint system, if a passenger on the school pupil activity bus fails to use or improperly uses the passenger restraint system. *(AD '02)*

27317. Previously Deployed Air Bag - Installation, Reinstallation or Distribution Prohibited

A person who installs, reinstalls, rewires, tampers with, alters, or modifies for compensation, a vehicle's computer system or supplemental restraint system, including, but not limited to, the supplemental restraint system's on-board system performance indicators, so that it falsely indicates the supplemental restraint system is in proper working order, or who knowingly distributes or sells a previously deployed air bag or previously deployed air bag component that will no longer meet the original equipment manufacturing form or function for proper operation, is guilty of a misdemeanor punishable by a fine of up to five thousand dollars ($5,000) or by imprisonment in a county jail for up to one year, or by both the fine and imprisonment. *(AM '12)*

27360. Child Restraint Requirements: Under 8 Years of Age

(a) Except as provided in Section 27363 a parent, legal guardian, or driver shall not transport on a highway in a motor vehicle, as defined in paragraph (1) of subdivision (3) of Section 27315, a child or ward who is under eight years of age, without properly securing that child in a rear seat in an appropriate child passenger restraint system meeting applicable federal motor vehicle safety standards.

(b) Subdivision (a) does not apply to a driver if the parent or legal guardian of the child is also present in the motor vehicle and is not the driver. *(RP-AD '11)*

27360.5. Child Safety Belt Requirements: 8 Years of Age or Older to Less than 16 Years of Age

(a) A parent, legal guardian, or driver shall not transport on a highway in a motor vehicle, as defined in paragraph (1) of subdivision (c) of Section 27315, a child or ward who is eight years of age or older, but less than 16 years of age, without properly securing that child or ward in an appropriate child passenger restraint system or safety belt meeting applicable federal motor vehicle safety standards.

(b) Subdivision (a) does not apply to a driver if the parent or legal guardian of the child is also present in the motor vehicle and is not the driver. *(RP-AD '11)*

27361. Notice to Appear for Violation

A law enforcement officer reasonably suspecting a violation of Section 27360 or 27360.5, or both of those sections, may stop a vehicle transporting a child appearing to the officer to be within the age specified in Section 27360 or 27360.5. The officer may issue a notice to appear for a violation of Section 27360 or 27360.5. *(AM '11)*

27362.1. Child Passenger Restraint System Involved in Accident; Sale Prohibited

(a) No individual may sell or offer for sale a child passenger restraint system that was in use by a child during an accident involving a motor vehicle.

(b) A violation of this section shall be punished by a fine of one hundred dollars ($100). *(AD '02)*

27363. Exemption; Medical Conditions or Size

(a) The court may exempt from the requirements of this article any class of child by age, weight, or size if it is determined that the use of a child passenger restraint system would be impractical by reason of physical unfitness, medical condition, or size. The court may require satisfactory proof of the child's physical unfitness, medical condition, or size and that an appropriate special needs child passenger restraint system is not available.

(b) In case of a life-threatening emergency, or when a child is being transported in an authorized emergency vehicle, if there is no child passenger restraint system available, a child may be transported without the use of that system, but the child shall be secured by a seatbelt.

(c) A child weighing more than 40 pounds may be transported in the backseat of a vehicle while wearing only a lap safety belt when the backseat of the vehicle is not equipped with a combination lap and shoulder safety belt.

(d) Notwithstanding Section 27360, a child or ward under eight years of age who is four feet nine inches in height or taller may be properly restrained by a safety belt, as defined in paragraph (2) of subdivision (d) of Section 27315, rather than by a child passenger restraint system.

(e) Notwithstanding Section 27360, a child or ward under eight years of age may ride properly secured in an appropriate child passenger restraint system meeting applicable federal motor vehicle safety standards in the front seat of a motor vehicle under any of the following circumstances:

(1) There is no rear seat.

(2) The rear seats are side-facing jump seats.

(3) The rear seats are rear-facing seats.

(4) The child passenger restraint system cannot be installed properly in the rear seat.

(5) All rear seats are already occupied by children seven years of age or under.

(6) Medical reasons necessitate that the child or ward not ride in the rear seat. The court may require satisfactory proof of the child's medical condition.

(f) Notwithstanding subdivision (e), a child shall not be transported in a rear-facing child passenger restraint system in the front seat of a motor vehicle that is equipped with an active frontal passenger airbag. *(AM '11)*

27365. Child Seat Restraints - Rental Vehicles

(a)(1) A car rental agency in California shall inform each of its customers of Section 27360 by posting, in a place conspicuous to the public in each established place of business of the agency, a notice not smaller than 15 by 20 inches which states the following:

"CALIFORNIA LAW REQUIRES ALL CHILDREN UNDER 8 YEARS OF AGE TO BE TRANSPORTED IN THE REAR SEAT OF THE VEHICLE IN A CHILD RESTRAINT SYSTEM. THIS AGENCY IS REQUIRED TO PROVIDE FOR RENTAL OF A CHILD RESTRAINT SYSTEM IF YOU DO NOT HAVE A CHILD RESTRAINT SYSTEM YOURSELF."

(2) The posted notice specified in paragraph (1) is not required if the car rental agency's place of business is located in a hotel that has a business policy prohibiting the posting of signs or notices in any area of the hotel. In that case, a car rental agency shall furnish a written notice to each customer that contains the same information as required for the posted notice.

(b) Every car rental agency in California shall have available for, and shall, upon request, provide for rental to, adults traveling with children under eight years of age, child passenger restraint systems that are certified by the manufacturer to meet applicable federal motor vehicle safety standards for use by children, are in good and safe condition, with no missing original parts, and are not older than five years.

(c) A violation of this section is an infraction punishable by a fine of one hundred dollars ($100). *(AM '11)*

27368. Applicability of Article to Fully Enclosed 3-Wheel Motor Vehicle

This article applies to child passengers in a fully enclosed three-wheeled motor vehicle that is not less than seven feet in length and not less than four feet in width, and has an unladen weight of 900 pounds or more.

27400. Wearing of Headsets or Earplugs

A person operating a motor vehicle or bicycle may not wear a headset covering, or earplugs in, both ears. This prohibition does not apply to any of the following:

(a) A person operating authorized emergency vehicles, as defined in Section 165.

(b) A person engaged in the operation of either special construction equipment or equipment for use in the maintenance of any highway.

(c) A person engaged in the operation of refuse collection equipment who is wearing a safety headset or safety earplugs.

(d) A person wearing personal hearing protectors in the form of earplugs or molds that are specifically designed to attenuate injurious noise levels. The plugs or molds shall be designed in a manner so as to not inhibit the wearer's ability to hear a siren or horn from an emergency vehicle or a horn from another motor vehicle.

(e) A person using a prosthetic device that aids the hard of hearing. *(AM '03)*

27450. Thickness of Solid Tire

When any vehicle is equipped with any solid tire, the solid tire shall have a minimum thickness of resilient rubber as follows:

(a) If the width of the tire is three inches but less than six inches, one inch thick.

(b) If the width of the tire is six inches but not more than nine inches, 1¼ inches thick.

(c) If the width of the tire is more than nine inches, 1½ inches thick.

27453. Dual Solid Tires

There shall not be an average difference greater than 1/8 inch between the outside diameters of each single tire composing a dual solid rubber tire.

27454. Protuberances on Tires: Exceptions

A tire on a vehicle upon a highway shall not have on its periphery any block, stud, flange, cleat, ridge, bead, or any other protuberance of metal or wood that projects beyond the tread of the traction surface of the tire.

This section does not apply to any of the following:

(a) Tire traction devices of reasonable size used to prevent skidding when upon wet surfaces or when upon snow or ice.

(b) Pneumatic tires that have embedded therein wire not to exceed 0.075 of an inch in diameter and that are constructed so that under no conditions will the percentage of metal in contact with the roadway exceed 5 percent of the total tire area in contact with the roadway, except that during the first 1,000 miles of use or operation of the tire, the metal in contact with the roadway may exceed 5 percent of the tire area in contact with the roadway, but shall in no event exceed 20 percent of the area.

(c) Vehicles operated upon unimproved roadways when necessary in the construction or repair of highways.

(d) Traction engines or tractors when operated under the conditions of a permit first obtained from the Department of Transportation.

(e)(1) Pneumatic tires containing metal-type studs of tungsten carbide or other suitable material that are inserted or constructed so that under no condition will the number of studs or the percentage of metal in contact with the roadway exceed 3 percent of the total tire area in contact with the roadway, between November 1 and April 30 of each year. A vehicle may be equipped year-round with tires that have studs that retract pneumatically or mechanically when not in use, if the studs are retracted between May 1 and October 31 of each year. A tire on a vehicle shall not be worn to a point at which the studs protrude beyond the tire tread when retracted.

(2) The commissioner, after consultation with the Department of Transportation, may extend the period during which the studded pneumatic tires may be used with studs deployed or inserted in areas of the state for the protection of the public because of adverse weather conditions.

(f) Pneumatic tires used on an authorized emergency vehicle, as defined in Section 165, containing metal-type studs of tungsten carbide or other suitable material, if the studs are inserted or constructed so that under no conditions will the number of studs or the percentage of metal in contact with the roadway exceed 3 percent of the total tire area in contact with the roadway. Notwithstanding subdivision (e), authorized emergency vehicles are permitted the unrestricted use of studded pneumatic tires throughout the year. *(AM '08)*

27455. Inner Tubes

(a) On and after January 1, 1975, no person shall sell or offer for sale an inner tube for use in a radial tire unless, at the time of manufacture, the tube valve stem is colored red or is distinctly marked in accordance with rules and regulations adopted by the department, taking into consideration the recommendations of manufacturers of inner tubes.

(b) No person shall install an inner tube in a radial tire unless the inner tube is designed for use in a radial tire.

27459. Tire Traction Devices or Snow-Tread Tires

No person shall operate any motor vehicle, trailer or semitrailer upon any portion of a highway without tire traction devices when that portion of the highway is signed for the requirement of tire chains. In any case where a passenger vehicle or motortruck having an unladen weight of 6,000 pounds or less may be required by the California Department of Transportation or local authorities to be equipped with tire chains, the chains shall be placed on at least two drive wheels, or the department or local authorities may provide, in the alternative, that the vehicle may be equipped with snow-tread tires on at least two drive wheels when the weather and surface conditions at the time are such that the stopping, tractive, and cornering abilities of the snow-tread tires are adequate. The snow-tread tires shall be of a type and design manufactured for use on snow as a replacement for tire chains, shall be in good condition, and shall bear the marking of M-S, M/S, or other marking indicating that the tire was manufactured for use on snow, or, in the case of tires purchased before January 1, 1987, shall either bear the markings or, in the opinion of the inspecting officer, comply with the tread pattern requirements of Section 558.

27459.5. Sale of Tire Traction Devices

(a) No person shall sell, offer for sale, lease, install, or replace on a vehicle for use on a highway, any tire traction devices which are not in compliance with requirements specified in Section 605.

(b) Every manufacturer who sells, offers for sale, or manufactures for use upon a vehicle, tire traction devices subject to the requirements of Section 605 shall, before the device is offered for sale, have laboratory test data showing compliance with those requirements. Tests may be conducted by the manufacturer.

27460. Four-Wheel Drive Vehicles

Any passenger vehicle or motor truck having an unladen weight of 6,500 pounds or less and operated and equipped with four-wheel drive and with snow-tread tires on all four drive wheels may be operated upon any portion of a highway without tire traction devices, notwithstanding the fact that such highway is signed for the requirement of those devices and provided that tire traction devices for at least one set of drive wheels are carried in or upon such vehicle. The snow tread tires shall meet the requirements specified in Section 27459 of this code, and such vehicle shall not, when so operated, tow another vehicle except as may be necessary to move a disabled vehicle from the roadway.

No person shall use such tires on four-wheel drive vehicles in place of tire traction devices whenever weather and roadway conditions at the time are such that the stopping, tractive and cornering abilities of the tires are not adequate or whenever the California Department of Transportation or local authorities, in their respective jurisdictions, place signs prohibiting their operation unless equipped with tire traction devices.

27460.5. Sale of Recut or Regrooved Tires

No person shall knowingly sell or offer or expose for sale any motor vehicle tire except a commercial vehicle tire, or any motor vehicle equipped with any tire except a commercial vehicle tire, which has been recut or regrooved. For purposes of this section a recut or regrooved tire is an unretreaded or unrecapped tire into which new grooves have been cut or burned.

27461. Use of Recut or Regrooved Tires

No person shall cause or permit the operation of and no driver shall knowingly operate any motor vehicle except a commercial vehicle, on any street or highway, which is equipped with one or more recut or regrooved tires. For purposes of this section a recut or regrooved tire is an unretreaded or unrecapped tire into which new grooves have been cut or burned.

27465. Tread Depth of Pneumatic Tires

(a) No dealer or person holding a retail seller's permit shall sell, offer for sale, expose for sale, or install on a vehicle axle for use on a highway, a pneumatic tire when the tire has less than the tread depth specified in subdivision (b). This subdivision does not apply to any person who installs on a vehicle, as part of an emergency service rendered to a disabled vehicle upon a highway, a spare tire with which such disabled vehicle was equipped.

(b) No person shall use on a highway a pneumatic tire on a vehicle axle when the tire has less than the following tread depth, except when temporarily installed on a disabled vehicle as specified in subdivision (a):

(1) One thirty-second of an inch tread depth in any two adjacent grooves at any location of the tire, except as provided in paragraphs (2) and (3).

(2) Four thirty-second of an inch tread depth at all points in all major grooves on a tire on the steering axle of any motor vehicle specified in Section 34500, and two thirty-second of an inch tread depth at all points in all major grooves on all other tires on the axles of these vehicles.

(3) Six thirty-second of an inch tread depth at all points in all major grooves on snow tires used in lieu of tire traction devices in posted chain control areas.

(c) The measurement of tread depth shall not be made where tie bars, humps, or fillets are located.

(d) The requirements of this section shall not apply to implements of husbandry.

(e) The department, if it determines that such action is appropriate and in keeping with reasonable safety requirements, may adopt regulations establishing more stringent tread depth requirements than those specified in this section for those vehicles defined in Sections 322 and 545, and may adopt regulations establishing tread depth requirements different from those specified in this section for those vehicles listed in Section 34500.

27501. Pneumatic Tires Which Do Not Conform to Regulations

(a) No dealer or person holding a retail seller's permit shall sell, offer for sale, expose for sale, or install on a vehicle for use on a highway, a pneumatic tire which is not in compliance with regulations adopted pursuant to Section 27500. This subdivision shall not apply to any person who installs on a vehicle, as part of an emergency service rendered to a vehicle upon a highway, a spare tire with which such disabled vehicle was equipped.

(b) No person shall use on a highway a pneumatic tire which is not in conformance with such regulations.

27600. Fenders and Mudguards

No person shall operate any motor vehicle having three or more wheels, any trailer, or semitrailer unless equipped with fenders, covers, or devices, including flaps or splash aprons, or unless the body of the vehicle or attachments thereto afford adequate protection to effectively minimize the spray or splash of water or mud to the rear of the vehicle and all such equipment or such body or attachments thereto shall be at least as wide as the tire tread. This section does not apply to those vehicles exempt from registration, trailers and semitrailers having an unladen weight of under 1,500 pounds, or any vehicles manufacture and first registered prior to January 1, 1971, having an unladen weight of under 1,500 pounds.

27602. Television

(a) A person shall not drive a motor vehicle if a television receiver, a video monitor, or a television or video screen, or any other similar means of visually displaying a television broadcast or video signal that produces entertainment or business applications, is operating and is located in the motor vehicle at a point forward of the back of the driver's seat, or is operating and the monitor, screen, or display is visible to the driver while driving the motor vehicle.

(b) Subdivision (a) does not apply to the following equipment when installed in a vehicle:

(1) A vehicle information display.

(2) A global positioning display.

(3) A mapping display.

(4) A visual display used to enhance or supplement the driver's view forward, behind, or to the sides of a motor vehicle for the purpose of maneuvering the vehicle.

(5) A television receiver, video monitor, television or video screen, or any other similar means of visually displaying a television broadcast or video signal, if that equipment satisfies one of the following requirements:

(A) The equipment has an interlock device that, when the motor vehicle is driven, disables the equipment for all uses except as a visual display as described in paragraphs (1) to (4), inclusive.

(B) The equipment is designed, operated, and configured in a manner that prevents the driver of the motor vehicle from viewing the television broadcast or video signal while operating the vehicle in a safe and reasonable manner.

(6) A mobile digital terminal that is fitted with an opaque covering that does not allow the driver to view any part of the display while driving, even though the terminal may be operating, installed in a vehicle that is owned or operated by any of the following:

(A) An electrical corporation, as defined in Section 218 of the Public Utilities Code.

(B) A gas corporation, as defined in Section 222 of the Public Utilities Code.

(C) A sewer system corporation, as defined in Section 230.6 of the Public Utilities Code.

(D) A telephone corporation, as defined in Section 234 of the Public Utilities Code.

(E) A water corporation, as defined in Section 241 of the Public Utilities Code.

(F) A local publicly owned electric utility, as defined in Section 224.3 of the Public Utilities Code.

(G) A city, joint powers agency, or special district, if that local entity uses the vehicle solely in the provision of sewer service, gas service, water service, or wastewater service.

(c) Subdivision (a) does not apply to a mobile digital terminal installed in an authorized emergency vehicle or to a motor vehicle providing emergency road service or roadside assistance.

(d) Subdivision (a) does not apply to a mobile digital terminal installed in a vehicle when the vehicle is deployed in an emergency to respond to an interruption or impending interruption of electrical, natural gas, telephone, sewer, water, or wastewater service, and the vehicle is owned or operated by any of the following:

(1) An electrical corporation, as defined in Section 218 of the Public Utilities Code.

(2) A gas corporation, as defined in Section 222 of the Public Utilities Code.

(3) A sewer system corporation, as defined in Section 230.6 of the Public Utilities Code.

(4) A telephone corporation, as defined in Section 234 of the Public Utilities Code.

(5) A water corporation, as defined in Section 241 of the Public Utilities Code.

(6) A local publicly owned electric utility, as defined in Section 224.3 of the Public Utilities Code.

(7) A city, joint powers agency, or special district, if that local entity uses the vehicle solely in the provision of sewer service, gas service, water service, or wastewater service. *(AM '03, '04, '09-'10)*

27603. Color Required for Former Schoolbus

When a motor vehicle formerly used as a schoolbus is sold to any person and is used exclusively for purposes other than the transportation of pupils pursuant to Article 3 of Chapter 5 of Part 23 of the Education Code, it shall be painted by the purchaser a color different than that prescribed by the CHP for schoolbuses before it is operated on any street or highway other than to have the vehicle painted or moved to a place of storage.

The provisions of this section shall not apply where the ownership of a schoolbus is transferred to a nonprofit organization under a contractual arrangement under which the ownership is required to be retransferred to the original owner within 90 days of the date of the original transfer.

27604. Painting of Former Law Enforcement Vehicle

When a motor vehicle, painted, as required by Section 40800, and formerly used in the enforcement of the provisions of Division 10 or 11, is sold to any person and is used for purposes other than law enforcement, the vehicle shall be painted or partially painted by the seller or agency formerly using such vehicle so that it will no longer resemble a vehicle complying with Section 40800 and any insignia or other marking of the vehicle identifying it as a traffic law enforcement vehicle shall be removed by the seller or agency formerly using such vehicle before it shall be operated on any street or highway, other than to have the vehicle moved to be painted or to a place of storage.

The provisions of this section do not apply to former law enforcement vehicles, without insignia, which are painted one solid color, or which are used exclusively for movie or television production and display signs stating "movie car" prominently on the doors, or which are motorcycles, as defined in Section 400, without insignia.

27605. Vehicle Resembling Law Enforcement Vehicle

No person shall own or operate a motor vehicle painted in the manner described in Section 40800 to resemble a motor vehicle used by a peace officer or traffic officer on duty for the primary purpose of enforcing the provisions of Division 10 or Division 11 pursuant to Section 40800.

The provisions of this section shall not apply to vehicles which are painted one solid color or to vehicles first registered on or before January 1, 1979. These provisions shall not apply to vehicles which are any of the following:

(a) Owned by vehicle manufacturers or dealers.

(b) Used by law enforcement agencies in the enforcement of the provisions of Division 10 or Division 11.

(c) Owned by persons or companies who use the vehicles exclusively for movie or television production and display signs stating "movie car"prominently on the doors,

(d) Owned by persons or companies who use the vehicles exclusively for funeral escort purposes.

(e) Motorcycles, as defined in Section 400, without insignia.

27606. Illegal Use of Light Bars

(a) No person shall own or operate a motor vehicle which is equipped with a light bar, or facsimile thereof to resemble a motor vehicle used by a peace officer or traffic officer while on duty within that jurisdiction for the primary purpose of enforcing Division 10 or Division 11 pursuant to Section 40800.

(b) For purposes of this section the following definitions apply:

(1) A "light bar"means any light or device affixed to or mounted upon the roof of a vehicle and extending the width of the roof, or a substantial portion thereof which emits amber, red, or blue, or any combination of those lights.

(2) A "facsimile of a light bar"is any device designed or contrived to resemble a light bar regardless of the degree of light emission or lack thereof.

27700. Required Equipment

(a) Tow trucks shall be equipped with and carry all of the following:

(1) One or more brooms, and the driver of the tow truck engaged to remove a disabled vehicle from the scene of an accident shall remove all glass and debris deposited upon the roadway the disabled vehicle which is to be towed.

(2) One or more shovels, and whenever practical the tow truck driver engaged to remove any disabled vehicle shall spread dirt upon that portion of the roadway where oil or grease has been deposited by the disabled vehicle.

(3) One or more fire extinguishers of the dry chemical or carbon dioxide type with an aggregate rating of at least 4-B,C units and bearing the approval of a laboratory nationally recognized as properly equipped to make the approval.

(b) A person licensed as a repossession agency pursuant to Chapter 11 of Division 3 of the Business and Professions Code is exempt from this section.

27800. Passengers: Equipment and Usage

It is unlawful for a driver of a motorcycle or a motorized bicycle to carry any other person thereon, except on a seat securely fastened to the machine at the rear of the driver and provided with footrests, or in a sidecar attached to a motorcycle and designed for the purpose of carrying a passenger. Every passenger on a motorcycle or a motorized bicycle shall keep his feet on the footrests while such vehicle is in motion.

27801. Required Position of Equipment

A person shall not drive a two-wheel motorcycle that is equipped with either of the following:

(a) A seat so positioned that the driver, when sitting astride the seat, cannot reach the ground with his or her feet.

(b) Handlebars so positioned that the hands of the driver, when upon the grips, are more than six inches above his or her shoulder height when sitting astride the seat. *(AM '04)*

27802. Safety Helmet Regulations

(a) The department may adopt reasonable regulations establishing specifications and standards for safety helmets offered for sale, or sold, for use by drivers and passengers of motorcycles and motorized bicycles as it determines are necessary for the safety of those drivers and passengers. The regulations shall include, but are not limited to, the requirements imposed by Federal Motor Vehicle Safety Standard No. 218 (49 C.F.R. Sec. 571.218) and may include compliance with that federal standard by incorporation of its requirements by reference. Each helmet sold or offered for sale for use by drivers and passengers of motorcycles and motorized bicycles shall be conspicuously labeled in accordance with the federal standard which shall constitute the manufacturer's certification that the helmet conforms to the applicable federal motor vehicle safety standards.

(b) No person shall sell, or offer for sale, for use by a driver or passenger of a motorcycle or motorized bicycle any safety helmet which is not of a type meeting requirements established by the department.

27803. Safety Helmets Required

(a) A driver and any passenger shall wear a safety helmet meeting requirements established pursuant to Section 27802 when riding on a motorcycle, motor-driven cycle, or motorized bicycle.

(b) It is unlawful to operate a motorcycle, motor-driven cycle, or motorized bicycle if the driver or any passenger is not wearing a safety helmet as required by subdivision (a).

(c) It is unlawful to ride as a passenger on a motorcycle, motor-driven cycles, or motorized bicycle if the driver or any passenger is not wearing a safety helmet as required by subdivision (a).

(d) This section applies to persons who are riding on motorcycles, motor-driven cycles, or motorized bicycles operated on the highways.

(e) For the purposes of this section, "wear a safety helmet" or "wearing a safety helmet" means having a safety helmet meeting the requirements of Section 27802 on the person's head that is fastened with the helmet straps and that is of a size that fits the wearing person's head securely without excessive lateral or vertical movement.

(f) It is the intent of the Legislature in enacting this section, to ensure that all persons are provided with an additional safety benefit while operating or riding a motorcycle, motor-driven cycle, or motorized bicycle.

27900. Identification Required

(a) Every motor vehicle or combination of vehicles used to carry the property of others for hire or used to carry passengers for hire, any truck or truck tractor having three or more axles or any truck tractor with a semitrailer, and all commercial motor vehicles, as defined in subdivision (c) of Section 34601, shall have displayed on both sides of each vehicle or on both sides of one of the vehicles in each combination of vehicles the name or trademark of the person under whose authority the vehicle or combination of vehicles is being operated.

(b) A vehicle or combination of vehicles listed in subdivision (a) that is operated under a rental agreement with a term of not more than 30 calendar days shall meet all of the following requirements:

(1) Have displayed on both sides of each vehicle or on both sides of one of the vehicles in each combination of vehicles the name or trademark of the lessor.

(2) Have displayed on both sides of each vehicle or on both sides of one of the vehicles in each combination of vehicles any of the following numbers issued to the lessor:

(A) The carrier identification number issued by the United States Department of Transportation.

(B) A valid operating authority number.

(C) A valid motor carrier of property number.

(3)(A) Have in the vehicle or combination of vehicles a copy of the rental agreement entered into by the lessor and the vehicle operator.

(B) The rental agreement shall be available for inspection immediately upon the request of any authorized employee of the department or any regularly employed and salaried police officer or deputy sheriff, or any reserve police officer or reserve deputy sheriff listed in Section 830.6 of the Penal Code.

(C) If the rented vehicle or combination of vehicles is operated in conjunction with a commercial enterprise, the rental agreement shall include the operator's carrier identification number or motor carrier of property permit number.

(c) A vehicle or combination of vehicles that is in compliance with Section 390.21 of Title 49 of the Code of Federal Regulations shall be deemed to be in compliance with subdivision (b).

(d) All names, trademarks, and other identifiers for companies no longer in business, no longer operating with the same name, or no longer operating under the same operating authority, shall be removed from or covered over on every motor vehicle or combination of vehicles listed in subdivision (a), within 60 days from the change of company ownership or operation. Those vehicles or combinations of vehicles shall be remarked pursuant to subdivision (a) before they may be operated on the highways. *(AM '98; '03)*

27901. Name and Trademark
The display of the name or trademark shall be in letters in sharp contrast to the background and shall be of such size, shape, and color as to be readily legible during daylight hours from a distance of 50 feet.

This section does not prohibit additional displays not inconsistent with this article.

27903. Designation of Cargo
(a) Subject to Section 114765 of the Health and Safety Code, any vehicle transporting any explosive, blasting agent, flammable liquid, flammable solid, oxidizing material, corrosive, compressed gas, poison, radioactive material, or other hazardous materials, of the type and in quantities that require the display of placards or markings on the vehicle exterior by the United States Department of Transportation regulations (49 C.F.R., Parts 172, 173, and 177), shall display the placards and markings in the manner and under conditions prescribed by those regulations of the United States Department of Transportation.

(b) This section does not apply to the following:

(1) Any vehicle transporting not more than 20 pounds of smokeless powder or not more than five pounds of black sporting powder or any combination thereof.

(2) An authorized emergency vehicle as defined in paragraph (1) of subdivision (b) of Section 165, operated by a peace officer as defined in Sections 830.1 and 830.2 of the Penal Code, when transportation is required within the scope and course of law enforcement explosives detection or removal duties, provided one of the following conditions applies:

(A) The law enforcement agency operating the vehicle complies with regulations adopted by the California Highway Patrol pursuant to subdivision (b) of Section 34501, notwithstanding Section 34500 and subdivision (a) of Section 34501.

(B) The peace officer possesses an exemption issued by the commissioner, who may require additional transportation restrictions as deemed appropriate. *(AM '02)*

27904. Pilot Cars: Company Name
There shall be displayed in a conspicuous place on both the right and left sides of a pilot car a sign showing the name of the company which owns or operates the pilot car. The name shall contrast with the background and shall be of a size, shape, and color as to be readily legible during daylight hours from a distance of 50 feet. Additional markings which do not interfere with the legibility of the name may also be displayed.

27904.5. Pilot Cars: Warning Signs
Subject to Section 35783.5, a pilot car shall display neat, clean, and legible signs containing the word "OVERSIZE."The words "OVERSIZE LOAD,""WIDE LOAD,"or "LONG LOAD"may be substituted as applicable. The sign shall be a minimum of 48 inches above the ground and shall be legible at 45 degrees from either side when read from the front or rear. The sign shall have a bright yellow background with a minimum projected area of 440 square inches. The lettering shall be black with a 1-inch minimum brush stroke width and a 6-inch minimum letter height.

27905. Fire Departments
It is unlawful to display on a vehicle any sign with the words "fire"or "fire department"thereon, except on vehicles owned and operated by a regularly organized fire department, fire district, forestry service, or the State Fire Marshal's Office, and on the privately owned vehicles of any regular member of any such fire departments.

27906. Schoolbuses
(a) Every schoolbus, while being used for the transportation of school pupils at or below the 12th-grade level shall bear upon the front and rear of the bus a plainly visible sign containing the word "schoolbus"in letters not less than eight inches in height. The letters on schoolbus signs shall be of proportionate width.

Except as provided in subdivision (b), no other vehicle shall display a sign containing the word "schoolbus."

(b) Notwithstanding subdivision (a), a schoolbus which is also used to transport persons of any age who are developmentally disabled, as defined by the Lanterman Developmental Disabilities Services Act (Division 4.5 of the Welfare and Institutions Code), may display a sign containing the word "schoolbus" while transporting those persons to or from vocational, prevocational, or work training centers sponsored by the State Department of Developmental Services.

(c) Every schoolbus, when operated for the transportation of school pupils at or below the 12th-grade level, shall bear upon the rear of the bus, below the rear windows, a plainly visible sign containing the words "Stop When Red Lights Flash" in letters not less than six inches in height. The letters on schoolbus signs shall be of proportionate width.

27906.5. Youth Buses

Every youth bus, when operated for the transportation of school pupils, shall bear, upon the front and rear of the youth bus, a plainly visible sign containing the words "YOUTH BUS" in letters not less than eight inches in height. The letters on youth bus signs shall be of proportionate width and the letters shall be in sharp contrast to the background.

27907. Tow Trucks

There shall be displayed in a conspicuous place on both the right and left side of a tow truck, a repossessor's tow vehicle, or an automobile dismantler's tow vehicle used to tow or carry vehicles a sign showing the name of the company or the owner or operator of the tow truck or tow vehicle. The sign shall also contain the business address and telephone number of the owner or driver. The letters and numbers of the sign shall not be less than 2 inches in height and shall be in contrast to the color of the background upon which they are placed.

A person licensed as a repossession agency pursuant to Chapter 11 (commencing with Section 7500) of Division 3 of the Business and Professions Code, or a registrant of the agency, may use the license number issued to the agency by the Department of Consumer Affairs in lieu of a name, business address, and telephone number. *(AM '99)*

27908. Taxicab Signs

(a) In every taxicab operated in this state there shall be a sign of heavy material, not smaller than 6 inches by 4 inches, or such other size as the agency regulating the operation of the taxicab provides for other notices or signs required to be in every taxicab, securely attached and clearly displayed in view of the passenger at all times, providing in letters as large as the size of the sign will reasonably allow, all of the following information:

(1) The name, address, and telephone number of the agency regulating the operation of the taxicab.

(2) The name, address, and telephone number of the firm licensed or controlled by the agency regulating the operation of the taxicab.

(b) In the event more than one local regulatory agency has jurisdiction over the operation of the taxicab, the paragraph (1) of subdivision (a) shall provide the name, address, and telephone number of the agency having jurisdiction in the area where the taxicab operator conducts its greatest volume of business; or, if this cannot readily be ascertained, the agency having jurisdiction in the area where the taxicab operator maintains its offices or primary place of business, provided that the operator conducts a substantial volume of business in such area; or, if neither of the foregoing provisions apply, any agency having jurisdiction of an area where the taxicab operator conducts a substantial volume of business.

(c) As used in this section, "taxicab" means a passenger vehicle designed for carrying not more than eight persons, excluding the driver, and used to carry passengers for hire. "Taxicab" shall not include a charter-party carrier of passengers within the meaning of the Passenger Charter-party Carriers' Act, Chapter 8 of Division 2 of the Public Utilities Code.

27909. Transporting Liquefied Petroleum or Natural Gas

Any vehicle which carries liquefied petroleum gas fuel or natural gas, in a tank attached to a vehicle, in any concealed area, including trunks, compartments, or under the vehicle, shall display on the exterior of the vehicle the letters "CNG,""LNG,"or "LPG,"whichever type fuel is utilized, in block letters at least one inch high. The letters shall be of contrasting color and shall be placed as near as possible to the area of the location of the tank. Any vehicle fueled by liquefied petroleum gas fuel or by natural gas may also comply with this section by displaying on each side of the vehicle words or letters at least 0.25 inch high indicating that the vehicle is fueled by liquefied petroleum gas or natural gas. It is unlawful to dispense liquefied petroleum gas fuel or natural gas into any tank in a concealed area of any vehicle registered in Calif., unless the vehicle complies with the requirements of this section.

28000. Refrigerator Vans

Every refrigerator van equipped with one or more doors designed to lock automatically upon closure shall have at least one door which can be opened from inside the van as an emergency means of exit.

For the purposes of this article, "refrigerator van"means any motor truck, semitrailer, or trailer, with a fully enclosed cargo body having an enclosed volume of 15 cubic feet or more, which utilizes a mechanical refrigeration system to reduce the temperature within the enclosed portion of the vehicle to 32 degrees Fahrenheit or less, or which provides refrigeration by the use of dry ice.

28050. True Mileage Driven

It is unlawful for any person to advertise for sale, to sell, to use, or to install on any part of a motor vehicle or on an odometer in a motor vehicle any device which causes the odometer to register any mileage other than the true mileage driven. For the purposes of this section the true mileage driven is that mileage driven by the car as registered by the odometer within the manufacturer's designed tolerance.

28050.5. Operation With Nonfunctional Odometer Prohibited

It is unlawful for any person with the intent to defraud to operate a motor vehicle on any street or highway knowing that the odometer of such vehicle is disconnected or nonfunctional.

28051. Unlawful to Alter Indicated Mileage

It is unlawful for any person to disconnect, turn back, or reset the odometer of any motor vehicle with the intent to alter the number of miles indicated on the odometer gauge.

28051.5. Device to Turn Back or Reset Odometer

It is unlawful for any person to advertise for sale, to sell, or to use, any device designed primarily for the purpose of turning back or resetting the odometer of any motor vehicle to reduce the number of miles indicated on the odometer gauge.

28053. Repair of Odometer: Required Information

(a) Nothing in this article prevents the service, repair, or replacement of an odometer, if the mileage indicated thereon remains the same as before the service, repair, or replacement. If the odometer is incapable of registering the same mileage as before the service, repair, or replacement, the odometer shall be adjusted to read zero and a notice in writing shall be attached to the left doorframe of the vehicle by the person performing the service, repair, or replacement specifying the mileage prior to the service, repair or replacement of the odometer and the date on which it was serviced, repaired, or replaced.

(b) No person shall fail to adjust an odometer or affix a notice regarding the adjustment as required by subdivision (a).

(c) No person shall, with intent to defraud, remove or alter any notice affixed to a vehicle pursuant to subdivision (a).

28060. Recreational Vehicles and Campers

(a) No person shall sell or offer for sale a new recreational vehicle or new camper which is equipped with cooking equipment or heating equipment, and no dealer or person holding a retail seller's permit shall sell or offer for sale a use recreational vehicle or a used camper which is equipped with cooking or heating equipment, unless such new or used vehicle or new or used camper is equipped with at least one fire extinguisher, filled and ready for use, of the dry chemical or carbon dioxide type with an aggregate rating of at least 4-B:C units, which meets the requirements specified in Section 13162 of the Health and Safety Code.

(b) The operator of a recreational vehicle, or a vehicle to which a camper is attached, which recreational vehicle or camper is equipped with a fire extinguisher as required by subdivision (a), shall carry such fire extinguisher in such recreational vehicle or camper and shall maintain the fire extinguisher in an efficient operating condition.

(c) As used in this section:

(1) "Cooking equipment"means a device designed for cooking which utilizes combustible material, including, but not limited to, materials such as charcoal or any flammable gas or liquid, and "heating equipment"means a device designed for heating which utilizes combustible material, including, but not limited to, materials such as charcoal or any flammable gas or liquid.

(2) "Recreational vehicle"has the same meaning as defined in Section 18010.5 of the Health and Safety Code.

28071. Passenger Vehicle Bumper Requirements

Every passenger vehicle registered in this state shall be equipped with a front bumper and with a rear bumper. As used in this section, "bumper"means any device designed and intended by a manufacturer to prevent the front or rear of the body of the vehicle from coming into contact with any other motor vehicle. This section shall not apply to any passenger vehicle that is required to be equipped with an energy absorption system pursuant to either state or federal law, or to any passenger vehicle which was not equipped with a front or rear bumper, or both, at the time that it was first sold and registered under the laws of this or any other state or foreign jurisdiction.

28080. Camper Passenger Signaling Device

(a) Every motor vehicle upon which a camper is mounted shall be equipped with an audible or visual signaling device which can be activated from inside the camper and which is constructed so as to allow any person inside the camper to gain the attention of the driver of the motor vehicle. In no event shall a horn, as required by Section 27000, be used to comply with this subdivision.

(b) No person shall drive a motor vehicle upon which is mounted a camper containing any passenger unless the motor vehicle is equipped as required by subdivision (a).

28085. Vehicle Theft Alarm Requirements

Any motor vehicle may be equipped with a theft alarm system which flashes the lights of the vehicle, or sounds an audible signal, or both, and which operates as follows:

(a) The system may flash any of the lights required or permitted on the vehicle.

(b) The system may sound an audible signal.

(c) No vehicle shall be equipped with a theft alarm system which emits the sound of a siren.

28100. Warning flags

A pilot car shall display at least one red warning flag on each side of the vehicle. The flags shall be a minimum of 16 inches square, and shall be mounted so as to be visible from both the front and rear of the vehicle. The flags shall be removed or covered when the vehicle is not operating as a pilot car.

28101. Additional Requirements

In addition to the lighting, sign, and flag requirements in Sections 25270, 27904, 27904.5, and 28100, a pilot car shall meet all of the following requirements:

(a) Be a vehicle not less than 60 inches in width.

(b) Be equipped with all of the following:

(1) One STOP/SLOW paddle.

(2) One orange vest, shirt, or jacket.

(3) One red hand flag (24 inches square).

(4) One two-way radio communication device.

28103.   Penalty
It is unlawful and an infraction for any person to violate any provision of this article or to fail to have any required equipment in good working order.

28150.   Electronic Speed Measurement - Jamming Devices Prohibited
(a) No vehicle shall be equipped with any device that is designed for, or is capable of, jamming, scrambling, neutralizing, disabling, or otherwise interfering with radar, laser, or any other electronic device used by a law enforcement agency to measure the speed of moving objects.

(b) No person shall use, buy, possess, manufacture, sell, or otherwise distribute any device that is designed for jamming, scrambling, neutralizing, disabling, or otherwise interfering with radar, laser, or any other electronic device used by a law enforcement agency to measure the speed of moving objects.

(c) Except as provided in subdivision (d), a violation of subdivision (a) or (b) is an infraction.

(d) When a person possesses four or more devices in violation of subdivision (b), the person is guilty of a misdemeanor.

(e) Notwithstanding any other provision of law, a person who has a valid federal license for operating the devices described in this section may transport one or more of those devices if the license is carried in the vehicle transporting the device at all times when the device is being transported. *(AD '98)*

DIVISION 13. TOWING AND LOADING EQUIPMENT

CHAPTER 1. TOWING EQUIPMENT

29000.   Application of Chapter
Unless specified, this chapter does not apply to tow trucks or to the drawbar or other connection between a motor vehicle and a pole or pipe dolly or logging dolly or to any lawful trailer used as a pole or pipe dolly.

29001.   Fifth Wheel Connecting Device
The upper and lower halves of every fifth wheel connecting device on any semitrailer and truck-tractor or auxiliary dolly shall be securely affixed to the vehicles to prevent shifting of the device on the vehicle to which it is attached.

29002.   Fifth Wheel Locking Device
Every fifth wheel mechanism, including adapters, shall be equipped with a locking device which will not permit the upper and lower halves to be separated without the operation of a positive manual release. The manual release shall be designed, installed, and maintained so that it cannot be accidentally operated. Automatic locking devices on fifth wheels designed and constructed to be readily separable are required on any vehicle first required to be registered in this state after January 1, 1954.

29003.   Hitch, Coupling Device or Connection, or Tow Dolly
(a) Every hitch or coupling device used as a means of attaching the towed and towing vehicles shall be properly and securely mounted and be structurally adequate for the weight drawn. The mounting of the hitch or coupling device on the towing and towed vehicle shall include sufficient reinforcement or bracing of the frame to provide sufficient strength and rigidity to prevent undue distortion of the frame.

(b) The drawbar, tongue, or other connection between the towing and towed vehicles shall be securely attached and structurally adequate for the weight drawn.

(c) The raised end of any motor vehicle being transported by another motor vehicle using a tow dolly shall be secured to the tow dolly by two separate chains, cables, or equivalent devices adequate to prevent shifting or separation of the towed vehicle and the tow dolly.

29004.   Towed Vehicle
(a)(1) Except as required under paragraph (2), a towed vehicle shall be coupled to the towing vehicle by means of a safety chain, cable, or equivalent device in addition to the regular drawbar, tongue, or other connection.

(2) A vehicle towed by a tow truck shall be coupled to the tow truck by means of at least two safety chains in addition to the primary restraining system. The safety chains shall be securely affixed to the truck frame, bed, or towing equipment, independent of the towing sling, wheel lift, or under-reach towing equipment.

(3) A vehicle transported on a slide back carrier tow truck a trailer shall be secured by at least four tiedown chains, straps, or an equivalent device, independent of the winch or loading cable. This subdivision does not apply to vehicle bodies that are being transported in compliance with Sections 393.100 to 393.136, inclusive, of Title 49 of the Code of Federal Regulations.

(b) All safety connections and attachments shall be of sufficient strength to control the towed vehicle in the event of failure of the regular hitch, coupling device, drawbar, tongue, or other connection. All safety connections and attachments also shall have a positive means of ensuring that the safety connection or attachment does not become dislodged while in transit.

(c) No more slack may be left in a safety chain, cable, or equivalent device than is necessary to permit proper turning. When a drawbar is used as the towing connection, the safety chain, cable, or equivalent device shall be connected to the towed and towing vehicle and to the drawbar so as to prevent the drawbar from dropping to the ground if the drawbar fails.

(d) Subdivision (a) does not apply to a semitrailer having a connecting device composed of a fifth wheel and kingpin assembly, and does not apply to a towed motor vehicle when steered by a person who holds a license for the type of vehicle being towed.

(e) For purposes of this section, a "tow truck" includes both of the following:

(1) A repossessor's tow vehicle, as defined in subdivision (b) of Section 615.

(2) An automobile dismantler's tow vehicle, as defined in subdivision (c) of Section 615.

(f) A vehicle towed by a repossessor's tow vehicle, as defined in subdivision (b) of Section 615, is exempt from the multisafety chain requirement of paragraph (2) of subdivision (a) so long as the vehicle is not towed more than one mile on a public highway and is secured by one safety chain. *(AM '12)*

29005. Drawbar Length
When one vehicle is towing another, the drawbar or other connection shall not exceed 15 feet.

29006. Coupling of Towed Vehicles
(a) No person shall operate a vehicle towing another motor vehicle upon a freeway unless the towing vehicle is coupled to the towed vehicle by a rigid structure attached securely to the vehicles by nonrigid means.

(b) The requirements of subdivision (a) are not applicable to a vehicle towing a motor vehicle which has been disabled and is being towed from the point of disablement to the nearest and most accessible exit from the freeway.

29009. Dolly Supporting Special Construction Equipment
The requirements of Section 29004 do not apply to a dolly used to support a portion of special construction equipment, as defined in Section 565, which, due to its size or weight is being operated under the authority of a permit issued by the California Department of Transportation, if the dolly is secured to the construction equipment, and the construction equipment is secured to the towing vehicle, by chain, cable, or equivalent devices of sufficient strength to control the construction equipment and dolly.

CHAPTER 2. LOGS & POLES

29200. Regulations Governing
(a) The department shall adopt regulations relating to the safe loading, securement, and transporting of logs and poles. The regulations shall include provisions prescribing the types of bunks and bunk stakes which may be used in combination in transporting logs and poles.

(b) In adopting these regulations the department shall consider the type of vehicle to be used, the construction of loads, and the types of binders, stakes, and restraining devices required to securely contain the load.

(c) It is unlawful to fail to comply with any provisions of these regulations.

29201. Exemption of Pole Dolly
The provisions of this chapter do not apply to the transportation of poles on a pole dolly by public utility companies or local public agencies engaged in the business of supplying electricity or telephone service, by the California Department of Transportation, or by a licensed contractor in the performance of work for a utility, the California Department of Transportation, or a local public agency, when such transportation is between storage yards or between a storage yard and job location where such poles are to be used, but in no event shall more than nine poles be transported on any dolly if any such pole exceeds a length of 30 feet. If poles 30 feet or less in length are transported by pole or pipe dolly not more than 18 poles shall be so transported. Poles shall be adequately secured when being transported on a dolly to prevent shifting or spilling of loads.

CHAPTER 3. LUMBER & LUMBER PRODUCTS

29800. Regulations Governing
(a) The department shall adopt regulations relating to the safe loading, securement and transporting of lumber and lumber products including, but not limited to, ties, laths, grapestakes, fenceposts, plywood and shingles.

(b) In adopting these regulations the department shall consider the type of vehicle to be used, the construction of loads and the type of binders, stakes and restraining devices required to contain the load.

(c) It is unlawful to fail to comply with any provisions of these regulations.

CHAPTER 4. BALED HAY

30800. Baled Hay and Straw Regulations
(a) The CHP shall adopt and enforce regulations relating to the safe loading, securement, and transporting of baled hay and baled straw. In adopting these regulations, the department shall take into consideration the nature of the load to be transported, the type of vehicle to be used, and the different types of binders required to securely fasten loads to prevent their improper release.

(b) No person shall transport or cause to be transported any baled hay or baled straw in violation of the regulations promulgated hereunder.

CHAPTER 5. TRANSPORTING OTHER LOADS

31301. Caldecott Tunnel Restriction
(a) No person shall transport any explosive substance, flammable liquid, liquefied petroleum gas or poisonous gas in a tank truck, trailer, or semitrailer through the Caldecott Tunnel located on State Highway, Route 24, near the Alameda-Contra Costa County boundary, connecting Oakland with Contra Costa County in the East Bay area at any time other than between the hours of 3 a.m. to 5 a.m.

(b) the California Department of Transportation may, in compliance with the requirements of Article 1 of Division 11, determine and declare a reduced speed limit, lower than the maximum speed of 55 miles per hour, found most appropriate for traffic safety between the hours of 3 a.m. and 5 a.m.

(c) Nothing in this section shall be construed as a limitation or restriction on the power of the California Department of Transportation, conferred by any other provision of law, to adopt regulations with regard to the movement of vehicles, including, but not limited to, tank truck vehicles transporting any cargo specified under subdivision (a) through the Caldecott Tunnel.

If, pursuant to any such other law, the California Department of Transportation adopts or amends regulations after the effective date of this section, which adopted or amended regulations govern the movement of vehicles subject to subdivision (a), then on the operative date of those regulations, this section shall no longer be operative.

31303. Hazardous Waste and Materials: Transportation Requirements: Penalties

(a) The provisions of this section apply to the highway transportation of hazardous materials and hazardous waste for which the display of placards or markings is required pursuant to Section 27903. This section does not apply to hazardous materials being transported on specified routes pursuant to Section 31616 or 33000.

(b) Unless restricted or prohibited pursuant to Section 31304, the transportation shall be on state or interstate highways which offer the least overall transit time whenever practicable.

(c) The transporter shall avoid, whenever practicable, congested thoroughfares, places where crowds are assembled, and residence districts as defined in Section 515.

(d) Vehicles used for the transportation shall not be left unattended or parked overnight in a residence district as defined in Section 515.

(e) When transporting hazardous waste pursuant to Section 25169.3 of the Health and Safety Code, all provisions of the waste hauler transportation safety plan, as approved by the State Department of Health Services, shall be complied with.

(f) Transportation which deviates from the routes required by this section shall not be excused on the basis of operating convenience.

(g) Notwithstanding subdivisions (b) and (c), vehicles engaged in the transportation may also use any of the following highways:

(1) Highways which provide necessary access to local pickup or delivery points consistent with safe vehicle operation.

(2) Highways which provide reasonable access to fuel, repairs, rest, or food facilities that are designed and intended to accommodate commercial vehicle parking, when that access is consistent with safe vehicle operation and when the facility is within one-half road mile of points of entry or exit from the state or interstate highway being used.

(3) Highways restricted or prohibited pursuant to this section when no other lawful alternative exists.

31307. Unlawful Operation: Penalties

(a) It is unlawful for the owner of any vehicle or the authorized agent of the owner to drive, or to direct or knowingly permit the driving of, the vehicle in violation of Section 31303 or 31304. Violation of any of these sections is a misdemeanor punishable as follows:

For a first violation, a fine not exceeding five hundred dollars ($500), imprisonment in the county jail not exceeding 60 days, or both the fine and imprisonment.

(2) For a second violation within a 12-month period, a fine not exceeding one thousand dollars ($1,000), imprisonment in the county jail not exceeding 60 days, or both the fine and imprisonment.

(3) For a third or subsequent violation within a 12-month period, a fine not exceeding two thousand five hundred dollars ($2,500), imprisonment in the county jail not exceeding 120 days, or both the fine and imprisonment.

(b) Additionally, upon recommendation of the CHP, three or more violations of these sections constitute grounds for suspension or revocation of registration, or denial of an application for registration under Section 25163 of the Health and Safety Code by the State Department of Health Services. Proceedings in these cases shall be subject to Chapter 5 of Part 1 of Division 3 of Title 2 of the Government Code.

31309. Hazardous Materials Placards

Notwithstanding Section 34500 and subdivision (a) of Section 34501, the transportation of hazardous materials in a manner requiring that placards be displayed on the transporting vehicle pursuant to Section 27903, shall comply with regulations adopted by the California Highway Patrol pursuant to subdivision (b) of Section 34501.

31400. Equipment Required - Transporting Workmen

Trucks used primarily or regularly for the transportation of workmen shall be:

(a) Equipped with seats securely fastened to the vehicle.

(b) Equipped, if a motortruck, with a railing or other suitable enclosure on the sides and end of the vehicle not less than 46 inches above the floor of the vehicle.

(c) Equipped with steps, stirrups, or other equivalent devices so placed and arranged that the vehicle may be safely mounted and dismounted.

31401. Farm Labor Vehicles

(a) The department shall adopt regulations designed to promote the safe operation of farm labor vehicles described in Section 322, including, but not limited to, vehicular design, equipment, passenger safety, and seating.

(b) The department shall inspect every farm labor vehicle described in Section 322 at least once annually to ascertain whether its construction, design, and equipment comply with all provisions of law. No person shall drive any farm labor vehicle described in Section 322 unless there is displayed therein a certificate issued by the department stating that on a stated day, which shall be within 13 months of the date of operation, an authorized employee of the department inspected the vehicle and found on the date of inspection the vehicle complied with applicable regulations relating to construction, design, and equipment. The commissioner shall provide by rule or regulation for the issuance and display of distinctive inspection certificates.

(c) The department may inspect any vehicle subject to these regulations in maintenance facilities, terminals, labor camps, or other private property of the vehicle owner or the farm labor contractor to insure compliance with the provisions of this code and regulations adopted pursuant to this section.

(d) The owner of any farm labor vehicle or any farm labor contractor, as defined in Section 1682 of the Labor Code, who rents a farm labor vehicle or who otherwise uses a farm labor vehicle to transport individuals is responsible for the inspection required under subdivision (b).

(e) An owner of any farm labor vehicle or any farm labor contractor who operates a farm labor vehicle under the circumstances described in subdivision (d) may not operate that vehicle unless the vehicle has a current certificate described in subdivision (b).

(f) It is unlawful to violate any provision of these regulations or this section. *(AM '99)*

31402. Operation of Unsafe Farm Labor Vehicle for Repairs

(a) No person may operate any farm labor vehicle except as may be necessary to return the unladen vehicle or combination of vehicles to the residence or place of business of the owner or driver, or to a garage, after notice by the department to the owner that the vehicle is in an unsafe condition or is not equipped as required by this code, or any regulations adopted thereunder, until the vehicle and its equipment have been made to conform with the requirements of this code, or any regulations adopted thereunder, and approved by the department.

(b)(1) A person who operates a farm labor vehicle in violation of this section while the vehicle is in a condition that presents an immediate safety hazard is guilty of a misdemeanor punishable by a fine of not less than one thousand dollars ($1,000) and not more than five thousand dollars ($5,000), or both that fine and a sentence of confinement for not more than six months in the county jail. No part of any fine imposed under this subdivision may be suspended.

(2) As used in this subdivision, an "immediate safety hazard" is any equipment violation described in subdivision (a) of Section 31401 or Section 31405, including any violation of a regulation adopted pursuant to that provision or those provisions.

(c) Any member of the Department of the California Highway Patrol may impound a farm labor vehicle operated in violation of this section pursuant to Section 34506.4. A farm labor vehicle shall not be impounded unless a member of that department determines that a person has failed to comply with subdivision (a) or a person fails to comply with a lawful out-of-service order, as described in subdivision (b) of Section 2800. *(AM '00)*

31403. Mechanic Certification of Farm Labor Vehicle

A farm labor vehicle known to an owner, farm labor contractor, or driver, to be unsafe, or not equipped as required by this code, or any regulations adopted thereunder, shall not be used for transporting any passengers until it is examined and repaired or equipped as required by this code, or any regulations adopted thereunder, and certified by a competent mechanic to be safe and lawfully equipped.

31405. Farm Labor Vehicles - Seatbelt Requirements; Unlawful Operation

(a) Except as authorized under paragraph (1) of subdivision (e), every farm labor vehicle issued an inspection certificate under Section 31401 shall be equipped at each passenger position with a Type 1 or Type 2 seatbelt assembly, conforming to the specifications set forth in Section 571.209 of Title 49 of the Code of Federal Regulations, that is anchored to the vehicle in a manner that conforms to the specifications of Section 571.210 of Title 49 of the Code of Federal Regulations.

(b) Except as authorized under paragraph (1) of subdivision (e), the department may not issue an initial inspection certificate under Section 31401 to any farm labor vehicle that is not equipped with a seatbelt assembly at each passenger position, as described in subdivision (a).

(c) The owner of a farm labor vehicle shall maintain all seatbelt assemblies and seatbelt assembly anchorages required under this section in good working order for the use of passengers.

(d) Except as authorized under paragraph (1) of subdivision (e) or subdivision (d) of Section 23116, no person may operate a farm labor vehicle on a highway unless that person and all passengers are properly restrained by a seatbelt assembly that conforms to this section.

(e)(1) Until January 1, 2007, this section does not apply to a farm labor vehicle that meets the definition in subdivision (a) of Section 233, meets all state and federal standards for safety and construction, and is not currently required to have seatbelts.

(2) On or after January 1, 2007, any farm labor vehicle that meets the conditions set forth in paragraph (1) shall be equipped at each passenger position with a seatbelt assembly as described in subdivision (a), unless exempted from this requirement under the regulations promulgated under Section 31401.

(f) The department shall adopt regulations to implement this section. *(AD '99; AM '00)*

31406. Farm Labor Vehicle Seating Requirements

(a) No person may be transported in a farm labor vehicle that does not have all passenger seating positions in compliance with Section 571.207 of Title 49 of the Code of Federal Regulations, as that provision exists now or may hereafter be amended.

(b) No person may install a seat or seating system in a farm labor vehicle unless that seat or seating system is in compliance with Section 571.207 of Title 49 of the Code of Federal Regulations, as that provision exists now or may hereafter be amended.

(c) This section shall become operative on March 31, 2002. *(AD '00)*

31407. Cutting Tools or Sharp Instruments in Farm Labor Vehicle; Storage Requirements

All cutting tools or tools with sharp edges carried in the passenger compartment of a farm labor vehicle shall be placed in securely latched containers that are firmly attached to the vehicle. All other tools, equipment, or materials carried in the passenger compartment shall be secured to the body of the vehicle to prevent their movement while the vehicle is in motion. Under no circumstances shall those tools, equipment, or materials obstruct an aisle or an emergency exit. *(AD '00)*

31408. Farm Labor Vehicle - Lighted Headlamps Required

No person may operate a farm labor vehicle on a highway unless both headlamps required under Section 24400 are lighted, regardless of the time of day. *(AD '99)*

31500. Trailers Transported Upon Other Vehicles

No vehicle upon which is loaded any trailer shall be driven or moved on any highway unless the trailer is securely bound to the vehicle in such a manner as to prevent the trailer from shifting, toppling over, or otherwise becoming unstable.

31501. Transportation of Log Trailers

Logging dollies being carried on trucks shall have at least one set of tires resting against a steel cross rail or rails and steel side chocks measuring not less than four inches from base to tip which shall be securely attached to the truck in a manner designed to prevent the forward and sideward movement of the dolly.

31520. Regulations Governing Baled Cotton, Paper, and Jute

(a) The department shall adopt and enforce regulations relating to the safe loading, securement, and transportation of loads consisting of baled cotton, baled paper, and baled jute.

(b) No person shall transport or cause to be transported any of these products in violation of the regulations promulgated hereunder.

31530. Regulations Governing Boxes

(a) The department shall adopt and enforce regulations relating to the safe loading, securement, and transportation of loads consisting of in excess of 100 empty wooden boxes not exceeding any of the following dimensions: 36 inches in length, 24 inches in width and 12 inches in height.

(b) It is unlawful to fail to comply with any provision of the regulations adopted by the department.

31540. Regulations Governing Tank Containers

(a) The department shall adopt and enforce such regulations as it determines are necessary for public safety regarding the transportation of:

(1) Freight van or tank containers which can be removed from the running gear or chassis of a truck or trailer, and

(2) Collapsible containers used to transport liquids on flatbed vehicles.

(b) It is unlawful to fail to comply with any provision of the regulations adopted by the department.

31560. Transportation of Waste Tires; Registration Requirement

(a) A person operating a vehicle, or combination of vehicles, in the transportation of 10 or more used tires or waste tires, or a combination of used tires and waste tires totaling 10 or more, as defined in Section 42950 of the Public Resources Code, shall be registered with the California Integrated Waste Management Board, unless specifically exempted, as provided in Chapter 19 (commencing with Section 42950) of Part 3 of Division 30 of the Public Resources Code and in regulations adopted by the board to implement that chapter.

(b) It is unlawful and constitutes an infraction for a person engaged in the transportation of 10 or more used tires or waste tires, or a combination of used tires and waste tires totaling 10 or more, to violate a provision of this article or Section 42951 of the Public Resources Code. *(AD '96; AM '08)*

DIVISION 14. TRANSPORTATION OF EXPLOSIVES

31602. License: Routes to Be Used

(a) It is a misdemeanor for any owner of a vehicle to drive or permit the driving of the vehicle on any public highway for the purpose of transporting any explosive as defined herein and within the scope of Section 31601 unless the owner then holds a valid license for the transportation of explosives as provided in this division, except such persons as are expressly exempted in this division.

(b) It is a misdemeanor for the owner, or authorized agent of the owner, of any vehicle transporting explosives to drive, or to permit the driving of the vehicle, or for the driver to drive such vehicle, upon any public highway, not designated in regulations adopted CHP as a route for the transportation of explosives, unless the use of the highway is required to permit delivery of, or the loading of, explosives at a point not on a highway designated as a route for the transportation of explosives, or unless the use of the highway is required to permit the vehicle to proceed to, and return from, a point designated as an inspection stop pursuant to this division.

(c) It is a misdemeanor for the driver of any vehicle transporting to stop at any place not designated as a safe stopping place unless the vehicle is disabled or except when necessary to avoid conflict with other traffic or to comply with the orders of a peace officer or an official traffic control device. A safe stopping place is any location designated by the CHP where the driver may stop for food, fuel or other necessary reasons and any location designated by the CHP as a safe parking place, a safe stopping place, or as an inspection stop for purposes of this division.

(d) In the event the owner of a vehicle leases the same to be used in the transportation of explosives for which a license is required, the lessee shall be deemed the owner for the purposes of this division.

31607. Inspection of Vehicle Transporting Explosives

(a) Any person operating or permitting the operation of a vehicle or combination of vehicles used in the transportation of explosives and subject to this division shall make or cause to be made an inspection of every said vehicle or combination of vehicles as hereinafter set forth.

(b) Such inspection as called for in Section 31608 shall be made immediately preceding the actual transportation of explosives by the vehicle and whenever there is an interchange of any vehicle operating in combination with any other vehicle in the transportation of explosives.

(c) Inspection of tires and brakes shall also be made enroute at suitable intervals, off the roadway, at inspection stops established by the CHP, at regular stops, terminal points, or driver-change points.

31609. Record of Inspection

Every person operating a vehicle or combination of vehicles in the transportation of explosives subject to this division shall complete a record of every inspection which is required under Sections 31607 and 31608 in such form as approved by the CHP showing the time and place of every inspection. The person making the inspection shall certify the fact in the record. The forms may be based upon the type used by the US DOT. The record of every inspection shall be made at the time such inspection is conducted.

The driver of the vehicle shall display the record upon demand of any member of the CHP or any police officer of a city who is on duty for the exclusive or main purpose of enforcing the provisions of this code.

31610. Requirements in Respect to Equipment

Every vehicle or combination of vehicles used in the transportation of explosives and subject to this division, in addition to any other equipment required by law, shall be equipped and maintained as required by this section.

(a) Brakes and the brake system shall be maintained in good and safe operating condition.

(b) The ignition and lighting systems shall be maintained in good operation.

(c) All tires shall be in good condition, properly matched and inflated. Except as may be necessary to cause immediate replacement, no vehicle shall be driven unless all tires in actual use on the vehicle are properly inflated.

(d) Fire extinguishers and other safety equipment prescribed by regulations adopted by the department pursuant to subdivision (f) of Section 34500 and 34501 shall be carried in each vehicle or combination of vehicles.

(e) No flare, fusee, oil lantern, or any signal device producing a flame shall be carried upon any vehicle or combination of vehicles.

31611. Instructions to Drivers

Every owner of a vehicle used in the transportation of explosives and subject to this division shall make available in each vehicle the latest map showing the routes which are to be used for the transportation of explosives which has been furnished for the vehicle by the CHP, a list of the safe stopping places prescribed by the regulations of the CHP for vehicles transporting explosives. The owner shall require that the driver be thoroughly familiar with the provisions of this division before operating any vehicle in the transportation of explosives.

31612. Shipping Instructions

Persons operating vehicles, or combinations of vehicles, in the transportation of explosives and subject to this division, shall not accept any explosives for transportation unless the shipment is accompanied by a bill of lading or other shipping paper supplied by the shipper, showing the kind of explosives and bearing a statement that they have been labeled and marked in accordance with regulations of the US DOT, and the bill of lading or other shipping paper shall be carried in the vehicle while enroute and shall be displayed upon demand of any member of the CHP or any police officer of a city who is on duty for the exclusive or main purpose of enforcing the provisions of this code.

31613. Certain Cargoes Prohibited
There shall not be included in any cargo of explosives any flammable liquids, acids, or corrosive liquids, oxidizers, or combustible materials, other than the explosives themselves, which may have such characteristics. Blasting caps or detonators shall not be transported upon the same vehicle with other explosives, nor shall electric blasting caps be transported upon any vehicle equipped with a radio transmitter. The foregoing provisions of this section shall be subject to such exceptions as are permitted by the US DOT loading chart for cargoes of explosives.

31614. Traffic Laws Applicable to Transportation of Explosives
The following provisions shall apply to any vehicle transporting explosives subject to this division:

(a) When transporting explosives through or into a city or any other congested area for which a route has not been designated by the CHP, drivers shall follow such routes as may be prescribed or established by local authorities.

(b) Where routes are not prescribed by local authority, every driver of a vehicle transporting explosives shall avoid, so far as practicable, and, where feasible, by rearrangement of routes, driving into or through congested thoroughfares, places where crowds are assembled, streetcar tracks, tunnels, viaducts, and dangerous crossings.

(c) No driver or other person in charge of any vehicle on any public or private property shall permit any explosive to be loaded into, or on, or to be unloaded from any motor vehicle with the engine running, and, whenever any loading operation is in progress, the parking brake on the motor vehicle shall be securely set and all reasonable precautions taken to prevent movement of the motor vehicle during loading or unloading.

(d) No driver or other person in charge of such vehicle shall operate or permit the operation of any vehicle transporting explosives unless all of that portion of the lading which consists of explosives is contained entirely within the body of the motor vehicle or within the horizontal outline thereof, without overhang or projection of any part of the load, and if such motor vehicle has a tailboard or tailgate it shall be closed and secured in place during such transportation.

(e) Every motor vehicle transporting explosives shall have either a closed body or have the explosive cargo covered with a fire- and water-resistant tarpaulin, and in either event, care shall be taken to protect the load from moisture and sparks. Subject to other exceptions as are permitted by the U. S. Department of Transportation regulations, explosives may be transported on flat-bed vehicles if the explosive portion of the load on each vehicle is packed in fire- and water-resistant containers or covered with a fire- and water-resistant tarpaulin.

(f) No person shall operate any vehicle transporting explosives past any fire of any kind burning on or near the highway until the driver ascertains that such passing can be made with safety.

(g) No motor vehicle transporting explosives shall be left unattended upon any street or highway except in extreme emergency. The vehicle shall be deemed attended whenever a driver or person in charge thereof is in or upon the vehicle or is in a position to observe the vehicle at all times. The driver or person in charge of a vehicle transporting explosives may, however, leave the vehicle unattended at any place designated as a safe parking place on the list of safe stopping places prepared by the CHP unless conditions exist, which are known to the driver, which make it unreasonable to do so.

(h) No driver or other person shall smoke or light any match or otherwise have or produce any fire or flame while in, upon, or near any vehicle transporting explosives.

(i) No person shall transport any explosives in a passenger vehicle, or bus, which is subject to this division.

DIVISION 14.1.
TRANSPORTATION OF HAZARDOUS MATERIAL

CHAPTER 1. LICENSING

32000.5. License to Transport Hazardous Material

(a) A motor carrier who directs the transportation of an explosive and a motor carrier who directs the transportation of a hazardous material, who is required to display placards pursuant to Section 27903, and a motor carrier who transports for a fee in excess of 500 pounds of hazardous materials of the type requiring placards pursuant to Section 27903, shall be licensed in accordance with this code, unless specifically exempted by this code or regulations adopted pursuant to this code. This license shall be available for examination and shall be displayed in accordance with the regulations adopted by the commissioner.

(b)(1) Except as provided in Section 32001, this division shall not apply to a person hauling only hazardous waste, as defined in Section 25115 or 25117 of the Health and Safety Code, and who is registered pursuant to subdivision (a) of Section 25163 of the Health and Safety Code or who is exempt from that registration pursuant to subdivision (b) of that section.

(2) A motor carrier that is transporting a hazardous waste and is required to display placards pursuant to Section 27903 shall comply with all provisions of Section 32001 except paragraph (3) of subdivision (c) of that section.

(c) This division does not apply to implements of husbandry, as defined in Section 36000.

(d) This division does not apply to the hauling of division 1.3 explosives classified as special fireworks or to division 1.4 explosives classified as common fireworks by the United States Department of Transportation if those fireworks are transported by a motor carrier under the authority of, and in conformance with, a license issued to the motor carrier by the State Fire Marshal pursuant to Part 2 (commencing with Section 12500) of Division 11 of the Health and Safety Code. In that case, a copy of the license shall be carried in the vehicle and presented to a peace officer upon request.

(e) (1) The department shall not issue a license to transport hazardous materials to a motor carrier unless each terminal from which hazardous materials carrying vehicles are operated is in compliance with Section 34501.12 and is currently rated satisfactory.

(2) The department shall adopt rules and regulations that provide for a temporary license to transport hazardous materials for a carrier who, within the previous three years, has not been issued an unsatisfactory rating as a result of an inspection conducted pursuant to Section 34501, 34501.12, or 34520.

(3) It is the intent of the Legislature that a carrier's license to transport hazardous materials should not be unreasonably hindered as a result of the department's verification and issuance process.

(f) This section does not prevent the department from issuing a new or initial license to transport hazardous materials to a motor carrier that applies for a license to transport hazardous materials and that, within the previous three years, has been issued an unsatisfactory rating as a result of an inspection conducted pursuant to Section 34501, 34501.12, or 34520, if the motor carrier has corrected the unsatisfactory rating before applying for the license to transport hazardous materials. *(AM '02, '07, '09)*

32001. Inspection of Containers: Requirements for Transporting

(a)(1) Any authorized employee of the department may inspect any sealed or unsealed vehicle, container, or shipment subject to this division in maintenance facilities, terminals, or other public or private property to ascertain the quantity and kind of hazardous material and to ensure compliance with the provisions of this code and regulations adopted pursuant to this code.

(2) If a seal is opened for inspection, the department shall reseal any vehicle, container, or shipment prior to further transportation.

(b) Unless specifically stated, nothing contained in this division shall be deemed to exempt any vehicle transporting a hazardous material subject to this division or the operator or any other person from other provisions of this code.

(c) No motor carrier shall direct the transportation of any shipment of a hazardous material in any vehicle unless all of the following are complied with:

(1) The vehicle is equipped as required by this code and applicable regulations adopted pursuant to law.

(2) The shipment complies with laws and regulations pertaining to the shipment or transportation of hazardous material.

(3) The motor carrier holds a valid license for the transportation of hazardous materials.

(4)(A) A vehicle or combination of vehicles required to display placards pursuant to Section 27903 is equipped with a two-way communication device, maintained in good working order, that enables the driver to contact the personnel responsible for the safety operations of the motor carrier in the event of an emergency.

(B) For the purposes of this section, "two-way communication device" means a radio, cellular telephone, or other similar device that permits communication between the driver and personnel responsible for the safety operations of the motor carrier.

(5)(A) The enclosed cargo body, when the display of placards is required pursuant to Section 27903, shall be locked and remain locked during transit of the hazardous materials so as to prevent any unauthorized entry and shall be opened only during loading, unloading, or at the direction of a peace officer, an authorized employee of the department, or a person authorized pursuant to Section 25185 of the Health and Safety Code.

(B) A driver transporting hazardous material in a locked cargo body shall verify that all locks are in place if the vehicle has been left unattended for any length of time. Each driver shall make a notation in his or her log book of the time and date that the verification occurred.

(C) For the purposes of this section, "cargo body" means a fully enclosed area that is an integral part of the vehicle and designed to encapsulate the entire load, such as a van body or an intermodal freight container, and does not mean a tank or flatbed type of vehicle.

(d) The commissioner may issue exemptions from the provisions of this section.

(e) Nothing in this section shall limit the ability of other state or local agencies to carry out their regulatory, enforcement, or emergency response duties under other provisions of law. *(AM 02)*

32002. Regulations: Penalty for Violation

(a) The commissioner may adopt any regulations that are necessary to administer this division. It is a misdemeanor for any motor carrier to violate this division or regulations adopted pursuant to this division.

(b) Notwithstanding subdivision (a), it is unlawful for the motor carrier or the person who directs the driver to operate a vehicle transporting hazardous material, when that transportation requires a license pursuant to this division, to cause the operation of the vehicle unless the motor carrier holds a valid license for the transportation of hazardous materials. A violation of this subdivision shall be punished as follows:

(1) For a first violation, by a fine of not less than two thousand dollars ($2,000).

(2) For a second or subsequent violation, by a fine of not less than four thousand dollars ($4,000).

CHAPTER 2. NOTIFICATION OF ROUTES

32050. Route Notification

(a) Prior to the transport of anhydrous hydrazine, methylhydrazine, dimethylhydrazine, Aerozine 50, fuming nitric acid, liquid fluorine, or nitrogen tetroxide in bulk packaging, except when that packaging contains only residue, outside the confines of a facility where that material was used or stored, or prior to the delivery of that bulk material to a carrier for transport, each carrier shall provide advance notification, in writing, of the shipment, to the department, which, in turn, shall notify the sheriff of each county and police chief of each city in which is located the proposed route. Notification shall be made through the Department of Justice's California Law Enforcement Telecommunications System. The sheriffs and police chiefs shall, in turn, make timely notification to the fire chiefs within their respective jurisdictions through a mutually agreed upon communications system.

(b) Subdivision (a) applies only to the extent that it does not conflict with federal law.

(c) For the purposes of this section, the following definitions apply:

(1) "Bulk packaging"has the same meaning as defined in Section 171.8 of Title 49 of the Code of Federal Regulations.

(2) "Fire chief"means the fire chief of each county and city fire department and the fire chief of each fire protection district serving a population greater than 15,000 in which is located the proposed route. This paragraph does not apply to any fire chief of a fire department or fire protection district that is composed of 50 percent or more volunteer firefighters.

(3) "Residue"has the same meaning as defined in Section 171.8 of Title 49 of the Code of Federal Regulations.

32052. Notification Periods

(a) The notification required by Section 32050 shall reach the department at least 72 hours before the beginning of the 48-hour period during which departure of the shipment of any material designated in Section 32050 is estimated to occur, and the department shall notify the sheriffs and the police chiefs as specified in subdivision (a) of Section 32050 at least 36 hours before the beginning of the 48-hour departure period specified in subdivision (a) of Section 32051, who shall notify the fire chiefs, as provided in Section 32050. A copy of the notification shall be retained by the department for three years.

(b) The carrier shall also notify, by telephone or telegram, the department if there are any changes in the scheduling of a shipment, in the routes to be used for shipment, or any cancellation of a shipment. The department shall, in turn, notify the sheriffs and the police chiefs specified in subdivision (a) of Section 32050 that would be affected by these changes in the scheduling of a shipment, in the routes to be used for a shipment, or the cancellation of a shipment, who shall notify the fire chiefs, as provided in Section 32050. The department shall maintain for three years a record of each telegram and telephonic notification.

DIVISION 14.3.
TRANSPORTATION OF INHALATION HAZARDS

32103. Transportation of Inhalation Hazards - Map and List of Inspection Stops, etc. in Vehicle

(a) Every motor carrier shall make available in each vehicle used in the transportation of inhalation hazards the latest map showing the routes to be used for the transportation of inhalation hazards and a list of the safe stopping places and inspection stops for vehicles transporting inhalation hazards as prescribed by regulations of the department. The carrier shall require that the driver be thoroughly familiar with this division before operating any vehicle in the transportation of inhalation hazards.

32104. Transportation of Inhalation Hazards - Driving on Undesignated Routes, etc.

(a) It is unlawful for the motor carrier or its authorized agent to drive or to permit the driving of any vehicle transporting inhalation hazards, or for the driver to drive the vehicle, upon any public highway not designated in regulations adopted by the department as a route for the transportation of inhalation hazards. This subdivision shall not apply when the use of the highway is required (1) to permit delivery of, or the loading of, inhalation hazards at a point not on a highway designated as a route for the transportation of inhalation hazards, or (2) to permit the vehicle to proceed to, and return from, an inspection stop, safe stopping place, or safe parking place.

(b) It is unlawful for the driver of any vehicle transporting inhalation hazards to stop at any place other than a safe stopping place, safe parking place, or an inspection stop unless the vehicle is disabled or except when necessary to avoid conflict with other traffic or to comply with the orders of a peace officer or an official traffic control device.

32105. Transportation of Inhalation Hazards - Avoid Heavily Populated or Congested Areas, etc.

(a) Unless there is no practicable alternative, every driver of a vehicle transporting inhalation hazards shall avoid, by prearrangement of routes, driving into or through heavily populated areas, congested thoroughfares, or places where crowds are assembled. Operating convenience is not a basis for determining whether it is practicable to operate a vehicle in accordance with this subdivision.

(b) No vehicle transporting inhalation hazards shall be left unattended upon any street or highway.

(c) Inspection of the following items of equipment shall be made immediately preceding the actual transportation of an inhalation hazard:

(1) Brakes and the brake system.

(2) Steering, connection devices, and lighting systems.

(3) All tires.

(4) All supplemental equipment as required by Section 32106.

(d) En route inspection of tires and brakes on vehicles transporting inhalation hazards shall be performed at the following locations:

(1) At an inspection stop at least every four hours or 150 miles traveled, whichever occurs first, or as close thereto as is practicable, depending upon the proximity of those inspection stops.

(2) Regardless of elapsed time or miles traveled, at the top of and prior to descending any grade upon which the Department of Transportation has declared a speed limit for trucks of less than 55 miles per hour as provided by Section 22407. The inspection shall be made off the roadway.

(3) Regardless of elapsed time or miles traveled, at any location designated in regulations of the department as a required inspection stop.

(e)(1) Every person operating a vehicle transporting an inhalation hazard shall complete a record of every inspection which is required pursuant to this section in the form approved by the department showing the time and place of every inspection.

(2) The record of every inspection shall be made at the time the inspection is conducted.

(3) The person making the inspection shall certify the fact in the record.

32106. Required Equipment and Maintenance

Every vehicle used in the transportation of an inhalation hazard, in addition to any other equipment required by law, shall be equipped and maintained as this section.

(a) Brakes and the brake system shall be maintained in good and safe operating condition.

(b) Steering, connection devices, and lighting systems shall be maintained in good operating condition.

(c) All tires shall be in good condition, properly matched and inflated. Except as may be necessary to cause immediate replacement, no vehicle shall be driven unless all tires in actual use on the vehicle are properly inflated.

(d) Fire extinguishers and other safety equipment prescribed by regulations adopted by the department pursuant to Section 34501 shall be carried in each vehicle or combination of vehicles.

32107. Other Required Equipment

Every vehicle, or combination of vehicles, transporting an inhalation hazard shall contain a self-contained breathing apparatus and equipment capable of immediate communication with emergency personnel.

DIVISION 14.5.
TRANSPORTATION OF RADIOACTIVE MATERIALS

33000. Radioactive Materials

Subject to the provisions of Section 25611 of the Health and Safety Code, the CHP, after consulting with the State Department of Health Services, shall adopt regulations specifying the time at which shipments may occur and the routes which are to be used in the transportation of cargoes of hazardous radioactive materials, as such materials are defined in regulations of the State Department of Health Services.

33002. Spent Radioactive Fuel: Notification

(a) Prior to the transport of any hazardous radioactive materials containing cargoes of commercially produced, spent radioactive fuel outside the confines of a facility where that material was used or stored, or prior to the delivery of these materials to a carrier for transport, each carrier shall provide advance notification, in writing, of the shipment to the Department of the California Highway Patrol, which, in turn, shall notify all of the following persons:

(1) The fire chiefs of each city and county fire department and the fire chiefs of each fire protection district serving a population greater than 15,000, which city, county, or fire protection district is located along the proposed route. The Department of the California Highway Patrol, however, shall notify only those fire chiefs who have requested, in writing, to be so notified. A fire chief may revoke this request, in writing, at any time.

This paragraph does not apply to any fire chief of a fire department or fire protection district that is composed of 50 percent or more volunteer firefighters.

(2) The police chiefs of each city where surface transportation would occur along the proposed route.

(b) Subdivision (a) applies only to the extent that it does not conflict with federal law.

(c) Each advance notification shall contain the following information:

(1) The name, address, and telephone number of the shipper, carrier, and receiver of the shipment.

(2) If the shipment originates within California, the point of origin of the shipment and the 48-hour period during which departure of the shipment is estimated to occur, the destination of the shipment within California, and the 48-hour period during which the shipment is estimated to arrive.

(3) If the shipment originates outside of California, the point of origin of the shipment and the 48-hour period during which the shipment is estimated to arrive at state boundaries, the destination of the shipment within California, and the 48-hour period during which the shipment is estimated to arrive.

(4) A telephone number and address for current shipment information.

(d) The Department of the California Highway Patrol shall design a standard notification form to include all of the information specified in subdivision (c) and shall make these forms available by April 1, 1984.

(e) The notification is required to reach the Department of the California Highway Patrol at least 72 hours before the beginning of the 48-hour period during which departure of the shipment is estimated to occur, and the Department of the California Highway Patrol shall notify the fire chiefs who have requested notification and the police chiefs specified in subdivision (a) at least 36 hours before the beginning of this 48-hour period. A copy of the notification shall be retained by the Department of the California Highway Patrol for three years.

(f) The carrier shall also notify, by telephone or telegram, the Department of the California Highway Patrol if there are any changes in the scheduling of a shipment, in the routes to be used for a shipment, or any cancellation of a shipment. The Department of the California Highway Patrol shall, in turn, notify the fire chiefs who have requested notification and the police chiefs specified in subdivision (a) who would be affected by these changes in the scheduling of a shipment, in the routes to be used for a shipment, or the cancellation of a shipment. The Department of the California Highway Patrol shall maintain for three years a record of each telegram and telephonic notification.

(g) Any person or agency that receives any information pursuant to this section shall not disseminate or reveal this information to any other person, state agency, city, county, or local agency unless the person or agency determines that disseminating or revealing this information is necessary to protect the public health and safety or the environment.

(h) The Governor shall appoint the fire chiefs eligible to request notification, as specified in paragraph (1) of subdivision (a), as the designated representatives of the Governor pursuant to paragraph (1) of subsection (c) of Section 73.21 of Title 10 of the Code of Federal Regulations for the purpose of receiving information classified as safeguards information pursuant to Part 73 of Title 10 of the Code of Federal Regulations.

(i) Any carrier who violates this section, in addition to any penalty provided by law, is subject to a civil penalty of not more than five hundred dollars ($500) for each violation. For purposes of this section, each day of a continuing violation is a separate and distinct violation.

When establishing the amount of civil liability pursuant to this subdivision, the court shall consider, in addition to other relevant circumstances, the following:

(1) The extent of the harm caused by the violation.

(2) The persistence of the violation.

(3) The number of prior violations by the same violator.

(4) The deterrent value of the penalty based on the financial resources of the violator.

DIVISION 14.7.
FLAMMABLE AND COMBUSTIBLE LIQUIDS

34100.   Violation a Misdemeanor [Renumbered from 34102]
A violation of this division or of any regulation adopted by the commissioner pursuant to this division is a misdemeanor. No person shall operate a tank vehicle upon a highway in violation of this division or of any regulation adopted by the commissioner pursuant to this division.

DIVISION 14.8.   SAFETY REGULATIONS

34501.   Matters Regulated
(a)(1) The department shall adopt reasonable rules and regulations that, in the judgment of the department, are designed to promote the safe operation of vehicles described in Section 34500, regarding, but not limited to, controlled substances and alcohol testing of drivers by motor carriers, hours of service of drivers, equipment, fuel containers, fueling operations, inspection, maintenance, recordkeeping, accident reports, and drawbridges. The rules and regulations shall not, however, be applicable to schoolbuses, which shall be subject to rules and regulations adopted pursuant to Section 34501.5.

The rules and regulations shall exempt local law enforcement agencies, within a single county, engaged in the transportation of inmates or prisoners when those agencies maintain other motor vehicle operations records which furnish hours of service information on drivers which are in substantial compliance with the rules and regulations. This exemption does not apply to any local law enforcement agency engaged in the transportation of inmates or prisoners outside the county in which the agency is located, if that agency would otherwise be required, by existing law, to maintain driving logs.

(2) The department may adopt rules and regulations relating to commercial vehicle safety inspection and out-of-service criteria. In adopting the rules and regulations, the commissioner may consider the commercial vehicle safety inspection and out-of-service criteria adopted by organizations such as the Commercial Vehicle Safety Alliance, other intergovernmental safety group, or the United States Department of Transportation. The commissioner may provide departmental representatives to that alliance or other organization for the purpose of promoting the continued improvement and refinement of compatible nationwide commercial vehicle safety inspection and out-of-service criteria.

(3) The commissioner shall appoint a committee of 15 members, consisting of representatives of industry subject to the regulations to be adopted pursuant to this section, to act in an advisory capacity to the department, and the department shall cooperate and confer with the advisory committee so appointed. The commissioner shall appoint a separate committee to advise the department on rules and regulations concerning wheelchair lifts for installation and use on buses, consisting of persons who use the wheelchair lifts, representatives of transit districts, representatives of designers or manufacturers of wheelchairs and wheelchair lifts, and representatives of the Department of Transportation.

(4) The department may inspect any vehicles in maintenance facilities or terminals, as well as any records relating to the dispatch of vehicles or drivers, and the pay of drivers, to assure compliance with this code and regulations adopted pursuant to this section.

(b) The department, using the definitions adopted pursuant to Section 2402.7, shall adopt regulations for the transportation of hazardous materials in this state, except the transportation of materials which are subject to other provisions of this code, that the department determines are reasonably necessary to ensure the safety of persons and property using the highways. The regulations may include provisions governing the filling, marking, packing, labeling, and assembly of, and containers that may be used for, hazardous materials shipments, and the manner by which the shipper attests that the shipments are correctly identified and in proper condition for transport.

(c) At least once every 13 months, the department shall inspect every maintenance facility or terminal of any person who at any time operates any bus. If the bus operation includes more than 100 buses, the inspection shall be without prior notice.

(d) The commissioner shall adopt and enforce regulations which will make the public or private users of any bus aware of the operator's last safety rating.

(e) It is unlawful and constitutes a misdemeanor for any person to operate any bus without the inspection specified in subdivision (c) having been conducted.

(f) The department may adopt regulations restricting or prohibiting the movement of any vehicle from a maintenance facility or terminal if the vehicle is found in violation of this code or regulations adopted pursuant to this section. *(AM '98)*

34501.2. Limitations: Driving Hours

(a) The regulations adopted under Section 34501 for vehicles engaged in interstate or intrastate commerce shall establish hours-of-service regulations for drivers of those vehicles that are consistent with the hours-of-service regulations adopted by the United States Department of Transportation in Part 395 of Title 49 of the Code of Federal Regulations, as those regulations now exist or are hereafter amended.

(b) The regulations adopted under Section 34501 for vehicles engaged in intrastate commerce that are not transporting hazardous substances or hazardous waste, as those terms are defined by regulations in Section 171.8 of Title 49 of the Code of Federal Regulations, as those regulations now exist or are hereafter amended, shall have the following exceptions:

(1) The maximum driving time within a work period shall be 12 hours for a driver of a truck or truck tractor, except for a driver of a tank vehicle with a capacity of more than 500 gallons transporting flammable liquid, who shall not drive for more than 10 hours within a work period.

(2) A motor carrier shall not permit or require a driver to drive, nor shall any driver drive, for any period after having been on duty for 80 hours in any consecutive eight days.

(3) A driver employed by an electrical corporation, as defined in Section 218 of the Public Utilities Code, a gas corporation, as defined in Section 222 of that code, a telephone corporation, as defined in Section 234 of that code, a water corporation, as defined in Section 241 of that code, or a public water district as defined in Section 20200 of the Water Code, is exempt from all hours-of-service regulations while operating a public utility or public water district vehicle.

(4) Any other exceptions applicable to drivers assigned to governmental fire suppression and prevention, as determined by the department.

(5) A driver employed by a law enforcement agency, as defined in Section 390.3(f)(2) of Title 49 of the Code of Federal Regulations, as that section now exists or is hereafter amended, during an emergency or to restore the public peace.

(c) The regulations adopted under Section 34501 for vehicles engaged in the transportation of farm products in intrastate commerce shall include all of the following provisions:

(1) A driver employed by an agricultural carrier, including a carrier holding a seasonal permit, or by a private carrier, when transporting farm products from the field to the first point of processing or packing, shall not drive for any period after having been on duty 16 hours or more following eight consecutive hours off duty and shall not drive for any period after having been on duty for 112 hours in any consecutive eight-day period, except that a driver transporting special situation farm products from the field to the first point of processing or packing, or transporting livestock from pasture to pasture, may be permitted, during one period of not more than 28 consecutive days or a combination of two periods totaling not more than 28 days in a calendar year, to drive for not more than 12 hours during any workday of not more than 16 hours. A driver who thereby exceeds the driving time limits specified in paragraph (2) of subdivision (b) shall maintain a driver's record of duty status, and shall keep a duplicate copy in his or her possession when

driving a vehicle subject to this chapter. These records shall be presented immediately upon request by any authorized employee of the department, or any police officer or deputy sheriff.

(2) Upon the request of the Director of Food and Agriculture, the commissioner may, for good cause, temporarily waive the maximum on-duty time limits applicable to any eight-day period when an emergency exists due to inclement weather, natural disaster, or an adverse economic condition that threatens to disrupt the orderly movement of farm products during harvest for the duration of the emergency. For purposes of this paragraph, an emergency does not include a strike or labor dispute.

(3) For purposes of this subdivision, the following terms have the following meanings:

(A) "Farm products"means every agricultural, horticultural, viticultural, or vegetable product of the soil, honey and beeswax, oilseeds, poultry, livestock, milk, or timber.

(B) "First point of processing or packing"means a location where farm products are dried, canned, extracted, fermented, distilled, frozen, ginned, eviscerated, pasteurized, packed, packaged, bottled, conditioned, or otherwise manufactured, processed, or preserved for distribution in wholesale or retail markets.

(C) "Special situation farm products"means fruit, tomatoes, sugar beets, grains, wine grapes, grape concentrate, cotton, or nuts. *(AM '00, '09)*

34501.3.   Motor Carriers: Unlawful Schedule

(a) No motor carrier shall schedule a run or permit or require the operation of any motor vehicle subject to this division between points within a period of time which would do either of the following:

(1) Necessitate the vehicle being operated at speeds greater than those prescribed by this code.

(2) Require the driver of the vehicle to exceed the applicable maximum hours of service.

(b) A logbook of a driver, which reflects a trip or trips between points within a period of time which would have necessitated excessive speed to complete, shall give rise to a rebuttable presumption that the driver exceeded the lawful speed limit.

(c) For a violation of paragraph (2) of subdivision (a), a first offense is punishable by a fine of not more than one thousand dollars ($1,000), a second offense by a fine of not more than two thousand five hundred dollars ($2,500), and a third or subsequent offense by a fine of not more than five thousand dollars ($5,000).

34501.8.   General Public Paratransit Vehicles: Inspection

(a) The Department of the California Highway Patrol shall inspect every general public paratransit vehicle, as defined in Section 336, at least once each year to certify that its condition complies with all provisions of law, including being equipped with a fire extinguisher, first-aid kit, and three-point tie downs for transporting wheelchair passengers.

(b) On or after July 1, 1989, no person shall drive any general public paratransit vehicle unless there is displayed therein a certificate issued by the Department of the California Highway Patrol stating that on a certain date, which shall be within 13 months of the date of operation, an authorized employee of the Department of the California Highway Patrol inspected the general public paratransit vehicle and found that on the date of inspection the general public paratransit vehicle complied with the applicable provisions of state law. The Commissioner of the California Highway Patrol shall provide, by rule or regulation, for the issuance and display of distinctive inspection certificates.

(c) The Commissioner of the California Highway Patrol shall determine a fee and method of collection for the annual inspection of general public paratransit vehicles. The fee, established by regulation, shall be sufficient to cover the cost to the department for general public paratransit vehicle inspections. All fees received shall be deposited in the Motor Vehicle Account in the State Transportation Fund.

This section shall become operative January 1, 1989.

34501.10.   Driver Records and Log Books: Location

The employer of any person required to keep log books, records of physical examination, and other driver records as may be required by the Department of the California Highway Patrol, the Department of Motor Vehicles, the Department of Toxic Substances Control, or the State Department of Health Services, shall register with the Department of the California Highway Patrol the address where the log books and other records are available for inspection.

34501.12. Inspection of Maintenance Facility or Terminal [Repeals 1-1-16]

(a) Notwithstanding Section 408, as used in this section and Sections 34505.5 and 34505.6, "motor carrier"means the registered owner of a vehicle described in subdivision (a), (b), (e), (f), or (g) of Section 34500, except in the following circumstances:

(1) The registered owner leases the vehicle to another person for a term of more than four months. If the lease is for more than four months, the lessee is the motor carrier.

(2) The registered owner operates the vehicle exclusively under the authority and direction of another person. If the operation is exclusively under the authority and direction of another person, that other person may assume the responsibilities as the motor carrier. If not so assumed, the registered owner is the motor carrier. A person who assumes the motor carrier responsibilities of another pursuant to subdivision (b) shall provide to that other person whose motor carrier responsibility is so assumed, a completed copy of a departmental form documenting that assumption, stating the period for which responsibility is assumed, and signed by an agent of the assuming person. A legible copy shall be carried in each vehicle or combination of vehicles operated on the highway during the period for which responsibility is assumed. That copy shall be presented upon request by an authorized employee of the department. The original completed departmental form documenting the assumption shall be provided to the department within 30 days of the assumption. If the assumption of responsibility is terminated, the person who had assumed responsibility shall so notify the department in writing within 30 days of the termination.

(b)(1) A motor carrier may combine two or more terminals that are not subject to an unsatisfactory compliance rating within the last 36 months for purposes of the inspection required by subdivision (d), subject to all of the following conditions:

(A) The carrier identifies to the department, in writing, each terminal proposed to be included in the combination of terminals for purposes of this subdivision prior to an inspection of the designated terminal pursuant to subdivision (d).

(B) The carrier provides the department, prior to the inspection of the designated terminal pursuant to subdivision (d), a written listing of all its vehicles of a type subject to subdivision (a), (b), (e), (f), or (g) of Section 34500 that are based at each of the terminals combined for purposes of this subdivision. The listing shall specify the number of vehicles of each type at each terminal.

(C) The carrier provides to the department at the designated terminal during the inspection all maintenance records and driver records and a representative sample of vehicles based at each of the terminals included within the combination of terminals.

(2) If the carrier fails to provide the maintenance records, driver records, and representative sample of vehicles pursuant to subparagraph (C) of paragraph (1), the department shall assign the carrier an unsatisfactory terminal rating and require a reinspection to be conducted pursuant to subdivision (h).

(3) For purposes of this subdivision, the following terms have the following meanings:

(A) "Driver records" includes pull notice system records, driver proficiency records, and driver timekeeping records.

(B) "Maintenance records"includes all required maintenance, lubrication, and repair records and drivers'daily vehicle condition reports.

(C) "Representative sample"means the following, applied separately to the carrier's fleet of motortrucks and truck tractors and its fleet of trailers:

Representative Fleet Size	Sample
1 or 2	All
3 to 8	3
9 to 15	4
16 to 25	6
26 to 50	9

51 to 90 14
91 or more 20

(c) Each motor carrier who, in this state, directs the operation of, or maintains, a vehicle of a type described in subdivision (a) shall designate one or more terminals, as defined in Section 34515, in this state where vehicles can be inspected by the department pursuant to paragraph (4) of subdivision (a) of Section 34501 and where vehicle inspection and maintenance records and driver records will be made available for inspection.

(d)(1) The department shall inspect, at least every 25 months, every terminal, as defined in Section 34515, of a motor carrier who, at any time, operates a vehicle described in subdivision (a).

(2) The department shall place an inspection priority on those terminals operating vehicles listed in subdivision (g) of Section 34500.

(3) As used in this section and in Sections 34505.5 and 34505.6, subdivision (f) of Section 34500 includes only those combinations where the gross vehicle weight rating ***of the towing vehicle exceeds 10,000 pounds, but does not include a pickup truck, and subdivision (g) of Section 34500 includes only those vehicles transporting hazardous material for which the display of placards is required pursuant to Section 27903, a license is required pursuant to Section 32000.5, or for which hazardous waste transporter registration is required pursuant to Section 25163 of the Health and Safety Code. Historical vehicles, as described in Section 5004, vehicles that display special identification plates in accordance with Section 5011, implements of husbandry and farm vehicles, as defined in Chapter 1 (commencing with Section 36000) of Division 16, and vehicles owned or operated by an agency of the federal government are not subject to this section or to Sections 34505.5 and 34505.6.

(e)(1) It is the responsibility of the motor carrier to schedule with the department the inspection required by subdivision (d). The motor carrier shall submit an application form supplied by the department, accompanied by the required fee contained in paragraph (2), for each terminal the motor carrier operates. This fee shall be submitted within 30 days of establishing a terminal. All fees submitted under paragraph (2) are nonrefundable.

(2)(A) The fee for each terminal is set forth in the following table:

Terminal Fleet Size	Required fee per terminal
1	$ 270
2	$ 375
3 to 8	$510
9 to 15	$615
16 to 25	$800
26 to 50	$1,040
51 to 90	$1,165
91 or more	$1,870

(B) In addition to the fee specified in subparagraph (A), the motor carrier shall submit an additional fee of three hundred fifty dollars ($350) for each of its terminals not previously inspected under the section.

(3) Except as provided in paragraph (5), the inspection term for each inspected terminal of a motor carrier shall expire 25 months from the date the terminal receives a satisfactory compliance rating, as specified in subdivision (h). Applications and fees for subsequent inspections shall be submitted not earlier than nine months and not later than seven months before the expiration of the motor carrier's then current inspection term. If the motor carrier has submitted the inspection application and the required accompanying fees, but the department is unable to complete the inspection within the 25-month inspection period, then no additional fee shall be required for the inspection requested in the original application.

(4) All fees collected pursuant to this subdivision, including delinquence fees, shall be deposited in the Motor Vehicle Account in the State Transportation Fund. An amount equal to the fees collected shall be available for appropriation by the Legislature from the Motor Vehicle Account to the department for the purpose of conducting truck terminal inspections and for the additional roadside safety inspections required by Section 34514.

(5) To avoid the scheduling of a renewal terminal inspection pursuant to this section during a carrier's seasonal peak business periods, the current inspection term of a terminal that has paid all required fees and has been rated satisfactory in its last inspection may be reduced by not more than nine months if a written request is submitted by the carrier to the department at least four months prior to the desired inspection month, or at the time of payment of renewal inspection fees in compliance with paragraph (3), whichever date is earlier. A motor carrier may request this adjustment of the inspection term during any inspection cycle. A request made pursuant to this paragraph shall not result in a fee proration and does not relieve the carrier from the requirements of paragraph (3).

(6) Failure to pay a fee required by this section, within the appropriate timeframe, shall result in additional delinquent fees as follows:

(A) For a delinquency period of more than 30 days and less than one year, the penalty is 60 percent of the required fee.

(B) For a delinquency period of one to two years, the penalty is 80 percent of the required fee.

(C) For a delinquency period of more than two years, the penalty is 160 percent of the required fee.

(7) Federal, state, and local public entities are exempt from the fee requirement of this section.

(f) It is unlawful for a motor carrier to operate a vehicle subject to this section without having submitted an inspection application and the required fees to the department as required by subdivision (e) or (h).

(g)(1) It is unlawful for a motor carrier to operate a vehicle subject to this section after submitting an inspection application to the department, without the inspection described in subdivision (d) having been performed and a safety compliance report having been issued to the motor carrier within the 25-month inspection period or within 60 days immediately preceding the inspection period.

(2) It is unlawful for a motor carrier to contract or subcontract with, or otherwise engage the services of, another motor carrier, subject to this section, unless the contracted motor carrier has complied with this section. A motor carrier shall not contract or subcontract with, or otherwise engage the services of, another motor carrier until the contracted motor carrier provides certification of compliance with this section. This certification shall be completed in writing by the contracted motor carrier. The certification, or a copy thereof, shall be maintained by each involved party for the duration of the contract or the period of service plus two years, and shall be presented for inspection immediately upon the request of an authorized employee of the department.

(h)(1) An inspected terminal that receives an unsatisfactory compliance rating shall be reinspected within 120 days after the issuance of the unsatisfactory compliance rating.

(2) A terminal's first required reinspection under this subdivision shall be without charge unless one or more of the following is established:

(A) The motor carrier's operation presented an imminent danger to public safety.

(B) The motor carrier was not in compliance with the requirement to enroll all drivers in the pull notice program pursuant to Section 1808.1.

(C) The motor carrier failed to provide all required records and vehicles for a consolidated inspection pursuant to subdivision (b).

(3) If the unsatisfactory rating was assigned for any of the reasons set forth in paragraph (2), the carrier shall submit the required fee as provided in paragraph (4).

(4) Applications for reinspection pursuant to paragraph (3) or for second and subsequent consecutive reinspections under this subdivision shall be accompanied by the fee specified in paragraph (2) of subdivision (e) and shall be filed within 60 days of issuance of the unsatisfactory compliance rating. The reinspection fee is nonrefundable.

(5) When a motor carrier's Motor Carrier of Property Permit or Public Utilities Commission operating authority is suspended as a result of an unsatisfactory compliance rating, the department shall not conduct a reinspection for permit or authority reinstatement until requested to do so by the Department of Motor Vehicles or the Public Utilities Commission, as appropriate.

(i) It is the intent of the Legislature that the department make its best efforts to inspect terminals within the resources provided. In the interest of the state, the Commissioner of the California Highway Patrol may extend for a period, not to exceed six months, the inspection terms beginning prior to July 1, 1990.

(j) Except as provided in paragraph (5), to encourage motor carriers to attain continuous satisfactory compliance ratings, the department may establish and implement an incentive program consisting of the following:

(1) After the second consecutive satisfactory compliance rating assigned to a motor carrier terminal as a result of an inspection conducted pursuant to subdivision (d), and after each consecutive satisfactory compliance rating thereafter, an appropriate certificate, denoting the number of consecutive satisfactory ratings, shall be awarded to the terminal, unless the terminal has received an unsatisfactory compliance rating as a result of an inspection conducted in the interim between the consecutive inspections conducted under subdivision (d), or the motor carrier is rated unsatisfactory by the department following a controlled substances and alcohol testing program inspection. The certificate authorized under this paragraph shall not be awarded for performance in the administrative review authorized under paragraph (2). However, the certificate shall include a reference to any administrative reviews conducted during the period of consecutive satisfactory compliance ratings.

(2) Unless the department's evaluation of the motor carrier's safety record indicates a declining level of compliance, a terminal that has attained two consecutive satisfactory compliance ratings assigned following inspections conducted pursuant to subdivision (d) is eligible for an administrative review in lieu of the next required inspection, unless the terminal has received an unsatisfactory compliance rating as a result of an inspection conducted in the interim between the consecutive inspections conducted under subdivision (d). An administrative review shall consist of all of the following:

(A) A signed request by a terminal management representative requesting the administrative review in lieu of the required inspection containing a promise to continue to maintain a satisfactory level of compliance for the next 25-month inspection term.

(B) A review with a terminal management representative of the carrier's record as contained in the department's files. If a terminal has been authorized a second consecutive administrative review, the review required under this subparagraph is optional, and may be omitted at the carrier's request.

(C) Absent any cogent reasons to the contrary, upon completion of the requirements of subparagraphs (A) and (B), the safety compliance rating assigned during the last required inspection shall be extended for 25 months.

(3) Not more than two administrative reviews may be conducted consecutively. At the completion of the 25-month inspection term following a second administrative review, a terminal inspection shall be conducted pursuant to subdivision (d). If this inspection results in a satisfactory compliance rating, the terminal shall again be eligible for an administrative review in lieu of the next required inspection. If the succession of satisfactory ratings is interrupted by a rating of other than satisfactory, irrespective of the reason for the inspection, the terminal shall again attain two consecutive satisfactory ratings to become eligible for an administrative review.

(4) As a condition for receiving the administrative reviews authorized under this subdivision in lieu of inspections, and in order to ensure that compliance levels remain satisfactory, the motor carrier shall agree to accept random, unannounced inspections by the department.

(5) Notwithstanding paragraphs (1) to (4), inclusive, a motor carrier of hazardous materials shall not be granted administrative review pursuant to this subdivision in lieu of a terminal inspection pursuant to subdivision (d) at any terminal from which hazardous materials carrying vehicles identified by paragraph (3) of subdivision (d) are operated.

(k) This section shall be known and may be cited as the Biennial Inspection of Terminals Program or BIT.

(l) The department shall, on or before January 1, 2016, adopt regulations establishing a performance-based truck terminal inspection priority selection system.

(m) This section shall remain in effect only until January 1, 2016, and as of that date is repealed, unless a later enacted statute, that is enacted before January 1, 2016, deletes or extends that date. *(AM-RP '13)*

34501.14. Grape Gondolas: Inspection

(a) Notwithstanding Section 34501.12, for purposes of this division, safety inspections of grape gondolas are governed by this section.

(b) Every registered owner of a grape gondola shall submit an application and the fee specified in subdivision (g) to the department for the initial inspection required by this section. The initial application shall be submitted on or before July 1, 1993. The inspection term for a grape gondola shall expire 25 months from the date the department conducts the inspection, and issues a certificate indicating the gondola has passed the inspection, and every 25 months thereafter. Applications and fees for subsequent inspections and certificates shall be submitted not later than seven months before the expiration of the then current inspection term. If the registered owner has submitted the inspection application and the required accompanying fees, but the department is unable to complete the inspection within the 25-month inspection period, then no additional fee shall be required for the inspection requested in the original application.

(c) On and after July 1, 1993, no person may operate any grape gondola without having submitted an inspection application and the required fees to the department as required by this section.

(d) On and after January 1, 1995, no person may operate any grape gondola, without the inspection described in subdivision (e) having been performed and a certificate having been issued to the owner.

(e) The safety inspection undertaken pursuant to this section shall be limited to an inspection of the brake system, steering, lights, connections, wheels and tires, frame, and suspension.

(f) For purposes of undertaking the inspection of grape gondolas under this section, the department shall schedule all inspections at one central location during a continuous eight-week period every odd-numbered year with at least two days of each week during that eight-week period devoted to the actual inspection. If the gondola does not pass its first inspection, it may be reinspected during the eight-week period at no additional cost.

(g) Fees shall be established by the department in an amount equal to the actual costs incurred by the department in carrying out this section, but not to exceed twenty-five dollars ($25) for each inspection or reinspection.

(h) As used in this section, "grape gondola" means a motor vehicle which has been permanently altered and is attached to a grape tank by two means. The first mean is by use of a kingpin on the trunk which is centered through a turntable assembly on the tank. The second means of attachment is through the use of a pair of horizontal crossarms between the drive axle and the rear tank axle. The tank is designed to pivot off of the chassis on two support arms during dumping, and is further designed to be specifically compatible with dumping facilities of the wineries.

(i) This section only applies to a grape gondola that is used under all of the following conditions:

(1) For 60 days or less during any calendar year.

(2) For not more than 500 miles in any calendar year.

(3) Only for the transportation of grapes.

34505. Tour Buses: Inspection

(a) Tour bus operators shall, in addition to the systematic inspection, maintenance, and lubrication services required of all motor carriers, require each tour bus to be inspected at least every 45 days, or more often if necessary to ensure safe operation. This inspection shall include, but not be limited to, all of the following:

(1) Brake adjustment.

(2) Brake system components and leaks.

(3) Steering and suspension systems.

(4) Tires and wheels.

(b) A tour bus shall not be used to transport passengers until all defects listed during the inspection conducted pursuant to subdivision (a) have been corrected and attested to by the signature of the operator's authorized representative.

(c) Records of inspections conducted pursuant to subdivision (a) shall be kept at the operator's maintenance facility or terminal where the tour bus is regularly garaged. The records shall be retained by the operator for one year, and shall be made available for inspection upon request by any authorized employee of the department. Each record shall include, but not be limited to, all of the following:

(1) Identification of the vehicle, including make, model, license number, or other means of positive identification.

(2) Date and nature of each inspection and any repair performed.

(3) Signature of operator's authorized representative attesting to the inspection and to the completion of all required repairs.

(4) Company vehicle number.

34506. Violations: Misdemeanors

It is a misdemeanor to fail to comply with any rule or regulation adopted by the CHP pursuant to Section 34501, 34501.5, 34508, or 34513 regarding any of the following:

(a) Hours of service of drivers.

(b) Hazardous material transportation.

(c) Schoolbus construction, design, color, equipment, maintenance, or operation.

(d) Youth bus equipment, maintenance, or operation.

(e) Tour bus equipment, maintenance, or operation.

(f) Equipment, maintenance, or operation of any vehicle described in subdivision (a), (b), (c), (d), (e), (f), or (g) of Section 34500.

(g) Equipment, maintenance, or operation of any school pupil activity bus.

34506.3. Violations: Infractions

Except as otherwise provided in this division, it is an infraction to fail to comply with any rule or regulation adopted by the department pursuant to this division.

34506.4. Removal of Certain Unsafe Vehicles

(a) Any member of the Department of the California Highway Patrol may remove from the highway and have placed in a storage facility, any vehicle described in subdivision (a) of Section 22406, subdivision (g) of Section 34500, and any motortruck with a gross vehicle weight rating of more than 10,000 pounds, which is in an unsafe condition.

(b) Any member of the Department of the California Highway Patrol may impound any farm labor vehicle operated in violation of subdivision (b) of Section 2800, subdivision (a) of Section 24002.5, or subdivision (a) of Section 31402, subject to the following requirements:

(1) A farm labor vehicle impounded for a first violation of subdivision (b) of Section 2800, subdivision (a) of Section 24002.5, or subdivision (a) of Section 31402 may be released within 24 hours upon delivery to the impounding authority of satisfactory proof that the vehicle will be legally moved or transported to a place of repair.

(2) A farm labor vehicle shall be impounded for not less than 10 days for a second violation of subdivision (b) of Section 2800, subdivision (a) of Section 24002.5, or subdivision (a) of Section 31402, or any combination of two of those provisions, if the original equipment or maintenance violation has not been repaired to comply with existing law. The farm labor vehicle shall be released after 10 days upon delivery to the impounding authority of satisfactory proof that the vehicle has been repaired to comply with existing law, or upon delivery to the impounding agency of satisfactory proof that the vehicle will be lawfully moved or transported to a place of repair.

(3) A farm labor vehicle shall be impounded for not less than 30 days for a third or subsequent violation of subdivision (b) of Section 2800, subdivision (a) of Section 24002.5, or subdivision (a) of Section 31402, or any combination of three or more of those provisions, if the original equipment or maintenance

violation has not been repaired to comply with existing law. The farm labor vehicle shall be released after 30 days upon delivery to the impounding authority of satisfactory proof that the vehicle has been repaired to comply with existing law, or upon delivery to the impounding agency of satisfactory proof that the vehicle will be lawfully moved or transported to a place of repair.

(c) All towing and storage fees for a vehicle removed under this section shall be paid by the owner. *(AM '00)*

34506.5. Forfeiture of Farm Labor Vehicle as Nuisance

(a) A farm labor vehicle is subject to forfeiture as a nuisance if it is driven on a highway in violation of subdivision (b) of Section 2800, subdivision (a) of Section 24002.5, or subdivision (a) of Section 31402 and has been impounded for a second or subsequent time pursuant to paragraph (3) of subdivision (b) of Section 34506.4.

(b)(1) A registered or legal owner of record at the time of impoundment may request a hearing to determine the validity of the impoundment pursuant to paragraph (1) or (2) of subdivision (n) of Section 14607.6.

(2) If it is determined that the necessary repairs had been completed and the farm labor vehicle complied with existing laws at the time of impoundment, the agency employing the person who directed the impoundment shall be responsible for the costs incurred for towing and storage.

(c) Procedures established in subdivisions (e), (f), (g), (h), (i), (j), (k), (l), (o), (p), (q), (r), (t), (u), and (v) of Section 14607.6 shall be utilized for the forfeiture of an impounded farm labor vehicle. *(Ad '00)*

34507. Display of Symbol

To assist the department in enforcing this division, a vehicle that is subject to this division and to the jurisdiction, control, and regulation of the Department of Motor Vehicles, the Public Utilities Commission, or the United States Secretary of the Department of Transportation shall have displayed prominently a distinctive identifying symbol as required by Section 34507.5.

34507.5. Carrier Identification Number

(a) A motor carrier, as defined in Section 408, a motor carrier of property, and a for-hire motor carrier of property, as defined in Section 34601, shall obtain a carrier identification number from the department. Application for a carrier identification number shall be on a form furnished by the department. Information provided in connection with an application for a carrier identification number shall be updated by a motor carrier upon request from the department.

(b) The carrier identification number assigned to the motor carrier under whose operating authority or motor carrier permit the vehicle or combination of vehicles is being operated shall be displayed on both sides of each vehicle, or on both sides of at least one motor vehicle in each combination of the following vehicles:

(1) Each vehicle set forth in Section 34500.

(2) A motortruck of two or more axles that is more than 10,000 pounds gross vehicle weight rating.

(3) Any other motortruck or motor vehicle used to transport property for compensation.

(c) A vehicle or combination of vehicles listed in subdivision (b) that is operated under a rental agreement with a term of not more than 30 calendar days shall meet all of the following requirements:

(1) Have displayed on both sides of each vehicle or on both sides of one of the vehicles in each combination of vehicles the name or trademark of the lessor.

(2) Have displayed on both sides of each vehicle or on both sides of one of the vehicles in each combination of vehicles any of the following numbers issued to the lessor:

(A) The carrier identification number issued by the United States Department of Transportation.

(B) A valid operating authority number.

(C) A valid motor carrier of property number.

(3)(A) Have in the vehicle or combination of vehicles a copy of the rental agreement entered into by the lessor and the vehicle operator.

(B) The rental agreement shall be available for inspection immediately upon the request of an authorized employee of the department, a regularly employed and salaried police officer or deputy sheriff, or a reserve police officer or reserve deputy sheriff listed pursuant to Section 830.6 of the Penal Code.

(C) If the rented vehicle or combination of vehicles is operated in conjunction with a commercial enterprise, the rental agreement shall include the operator's carrier identification number or motor carrier of property permit number.

(d) A vehicle or combination of vehicles that is in compliance with Section 390.21 of Title 49 of the Code of Federal Regulations shall be deemed to be in compliance with subdivision (c).

(e) This section does not apply to any of the following vehicles:

(1) A vehicle described in subdivision (f) of Section 34500, that is operated by a private carrier as defined in subdivision (d) of Section 34601, if the gross vehicle weight rating of the towing vehicle is 10,000 pounds or less, or the towing vehicle is a pickup truck, as defined in Section 471. This exception does not apply to a vehicle combination described in subdivision (k) of Section 34500.

(2) A vehicle described in subdivision (g) of Section 34500, that is operated by a private carrier as defined in subdivision (d) of Section 34601, if the hazardous material transportation does not require the display of placards pursuant to Section 27903, a license pursuant to Section 32000.5, or hazardous waste hauler registration pursuant to Section 25163 of the Health and Safety Code.

(3) A historical vehicle, as described in Section 5004, and a vehicle that displays special identification plates in accordance with Section 5011.

(4) An implement of husbandry as defined in Chapter 1 (commencing with Section 36000) of Division 16.

(5) A vehicle owned or operated by an agency of the federal government.

(6) A pickup truck, as defined in Section 471, and a two-axle daily rental truck with a gross vehicle weight rating of less than 26,001 pounds, when operated in noncommercial use.

(f) Subdivision (b) does not apply to the following:

(1) A vehicle that displays a valid identification number assigned by the United States Secretary of the Department of Transportation.

(2) A vehicle that is regulated by, and that displays a valid operating authority number issued by, the Public Utilities Commission, including a household goods carrier as defined in Section 5109 of the Public Utilities Code.

(3) A for-hire motor carrier of passengers.

(g) The display of the carrier identification number shall be in sharp contrast to the background, and shall be of a size, shape, and color that it is readily legible during daylight hours from a distance of 50 feet.

(h) The carrier identification number for a company no longer in business, no longer operating with the same name, or no longer operating under the same operating authority, identification number, or motor carrier permit shall be removed before sale, transfer, or other disposal of a vehicle marked pursuant to this section. *(AM '06)*

34507.6.   Bus: Carrier Identification Number

(a) Every operator of transportation service which is exempt from regulation as a charter-party carrier of passengers pursuant to subdivision (k) or (l) of Section 5353 of the Public Utilities Code, and which furnishes that transportation service in a bus, shall obtain a carrier identification number from the CHP Application for a carrier identification number shall be on a form furnished by the CHP.

(b)(1) The carrier identification number so obtained by the operator shall be displayed on both sides of each bus used in that transportation service.

(2) The display of the carrier identification number shall be in sharp contrast to the background, and shall be of a size, shape, and color as to be readily legible during daylight hours from a distance of at least 50 feet.

(3) The carrier identification number shall be removed before the sale, transfer, or other disposal of the bus.

34509. Vanpool Vehicles: Equipment and Inspection

Vanpool vehicles, as defined in Section 668, and vanpool vehicles when used for purposes other than traveling to and from a work location and transporting not more than 10 persons including the driver, shall be exempt from the regulations adopted pursuant to Section 34501, except that the following shall apply:

(a) The vanpool vehicle shall be equipped with an operable fire extinguisher which is of the dry chemical or carbon dioxide type with an aggregate rating of at least 4-B:C and which is securely mounted and readily accessible.

(b) The vanpool vehicle shall be equipped with a first aid kit, conforming to the minimum requirements for schoolbuses. First aid kits shall be readily visible, accessible, and plainly marked "First Aid Kit."

(c) The vanpool vehicle shall be regularly and systematically inspected, maintained, and lubricated in accordance with the manufacturer's recommendations, or more often if necessary to insure the safe operating condition of the vehicle. The maintenance shall include, as a minimum, an in-depth inspection of the vehicle's brake system, steering components, lighting system, and wheels and tires, to be performed at intervals of not more than every six months or 6,000 miles, whichever occurs first.

(d) Operators of vanpool vehicles shall document each systematic inspection, maintenance, and lubrication and repair performed for each vehicle under their control. Required records shall include services performed, the person performing the service, the date, and the mileage on the vehicle at the time of the repair. The records shall be maintained with the vehicle for one year, and shall be presented upon demand to any authorized representative of the CHP.

(e) Vanpool vehicles being operated pursuant to the exemptions specified in this section shall display, upon the rear and sides of the vehicle, a sign or placard, clearly visible and discernible for a distance of not less than 50 feet, indicating that the vehicle is being used as a vanpool vehicle.

34510. Display of Shipping Papers

Persons operating vehicles, or combinations of vehicles, in the transportation of hazardous material and subject to this division, shall carry in the vehicle while en route any shipping papers required to accompany the vehicle in accordance with regulations adopted pursuant to Section 2402. The bill of lading or other shipping paper shall be displayed upon demand of any member of the California Highway Patrol or any police officer of a city who is on duty for the exclusive or main purpose of enforcing the provisions of this code. *(AM '01)*

34516. Transportation of Food Products

(a) No person shall use or arrange for the use of a refrigerated motor vehicle, tank truck, dry van, or other motor vehicle, to provide transportation of food products for human consumption if the vehicle has been used to transport solid waste destined for landfills, or if precluded from use in accordance with subdivision (c).

(b) A violation of this section is a misdemeanor.

(c) If, pursuant to a federal statute having the same purposes as the act which added this section to the Public Utilities Code during the 1990 portion of the 1989-90 Regular Session, the United States Secretary of Transportation publishes a list of categories of solid waste or hazardous substances which he or she determines make food unsafe as a result of having been transported in a refrigerated motor vehicle, tank truck, dry van, or other motor vehicle also used to transport food products for human consumption, subdivisions (a) and (b) apply to those substances.

(d) A person or corporation charged with a violation of this section may avoid liability upon a showing by clear and convincing evidence that the transportation alleged to violate this section did not in fact endanger the public health, due to the specific protective or remedial actions taken by the person or corporation charged.

34517. Foreign Commercial Vehicle: Operate within Commercial Zones

(a) With respect to a commercial motor vehicle from another country, a person shall not operate the vehicle outside the boundaries of a designated commercial zone unless the required operating authority from the United States Secretary of the Department of Transportation has first been obtained.

(b) A violation of subdivision (a) is an infraction punishable by a fine of one thousand dollars ($1,000).

(c) Notwithstanding subdivision (b), a peace officer, as defined in Chapter 4.5 (commencing with Section 830) of Title 3 of Part 2 of the Penal Code, shall issue a citation for a violation of subdivision (a) to the driver of the vehicle and order the driver of the vehicle to return the vehicle to its country of origin. The peace officer may impound a vehicle cited pursuant to this section and its cargo until the citation and all charges related to the impoundment are cleared. The impoundment charges are the responsibility of the vehicle's owner.

(d) As used in this section, "designated commercial zone" means a commercial zone, as defined in Part 372 (commencing with Section 372.101) of Title 49 of the Code of Federal Regulations. *(AM '06)*

34518.   Prohibited Acts [Renumbered from 6855]

(a) A foreign motor carrier or foreign private motor carrier required to have a certificate of registration issued by the United States Secretary of the Department of Transportation pursuant to Part 368 (commencing with Section 368.1), or required to be registered pursuant to Part 365 (commencing with Section 365.101), of Title 49 of the Code of Federal Regulations shall not do any of the following:

(1) Operate in this state without the required certificate in the vehicle.

(2) Operate beyond the limitations or restrictions specified in the certificate as issued.

(3) Refuse to show the certificate upon request of a peace officer.

(4) Provide point-to-point transportation services, including express delivery services, within the United States for goods other than international cargo.

(b) A motor carrier required to be registered with the United States Secretary of the Department of Transportation pursuant to Section 13902 of Title 49 of the United States Code, Part 365 (commencing with Section 365.101), Part 390 (commencing with Section 390.1), or Section 392.9a of Title 49 of the Code of Federal Regulations shall not do any of the following:

(1) Operate in this state without the required registration.

(2) Operate beyond the limitations or restrictions specified in its registration.

(3) Operate in this state without the required operating authority.

(c) A violation of subdivision (a) or (b) is an infraction punishable by a fine of one thousand dollars ($1,000).

(d) A member of the Department of the California Highway Patrol may impound a vehicle operated in violation of subdivision (a) or (b) and its cargo, until the citation and all charges related to the impoundment are cleared. The impoundment charges are the responsibility of the vehicle's owner.

(e)(1) A motor carrier granted permanent operating authority pursuant to subdivision (a) shall not operate a vehicle on a highway, unless the vehicle is inspected by a Commercial Vehicle Safety Alliance-certified inspector every three months and displays a current safety inspection decal attesting to the successful completion of those inspections for at least three years after receiving permanent operating authority.

(2) Paragraph (1) does not apply to a motor carrier granted authority to operate solely in a commercial zone on the United States-Mexico International Border.

(f) As used in this section "limitations" or "restrictions" include definitions of "commercial zones," "municipality," "contiguous municipalities," "unincorporated area," and "terminal areas," in Part 372 (commencing with Section 372.101) of Title 49 of the Code of Federal Regulations. *(AM/RN '06; AM '10)*

34620.   Motor Carrier of Property: Illegal Operation

(a) Except as provided in subdivision (b) and Section 34622, a motor carrier of property shall not operate a commercial motor vehicle on any public highway in this state, unless it has complied with Section 34507.5 and has registered with the department its carrier identification number authorized or assigned thereunder, and holds a valid motor carrier permit issued to that motor carrier by the department. The department shall issue a motor carrier permit upon the carrier's written request, compliance with Sections 34507.5, 34630, and 34640, and subdivisions (e) and (h) of Section 34501.12 for motor carriers listed in that section, and the payment of the fee required by this chapter.

(b) A person shall not contract with, or otherwise engage the services of, a motor carrier of property, unless that motor carrier holds a valid motor carrier of property permit issued by the department. A motor carrier of property or broker of construction trucking services, as defined in Section 3322 of the Civil Code, shall not contract or subcontract with, or otherwise engage the services of, a motor carrier of property, until the contracted motor carrier of property provides certification in the manner prescribed by this section, of compliance with subdivision (a). This certification shall be completed by the contracted motor carrier of property and shall include a provision requiring the contracted motor carrier of property to immediately notify the person to whom they are contracted if the contracted motor carrier of property's permit is suspended or revoked. A copy of the contracted motor carrier of property's permit shall accompany the required certificate. The Department of the California Highway Patrol shall, by regulation, prescribe the format for the certificate and may make available an optional specific form for that purpose. The certificate, or a copy thereof, shall be maintained by each involved party for the duration of the contract or period of service plus two years, and shall be presented for inspection at the location designated by each carrier under Section 34501.10, immediately upon the request of an authorized employee of the Department of the California Highway Patrol.

(c)(1) A motor carrier of property shall not retrieve a vehicle through the use of a tow truck, as defined in subdivision (a) of Section 615, from the premises of another motor carrier of property until the retrieving motor carrier provides a copy of its motor carrier permit to the releasing motor carrier.

(2) A motor carrier of property shall not release a vehicle to another motor carrier of property utilizing a tow truck, as defined in subdivision (a) of Section 615, until the releasing motor carrier obtains a copy of the motor carrier permit from the retrieving motor carrier. The motor carrier releasing the vehicle shall maintain a copy of the motor carrier permit for a period of two years after the transaction, and, upon the request of an authorized employee of the Department of the California Highway Patrol, shall immediately present the permit for inspection at the location designated by the releasing motor carrier under Section 34501.10.

(3) This subdivision does not apply to a person licensed pursuant to the Collateral Recovery Act (Chapter 11 (commencing with Section 7500) of Division 3 of the Business and Professions Code). *(AM '13)*

34623. Highway Patrol to Have Exclusive Jurisdiction: Suspension of Permit [Repeals 1-1-16]
(a) The Department of the California Highway Patrol has exclusive jurisdiction for the regulation of safety of operation of motor carriers of property.

(b) The motor carrier permit of a motor carrier of property may be suspended for failure to do any of the following:

(1) Maintain any vehicle of the carrier in a safe operating condition or to comply with this code or with applicable regulations contained in Title 13 of the California Code of Regulations, if that failure is either a consistent failure or presents an imminent danger to public safety.

(2) Enroll all drivers in the pull notice system as required by Section 1808.1.

(3) Submit any application or pay any fee required by subdivision (e) or (h) of Section 34501.12 within the timeframes set forth in that section.

(c) The motor carrier permit of a motor carrier of property shall be suspended for failure to either (1) comply with the requirements of federal law described in subdivision (a) of Section 34520 of the Vehicle Code, or (2) make copies of results and other records available as required by subdivision (b) of that section. The suspension shall be as follows:

(1) For a serious violation, which is a willful failure to perform substance abuse testing in accordance with state or federal law:

(A) For a first offense, a mandatory five-day suspension.

(B) For a second offense within three years of a first offense, a mandatory three-month suspension.

(C) For a third offense within three years of a first offense, a mandatory one -year suspension.

(2) For a nonserious violation, the time recommended to the department by the Department of the California Highway Patrol.

(3) For the purposes of this subdivision, "willful failure"means any of the following:

(A) An intentional and uncorrected failure to have a controlled substances and alcohol testing program in place.

(B) An intentional and uncorrected failure to enroll an employed driver into the controlled substances and alcohol testing program.

(C) A knowing use of a medically disqualified driver, including the failure to remove the driver from safety-sensitive duties upon notification of the medical disqualification.

(D) An attempt to conceal legal deficiencies in the motor carrier's controlled substances and alcohol testing program.

(d) The department, pending a hearing in the matter pursuant to subdivision (f), may suspend a carrier's permit.

(e)(1) A motor carrier whose motor carrier permit is suspended pursuant to subdivision (b) may obtain a reinspection of its terminal and vehicles by the Department of the California Highway Patrol by submitting a written request for reinstatement to the department and paying a reinstatement fee as required by Section 34623.5.

(2) A motor carrier whose motor carrier permit is suspended for failure to submit any application or to pay any fee required by Section 34501.12 shall present proof of having submitted that application or have paid that fee to the Department of the California Highway Patrol before applying for reinstatement of its motor carrier permit.

(3) The department shall deposit all reinstatement fees collected from motor carriers of property pursuant to this section in the fund. Upon receipt of the fee, the department shall forward a request to the Department of the California Highway Patrol, which shall perform a reinspection within a reasonable time, or shall verify receipt of the application or fee or both the application and fee. Following the term of a suspension imposed under Section 34670, the department shall reinstate a carrier's motor carrier permit suspended under subdivision (b) upon notification by the Department of the California Highway Patrol that the carrier's safety compliance has improved to the satisfaction of the Department of the California Highway Patrol, or that the required application or fees have been received by the Department of the California Highway Patrol, unless the permit is suspended for another reason or has been revoked.

(f) Whenever the department suspends the permit of any carrier pursuant to subdivision (b), (c), or paragraph (3) of subdivision (i), the department shall furnish the carrier with written notice of the suspension and shall provide for a hearing within a reasonable time, not to exceed 21 days, after a written request is filed with the department. At the hearing, the carrier shall show cause why the suspension should not be continued. Following the hearing, the department may terminate the suspension, continue the suspension in effect, or revoke the permit. The department may revoke the permit of any carrier suspended pursuant to subdivision (b) at any time that is 90 days or more after its suspension if the carrier has not filed a written request for a hearing with the department or has failed to submit a request for reinstatement pursuant to subdivision (e).

(g) Notwithstanding any other provision of this code, no hearing shall be provided when the suspension of the motor carrier permit is based solely upon the failure of the motor carrier to maintain satisfactory proof of financial responsibility as required by this code, or failure of the motor carrier to submit an application or to pay fees required by Section 34501.12.

(h) A motor carrier of property may not operate a commercial motor vehicle on any public highway in this state during any period its motor carrier of property permit is suspended pursuant to this division.

(i)(1) A motor carrier of property whose motor carrier permit is suspended pursuant to this section or Section 34505.6, which suspension is based wholly or in part on the failure of the motor carrier to maintain any vehicle in safe operating condition, may not lease, or otherwise allow, another motor carrier to operate the vehicles of the carrier subject to the suspension, during the period of the suspension.

(2) A motor carrier of property may not knowingly lease, operate, dispatch, or otherwise utilize any vehicle from a motor carrier of property whose motor carrier permit is suspended, which suspension is based wholly or in part on the failure of the motor carrier to maintain any vehicle in safe operating condition.

(3) The department may immediately suspend the motor carrier permit of any motor carrier that the department determines to be in violation of paragraph (2).

(j) This section shall remain in effect only until January 1, 2016, and as of that date is repealed, unless a later enacted statute, that is enacted before January 1, 2016, deletes or extends that date. *(AM-RP '13)*

34660. Fines and Penalties Generally

(a) A motor carrier of property, after its motor carrier permit has been suspended by the department, who continues to operate as a motor carrier, either independently or for another motor carrier, is guilty of a misdemeanor, punishable by a fine of not more than two thousand five hundred dollars ($2,500), or by imprisonment in the county jail for not more than three months, or by both that fine and imprisonment.

(b) Each violation of this section is a separate and distinct offense, and, in the case of a continuing violation, each day's continuance of operation as a carrier in violation of this section is a separate and distinct offense.

(c) Upon finding that a motor carrier of property is willfully violating this section after being advised that it is not operating in compliance with the laws of this state, the court may issue an injunction to stop the carrier's continued operation.

(d) A member of the Department of the California Highway Patrol may impound a vehicle or combination of vehicles operated by a motor carrier of property, when the vehicle or combination of vehicles is found upon a highway, any public lands, or an offstreet parking facility and the motor carrier is found to be in violation of this section. For purposes of this subdivision, the vehicle shall be released to the registered owner or authorized agent only after the registered owner or authorized agent furnishes the Department of the California Highway Patrol with proof of current registration, a currently valid driver's license of the appropriate class to operate the vehicle or combination of vehicles, and proof of compliance with this division. The registered owner or authorized agent is responsible for all towing and storage charges related to the impoundment.

DIVISION 15.   SIZE, WEIGHT, AND LOAD

CHAPTER 2.   WIDTH

35100. Total Outside Width

(a) The total outside width of any vehicle or its load shall not exceed 102 inches, except as otherwise provided in this chapter.

(b) Notwithstanding any other provision of law, safety devices which the Secretary of Transportation determines to be necessary for the safe and efficient operation of motor vehicles shall not be included in the calculation of width as specified in subdivision (a).

(c) Any city or county may, by ordinance, prohibit a combination of vehicles of a total width in excess of 96 inches upon highways under its jurisdiction. The ordinance shall not be effective until appropriate signs are erected indicating the streets affected.

35100.1. Width Measurement

For purposes of subdivision (a) of Section 35100, the following apply:

(a) The metric equivalent of 102 inches, 2.6 meters, meets the requirement of Section 35100.

(b) The width measurement of any vehicle with side walls shall be made from the outside wall of the two opposite sides of the vehicle.

35101. Pneumatic Tires: Maximum Width: Performance Standards

When any vehicle is equipped with pneumatic tires, the maximum width from the outside of one wheel and tire to the outside of the opposite outer wheel and tire shall not exceed 108 inches, but the outside width of the body of the vehicle or the load thereon shall not exceed 102 inches.

Vehicles manufactured, reconstructed, or modified after the effective date of amendments to this section enacted during the 1983 portion of the 1983-84 Regular Session of the Legislature, to utilize the 102 inch maximum width dimension, shall be equipped with axles, tires, and wheels of sufficient width to adequately and safely stabilize the vehicle. The CHP shall conduct tests relating to the dynamic stability of vehicles utilizing body widths over 96 inches, up to and including 102 inches, to determine the necessity for establishing performance standards under the authority of Section 34500. Such standards if established shall be consistent with width standards established by or under the authority of the US DOT.

35102. Loose Loads-Agricultural Products
When any vehicle carries a load of loosely piled agricultural products such as hay, straw, or leguminous plants in bulk but not crated, baled, boxed, or sacked, such load of loosely piled material and any loading racks retaining the same shall not exceed 120 inches in width.

35103. Recreational Vehicles; Exceptions to Maximum Width Limits
(a) A vehicle used for recreational purposes may exceed the maximum width established under Section 35100 if the excess width is attributable to an appurtenance, excluding a safety device, that does not exceed six inches beyond either sidewall of the vehicle.

(b) For the purposes of subdivision (a), an appurtenance is an integral part of a vehicle and includes, but is not limited to, awnings, grab handles, lighting equipment, cameras, and vents. An appurtenance may not be used as a load carrying device. *(AD '03)*

35104. Vehicles Limited to 120-Inch Width
The limitations as to width do not apply, to the following vehicles except that these vehicles shall not exceed a width of 120 inches:

(a) Special mobile equipment.

(b) Special construction or highway maintenance equipment.

(c) Motor vehicles designed for, and used exclusively to, haul feed for livestock that are exempted from registration by subdivision (c) of Section 36102, except when operated on a highway during darkness.

35106. Motor Coaches and Buses
(a) Motor coaches or buses may have a maximum width not exceeding 102 inches.

(b) Notwithstanding subdivision (a), motor coaches or buses operated under the jurisdiction of the Public Utilities Commission in urban or suburban service may have a maximum outside width not exceeding 104 inches, when approved by order of the Public Utilities Commission for use on routes designated by it. Motor coaches or buses operated by common carriers of passengers for hire in urban or suburban service and not under the jurisdiction of the Public Utilities Commission may have a maximum outside width not exceeding 104 inches. *(AM '06)*

35109. Projecting Lights, Mirrors, or Devices
Lights, mirrors, or devices which are required to be mounted upon a vehicle under this code may extend beyond the permissible width of the vehicle to a distance not exceeding 10 inches on each side of the vehicle.

35110. Projecting Equipment
(a) Door handles, hinges, cable cinchers, chain binders, aerodynamic devices, and holders for the display of placards warning of hazardous materials may extend three inches on each side of the vehicle.

(b) For purposes of this section, "aerodynamic devices" means devices using technologies that minimize drag and improve airflow over an entire tractor-trailer vehicle. These include gap fairings that reduce turbulence between the tractor and trailer, side skirts that minimize wind under the trailer, and rear fairings that reduce turbulence and pressure drop at the rear of the trailer, provided that these devices shall not adversely impact the vehicle's swept width and turning characteristics and that the primary purpose of the device is not for advertising. *(AM '12)*

35111. Loads on Passenger Vehicles
No passenger vehicle shall be operated on any highway with any load carried thereon extending beyond the line of the fenders on its left side or more than six inches beyond the line of the fenders on its right side.

CHAPTER 3. HEIGHT

35250. Maximum Height: Exceptions

No vehicle or load shall exceed a height of 14 feet measured from the surface upon which the vehicle stands, except that a doubledeck bus may not exceed a height of 14 feet, 3 inches. Any vehicle or load which exceeds a height of 13 feet, 6 inches, shall only be operated on those highways where deemed to be safe by the owner of the vehicle or the entity operating the bus.

35252. Vertical Clearance Measuring Device

(a) A pilot car may operate a vertical clearance measuring device with a height in excess of 14 feet when escorting a permitted overheight load. The pilot car may also operate the vertical clearance measuring device when surveying a route for a permitted overheight load.

(b) Any vertical measuring device used by a pilot car shall be designed and operated so as to avoid any damages to overhead structures. The measuring device shall be securely affixed to the pilot car, and shall be operated in a manner that does not create a hazard to surrounding traffic.

(c) The operator of the pilot car shall not reduce the vehicle's speed more than 20 miles per hour below the posted speed limit on the roadway to measure overhead clearance, nor exit the vehicle to measure the clearance of overhead structures from a vantage point on or above the roadway.

CHAPTER 4. LENGTH

35400. General Limitation - Length

(a) A vehicle may not exceed a length of 40 feet.

(b) This section does not apply to any of the following:

(1) A vehicle used in a combination of vehicles when the excess length is caused by auxiliary parts, equipment, or machinery not used as space to carry any part of the load, except that the combination of vehicles shall not exceed the length provided for combination vehicles.

(2) A vehicle, when the excess length is caused by any parts necessary to comply with the fender and mudguard regulations of this code.

(3)(A) An articulated bus or articulated trolley coach that does not exceed a length of 60 feet.

(B) An articulated bus or articulated trolley coach described in subparagraph (A) may be equipped with a folding device attached to the front of the bus or trolley if the device is designed and used exclusively for transporting bicycles. The device, including any bicycles transported thereon, shall be mounted in a manner that does not materially affect efficiency or visibility of vehicle safety equipment, and shall not extend more than 36 inches from the front body of the bus or trolley coach when fully deployed. The handlebars of a bicycle that is transported on a device described in this subparagraph shall not extend more than 42 inches from the front of the bus.

(4) A semitrailer while being towed by a motortruck or truck tractor, if the distance from the kingpin to the rearmost axle of the semitrailer does not exceed 40 feet for semitrailers having two or more axles, or 38 feet for semitrailers having one axle if the semitrailer does not, exclusive of attachments, extend forward of the rear of the cab of the motortruck or truck tractor.

(5) A bus or house car when the excess length is caused by the projection of a front safety bumper or a rear safety bumper, or both. The safety bumper shall not cause the length of the vehicle to exceed the maximum legal limit by more than one foot in the front and one foot in the rear. For the purposes of this chapter, "safety bumper" means any device that is fitted on an existing bumper or which replaces the bumper and is constructed, treated, or manufactured to absorb energy upon impact.

(6) A schoolbus, when the excess length is caused by the projection of a crossing control arm. For the purposes of this chapter, "crossing control arm" means an extendable and retractable device fitted to the front of a schoolbus that is designed to impede movement of pupils exiting the schoolbus directly in front of the schoolbus so that pupils are visible to the driver while they are moving in front of the schoolbus. An operator of a schoolbus shall not extend a crossing control arm while the schoolbus is in motion. Except when activated, a crossing control arm shall not cause the maximum length of the schoolbus to be extended

by more than 10 inches, inclusive of any front safety bumper. Use of a crossing control arm by the operator of a schoolbus does not, in and of itself, fulfill his or her responsibility to ensure the safety of students crossing a highway or private road pursuant to Section 22112.

(7) A bus, when the excess length is caused by a device, located in front of the front axle, for lifting wheelchairs into the bus. That device shall not cause the length of the bus to be extended by more than 18 inches, inclusive of any front safety bumper.

(8) A bus, when the excess length is caused by a device attached to the rear of the bus designed and used exclusively for the transporting of bicycles. This device may be up to 10 feet in length, if the device, along with any other device permitted pursuant to this section, does not cause the total length of the bus, including any device or load, to exceed 50 feet.

(9) A bus operated by a public agency or a passenger stage corporation, as defined in Section 226 of the Public Utilities Code, used in transit system service, other than a schoolbus, when the excess length is caused by a folding device attached to the front of the bus which is designed and used exclusively for transporting bicycles. The device, including any bicycles transported thereon, shall be mounted in a manner that does not materially affect efficiency or visibility of vehicle safety equipment, and shall not extend more than 36 inches from the front body of the bus when fully deployed. The handlebars of a bicycle that is transported on a device described in this paragraph shall not extend more than 42 inches from the front of the bus. A device described in this paragraph may not be used on a bus that, exclusive of the device, exceeds 40 feet in length or on a bus having a device attached to the rear of the bus pursuant to paragraph (8).

(10)(A) A bus of a length of up to 45 feet when operating on those highways specified in subdivision (a) of Section 35401.5. The Department of Transportation or local authorities, with respect to highways under their respective jurisdictions, may not deny reasonable access to a bus of a length of up to 45 feet between the highways specified in subdivision (a) of Section 35401.5 and points of loading and unloading for motor carriers of passengers as required by the federal Intermodal Surface Transportation Efficiency Act of 1991 (P.L. 102-240).

(B) A bus operated by a public agency and on those highways specified in subparagraph (A) may be equipped with a folding device attached to the front of the bus that is designed and used exclusively for transporting bicycles. The device, including all bicycles transported thereon, may be mounted in a manner that does not materially affect efficiency or visibility of vehicle safety equipment, and may not extend more than 36 inches from the front body of the bus when fully deployed. The handlebars of a bicycle that is transported on a device described in this subparagraph may not extend more than 42 inches from the front of the bus. The total length of the bus, including the folding device or load, may not exceed 48.5 feet. A Route Review Committee, established under this subparagraph, shall review the routes where a public agency proposes to operate a 45-foot bus equipped with a front mounted bicycle rack. The Route Review Committee shall be comprised of one member from the public agency appointed by the general manager of the public agency; one member who is a traffic engineer and is employed and selected by the public agency that has jurisdiction over the largest proportional share of routes among all affected agencies; and one member appointed by the labor organization that is the exclusive representative of the bus drivers of the public agency. If there is no exclusive representative of the bus drivers, a bus driver member shall be chosen by a majority vote of the bus drivers employed by the agency. The members of the Route Review Committee shall be selected not more than 30 days after receipt of a public agency proposal to equip a 45-foot bus with a front mounted bicycle rack. The review shall include a field review of the proposed routes. The purpose of the Route Review Committee is to ensure the safe operation of a 45-foot bus that is equipped with a front mounted bicycle rack. The Route Review Committee, by a unanimous vote, shall make a determination of which routes are suitable for the safe operation of a 45-foot bus that is equipped with a front mounted bicycle rack. These determinations shall be consistent with the operating requirements specified in subparagraph (A). It is the intent of the Legislature that the field review required under this subparagraph include consultation with traffic engineers from affected public agencies that have jurisdiction over segments of the route or routes under review, to ensure coordination with all effected state and local public road agencies that may potentially be impacted due to the operation of a 45-foot bus with a front mounted bicycle rack.

(11)(A) A house car of a length of up to 45 feet when operating on the National System of Interstate and Defense Highways or when using those portions of federal aid primary system highways that have been qualified by the United States Secretary of Transportation for that use, or when using routes appropriately identified by the Department of Transportation or local authorities, with respect to highways under their respective jurisdictions.

(B) A house car described in subparagraph (A) may be operated on a highway that provides reasonable access to facilities for purposes limited to fuel, food, and lodging when that access is consistent with the safe operation of the vehicle and when the facility is within one road mile of identified points of ingress and egress to or from highways specified in subparagraph (A) for use by that vehicle.

(C) As used in this paragraph and paragraph (10), "reasonable access" means access substantially similar to that authorized for combinations of vehicles pursuant to subdivision (c) of Section 35401.5.

(D) Any access route established by a local authority pursuant to subdivision (d) of Section 35401.5 is open for access by a house car of a length of up to 45 feet. In addition, local authorities may establish a process whereby access to services by house cars of a length of up to 45 feet may be applied for upon a route not previously established as an access route. The denial of a request for access to services shall be only on the basis of safety and an engineering analysis of the proposed access route. In lieu of processing an access application, local authorities, with respect to highways under their jurisdiction, may provide signing, mapping, or a listing of highways, as necessary, to indicate the use of these specific routes by a house car of a length of up to 45 feet.

(c) The Legislature, by increasing the maximum permissible kingpin to rearmost axle distance to 40 feet effective January 1, 1987, as provided in paragraph (4) of subdivision (b), does not intend this action to be considered a precedent for any future increases in truck size and length limitations.

(d) Any transit bus equipped with a folding device installed on or after January 1, 1999, that is permitted under subparagraph (B) of paragraph (3) of subdivision (b) or under paragraph (9) of subdivision (b) shall be additionally equipped with any of the following:

(1) An indicator light that is visible to the driver and is activated whenever the folding device is in an extended position.

(2) Any other device or mechanism that provides notice to the driver that the folding device is in an extended position.

(3) A mechanism that causes the folding device to retract automatically from an extended position.

(e)(1) A person may not improperly or unsafely mount a bicycle on a device described in subparagraph (B) of paragraph (3) of subdivision (b), or in paragraph (9) or (10) of subdivision (b).

(2) Notwithstanding subdivision (a) of Section 23114 or subdivision (a) of Section 24002 or any other provision of law, when a bicycle is improperly or unsafely loaded by a passenger onto a transit bus, the passenger, and not the driver, is liable for any violation of this code that is attributable to the improper or unlawful loading of the bicycle. *(AM '01-'03)*

35400.6. Fifth-Wheel Travel Trailer Exceptions [Added Stats. 2013]
(a) Subdivision (a) of Section 35400 does not apply to a fifth-wheel travel trailer that does not exceed the following lengths:

(1) Forty-eight feet in length from the foremost point of the trailer to the rear extremity of the trailer.

(2)(A) For a fifth-wheel travel trailer with a single axle, 38 feet in length from the kingpin to the rearmost axle.

(B) For a fifth-wheel travel trailer with two or more axles, 40 feet in length from the kingpin to the rearmost axle.

(b) A manufacturer of a fifth-wheel travel trailer described by subdivision (a) shall include in the delivery documents the information necessary to register that fifth-wheel travel trailer, including its overall length pursuant to paragraph (1) of subdivision (a) and a declaration that its length is in compliance with subparagraph (A) or subparagraph (B) of paragraph (2) of subdivision (a). The dealer may reject acceptance of the fifth-wheel travel trailer if this documentation is not provided. *(AD '13)*

35401. Combinations of Vehicles

(a) Except as provided in subdivisions (b), (c), and (d), a combination of vehicles coupled together, including attachments, may not exceed a total length of 65 feet.

(b)(1) A combination of vehicles coupled together, including attachments, that consists of a truck tractor, a semitrailer, and a semitrailer or trailer, may not exceed a total length of 75 feet, if the length of neither the semitrailers nor the trailer in the combination of vehicles exceeds 28 feet 6 inches.

(2) A B-train assembly is excluded from the measurement of semitrailer length when used between the first and second semitrailers of a truck tractor-semitrailer-semitrailer combination of vehicles. However, if there is no second semitrailer mounted to the B-train assembly, it shall be included in the length measurement of the semitrailer to which it is attached.

(c)(1) A tow truck in combination with a single disabled vehicle or a single abandoned vehicle that is authorized to travel on the highways by this chapter is exempt from subdivision (a) when operating under a valid annual transportation permit.

(2) A tow truck, in combination with a disabled or abandoned combination of vehicles that are authorized to travel on the highways by this chapter, is exempt from subdivision (a) when operating under a valid annual transportation permit and within a 100-mile radius of the location specified in the permit.

(3) A tow truck may exceed the 100-mile radius restriction imposed under paragraph (2) if a single trip permit is obtained from the Department of Transportation.

(d) A city or county may, by ordinance, prohibit a combination of vehicles of a total length in excess of 60 feet upon highways under its respective jurisdiction. The ordinance may not be effective until appropriate signs are erected indicating either the streets affected by the ordinance or the streets not affected, as the local authority determines will best serve to give notice of the ordinance.

(e) A city or county, upon a determination that a highway or portion of highway under its jurisdiction cannot, in consideration of public safety, sustain the operation of trailers or semitrailers of the maximum kingpin to rearmost axle distances permitted under Section 35400, may, by ordinance, establish lesser distances consistent with the maximum distances that the highway or highway portion can sustain, except that a city or county may not restrict the kingpin to rearmost axle measurement to less than 38 feet on those highways or highway portions. A city or county considering the adoption of an ordinance shall consider, but not be limited to, consideration of, all of the following:

(1) A comparison of the operating characteristics of the vehicles to be limited as compared to operating characteristics of other vehicles regulated by this code.

(2) Actual traffic volume.

(3) Frequency of accidents.

(4) Any other relevant data.

In addition, the city or county may appoint an advisory committee consisting of local representatives of those interests that are likely to be affected and shall consider the recommendations of the advisory committee in adopting the ordinance. The ordinance may not be effective until appropriate signs are erected indicating the highways or highway portions affected by the ordinance.

This subdivision shall only become operative upon the adoption of an enabling ordinance by a city or county.

(f) Whenever, in the judgment of the Department of Transportation, a state highway cannot, in consideration of public safety, sustain the operation of trailers or semitrailers of the maximum kingpin to rearmost axle distances permitted under Section 35400, the director, in consultation with the Department of the California Highway Patrol, shall compile data on total traffic volume, frequency of use by vehicles covered by this subdivision, accidents involving these vehicles, and other relevant data to assess whether these vehicles are a threat to public safety and should be excluded from the highway or highway segment. The study, containing the conclusions and recommendations of the director, shall be submitted to the Secretary of the Business, Transportation and Housing Agency. Unless otherwise notified by the secretary, the director shall hold public hearings in accordance with the procedures set forth in Article 3 (commencing with Section 35650) of Chapter 5 for the purpose of determining the maximum kingpin to rear axle length, which shall be not less than 38 feet, that the highway or highway segment can sustain without unreasonable threat to the safety of the public. Upon the basis of the findings, the Director of Transportation shall declare in writing the maximum kingpin to rear axle lengths which can be maintained with safety upon the highway. Following the declaration of maximum lengths as provided by this subdivision, the Department of Transportation shall erect suitable signs at each end of the affected portion of the highway and at any other points that the Department of Transportation determines to be necessary to give adequate notice of the length limits.

The Department of Transportation, in consultation with the Department of the California Highway Patrol, shall compile traffic volume, geometric, and other relevant data, to assess the maximum kingpin to rearmost axle distance of vehicle combinations appropriate for those state highways or portion of highways, affected by this section, that cannot safely accommodate trailers or semitrailers of the maximum kingpin to rearmost axle distances permitted under Section 35400. The department shall erect suitable signs appropriately restricting truck travel on those highways, or portions of highways.

(g) This section shall become operative on January 1, 2010. *(AD '74; AM '82, '83, '84, '86, '88, '91, '02, '04; AM-RP-AD '06; AM '08)*

35401.3. Combination of Vehicles: Additional Exceptions

(a) Notwithstanding subdivisions (a) and (b) of Section 35401, a combination of vehicles designed and used to transport motor vehicles, camper units, or boats, which consists of a motortruck and stinger-steered semitrailer, shall be allowed a length of up to 70 feet if the kingpin is at least 3 feet behind the rear drive axle of the motortruck. This combination shall not be subject to subdivision (a) of Section 35411, but the load upon the rear vehicle of the combination shall not extend more than 6 feet 6 inches beyond the allowable length of the vehicle.

(b) A combination of vehicles designed and used to transport motor vehicles, camper units, or boats, which consists of a motortruck and stinger-steered semitrailer, shall be allowed a length of up to 75 feet if all of the following conditions are maintained:

(1) The distance from the steering axle to the rear drive axle of the motortruck does not exceed 24 feet.

(2) The kingpin is at least 5 feet behind the rear drive axle of the motortruck.

(3) The distance from the kingpin to the rear axle of the semitrailer does not exceed 34 feet except that the distance from the kingpin to the rear axle of a triple axle semitrailer does not exceed 36 feet.

This combination shall not be subject to subdivision (a) of Section 35411, but the load upon the rear vehicle of the combination shall not extend more than 6 feet 6 inches beyond the allowable length of the vehicle. *(AM '98, '00)*

35401.5. Additional Exceptions: Combination of Vehicles

(a) A combination of vehicles consisting of a truck tractor and semitrailer, or of a truck tractor, semitrailer, and trailer, is not subject to the limitations of Sections 35400 and 35401, when operating on the Dwight D. Eisenhower National System of Interstate and Defense Highways or when using those portions of federal-aid primary system highways that have been qualified by the United States Secretary of Transportation for that use, or when using routes appropriately identified by the Department of Transportation or local authorities as provided in subdivision (c) or (d), if all of the following conditions are met:

(1) The length of the semitrailer in exclusive combination with a truck tractor does not exceed 48 feet. A semitrailer not more than 53 feet in length shall satisfy this requirement when configured with two or more rear axles, the rearmost of which is located 40 feet or less from the kingpin or when configured with a single axle which is located 38 feet or less from the kingpin. For purposes of this paragraph, a motortruck used in combination with a semitrailer, when that combination of vehicles is engaged solely in the transportation of motor vehicles, camper units, or boats, is considered to be a truck tractor.

(2) Neither the length of the semitrailer nor the length of the trailer when simultaneously in combination with a truck tractor exceeds 28 feet 6 inches.

(b) Subdivisions (b), (d), and (e) of Section 35402 do not apply to combinations of vehicles operated subject to the exemptions provided by this section.

(c) Combinations of vehicles operated pursuant to subdivision (a) may also use highways not specified in subdivision (a) that provide reasonable access to terminals and facilities for purposes limited to fuel, food, lodging, and repair when that access is consistent with the safe operation of the combinations of vehicles and when the facility is within one road mile of identified points of ingress and egress to or from highways specified in subdivision (a) for use by those combinations of vehicles.

(d) The Department of Transportation or local authorities may establish a process whereby access to terminals or services may be applied for upon a route not previously established as an access route. The denial of a request for access to terminals and services shall be only on the basis of safety and an engineering analysis of the proposed access route. If a written request for access has been properly submitted and has not been acted upon within 90 days of receipt by the department or the appropriate local agency, the access shall be deemed automatically approved. Thereafter, the route shall be deemed open for access by all other vehicles of the same type regardless of ownership. In lieu of processing an access application, the Department of Transportation or local authorities with respect to highways under their respective jurisdictions may provide signing, mapping, or a listing of highways as necessary to indicate the use of specific routes as terminal access routes. For purposes of this subdivision, "terminal" means either of the following:

(1) A facility where freight originates, terminates, or is handled in the transportation process.

(2) A facility where a motor carrier maintains operating facilities.

(e) Nothing in subdivision (c) or (d) authorizes state or local agencies to require permits of terminal operators or to charge terminal operators fees for the purpose of attaining access for vehicles described in this section.

(f) Notwithstanding subdivision (d), the limitations of access specified in that subdivision do not apply to licensed carriers of household goods when directly enroute to or from a point of loading or unloading of household goods, if travel on highways other than those specified in subdivision (a) is necessary and incidental to the shipment of the household goods.

(g)(1) Notwithstanding Sections 35400 and 35401, a combination of vehicles consisting of a truck tractor semitrailer combination with a kingpin to rearmost axle measurement limit of not more than 46 feet, a trailer length of not more than 56 feet, and used exclusively or primarily in connection with motorsports, may operate on the routes identified in subdivision (a) as well as on any other routes authorized for that purpose by the Department of Transportation in consultation with the Department of the California Highway Patrol. As used in this subdivision, "motorsports" means an event, and all activities leading up to that event, including, but not limited to, administration, testing, practice, promotion, and merchandising, that is sanctioned under the auspices of the member organizations of the Automobile Competition Committee for the United States.

(2)(A) The Department of Transportation shall conduct a field test of the tractor truck semitrailer combination authorized under paragraph (1) for motorsport trucks with a trailer length of 56 feet to evaluate their performance on various segments of the National Network and transition routes. The Department of Transportation shall, no later than January 1, 2014, submit a report to the Legislature in compliance with Section 9795 of the Government Code that includes the results of the field test and a recommendation, in consultation with the Department of the California Highway Patrol, as to whether the 56 foot trailer length should be reauthorized.

(B) Notwithstanding Section 10231.5 of the Government Code, the requirement for submitting a report under this paragraph is inoperative on January 1, 2018.

(3) This subdivision shall remain in effect only until January 1, 2016, and as of that date is repealed, unless a later enacted statute, that is enacted before January 1, 2016, deletes or extends that date.

(h) The Legislature finds and declares both of the following:

(1) In authorizing the use of 53-foot semitrailers, it is the intent of the Legislature to conform with Section 31111(b)(1)(C) of Title 49 of the United States Code by permitting the continued use of semitrailers of the dimensions as those that were in actual and legal use on December 1, 1982, and does not intend this action to be a precedent for future increases in the parameters of any of those vehicles that would adversely affect the turning maneuverability of vehicle combinations.

(2) In authorizing the department to issue special transportation permits for motorsports, it is the intent of the Legislature to conform with Section 31111(b)(1)(F) of Title 49 of the United States Code. It is also the intent of the Legislature that this action not be a precedent for future increases in the distance from the kingpin to the rearmost axle of semitrailers and trailers that would adversely affect the turning maneuverability of vehicle combinations. *(AM '12)*

35406. Loads

(a) Except as provided in subdivision (b), the load on any vehicle operated alone, or the load upon the front vehicle of a combination of vehicles, shall not extend more than three feet beyond the foremost part of the front tires of the vehicle or the front bumper of the vehicle, if it is equipped with a front bumper.

(b) When the load is composed solely of vehicles, the load upon the front vehicle of a combination of vehicles shall not extend more than four feet beyond the foremost part of the front tires of the vehicle or the front bumper of the vehicle, if it is equipped with a front bumper.

35407.5. Heel-Boom Log Loader

Section 35406 and subdivisions (a) and (d) of Section 35407 do not apply to the booms or masts of a self-propelled heel-boom log loader first sold in this state prior to January 1, 1988, if all of the following conditions are met:

(a) A system of mirrors or other view enhancements permits the driver to see in any area blocked from view.

(b) The log loader is operated together with a four wheeled lead vehicle which remains a reasonable distance ahead to guide the movement of the log loader.

(c) Two-way radio communication equipment is maintained in good working condition on the log loader and the pilot car, and is used between those vehicles during movement upon any highway.

35408. Front Bumper

In no event shall a front bumper on a motor vehicle be constructed or installed so as to project more than two feet forward of the foremost part of either the fenders or cab structure or radiator, whichever extends farthest toward the front of such vehicle.

35410. Projections to the Rear

The load upon any motor vehicle alone or an independent load only upon a trailer or semitrailer shall not extend to the rear beyond the last point of support for a greater distance than that equal to two-thirds of the length of the wheelbase of the vehicle carrying such load, except that the wheelbase of a semitrailer shall be considered as the distance between the rearmost axle of the towing vehicle and the rearmost axle of the semitrailer.

35411. Combination of Vehicles: Loads

(a) Except as provided in subdivision (b), the load on any combination of vehicles shall not exceed 75 feet measured from the front extremity of the front vehicle or load to the rear extremity of the last vehicle or load.

(b) The load upon any combination of vehicles operating pursuant to Section 35401 or 35401.5, when the overall length of the combination of vehicles exceeds 75 feet, shall be confined within the exterior dimensions of the vehicles.

CHAPTER 5. WEIGHT

35550. Maximum Weight on Single Axle or Wheels

(a) The gross weight imposed upon the highway by the wheels on any one axle of a vehicle shall not exceed 20,000 pounds and the gross weight upon any one wheel, or wheels, supporting one end of an axle, and resting upon the roadway, shall not exceed 10,500 pounds.

(b) The gross weight limit provided for weight bearing upon any one wheel, or wheels, supporting one end of an axle shall not apply to vehicles the loads of which consist of livestock.

(c) The maximum wheel load is the lesser of the following:

(1) The load limit established by the tire manufacturer, as molded on at least one sidewall of the tire.

(2) A load of 620 pounds per lateral inch of tire width, as determined by the manufacturer's rated tire width as molded on at least one sidewall of the tire for all axles except the steering axle, in which case paragraph (1) applies.

35551. Computation of Allowable Gross Weight

(a) Except as otherwise provided in this section or Section 35551.5, the total gross weight in pounds imposed on the highway by any group of two or more consecutive axles shall not exceed that given for the respective distance. (See Code for tables)

(b) In addition to the weights specified in subdivision (a), two consecutive sets of tandem axles may carry a gross weight of 34,000 pounds each if the overall distance between the first and last axles of the consecutive sets of tandem axles is 36 feet or more. The gross weight of each set of tandem axles shall not exceed 34,000 pounds and the gross weight of the two consecutive sets of tandem axles shall not exceed 68,000 pounds.

(c) The distance between axles shall be measured to the nearest whole foot. When a fraction is exactly six inches, the next larger whole foot shall be used.

(d) Nothing contained in this section shall affect the right to prohibit the use of any highway or any bridge or other structure thereon in the manner and to the extent specified in Article 4 and Article 5 of this chapter.

(e) The gross weight limits expressed by this section and Section 35550 shall include all enforcement tolerances.

35551.5. Alternate Method of Computation of Allowable Gross Weight

(a) The provisions of this section shall apply only to combinations of vehicles which contain a trailer or semitrailer. Each vehicle in such combination of vehicles, and every such combination of vehicles, shall comply with either Section 35551 or with subdivisions (b), (c), and (d) of this section.

(b) The gross weight imposed upon the highway by the wheels on any one axle of a vehicle shall not exceed 18,000 pounds and the gross weight upon any one wheel, or wheels, supporting one end of an axle and resting upon the roadway, shall not exceed 9,500 pounds, except that the gross weight imposed upon the highway by the wheels on any front steering axle of a motor vehicle shall not exceed 12,500 pounds. The gross weight limit provided for weight bearing upon any one wheel, or wheels, supporting one end of an axle shall not apply to vehicles the loads of which consist of livestock. The following vehicles are exempt from the front axle weight limits specified in this subdivision:

(1) Trucks transporting vehicles.

(2) Trucks transporting livestock.

(3) Dump trucks.

(4) Cranes.

(5) Buses.

(6) Transit mix concrete or cement trucks, and trucks that mix concrete or cement at, or adjacent to, a jobsite.

(7) Motor vehicles that are not commercial vehicles.

(8) Vehicle operated by any public utility furnishing electricity, gas, water, or telephone service.

(9) Trucks or truck tractors with a front axle at least four feet to the rear of the foremost part of the truck or truck tractor, not including the front bumper.

(10) Trucks transporting garbage, rubbish, or refuse.

(11) Trucks equipped with a fifth wheel when towing a semitrailer.

(12) Tank trucks which have a cargo capacity of at least 1,500 gallons.

(13) Trucks transporting bulk grains or bulk livestock feed.

(c) The total gross weight with load imposed on the highway by any group of two or more consecutive axles of a vehicle in such combination of vehicles or of such combination of vehicles where the distance between the first and last axles of the two or more consecutive axles is 18 feet or less shall not exceed that given for the respective distance in the following table:

Distance in feet between first and last axles of group	Allowed load in pounds on group of axles
4	32,000
5	32,000
6	32,200
7	32,900
8	33,600
9	34,300
10	35,000
11	35,700
12	36,400
13	37,100
14	43,200
15	44,000
16	44,800
17	45,600
18	46,400

(d) The total gross weight with load imposed on the highway by any vehicle in such combination of vehicles or of such combination of vehicles where the distance between the first and last axles is more than 18 feet shall not exceed that given for the respective distances in the following table:

Distance in feet	Allowed load in pounds
19	47,200
20	48,000
21	48,800
22	49,600
23	50,400
24	51,200
25	55,250
26	56,100
27	56,950
28	57,800
29	58,650
30	59,500
31	60,350
32	61,200
33	62,050
34	62,900
35	63,750
36	64,600
37	65,450
38	66,300
39	68,000
40	70,000
41	72,000
42	73,280
43	73,280
44	73,280
45	73,280

```
46 . . . . . . . . . . . . . . . . . . . . . . . . . . . . . . . . . . . . . . . .73,280
47 . . . . . . . . . . . . . . . . . . . . . . . . . . . . . . . . . . . . . . . .73,280
48 . . . . . . . . . . . . . . . . . . . . . . . . . . . . . . . . . . . . . . . .73,280
49 . . . . . . . . . . . . . . . . . . . . . . . . . . . . . . . . . . . . . . . .73,280
50 . . . . . . . . . . . . . . . . . . . . . . . . . . . . . . . . . . . . . . . .73,280
51 . . . . . . . . . . . . . . . . . . . . . . . . . . . . . . . . . . . . . . . .73,280
52 . . . . . . . . . . . . . . . . . . . . . . . . . . . . . . . . . . . . . . . .73,600
53 . . . . . . . . . . . . . . . . . . . . . . . . . . . . . . . . . . . . . . . .74,400
54 . . . . . . . . . . . . . . . . . . . . . . . . . . . . . . . . . . . . . . . .75,200
55 . . . . . . . . . . . . . . . . . . . . . . . . . . . . . . . . . . . . . . . .76,000
56 or over . . . . . . . . . . . . . . . . . . . . . . . . . . . . . . . . .76,800
```

(e) The distance between axles shall be measured to the nearest whole foot. When a fraction is exactly six inches, the next larger whole foot shall be used.

(f) The gross weight limits expressed by this section shall include all enforcement tolerances.

(g) Nothing in this section shall affect the right to prohibit the use of any highway or any bridge or other structure thereon in the manner and to the extent specified in Article 4 (commencing with Section 35700) and Article 5 (commencing with Section 35750) of Chapter 5 of Division 15.

(h) The Legislature, in enacting this section, does not intend to increase, and this section shall not be construed to allow, statutory weights any greater than existed prior to January 1, 1976.

35552. Vehicles Transporting Logs

(a) This section applies only to trucks and vehicle combinations while transporting loads composed solely of logs.

(b) One set of tandem axles of such a truck or vehicle combination shall be deemed to be in compliance with Section 35551 if the total gross weight of 34,000 pounds on such a set that is permitted by Section 35551 is not exceeded by more than 1,500 pounds. In addition, such a truck and vehicle combination that has two consecutive sets of tandem axles shall be deemed to be in compliance with Section 35551 if such consecutive sets of tandem axles do not carry a combined total gross weight of more than 69,000 pounds, if the total gross weight on any one such set does not exceed 35,500 pounds, and if the overall distance between the first and last axle of such consecutive sets of tandem axles is 34 feet or more. All such truck and vehicle combinations shall be subject to all other provisions of Section 35551 or any other provision made applicable to the total gross weight of such a truck or vehicle combination in lieu of Section 35551.

(c) The gross weight limits expressed in this section shall include all enforcement tolerances.

(d) If any total gross weight permitted by this section is exceeded, the allowed weight in pounds set forth in subdivision (a) of Section 35551 shall be the maximum permitted weight for purposes of determining the amount of fine for such violation as specified in the table in Section 42030; except that, whenever the violation is for exceeding the total gross weight for two consecutive sets of tandem axles, and if the overall distance between the first and last axle of such sets is 34 feet or more, the allowed weight on the two consecutive sets shall be 68,000 pounds.

(e) This section shall have no application to highways which are a part of the National System of Interstate and Defense Highways (as referred to in subdivision (a) of Section 108 of the Federal-aid Highway Act of 1956).

This section may be cited as the Christensen-Belotti Act.

35554. Gross Weight Limit for Bus Axle [Repeals 1-1-2015; A Second Version Follows]]

(a)(1) Notwithstanding Section 35550, the gross weight on any one axle of a bus shall not exceed 20,500 pounds.

(2) A transit bus procured through a solicitation process pursuant to which a solicitation was issued before January 1, 2013, or though a solicitation process pursuant to subdivision (d) is not subject to this subdivision.

(b) A transit bus is not subject to Section 35550.

(c) A transit bus shall not operate on the Dwight D. Eisenhower System of Interstate and Defense Highways in excess of the weight limitation for transit buses specified in federal law.

(d)(1) A publicly owned or operated transit system or an operator of a transit system under contract with a publicly owned or operated transit system shall not procure, through a solicitation process pursuant to which a solicitation is issued on or after January 1, 2013, a transit bus whose weight on any single axle exceeds 20,500 pounds except as follows:

(A) It may procure and operate a new bus exceeding 20,500 pounds that is of the same or lesser weight than the bus it is replacing.

(B) It may procure and operate a new transit bus exceeding 20,500 pounds in order to incorporate a new fleet class into its inventory if its governing board adopts a finding at a public hearing that the fleet class expansion or change in fleet classes is necessary to address a need to serve a new or existing market pursuant to its most recently adopted short-range transit plan, or to meet a federal, state, or regional statutory or regulatory requirement, and includes a consideration of vehicle needs and fleet size.

(2) If the governing board of the publicly owned or operated transit system holds a public hearing to consider a procurement made pursuant to subparagraph (A) or (B) of paragraph (1), the board shall provide written notice to those cities and counties on whose roads the bus would travel of the public hearing at which this procurement is to be considered and shall place in the public record any comment of concern the board receives about the procurement.

(3) For purposes of this subdivision "fleet class" means a group of transit buses designated by a publicly owned or operated transit system or an operator under contract with a publicly owned or operated transit system that owns those transit buses, if the transit buses have a combination of two or more of the following similar defining characteristics:

(A) Length.

(B) Seating capacity.

(C) Number of axles.

(D) Fuel or power system.

(E) Width.

(F) Structure.

(G) Equipment package.

(e) This section shall remain in effect only until January 1, 2015, and as of that date is repealed, unless a later enacted statute, that is enacted before January 1, 2015, deletes or extends that date. *(AM-RP-'12; A new version will be added 1-31-14)*

35555. Gross Weight Limit for Cotton Module Mover

(a) During the period commencing September 15 of each year and ending March 15 of the following year, the weight limitations of Section 35551 do not apply to any cotton module mover or any truck tractor pulling a semitrailer that is a cotton module mover, when operated as follows:

(1) Laterally across a state highway at grade of the state highway.

(2) Upon any county highway within the Counties of Butte, Colusa, Fresno, Glenn, Imperial, Kern, Kings, Madera, Merced, Riverside, Sacramento, San Benito, San Bernardino, San Joaquin, Stanislaus, Sutter, Tehama, Tulare, Yolo, and Yuba, except as prohibited or limited on county highways or portions thereof by resolution of the county board of supervisors having jurisdiction.

(b) A cotton module mover may be operated upon a state highway within the counties and during the period set forth in subdivision (a) if all of the following are met:

(1) The operator is in possession of a driver's license of the class required for operation of the mover.

(2) The mover is operated in compliance with Sections 24002 and 24012; Article 1 (commencing with Section 24250) of, Article 3 (commencing with Section 24600) of, Article 4 (commencing with Section 24800) of, Article 5 (commencing with Section 24950) of, Article 6 (commencing with 25100) of, Article 9 (commencing with 25350) of, Article 11 (commencing with 25450) of, Chapter 2 of Division 12; and Article 2 (commencing with 26450) and Article 3 (commencing with 26502) of Chapter 3 of Division 12.

(3) The mover does not exceed the maximum allowable gross axle weight for tandem axles set forth in Section 35551 by more than 6,000 pounds.

(4) The operator of a mover that exceeds the maximum allowable gross axle weight for tandem axle vehicles as set forth in Section 35551 shall possess a commercial driver's license as defined in subdivision (a) of Section 15210.

(c) This section does not apply to those highways designated by the United States Department of Transportation as national network routes. *(AD '80; AM '01)*

35655.   Violation of Decreased Restriction

(a) No person shall drive a vehicle on any state highway when the weight of the vehicle and load is greater than the maximum weight which the highway will sustain. Violations of this subdivision shall be punished in accordance with the schedule of fines set forth in Section 42030.

(b) Upon the trial of any person charged with a violation with respect to signs erected under Section 35654, proof of the determination and the maximum weight by the California Department of Transportation and the existence of the signs constitutes prima facie evidence of the maximum weight which the state highway will sustain.

35655.5.   Maximum Gross Weight; Portions of I-580

(a) Notwithstanding this article or any other provision of law, no vehicle, as described in Sections 410 and 655, with a gross weight of 9,000 pounds or more, shall be operated on the segment of Interstate Route 580 (I-580) that is located between Grand Avenue in the City of Oakland and the city limits of the City of San Leandro. This subdivision does not apply to passenger buses or paratransit vehicles.

(b) The Department of Transportation shall erect suitable signs at each end of the portion of highway described in subdivision (a) and at any other points that the department deems necessary to give adequate notice of the weight limit imposed under this section. *(AD '00)*

35753.   Violation of Decreased Restrictions

(a) No person shall drive a vehicle over any bridge, causeway, viaduct, trestle, or dam constituting a part of a highway when the weight of the vehicle and load thereon is greater than the maximum weight which the bridge or other structure with safety to itself will sustain. Violations of this subdivision shall be punished in accordance with the schedule of fines set forth in Section 42030.

(b) Upon the trial of any person charged with a violation with respect to a weight restriction sign erected pursuant to Section 35752, proof of the determination of the maximum weight by the California Department of Transportation and the existence of the weight restriction signs constitute prima facie evidence of the maximum weight which the bridge or other structure with safety to itself will sustain.

35783.   Possession of Permit

Every permit shall be carried in the vehicle or combination of vehicles to which it refers and shall be open to inspection of any peace officer, traffic officer, authorized agent of the California Department of Transportation, or an other officer or employee charged with the care or protection of such highways.

35783.5.   Removal or Covering of Warning Signs

Warning signs required by the terms of a permit shall either be removed from the vehicle or covered from the view of other motorists whenever the vehicle is operating without the load that required the permit.

35784.   Violation of Permit Misdemeanor: Exception

(a) Except as provided in subdivision (b), it is unlawful for any person to violate any of the terms or conditions of any special permit.

(b) In an incorporated city where compliance with the route described in a special permit would result in a violation of local traffic regulations, the permittee may detour from the prescribed route to avoid violating the local traffic regulations if the permittee returns as soon as possible to the prescribed route. A detour under this subdivision shall be made only on nonresidential streets.

(c) If a violation under subdivision (a) consists of an extralegal load not being on the route described in the special permit, and the violation is directly caused by the action of an employee under the supervision of or by the action of any independent contractor working for, a permittee subject to this section, the employee or independent contractor the violation is guilty of a misdemeanor. This subdivision applies only if the employee or independent contractor has been provided written direction on the route to travel and has not been directed to take a different route by a peace officer.

(d) The guilt of an employee or independent contractor under subdivision (c) shall not extend to the permittee employing that person unless the permittee is separately responsible for an action causing the violation.

(e) A violation of equipment requirements contained in Division 12, by any person operating a pilot car shall not be considered a violation of any terms or conditions of a special permit under subdivision (a).

(f)(1) Any person convicted of a violation of the terms and conditions of a special permit shall be punished by a fine not exceeding five hundred dollars ($500) or by imprisonment in the county jail for a period not exceeding six months, or by both that fine and imprisonment.

(2) In addition, if the violation involves weight in excess of that authorized by the permit, an additional fine shall be levied as specified in Section 42030 on the amount of weight in excess of the amount authorized by the permit.

35785. Hauling of Saw Logs
(a) The axle weight limitations imposed in Sections 35550 and 35551 shall not apply to the transportation of a single saw log which does not exceed 8 feet in diameter and 21 feet in length or 6 feet in diameter and 33 feet in length, if such log is hauled on a combination of vehicles consisting of a three-axle truck and a two-axle logging dolly under permit issued by the California Department of Transportation or by local authorities with respect to highways under their respective jurisdictions. Such permit may be granted for not more than thirty (30) days and may be revocable upon notice by the department or local authorities, as the case may be.

(b) When so transported, the vehicle shall not be operated over any bridge or causeway at a speed of more than 15 miles per hour or on the highway at more than 25 miles per hour, on routes designated in the permit. Diameter measurements of the logs shall be made on the large end.

35786. Use of Truck Booster Power Units
Truck booster power units may be used to aid in propelling or moving any motor truck or lawful combination of motor vehicles upon a highway upon an ascending or descending grade, subject to the following conditions:

(a) A permit for such operation must be obtained as provided in this article.

(b) The truck booster power unit shall be operated only on such highways and at such times and according to such conditions and requirements as may be specified in the permit.

35789. Building Mover's Notice to Railroad
Any housemoving contractor or other person who by contract or otherwise moves or transports a dwelling house or other building across railroad tracks shall furnish to the division or district superintendent of the railroad company operating such tracks written notice of intention to make such movement at least 36 hours prior to doing so. The written notice of intention to make such a movement shall contain the name of the street, highway or road over which such dwelling house or other building will be moved across the railroad tracks, the approximate time of day such movement will be made and such other information as may be necessary to enable the railroad company to take precautionary measures to avoid a collision by a train with such dwelling house or other building.

35790. Overwidth Manufactured Homes
(a) The Department of Transportation or local authorities with respect to highways under their respective jurisdictions may, upon application in writing and if good cause appears, issue a special or annual permit in writing authorizing the applicant to move any manufactured home in excess of the maximum width but not exceeding 14 feet in total width, exclusive of lights and devices provided for in Sections 35109 and 35110, upon any highway under the jurisdiction of the party granting the permit.

(b) A public agency, in the exercise of its discretion in granting permits for the movement of overwidth manufactured homes, and in considering the individual circumstances of each case, may use merchandising or relocation of residence as a basis for movement for good cause.

(c)(1) The application for a special permit shall specifically describe the manufactured home to be moved and the particular highways over which the permit to operate is requested.

(2) The application for an annual permit shall specifically describe the power unit to be used to tow the overwidth manufactured homes and the particular highways over which the permit to operate is requested. The annual permit shall be subject to all of the conditions of this section and any additional conditions imposed by the public agency.

(d) The Department of Transportation or local authority may establish seasonal or other time limitations within which a manufactured home may be moved on the highways indicated, and may require an undertaking or other security as it deems necessary to protect the highways and bridges from injury or to provide indemnity for any injury resulting from the operation.

(e) Permits for the movement of manufactured homes under this section shall not be issued except to transporters or licensed manufacturers and dealers and only under the following conditions:

(1) The manufactured home for which the permit is issued shall comply with Sections 35550 and 35551.

(2) In the case of a permit issued on an individual or repetitive trip basis, the applicant has first received the approval of a city or county if the trip will include movement on streets or highways under the jurisdiction of the city or county. The application for such a permit shall indicate the complete route of the proposed move and shall specify all cities and counties that have approved the move. This paragraph shall not be construed to require the Department of Transportation to verify the information provided by an applicant with respect to movement on streets or highways under local jurisdiction.

(3) It is a violation of any permit, which is issued by the Department of Transportation and authorizes a move only on a state highway, for that move to be extended to a street or highway under the jurisdiction of a city or county unless the move has been approved by the city or county.

(f) The Department of Transportation, in cooperation with the Department of the California Highway Patrol, or the local authority may establish additional reasonable permit regulations as they may deem necessary in the interest of public safety, which regulations shall be consistent with this section.

(g) Every permit, the consent form or forms as required by Section 18099.5 of the Health and Safety Code, and a copy of the tax clearance certificate, certificate of origin, or dealer's notice of transfer, when the certificate or notice is required to be issued, shall be carried in the manufactured home or power unit to which it refers and shall be open to inspection by any peace officer or traffic officer, any authorized agent of the Department of Transportation, or any other officer or employee charged with the care and protection of the highways.

(h) It is unlawful for any person to violate any of the terms or conditions of any permit.

35790.1. Manufactured Home; Conditions and Specifications to Move

In addition to the requirements and conditions contained in Section 35790 and notwithstanding any other provision of law, all of the following conditions and specifications shall be complied with to move any manufactured home, as defined in Section 18007 of the Health and Safety Code, that is in excess of 14 feet in total width, but not exceeding 16 feet in total width, exclusive of lights and devices provided for in Sections 35109 and 35110, upon any highway under the jurisdiction of the entity granting the permit:

(a) For the purposes of width requirements under this code, the overall width of manufactured housing specified in this section shall be the overall width, including roof overhang, eaves, window shades, porch roofs, or any other part of the manufactured house that cannot be removed for the purposes of transporting upon any highway.

(b) Unless otherwise exempted under this code, all combinations of motor vehicles and manufactured housing shall be equipped with service brakes on all wheels. Service brakes required under this subdivision shall be adequate, supplemental to the brakes on the towing vehicle, to enable the combination of vehicles to comply with the stopping distance requirements of Section 26454.

(c) In addition to the requirements contained in Section 26304, the breakaway brake device on any manufactured housing unit equipped with electric brakes shall be powered by a wet cell rechargeable battery that is of the same voltage rating as the brakes and has sufficient charge to hold the brakes applied for not less than 15 minutes.

(d) Notwithstanding any other provision of this code, the weight imposed upon any tire, wheel, axle, drawbar, hitch, or other suspension component on a manufactured housing unit shall not exceed the manufacturer's maximum weight rating for the item or component.

(e) In addition to the requirements in subdivision (d), the maximum allowable weight upon one manufactured housing unit axle shall not exceed 6,000 pounds, and the maximum allowable weight upon one manufactured housing unit wheel shall not exceed 3,000 pounds.

(f) Manufactured housing unit tires shall be free from defects, have at least 2/32 of an inch tread depth, as determined by tire tread wear indicators, and shall comply with specifications and requirements contained in Section 3280.904(b)(8) of Title 24 of the Code of Federal Regulations.

(g) Manufactured housing unit manufacturers shall provide transporters with a certification of compliance document, certifying the manufactured housing unit complies with the specifications and requirements contained in subdivisions (d), (e), and (f). Each certification of compliance document shall identify, by serial or identification number, the specific manufactured housing unit being transported and shall be signed by a representative of the manufacturer. Each transporter of manufactured housing units shall have in his or her immediate possession a copy of the certification of compliance document and shall make the document available upon request by any member of the Department of the California Highway Patrol, any authorized employee of the Department of Transportation, or any regularly employed and salaried municipal police officer or deputy sheriff.

(h) Manufactured housing unit dealers shall provide transporters with a certification of compliance document, specifying that all modifications, equipment additions, or loading changes by the dealer have not exceeded the gross vehicle weight rating of the manufactured housing unit or the axle and wheel requirements contained in subdivisions (d), (e), and (f). Each certification of compliance document shall identify, by serial or identification number, the specific manufactured housing unit being transported and shall be signed by a representative of the dealer. Each transporter of manufactured housing units shall have in his or her immediate possession a copy of the certification of compliance document and shall make the document available upon request by any member of the Department of the California Highway Patrol, any authorized employee of the Department of Transportation, any regularly employed and salaried municipal police officer or deputy sheriff, or any reserve police officer or reserve deputy sheriff listed under Section 830.6 of the Penal Code.

(i) Transporters of manufactured housing units shall not transport any additional load in, or upon, the manufactured housing unit that has not been certified by the manufactured housing unit's manufacturer or dealer.

(j) Every hitch, coupling device, drawbar, or other connections between the towing unit and the towed manufactured housing unit shall be securely attached and shall comply with Subpart J of Part 3280 of Title 24 of the Code of Federal Regulations.

(k) Manufactured housing units shall be equipped with an identification plate, specifying the manufacturer's name, the manufactured housing unit's serial number, the gross vehicle weight rating of the manufactured housing unit, and the gross weight of the cargo that may be transported in or upon the manufactured housing unit without exceeding the gross vehicle weight rating. The identification plate shall be permanently attached to the manufactured housing unit and shall be positioned adjacent to, and meet the same specifications and requirements applicable to, the certification label required by Subpart A of Part 3280 of Title 24 of the Code of Federal Regulations.

(l) Manufactured housing units shall be subject to all lighting requirements contained in Sections 24603, 24607, 24608, and 24951. When transported during darkness, manufactured housing units shall additionally be subject to Sections 24600 and 25100.

(m) Manufactured housing units shall have all open sides covered by plywood, hard board, or other rigid material, or by other suitable plastics or flexible material. Plastic or flexible side coverings shall not billow or flap in excess of six inches in any one place. Units that are opened on both sides may be transported empty with no side coverings.

(n) Transporters of manufactured housing units shall make available all permits, licenses, certificates, forms, and any other relative document required for the transportation of manufactured housing upon request by any member of the Department of the California Highway Patrol, any authorized employee of the Department of Transportation, any regularly employed and salaried municipal police officer or deputy sheriff, or any reserve police officer or reserve deputy sheriff listed under Section 830.6 of the Penal Code.

(o) The Department of Transportation, in cooperation with the Department of the California Highway Patrol, or the local authority, shall require   pilot car or special escort services for the movement of any manufactured housing unit pursuant to this section, and may establish additional reasonable permit regulations, including special routing requirements, as necessary in the interest of public safety and consistent with this section.

(p) The Department of Transportation shall not issue a permit to move a manufactured home that is in excess of 14 feet in total width unless that department determines that all of the conditions and specifications set forth in this section have been met. *(AM '00, '03)*

DIVISION 16. IMPLEMENTS OF HUSBANDRY

CHAPTER 2. REGISTRATION

36102.   Other Farm Vehicles: Identification Required
The following vehicles are exempt from registration if they have and display identification plates, as specified in Section 5014; and these vehicles, except when operated pursuant to subdivision (k) of Section 36005, shall not be deemed to be implements of husbandry and they shall be subject to all equipment and device requirements as if registered:

(a) An automatic bale wagon operated unladen on a highway.

(b) An automatic bale wagon when transporting baled hay or straw for a distance of not more than five continuous road miles on a highway from one parcel of property owned, leased, or controlled by a farmer to another parcel of property owned, leased, or controlled by such farmer.

(c) A motor vehicle which is designed for, and used exclusively to, haul feed for livestock and which is owned and operated exclusively by a farmer or an employee of a farmer. A vehicle exempted by this subdivision may be operated only on those highways that are maintained by local authorities, only pursuant to a permit issued as provided in Section 35780 by the local authority having jurisdiction over the highways used, and only for a distance of not more than five continuous road miles from one parcel of property owned, leased, or controlled by the farmer to another parcel of property owned, leased, or controlled by the farmer. This subdivision does not apply to transportation for compensation.

CHAPTER 3. DRIVERS' LICENSES

36300.   Implement of Husbandry Operation
Any person, while driving or operating an implement of husbandry incidentally operated or moved over a highway is not required to obtain a driver's license; except that the driver of any farm tractor while being used to draw a farm trailer carry farm produce between farms or from a farm to a processing or handling point and return, and the driver of an automatic bale wagon which is being operated as specified in Section 36102, but is not being operated as provided in subdivision (k) of Section 36005, shall be in possession of a driver's license of the appropriate class other than a junior permit.

36305. Implement of Husbandry: Driver's License Required
The driver of any implement of husbandry shall possess a valid class C driver's license when operating a combination of vehicles at a speed in excess of 25 miles per hour or towing any implement of husbandry as specified in subdivision (d), (e), or (j) of Section 36005.

CHAPTER 4. SPEED LAWS

36400. Lift-Carrier Limit
No person shall move or drive a lift-carrier or other vehicle designed and used exclusively for the lifting and carrying of implements of husbandry or tools used exclusively for the production or harvesting of agricultural products at a speed in excess of 35 miles per hour.

CHAPTER 5. EQUIPMENT

36508. New Implement of Husbandry
After July 1, 1970, no new implement of husbandry designed or intended by the manufacturer to be operated or moved at a speed not in excess of 25 miles per hour shall be sold in this state unless it is equipped by the manufacturer with a slow-moving vehicle emblem as prescribed by Section 24615, and such an emblem shall thereafter be displayed and maintained on such implement of husbandry while the implement is able to be operated upon a public highway.

36509. Warning Lights or Flags
(a) An implement of husbandry, a farm vehicle, or any vehicle escorting or towing an implement of husbandry or farm vehicle, may display flashing amber warning lamps or flashing amber turn signals:
(1) When the vehicle is required to display a "slow moving vehicle"emblem as defined in Section 24615.
(2) When the width, length, height or speed of the vehicle may cause a hazard to other traffic on the highway.
(b) An implement of husbandry, a farm vehicle, or any vehicle towing an implement of husbandry or farm vehicle, when the load upon the vehicle exceeds 120 inches in width, shall display either:
(1) Flashing amber warning lamps.
(2) Flashing amber turn signals.
(3) During daylight hours, red flags, each of which shall be not less than 16 inches square, mounted at the left and right outer extremities of the vehicle or load whichever has the greater horizontal dimension.

36510. Stopping Distance Requirements
Implements of husbandry are not subject to stopping distance requirements contained in Section 26454, but if any such vehicle cannot be stopped within 32 feet from an initial speed of 15 miles per hour, it shall not be operated at a speed in excess of that permitting a stop in 32 feet.

CHAPTER 6. SIZE, WEIGHT, AND LOAD

36600. Width Exemptions and Limitations
(a) The limitations as to width as set forth in Chapter 2 of Division 15 do not apply to implements of husbandry incidentally operated, transported, towed, or otherwise moved over a highway.
(b) Notwithstanding subdivision (a), when an implement of husbandry is transported or moved over a highway which is a part of the National System of Interstate and Defense Highways (as referred to in Section 108 of the Federal-aid Highway Act of 1956) as a load on another vehicle, if the load exceeds 102 inches in width, the vehicle and load shall not be operated for a distance in excess of 25 miles from the point of origin of the trip. The operator of the transporting vehicle shall be a farmer or a person regularly employed by a farmer or farm corporation, and the operator transporting the load shall have in his or her immediate possession a writing signed by the farmer or farm corporation agent which states the origin and destination of the trip.

(c) Notwithstanding subdivision (a), when an implement of husbandry is transported or moved over any other highway as a load on another vehicle, if the load exceeds 120 inches in width, the vehicle and load shall not be operated for a distance in excess of 25 miles from the point of origin of the trip. The operator of the transporting vehicle shall be a farmer or a person employed by a farmer or farm corporation, and the operator transporting the load shall have in his or her immediate possession a writing signed by the farmer or farm corporation agent which states the origin and destination of the trip.

36605. Width Exemption: Trailers and Semitrailers

The limitations as to width, as set forth in Chapter 2 of Division 15, do not apply to any trailer or semitrailer, including lift carriers and tip-bed trailers, used exclusively for the transportation of implements of husbandry or tools used exclusively for the production or harvesting of agricultural products by farmers or implement dealers, except as follows:

(1) With respect to any trailer or semitrailer transporting a grain-harvesting combine, that vehicle shall not exceed a width of 144 inches.

(2) With respect to any other vehicle described in this section, that vehicle, or the load on that vehicle when that load consists of tools, shall not exceed a width of 120 inches.

(3) With respect to any trailer or semitrailer described in subdivision (c) of Section 36005, that vehicle, when towed upon a highway shall not exceed a width of 174 inches and shall be subject to subdivisions (b) and (c) of Section 36600.

36606. Width Exemption: Automatic Bale Wagons

(a) The limitations as to width, as set forth in Chapter 2 of Division 15, do not apply to automatic bale wagons while operated as specified in Section 36102, except that such vehicles or the load thereon may not exceed 120 inches in width.

(b) This section shall have no application to highways which are a part of the National System of Interstate and Defense Highways (as referred to in subdivision (a) of Section 108 of the Federal-Aid Highway Act of 1956).

36610. Height Exemptions and Limitations

(a) The limitations as to height of vehicles contained in Chapter 3 of Division 15 do not apply to implements of husbandry incidentally operated, transported, towed, or otherwise moved over a highway.

(b) Notwithstanding subdivision (a), when an implement of husbandry is transported or moved over a highway as a load on another vehicle and the load exceeds 14 feet in height, the vehicle and load shall not be operated for a distance in excess of 25 miles from the point of origin of the trip. The operator of the transporting vehicle shall be a farmer or a person regularly employed by a farmer or farm corporation, and the operator transporting the vehicle shall have in his or her immediate possession a writing signed by the farmer or farm corporation agent which states the origin and destination of the trip.

CHAPTER 7. OTHER REQUIREMENTS

36705. Automatic Bale Wagon: Operation During Darkness

No automatic bale wagon exceeding 96 inches in width or carrying a load in excess of 100 inches in width may be operated on any highway during darkness.

DIVISION 16.5. OFF-HIGHWAY VEHICLES

CHAPTER 2. REGISTRATION, ETC.

38010. Issuance and Display of Identification Plates

(a) Except as otherwise provided in subdivision (b), every motor vehicle specified in Section 38012 that is not registered under this code because it is to be operated or used exclusively off the highways, except as provided in this division, shall be issued and display an identification plate or device issued by the department.

(b) Subdivision (a) does not apply to any of the following:

(1) Motor vehicles specifically exempted from registration under this code, including, but not limited to, motor vehicles exempted pursuant to Sections 4006, 4010, 4012, 4013, 4015, 4018, and 4019.

(2) Implements of husbandry.

(3) Motor vehicles owned by the state, or any county, city, district, or political subdivision of the state, or the United States.

(4) Motor vehicles owned or operated by, or operated under contract with a utility, whether privately or publicly owned, when used as specified in Section 22512.

(5) Special construction equipment described in Section 565, regardless of whether those motor vehicles are used in connection with highway or railroad work.

(6) A motor vehicle with a currently valid special permit issued under Section 38087.5 that is owned or operated by a nonresident of this state and the vehicle is not identified or registered in a foreign jurisdiction. For the purposes of this paragraph, a person who holds a valid driver's license issued by a foreign jurisdiction is presumed to be a nonresident.

(7) Commercial vehicles weighing more than 6,000 pounds unladen.

(8) Any motorcycle manufactured in the year 1942 or prior.

(9) Four-wheeled motor vehicles operated solely in organized racing or competitive events upon a closed course when those events are conducted under the auspices of a recognized sanctioning body or by permit issued by the local governmental authority having jurisdiction.

(10) A motor vehicle with a currently valid identification or registration permit issued by another state. *(AM '99)*

38020. Identification Required

Except as otherwise provided in this division, no person shall operate, transport, or leave standing any off-highway motor vehicle subject to identification under this code which is not registered under the provisions of Division 3 (commencing with Section 4000), unless it is identified under the provisions of this chapter. A violation of this section is an infraction. Riding in violation of seasons established by Section 2412(f) and 2415 of Title 13 of the California Code of Regulations constitutes a violation of this section. This section shall not apply to the operation, transportation, or leaving standing of an off-highway vehicle pursuant to a valid special permit. *(AM '04)*

38025. Operation on Highway

In accordance with subdivision (c) of Section 4000, a motor vehicle issued a plate or device pursuant to Section 38160 may be operated or driven upon a highway but only as follows:

(a) On a two-lane highway, only to cross the highway at an angle of approximately 90 degrees to the direction of the roadway and at a place where a quick and safe crossing may be made, or only when the roadway is not maintained by snow removal equipment and is closed to motor vehicles that are subject to registration pursuant to Division 3 (commencing with Section 4000), or only to cross a highway in the manner specified in subdivision (b).

(b) With respect to the crossing of a highway having more than two lanes, or a highway having limited access, a motor vehicle may cross a highway but only at a place designated by the Department of Transportation or local authorities with respect to a highway under their respective jurisdictions as a place where a motor vehicle, or specified types of motor vehicle, may cross a highway, and a vehicle shall cross the highway only at that designated place and only in a quick and safe manner.

(c) The Department of Transportation and local authorities with respect to a highway under their respective jurisdictions may designate, by the erection of an appropriate sign of a type approved by the Department of Transportation, a place where a motor vehicle, or specified type of motor vehicle, may cross a highway having more than two lanes or having limited access.

(d) A motor vehicle identified pursuant to Section 38010 may be towed upon a highway, but not driven, if the vehicle displays a plate or device issued pursuant to Section 38160.

(e) A motorcycle identified pursuant to Section 38010 may be pushed upon a highway, but not ridden, if the motorcycle has displayed upon it a plate or device issued pursuant to Section 38160.

(f) A peace officer, as defined in Chapter 4.5 (commencing with Section 830) of Title 3 of Part 2 of the Penal Code, may operate or drive an off-highway vehicle identified pursuant to Section 38010 upon a highway in an emergency response situation. *(AM '03)*

38026. Designating Highways: Combined Use

(a) In addition to Section 38025 and after complying with subdivision (c) of this section, if a local authority, an agency of the federal government, or the Director of Parks and Recreation finds that a highway, or a portion of a highway, under the jurisdiction of the authority, agency, or the director, as the case may be, is located in a manner that provides a connecting link between off-highway motor vehicle trail segments, between an off-highway motor vehicle recreational use area and necessary service facilities, or between lodging facilities and an off-highway motor vehicle recreational facility and if it is found that the highway is designed and constructed so as to safely permit the use of regular vehicular traffic and also the driving of off-highway motor vehicles on that highway, the local authority, by resolution or ordinance, agency of the federal government, or the Director of Parks and Recreation, as the case may be, may designate that highway, or a portion of a highway, for combined use and shall prescribe rules and regulations therefor. A highway, or portion of a highway, shall not be so designated for a distance of more than three miles, except as provided in Section 38026.1. A freeway shall not be designated under this section.

(b) The Off-Highway Motor Vehicle Recreation Commission may propose highway segments for consideration by local authorities, an agency of the federal government, or the Director of Parks and Recreation for combined use.

(c) Prior to designating a highway or portion of a highway on the motion of the local authority, an agency of the federal government, or the Director of Parks and Recreation, or as a recommendation of the Off-Highway Motor Vehicle Recreation Commission, a local authority, an agency of the federal government, or the Director of Parks and Recreation shall notify the Commissioner of the California Highway Patrol, and shall not designate any segment pursuant to subdivision (a) which, in the opinion of the commissioner, would create a potential traffic safety hazard.

(d)(1) A designation of a highway, or a portion of a highway, under subdivision (a) shall become effective upon the erection of appropriate signs of a type approved by the Department of Transportation on and along the highway, or portion of the highway.

(2) The cost of the signs shall be reimbursed from the Off-Highway Vehicle Trust Fund, when appropriated by the Legislature, or by expenditure of funds from a grant or cooperative agreement made pursuant to Section 5090.50 of the Public Resources Code. *(AM '11)*

38026.5. Operation on Designated Highways

(a) In accordance with subdivision (c) of Section 4000, a motor vehicle issued a plate or device pursuant to Section 38160 may be operated or driven on a local highway, or a portion of the local highway, that is designated pursuant to Section 38026 or 38026.1 if the operation is in conformance with this code and the vehicle complies with off-highway vehicle equipment requirements specified in this division.

(b) Notwithstanding subdivision (a), it is unlawful for a person using an off-highway vehicle on a combined-use highway to do any of the following:

(1) Operate an off-highway motor vehicle on the highway during the hours of darkness.

(2) Operate a vehicle on the highway that does not have an operational stoplight.

(3) Operate a vehicle on the highway that does not have rubber tires.

(4) Operate a vehicle without a valid driver's license of the appropriate class for the vehicle operation in possession.

(5) Operate a vehicle on the highway without complying with Article 2 (commencing with Section 16020) of Chapter 1 of Division 7. *(AM '11)*

38060. Change of Address

(a) Whenever any person, after making application for identification of an off-highway motor vehicle subject to identification, or after the identification either as owner or legal owner, moves or acquires a new address different from the address shown in the application or upon the certificate of ownership or identification certificate, that person shall, within 10 days thereafter, notify the department of his or her old and new addresses.

(b) Any owner having notified the department as required in subdivision (a), shall immediately mark out the former on the face of the certificate an write with pen and ink or type the new on the face of the certificate immediately below the former address and initial the entry.

38085. Identification Certificate Kept with Vehicle

(a) Every owner upon receipt of an identification certificate shall maintain the same or a facsimile copy thereof with the vehicle for which it is issued at all times when the vehicle is operated or transported.

(b) The provisions of this section do not apply when an identification certificate is removed from the vehicle for the purpose of application for renewal or transfer of identification.

38090. Stolen, Lost, or Damaged Identification Plates and Certificates

If any identification certificate or identification plate or device is stolen, lost, mutilated or illegible, the owner of the vehicle for which the same was issued, as shown by the records of the department, shall immediately make application for and may, upon furnishing information satisfactory to the department, obtain a duplicate or substitute or a new identification under a new number, as determined to be most advisable by the department. An application for a duplicate identification certificate is not required in conjunction with any other application.

38095. Stolen, Lost, or Damaged Certificate of Ownership

If any certificate of ownership is stolen, lost, mutilated or illegible, the legal owner or, if none, the owner of the vehicle for which the same was issued as shown by the records of the department shall immediately make application for and may, upon furnishing information satisfactory to the department, obtain a duplicate.

38170. Off-Highway Vehicles: I.D. Plate Display & Location

(a) Every off-highway motor vehicle subject to identification shall have displayed upon it the identification number assigned to the vehicle for which it is issued, together with the word "California"or the abbreviation "CAL"and the year number for which it is issued or a suitable device issued by the department for validation purposes, which device shall contain the year for which it is issued.

(b) The identification plate or device shall at all times be securely fastened to the vehicle for which it is issued and shall be mounted or affixed in a position to be clearly visible, and shall be maintained in a condition so as to be clearly legible. No covering shall be used on the identification plate or device.

(c) All identification plates or devices issued on or after January 1, 1996, shall be displayed as follows:

(1) On the left fork leg of a motorcycle, either horizontal or vertical, and shall be visible from the left side of the motorcycle.

(2) On the left quadrant of the metal frame member of sand rails, rail-type buggies, and dune buggies, visible from the rear of the vehicle.

(3) On the left rear quadrant on permanent plastic or metal frame members of all-terrain vehicles, visible to outside inspections.

(4) On the left tunnel on the back quadrant of snowmobiles.

38205. Application for Transfer

Whenever any person has received as transferee a properly endorsed certificate of ownership, he or she shall, within 10 days thereafter, endorse the ownership certificate as required and forward the ownership certificate with the proper transfer fee and, if required under Section 38120, any other fee due and thereby make application for transfer of identification. The certificate of ownership shall contain a space for the applicant's driver's license or identification card number, and the applicant shall furnish that number, if any, in the space provided.

38280. Traffic Signs, Signals and Markings - Federal, State, and Local Authority

Federal, state, or local authorities having jurisdiction over public lands may place or cause to be placed and maintained, such appropriate signs, signals and other traffic control devices as may be necessary to properly indicate and carry out any provision of law or any duly adopted regulation of such governmental authority or to warn or guide traffic.

CHAPTER 5. OFF-HIGHWAY VEHICLE OPERATING RULES

38300. Unlawful to Disobey Sign, Signal, or Traffic Control Device

It is unlawful for the driver of any vehicle to disobey any sign, signal, or traffic control device placed or maintained pursuant to Section 38280.

38301. Unlawful to Violate Special Regulations

(a) It is unlawful to operate a vehicle in violation of special regulations which have been promulgated by the governmental agency having jurisdiction over public lands, including, but not limited to, regulations governing access, routes of travel, plants, wildlife, wildlife habitat, water resources, and historical sites.

(b) A person who operates a motor vehicle in an area closed to that vehicle is guilty of a public offense and shall be punished as follows:

(1) Except as provided in paragraphs (2) and (3), the offense is an infraction punishable by a fine not exceeding fifty dollars ($50).

(2) For a second offense committed within seven years after a prior violation for which there was a conviction punishable under paragraph (1), the offense is an infraction punishable by a fine not exceeding seventy-five dollars ($75).

(3) For a third or subsequent offense committed within seven years after two or more prior violations for which there were convictions punishable under this section, the offense is punishable by a fine not exceeding one hundred fifty dollars ($150). In addition to the fine, the court may assess costs sufficient to repair property damage resulting from the violation. *(AM '07)*

38301.3. Prohibited Entry Into Federal or State Wilderness Area; Penalties

Notwithstanding subdivision (d) of Section 5008 of the Public Resources Code, or any other provision of state law, and to the extent authorized under federal law, a person who violates a state or federal regulation that prohibits entry of a motor vehicle into all or portions of an area designated as a federal or state wilderness area is guilty of a public offense and shall be punished as follows:

(a) Except as provided in subdivisions (b) and (c), the offense is an infraction punishable by a fine not exceeding one hundred fifty dollars ($150).

(b) For a second offense committed within seven years after a prior violation for which there was a conviction punishable under subdivision (a), the offense is an infraction punishable by a fine not exceeding two hundred twenty-five dollars ($225).

(c)(1) For a third or subsequent offense committed within seven years after two or more prior violations for which there were convictions punishable under this section, the offense is a misdemeanor punishable by a fine not exceeding three hundred dollars ($300) or by imprisonment in the county jail not exceeding 90 days, or by both that fine and imprisonment.

(2) In addition to the fine imposed under paragraph (1), the court may order impoundment of the vehicle used in the offense under the following conditions:

(A) The person convicted under this subdivision is the owner of the vehicle.

(B) The vehicle is subject to Section 4000 or 38010.

(3) The period of impoundment imposed pursuant to this subdivision shall be not less than one day nor more than 30 days. The impoundment shall be at the owner's expense. *(AD '05)*

38302. Unlawful to Place Unauthorized Signs

It is unlawful for any person to place or erect any sign, signal, or traffic control device for off-highway traffic upon public lands unless authorized by law.

38304. Ability to Reach and Operate Controls

The operator of an off-highway motor vehicle shall be able to reach and operate all controls necessary to safely operate the vehicle.

38304.1. Knowingly Grant Permission or Allow Child Under 14 to Operate Controls of Off-Highway Vehicle

(a) Neither a parent or guardian of a child who is under 14 years of age, nor an adult who is authorized by the parent or guardian to supervise that child, shall grant permission to, or knowingly allow, that child to operate an off-highway motor vehicle in a manner that violates Section 38304.

(b) A person convicted of a violation of subdivision (a) is punishable as follows:

(1) For a first conviction, the court shall impose a fine of thirty-five dollars ($35).

(2) For a second conviction, a fine of not less than thirty-five dollars ($35) nor more than fifty dollars ($50).

(3) For a third or any subsequent conviction, a fine of not less than fifty dollars ($50) nor more than seventy-five dollars ($75). *(AD '09)*

38305. Basic Speed Law

No person shall drive an off-highway motor vehicle at a speed greater than is reasonable or prudent and in no event at a speed which endangers the safety of other persons or property.

38310. Prima Facie Speed Limit

The prima facie speed limit within 50 feet of any campground, campsite, or concentration of people or animals shall be 15 miles per hour unless changed as authorized by this code and, if so changed, only when signs have been erected giving notice thereof.

38312. Starting Parked Vehicles

No person shall place in motion an off-highway motor vehicle that is stopped, standing, or parked until such movement can be made with reasonable safety.

38314. Turning Movements

No person shall turn an off-highway motor vehicle from a direct course or move right or left until such movement can be made with reasonable safety.

38316. Reckless Driving

(a) It is unlawful for any person to drive any off-highway motor vehicle with a willful and wanton disregard for the safety of other persons or property.

(b) Any person who violates this section shall, upon conviction thereof be punished by imprisonment in the county jail for not less than five days nor more than 90 days or by fine of not less than fifty dollars ($50) nor more than five hundred dollars ($500) or by both such fine and imprisonment, except as provided in Section 38317.

38317. Reckless Driving Causing Bodily Injury

Whenever reckless driving of an off-highway motor vehicle proximately causes bodily injury to any person, the person driving the vehicle shall, upon conviction thereof be punished by imprisonment in the county jail for not less than 30 days nor more than six months or by fine of not less than one hundred dollars ($100) nor more than one thousand dollars ($1,000) or by both such fine and imprisonment.

38318. Throwing Substances at Off-Highway Motor Vehicles

(a) Any person who throws any substance at an off-highway motor vehicle or occupant thereof is guilty of a misdemeanor and be punished pursuant to Section 42002 by a fine of not more than one thousand dollars ($1,000) or by imprisonment in the county jail for not more than six months, or by both the fine and imprisonment.

(b) Any person who, with intent to do great bodily injury, maliciously and willfully throws or projects any rock, brick, bottle, metal, or this other missile, projects any other substance capable of doing serious bodily harm, or discharges a firearm at an off-highway motor vehicle or occupant thereof is guilty of a felony.

38318.5.   Malicious Acts

(a) Any person who maliciously removes or alters trail, danger, or directional markers or signs provided for the safety or guidance of off-highway motor vehicles is guilty of a misdemeanor and shall be punished pursuant to Section 42002 by a fine of not more than one thousand dollars ($1,000) or by imprisonment in the county jail for not more than six months, or by both the fine and imprisonment.

(b) Any person who, with intent to do great bodily injury (1) proximately causes great bodily injury to any person as a result of acts prohibited by subdivision (a), or (2) erects or places any cable, chain, rope, fishing line, or other similar material which is unmarked or intentionally placed, or both, for malicious purpose is guilty of a felony.

(c) Any person convicted under subdivision (a) or (b) shall, if the violation proximately causes one or more adverse environmental impacts, also be liable in civil damages for the cost of mitigation, restoration, or repair thereof, in addition to any other liability imposed by law.

38319.   Operation Causing Damage

No person shall operate, nor shall an owner permit the operation of, an off-highway motor vehicle in a manner likely to cause malicious or unnecessary damage to the land, wildlife, wildlife habitat or vegetative resources.

38320.   Throwing, Depositing, or Dumping Matter

(a) No person shall throw or deposit, nor shall the registered owner or the driver, if such owner is not then present in the vehicle, aid or abet in the throwing or depositing, upon any area, public or private, any bottle, can, garbage, glass, nail, offal, paper, wire, any substance likely to injure or kill wild or domestic animal or plant life or damage traffic using such area, or any noisome, nauseous or offensive matter of any kind.

(b) No person shall place, deposit or dump, or cause to be placed, deposited or dumped, any rocks or dirt in or upon any area, public or private, without the consent of the property owner or public agency having jurisdiction over the area.

(c) Any person who violates this section shall, upon conviction thereof, be punished by a fine of not less than fifty dollars ($50). No part of such fine shall be suspended. The court may permit the fine required by this section to be paid in installments if the court determines that the defendant is unable to pay the fine in one lump sum.

CHAPTER 6.   OFF-HIGHWAY VEHICLE EQUIPMENT

38330.   Vehicle Not Equipped or Unsafe

It is unlawful to operate any vehicle or combination of vehicles which is in an unsafe condition, which is not equipped as required by this chapter or the equipment regulations of the governmental agency having jurisdiction over public lands or which is not safely loaded.

38335.   Headlamps

When operated from one-half hour after sunset to one-half hour before sunrise, each motor vehicle shall be equipped with at least one lighted white headlamp directed toward the front of the vehicle. Such lamp shall be of an intensity sufficient to reveal persons and vehicles at a distance of at least 200 feet.

38345.   Taillamps

When operated from one-half hour after sunset to one-half hour before sunrise, each motor vehicle which is not in combination with any other vehicle shall be equipped with at least one lighted red taillamp which shall be clearly visible from the rear.

(a) Every such vehicle or vehicles at the end of a combination of vehicles shall be equipped with one lighted red taillamp when operated from one-half hour after sunset to one-half hour before sunrise.

38346.   Flashing or Steady Red or Blue Warning Light Prohibited; Exception

A person shall not display a flashing or steady burning red or blue warning light on an off-highway motor vehicle except as permitted by Section 21055 or when an extreme hazard exists. *(AD '04)*

38375.　Siren Prohibited

(a) An off-highway motor vehicle, except an authorized emergency vehicle, shall not be equipped with a siren.

(b) A person driving an off-highway motor vehicle, except the driver of an authorized emergency vehicle as permitted by Section 21055, shall not use a siren. *(AD '04)*

38355.　Service Brakes Required

(a) Except as provided in subdivision (b), every motor vehicle shall be equipped with a service brake system which is in good working order and adequate to control the movement of, and to stop and hold to the limit of traction of, such vehicle or combination of vehicles under all conditions of loading and upon any grade on which it is operated.

(b) Any motor vehicle, such as an air-cushioned vehicle, which is unable to comply with the requirements of this section due to the this method of operation, is exempt, if the operator is able to exercise safe control over the movement of such vehicle.

38365.　Mufflers and Exhaust Systems

(a) Every off-highway motor vehicle, as defined in Section 38306, shall at all times be equipped with an adequate muffler in constant operation and properly maintained so as to meet the requirements of Section 38370, and no muffler or exhaust system shall be equipped with a cutout, bypass, or similar device.

(b) The provisions of subdivision (a) shall not be applicable to vehicles being operated off the highways in an organized racing or competitive event upon a closed course or in a hill climb or drag race, which is conducted under the auspices of a recognized sanctioning body or by permit issued by the local governmental authority having jurisdiction.

38366.　Spark Arrester

(a) Notwithstanding Section 4442 of the Public Resources Code, and except for vehicles with mufflers as provided in Article 2 of Chapter 5 of Division 12, no person shall use or allow to be used or operated, any off-highway motor vehicle, as defined in Section 38006, on any forest-covered land, brush-covered land, or grass-covered land unless the vehicle is equipped with a spark arrester maintained in effective working order.

(b) A spark arrester affixed to the exhaust system of a vehicle subject to this section shall not be placed or mounted in such a manner as to allow flames or heat from the exhaust system to ignite any flammable material.

(c) A spark arrester is a device constructed of nonflammable materials specifically for the purpose of removing and retaining carbon and other flammable particles over 0.0232 of an inch in size from the exhaust flow of an internal combustion engine or which is qualified and rated by the United States Forest Service.

(d) Subdivision (a) shall not be applicable to vehicles being operated off the highway in an organized racing or competitive event upon a closed course, which is conducted under the auspices of a recognized sanctioning body and by permit issued by the fire protection authority having jurisdiction.

38375.　Siren Prohibited

(a) An off-highway motor vehicle, except an authorized emergency vehicle, shall not be equipped with a siren.

(b) A person driving an off-highway motor vehicle, except the driver of an authorized emergency vehicle as permitted by Section 21055, shall not use a siren. *(AD '04)*

38390.　Pollution Control Device

No person shall operate or maintain in a condition of readiness for operation any off-highway motor vehicle which is required to be equipped with a motor vehicle pollution control device under Part 5 of the Health and Safety Code or with any other certified motor vehicle pollution control device required by any other state law or any rule or regulation adopted pursuant to such law, or required to be equipped with a motor vehicle pollution control device pursuant to the Clean Air Act (42 U.S.C. 1557 et seq.) and the standards and regulations promulgated thereunder, unless it is equipped with the required motor vehicle pollution control device which is correctly installed and in operating condition. No person shall disconnect, modify, or alter any such required device. Notwithstanding Section 43107 of the Health and Safety Code, this section shall apply only to off-highway motor vehicles of the 1978 or later model year.

38391. Modification Devices
No person shall install, sell, offer for sale, or advertise any device, apparatus, or mechanism intended for use with, or as a part of, any required off-highway motor vehicle pollution control device or system which alters or modifies the original design or performance of any such motor vehicle pollution control device or system.

38393. Operation after Notice
No person shall operate an off-highway motor vehicle after notice by a traffic officer or other authorized public officer that such vehicle is not equipped with the required certified motor vehicle pollution control device correctly installed in operating condition, except as may be necessary to return the vehicle to the residence or place of business of the owner or driver or to a garage, until the vehicle has been properly equipped with such a device.

CHAPTER 7. ALL-TERRAIN VEHICLES

38503. Conditions for Operating: Minors
No person under the age of 18 years, on and after January 1, 1990, shall operate an all-terrain vehicle on public lands of this state unless the person satisfies one of the following conditions:

(a) The person is taking a prescribed safety training course under the direct supervision of a certified all-terrain vehicle safety instructor.

(b) The person is under the direct supervision of an adult who has in their possession an appropriate safety certificate issued by this state, or issued under the authority of another state.

(c) The person has in possession an appropriate safety certificate issued by this state or issued under the authority of another state.

38504. Conditions for Operating: Additional Requirements
No person under 14 years of age, on and after January 1, 1990, shall operate an all-terrain vehicle on public lands of this state unless the person satisfies one of the conditions set forth in Section 38503 and, in addition, is accompanied by and under the direct supervision of a parent or guardian or is accompanied by and under the direct supervision of an adult who is authorized by the parent or guardian.

38504.1. Allow Operation of ATV by Person Under Age 14; Penalties
(a) Neither a parent or guardian of a child who is under 14 years of age, nor an adult who is authorized by the parent or guardian to supervise that child shall grant permission to, or knowingly allow, that child to operate an all-terrain vehicle in a manner that violates Section 38504.

(b) A person convicted of a violation of subdivision (a) is punishable as follows:

(1) For a first conviction, the court shall either impose a fine of one hundred twenty-five dollars ($125) or order the person to take or retake and complete an all-terrain vehicle safety training course pursuant to Section 38501. If ordered to take or retake and complete the safety training course, the person shall provide the court a copy of the all-terrain vehicles safety certificate issued as a result of that completion.

(2) For a second conviction, a fine of not less than one hundred twenty-five dollars ($125) nor more than two hundred fifty dollars ($250).

(3) For a third or any subsequent conviction, a fine of not less than two hundred fifty dollars ($250) nor more than five hundred dollars ($500). *(AD '06)*

38505. Safety Helmet Required
No person, on and after January 1, 1989, shall ride, or be otherwise propelled on an all-terrain vehicle on public lands unless the person wears a safety helmet meeting requirements established for motorcycles and motorized bicycles, pursuant to Section 27802.

38506. Passengers Prohibited

No operator of an all-terrain vehicle may carry a passenger when operating on public lands.

However, the operator of an all-terrain vehicle, that is designed for operation off of the highway by an operator with no more than one passenger, may carry a passenger when operating on public lands. *(AM '03)*

38603. Use of Manufacturer-Provided Passenger Seat Required; Operator Responsibility

(a) A person operating a recreational off-highway vehicle with a model year of 2014 or later shall not allow a passenger to occupy a separate seat location not designed and provided by the manufacturer for a passenger.

(b) ***Seats that are installed in a separate seat location not designed and provided by the manufacturer for a passenger in vehicles with model year of 2013 or earlier may be occupied by a passenger if the occupant of the seat is fully contained inside of the vehicle's rollover protection structure at all times while the vehicle is being operated. *(AM '13)*

38604. Passenger Able to Grasp Occupant Handhold; Operator Requirement

(a) A person operating a recreational off-highway vehicle shall not ride with a passenger, unless the passenger, while seated upright with his or her back against the seatback***, can grasp the occupant handhold with the seatbelt and shoulder belt or safety harness properly fastened.

(b) For purposes of this chapter, "occupant handhold" means any factory or aftermarket device grasped by an occupant to provide support and to assist in keeping arms and hands within the recreational off-highway vehicle. The steering wheel shall be considered an occupant handhold for the recreational off-highway vehicle operator.

(c) Occupant handholds shall be designed to allow the recreational off-highway vehicle passenger to exit the vehicle without interference from the handholds. *(AM '13)*

DIVISION 16.7.
BICYCLE REGISTRATION AND LICENSING

39002. License Requirement

(a) A city or county, which adopts a bicycle licensing ordinance or resolution, may provide in the ordinance or resolution that no resident shall operate any bicycle, as specified in the ordinance, on any street, road, highway, or other public property within the jurisdiction of the city or county, as the case may be, unless the bicycle is licensed in accordance with this division.

(b) It is unlawful for any person to tamper with, destroy, mutilate, or alter any license indicia or registration form, or to remove, alter, or mutilate the serial number, or the identifying marks of a licensing agency's identifying symbol, on any bicycle frame licensed under this division.

39006. Information Required Upon Retail Sale

(a) Each bicycle retailer and each dealer shall supply to each purchaser preregistration form provided by the licensing agency and shall include on the sales check or receipt given to the purchaser, a record of the following information: name of retailer, address of retailer, year and make of the bicycle, serial number of bicycle if delivered to the purchaser in an assembled state, general description of the bicycle, name of purchaser, and address of purchaser. A copy of the preregistration form shall be filled out and forwarded by the purchaser to the appropriate licensing agency within 10 days from the date of sale.

(b) For the purposes of this division, a bicycle dealer is any person who sells, gives away, buys, or takes in trade for the purpose of resale, more than five bicycles in any one calendar year, whether or not such bicycles are owned by such person. "Bicycle dealer" also includes agents or employees of such person.

39007. Serial Numbers

After December 31, 1976, no bicycle retailer shall sell any new bicycle in this state unless such bicycle has legibly and permanently stamped or cast on its frame a serial number, no less than one inch in size, and unique to the particular bicycle of each manufacturer. The serial number only shall be stamped or cast in the head of the frame, either side of the seat tube, the toeplate or the bottom sprocket (crank) housing.

39008. Recordation of Transfer

(a) Whenever any person sells or otherwise disposes of a bicycle, he shall endorse upon the registration certificate previously issued for such bicycle a written transfer of same, setting forth the name, address, telephone number of the transferee, date of transfer, and signature of the transferor, and shall deliver the registration certificate, so endorsed, to the licensing agency within 10 days.

(b) Any person who purchases or otherwise acquires possession of a bicycle shall within 10 days of taking possession apply for the transfer of license to his own name. Cities and counties may establish rules and regulations to govern and enforce the provisions of this section.

39009. Notification of Change of Address; Duplicate License or Registration Form

(a) Whenever the owner of a bicycle licensed pursuant to an ordinance or resolution of a city or county changes his address, he shall within 10 days notify the appropriate licensing agency of the old and new address.

(b) In the event that any bicycle license indicia or registration form issued pursuant to the provisions of this division is lost, stolen, or mutilated, the licensee of such bicycle shall immediately notify the licensing agency, and, within 10 days after such notification, shall apply to the licensing agency for a duplicate license indicia or registration form. Thereupon, the licensing agency shall issue to such licensee a replacement indicia or registration form upon payment to the licensing agency of the appropriate fee.

DIVISION 17. OFFENSES AND PROSECUTION

40001. Owner's Responsibility

(a) It is unlawful for the owner, or any other person, employing or otherwise directing the driver of any vehicle to cause the operation of the vehicle upon a highway in any manner contrary to law.

(b) It is unlawful for an owner to request, cause, or permit the operation of any vehicle that is any of the following:

(1) Not registered or for which any fee has not been paid under this code.

(2) Not equipped as required in this code.

(3) Not in compliance with the size, weight, or load provisions of this code.

(4) Not in compliance with the regulations promulgated pursuant to this code, or with applicable city or county ordinances adopted pursuant to this code.

(5) Not in compliance with the provisions of Part 5 (commencing with Section 43000) of Division 26 of the Health and Safety Code and the rules and regulations of the State Air Resources Board.

(c) Any employer who violates an out-of-service order, that complies with Section 396.9 of Title 49 of the Code of Federal Regulations, or who knowingly requires or permits a driver to violate or fail to comply with that out-of-service order, is guilty of a misdemeanor.

(d) An employer who is convicted of allowing, permitting, requiring, or authorizing a driver to operate a commercial motor vehicle in violation of any statute or regulation pertaining to a railroad-highway grade crossing is subject to a fine of not more than ten thousand dollars ($10,000).

(e) Whenever a violation is chargeable to the owner or lessee of a vehicle pursuant to subdivision (a) or (b), the driver shall not be arrested or cited for the violation unless the vehicle is registered in a state or country other than California, or unless the violation is for an offense that is clearly within the responsibility of the driver.

(f) Whenever the owner, or lessee, or any other person is prosecuted for a violation pursuant to this section, the court may, on the request of the defendant, take appropriate steps to make the driver of the vehicle, or any other person who directs the loading, maintenance, or operation of the vehicle, a codefendant. However, the court may make the driver a codefendant only if the driver is the owner or lessee of the vehicle, or the driver is an employee or a contractor of the defendant who requested the court to make the driver a codefendant. If the codefendant is held solely responsible and found guilty, the court may dismiss the charge against the defendant.

(g) In any prosecution under this section, it is a rebuttable presumption that any person who gives false or erroneous information in a written certification of actual gross cargo weight has directed, requested, caused, or permitted the operation of a vehicle in a manner contrary to law in violation of subdivision (a) or (b), or both. *(AM '01, '04)*

40008. Reckless Driving, Following To Closely or Interfering with Driver's Controls to Capture Visual Image, Sound Recording or other Physical Impression for Commercial Purpose

(a) Notwithstanding any other provision of law, except as otherwise provided in subdivision (c), any person who violates Section 21701, 21703, or 23103, with the intent to capture any type of visual image, sound recording, or other physical impression of another person for a commercial purpose, is guilty of a misdemeanor and not an infraction and shall be punished by imprisonment in a county jail for not more than six months and by a fine of not more than two thousand five hundred dollars ($2,500).

(b) Notwithstanding any other provision of law, except as otherwise provided in subdivision (c), any person who violates Section 21701, 21703, or 23103, with the intent to capture any type of visual image, sound recording, or other physical impression of another person for a commercial purpose and who causes a minor child or children to be placed in a situation in which the child's person or health is endangered, is guilty of a misdemeanor and not an infraction and shall be punished by imprisonment in a county jail for not more than one year and by a fine of not more than five thousand dollars ($5,000).

(c) Pursuant to Section 654 of the Penal Code, an act or omission described in subdivision (a) or (b) that is punishable in different ways by different provisions of law shall be punished under the provision that provides for the longest potential term of imprisonment, but in no case shall the act or omission be punished under more than one provision. An acquittal or conviction and sentence under any one provision bars a prosecution for the same act or omission under any other provision. *(AD '10)*

40200.1. Simultaneous Notice of Parking Violation Notice to Appear Prohibited

A person shall not be subject to both a notice of parking violation and a notice to appear for the same violation. *(AD '09)*

Article 4. Procedure on Toll Evasion Violations

40250. Toll Evasion Violations

(a) Except where otherwise specifically provided, a violation of a statute, regulation, or ordinance governing the evasion of tolls on toll facilities under this code, under a federal or state statute or regulation, or under an ordinance enacted by a local authority including a joint powers authority, or a district organized pursuant to Part 3 (commencing with Section 27000) of Division 16 of the Streets and Highways Code is subject to a civil penalty. The enforcement of a civil penalty is governed by the civil administrative procedures set forth in this article.

(b) Except as provided in Section 40264, the registered owner, driver, rentee, or lessee of a vehicle cited for a toll evasion violation of a toll facility, under an applicable statute, regulation, or ordinance shall be jointly and severally liable for the toll evasion penalty imposed under this article, unless the owner can show that the vehicle was used without the express or implied consent of that person. A person who pays a toll evasion penalty, a civil judgment, costs, or administrative fees pursuant to this article has the right to recover the same from the driver, rentee, or lessee.

(c) The driver of a vehicle who is not the vehicle owner but who uses or operates the vehicle with the express or implied permission of the owner is the agent of the owner to receive a notice of a toll evasion violation served in accordance with this article and may contest the notice of violation.

(d) If the driver of the vehicle is in violation of a statute, regulation, or ordinance governing toll evasion violations, and if the driver is arrested pursuant to Article 1 (commencing with Section 40300) of Chapter 2, this article does not apply.

(e) For the purposes of this article, the following definitions apply:

(1) "Issuing agency"is an entity, public or private, authorized to collect tolls.

(2) "Registered owner"is either of the following:

(A) A person described in Section 505.

(B) A person registered as the owner of the vehicle by the appropriate agency or authority of another state, the District of Columbia, or a territory or possession of the United States. *(AM '07)*

40254. Toll Evasion: Notice of Violation

(a) If a vehicle is found, by automated devices, by visual observation, or otherwise, to have evaded tolls on any toll road or toll bridge, and subdivision (d) of Section 40250 does not apply, an issuing agency or a processing agency, as the case may be, shall, within 21 days of the violation, forward to the registered owner a notice of toll evasion violation setting forth the violation, including reference to the section violated, the approximate time thereof, and the location where the violation occurred. If accurate information concerning the identity and address of the registered owner is not available to the processing agency within 21 days of the violation, the processing agency shall have an additional 45 calendar days to obtain such information and forward the notice of toll evasion violation. Where the registered owner is a repeat violator, the processing agency shall forward the notice of toll evasion violation within 90 calendar days of the violation. "Repeat violator"means any registered owner for whom more than five violations have been issued pursuant to this section in any calendar month within the preceding 12-month period. The notice of toll evasion violation shall also set forth the following:

(1) The vehicle license plate number.

(2) If practicable, the registration expiration date and the make of the vehicle.

(3) A clear and concise explanation of the procedures for contesting the violation and appealing an adverse decision pursuant to Sections 40255 and 40256.

(b) Once the authorized person has notified the processing agency of a toll evasion violation, the processing agency shall prepare and forward the notice of violation to the registered owner of the vehicle cited for the violation. Any person, including the authorized person and any member of the person's department or agency, or any peace officer who, with intent to prejudice, damage, or defraud, is found guilty of altering, concealing, modifying, nullifying, or destroying, or causing to be altered, concealed, modified, nullified, or destroyed, the face of the original or any copy of a notice that was retained by the authorized person before it is filed with the processing agency or with a person authorized to receive the deposit of the toll evasion violation is guilty of a misdemeanor.

(c) If, after a copy of the notice of toll evasion violation has been sent to the registered owner, the issuing person determines that, due to a failure of proof of apparent violation, the notice of toll evasion violation should be dismissed, the issuing agency may recommend, in writing, that the charges be dismissed. The recommendation shall cite the reasons for the recommendation and shall be filed with the processing agency.

(d) If the processing agency makes a finding that there are grounds for dismissal, the notice of toll evasion violation shall be canceled pursuant to Section 40255.

(e) Under no circumstances shall a personal relationship with any law enforcement officer, public official, law enforcement agency, processing agency or toll operating agency or entity be grounds for dismissal of the violation.

The processing agency shall use its best efforts to obtain accurate information concerning the identity and address of the registered owner for the purpose of forwarding a notice of toll evasion violation pursuant to subdivision (a). *(AM '02)*

CHAPTER 2. PROCEDURES ON ARRESTS

40300.5. Arrest Without Warrant

In addition to the authority to make an arrest without a warrant pursuant to paragraph (1) of subdivision (a) of Section 836 of the Penal Code, a peace officer may, without a warrant, arrest a person when the officer has reasonable cause to believe that the person had been driving while under the influence of an alcoholic beverage or any drug, or under the combined influence of an alcoholic beverage and any drug when any of the following exists:

(a) The person is involved in a traffic accident.

(b) The person is observed in or about a vehicle that is obstructing a roadway.

(c) The person will not be apprehended unless immediately arrested.

(d) The person may cause injury to himself or herself or damage property unless immediately arrested.

(e) The person may destroy or conceal evidence of the crime unless immediately arrested.

40300.6. Place of Arrest: Driving Under the Influence

Section 40300.5 shall be liberally interpreted to further safe roads and the control of driving while under the influence of an alcoholic beverage or any drug in order to permit arrests to be made pursuant to that section within a reasonable time and distance away from the scene of a traffic accident.

The enactment of this section during the 1985-86 Regular Session of the Legislature does not constitute a change in, but is declaratory of, the existing law.

40301. Procedure

Except as provided in this chapter, whenever a person is arrested for any violation of this code declared to be a felony, he shall be dealt with in like manner as upon arrest for the commission of any other felony.

40302. Mandatory Appearance

Whenever any person is arrested for any violation of this code, not declared to be a felony, the arrested person shall be taken without unnecessary delay before a magistrate within the county in which the offense charged is alleged to have been committed and who has jurisdiction of the offense and is nearest or most accessible with reference to the place where the arrest is made in any of the following cases:

(a) When the person arrested fails to present his driver's license or other satisfactory evidence of his identity for examination.

(b) When the person arrested refuses to give his written promise to appear in court.

(c) When the person arrested demands an immediate appearance before a magistrate.

(d) When the person arrested is charged with violating Section 23152.

40302.5. Arrest of Minor

Whenever any person under the age of 18 years is taken into custody in connection with any traffic infraction case, and he is not taken directly before a magistrate, he shall be delivered to the custody of the probation officer. Unless sooner released, the probation officer shall keep the minor in the juvenile hall pending his appearance before a magistrate. When a minor is cited for an offense not involving the driving of a motor vehicle, the minor shall not be taken into custody pursuant to subdivision (a) of Section 40302 solely for failure to present a driver's license.

40303. Optional Appearance Before a Magistrate

(a) Whenever a person is arrested for any of the offenses listed in subdivision (b) and the arresting officer is not required to take the person without unnecessary delay before a magistrate, the arrested person shall, in the judgment of the arresting officer, either be given a 10 days' notice to appear, or be taken without unnecessary delay before a magistrate within the county in which the offense charged is alleged to have been committed and who has jurisdiction of the offense and is nearest or most accessible with reference to the place where the arrest is made. The officer may require that the arrested person, if he or she does not have satisfactory identification, place a right thumbprint, or a left thumbprint or fingerprint if the person has a missing or disfigured right thumb, on the 10 days' notice to appear when a 10 days' notice is provided. Except for law enforcement purposes relating to the identity of the arrestee, a person or entity shall not sell, give away, allow the distribution of, include in a database, or create a database with, this print.

(b) Subdivision (a) applies to the following offenses:

(1) Section 10852 or 10853, relating to injuring or tampering with a vehicle.

(2) Section 23103 or 23104, relating to reckless driving.

(3) Subdivision (a) of Section 2800, insofar as it relates to a failure or refusal of the driver of a vehicle to stop and submit to an inspection or test of the lights upon the vehicle pursuant to Section 2804, that is punishable as a misdemeanor.

(4) Subdivision (a) of Section 2800, insofar as it relates to a failure or refusal of the driver of a vehicle to stop and submit to a brake test that is punishable as a misdemeanor.

(5) Subdivision (a) of Section 2800, relating to the refusal to submit vehicle and load to an inspection, measurement, or weighing as prescribed in Section 2802 or a refusal to adjust the load or obtain a permit as prescribed in Section 2803.

(6) Subdivision (a) of Section 2800, insofar as it relates to a driver who continues to drive after being lawfully ordered not to drive by a member of the Department of the California Highway Patrol for violating the driver's hours of service or driver's log regulations adopted pursuant to subdivision (a) of Section 34501.

(7) Subdivision (b), (c), or (d) of Section 2800, relating to a failure or refusal to comply with a lawful out-of-service order.

(8) Section 20002 or 20003, relating to duties in the event of an accident.

(9) Section 23109, relating to participating in a speed contest or exhibition of speed.

(10) Section 14601, 14601.1, 14601.2, or 14601.5, relating to driving while the privilege to operate a motor vehicle is suspended or revoked.

(11) When the person arrested has attempted to evade arrest.

(12) Section 23332, relating to persons upon vehicular crossings.

(13) Section 2813, relating to the refusal to stop and submit a vehicle to an inspection of its size, weight, and equipment.

(14) Section 21461.5, insofar as it relates to a pedestrian who, after being cited for a violation of Section 21461.5, is, within 24 hours, again found upon the freeway in violation of Section 21461.5 and thereafter refuses to leave the freeway after being lawfully ordered to do so by a peace officer and after having been informed that his or her failure to leave could result in his or her arrest.

(15) Subdivision (a) of Section 2800, insofar as it relates to a pedestrian who, after having been cited for a violation of subdivision (a) of Section 2800 for failure to obey a lawful order of a peace officer issued pursuant to Section 21962, is within 24 hours again found upon the bridge or overpass and thereafter refuses to leave after being lawfully ordered to do so by a peace officer and after having been informed that his or her failure to leave could result in his or her arrest.

(16) Section 21200.5, relating to riding a bicycle while under the influence of an alcoholic beverage or a drug.

(17) Section 21221.5, relating to operating a motorized scooter while under the influence of an alcoholic beverage or a drug.

(c)(1) A person contesting a charge by claiming under penalty of perjury not to be the person issued the notice to appear may choose to submit a right thumbprint, or a left thumbprint if the person has a missing or disfigured right thumb, to the issuing court through his or her local law enforcement agency for comparison with the one placed on the notice to appear. A local law enforcement agency providing this service may charge the requester no more than the actual costs. The issuing court may refer the thumbprint submitted and the notice to appear to the prosecuting attorney for comparison of the thumbprints. When there is no thumbprint or fingerprint on the notice to appear, or when the comparison of thumbprints is inconclusive, the court shall refer the notice to appear or copy thereof back to the issuing agency for further investigation, unless the court finds that referral is not in the interest of justice.

(2) Upon initiation of the investigation or comparison process by referral of the court, the court shall continue the case and the speedy trial period shall be tolled for 45 days.

(3) Upon receipt of the issuing agency's or prosecuting attorney's response, the court may make a finding of factual innocence pursuant to Section 530.6 of the Penal Code if the court determines that there is insufficient evidence that the person cited is the person charged and shall immediately notify the Department of Motor Vehicles of its determination. If the Department of Motor Vehicles determines the citation

or citations in question formed the basis of a suspension or revocation of the person's driving privilege, the department shall immediately set aside the action.

(4) If the prosecuting attorney or issuing agency fails to respond to a court referral within 45 days, the court shall make a finding of factual innocence pursuant to Section 530.6 of the Penal Code, unless the court finds that a finding of factual innocence is not in the interest of justice.

(5) The citation or notice to appear may be held by the prosecuting attorney or issuing agency for future adjudication should the arrestee who received the citation or notice to appear be found. *(AM '06)*

40303.5. Notice to Correct Violation for Specified Infractions

Whenever any person is arrest for any of the following offenses, the arresting officer shall permit the arrested person to execute a notice containing a promise to correct the violation in accordance with the provisions of Section 40610 unless the arresting officer finds that any of the disqualifying conditions specified in subdivision (b) of Section 40610 exist:

(a) Any registration infraction set forth in Division 3, (commencing with Section 4000).

(b) Any driver's license infraction set forth in Division 6, (commencing with Section 12500), and subdivision (a) of Section 12951, relating to possession of driver's license.

(c) Section 21201, relating to bicycle equipment.

(d) Any infraction involving equipment set forth in Division 12 (commencing with Section 24000), Division 13 (commencing with Section 29000), Division 14.8 (commencing with Section 34500), Division 16 (commencing with Section 36000), Division 16.5 (commencing with Section 38000), and Division 16.7 (commencing with Section 39000).

40305. Offense by Nonresident

(a) Whenever a nonresident is arrested for violating any section of this code while driving a motor vehicle and does not furnish satisfactory evidence of identity and an address within this state at which he or she can be located, he or she may, in the discretion of the arresting officer, be taken immediately before a magistrate within the county where the offense charged is alleged to have been committed, and who has jurisdiction over the offense and is nearest or most accessible with reference to the place where the arrest is made. If the magistrate is not available at the time of the arrest and the arrested person is not taken before any other person authorized to receive a deposit of bail, and if the arresting officer does not have the authority or is not required to take the arrested person before a magistrate or other person authorized to receive a deposit of bail by some other provision of law, the officer may require the arrested person, if he or she has no satisfactory identification, to place a right thumbprint, or a left thumbprint or fingerprint if the person has a missing or disfigured right thumb, on the notice to appear as provided in Article 2 (commencing with Section 40500).

Except for law enforcement purposes relating to the identity of the arrestee, no person or entity may sell, give away, allow the distribution of, include in a database, or create a database with, this print.

(b)(1) A person contesting a charge by claiming under penalty of perjury not to be the person issued the notice to appear may choose to submit a right thumbprint, or a left thumbprint if the person has a missing or disfigured right thumb, to the issuing court through his or her local law enforcement agency for comparison with the one placed on the notice to appear. A local law enforcement agency providing this service may charge the requester no more than the actual costs. The issuing court may refer the thumbprint submitted and the notice to appear to the prosecuting attorney for comparison of the thumbprints. When there is no thumbprint or fingerprint on the notice to appear, or when the comparison of thumbprints is inconclusive, the court shall refer the notice to appear or copy thereof back to the issuing agency for further investigation, unless the court finds that referral is not in the interest of justice.

(2) Upon initiation of the investigation or comparison process by referral of the court, the court shall continue the case and the speedy trial period shall be tolled for 45 days.

(3) Upon receipt of the issuing agency's or prosecuting attorney's response, the court may make a finding of factual innocence pursuant to Section 530.6 of the Penal Code if the court determines that there is insufficient evidence that the person cited is the person charged and shall immediately notify the Depart-

ment of Motor Vehicles of its determination. If the Department of Motor Vehicles determines the citation or citations in question formed the basis of a suspension or revocation of the person's driving privilege, the department shall immediately set aside the action.

(4) If the prosecuting attorney or issuing agency fails to respond to a court referral within 45 days, the court shall make a finding of factual innocence pursuant to Section 530.6 of the Penal Code, unless the court determines that a finding of factual innocence is not in the interest of justice.

(5) The citation or notice to appear may be held by the prosecuting attorney or issuing agency for future adjudication should the arrestee who received the citation or notice to appear be found. *(AM '03)*

40305.5. Offense by Nonresident: Commercial Vehicles

(a) If a nonresident is arrested for violating this code while driving a commercially registered motor vehicle, excluding house cars, with an unladen weight of 7,000 pounds or more, and does not furnish satisfactory evidence of identity and an address within this state at which he or she can be located, the arresting officer may, in lieu of the procedures set forth in Section 40305, accept a guaranteed traffic arrest bail bond certificate, and the nonresident shall be released from custody upon giving a written promise to appear as provided in Article 2 (commencing with Section 40500). The officer may require the arrested person, if he or she has no satisfactory identification, to place a right thumbprint, or a left thumbprint or fingerprint if the person has a missing or disfigured right thumb, on the notice to appear as provided in Article 2 (commencing with Section 45000). Except for law enforcement purposes relating to the identity of the arrestee, a person or entity shall not sell, give away, allow the distribution of, include in a database, or create a database with, this print.

(b) Every guaranteed traffic arrest bail bond certificate shall contain all of the following information:

(1) The name and address of the surety and of the issuer, if other than the surety.

(2) The name, address, driver's license number and signature of the individual covered by the certificate.

(3) The maximum amount guaranteed.

(4) Exclusions from coverage.

(5) A statement that the issuing company guarantees the appearance of a person to whom a guaranteed traffic arrest bail bond certificate is issued and, in the event of the failure of the person to appear in court at the time of trial, the issuing company shall pay any fine or forfeiture imposed on the person, not to exceed the amount stated on the certificate.

(6) The expiration date of the certificate.

(c) A guaranteed traffic arrest bail bond certificate may be issued by a surety admitted in this state. The certificate may also be issued by an association of motor carriers if all of the following conditions are met:

(1) The association is incorporated, or authorized to do business, in this state.

(2) The association is covered by a guaranteed traffic arrest bail bond issued by a surety admitted in this state.

(3) The association agrees to pay fines or bail assessed against the guaranteed traffic arrest bail bond certificate.

(4) The surety guarantees payment of fines or bail assessed against the guaranteed traffic arrest bail bond certificates issued by the association.

(d) The arresting officer shall file the guaranteed traffic arrest bail bond certificate with the notice to appear required to be filed by Section 40506.

(e) A "guaranteed traffic arrest bail bond certificate" is a document that guarantees the payment of fines or bail assessed against an individual for violation of this code, except driving while under the influence of alcohol or drugs, driving without a license or driving with a suspended or revoked license, operating a motor vehicle without the permission of the owner, or any violation punishable as a felony.

(f) A "guaranteed traffic arrest bail bond" is a bond issued by a surety guaranteeing the obligations of the issuer of guaranteed traffic arrest bail bond certificates. The bond shall be in the amount of fifty thousand dollars ($50,000) and shall be filed with the Secretary of State. Any court in this state may assess against the surety the amount of covered fines or bail that the issuer of a guaranteed traffic arrest bail bond certificate fails to pay.

(g)(1) A person contesting a charge by claiming under penalty of perjury not to be the person issued the notice to appear may choose to submit a right thumbprint, or a left thumbprint if the person has a missing or disfigured right thumb, to the issuing court through his or her local law enforcement agency for comparison with the one placed on the notice to appear. A local law enforcement agency providing this service may charge the requester no more than the actual costs. The issuing court may refer the thumbprint submitted and the notice to appear to the prosecuting attorney for comparison of the thumbprints. If there is no thumbprint or fingerprint on the notice to appear or the comparison of thumbprints is inconclusive, the court shall refer the notice to appear or copy of the notice to appear back to the issuing agency for further investigation, unless the court finds that referral is not in the interest of justice.

(2) Upon initiation of the investigation or comparison process by referral of the court, the court shall continue the case and the speedy trial period shall be tolled for 45 days.

(3) Upon receipt of the issuing agency's or prosecuting attorney's response, the court may make a finding of factual innocence pursuant to Section 530.6 of the Penal Code if the court determines that there is insufficient evidence that the person cited is the person charged and shall immediately notify the Department of Motor Vehicles of its determination. If the Department of Motor Vehicles determines the citation or citations in question formed the basis of a suspension or revocation of the person's driving privilege, the department shall immediately set aside the action.

(4) If the prosecuting attorney or issuing agency fails to respond to a court referral within 45 days, the court shall make a finding of factual innocence pursuant to Section 530.6 of the Penal Code, unless the court determines that a finding of factual innocence is not in the interest of justice.

(5) The citation or notice to appear may be held by the prosecuting attorney or issuing agency for future adjudication should the arrestee who received the citation or notice to appear be found. *(AM '11)*

40312. Arrest Prohibition: Receipt for Fine
A peace officer shall not arrest, on the basis of an outstanding warrant arising from a violation of this code, any person who presents to the peace officer a receipt, from a proper official of the court, indicating that the person has paid the fine for the violation that caused the warrant to be issued. The receipt shall contain sufficient information to identify the name and number of the court issuing the receipt, the date the case was adjudicated or the fine was paid, the case number or docket number, and the violations disposed of.

40500. Notice to Appear
(a) Whenever a person is arrested for any violation of this code not declared to be a felony, or for a violation of an ordinance of a city or county relating to traffic offenses and he or she is not immediately taken before a magistrate, as provided in this chapter, the arresting officer shall prepare in triplicate a written notice to appear in court or before a person authorized to receive a deposit of bail, containing the name and address of the person, the license number of his or her vehicle, if any, the name and address, when available, of the registered owner or lessee of the vehicle, the offense charged and the time and place when and where he or she shall appear. If the arrestee does not have a driver's license or other satisfactory evidence of identity in his or her possession, the officer may require the arrestee to place a right thumbprint, or a left thumbprint or fingerprint if the person has a missing or disfigured right thumb, on the notice to appear. Except for law enforcement purposes relating to the identity of the arrestee, no person or entity may sell, give away, allow the distribution of, include in a database, or create a database with, this print.

(b) The Judicial Council shall prescribe the form of the notice to appear.

(c) Nothing in this section requires the law enforcement agency or the arresting officer issuing the notice to appear to inform any person arrested pursuant to this section of the amount of bail required to be deposited for the offense charged.

(d) Once the arresting officer has prepared the written notice to appear, and has delivered a copy to the arrested person, the officer shall deliver the remaining original and all copies of the notice to appear as provided by Section 40506.

Any person, including the arresting officer and any member of the officer's department or agency, or any peace officer, who alters, conceals, modifies, nullifies, or destroys, or causes to be altered, concealed, modified, nullified, or destroyed, the face side of the remaining original or any copy of a citation that was retained by the officer, for any reason, before it is filed with the magistrate or with a person authorized by the magistrate or judge to receive a deposit of bail, is guilty of a misdemeanor.

If, after an arrested person has signed and received a copy of a notice to appear, the arresting officer or other officer of the issuing agency, determines that, in the interest of justice, the citation or notice should be dismissed, the arresting agency may recommend, in writing, to the magistrate or judge that the case be dismissed. The recommendation shall cite the reasons for the recommendation and be filed with the court.

If the magistrate or judge makes a finding that there are grounds for dismissal, the finding shall be entered on the record and the infraction or misdemeanor dismissed.

Under no circumstances shall a personal relationship with any officer, public official, or law enforcement agency be grounds for dismissal.

(e)(1) A person contesting a charge by claiming under penalty of perjury not to be the person issued the notice to appear may choose to submit a right thumbprint, or a left thumbprint if the person has a missing or disfigured right thumb, to the issuing court through his or her local law enforcement agency for comparison with the one placed on the notice to appear. A local law enforcement agency providing this service may charge the requester no more than the actual costs. The issuing court may refer the thumbprint submitted and the notice to appear to the prosecuting attorney for comparison of the thumbprints. When there is no thumbprint or fingerprint on the notice to appear, or when the comparison of thumbprints is inconclusive, the court shall refer the notice to appear or copy thereof back to the issuing agency for further investigation, unless the court determines that referral is not in the interest of justice.

(2) Upon initiation of the investigation or comparison process by referral of the court, the court shall continue the case and the speedy trial period shall be tolled for 45 days.

(3) Upon receipt of the issuing agency's or prosecuting attorney's response, the court may make a finding of factual innocence pursuant to Section 530.6 of the Penal Code if the court determines that there is insufficient evidence that the person cited is the person charged and shall immediately notify the Department of Motor Vehicles of its determination. If the Department of Motor Vehicles determines the citation or citations in question formed the basis of a suspension or revocation of the person's driving privilege, the department shall immediately set aside the action.

(4) If the prosecuting attorney or issuing agency fails to respond to a court referral within 45 days, the court shall make a finding of factual innocence pursuant to Section 530.6 of the Penal Code, unless the court determines that a finding of factual innocence is not in the interest of justice.

(5) The citation or notice to appear may be held by the prosecuting attorney or issuing agency for future adjudication should the arrestee who received the citation or notice to appear be found. *(AM '03)*

40504. Delivery of Notice

(a) The officer shall deliver one copy of the notice to appear to the arrested person and the arrested person in order to secure release must give his or her written promise to appear in court or before a person authorized to receive a deposit of bail by signing two copies of the notice which shall be retained by the officer, and the officer may require the arrested person, if this person has no satisfactory identification, to place a right thumbprint, or a left thumbprint or fingerprint if the person has a missing or disfigured right thumb, on the notice to appear. Thereupon, the arresting officer shall forthwith release the person arrested from custody. Except for law enforcement purposes relating to the identity of the arrestee, no person or entity may sell, give away, allow the distribution of, include in a database, or create a database with, this print.

(b) Any person who signs a written promise to appear with a false or fictitious name is guilty of a misdemeanor regardless of the disposition of the charge upon which he or she was originally arrested.

(c)(1) A person contesting a charge by claiming under penalty of perjury not to be the person issued the notice to appear may choose to submit a right thumbprint, or a left thumbprint if the person has a missing or disfigured right thumb, to the issuing court through his or her local law enforcement agency for comparison with the one placed on the notice to appear. A local law enforcement agency providing this service may charge the requester no more than the actual costs. The issuing court may refer the thumbprint submitted and the notice to appear to the prosecuting attorney for comparison of the thumbprints. When there is no thumbprint or fingerprint on the notice to appear, or when the comparison of thumbprints is inconclusive, the court shall refer the notice to appear or copy thereof back to the issuing agency for further investigation, unless the court finds that referral is not in the interest of justice.

(2) Upon initiation of the investigation or comparison process by referral of the court, the court shall continue the case and the speedy trial period shall be tolled for 45 days.

(3) Upon receipt of the issuing agency's or prosecuting attorney's response, the court may make a finding of factual innocence pursuant to Section 530.6 of the Penal Code if the court determines that there is insufficient evidence that the person cited is the person charged and shall immediately notify the Department of Motor Vehicles of its determination. If the Department of Motor Vehicles determines the citation or citations in question formed the basis of a suspension or revocation of the person's driving privilege, the department shall immediately set aside the action.

(4) If the prosecuting attorney or issuing agency fails to respond to a court referral within 45 days, the court shall make a finding of factual innocence pursuant to Section 530.6 of the Penal Code, unless the court finds that a finding of factual innocence is not in the interest of justice.

(5) The citation or notice to appear may be held by the prosecuting attorney or issuing agency for future adjudication should the arrestee who received the citation or notice to appear be found. *(AM '03)*

40508. Violation of Promise to Appear or Pay Fine

(a) A person willfully violating his or her written promise to appear or a lawfully granted continuance of his or her promise to appear in court or before a person authorized to receive a deposit of bail is guilty of a misdemeanor regardless of the disposition of the charge upon which he or she was originally arrested.

(b) A person willfully failing to pay bail in installments as agreed to under Section 40510.5 or a lawfully imposed fine for a violation of a provision of this code or a local ordinance adopted pursuant to this code within the time authorized by the court and without lawful excuse having been presented to the court on or before the date the bail or fine is due is guilty of a misdemeanor regardless of the full payment of the bail or fine after that time.

(c) A person willfully failing to comply with a condition of a court order for a violation of this code, other than for failure to appear or failure to pay a fine, is guilty of a misdemeanor, regardless of his or her subsequent compliance with the order.

(d) If a person convicted of an infraction fails to pay bail in installments as agreed to under Section 40510.5, or a fine or an installment thereof, within the time authorized by the court, the court may, except as otherwise provided in this subdivision, impound the person's driver's license and order the person not to drive for a period not to exceed 30 days. Before returning the license to the person, the court shall endorse on the reverse side of the license that the person was ordered not to drive, the period for which that order was made, and the name of the court making the order. If a defendant with a class C or M driver's license satisfies the court that impounding his or her driver's license and ordering the defendant not to drive will affect his or her livelihood, the court shall order that the person limit his or her driving for a period not to exceed 30 days to driving that is essential in the court's determination to the person's employment, including the person's driving to and from his or her place of employment if other means of transportation are not reasonably available. The court shall provide for the endorsement of the limitation on the person's license. The impounding of the license and ordering the person not to drive or the order limiting the person's driving does not constitute a suspension of the license, but a violation of the order constitutes contempt of court. *(AM '03, '07)*

40519. Trial Scheduling; Written Not Guilty

(a) Any person who has received a written notice to appear for an infraction may, prior to the time at which the person is required to appear, make a deposit and declare the intention to plead not guilty to the clerk of the court named in the notice to appear. The deposit shall be in the amount of bail established pursuant to Section 1269b of the Penal Code, together with any assessment required by Section 42006 of this code or Section 1464 of the Penal Code, for the offense charged, and shall be used for the purpose of guaranteeing the appearance of the defendant at the time and place scheduled by the clerk for arraignment and for trial, and to apply toward the payment of any fine or assessment prescribed by the court in the event of conviction. The case shall thereupon be set for arraignment and trial on the same date, unless the defendant requests separate arraignment. A deposit of bail under this section does not constitute entry of a plea or a court appearance. A plea of not guilty under this section must be made in court at the arraignment.

(b) Any person who has received a written notice to appear may, prior to the time at which the person is required to appear, plead not guilty in writing in lieu of appearing in person. The written plea shall be directed to the court named in the notice to appear and, if mailed, shall be sent by certified or registered mail postmarked not later than five days prior to the day upon which appearance is required. The written plea and request to the court or city agency shall be accompanied by a deposit consisting of the amount of bail established pursuant to Section 1269b of the Penal Code, together with any assessment required by Section 42006 of this code or Section 1464 of the Penal Code, for that offense, which amount shall be used for the purpose of guaranteeing the appearance of the defendant at the time and place set by the court for trial and to apply toward the payment of any fine or assessment prescribed by the court in the event of conviction. Upon receipt of the plea and deposit, the case shall be set for arraignment and trial on the same date, unless the defendant requests separate arraignment. Thereafter, the case shall be conducted in the same manner as if the defendant had appeared in person, had made his or her plea in open court, and had deposited that sum as bail. The court or the clerk of the court shall notify the accused of the time and place of trial by first-class mail postmarked at least 10 days prior to the time set for the trial. Any person using this procedure shall be deemed to have waived the right to be tried within the statutory period.

(c) Any person using the procedure set forth in subdivision (a) or (b) shall be deemed to have given a written promise to appear at the time designated by the court for trial, and failure to appear at the trial shall constitute a misdemeanor. *(AM '09)*

40600. Notice of Violation; Reasonable Cause for Issuance

(a) Notwithstanding any other provision of law, a peace officer who has successfully completed a course or courses of instruction, approved by the Commission on Peace Officer Standards and Training, in the investigation of traffic accidents may prepare, in triplicate, on a form approved by the Judicial Council, a written notice to appear when the peace officer has reasonable cause to believe that any person involved in a traffic accident has violated a provision of this code not declared to be a felony or a local ordinance and the violation was a factor in the occurrence of the traffic accident.

(b) A notice to appear shall contain the name and address of the person, the license number of the person's vehicle, if any, the name and address, when available, of the registered owner or lessee of the vehicle, the offense charged, and the time and place when and where the person may appear in court or before a person authorized to receive a deposit of bail. The time specified shall be at least 10 days after the notice to appear is delivered.

(c) The preparation and delivery of a notice to appear pursuant to this section is not an arrest.

(d) For purposes of this article, a peace officer has reasonable cause to issue a written notice to appear if, as a result of the officer's investigation, the officer has evidence, either testimonial or real, or a combination of testimonial and real, that would be sufficient to issue a written notice to appear if the officer had personally witnessed the events investigated.

(e) As used in this section, "peace officer"means any person specified under Section 830.1 or 830.2 of the Penal Code, or any reserve police officer or reserve deputy sheriff listed in Section 830.6 of the Penal Code, with the exception of members of the California National Guard.

(f) A written notice to appear prepared on a form approved by the Judicial Council and issued pursuant to this section shall be accepted by any court. *(AM '03)*

40610. Notice to Correct Violation

(a)(1) Except as provided in paragraph (2), if, after an arrest, accident investigation, or other law enforcement action, it appears that a violation has occurred involving a registration, license, all-terrain vehicle safety certificate, or mechanical requirement of this code, and none of the disqualifying conditions set forth in subdivision (b) exist and the investigating officer decides to take enforcement action, the officer shall prepare, in triplicate, and the violator shall sign, a written notice containing the violator's promise to correct the alleged violation and to deliver proof of correction of the violation to the issuing agency.

(2) If any person is arrested for a violation of Section 4454, and none of the disqualifying conditions set forth in subdivision (b) exist, the arresting officer shall prepare, in triplicate, and the violator shall sign, a written notice containing the violator's promise to correct the alleged violation and to deliver proof of correction of the violation to the issuing agency. In lieu of issuing a notice to correct violation pursuant to this section, the officer may issue a notice to appear, as specified in Section 40522.

(b) Pursuant to subdivision (a), a notice to correct violation shall be issued as provided in this section or a notice to appear shall be issued as provided in Section 40522, unless the officer finds any of the following:

(1) Evidence of fraud or persistent neglect.

(2) The violation presents an immediate safety hazard.

(3) The violator does not agree to, or cannot, promptly correct the violation.

(c) If any of the conditions set forth in subdivision (b) exist, the procedures specified in this section or Section 40522 are inapplicable, and the officer may take other appropriate enforcement action.

(d) Except as otherwise provided in subdivision (a), the notice to correct violation shall be on a form approved by the Judicial Council and, in addition to the owner's or operator's address and identifying information, shall contain an estimate of the reasonable time required for correction and proof of correction of the particular defect, not to exceed 30 days, or 90 days for the all-terrain vehicle safety certificate. *(AM '04)*

40614. Sign with False or Fictitious Name

Any person who signs a notice to correct or a certificate of correction with a false or fictitious name is guilty of a misdemeanor.

40616. Fail to Correct or Deliver Proof

Any person willfully violating a written promise to correct or willfully failing to deliver proof of correction of violation is guilty of a misdemeanor. Proof of correction may consist of a certification by an authorized representative of one of the following agencies that the alleged violation has been corrected:

(a) Brake, lamp, smog device, or muffler violations may be certified as corrected by any station licensed to inspect and certify for the violation pursuant to Article 8 of Chapter 20.3 of Division 3 of the Business and Professions Code and Section 27150.2.

(b) Driver license and registration violations may be certified as corrected by the department or by any clerk or deputy clerk of a court.

(c) Any violation may be certified as corrected by a police department, the CHP, sheriff, marshal, or other law enforcement agency regularly engaged in enforcement of the Vehicle Code.

This page intentionally left blank.

Asterisks (***) Denote Text Deleted By Legislation

SELECTED PROVISIONS FROM THE FOLLOWING CALIFORNIA CODES

Business & Professions

Fish & Game

Food & Agricultural

Harbors & Navigation

Health & Safety

Public Resources

Public Utilities

Streets & Highways

BUSINESS AND PROFESSIONS CODE

25661.   Minor Possessing or Using False I. D.

(a) Any person under the age of 21 years who presents or offers to any licensee, his or her agent or employee, any written, printed, or photostatic evidence of age and identity which is false, fraudulent or not actually his or her own for the purpose of ordering, purchasing, attempting to purchase or otherwise procuring or attempting to procure, the serving of any alcoholic beverage, or who has in his or her possession any false or fraudulent written, printed, or photostatic evidence of age and identity, is guilty of a misdemeanor and shall be punished by a fine of at least two hundred fifty dollars ($250), no part of which shall be suspended; or the person shall be required to perform not less than 24 hours nor more than 32 hours of community service during hours when the person is not employed and is not attending school, or a combination of fine and community service as determined by the court. A second or subsequent violation of this section shall be punished by a fine of not more than five hundred dollars ($500), or the person shall be required to perform not less than 36 hours or more than 48 hours of community service during hours when the person is not employed or is not attending school, or a combination of fine and community service, as the court deems just. It is the intent of the Legislature that the community service requirements prescribed in this section require service at an alcohol or drug treatment program or facility or at a county coroner's office, if available, in the area where the violation occurred or where the person resides.

(b) The penalties imposed by this section do not preclude prosecution or the imposition of penalties under any other provision of law, including, but not limited to, Section 13202.5 of the Vehicle Code. *(AM '07)*

25662.   Possession of Alcohol by Minor

(a) Except as provided in Section 25667, any person under the age of 21 years who has any alcoholic beverage in his or her possession on any street or highway or in any public place or in any place open to the public is guilty of a misdemeanor and shall be punished by a fine of two hundred fifty dollars ($250) or the person shall be required to perform not less than 24 hours or more than 32 hours of community service during hours when the person is not employed or is not attending school. A second or subsequent violation shall be punishable as a misdemeanor and the person shall be fined not more than five hundred dollars ($500), or required to perform not less than 36 hours or more than 48 hours of community service during hours when the person is not employed or is not attending school, or a combination of fine and community service as the court deems just. It is the intent of the Legislature that the community service requirements prescribed in this section require service at an alcohol or drug treatment program or facility or at a county coroner's office, if available, in the area where the violation occurred or where the person resides. This section does not apply to possession by a person under the age of 21 years making a delivery of an alcoholic beverage in pursuance of the order of his or her parent, responsible adult relative, or any other adult designated by the parent or legal guardian, or in pursuance of his or her employment. That person shall have a complete defense if he or she was following, in a timely manner, the reasonable instructions of his or her parent, legal guardian, responsible adult relative, or adult designee relating to disposition of the alcoholic beverage.

(b) Unless otherwise provided by law, where a peace officer has lawfully entered the premises, the peace officer may seize any alcoholic beverage in plain view that is in the possession of, or provided to, a person under the age of 21 years at social gatherings, when those gatherings are open to the public, 10 or more persons under the age of 21 years are participating, persons under the age of 21 years are consuming alcoholic beverages, and there is no supervision of the social gathering by a parent or guardian of one or more of the participants.

Where a peace officer has seized alcoholic beverages pursuant to this subdivision, the officer may destroy any alcoholic beverage contained in an opened container and in the possession of, or provided to, a person under the age of 21 years, and, with respect to alcoholic beverages in unopened containers, the officer shall impound those beverages for a period not to exceed seven working days pending a request for the release of those beverages by a person 21 years of age or older who is the lawful owner or resident of the property upon which the alcoholic beverages were seized. If no one requests release of the seized alcoholic beverages within that period, those beverages may be destroyed.

(c) The penalties imposed by this section do not preclude prosecution or the imposition of penalties under any other provision of law, including, but not limited to, Section 13202.5 of the Vehicle Code. *(AM '10)*

25667. Persons Under the Age of 21 Years Immune from Prosecution

(a) Any person under the age of 21 years shall be immune from criminal prosecution under subdivision (a) of Section 25662 and subdivision (b) of Section 25658, where the person establishes all of the following:

(1) The underage person called 911 and reported that either himself or herself or another person was in need of medical assistance due to alcohol consumption.

(2) The underage person was the first person to make the 911 report.

(3) The underage person, who reported that another person was in need of medical assistance, remained on the scene with the other person until that medical assistance arrived and cooperated with medical assistance and law enforcement personnel on the scene.

(b) This section shall not provide immunity from criminal prosecution for any offense that involves activities made dangerous by the consumption of alcoholic beverages, including, but not limited to, a violation of Section 23103 of the Vehicle Code, as specified by Section 23103.5 of the Vehicle Code, or a violation of Sections 23152 and 23153 of the Vehicle Code. *(AD '10)*

FISH AND GAME CODE

2005. Use of Lights; Sniperscopes

(a) Except as otherwise authorized by this section, it is unlawful to use an artificial light to assist in the taking of game birds, game mammals, or game fish, except that this section shall not apply to sport fishing in ocean waters or other waters where night fishing is permitted if the lights are not used on or as part of the fishing tackle, commercial fishing, nor to the taking of mammals, the taking of which is governed by Article 2 (commencing with Section 4180) of Chapter 3 of Part 3 of Division 4.

(b) It is unlawful for any person, or one or more persons, to throw or cast the rays of any spotlight, headlight, or other artificial light on any highway or in any field, woodland, or forest where game mammals, fur-bearing mammals, or nongame mammals are commonly found, or upon any game mammal, fur-bearing mammal, or nongame mammal, while having in his or her possession or under his or her control any firearm or weapon with which that mammal could be killed, even though the mammal is not killed, injured, shot at, or otherwise pursued.

(c) It is unlawful to use or possess at any time any infrared or similar light used in connection with an electronic viewing device or any night vision equipment, optical devices, including, but not limited to, binoculars or scopes, that use light-amplifying circuits that are electrical or battery powered, to assist in the taking of birds, mammals, amphibians, or fish.

(d) The provisions of this section do not apply to any of the following:

(1) The use of a hand -held flashlight no larger, nor emitting more light, than a two-cell, three-volt flashlight, provided that light is not affixed in any way to a weapon, or to the use of a lamp or lantern that does not cast a directional beam of light.

(2) Headlights of a motor vehicle operated in a usual manner where there is no attempt or intent to locate a game mammal, fur-bearing mammal, or nongame mammal.

(3) To the owner, or his or her employee, of land devoted to the agricultural industry while on that land, or land controlled by such an owner and in connection with the agricultural industry.

(4) To those other uses as the commission may authorize by regulation.

(e) A person shall not be arrested for violation of this section except by a peace officer. *(AM '07)*

2006. Loaded Rifle or Shotgun in Vehicle

(a) It is unlawful to possess a loaded rifle or shotgun in any vehicle or conveyance or its attachments which is standing on or along or is being driven on or along any public highway or other way open to the public.

(b) A rifle or shotgun shall be deemed to be loaded for the purposes of this section when there is an unexpended cartridge or shell in the firing chamber but not when the only cartridges or shells are in the magazine.

(c) The provisions of this section shall not apply to peace officers or members of the Armed Forces of this state or the United States, while on duty or going to or returning from duty. *(AM '11)*

2016. Unlawful Entry Onto Lands Fenced, Posted or Under Cultivation To Discharge Firearm, Take Game, Etc.; Sign Requirements; Permissions

It is unlawful to enter any lands under cultivation or enclosed by a fence, belonging to, or occupied by, another, or to enter any uncultivated or unenclosed lands, including lands temporarily inundated by waters flowing outside the established banks of a river, stream, slough, or other waterway, where signs forbidding trespass or hunting, or both, are displayed at intervals not less than three to the mile along all exterior boundaries and at all roads and trails entering those lands, for the purpose of discharging any firearm or taking or destroying any mammal or bird, including any waterfowl, on those lands without having first obtained written permission from the owner, or his or her agent, or the person in lawful possession of, those lands. Signs may be of any size and wording that will fairly advise persons about to enter the land that the use of the land is so restricted. *(AM '12)*

3002. Shooting From Vehicles

It is unlawful to shoot at any game bird or mammal, including a marine mammal as defined in Section 4500, from a powerboat, sailboat, motor vehicle, or airplane.

3003.5. Illegal Herding with Motorized Vehicles

It is unlawful to pursue, drive, or herd any bird or mammal with any motorized water, land, or air vehicle, including, but not limited to, a motor vehicle, airplane, powerboat, or snowmobile, except in any of the following circumstances:

(a) On private property by the landowner or tenant thereof to haze birds or mammals for the purpose of preventing damage by that wildlife to private property.

(b) Pursuant to a permit from the department issued under regulations as the commission may prescribe.

(c) In the pursuit of agriculture. *(AM '07)*

3004. Discharge of Deadly Weapons within 150 Yards of Buildings; Exceptions

(a) It is unlawful for any person, other than the owner, person in possession of the premises, or a person having the express permission of the owner or person in possession of the premises, to hunt or to discharge while hunting, any firearm or other deadly weapon within 150 yards of any occupied dwelling house, residence, or other building or any barn or other outbuilding used in connection therewith. The 150-yard area is a "safety zone."

(b) It is unlawful for any person to intentionally discharge any firearm or release any arrow or crossbow bolt over or across any public road or other established way open to the public in an unsafe and reckless manner. *(AM '07, '09)*

FOOD AND AGRICULTURAL CODE

5341.5. Certificate of Inspection

(a) Every operator of a motor vehicle entering the state with a shipment of any agricultural commodity shall cause the vehicle and the shipment to be inspected, and shall obtain a certificate of inspection, at the plant quarantine inspection station nearest the point of entry into the state.

(b) Failure to obtain the required certificate of inspection shall subject the operator of the vehicle and the registered owner of the vehicle, if a different person or legal entity, to separate civil penalties of not more than two thousand five hundred dollars ($2,500) for each violation. In determining the severity of the penalty to be imposed, the court shall consider any prior violations of the same nature within the preceding 24 months, the commodity being transported, and any evidence, including deviation from normal and usual routes, that the operator of the vehicle intentionally avoided inspection.

(c) Inspection shall not be required when the operator of the vehicle would be required to travel a distance of 15 miles or more from normal and usual routes for the particular trip to obtain the required inspection and certification, or when weather conditions or road closures on normal and usual routes prevent travel to the nearest plant quarantine inspection station.

(d) Violation of this section is a separate offense from violation of any other provision of this code and proceedings under this section shall not be deemed to prevent separate proceedings for any other offense.

(e) Proceedings under this section may be brought by the secretary or, with the secretary's concurrence, by the district attorney of the county in which the violation occurred. The civil penalty shall be awarded to the agency which brings the enforcement action for use by that agency in enforcing the provisions of this code.

(f) The secretary may, by regulation or executive order, as the secretary deems advisable, permit exceptions for certain commodities, areas, and times consistent with the purposes of this division, patterns of local traffic near border areas, and availability of inspection stations.

(g) Persons holding a valid permit to transport cattle pursuant to Section 21067 are exempt from this section. *(AM '10)*

5344. Plant Quarantine and Pest Control
It is unlawful for the operator of any vehicle to fail to stop the vehicle at an inspection station or upon demand of a clearly identified plant quarantine officer, or officers authorized pursuant to Section 5348 to cite persons for violations committed pursuant to this article, for the purpose of determining whether any quarantine which is established pursuant to any provision of this division is being violated.

5345. Operation of Vehicle in Violation of Quarantine
It is unlawful for any person to operate upon any highway in this state any vehicle which, in violation of Section 5344, was not stopped as required by that section, if the person who is operating such vehicle knows of such violation of Section 5344. The violation of this section continues unless and until one of the following occurs:

(a) A period of 24 hours has elapsed following the violation of Section 5344.

(b) The operator who violated Section 5344 has been apprehended and the vehicle which is involved has been inspected and released from quarantine by any authorized state plant quarantine officer. An operator who is so apprehended does Not violate this section by reason of operating the vehicle enroute to the closest inspection station immediately following his apprehension for violation of Section 5344, nor does any other person, who operates the vehicle for such purpose, violate this section.

9702. Animal Quarantine Inspection; Failure to Stop
It is unlawful for the operator of any vehicle to fail to stop the vehicle upon demand of a clearly identified animal health quarantine officer when the officer orders the operator to stop for the purpose of determining whether any quarantine which is established pursuant to this chapter is being violated and the officer has reasonable cause to believe that the vehicle is being used in connection with a quarantine violation.

16151. Disposal of Garbage; Exceptions
It is unlawful for any person to throw, discharge, deposit, remove, or carry garbage, or cause, suffer, or procure garbage to be thrown, discharged, deposited, removed, or carried, from any vessel, aircraft, or any other vehicle into any territorial waters, or onto land within the state, except for any of the following:

(a) Immediate burning in incinerators.

(b) Approved treatment or approved disposal under the supervision and pursuant to the regulations of the director.

(c) Delivery to a garbage collector that, for the purpose of accepting garbage, is licensed by the director or by the federal government.

16901. Animals on Railroad Tracks

It is unlawful for any person to do any of the following:

(a) Lead, drive, or conduct any animal along the track of a railroad, unless the railroad is built within the limits of a public highway or public place.

(b) Permit any animal to be placed within the fences of a railroad for grazing or other purposes if he has the right to prevent it.

16902. Animals at large

A person that owns or controls the possession of any livestock shall not willfully or negligently permit any of the livestock to stray upon, or remain unaccompanied by a person in charge or control of the livestock upon, a public highway, if both sides of the highway are adjoined by property which is separated from the highway by a fence, wall, hedge, sidewalk, curb, lawn, or building.

16903. Drive Livestock on Highway During Nighttime

It is unlawful for any person to drive any livestock upon, over, or across any public highway between the hours of sunset and sunrise unless he keeps a sufficient number of herders on continual duty to open the road so as to permit the passage of vehicles.

HARBORS AND NAVIGATION CODE

655. Operate Vessel Recklessly or While Under the Influence

(a) No person shall use any vessel or manipulate water skis, an aquaplane, or a similar device in a reckless or negligent manner so as to endanger the life, limb, or property of any person. The department shall adopt regulations for the use of vessels, water skis, aquaplanes, or similar devices in a manner that will minimize the danger to life, limb, or property consistent with reasonable use of the equipment for the purpose for which it was designed.

(b) No person shall operate any vessel or manipulate water skis, an aquaplane, or a similar device while under the influence of an alcoholic beverage, any drug, or the combined influence of an alcoholic beverage and any drug.

(c) No person shall operate any recreational vessel or manipulate any water skis, aquaplane, or similar device if the person has an alcohol concentration of 0.08 percent or more in his or her blood.

(d) No person shall operate any vessel other than a recreational vessel if the person has an alcohol concentration of 0.04 percent or more in his or her blood.

(e) No person shall operate any vessel, or manipulate water skis, an aquaplane, or a similar device who is addicted to the use of any drug. This subdivision does not apply to a person who is participating in a narcotic treatment program approved pursuant to Article 3 (commencing with Section 11875) of Chapter 1 of Part 3 of Division 10.5 of the Health and Safety Code.

(f) No person shall operate any vessel or manipulate water skis, an aquaplane, or a similar device while under the influence of an alcoholic beverage, any drug, or under the combined influence of an alcoholic beverage and any drug, and while so operating, do any act forbidden by law, or neglect any duty imposed by law in the use of the vessel, water skis, aquaplane, or similar device, which act or neglect proximately causes bodily injury to any person other than himself or herself.

(g) Notwithstanding any other provision of law, information, verbal or otherwise, which is obtained from a commissioned, warrant, or petty officer of the United States Coast Guard who directly observed the offense may be used as the sole basis for establishing the necessary reasonable cause for a peace officer of this state to make an arrest pursuant to the United States Constitution, the California Constitution, and Section 836 of the Penal Code for violations of subdivisions (b), (c), (d), and (e) of this section.

Asterisks (***) Denote Text Deleted By Legislation

(h) In any prosecution under subdivision (c), it is a rebuttable presumption that the person had 0.08 percent or more, by weight, of alcohol in his or her blood at the time of operation of a recreational vessel if the person had an alcohol concentration of 0.08 percent or more in his or her blood at the time of the performance of a chemical test within three hours after the operation.

(i) In any prosecution under subdivision (d), it is a rebuttable presumption that the person had 0.04 percent or more, by weight, of alcohol in his or her blood at the time of operation of a vessel other than a recreational vessel if the person had an alcohol concentration of 0.04 percent or more in his or her blood at the time of the performance of a chemical test within three hours after the operation.

(j) Upon the trial of any criminal action, or preliminary proceeding in a criminal action, arising out of acts alleged to have been committed by any person who was operating a vessel or manipulating water skis, an aquaplane, or a similar device while under the influence of an alcoholic beverage in violation of subdivision (b) or (f), the amount of alcohol in the persons blood at the time of the test, as shown by a chemical test of that persons blood, breath, or urine, shall give rise to the following presumptions affecting the burden of proof:

(1) If there was at that time less than 0.05 percent, by weight, of alcohol in the persons blood, it shall be presumed that the person was not under the influence of an alcoholic beverage at the time of the alleged offense.

(2) If there was at that time 0.05 percent or more, but less than 0.08 percent, by weight, of alcohol in the persons blood, that fact shall not give rise to any presumption that the person was or was not under the influence of an alcoholic beverage, but the fact may be considered with other competent evidence in determining whether the person was under the influence of an alcoholic beverage at the time of the alleged offense.

(3) If there was at that time 0.08 percent or more, by weight, of alcohol in the persons blood, it shall be presumed that the person was under the influence of an alcoholic beverage at the time of the alleged offense.

(k) This section does not limit the introduction of any other competent evidence bearing upon the question whether the person ingested any alcoholic beverage or was under the influence of an alcoholic beverage at the time of the alleged offense.

(l) This section applies to foreign vessels using waters subject to state jurisdiction. (AM '97)

HEALTH AND SAFETY CODE

12101.   Explosives - Permit Required

(a) No person shall do any one of the following without first having made application for and received a permit in accordance with this section:

(1) Manufacture explosives.

(2) Sell, furnish, or give away explosives.

(3) Receive, store, or possess explosives.

(4) Transport explosives.

(5) Use explosives.

(6) Operate a terminal for handling explosives.

(7) Park or leave standing any vehicle carrying explosives, except when parked or left standing in or at a safe stopping place designated as such by the Department of the California Highway Patrol under Division 14 (commencing with Section 31600) of the Vehicle Code.

(b) Application for a permit shall be made to the appropriate issuing authority.

(c)(1) A permit shall be obtained from the issuing authority having the responsibility in the area where the activity, as specified in subdivision (a), is to be conducted.

(2) If the person holding a valid permit for the use or storage of explosives desires to purchase or receive explosives in a jurisdiction other than that of intended use or storage, the person shall first present the permit to the issuing authority in the jurisdiction of purchase or receipt for endorsement. The issuing authority may include any reasonable restrictions or conditions which the authority finds necessary for the prevention of fire and explosion, the preservation of life, safety, or the control and security of explosives

within the authority's jurisdiction. If, for any reason, the issuing authority refuses to endorse the permit previously issued in the area of intended use or storage, the authority shall immediately notify both the issuing authority who issued the permit and the Department of Justice of the fact of the refusal and the reasons for the refusal.

(3) Every person who sells, gives away, delivers, or otherwise disposes of explosives to another person shall first be satisfied that the person receiving the explosives has a permit valid for that purpose. When the permit to receive explosives indicates that the intended storage or use of the explosives is other than in that area in which the permittee receives the explosives, the person who sells, gives away, delivers, or otherwise disposes of the explosives shall ensure that the permit has been properly endorsed by a local issuing authority and, further, shall immediately send a copy of the record of sale to the issuing authority who originally issued the permit in the area of intended storage or use. The issuing authority in the area in which the explosives are received or sold shall not issue a permit for the possession, use, or storage of explosives in an area not within the authority's jurisdiction.

(d) In the event any person desires to receive explosives for use in an area outside of this state, a permit to receive the explosives shall be obtained from the State Fire Marshal.

(e) A permit may include any restrictions or conditions which the issuing authority finds necessary for the prevention of fire and explosion, the preservation of life, safety, or the control and security of explosives.

(f) A permit shall remain valid only until the time when the act or acts authorized by the permit are performed, but in no event shall the permit remain valid for a period longer than one year from the date of issuance of the permit.

(g) Any valid permit which authorizes the performance of any act shall not constitute authorization for the performance of any act not stipulated in the permit.

(h) An issuing authority shall not issue a permit authorizing the transportation of explosives pursuant to this section if the display of placards for that transportation is required by Section 27903 of the Vehicle Code, unless the driver possesses a license for the transportation of hazardous materials issued pursuant to Division 14.1 (commencing with Section 32000) of the Vehicle Code, or the explosives are a hazardous waste or extremely hazardous waste, as defined in Sections 25117 and 25115 of the Health and Safety Code, and the transporter is currently registered as a hazardous waste hauler pursuant to Section 25163 of the Health and Safety Code.

(i) An issuing authority shall not issue a permit pursuant to this section authorizing the handling or storage of division 1.1, 1.2, or 1.3 explosives in a building, unless the building has caution placards which meet the standards established pursuant to subdivision (g) of Section 12081.

(j)(1) A permit shall not be issued to a person who meets any of the following criteria:

(A) He or she has been convicted of a felony.

(B) He or she is addicted to a narcotic drug.

(C) He or she is in a class prohibited by state or federal law from possessing, receiving, owning, or purchasing a firearm.

(2) For purposes of determining whether a person meets any of the criteria set forth in this subdivision, the issuing authority shall obtain two sets of fingerprints on prescribed cards from all persons applying for a permit under this section and shall submit these cards to the Department of Justice. The Department of Justice shall utilize the fingerprint cards to make inquiries both within this state and to the Federal Bureau of Investigation regarding the criminal history of the applicant identified on the fingerprint card.

This paragraph does not apply to any person possessing a current certificate of eligibility issued pursuant to paragraph (4) of subdivision (a) of Section 12071 or to any holder of a dangerous weapons permit or license issued pursuant to Section 12095, 12230, 12250, 12286, or 12305 of the Penal Code.

(k) An issuing authority shall inquire with the Department of Justice for the purposes of determining whether a person who is applying for a permit meets any of the criteria specified in subdivision (j). The Department of Justice shall determine whether a person who is applying for a permit meets any of the criteria specified in subdivision (j) and shall either grant or deny clearance for a permit to be issued pursuant to the determination. The Department of Justice shall not disclose the contents of a person's records to any person who is not authorized to receive the information in order to ensure confidentiality. If an applicant becomes ineligible to hold a permit, the Department of Justice shall provide to the issuing authority any subsequent arrest and conviction information supporting that ineligibility. *(AM '08, '09)*

13002. Throwing Lighted Substance

(a) Every person is guilty of a misdemeanor who throws or discharges any lighted or nonlighted cigarette, cigar, match, or any flaming or glowing substance, or any substance or thing which may cause a fire upon any highway, including any portion of the right-of-way of any highway, upon any sidewalk, or upon any public or private property. This subdivision does not restrict a private owner in the use of his or her own private property, unless the placing, depositing, or dumping of the waste matter on the property creates a public health and safety hazard, a public nuisance, or a fire hazard, as determined by a local health department, local fire department or fire district, or the Department of Forestry and Fire Protection, in which case this section applies.

(b) Every person convicted of a violation of this section shall be punished by a mandatory fine of not less than one hundred dollars ($100) nor more than one thousand dollars ($1,000) upon a first conviction, by a fine of not less than five hundred dollars ($500) nor more than one thousand dollars ($1,000) upon a second conviction, and by a mandatory fine of not less than seven hundred fifty dollars ($750) nor more than one thousand dollars ($1,000) upon a third or subsequent conviction.

The court may, in addition to the fine imposed upon a conviction, require as a condition of probation, in addition to any other condition, that any person convicted of a violation of this section pick up litter at a time and place within the jurisdiction of the court for not less than eight hours.

25163. Transport Hazardous Waste Without Permit

(a)(1) Except as otherwise provided in subdivisions (b), (c), (e), and (f), it is unlawful for any person to carry on, or engage in, the transportation of hazardous wastes unless the person holds a valid registration issued by the department, and it is unlawful for any person to transfer custody of a hazardous waste to a transporter who does not hold a valid registration issued by the department. A person who holds a valid registration issued by the department pursuant to this section is a registered hazardous waste transporter for purposes of this chapter. Any registration issued by the department to a transporter of hazardous waste is not transferable from the person to whom it was issued to any other person.

(2) Any person who transports hazardous waste in a vehicle shall have a valid registration issued by the department in his or her possession while transporting the hazardous waste. The registration certificate shall be shown upon demand to any representative of the department, officer of the Department of the California Highway Patrol, any local health officer, or any public officer designated by the department. Any person registered pursuant to this section may obtain additional copies of the registration certificate from the department upon the payment of a fee of two dollars ($2) for each copy requested, in accordance with Section 12196 of the Government Code.

(3) The hazardous waste information required and collected for registration pursuant to this subdivision shall be recorded and maintained in the management information system operated by the Department of the California Highway Patrol.

(b) Persons transporting only septic tank, cesspool, seepage pit, or chemical toilet waste that does not contain a hazardous waste originating from other than the body of a human or animal and who hold an unrevoked registration issued by the health officer or the health officer's authorized representative pursuant to Article 1 (commencing with Section 117400) of Chapter 4 of Part 13 of Division 104 are exempt from the requirements of subdivision (a).

(c) Except as provided in subdivision (f), persons transporting hazardous wastes to a permitted hazardous waste facility for transfer, treatment, recycling, or disposal, which wastes do not exceed a total volume of five gallons or do not exceed a total weight of 50 pounds, are exempt from the requirements of subdivision (a) and from the requirements of Section 25160 concerning possession of the manifest while transporting hazardous waste, upon meeting all of the following conditions:

(1) The hazardous wastes are transported in closed containers and packed in a manner that prevents the containers from tipping, spilling, or breaking during the transporting.

(2) Different hazardous waste materials are not mixed within a container during the transporting.

(3) If the hazardous waste is extremely hazardous waste or acutely hazardous waste, the extremely hazardous waste or acutely hazardous waste was not generated in the course of any business, and is not more than 2.2 pounds.

(4) The person transporting the hazardous waste is the producer of that hazardous waste, and the person produces not more than 100 kilograms of hazardous waste in any month.

(5) The person transporting the hazardous waste does not accumulate more than a total of 1,000 kilograms of hazardous waste onsite at any one time.

(d) Any person registered as a hazardous waste transporter pursuant to subdivision (a) is not subject to the registration requirements of Chapter 6 (commencing with Section 25000), but shall comply with those terms, conditions, orders, and directions that the health officer or the health officer's authorized representative may determine to be necessary for the protection of human health and comfort, and shall otherwise comply with the requirements for statements as provided in Section 25007. Violations of those requirements of Section 25007 shall be punished as provided in Section 25010. Proof of registration pursuant to subdivision (a) shall be submitted by mail or in person to the local health officer in the city or county in which the registered hazardous waste transporter will be conducting the activities described in Section 25001.

(e) Any person authorized to collect solid waste, as defined in Section 40191 of the Public Resources Code, who unknowingly transports hazardous waste to a solid waste facility, as defined in Section 40194 of the Public Resources Code, incidental to the collection of solid waste is not subject to subdivision (a).

(f) Any person transporting household hazardous waste or a conditionally exempt small quantity generator transporting hazardous waste to an authorized household hazardous waste collection facility pursuant to Section 25218.5 is exempt from subdivision (a) and from paragraph (1) of subdivision (d) of Section 25160 requiring possession of the manifest while transporting hazardous waste. *(AM '00)*

25189.5. Disposal of Hazardous Waste

(a) The disposal of any hazardous waste, or the causing thereof, is prohibited when the disposal is at a facility which does not have a permit from the department issued pursuant to this chapter, or at any point which is not authorized according to this chapter.

(b) Any person who is convicted of knowingly disposing or causing the disposal of any hazardous waste, or who reasonably should have known that he or she was disposing or causing the disposal of any hazardous waste, at a facility which does not have a permit from the department issued pursuant to this chapter, or at any point which is not authorized according to this chapter shall, upon conviction, be punished by imprisonment in a county jail for not more than one year or by imprisonment pursuant to subdivision (h) of Section 1170 of the Penal Code.

(c) Any person who knowingly transports or causes the transportation of hazardous waste, or who reasonably should have known that he or she was causing the transportation of any hazardous waste, to a facility which does not have a permit from the department issued pursuant to this chapter, or at any point which is not authorized according to this chapter, shall, upon conviction, be punished by imprisonment in a county jail for not more than one year or by imprisonment pursuant to subdivision (h) of Section 1170 of the Penal Code.

(d) Any person who knowingly treats or stores any hazardous waste at a facility which does not have a permit from the department issued pursuant to this chapter, or at any point which is not authorized according to this chapter, shall, upon conviction, be punished by imprisonment in a county jail for not more than one year or by imprisonment pursuant to subdivision (h) of Section 1170 of the Penal Code.

(e) The court also shall impose upon a person convicted of violating subdivision (b), (c), or (d), a fine of not less than five thousand dollars ($5,000) nor more than one hundred thousand dollars ($100,000) for each day of violation, except as further provided in this subdivision. If the act which violated subdivision (b), (c), or (d) caused great bodily injury, or caused a substantial probability that death could result, the person convicted of violating subdivision (b), (c), or (d) may be punished by imprisonment pursuant to subdivision (h) of Section 1170 of the Penal Code for one, two, or three years, in addition and consecutive to the term specified in subdivision (b), (c), or (d), and may be fined up to two hundred fifty thousand dollars ($250,000) for each day of violation.

(f) For purposes of this section, except as otherwise provided in this subdivision, "each day of violation" means each day on which a violation continues. In any case where a person has disposed or caused the disposal of any hazardous waste in violation of this section, each day that the waste remains disposed of in violation of this section and the person has knowledge thereof is a separate additional violation, unless the person has filed a report of the disposal with the department and is complying with any order concerning the disposal issued by the department, a hearing officer, or court of competent jurisdiction. *(AM '11)*

25189.6. Hazardous Waste; Handle, Treat, Transport, etc. in Reckless Manner

(a) Any person who knowingly, or with reckless disregard for the risk, treats, handles, transports, disposes, or stores any hazardous waste in a manner which causes any unreasonable risk of fire, explosion, serious injury, or death is guilty of a public offense and shall, upon conviction, be punished by a fine of not less than five thousand dollars ($5,000) nor more than two hundred fifty thousand dollars ($250,000) for each day of violation, or by imprisonment in a county jail for not more than one year, or by imprisonment pursuant to subdivision (h) of Section 1170 of the Penal Code, or by both that fine and imprisonment.

(b) Any person who knowingly, at the time the person takes the actions specified in subdivision (a), places another person in imminent danger of death or serious bodily injury, is guilty of a public offense and shall, upon conviction, be punished by a fine of not less than five thousand dollars ($5,000) nor more than two hundred fifty thousand dollars ($250,000) for each day of violation, and by imprisonment pursuant to subdivision (h) of Section 1170 of the Penal Code for three, six, or nine years. *(AM '11)*

25190. Violate Provisions of Chapter; Penalties

Except as otherwise provided in Sections 25189.5, 25189.6, 25189.7, and 25191, any person who violates any provision of this chapter, or any permit, rule, regulation, standard, or requirement issued or adopted pursuant to this chapter, is, upon conviction, guilty of a misdemeanor and shall be punished by a fine of not more than one thousand dollars ($1,000) or by imprisonment for up to six months in a county jail or by both that fine and imprisonment.

If the conviction is for a second or subsequent violation, the person shall, upon conviction, be punished by imprisonment in the county jail for not more than one year or by imprisonment pursuant to subdivision (h) of Section 1170 of the Penal Code for 16, 20, or 24 months. The court shall also impose upon the person a fine of not less than five thousand dollars ($5,000) or more than twenty-five thousand dollars ($25,000). *(AM '11)*

25191. Conceal Dangers of Hazardous Materials; Transport or Store Same Without Proper Manifest

(a)(1) Any person who knowingly does any of the acts specified in subdivision (b) shall, upon conviction, be punished by a fine of not less than two thousand dollars ($2,000) or more than twenty-five thousand dollars ($25,000) for each day of violation, or by imprisonment in a county jail for not more than one year, or by both that fine and imprisonment.

(2) If the conviction is for a second or subsequent violation of subdivision (b), the person shall be punished by imprisonment pursuant to subdivision (h) of Section 1170 of the Penal Code for 16, 20, or 24 months, or in a county jail for not more than one year, or by a fine of not less than two thousand dollars ($2,000) or more than fifty thousand dollars ($50,000) for each day of violation, or by both that fine and imprisonment.

(3) Each day or partial day that a violation occurs is a separate violation.

(b) A person who does any of the following is subject to the punishment prescribed in subdivision (a):

(1) Makes any false statement or representation in any application, label, manifest, record, report, permit, notice to comply, or other document filed, maintained, or used for the purposes of compliance with this chapter.

(2) Has in his or her possession any record relating to the generation, storage, treatment, transportation, disposal, or handling of hazardous waste required to be maintained pursuant to this chapter, that has been altered or concealed.

(3) Destroys, alters, or conceals any record relating to the generation, storage, treatment, transportation, disposal, or handling of hazardous waste required to be maintained pursuant to this chapter.

(4) Withholds information regarding a real and substantial danger to the public health or safety when that information has been requested by the department, or by a local officer or agency authorized to enforce this chapter pursuant to subdivision (a) of Section 25180, and is required to carry out the responsibilities of the department or the authorized local officer or agency pursuant to this chapter in response to a real and substantial danger.

(5) Except as otherwise provided in this chapter, engages in transportation of hazardous waste in violation of Section 25160 or 25161, or subdivision (a) of Section 25163, or in violation of any regulation adopted by the department pursuant to those provisions, including, but not limited to, failing to complete or provide the manifest in the form and manner required by the department.

(6) Except as otherwise provided in this chapter, produces, receives, stores, or disposes of hazardous waste, or submits hazardous waste for transportation, in violation of Section 25160 or 25161 or any regulation adopted by the department pursuant to those sections, including, but not limited to, failing to complete, provide, or submit the manifest in the form and manner required by the department.

(7) Transports any waste, for which there is provided a manifest, if the transportation is in violation of this chapter or the regulations adopted by the department pursuant thereto.

(8) Violates Section 25162.

(c)(1) The penalties imposed pursuant to subdivision (a) on any person who commits any of the acts specified in paragraph (5), (7), or (8) of subdivision (b) shall be imposed only (A) on the owner or lessee of the vehicle in which the hazardous wastes are unlawfully transported, carried, or handled or (B) on the person who authorizes or causes the transporting, carrying, or handling. These penalties shall not be imposed on the driver of the vehicle, unless the driver is also the owner or lessee of the vehicle or authorized or caused the transporting, carrying, or handling.

(2) If any person other than the person producing the hazardous waste prepares the manifest specified in Section 25160, that other person is also subject to the penalties imposed on a person who commits any of the acts specified in paragraph (6) of subdivision (b).

(d) Any person who knowingly does any of the following acts, each day or partial day that a violation occurs constituting a separate violation, shall, upon conviction, be punished by a fine of not more than five hundred dollars ($500) for each day of violation, or by imprisonment in the county jail for not to exceed six months, or by both that fine and imprisonment:

(1) Carries or handles, or authorizes the carrying or handling of, a hazardous waste without having in the driver's possession the manifest specified in Section 25160.

(2) Transports, or authorizes the transportation of, hazardous waste without having in the driver's possession a valid registration issued by the department pursuant to Section 25163.

(e) Whenever any person is prosecuted for a violation pursuant to paragraph (5), (6), (7), or (8) of subdivision (b), subdivision (d), or subdivision (c) of Section 25189.5, the prosecuting attorney may take appropriate steps to make the owner or lessee of the vehicle in which the hazardous wastes are unlawfully transported, carried, or handled, the driver of the vehicle, or any other person who authorized or directed the loading, maintenance, or operation of the vehicle, who is reasonably believed to have violated these provisions, a codefendant. If a codefendant is held solely responsible and found guilty, the court may dismiss the charge against the person who was initially so charged. *(AM '11)*

Article 2.5 Marco Firebaugh Memorial Children's Health and Safety Act of 2007

118947.   Marco Firebaugh Memorial Children's Health and Safety Act of 2007
This act shall be known, and may be cited, as the Marco Firebaugh Memorial Children's Health and Safety Act of 2007.

118948.   Smoke In Motor Vehicle When A Minor Is Present
   (a) It is unlawful for a person to smoke a pipe, cigar, or cigarette in a motor vehicle, whether in motion or at rest, in which there is a minor.
   (b) For the purposes of this section, "to smoke"means to have in one's immediate possession a lighted pipe, cigar, or cigarette containing tobacco or any other plant.
   (c) A violation of this section is an infraction punishable by a fine not exceeding one hundred dollars ($100) for each violation.

118949.   Officers Shall Not Stop Vehicle Solely To Check For Such Violation
   A law enforcement officer shall not stop a vehicle for the
sole purpose of determining whether the driver is in violation of
this article.

PUBLIC RESOURCES CODE

5091.15.   Snow Park Permit
   (a) Except as provided in this section, no person shall, from November 1 of any year to May 30 of the next year or for a shorter time as determined by the department, park a vehicle in a designated parking area unless the vehicle displays a parking permit issued by the department. Overnight camping in a vehicle parked in a designated parking area may be authorized by the department when it determines that the use is for a recreational activity, is safe and prudent, and is of limited duration.
   (b) No parking permit shall be required under this section for a vehicle owned and operated by the United States, another state or political subdivision thereof, or by this state or by a city, county, district, or political subdivision thereof.
   (c) The fee for the issuance of a parking permit under this chapter shall be determined by the department. The department shall hold at least one public hearing and notify the Legislature at least 30 days prior to any proposal to change the fees.
   (d) A person who violates this section is guilty of an infraction punishable by a fine of seventy-five dollars ($75). Unless the peace officer issuing the citation witnesses the parking of the vehicle, a rebuttable presumption exists that a vehicle parked in violation of this section was parked by the registered owner of the vehicle. If the parking of the vehicle is witnessed by the peace officer, the operator of the vehicle is in violation of this section.
   (e) The department may negotiate reciprocity agreements with other states having similar programs if the agreements are in the best interests of the California SNO-PARK program.
   (f) The department may contract with appropriate agencies for law enforcement, including, but not limited to, the Department of the California Highway Patrol, the county sheriffs, and the United States Department of Agriculture Forest Service. Enforcement activities may be funded with moneys appropriated from the Winter Recreation Fund. *(AM '01, '07)*

PUBLIC UTILITIES CODE

2119.   PUC Symbol: Display Required
   Every passenger stage corporation, highway common carrier, or cement carrier,
and every officer, director, agent, or employee of a passenger stage
corporation, highway common carrier, or cement carrier, who displays on any
vehicle any identifying symbol other than one prescribed by the commission

Asterisks (***) Denote Text Deleted By Legislation

pursuant to Section 1038.5 or 1068, or who fails to remove an identifying symbol when required by the commission, is guilty of a misdemeanor and is punishable by a fine of not more than one thousand dollars ($1,000), by imprisonment in the county jail for not more than one year, or by both.

5311. Household Goods Carrier

(a) Every household goods carrier and every officer, director, agent, or employee of any household goods carrier who violates or who fails to comply with, or who procures, aids, or abets any violation by any household goods carrier of any provision of this chapter, or who fails to obey, observe, or comply with any order, decision, rule, regulation, direction, demand, or requirement of the commission, or of any operating permit issued to any household goods carrier, or who procures, aids, or abets any household goods carrier in its failure to obey, observe, or comply with any such order, decision, rule, regulation, direction, demand, requirement, or operating permit, is guilty of a misdemeanor, and is punishable by a fine of not more than two thousand five hundred dollars ($2,500) or by imprisonment in the county jail for not more than three months, or both. If a violation is willful, each willful violation is punishable by a fine of not more than ten thousand dollars ($10,000) or by imprisonment in the county jail for not more than one year, or both. If the violation involves operating or holding one's self out as a household goods carrier without a permit, the fine shall be not less than one thousand dollars ($1,000).

(b) Any person who violates subdivision (a) of Section 5133, is guilty of a misdemeanor, and is punishable by a fine of not more than ten thousand dollars ($10,000), by imprisonment in the county jail for not more than one year, or both, for each violation. *(AM '12)*

21403. Aircraft: Flight at Low Altitudes; Use of Public Highway or Road

(a) Flight in aircraft over the land and waters of this state is lawful, unless at altitudes below those prescribed by federal authority, or unless conducted so as to be imminently dangerous to persons or property lawfully on the land or water beneath. The landing of an aircraft on the land or waters of another, without his or her consent, is unlawful except in the case of a forced landing or pursuant to Section 21662.1. The owner, lessee, or operator of the aircraft is liable, as provided by law, for damages caused by a forced landing.

(b) The landing, takeoff, or taxiing of an aircraft on a public freeway, highway, road, or street is unlawful except in the following cases:

(1) A forced landing.

(2) A landing during a natural disaster or other public emergency if the landing has received prior approval from the public agency having primary jurisdiction over traffic upon the freeway, highway, road, or street.

(3) When the landing, takeoff, or taxiing has received prior approval from the public agency having primary jurisdiction over traffic upon the freeway, highway, road or street.

The prosecution bears the burden of proving that none of the exceptions apply to the act which is alleged to be unlawful.

(c) The right of flight in aircraft includes the right of safe access to public airports, which includes the right of flight within the zone of approach of any public airport without restriction or hazard. The zone of approach of an airport shall conform to the specifications of Part 77 of the Federal Aviation Regulations of the Federal Aviation Administration, Department of Transportation.

21407.1. Operate Aircraft or Sport Parachute While Under the Influence

of Alcoholic Beverage or Drug

(a) It is unlawful for any person, who is under the influence of an alcoholic beverage or any drug, or the combined influence of an alcoholic beverage and any drug, to operate an aircraft in the air, or on the ground or water, or to engage in parachuting for sport.

(b) No person shall operate an aircraft in the air or on the ground or water who has 0.04 percent or more, by weight, of alcohol in his or her blood.

21661. Applicability of Article

This article does not apply to any temporary seaplane landing site, ultra light vehicle flight park, or to airports owned or operated by the United States. To the extent necessary, the department may exempt any other class of airports, pursuant to a reasonable classification or grouping, from any rule or requirement thereof, adopted pursuant to this article, if it finds that its application would be an undue burden on the class and is not required in the interest of public safety.

This section shall become operative on January 1, 1989.

21662.1. Designation of Landing and Take Off Area; Medical Emergencies

(a) At or as near as practical to the site of a medical emergency and at a medical facility, an officer authorized by a public safety agency may designate an area for the landing and taking off of an emergency service helicopter, in accordance with regulations established not later than January 1, 1989, pursuant to Section 21243.

(b) "Public safety agency"means any city, county, state agency, or special purpose district authorized to arrange for emergency medical services.

STREETS AND HIGHWAYS CODE

35. Vista Point

"Vista point"means any signed roadside area on the state highway system developed and maintained by the department for the purpose of providing the motorist with a place to stop to view the scenic panorama or points of visual interest.

225.5. Vending at Vista Point or Roadside Rest Area

(a) Notwithstanding Section 22520.5 or 22520.6 of the Vehicle Code, and except as specifically authorized by this article, no person shall display, sell, offer for sale, or otherwise vend or attempt to vend any merchandise, foodstuff, or service within any vista point or safety roadside rest area.

(b) No person shall solicit money within any vista point or safety roadside rest for any purpose.

(c) When requested by a uniformed member of the Department of the California Highway Patrol, or other peace officer, any person or persons and any property may be relocated to a specified area of a vista point or rest area, or may be required to quit the premises, as directed by that officer, if, in the opinion of the officer, the person's presence or activity or the presence of the property, creates, or may reasonably be expected to create, a safety problem, hazard, or nuisance, either on or near the vista point or safety roadside rest area.

(d) To the extent the provisions of any regulations adopted by the department conflict with this section, those provisions are void, and permission given pursuant to those provisions for a person to engage in activities prohibited by subdivision (a) or (b) of this section is revoked.

725. State Highway: Drain Water, Obstruct Natural Water Flow, etc.

It is unlawful for any person to do any of the following acts:

(a) Drain water, or permit water to be drained, from his lands onto any state highway by any means which results in damage to the highway.

(b) Obstruct any natural water course so as to:

(1) Prevent, impede or restrict the natural flow of waters from any state highway into and through such water course, unless other adequate and proper drainage is provided.

(2) Cause waters to be impounded within any State highway, to the damage of the highway.

(3) Cause interference with, or damage or hazard to public travel.

(c) Store or distribute water for any purpose so as to permit it to overflow onto, to saturate by seepage, or to obstruct any State highway, to the damage of the highway.

731. Vending From State Highway

Any vehicle or structure parked or placed wholly or partly within any state highway, for the purpose of selling the same or of selling therefrom or therein any article, service or thing, is a public nuisance and the department may immediately remove that vehicle or structure from within any highway.

Any person parking any vehicle or placing any structure wholly or partly within any highway for the purpose of selling that vehicle or structure, or of selling therefrom or therein any article or thing, and any person selling, displaying for sale, or offering for sale any article or thing either in or from that vehicle or structure so parked or placed, and any person storing, servicing, repairing or otherwise working upon any vehicle, other than upon a vehicle which is temporarily disabled, is guilty of a misdemeanor.

The California Highway Patrol and all peace officers from local law enforcement agencies may enforce the provisions of this chapter with respect to highways under their respective jurisdiction and shall cooperate with the department to that end. Whenever any member of the California Highway Patrol or any peace officer from a local law enforcement agency removes a vehicle from a highway under the provisions of this section, then all of the provisions of Article 3 (commencing with Section 22850), Chapter 10, Division 11 of the Vehicle Code with reference to the removal of a vehicle from a highway shall be applicable.

This section does not prohibit a seller from taking orders or delivering any commodity from a vehicle on that part of any state highway immediately adjacent to the premises of the purchaser; prohibit an owner or operator of a vehicle, or a mechanic, from servicing, repairing or otherwise working upon any vehicle which is temporarily disabled in a manner and to an extent that it is impossible to avoid stopping that vehicle within the highway; or prohibit coin-operated public telephones and related telephone structures in park and ride lots, vista points, and truck inspection facilities within state highway rights-of-way for use by the general public. *(AM '07)*

1487. Injure or Obstruct County Highway by Ditch or Dam

A person who, by means of ditches or dams, obstructs or injures any county highway, diverts any watercourse into any county highway, or drains water from his or her land upon any county highway, to the injury of the highway, shall, upon notice by the road commissioner, immediately cease and discontinue the obstruction and injury, and shall repair the highway at his or her own expense. He or she is liable to a penalty of three hundred fifty dollars ($350) for each day the obstruction or injury remains, recoverable as provided in Section 1496, and is also guilty of a misdemeanor. *(AM '03)*

1492. Willful Removal of Mile-Board, Milestone or Guide-Pose

Any person who willfully removes or injures any mile-board, milestone or guide-post, or any inscription thereon, erected on any county highway, is liable for a penalty of ten dollars, recoverable as provided in section 1496, for every such offense, and is also guilty of a misdemeanor.

2559. Motorist Aid Call Box: Remove, Damage, Interfere with Use of

It is a misdemeanor for any person to remove, damage, interfere with the use of, or obstruct any motorist aid call box provided pursuant to this chapter without the consent of the authority.

A person convicted under this section may be required by the court to pay to the service authority the costs of repairing or replacing the call box, in addition to any other penalty.

INDEX

A

ABANDON VEHICLE PRESUMPTION, 22524
ABANDONED VEHICLES; REMOVAL, 22669
ABANDONING VEHICLE PROHIBITED, 22523
ACCIDENT(S) INFORMATION, INVESTIGATIONS, REPORT FORMS
  Civil Liability; Application of Division, 20000
  Coroner's Report, 20011
  Counter Reports; No Determination of Fault, 20015
  Driver Incapacity to Report, 16003
  Driver Unable to Report, 20010
  Driver Without License, 20006
  Duty to Report, 20008
  Duty to Stop at Scene, 20001
  Duty Upon Death, 20004
  Duty Upon Injury or Death, 20003
  Duty Where Property Damaged, 20002
  Employer's Vehicle; Driver Duty to Report, 16002
  Failure to Report; Mandatory Suspension of License, 16004
  Information, 2408
  Investigation, 2412
  Report, 16000
  Report Forms, 2407
  Reportable Off-Highway, 16000.1
  Reports as Evidence, 20013
  Reports Confidential, 20012
  Supplemental Reports, 20009
  Use of Reports, 20014
ACETYLENE LAMPS, 25450
ACETYLENE LAMPS ON MOTORCYCLES, 25451
ACQUISITION OF VEHICLE BY MINOR; DRIVER'S LICENSE REQUIRED, 15500
ADDITIONAL REQUIREMENTS; OFF-HIGHWAY MOTOR VEHICLE, 38504
ADDITIONAL WARNING LIGHTS ON EMERGENCY VEHICLES, 25259
ADDRESS CHANGE; DRIVER'S LICENSE, 14600
ADDRESS OF PEACE OFFICER; CONFIDENTIAL RECORDS, 1808.2
ADDRESS OF RESIDENCE; CONFIDENTIAL RECORDS, 1808.21
ADDRESS; NOTICE OF CHANGE, 4159
AERIAL LIFT VEHICLE WARNING LIGHTS, 25260.3
AFFIRMATION; OATH, 16
AGE FOR DRIVING SCHOOLBUS, 12516
AGE LIMIT; DRIVING FOR HIRE OR TRUCK DRIVING, 12515
AIR BAG; PREVIOUSLY DEPLOYED; INSTALLATION, REINSTALLATION OR DISTRIBUTION PROHIBITED, 27317
AIR BRAKES, 108
AIR BRAKES; RESTRICTION, 15260
AIR BRAKES; RESTRICTION, 15260
AIR POLLUTION CONTROL DEVICE, 27156
AIRCRAFT REFUELING VEHICLE, 4021
ALCOHOL
  Abuse Education & Prevention Assessment, 23196
  Alcohol or Drug Education Program; Minor, 23154
  Alcoholic Beverage, 109
  Alcoholic Beverages; Possession of; Exceptions, 23229
  Blood Alcohol Volume of Minor Driver, 23140
  Education Program; Minor, 23141
  Education Program; When Required of Minor, 23142

  Limousine; Possession in; Passengers Under Age 21, 23229.1
  Vehicle; Person Under 21, 23224, 25662
ALCOHOL SCREENING, PRELIMINARY, 13389
ALLEY, 110
ALTERATIONS TO VEHICLES, 9406
ALTERED LICENSE PLATES, 4464
ALTERING INDICATED MILEAGE, 28051
ALTERING OR CHANGING VEHICLE IDENTIFICATION, 10750
AMBULANCE LAMPS & SIRENS, 25806
AMBULANCE OR ARMORED CAR LICENSE, 2510
AMBULANCE OR ARMORED CAR LICENSE ELIGIBILITY, 2511
ANIMAL(S)
  Animal Control Vehicle Warning Lamps, 25271.5
  Animals & Vehicles Prohibited on Certain Public Grounds, 21113
  Animals, Vehicles, Bicycles, & Motorized Bicycles; Vehicular Crossings, 23330
  Carrying in Motor Truck, 23117
  Riding or Driving, 21050
ANTISIPHONING DEVICE FOR METHANOL & ETHANOL VEHICLES, 28110
APPEARANCE BY COUNSEL, 40507
APPLICATION, 4300
APPLICATION FOR RENEWAL OF REGISTRATION, 4602
APPLICATION OF DIVISION, 36800
APPLICATION OF OTHER PROVISIONS; HUSBANDRY IMPLEMENTS, 36700
APPRAISERS, 22855
APPROACHING VEHICLES, 21660
ARMED FORCES; PERSONS IN, 12817
ARMORED CAR, 21713
ARMORED CARS; RED LIGHTS, 25262
ARMORED CARS; SIRENS, 27003
ARRAIGNMENT FOR OTHER VIOLATIONS, 40311
ARREST(S)
  Application of Chapter, 40300
  CHP; Discretionary Procedure, 40304
  Driving Under the Influence, 40300.6
  Felony; Procedure, 40301
  Immediate, When Permitted, 23109.2
  Minor, 40302.5
  Misdemeanor; Mandatory Appearance, 40302
  Prohibition; Receipt for Fine, 40312
  Quota Defined, 41600
  Quota Prohibited, 41602
  Warrant; Bail, 40304.5
  Without Warrant, 40300.5
ASSISTANCE TO MOTORISTS, 20018
ATV, UNSUPERVISED OPERATION BY PERSON UNDER 14, 38504.1
AUTOETTE, 175, 4000.5
AUTOMATIC BALE WAGON; OPERATION DURING DARKNESS, 36705
AUXILIARY DOLLIES; BRAKES, 26305
AUXILIARY DRIVING & PASSING LAMPS, 24402
AUXILIARY GASOLINE TANKS, 27156.1
AUXILIARY LAMPS; OFF-HIGHWAY USE, 24411
AXLE, 230

B

BACKING PARKED VEHICLES, 22106

347

S

INDEX

This page intentionally left blank.